An Illustrated Glossary of
Early Southern Architecture and Landscape

B. Cole sculp.

Enter'd in the Hall Book.

An Illustrated Glossary
of
Early Southern Architecture
and Landscape

CARL R. LOUNSBURY

Editor

With editorial assistance by
Vanessa E. Patrick

Prepared at
The Colonial Williamsburg Foundation

"Dictionaries are like watches; the worst is better than none,
and the best cannot be expected to go quite true."
—SAMUEL JOHNSON

New York   Oxford
Oxford University Press
1994

To my colleagues in the Vernacular Architecture Forum
and to my friends in the Architectural Research Department
at the Colonial Williamsburg Foundation.

Oxford University Press

Oxford   New York   Toronto
Delhi   Bombay   Calcutta   Madras   Karachi
Kuala Lumpur   Singapore   Hong Kong   Tokyo
Nairobi   Dar es Salaam   Cape Town
Melbourne   Auckland   Madrid

and associated companies in
Berlin   Ibadan

Published by Oxford University Press, Inc.,
200 Madison Avenue, New York, NY 10016

Oxford is a registered trademark of Oxford University Press

Library of Congress Cataloging-in-Publication Data
An illustrated glossary of early southern architecture and landscape
Carl R. Lounsbury, editor; with editorial assistance by Vanessa E. Patrick.
p. cm. "Prepared at the Colonial Williamsburg Foundation."
Includes bibliographical references.
ISBN 0-19-507992-2
1. Architecture, Colonial—Southern States—Dictionaries.
I. Lounsbury, Carl. II. Patrick, Vanessa Elizabeth.
III. Colonial Williamsburg Foundation.
NA727.I44   1994
720'.975'03—dc20   93-25433

Frontispiece art from *The Art of Sound Buildings*, by William Halfpenny,
London, 1725. Title-page quotation from *Anecdotes of the Late*
Samuel Johnson, by Hester Thrale Piozzi, 1786.

Printing (last digit): 9 8 7 6 5 4 3 2 1

Printed in the United States of America
on acid-free paper

PREFACE

The story of early southern architecture can be traced in the language of its builders and users. This work documents the transfer of English building terminology to the southern mainland colonies in the 17th and 18th centuries and explores the subsequent growth of a regional vernacular through the early national period. The glossary defines and analyzes the various and sometimes changing meanings and usages of the South's building and landscape vocabulary. It is a compilation of nearly fifteen hundred words and terms known to have been in use from the 1610s through the 1820s in the region encompassing Delaware in the north, Georgia in the south, and the newly settled western regions of Kentucky and Tennessee.

Although there is no obvious termination date for a glossary of this kind, concluding it at the beginning of the second quarter of the 19th century makes sense for a number of reasons. The expansion of the economy stimulated a building boom throughout much of the South. Substantial, well-finished dwellings replaced old, impermanent housing on farms and in villages across the region. Cities expanded beyond their tiny colonial boundaries as new public and commercial buildings rose on public squares and cheek by jowl along broad thoroughfares. Although preindustrial building technology continued to thrive throughout the South well into the late 19th century, the 1820s and 1830s witnessed the rise of professional contracting firms whose scale, organization, and scope of operations far exceeded anything of the preceding generations. New materials and the beginning of standardized building practices, foreshadowed by the use of steam machinery and the mechanization of the joiner's profession, had a subtle but profound influence on the builder's vocabulary. The growth of a literate public with an interest in the art of building meant that the language of architecture was no longer confined to those engaged in the design and construction of buildings. The publication of American builders' books and Noah Webster's dictionaries (1806, 1828) hastened changes in regional spellings and introduced a number of northern terms. Newspapers and journals regularly described and commented on the new buildings that were reshaping the southern landscape. Finally, the number of surviving documents concerned with building after 1825 is massive. Any historian wishing to examine a fair representation of all these documents throughout the region faces an overwhelming task, especially if the new states and territories along the Gulf Coast were included. The strength of this book lies in its thorough sampling of all types of evidence from the period prior to this flood of antebellum material.

This work is intended to serve a broad audience, ranging from those with the most casual interest in architecture to professionals in the field. Although architectural historians, archaeologists, conservators, preservationists, geographers, curators, architects, and others study early buildings for different reasons, all have need for a standard reference source that provides explanations of common as well as unfamiliar architectural terms. A cursory perusal of the words and phrases contained in this book reveals a wide discrepancy between historical usage and the language of modern architectural analysis. Although this glossary does not pretend to be a panacea for linguistic confusion, it does offer a clear guide to the language of building used by early Southerners. I am fully aware, as Dr. Johnson noted in the preface to his *Dictionary of the English Language* (1755), that "this recommendation of steadiness and uniformity does not proceed from an opinion, that particular combinations of letters have much influence on human happiness; or that truth may not be successfully taught by modes of spelling fanciful and erroneous; I am not yet so lost in lexicography, as to forget that *words are the daughters of earth, and that things are the sons of heaven.* Language is only the instrument of science, and words are but the signs of ideas: I wish, however, that the instrument might be less apt to decay, and that signs might be permanent, like the things which they denote."

Users of this glossary may find it helpful in a number of ways. It contains information about construction technology and building types that rarely appears in published architectural dictionaries. It includes a full range of building vocabulary prevalent in early America, much of which is now simply unfamiliar to modern researchers and surveyors. Readers can refer to it to define archaic terms found in early documents, to verify the use of specific words at different periods of time, to identify names of architectural details, to recognize how architectural terminology has been used and modified over time, and, by comparison with other parts of the country, to identify regional patterns in the usage of such terms. After a brief definition, most words and phrases are followed by one or more citations from primary sources. Since by their very nature dictionaries are atomistic structures, these citations are intended to illustrate how each word or phrase was used in context to give some idea of how they were combined or integrated into design ideas or methods of building. Although I have by no means exhausted the primary source material, I have sought out examples of a term's earliest appearance, duration of use, and geographic range.

This glossary should stir the interests of linguists and lexicographers concerned with the development of distinctive American terminology and the emergence of regional variations in the 18th and 19th centuries. The first two volumes of the *Dictionary of American Regional English* (1985, 1991), edited by Frederic Cassidy and Joan Hall, and Richard Lederer's *Colonial American English* (1985) are masterful compilations of the American vernacular, but contain few references to building. Next to farming, the building trades were one of the largest and most important sources of employment in early America. Although much of the language used by the thousands of skilled craftsmen and laborers was highly technical in nature, the universality of building meant that much of the vocabulary found its way into everyday usage. The transformation of English into a distinctly American English can be discerned in the words used by America's early builders. Similarly, the emergence of regional dialects and expressions appears in the common spellings and names attached to architectural features and construction practices. The various names given to common building types—for example, *henhouses* in the Chesapeake, *fowl houses* in the Carolina lowcountry—suggest strong subregional differences.

Although there are several glossaries currently in print covering general building terminology, none specifically treats the origins and development of colonial American architecture. *A Dictionary of Architecture* (1992) by Nikolaus Pevsner, John Fleming, and Hugh Honour is an excellent example of a concise, yet broad-ranging reference work. Perhaps still unsurpassed is Russell Sturgis's multivolume *Illustrated Dictionary of Architecture and Building,* first published in 1901–1902. Ambitious in scope, lavishly illustrated, and well written, it is concerned with academic architecture and says little about the kinds of buildings constructed by Americans in the colonial period. Closer in spirit to this glossary are James Stevens Curl's *English Architecture* (1987) and Glen Pride's *Glossary of Scottish Building* (1990). The latter deals at length with vernacular building practices and is a rich source of archaic building terms.

Reference works limited to American architecture are scarce. The handful of glossaries that claim to cover colonial terminology are limited in scope and do little to explain the changes that took place in the architectural vocabulary during the early period. Instead, publications such as Norman Isham's *A Glossary of Colonial Architectural Terms* (1967) present a hodgepodge of colonial and modern terms and definitions. They also tend to be inadequately illustrated, and none consistently cites original examples of word usage. Although this glossary covers only the South, a sampling of primary source material from New England and mid-Atlantic states suggests a substantial body of common usage in those regions. A common British heritage and the introduction of English architectural publications ensured a large degree of similarity and continuity. However, differences in construction techniques and building types among these regions argues for a small but important body of words and phrases that set the South apart from its northern neighbors. Establishing these fine distinctions is necessary if the complex texture of past thinking about building in these very different parts of the country is to be recovered. Recognizing variations in a turn of a phrase or discovering the timing of the appearance of a certain term may reveal something of the regional contrasts in early American design.

The terms selected for this glossary are limited to the English language except in the few instances where foreign words were adopted by English-speaking settlers. Although the sounds of German, French, Swedish, Dutch, Spanish, Welsh, Gaelic, and the myriad of African and Indian languages reverberated over the South, the dominant political and social culture was English.

The present work reflects that reality. The contributions that non-English-speaking Europeans, Native Americans, and African-Americans made to the development of American English in the 17th, 18th, and early 19th centuries remains to be charted. I eagerly await others to take up the challenge so that regional and ethnic variations may be assessed in a systematic manner.

A project as large as this one could not have been accomplished without the aid of numerous individuals and the resources of many institutions. The research and much of the writing were made possible by grants from the National Endowment for the Humanities (Grant RT-21027–89), the Richard Gwathmey and Caroline T. Gwathmey Memorial Trust, and the Graham Foundation for Advanced Studies in the Fine Arts. Since the early 1980s, the Architectural Research Department at the Colonial Williamsburg Foundation has accumulated a large file of architectural terms gleaned from documentary research in county court and parish vestry books. In the past few years, this body of material has been substantially increased with the addition of information contained in various other documents from the colonial and early national periods. This created a solid base from which to develop a comprehensive glossary of early building terms. It contained many detailed specifications for all types of buildings that name and describe framing members, construction techniques, and detail finishes.

Although the glossary reflects the weight of years of research in the records of Britain's largest colony in North America, an effort was made to examine as much representative and analogous evidence from the other colonies and states of the Old South in order to strengthen the regional coverage. Perhaps the foremost repository of source material pertaining to the architecture and decorative arts in this region is at the Museum of Early Southern Decorative Arts in Winston-Salem. Frank Horton, Brad Rauschenburg, and Martha Rowe kindly opened to editorial assistant Vanessa Patrick and me their voluminous files, which we devoured with great relish on several trips. We have also benefited from the massive amount of material on North Carolina collected by Catherine Bishir and others. Orlando Ridout V helped us with primary sources in Maryland and the District of Columbia and sent us his transcripts of court orphans records. Bernard Herman contributed similar material from all three Delaware counties, while in South Carolina, Jonathan Poston, Thomas Savage, Robert Leath, and Louis Nelson expedited our investigation of records in various institutions in Charleston. Patricia Cooper very kindly dispatched records of Georgia plantation accounts. Camille Wells augmented the Virginia material with transcripts from the Jonathan Clark survey of lands on the western frontier and many newspaper advertisements. Travis McDonald passed along material from Thomas Jefferson's correspondence and papers. Barbara Sarudy very generously supplied garden references from across the South. Robert Alexander, John Barden, Charles Brownell, Richard Candee, Barbara Carson, Al Chambers, Claire Dempsey, Michael Dwyer, Linda Goldstein, Bryan Green, Murray Howard, Andy Ladigo, John Larson, Susan Lounsbury, Bill Macintire, Turk McCleskey, George McDaniel, Peter Sandbeck, Russell Steele, Dell Upton, Donna Ware, Mitch Wilds, James T. Wollen, Jr., and Garland Wood contributed material and provided leads that made the inventory of resources for this project far richer.

In conducting research in national, state, city, and county archives, all those involved in this work enjoyed the assistance and friendly support of the staffs at those institutions. Many thanks go to those who helped locate documents and illustrations and answer our queries at the Charleston Library Society, Charleston Museum, College of Charleston, College of William and Mary, Duke University Library, Georgia Historical Society, Gibbes Museum of Art, Historic Charleston Foundation, Library of Congress, Maryland Historical Society, Maryland State Archives, Massachusetts Historical Society, Mount Vernon Ladies' Association, North Carolina Division of Archives and History, Octagon Museum, South Carolina Historical Society, Southern Historical Collection, University of Virginia, Virginia State Archives, Virginia Historical Society, and the Winterthur Museum. We owe a debt of appreciation to our own library staff at the Colonial Williamsburg Foundation. Susan Berg, John Ingram, Mary Keeling, Cathy Grosfils, Suzanne Brown, Lois Danuser, and Liz Ackert enabled us to work smoothly through our extensive collection of accounts, diaries, 18th-century architectural books, newspapers, and other primary sources and promptly filled our many requests for interlibrary loans and photographs. Microfilm material from our own and other repositories made it possible to keep an army of student interns involved over the past few years. Cameron Arnold, Nicole Bliss, Charmian Combs, Lori Cousins, Matt Dalbey, Michelle Deleiden, Susan Gilliam, Deborah Hutton, Doug Jacobs, Beth Ann Spyrison, and Hampton Tucker spent many delightful hours examining these sources. David Hurley helped design many of the accompanying illustrations and Kathleen Maloney provided an invaluable service in creating the bibliography. David Beatty exhibited his drafting skills in producing many of the final drawings in the glossary. I am truly indebted to Marilyn Melchor, who very kindly volunteered her services and spent more than two years perusing church records and newspapers.

The task of collecting all this material and retrieving it in a systematic manner was made easy for me by James Garrett of the Colonial Williamsburg library staff and later by Mark Ferguson and Beth Nagle of Information Systems who devised a useful computerized database storage system. Helen Tate very patiently entered more than twenty-five thousand references into this electronic storage system, and I greatly appreciated her fortitude as well as admired her skills in reading atrocious handwriting, both mine and my colonial predecessors.

From the very beginning of this project, there has been a central core of individuals on whom I have relied for guidance, depending on their knowledge of building practices and manuscript sources in their respective states and fields of expertise. This advisory group consisted of Catherine Bishir of the North Carolina Division of Archives and History, Bernard Herman of the University of Delaware, Carter Hudgins of Mary Washington College, Orlando Ridout V of the Maryland Historical Trust, and Gary Stanton, formerly of the McKissick Museum in Columbia and now at Mary Washington College. This group helped shape the nature of the project, kept me informed of valuable sources, kindly provided material from their own files, furnished drawings and other illustrations, and read the manuscript in its various stages of formation. Two unofficial members of this group included Barbara Sarudy of Monkton, Maryland, and Jonathan Poston of the Historic Charleston Foundation, who also provided invaluable assistance in the research and writing of this glossary. Professor Sarudy wrote or edited many of the landscape terms. At Oxford University Press, Linda Halvorson Morse provided early support for the project. Claude Conyers offered reassurance and Jeffrey Edelstein efficiently negotiated the manuscript through production and publication.

I am last but not least appreciative of all the time and support given me by my colleagues at the Colonial Williamsburg Foundation. Sharon Thelin, Sarah Houghland, Annie Davis, Grant Healey, and Al Louer in the Development Department improved grant proposals and found the monetary support that made this work over the past five years feasible. In the Research Division, Cary Carson provided valuable guidance and, along with Wendy Sumerlin, managed to keep the project financially secure and on a reasonable schedule. Rosemary Brandau, Betty Leviner, Roberta Reid, Thomas Taylor, John Davis, and Margaret Pritchard vetted several parts of the glossary in their respective areas of expertise. Lorena Walsh, Patricia Gibbs, Kevin Kelly, Mick Nichols, David Konig, and Lou Powers answered many questions about various aspects of colonial and Southern history. I am especially grateful to Meredith Moodey for her encouragement. Without the editorial and secretarial skills of Ethel Hawkins and Helen Tate, this work would have lagged far longer. Finally, I am indebted beyond measure to my colleagues in the Architectural Research Department for their substantial contributions to this work. Edward Chappell, Willie Graham, Vanessa Patrick, and Mark R. Wenger contributed to this project in every way, from providing obscure references and apt illustrations to writing definitions when deadlines loomed. Jeffrey Bostetter's fine drafting dexterity was employed in producing many of the original drawings for the text. I have benefitted greatly from the diligence of Vanessa Patrick's editorial assistance. I consider myself very fortunate to have worked with such an agreeable group of individuals, whose prodigious knowledge of early American architecture I have come to admire with the greatest respect.

Carl R. Lounsbury
Williamsburg
February 1993

INTRODUCTION

Most architectural dictionaries define a timeless, universal language of building. In contrast, this glossary is rooted in a particular time and place: the old South in the period from first settlement to the second quarter of the 19th century. From the fortified earthfast dwellings of John Smith's Jamestown to the intellectualized landscape of Thomas Jefferson's Monticello, southern architectural forms and landscape underwent a revolutionary metamorphosis. So too did the language of building from Smith to Jefferson. It had been founded upon the workaday grammar of English artisans but was altered by new world conditions and the slow absorption of the self-conscious, scholarly grammar of classical architecture. This academic language of Renaissance scholars and gentlemen had scarcely affected the vernacular of English builders in the period of initial settlement in the 17th century. By the time of Thomas Jefferson's death in 1826, it had made strong inroads in the contracts, accounts, and conversations of builders and clients. However, as late as the 1820s, the arcane grammar and rules of the classical orders had by no means displaced the less explicit but well understood language of the trades expressed in terms of *workmanlike* craftsmanship.

Because the language of building reflects the currency of certain design ideas and architectural forms at any given period, it is possible to observe fundamental shifts in the way Southerners thought and wrote about building during the first two hundred years of settlement. Although immigrants to the new world in the early 17th century brought English tools, skills, and habits of building to their task of constructing shelters, dwellings, agricultural structures, public buildings, and fortifications, economic, social, and environmental conditions that shaped the early colonies in the Chesapeake and the Carolinas subtly but substantially transformed their methods.

Architecturally, Britain at the time of the settlement of North America was a land marked by many strong regional contrasts. From the west country to East Anglia, in expanding London and the populous home counties, and stretching northward to the remote dales of Yorkshire and beyond, the domestic architecture of England diverged widely in plan, room uses, materials, construction methods, and finishes. Regional distinctions were evident in the names given to various rooms and parts of the house. The principal, all-purpose room known as the *hall* in the south and the *house* throughout much of the north was also called *forehouse*, *fireroom*, and *housebody* in many localities. In the north of England and in Scotland, a *gable* was called a *gavel* while in the southwest, the French term *pignon* was widely used.[1] Variations also appeared in the terms given framing members. A *teazle post* was a principal post in Yorkshire while a *span piece* was a Devonshire term for a roof collar.[2] Many builders referred to small upright timbers set between posts as *studs*, but *punch* or *puncheon* was also widely in circulation. In the 17th century, the term *quarter* began to supersede *puncheon* on the building site.[3] The latter term survived a transatlantic crossing and occasionally entered into colonial contractual agreements.

In the century prior to North American settlement, the English erected more and more solidly constructed dwellings, replacing impermanent structures. Many people improved older houses by the insertion of floors over rooms once open to the roof. The construction of masonry chimney stacks in place of wooden ones or open hearths provided more efficient heating and the introduction of window glass, paneling, and decorative plasterwork lightened, brightened, warmed, and enhanced many interiors. New terms such as *wainscot* and *casement* entered into the vocabulary to describe certain features of these improvements. More houses acquired service rooms for food preparation, storage, and domestic manufacturing. *Dairies*, *bakehouses*, and *butteries* emerged as essential elements in many dwellings. This transformation of domestic life from the old communal patterns of the open hall of a medieval household into a more comfortable, private, and specialized house did not occur evenly across Britain. In some of the wealthy areas such as the southeast, such developments had occurred some fifty to one hundred years before the settlement

---

1. L. F. Salzman, *Building in England down to 1540: A Documentary History* (Oxford: Clarendon Press, 1952), p. 214.
2. *Vernacular Architecture* 1 (1970), p. 16.
3. Salzman, *Building in England*, pp. 205–206.

of Jamestown in 1607. Elsewhere, such as in the pastoral highlands of the north, age-old patterns continued with few signs of change.

Layered over this body of indigenous architecture and regional building vocabulary was a new interest in foreign forms and ways of thinking about building. At the top level of society on the country estates owned by the aristocracy and in the buildings constructed by the cognoscenti associated with the royal court as well as the planned developments in the city of Westminster, the Renaissance rediscovery of the form and language of classical architecture of antiquity began to influence ideas about design. Although books explaining the rules and forms of this architectural grammar would be an important transmitter of this language to America in the late colonial and early republican era, the first signs of the impact of Renaissance classicism on English vernacular practices and thus on early American building appeared much earlier. These ideas grew slowly but steadily throughout the 17th century, influencing everything from the overall form of buildings and placement of apertures to the pattern of interior finishes and the shape of molding profiles. Misapplication of this language also made its way into use. Although the Italian name for an open square was *piazza*, the English used the term to describe the ground-floor arcade that surrounded the squares at Covent Garden and the Royal Exchange. In this sense, the term was appropriated in the late 17th century by Chesapeake colonists to refer to the arcaded space of public buildings.

The geographical diversity of England, combined with the dynamic trends in its architecture, provided the first settlers of the Chesapeake with a rich mixture of alternatives in construction technologies, building types, and words to describe domestic and public spaces. The development of a plantation society in the Chesapeake by the middle of the 17th century and the consequent emergence of a creole culture fostered the growth of a distinctive vernacular building tradition based mainly on impermanent construction techniques. Although buildings such as Bacon's Castle (1665) in Surry County, Virginia, and Arlington, the home of Custis family on the Eastern Shore of the colony, resembled in plan, construction, and scale some buildings erected by the minor gentry and prosperous farmers in many parts of England, most farmhouses and public structures erected by this dispersed agricultural society varied significantly from standard English patterns. By the middle of the 17th century, immigrants to the southern colonies acknowledged this difference between well-framed, *English houses* with beaded and chamfered beams fastened with strong joints and a cheaper and more prevalent form of riven carpentry. Early contracts often described buildings as a system of repetitive units fabricated of so many *lengths of boards* held together by a rudimentary framing system. The lower part of this hewn and riven frame was secured into posts or sills that sat in or on the ground. The colonists rarely considered these buildings—known as *earthfast* constructions by modern scholars and as *Virginia houses* by contemporaries—as anything more than inferior but necessary structures. In this earthfast system, the placement of apertures and fabrication of other major elements, which later craftsmen and builders would carefully design and provide decorative finishes, were left to the discretion of *clapboard carpenters*. Rarely did building agreements specify finish details. The paucity of skilled joiners in the records before the last quarter of the 17th century testifies to the pervasiveness of this simple quality of construction and finish.

The use of simplified construction techniques should not mask the radical restructuring that was taking place in the arrangement and function of rooms in domestic and public architecture. For most of the 17th century, southern colonists experimented with many English houses types, juggling elements to fit the needs of a plantation culture dependent upon servant and slave labor. Mounting evidence from the archaeological record of early Chesapeake sites reveals a tremendous range of house forms and construction methods.[4] Lobby-entry houses, common in many parts of southern England and long associated with the early New England landscape, were erected in the Chesapeake in the second half of the century. However, the dozens of house types characteristic of the English inheritance gradually were pared down to a few well-considered options. By the beginning of the 18th century, Southerners had completely rethought the configuration of the English house, consigning many service spaces

4. See Cary Carson, et al., "Impermanent Architecture in the Southern American Colonies," *Winterthur Portfolio* 16 (Summer/Autumn 1981): 135–196.

such as the kitchen, pantry, and buttery to detached structures or *outhouses*. The documentary record does not initially give full voice to this reorientation of domestic spaces. Only by the careful reading of contractual agreements and estate inventories can the movement of functions out of the main living space be detected. Occasionally, the emergence of new building types and names such as *smokehouse* and *wash house* or the disappearance of certain room names such as *buttery* make explicit this transformation.

The language of building changed dramatically in the last decades of the 17th century and the first two or three of the next century. One can follow this growing influence of Renaissance ideas on early American building in the appearance and acceptance of its words and phrases in contracts and accounts. Fashionable words such as *architecture, modillion, architrave,* and *fretwork* embellish the descriptions of new dwellings and the specifications for churches and courthouses. These words reflect a new desire to disguise the structural frame of a building beneath applied decorative elements. Exposed framing members, carefully finished with carved moldings, beads, and chamfers, disappeared, replaced by smooth planar surfaces and works of the joiner's art. The juncture of rafters, wallplate, and joists at the eaves were enclosed by *cornices*. Doorposts received decorative *frontispieces*. Interior walls were sheathed with wainscoting or plaster while corner posts were encased or *guttered* to hide their presence. Complex and sometimes intricately carved *chimney pieces* replaced chamfered *manteltrees*. Contracts grew longer as Southerners made specific choices of finish treatments and fashionable new items such as sash windows and paneled wainscoting. Specifications also clearly indicate that by the use of terms such as *out to out, in the clear,* and *pitch,* buildings began to be thought of in three dimensions with a concern for their overall appearance. Design drawings (mainly plans) now accompanied articles of agreement for the first time, fixing the relationship of apertures, chimneys, and partition walls according to the architectural principles of proportion and symmetry, hallmarks of a style that modern architectural historians have variously named classical, academic, or Georgian.

By the middle of the 18th century, Southerners began to import an ever-growing number of English architectural books that provided builders and some clients with the images and the precepts of classical design. This classical language of architecture, with its accompanying set of rules governing the shape, proportioning, and combination of elements, received a strong boost from professionally trained craftsmen who immigrated from the British Isles. Cognizant of its cachet and the desire among the wealthiest colonists to emulate cosmopolitan tastes, joiners, cabinetmakers, and bricklayers made the self-conscious language and knowledge of Georgian architecture an essential element of their workshops and practice. In 1769, Ezra Waite, "Civil Architect, House-builder in general, and Carver, from London," proclaimed in the newspaper his ability to provide such expertise. He offered proof of his talents and understanding of the intricacies of this system in the *tabernacle frames,* cornices, architraves, and other carved woodwork he fabricated for Miles Brewton's house in Charleston. He appealed to men of good taste that "if on inspection of the above mentioned work, and twenty-seven years experience, both in theory and practice, in noblemen and gentlemen's seats, be sufficient to recommend, he flatters himself to give satisfaction to any gentleman, either by plans, sections, elevations, or executions."[5] However, this wave of fashion, which Waite exemplified and rode full crest, did not wash away the older language and practice of traditional building. Classical *cyma* and *ovolo* moldings remained *ogees* and *quarter rounds* to the builders who worked on the best churches in Charleston as well as simple farmhouses in North Carolina and Delaware. Acknowledging the forms of classical design, the language of building nonetheless remained distinctly vernacular except among cabinetmakers, some joiners, and other craftsmen like Waite and John Hawks, the architect of Tryon's Palace in New Bern, for whom high fashion created choices of finishes and details and dictated the calling out of explicit design features.

Provincial architecture was not a diminished image of metropolitan design ideas, diluted or distorted by rude or ill-trained artisans unable to comprehend the sophistication and complexity of the original forms. Rather, Southern architecture was selective in nature: colonists carefully chose those aspects of the metropolitan and academic

---

5. *South Carolina Gazette and Country Journal,* August 22, 1769.

corpus that suited their own peculiar needs and desires.[6] Academic design concepts and the language that accompanied these ideas did not displace the local vernacular but became intricately woven into the native building tradition, creating distinctive regional forms. Many features of this 18th-century academic architecture—such as rubbed brickwork, hipped roofs, and oval windows—merged with local elements and practices from the previous century so that the great houses, courthouses, and churches constructed in the late colonial period were blends of Anglo-Georgian ideals and creole building practices. Colonial merchants and planters built double-pile dwellings but arranged and used their rooms in a manner that diverged from English practices. In Virginia, county courthouses incorporated elements and images borrowed from English public buildings in such a manner as to devise a unique regional building type.[7]

Colonial Charleston, Annapolis, Williamsburg, and New Bern were not merely smaller and less lavish reflections of Georgian London. Among other features, open porches or *piazzas*, wood shingles, and beaded weatherboards set them apart. Social conditions, levels of wealth, access to materials, technological capabilities, craft skills, climate, and topography shaped each area's response to building forms. Unlike the production of some artifacts such as ceramics, fabrics, silver, and even furniture, which served simple functions and were made by one or only a handful of individuals in a few operations, the process of designing, building, and furnishing a house was a complex one involving the participation of dozens of people in various and ever-changing combinations and circumstances. Small elements such as a window architrave or even more complex pieces such as a mantel or paneled door may show few variations from examples illustrated in imported builders' books, but their execution, treatment, and combination with other elements almost in-

variably reveal local or regional patterns. Architrave moldings, balusters, paneled dados, and other Georgian details might attest to the superficial resemblances of dwellings in 18th-century Bristol and Charleston, but differences in materials, construction, scale, plans, and the arrangement of buildings in the landscape made the architectural character of the two ports as distinct as the accents of their inhabitants.

Regional variations remained firmly entrenched in the building process because much of the design and fabrication of buildings was left in the hands of skilled craftsmen. The thousand and one decisions about any building—the finish of a piece of material, the arrangement of the archwork over an aperture, or the detailing of a staircase—continued to be resolved by joiners, carpenters, and bricklayers on the job site. Although building specifications grew in their list of particulars as clients indicated their choices of treatments and details, many fundamental as well as minor elements were left to the traditional rules governing the execution of workmanlike craftsmanship.[8] Contracts may have required good, well-fired bricks and hard lime mortar but rarely did they specify types of brick bonding, mortar joint widths and finishes, or range of brick colors. It was understood by longstanding experience what was expected and any variation from time-honored practices of a particular locality required explicit explanation. Thus, the uniformity in color of the brickwork in Charleston in the late colonial period distinguishes it from the characteristic penchant for variegated surfaces in the Chesapeake. Each region had evolved its own standards of practice. While the dimensioning of framing members was frequently included in specifications, less was said about the spacing of studs, posts, joists, and rafters or the types of joints used to secure these elements together. What was not spelled out was left to custom, so that tradition continued to shape the form and finish of most buildings erected in the colonial period.

A hallmark of 18th-century southern architecture was the growth in the specialization of building types and room uses. At the beginning of the century, there were few distinguishing features that

6. Dell Upton, "Vernacular Domestic Architecture in Eighteenth-Century Virginia," *Winterthur Portfolio* 17 (Summer/Autumn 1982): 95–119.

7. Carl Lounsbury, "The Structure of Justice: The Courthouses of Colonial Virginia," in *Perspectives in Vernacular Architecture III*, edited by Thomas Carter and Bernard Herman (Columbia: University of Missouri Press, 1989), pp. 214–226; and "'An Elegant and Commodious Building': William Buckland and the Design of the Prince William County Courthouse," *Journal of the Society of Architectural Historians* 46 (September 1987): 228–240.

8. See Catherine W. Bishir, "Good and Sufficient Language for Building," in *Perspectives in Vernacular Architecture IV*, edited by Thomas Carter and Bernard Herman (Columbia: University of Missouri Press, 1991), pp. 44–52.

differentiated the exterior of a store from a dwelling or a courthouse from a stable. The hull of the same wooden frame could have been used for any one of them and the similarity of size, scale, and finish treatment belied any functional differences. Rearrangement of the furniture or movement of a partition wall could turn a dwelling into a courthouse or a store into a stable. Gradually, the growth of highly specialized functions requiring specific furniture, spatial arrangements, light, finishes, and details transformed people's perceptions of the nature and form of public, commercial, agricultural, and domestic structures. Courthouses acquired large-scale openings, arcades, and cupolas on their exteriors and specialized fittings for officials on the inside. Store owners constructed buildings with large apertures or bow windows on the front of the shop but few or no openings along side walls, which were lined with shelves. Large trade signs hung from shop fronts and long sales counters inside provided additional space for merchants to display their wares. Many fashionable taverns shed their domestic appearance by the construction of an enclosed bar, and their plans accommodated large public entertaining rooms that sometimes rivaled the best merchant houses with their marble chimney pieces and other genteel decorations and furnishings. Churches grew in scale and acquired cupolas and steeples. The architecture of city and countryside became more diversified as specialized functions shaped the form, finish, and materials of many structures. In the course of the century, theaters, warehouses, schools, exchanges, smokehouses, dairies, and kitchens became recognizable building types.

Domestic architecture shared in this growing specialization of space as Southerners reordered the manner in which they worked, slept, dined, and socialized in their dwellings. In the century before the Revolution, room configurations and uses underwent profound alterations driven by needs for personal privacy and functional segregation. Throughout the 17th century and much of the next, most individuals occupied multipurpose, communal living spaces where household chores, entertaining, eating, and sleeping occurred within one or two rooms. The communal nature of these rooms was evident in the nonspecialized goods and furnishings that filled them. Benches, chairs, and tables served many pur-

poses. Owing to the growth of genteel refinement that redefined the rules of personal and public behavior, the advent of a consumer revolution that resulted in the importation or manufacture of thousands of household and personal goods, and changes in the dynamics of familial behavior, there was a growing tendency to rearrange and segregate domestic activity into discrete locations. A new emphasis on entertaining guests away from the daily chores of household work led to the setting aside of rooms for the reception of visitors. Such rooms contained specialized implements for their entertainment such as new forms of seating furniture, tea sets, and fashionable dining equipage. To underscore the social importance of these new entertaining spaces, *dining rooms, drawing rooms,* and *saloons* received the best architectural finishes, having carved chimney pieces, paneled wainscoting, paperhangings, or built-in buffets in which to display costly china and glass. Other specialized rooms and spaces appeared to contain separate activities such as a *library* or *nursery,* or to segregate visitors and servants from members of the family such as the *passage* and *servants' hall.* With the growing concern for individual space, the number of *bedchambers* in large houses began to increase.[9] As in other spheres, these changes in the dynamics of domestic life spawned a wealth of new terms and names for rooms. Although English terminology provided the precedent, Southerners appropriated these terms to describe their own peculiar circumstances.

In the decades following the Revolution, bookish men such as Thomas Jefferson and a rising generation of professional architects led by Benjamin Henry Latrobe, Robert Mills, and William Nichols attempted to move building to a level of self-conscious complexity and refinement that required a degree of specificity previously unseen. These men saw buildings as exemplars of taste and in their view the South along with the rest of the new nation had few monuments worthy of its political and cultural ideals. What they saw as ill-proportioned public buildings and unassuming dwellings exposed a wide gulf between the ideal

9. See Mark R. Wenger, "The Central Passage in Virginia: Evolution of an Eighteenth-Century Living Space," in *Perspectives in Vernacular Architecture II,* edited by Camille Wells (Columbia: University of Missouri Press, 1986), pp. 137–149; and "The Dining Room in Early Virginia," in *Perspectives in Vernacular Architecture III,* edited by Thomas Carter and Bernard Herman (Columbia: University of Missouri Press, 1989), pp. 149–159.

and the traditional. Jefferson was a harsh judge of the older forms. In *Notes on the State of Virginia,* his criticism of the second capitol in Williamsburg (1753) expressed this dissatisfaction. The two-story building was "a light and airy structure, with a portico in front of two orders, the lower of which, being Doric, is tolerably just in its proportions and ornaments, save only that the intercolumnations are too large. The upper Ionic is much too small for that on which it is mounted, its ornaments not proper to the order, nor proportioned within themselves. It is crowned with a pediment, which is too large for its span. Yet on the whole, it is the most pleasing piece of architecture we have."[10] The harmony was in the details and anything that failed to measure up to such rigorous standards was repudiated as naive at best and barbaric at worst. In his travels throughout the upper South, Latrobe observed numerous examples of the misapplication of classical detailing and took time to sketch an improperly designed Tuscan entablature on the Loudoun County courthouse in Leesburg, Virginia.[11] A few builders and carpenters recognized and understood these new rules of classical scholarship, but the accompanying grammar was scarcely evident in their designs or in the contractual language that described their work. Although terms such as *caulicole, gutta, intercolumniation, list, module, parastata, peripteral,* and *socle* had been used and illustrated in English architec-

tural books since the beginning of the 18th century, few except John Hawks in New Bern tried to apply the rules or terms of classical architecture to the world of building design. Jefferson was one of the first individuals to grasp the nuances of proportioning and detailing inherent in this system and tried to impose order on the orders in South. His understanding of this arcane knowledge was embodied and expressed in the use of this specialized language.

Older vernacular ways of conveying information no longer suited these heralds of sophisticated international design. In the state capitol in Richmond and the nation's capitol in Washington, Jefferson and Latrobe invoked design sources that stood well beyond the local or even regional building tradition. Professional architects left little to chance as contracts called for builders to follow specific designs and detailed working drawings.[12]

The architect's drawing dislodged the job site methods of the carpenter's rule as the arbiter of form. Relaxed attitudes toward classical proportioning had no place in a world where capitals and entablatures were based on specific classical examples that had been measured and drawn in painstaking detail. Latrobe and the growing coterie of professional architects soon expanded the southern architectural vocabulary. However, in doing so, these practitioners built on a vast substructure of traditional terms that reflected a solidly rooted vernacular building process, one that would flourish well into the 19th century.

---

10. Thomas Jefferson, *Notes on the State of Virginia,* edited by W. Peden (Chapel Hill: University of North Carolina Press, 1955), pp. 152–153.

11. Edward C. Carter II, John C. Van Horne, and Charles E. Brownell, eds., *Latrobe's View of America, 1795–1820* (New Haven, Yale University Press, 1985), p. 334.

12. See Catherine W. Bishir, Charlotte V. Brown, Carl R. Lounsbury, and Ernest H. Wood III, *Architects and Builders in North Carolina: A History of the Practice of Building* (Chapel Hill: University of North Carolina Press, 1990), pp. 120–128.

An Illustrated Glossary of
Early Southern Architecture and Landscape

abacus The uppermost member of a capital, often a square slab but sometimes molded and ornamented, on top of which rests the lower part of the entablature.

> 1802 Carpenter's accounts for John Tayloe's Washington town house included charge for "Abacus's 10/2 Bases 10/...2 plints 5/...2 Capitel Columns 10/." Tayloe Papers, VHS.
>
> 1819 In ordering marble from Italy for the University of Virginia, Thomas Jefferson preferred that the Corinthian capitals should "have only the ovolo of the abacus carved." Lambeth and Manning, *Thomas Jefferson as an Architect*.

abutment A large mass such as a pier or wall, generally of masonry, that counteracts the thrust of an arch or vault.

> 1811 Specifications for a wharf in Hampton, Virginia, stated that "the corners and abutments of the logs should be fastened with inch square Iron bolts." Elizabeth City Co., Va., Deed and Will Book 1809–1818.
>
> 1826 The cracks in the tower and portico of a church were "caused by the removal of that mass of brick work which filled up the space, now occupied by the tower stair, as thereby the North Arch of the Vestibule lost a main part of one of its Abutments, which produced in it a tendency to spread." St. Philip's Parish, Charleston, S.C., Vestry Book.

abacus
Fullerton House, 15 Legare Street, Charleston, S.C.

academy A secondary school or institution of higher learning. In architecture, a building housing such a school. By the end of the 18th century, most large towns in the South had one or more academies, many of which were located in purpose-built, two-story brick and frame structures. See also **schoolhouse**.

> 1766 In New Bern, "the schoolhouse is at length inclosed & . . . is a large & decent Edifice for such a young country, forty five feet in Length & Thirty in Breadth. . . . Twould give me great satisfaction to see a little flourishing Academy in this place." SPG Letterbook B, SPGFP.
>
> 1800 An "Academy in the town of Edenton" was to be built "52 feet long 21 feet wide, 2 stories high with two rooms on each floor and a passage of 10 feet wide." *Encyclopedian Instructor and Farmers Gazette*.
>
> 1816 "SEALED proposals will be received in Sparta [Georgia] . . . for building an ACADEMY . . . of the following dimensions: 52 feet long by 25 feet wide—22 feet pitch including the floors—the ground floor to have two rooms; the upper floors two rooms—two flights of stairs." Washington, Ga., *The News*.

acanthus A common herbaceous plant of the Mediterranean region, traditionally considered the inspiration for the Corinthian capital. A stylized representation of the plant's large, scalloped, pointed leaves and spiny stalks also appears in the Composite order. Carved, molded, or cast acanthus ornament was also applied to such elements as friezes, keystones, and consoles.

acanthus
Pavilion 3, University of Virginia

acroteria (acroterion, acroterium) The pedestals on the sides and apex of pediments on which statues are placed. Sometimes the term refers to the statues on the pedestals as well.

adz (adze, ads, adds) A cutting tool with the metal blade set at right angles to the wooden handle. Carpenters used a long-handled adz to remove large surface areas when squaring timbers. Coopers employed a short-handled adz to cut the bevel edges at the top and bottom of a barrel or cask.

air hole A small opening in masonry foundations intended to provide ventilation to preserve wood framing and flooring.

air hole
Tuckahoe, Goochland County, Va.

1727 It was noted that a "Workman [was] to make air holes through the church wall to preserve the floor." St. Helena's Parish, S.C., Vestry Book.

1770 In Richmond County, Virginia, a planter noted that "my prize house has been hanging too many plants on a stick, for in spite of every thing but scaffolding it will everyday grow wet and funkey, though I have large air holes cut every where." *Diary of Landon Carter*, 1.

1794 At Mount Vernon, George Washington observed that "when this last work is done, that is, underpinning the house, it must be remembered that air holes is left in it, to prevent the Sleepers from rotting." *MLIHS*, 4.

1813 Foundations of a jail were to have "are Holes at the distance of three feet all round the wall of 4 Inches wide and 2 1/2 Inches in highth." Wayne Co., N.C., Miscellaneous Court Records, NCA&H.

aisle (aile, isle, ile)   **1.** A passage in a church between seats or pews. The term was in use in the South by the early 18th century and is thought to have been confused with the more customary term *alley*. However, by the beginning of the 19th century, it supplanted *alley* to describe such a passageway. See also **alley** (1).

1703 An order was made "to brick the Ile of the Brick Church from dore to dore." St. Peter's Parish, New Kent Co., Va., Vestry Book.

1734 In a new church "the Isle [is to be] Eight foot wide Laid with Portland Stone and Bristol Marble." Bristol Parish, Prince George Co., Va., Vestry Book.

1765 Charleston merchant Gabriel Manigault "made a present of 950 red tile for flooring the Iles" of Pompion Hill chapel in St. Thomas's Parish, South Carolina. SPG Letterbook B, SPGFP.

1784 It was ordered that "as soon as the Gallery be compleated that all Negros and other servants be required to take their seat in those places and by no means be permitted to sit in the Isles or about the Door ways." Congregational Church, Charleston, S.C., Record Book.

2. A division within a church, generally divided longitudinally by a row of columns, pillars, or an arcade. The usage of the term in this sense rarely appeared before the 19th century.

alabaster   A fine, translucent variety of sulphate of lime, generally white in color. It was used in architecture for decorative ornament.

1803 For sale: "A few handsome Italian Marble chimney pieces with Jams and Alabaster Chimney Ornaments." *Alexandria Advertiser and Commercial Intelligencer*.

alcove   **1.** A small recessed space opening into a room, generally as a place for a bed in a bedchamber.

1808 A workman described the progress of construction at Thomas Jefferson's house at Poplar Forest in Bedford County, Virginia: "Mr. Perry has laid the flow in west rooms and is now studing the alcove" in the bed chamber. Coolidge Collection, Massachusetts Historical Society.

2. A recess or niche in a garden or pleasure ground.   The term originally referred to an area surrounded by a wall or hedge, but in the late 18th century came to refer to any covered retreat like a bower or summerhouse.

1801 At John Burgwin's plantation near Wilmington, North Carolina, "the Gardens were large . . . There was alcoves and summer houses at the termination of each walk, seats under trees in the more shady recesses of the Big Garden." *Autobiography and Diary of Mrs. Eliza Clitherall*.

ale house   **1.** A house where beer, liquors, and other spirituous drinks are sold. The term appears infrequently in the 17th century and rarely in the 18th century. See also **ordinary, tavern**.

1663 Virginia legislators debated "whether it was not more profitable to purchase [a building for a statehouse] then to continue for ever at the expence, accompanied with the dishonour of all our laws being made and our judgments given in ale-houses." Hening, *Statutes at Large*, 2.

2. A building used for the storage or manufacture of beer and ale. The meaning of the term in this second sense is rare.

> **1829** On a plantation was "one ale house four by five" feet in size. Sussex Co., Del., Orphans Court Valuations P.

alley (allée ally)   **1.** A passage in a church between seats and pews. By the early 18th century, the term used in this sense was often replaced by *aisle*. At the end of the century it had all but disappeared. See also **aisle** (2).

> **1683** It was ordered that "new pavement [be] laid in the chancell and alley" of the Great Church. Christ Church Parish, Middlesex Co., Va., Vestry Book.
> **1690** A craftsman was "to lay ye Chancel and Ally with plank." St. Peter's Parish, New Kent Co., Va., Vestry Book.
> **1752** In a new church "the Alleys [are] to be laid with Flag Stones or Tyle made for that Purpose." Trinity Parish, Charles Co., Md., Vestry Book.

2. A narrow passage between buildings, or a narrow street or lane.

> **1796** In laying off a new residential square, city ordinance required that "there shall be a foot way five feet wide upon each side of each alley paved with brick and the remainder of each of the said alleys paved with a proper paving stone." Alexandria, Va., Hustings Court Order Book 1796–1797.
> **1804** An order was issued to "employ a Bricklayer to repair the Foot pavement at the Corner of Saint Michael's Alley." St. Michael's Parish, Charleston, S.C., Vestry Book.

3. In a formal garden or pleasure ground, a walkway bordered with single or double rows of trees or hedges. The term sometimes referred to the walkway space in the garden between beds of plants bordered by low-growing shrubs.

> **1753** A garden in Charleston was "genteelly laid out in walks and alleys with flower-knots, & laid round with bricks." *South Carolina Gazette.*

almshouse   A building or group of buildings erected for the charitable reception of the poor. Although the term appears throughout the South, the more common name given to this public-supported institution was *poorhouse*. See also **poorhouse, workhouse.**

> **1707** Workmen were paid "for building an almshouse." St. Paul's Parish, Hanover Co., Va., Vestry Book.
> **1754** Vestry ordered "that the alms house that is to be built in Suffolk town be raised two feet in the walls all round so that the floors be ten feet from the ceiling." Upper Parish, Nansemond Co., Va., Vestry Book.
> **1766** A notation in a vestry book read: "Agreed that Sarah Nelmes to have the room over the room where Mrs. Brathwait resides in the old Alms House." St. Philip's Parish, Charleston, S.C., Vestry Book.
> **1770** An Advertisement was placed for "any Persons willing to undertake the building of an Alms and Work-House, for the Use of the Poor and vagrants" of Anne Arundel County, Maryland. *Maryland Gazette.*

altar (alter)   Specifically, an elevated table; more generally, a raised area where sacrificial and commemorative offerings are made to a deity. In some Christian churches that celebrated the eucharist or communion service, the altar was the consecrated place for this act. In colonial America, Anglican liturgical requirements called for the altar to be enclosed by a railing or balustrade on a raised platform in the east end of the church or chapel. Southern Anglicans primarily used the term *altar* to refer to the area where the service occurred and preferred the term *communion table* to describe the furniture on which it was celebrated. By contrast, other denominations and sects placed their altars or communion tables in a variety of locations, usually near the pulpit, and only infrequently enclosed them with balustrades or raised them off the church floor.

> 1715   The "Oiles & Alter" were to be laid "Herring-Bone Fashion" with brick in a parish church. St. Paul's Parish, Kent Co., Md., Vestry Book.
>
> 1734   An Anglican church was to have "a Compas alter with railes and banestered and a table." Blisland Parish, James City and New Kent Cos., Va., Vestry Book.
>
> 1763   In the east end of a church, "the alter [was] to be neatly wainscotted with good pine plank as high as the windows." Wicomico Parish, Northumberland Co., Va., Vestry Book.
>
> 1793   The minister was to "chuse freely a text from the Bible to preach upon, but to read the Gospel and Epistle from the Altar." St. John's Lutheran Church, Charleston, S.C., Minute Book.

altarpiece

altarpiece (alter piece, aulter peace)   A decorative sculpture, painting, or tablet placed behind or over an altar; a reredos. Required by church law in colonial Anglican worship, altarpieces consisted of tablets containing the Ten Commandments and, frequently, the Lord's Prayer and Apostles' Creed. Sometimes these tablets were elaborately carved architectural screens with pilasters and pediments.

> 1719   The churchwarden was ordered "to divide the Altar piece and sett up the same each side of the east window." Christ Church Parish, Middlesex Co., Va., Vestry Book.
>
> 1727   St. James, Goose Creek, South Carolina, had an "alter piece decently beautified with paintings and guildings grave and commendable." SPG Letterbook A, SPGFP.
>
> 1739   The vestry ordered "the Aulter peace to be Neatly Painted: the Ground work of the Pannels to be Jappand; the Creed, Lords Prayor & Ten Commandments to be Done in a Leagable hand in fair Gold letters and All Carvingwork to be Guilded." Petsworth Parish, Gloucester Co., Va., Vestry Book.
>
> 1771   "The dimentions of the alterpeace mentioned in the Articles with the undertaker for building the New Church are not according to the proportions of Architecture, the said undertaker is authorized and desired to make the same according to the true proportions of the Ionic order." Truro Parish, Fairfax Co., Va., Vestry Book.

American bond   See **bond.**

amphitheater (amphitheatre)   An open or enclosed circular or oval building with tiers of seats around a central open area, used for theatrical performances, exhibitions, games, and other public entertainments. Also any room that has such an arrangement of tiered seats and central stage.

> 1783   At one end of the ground floor in the statehouse in Annapolis, "there are raised seats in the form of an amphitheater designed for the meetings of the high courts." Schöepf, *Travels in the Confederation.*
>
> 1813   It was advertised in Charleston that at the "Amphitheatre. THIS EVENING . . . will be exhibited a grand and brilliant representation of Feats of HORSEMANSHIP." *City Gazette and Commercial Advertiser.*

ancone   A scroll-shaped bracket or console supporting a cornice, mantel shelf, or the entablature over a door, window, or niche. See also **bracket.**

andiron (an iron, handiron)   One of a pair of long metal bars raised on short feet and terminated at the front end by a longer upright piece, often decoratively treated, used for holding logs in a fireplace. Andirons typically appear in inventories of fireplace tools. The terms *dog* and *dog iron* also appear in colonial and early national records to describe this implement.

> **1776** "Mr. Edmund Bull gave his acct. for making a pr of Andirons & Tongs & Shovel." St. George's Parish, Harford Co., Md., Vestry Book.
> **1814** An order appeared as follows: "Sheriff to purchase two pair of and irons for the use of the jury rooms of the courthouse." Goochland Co., Court Order Book 1813–1819.

angle brace A piece of scantling set diagonally between two framing members to provide structural rigidity. The most common angle braces are downbraces and upbraces that run from a post to a sill or from a post to a plate or girder. See **brace** (1).

angle joist A joist running diagonally from an internal girder to the corner intersection of two wall plates, used to support the feet of hip rafters. See also **dragon beam**.

> **1790** Carpenter's bill for Hampton in Baltimore County, Maryland, included "18 sqr 72 ft of fraiming angle joice @ 15s pr sqr." *MHM*, 33.

angle rafter A rafter at the junction of two planes of a hip roof, more commonly called a hip rafter. See also **hip rafter.**

annulet A small fillet encircling the shaft of a column. In particular, it is one of a series of fillets just below the echinus of a Doric capital.

annulet
Pavilion 10, University of Virginia

anta (*pl.* antae; in antis) A pilaster or pillar at the corner of a building, especially associated with a portico. Its base and capital often differ from the order appearing elsewhere in the building. The plural form of the term is most commonly used. The phrase *in antis* describes a portico that recedes into, rather than projects from, a building. Its columns range with the front wall of the structure and are set between the antae at each outer corner. *Antae* and *in antis* begin to appear in the literature of American building in the first half of the 19th century. See also **parastatae.**

antechamber, anteroom A room that serves as an entrance and waiting area for a larger, more important room.

> **1734** "ANTE-CHAMBER: An outer Chamber, before the principal Chamber of an Apartment, where the Servants wait, and Strangers stay till the Person to be spoken withal is at Leisure, &c." *Builder's Dictionary*.
> **1814** The Governor's House in Raleigh was "to be somewhat similar in plan (tho' not in decorations) to Mr. Wickham's superb house in Richmond. The front 70 feet, depth 50 feet, and two stories high, besides the basement story. In front is a portico by which you enter the anti-chamber; from this you pass into the rotunda in the centre of the building, which is lighted by a lantern window in the roof." *The Star*.

anthemion A classical floral design loosely resembling the honeysuckle or palmette often found as a running ornament on friezes.

anthemion

apartment 1. A room or set of rooms in a dwelling or building set apart for the specific use of a person or for a particular function.

> **1697** Plans were made for "erecting a state house for the administration of Justice . . . in which we comprehend convenient apartments for all the offices of business in Annapolis, Maryland." Fulham Papers II, Lambeth Palace Library.
> **1787** A tavern "consisted of two Apartments, one was the sitting Room, the floor was of Clay or dirt. . . . The other Apartment was floored with Boards." Attmore, *Journal of a Tour to North Carolina.*

1814 Invitation to bid on the construction of a public jail in Wilkesboro, North Carolina, noted that the "jail is to be forty feet long and thirty feet wide- to be built of hewed timber and brick, with a stone foundation; to contain apartments for Debtors, Women, Criminals and Negroes, as the law requires; and also an apartment for the residence of the Jailor." *Raleigh Star.*

2. A separate division in a piece of furniture; a compartment.

1805 Orders for a courthouse included "a new Barr with double seats as required banister'd in front with apartments beneath. The top of them for papers, hats, etc." Loudoun Co., Va., Court Order Book 1805–1806.

aperture An opening or hole within a solid.

1755 "APERTURES—from the Latin signifying Opening, but in Architecture tis used to signify Doors, Windows, Stair-Cases, Chimnies, or other Conduits and in short all inlets and outlets for men, light, smoak, and etc." Salmon, *Palladio Londinensis.*
1803 In the specifications for a church, architect Robert Mills noted that "the requisite Apertures [are] to be made" in the brick walls. Johns Island Church Specifications, Library Society of Charleston.

apothecary shop A store or shop where drugs, spices, and other medicinal treatments were prepared and sold.

1816 The growing town of Lynchburg, Virginia, had "4 Apothecarie's Shops" in it. *Lynchburg Press.*

appentice See **pent.**

apprentice A young person who is legally bound to a craftsman for a specified period of time in order to learn the skills of a particular trade. First appearing in the third quarter of the 17th century in the Chesapeake, the apprenticeship system in the building trades evolved out of ancient English practice that promoted training through practical experience. When an apprentice entered into the service of a master craftsman, an indenture was usually drawn up that specified the obligation of each party. The master was to provide food, clothing, and lodging and promised to teach the youth the rudiments of his craft, as well as to read and write. The apprentice (who entered into service anywhere from the age of five or six, if the child were an orphan or bastard, to the more customary age of fourteen or fifteen) was instructed in all aspects of his trade, from the most subtle forms of design to the dull and repetitive tasks of fabrication. See also **master.**

1663 "Mathew Shipp & Thomas Manning were by Indenture bound Apprentices unto Richard Church for to learne the trade of a Carpenter . . . the sd Church imploainge them to worke in the ground contrary to agreement." Norfolk Co., Va., Will and Deed Book 1656–1666.
1695 "John Bentley, son of Richard Bentley, decd. with consent of his mother" apprenticed himself to Anthony Dawson, carpenter. Bentley agreed not to "absent himself from his masters service day nor night without consent from his said master, he shall not contract matrimony nor use no unlawful gaming as cards or dice. . . . Anthony Dawson must give sufficient meet, Drink, washing & Lodging & clothing for the term and also use his best endeavors to learn his said apprentice the full art & mistery of the carpenters trade, and also to endeavor to teach him to Read & to write & to deliver to him a Mare filly in May in the year 1698." Perquimans Co., N.C., Deed Book A.
1749 "John Chiles binds himself an apprentice to Mourning Richards for four years and ten months. Richards obliges himself to teach the sd Chiles the joiners trade and to find him sufficient clothing, meat, drink, washing, and lodging, and also to have him taught to read and write." Caroline Co., Va., Court Order Book 1746–1754.

1777 A carpenter charged his client 3 shillings a day for the work of his journeyman and "for work by my apprentis Stophel Heanat 2sh a day." Joseph Doll Ledger A, Frederick, Md.

apse A semicircular or polygonal space in a building, often forming a domed recess. In the early South, the east end of a few churches, county courthouses, and other public buildings terminated at one end in an apsidal projection. However, these semicircular and polygonally shaped areas enclosing an altar or magistrates' platform were rarely referred to as apses. Rather specifications generally called them arched, curved, or semicircular ends. See also **arch.**

1750 Specifications for a church noted that "the Gable end for the Chancel [are] to be arched the Arch Juting out wards in proportion to the dimentions" of the body. St. George's Parish, Harford Co., Md., Vestry Book.

1770 Specifications for a church stated that it was to be "thirty feet Wide within the Walls with a SimiCircle projected from the East end of the said Church of the Radius of Eleven feet from the Center of the outside of the Wall to be carried up with the end wall and united Circular by therewith at the distance of five feet from each Corner of the East end of the said Church." St. John's Parish, Queen Anne's Co., Md., Vestry Book.

aqueduct (aquaduct) An elevated or underground conduit for conveying water from place to place. See also **gutter.**

1621 Among the public works considered by the Virginia Company was the "building of Bridges, makinge of Highways, and Aquaductes." *Virginia Company Records,* 1.

1788 A workman was hired to "fix proper & sufficient Gutters or Aqueducts to convey the Water from the roof" of a church "into four leaden pipes to be fixed at the four Corners." St. Michael's Parish, Charleston, S.C., Vestry Book.

1812 Winchester, Virginia, was "watered by aqueducts, which are in every corner of the streets." *Diary of Elbridge Gerry.*

araeostyle See **intercolumniation.**

arbor (arbour, harbour) **1.** An impermanent shelter consisting of a leafy, shaded recess formed by tree branches, a trellis, or lattice work, sometimes found in gardens and pleasure grounds; also a shaded alley or walk. See also **bower.**

1746 The English victory at Culloden was celebrated in the village of Newcastle in Hanover County, Virginia, "where a handsome Dinner was provided; a long Arbour was set up, in which 50 Gentlemen and Ladies din'd." *Virginia Gazette.*

arbor (1) (*Left*) Charles Fraser, arbor, unknown location, South Carolina, 1796

arbor (2) (*Right*) Religious encampment, Virginia, early 19th century

1781 At an encampment of the British army in Hanover County, Virginia, "there was not one Tent . . . all of them lying under temporary sheds or arbours, made with boughs of Trees, fence rails etc." *VMHB*, 79.
1784 At a barbeque in Westmoreland County, Virginia, "We then dine[d] sumptuously under a large shady tree or an arbour made of green bushes." *Magazine of American History*, 1.

2. An open-air area where church congregations or revival gatherings met for preaching and communal services. Church arbors often consisted of covered shelters made from trees, branches, and vines supported on a framework under which ministers preached and some listeners gathered. In the early 19th century the temporary and rustic nature of such arbors was sometimes lost as congregations and camp meeting sponsors converted the canvas tents and preaching sheds of camp meeting grounds into more substantial and permanent structures. The large, framed, open preaching sheds continued to be called *arbors*, and the small wooden houses around them *tents*.

1713 A vestry paid its sexton "for building an Arbor." Christ Church Parish, Middlesex Co., Va., Vestry Book.
1737 "Seates & harbour" were constructed in a parish churchyard. Blisland Parish, James City and New Kent Cos., Va., Vestry Book.
1773 Baptists gathered for "a church meeting . . . at Clays arber." Chesterfield Co., Va., Baptist Church Minute Book.

arcade A covered walk or space open at one or both sides and supported by a series of arched openings. Arcades first appear in Virginia in the late 17th century in public buildings. By the second quarter of the 18th century, following the precedent set by the arcaded space linking the two wings of the capitol in Williamsburg, a number of county courthouses in the colony were erected with arcaded fronts. Throughout the colonial period, such arcades were often referred to as piazzas. Elsewhere, arcades could be found at the basement level of many open porches on dwellings and as links between main buildings and subsidiary structures. The term gained wider currency in the early 19th century. See also **piazza** (1).

1755 "ARCADE—A Range of arches with open places to walk, as that of Covent Garden, the Royal Exchange, and etc." Salmon, *Palladio Londinensis*.
1787 The two wings at Tryon's Palace in New Bern were "connected with the principal Building by a circular arcade reaching from each of the front Corners to the corner of the Wing." Attmore, *Journal of a Tour to North Carolina*.
1829 Specifications stated that the Madison County, Virginia, courthouse was "to be of brick 40 feet by 50 feet from out to out, including an arcade in the front 10 feet in the clear." Malcolm Crawford Papers, VSL.

arch **1.** Any architectural element or part of a building in the form of a curve. See also **compass.**

1679 The ceiling of a church was to take the form of "arches under neath the roof." Accomack Co., Va., Will, Deed, and Order Book 1678–1682.
1692 A courtroom was "to be ceiled and arched with good thin clapboards." Princess Anne Co., Va., Court Order Book 1691–1709.
1750 A brick church was planned to be 57-by-35 feet with "the Gable end for the Chancel to be arched the Arch Juting outwards in proportion to the dimentions . . . with a window in the Arch of ye Chancel End." St. George's Parish, Harford Co., Md., Vestry Book.

2. The arrangement of masonry or other material in the form of a curve to span an opening. The arch is composed of a series of discrete, wedge-shaped blocks known as voussoirs, whose narrower side

arcade
Pavilion 7, University of Virginia

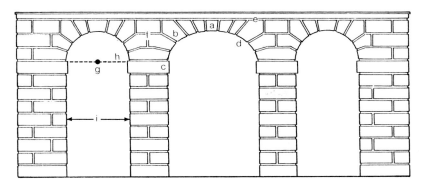

arch (2) Courthouse, Charleston, S.C., 1792. Elements of an arch: (a) keystone, (b) voussoir, (c) impost, (d) intrados, (e) extrados, (f) spandrel, (g) center, (h) spring line, (i) span

forms the intrados, or lower part of the opening, and that support one another by their mutual pressure. The uppermost voussoir at the center of the arch is the keystone. The solid part on which the arch is supported is the abutment. The springing or impost of the arch is the point where it meets the abutting support. Sometimes this point is accentuated by impost blocks consisting of decorative capitals, architraves, or simple masonry units projecting beyond the surface of the arch voussoirs. An archivolt is the decorative molded band or architrave that follows the outer curve or extrados of the arch. Arches varied widely in shape from flat to extremely acute, pointed ones. The most common were the flat or straight arch; segmental arches based on a segment of a circle; semicircular or compass-headed arches whose intrados is a semicircle; and elliptical arches whose intrados is formed by a number of center points or a semiellipse. Relieving arches located in cellars led some Delaware inventory takers to describe cellars as arch rooms. See also **abutment, arcade, archivolt, compass, extrados, impost, intrados, keystone, piazza** (1), **straight arch, vault, voussoir.**

1674 The porch on the Maryland statehouse was "to have an arch in front six foote wide in the Cleere and Eleven foote high to the Keystone of the Arch with two Arches on each side." *Archives of Maryland,* 2.

1736 Plans for a courthouse included "to have Eight Arches or Piazas in the outside wall frunting ye Courte." Spotsylvania Co., Va., Will Book 1722–1749.

1749 An agreement was made "to build a Roman Arch in the new Courthouse according to the plan lodg'd." Richmond Co., Va., Court Order Book 1746–1752.

1751 "Instead of Square Arches to the windows" in a church, they were to "have compass heads." Upper Parish, Nansemond Co., Va., Vestry Book.

1789 In New Bern, "the court-house is raised on brick arches, so as to render the lower part a convenient market-place." Morse, *American Geography.*

1811 Masonry work on a Baltimore town house included "cutting & setting 15 ft. Elliptical, rubbed, gauged arches @ 150 cts pr ft $22.50." Riddell Accounts, Pleasants Papers, MHS.

architect (architectus, architector) An individual engaged in the design and the supervision of construction of buildings and structures. The term was applied broadly throughout the colonial and early national period to individuals of diverse training, skills, and knowledge of architecture, each of whom played a variety of roles in the building process. The notion of an architect as a specially trained designer, highly conscious of the tradition and rules of architectural forms and tastes and whose primary responsibility was to provide the design of a building in a series of detailed measured drawings, held little currency in early America. It was not until the late 18th and early 19th centuries that men such as John Hawks, Benjamin Henry Latrobe, Robert Mills, and William Nichols played a distinctive new role and gave a modern meaning to the term. An architect was defined much more loosely, as design responsibilities and ornamental details for most projects lay in the hands of many individuals, from the client to the craftsman. Generally, the term was applied to any undertaker who was competent enough to direct construction of the most complex of buildings and who had some ability to conceive and execute a set of basic design drawings. Almost everyone described as an architect in the 18th and early 19th centuries had been trained in one of the building trades. Rounding out the group of recognized architects in this early period were a few men of higher social standing without craft training, who became engaged in design and building as contractual entrepreneurs. In this sense, the terms *architect* and *master builder* were nearly synonymous. See also **builder, contractor, undertaker.**

1680 Specifications for a courthouse noted "that all the several timbers thereto be good proportion & such regular scantling as shall be reasonably advised by any good Archytecktare." Talbot Co., Md., Judgement Book 1675–1682.

1740 Articles of agreement were made with "William Walker undertaker and Arthiteck of the County of Stafford for building certain bridges." Richmond Co., Va., Account Book 1724–1783.

1767 "ARTICLES OF AGREEMENT . . . between His Excellency William Tryon Esquire Captain General Governor and Commander in Chief in and over the province of North Carolina of the one part, and John Hawks of Newbern, architect of the other part" were signed to build a dwelling for the governor in New Bern, North Carolina, for a salary of £300 per annum. Carrying out the work would "be most effectually promoted by the constant inspection superintendence and industry of a person acquainted with the value of the work, qualified to adapt the proportions, experienced to direct the quality and choice of materials, and of ability to judge of the performance of the several artificers and tradesmen, to be employed in the said Building; His Excellency therefore desirous of facilitating the progress of the said undertaking, hath acceded to the proposals made by the said John Hawks on whose skill and integrity he relyes, for the faithful observance of the several covenants and agreements." *Correspondence of William Tryon,* 1.

1769 In Charleston, "EZRA WAITE, Civil Architect, House-builder in general, and Carver, from London, HAS finished the architecture, conducted the execution thereof, in the joiners way . . . of MILES BREWTON, Esquire's House." *South Carolina Gazette.*

1798 There was to be constructed a "Penitentiary in Richmond. . . . Proposals will be received &c. for executing the following Carpenters and Joiners Work . . . 2. Framing the principal roofs according to directions and drawings to be given by the Architect." *The Correspondence and Miscellaneous Papers of Benjamin Henry Latrobe,* 1.

1798 "As . . . both the employment of an architect and its concomitant expence appears to be new to the public Works of this State, I take the liberty to trouble you with the following explanatory remarks. . . . It is in France, Germany, and England the established custom of Architects . . . to charge for their works: 1. a commission of 5 Per Cent of the whole amount of the expence incurred in executing their design; 2. a certain sum for fair drawings, if furnished, according to their difficulty, number, or beauty; 3. if the work be at a distance from the usual residence of the Architect, all travelling expences, and a certain sum per day for loss of time." *The Correspondence and Miscellaneous Papers of Benjamin Henry Latrobe,* 1.

architecture The art, science, and practice of designing and constructing buildings and other structures. As it was used in early America, the term encompassed a broad range of interests and perspectives, from a concern for aesthetics, chiefly in the application of certain classical rules to the design of buildings and the shape and arrangement of ornaments, to the consideration of the functional aspects of building, including the arrangement and accommodation of spaces as well as the structural principles of materials and construction methods. Occasionally in the 18th century, users of the term would drop the last syllable.

> **1699** Specifications for St. Anne's Church in Annapolis noted that "if the demensions here incerted and the Scantlings of the timber here proposed shall not appear to be According to the Rules of Architecture then to Conforme the Same to such Rules." *Archives of Maryland, 22.*
> **1717** The estate of Richard Brown included "A chest of Carpenters tooles . . . [and] Andr Polados book of Architect." Lancaster Co., Va., Will and Inventory Book 1709–1727.
> **1743** "Having taken no notice for a while what Steps were taken towards building our Church" in Savannah, Georgia, "I well knowing my own Incapacity in Architecture did not Venture without proper help to form a plan, and Assign the just Dimensions." *The Journal of William Stephens 1743–1745.*
> **1752** In Charleston, St. Michael's Church "will be built on the Plan of one of Mr. Gibson's Designs; and, 'tis tho't, will exhibit a fine Piece of Architecture when compleated." *South Carolina Gazette.*
> **1755** As money was running out to construct St. Michael's in Charleston, a member of the building committee noted that the church was "made of such Dimensions as would the better accommodate a growing Town, & with such decent Ornaments of Architecture as are suitable to the Public Use of divine worship." Williams, *St. Michael's.*
> **1771** "It appears that the dimentions of the alterpeace mentioned in the Articles with the undertaker for building the New Church are not according to the proportions of Architecture." Truro Parish, Fairfax Co., Va., Vestry Book.
> **1771** At St. John's Church in Granville County, North Carolina, "there shall be no Joists but end Joists except such Short Joists as are Necessary According to the Rules of Architecture in framing a Cove Arch or Concave Roof." Francis Hawks Collection, Church Historical Society, Austin.
> **1777** "MARDUN V. EVINGTON . . . would be glad to be employed as a master workman in the various branches of architecture, either in publick or private buildings, from the most elegant and superb, down to the gentleman's plain country seat." *Virginia Gazette.*

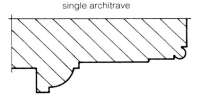

single architrave

architrave (architrive)   **1.** The lowest division of the entablature that rests on the abaci of columns.

> **1790** A carpenter's work at Hampton in Baltimore included "16 plain pilaster under architraves." *MHM, 33.*
> **1798** At the White House in Washington, "the stone work has been carried up from the window heads of the 3d story, to the level of the roof, including the architrave, frieze, and cornice." *The Observatory.*

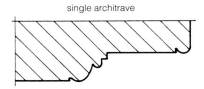

single architrave

2. The linear ornamental moldings and bands that surround a window, door, panel, niche, or other opening. A *single architrave* consisted of a bead at the opening, followed by a broad band and terminated by a raised molding with a fillet on the outside. The more elaborate *double architrave*, generally used in superior spaces, had two bands in different planes separated most commonly by a cyma or ovolo molding. Distinctions between single and double architraves expressed a clear sense of hierarchy between simple and elaborate finish within a building or even a room. See also **archivolt, banded architrave, facing.**

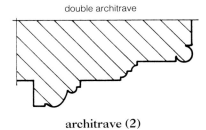

double architrave

architrave (2)

> **1711** Building specifications called for courthouse "Lights over the door worked with Archytrive on the sd Doore Case the front to have archytrive Transome windows all the other windows to be plain tramsome windows." Talbot Co., Md., Land Records RF No. 12.
> **1746** Plans for Charles Pinckney's dwelling in Charleston called for "6, six panneld doors the frames or cases double architraved." Huger Smith, *Dwelling Houses of Charleston.*

1783 In the drawing room of the Governor's House in New Bern, there were "kneed architraves to the windows." Hawks Letter, Miranda Papers, Academia Nacional de la Historia, Caracas.

1802 The ground floor of a dwelling house in Washington was "finished Plaine" with "Single faced arcatrives Round Doors & windows," while the principal rooms in the second story had "Double faced arcatrives Round doors & windows." INA Records, CIGNA Archives.

1828 "All the windows and door frames" in a Virginia courthouse were "to be finished on the out and inside, with double raised architraves, plain jambs and window seats." Malcolm Crawford Papers, VSL.

archivolt The continuous curved architrave molding of an arch. The term was rarely used, as most builders called an *archivolt* a *circular architrave*. See also **arch** (2), **architrave** (2).

area An excavated open space in front of a building that provides light and access for a subterranean or partially submerged cellar, usually enclosed by a fence or palisade.

c. 1767 Architect John Hawks's drawing of the ground-floor plan of the Governor's House in New Bern noted that the space extending across the front facade was to have an "area" for access into the service rooms in the cellar. Public Records Office, London.

1802 The bill for blacksmith's work at the Tayloe house in Washington, D.C., included "2 rails & Bannister 330 lb . . . 2 ramps for areas 47 lb . . . 1 Rail & Bannisters for Kitchen . . . 6 Ramps 123 lb . . . 4 Bannisters 24 lb . . . 3 Braces for area." Tayloe Papers, VHS.

armature Embedded skeletal framework of wood or iron used to strengthen and consolidate decorative plasterwork.

armory (armoury) A building or place where arms and other munitions are stored or manufactured. See also **magazine, powder house.**

1767 In Charleston, a new watch house was to be built "in Broad Street, between the public armory, statehouse, St. Michael's church and the market." *South Carolina Gazette.*

1812 At Harper's Ferry, an English traveler observed "a manufactory of arms of which 13,000 stand were lying ready in the armoury." Foster, *Jeffersonian America.*

1817 In Annapolis, "the armory is tastefully arranged, and the arms in excellent order." *The Diaries of Martha Ogle Forman.*

arris A sharp edge made at the junction of two surfaces, such as between flutes on a Doric column.

1773 The windows in the debtors room in a prison in Edenton, North Carolina were to be secured by "7 upright Inch and quarter Iron Bars set arris and let thro' flat bars two or three in number." Hawks Papers, SHC.

arsenal A building or place containing arms and other military equipment; an armory used for the storage or manufacture of arms. See also **armory, magazine.**

1784 Payment was made for guarding "the Arsenal" in the attic of the South Carolina statehouse in Charleston. South Carolina Treasury Records, Journal 1783–1791. SCA&H.

1798 "I had understood that it was the intention of the Government to erect an Arsenal and a Manufactory of arms at Harpers ferry." *Virginia Journals of Benjamin Henry Latrobe,* 2.

artificial lake, pond A man-made body of water constructed in a pleasure ground near a dwelling, for recreation, food, ice, and beauty.

1736 A plantation for sale near Charleston contained "an artificial fish-pond, always supplied by fresh springs, and well stored with several sorts of fish." *South Carolina Gazette.*

1806 At Riversdale in Prince George's County, Maryland, "Birch drew us a plan for the grounds. He thinks an artificial lake would be better on the south of the house than on the north since the terrain is better adapted." Two years later, the "lake just finished, which looks like a large river on the southern side, gives a very beautiful effect and furnishes us at the same time with fish and ice for our ice-house." *Letters of Rosalie Stier Calvert.*

ash Any of a variety of hardwood trees of the genus *Fraxinus* commonly found throughout the South. Ash flooring and scantling were occasionally employed in building, but the wood was more commonly used for spokes, handles, and furniture.

1709 "Of Ash we have two sorts, agreeing nearly with the English in Grain. One of our sorts is tough, like the English, but differs something in the Leaf, and much more in the Bark." Lawson, *A New Voyage to Carolina.*

1774 "Plank and Scantling to be sold" at a "Saw Mill, near Aylett's Warehouse, Mattapony River" in King William County, Virginia, included "White Oak, Black Walnut, Sweet Gum, Ash, Poplar, Birch." *Virginia Gazette.*

ash house An outbuilding for the storage of ash, used in making soap or in gardens.

1824 An orphan's estate in Delaware had on it "one framed ash house five feet by three." Sussex Co., Del., Orphans Court Valuations N.

ashlar
Mount Airy, Richmond County, Va.

ashlar (ashler) Squared and finished building stone.

1801 Stonecutters' accounts for work on John Tayloe's Washington, D.C., residence included "Moulded Astragle Steps & Landings . . . Circular ends and Scrools . . . Ashler to Steps." Tayloe Papers, VHS.

1805 At the Capitol in Washington, "the Wall North of the return [is] to be carried up with plain Ashler." *The Correspondence and Miscellaneous Papers of Benjamin Henry Latrobe*, 1.

ashler (ashlering, ashlin, ashling) Short upright stud between the sloping rafter and flooring in a garret that forms the knee wall.

1726 There is a notation for "ASHLERING - quartering in Garrets about 2 1/2 or 3 feet high, perpendicular to the Floor, up to the under side of the rafters." Neve, *City and Country Purchaser*, London.

1730 Carpenters were "to put up Ceiling Joyce and ashlers for the plaistering above stairs" of an Anglican parsonage house. Prince Frederick, Winyah Parish, S.C., Vestry Book.

1745 Repairs to a glebe house garret called for "ashlers to be put up around the whole house & well plaister'd & white wash'd." Christ Church Parish, Lancaster Co., Va., Vestry Book.

1790 At Hampton in Baltimore County, a carpenter's bill noted: "To work in the garrot . . . to 34 feet ashlins under dormont windows at 3d [and] to 30 sqr 60 feet of squir joint rough flooring under ashlins." *MHM*, 33.

ashler
Cupola House, Edenton, N.C.

assembly room A room or suite of rooms in a tavern, hotel, market house, or town hall where social gatherings such as balls and other entertainments were held. Following an English fashion that developed in the 1710s, public assemblies appeared in the southern colonies by the middle of the 18th century, when a few enterprising tavernkeepers and corporations erected purpose-built structures or rooms for meetings of polite society. Generally consisting of a large ballroom with smaller ancillary rooms, assembly rooms were first used for balls, conversation, cards, and tea. These assemblies were either private affairs or open to the public through subscription tickets. Gradually, the range of entertainments expanded to include theatrical performances, concerts, magic shows, lectures, and public dinners. See also **ballroom, long room.**

> 1766 Property was sold in Annapolis "for the use of a Public Ball House or Assembly Rooms thereon to be built." Anne Arundel Co., Md., Land Record Book 1763–1768.
>
> 1771 "For the BENEFIT of Mr. SCHNEIDER, At the Assembly Room in ANNAPOLIS, Will be a BALL. . . . Ticket One Dollar, which admits One Person." *Maryland Gazette.*
>
> 1772 In Charleston, a "CONCERT . . . AT PIKE'S NEW ASSEMBLY-ROOM, Will be performed. . . . The whole Sum that may be raised on this Occasion, to be laid out for a covered WAY and elegant PORTICO next the Street; thereby to enable Ladies and Gentlemen always to go to the New Suit of Rooms without being incommoded by the Weather." *South Carolina Gazette.*
>
> 1786 A three-story brick house for rent in Richmond had on the third floor three rooms "so constructed that they may occasionally be thrown into one large Assembly Hall 60 by 24 with a fireplace in each end." *Virginia Gazette.*
>
> 1788 In Wilmington, North Carolina, "last evening a polite and numerous audience were most agreeably amused at the Assembly Room in the Borough Tavern, with Mr. Godwin's Lecture on Heads." *The Wilmington Centinel and General Advertiser.*

astragal A small, convex, half-round molding that projects beyond the adjoining surface. Generally found in conjunction with other moldings such as a cavetto, cyma, or an ovolo.

> 1802 Washington, D.C., stonecutters Shaw & Birth charged John Tayloe for "312 [feet] 1 [inch] Moulded Astragle Steps & Landings [at] 6/6...101.8.6...34 [feet] 6 [inches] Circular ends and Scrools [at] 10/...79 [feet] Ashler to Steps [at] 5/9." The preceding December, plasterer William Fox charged for "989 [feet] Run of frieze...6/2...989 [feet] Astragal & ribbon 1/." Tayloe Papers, VHS.
>
> 1811 Work on Montpelier in Orange County, Virginia, included the construction of "framed door jambs 3/4 ogee & quarter round with astra gals." Cocke Papers, UVa.
>
> 1823 In building the Rotunda at the University of Virginia, Thomas Jefferson wrote to a factor in Italy informing him that "our columns being of brick, in which no moulding can be worked it is necessary to subjoin to the capitel the astragal of the column making it a part of the same block, and the term astragal is meant to include (besides it's halfround member or torus) the cavetto & listel below it . . . and which will be seen in the same plate of Palladio's." Lambeth and Manning, *Thomas Jefferson as an Architect.*

astylar Without columns or pilasters.

asylum A building for the care and treatment of the insane. The term in this sense comes into use in the early 19th century. See also **hospital** (2).

attic (attick) The uppermost story of a building, and sometimes specifically a low story above an exterior entablature or cornice. The latter was also called an attic story. The term was seldom used until the 19th century, and then primarily by commentators versed in classical architecture or when neoclassically designed buildings included such spaces. See also **garret, loft.**

> 1802 John Tayloe's Washington, D.C., residence, known today as the Octagon, was originally designed as a three-story house with a nearly flat roof concealed behind parapet walls. The original roof leaked and circa 1817 was covered over with a more conventional roof. In the original carpentry accounts, the "attic" is the third story, demarcated by a stone belt course on the exterior and having conventional

ceiling heights, in contrast to grander room proportions on the lower stories. The carpenter billed Tayloe for "taking down Partition in attic and making a doorway thru same into Mʳ Ogles room." Tayloe Papers, VHS.

1805 Advertisement for a dwelling house in Chestertown, Maryland, noted that "in the third or attic story are four rooms and a clothes press, with passages as in the second story, and a flush garret above." *Republican Star or Eastern Shore General Advertiser.*

1808 Monticello in Albemarle County, Virginia, was described as including "in the centre of the S.W. side, over the parlor . . . an attic story, terminated with a dome, which has a fine effect, and forms a beautiful room inside." Caldwell, *A Tour Through Part of Virginia in the Summer of 1808.*

Attic base See **base** (2).

auger (augur, augre) A tool consisting of a short iron blade with a perpendicular wooden handle used for boring large holes. Carpenters typically used augers, whose blade diameters generally ranged from one half to two inches, to bore treenail holes in framing members and dowel holes in flooring.

avenue A wide, straight roadway or an approach to a rural dwelling or a public building, lined with single or double rows of trees. Avenues were usually wide enough for a horse or carriage to pass, some were much wider, and many were the width of the building and broader than subsidiary intersecting ones. As was done at Gunston Hall in Fairfax County, Virginia, the perspective was occasionally manipulated to extend the apparent length of an avenue by gradually narrowing the avenue towards the far end. The term also referred to a public, tree-lined street in a town.

1733 Germanna, Virginia, "consists of Col. Spotswood's enchanted castle. . . . There had also been a chapel about a bow-shot from the colonel's house, at the end of an avenue of cherry trees." Byrd, *A Journey to the Land of Eden.*

1737 It was "Ordered that there be paid to Mr. Philip Finch the sum of ten pounds for laying and planting the Avenue to the Governors House" in Williamsburg. *Executive Journals of the Council of Colonial Virginia*, 4.

1743 "I . . . cant say one word of the other seat I saw in this ramble" near Charleston "except the Count's large double row of Oaks on each side of the Avenue that leads to the house." *Letterbook of Eliza Lucas Pinckney.*

1773 "Due east of the Great House" at Nomini Hall in Westmoreland County, Virginia, "are two Rows of tall flourishing, beautiful Poplars, these Rows are something wider than the House & are about 300 yards Long. . . . These Rows of Poplars form an extremely pleasant avenue." *Journal & Letters of Philip Vickers Fithian.*

1778 "For sale" in Charleston were "Magnolia or Laurels fit for Avenues . . . any height from three feet to twenty." *South Carolina and American General Gazette.*

avenue
Charles Fraser, Golden Grove, Stono, S.C.

aviary A cage or enclosed space in which birds are kept.

1772 A plantation to be rented on the Ashley River near Charleston contained "two well contrived AVIARIES." *South Carolina and American General Gazette.*

awl A pointed tool used for piercing small holes. Unlike a gimlet, which cuts through a material in a screw fashion, an awl bores a hole. Brad awls were used by carpenters to start pilot holes for nails and screws.

awning A protective screen of canvas or other material hung either as a roof or as a sloping projection from windows and doors.

1624 At Jamestown, the first settlers "did hang an awning (which is an old saile) to

. . . trees to shadow us from the Sunne." *Complete Works of Captain John Smith.*

1744 In Philadelphia, "the people commonly use awnings of painted cloth or duck over their shop doors and windows." *The Itinerarium of Dr. Alexander Hamilton.*

ax (axe, falling axe) A tool with a bladed iron or steel head and a wooden handle used to chop, hew, and split wood and finish stone. Among the most important types of this most basic tool in the woodworking trades was the felling ax, with a long handle and a narrow blade used to cut down trees. The broad ax, with a shorter, offset handle and large, chisel-edged blade, was used for squaring logs. Mortising axes had long narrow blades that were suitable for chopping inside a mortise hole.

back See **chimney back.**

backband A fillet at the outer edge of an architrave that returns to the face of the wall. See also **architrave (2), band.**

back building, backhouse A detached or contiguous subsidiary structure standing behind the main building.

1711 The courthouse was "to be thirty foot long in the clear and twenty foot wide in the clear with a back building for the Seat of Judicature of twelve foot and eighteen foot in the clear." Talbot Co., Md., Land Records Book No. 12, MSA.

1735 "To be Lett A Very good Dwelling-house, with convenient Back-houses." *South Carolina Gazette.*

1738 Survey of a plantation noted that there was "one old dwelling house in length 36 feet and 16 feet in width with an old back building 20 feet in length and 16 in width." Queen Anne's Co., Md., Deed Book B.

1748 "JOHN CLIFFORD has a House to lett, in King-street, with a Billiard-Table in a Back-house." *South Carolina Gazette.*

bagnio (bannio) A bathhouse or place arranged for bathing, sweating, and cleansing the body. See also **bath house.**

1720 An estimate was made for "finishing the Bannio" at the Governor's House in Williamsburg. *Journals of the House of Burgesses*, 5.

bakehouse A building used for baking, usually containing an oven and sometimes other necessary fittings like shelves and tables. Bakehouses appeared almost exclusively in urban locations, most often in proximity to the owner's dwelling house. They served mainly commercial rather than domestic purposes. The term is rarely encountered before the mid-18th century. See also **oven.**

1759 An Advertisement for a half-acre lot in Alexandria, Virginia, stated that it contained four houses, a meat house, a well, a paled garden, and "a Bake House 16 by 16, with a Shed 16 by 6, having a large Oven adjoining." *Maryland Gazette.*

1796 In Charleston, "a small bake-house, belonging to Mr. Gromet, in Market-square, was discovered to be on fire." *Columbian Herald.*

1800 An ordinance "for preventing as much as may be, accidents which may happen by fire in Savannah" prohibited "bakers of bread to carry on their trades within the City, unless their bake houses shall be built and paved with brick or stone, covered with tile or slate, or their situation should be so remote and attended with such security to adjacent buildings, as to be approved of by the fire masters." *Columbian Museum and Savannah Advertiser.*

balcony A platform enclosed with a low parapet, railing, or balustrade and projecting from a wall, usually in front of a window or other opening. Balconies generally appeared on the exteriors of buildings and were either cantilevered or supported on some variety of bracket or post. The term came into common usage in the southern colonies around the middle of the 18th century. See also **gallery** (1), **loft** (2), **piazza** (2).

> 1705 Specifications for the capitol building in Williamsburg stated that "each side of the said building, shall have a circular porch, with an iron balcony upon the first floor over it." Hening, *Statutes at Large*, 3.
> 1763 Dr. George Milligen Johnston described the dwelling houses of Charleston as having "a Genteel Appearance, though generally incumbered with Balconies or Piazzas." *A Short Description of the Province of South-Carolina.*
> 1790 Residents of Wilmington, North Carolina, objected to being "restrained from building or repairing covered Piazzas or Balconies, to their houses, situate on the streets . . . such [elements] are not only really useful . . . but in this hot Climate, are essentially necessary to the Health and convenience of the Inhabitants." Legislative Papers, NCA&H.

baldachin An ornamental canopy supported by columns or suspended from overhead that covers a freestanding altar or throne.

bald cypress See **cypress.**

bale house A warehouse for the storage of goods. For a more detailed description see **warehouse.**

> 1766 Property advertized for rent or for sale in Alexandria, Virginia, included a dwelling "and several other good Houses, viz. a Store house and a Bale House." *Maryland Gazette.*

ballroom (ball room, ball house) A large room in a dwelling, tavern, or public building such as a town hall or market house designed for dancing, concerts, and similar entertainments. As the fashion for assemblies grew in the South in the middle of the 18th century, merchants, planters, tavernkeepers, and corporations added or incorporated large rooms for dancing and assembled gatherings. See also **assembly room, long room.**

> 1774 Nomini Hall, the home of Robert Carter in Westmoreland County, Virginia, had on the ground floor two dining rooms, a study, and "a Ball-Room thirty Feet long." *Journal and Letters of Philip Vickers Fithian.*
> 1788 The corporation of Fredericksburg, Virginia, rented the upper space of the market house to "David Blair for the ball room 6 nights for the Assembly [for] £3." Fredericksburg City Council Minute Book 1782–1801.
> 1797 "THE Ladies of Alexandria and its vicinity on both sides of the Potomac, are respectfully invited to a BALL, to be held at Mr. Gadsby's Ball Room . . . to celebrate the Anniversary of the birth of the President of the United States." *Columbia Mirror and Alexandria Gazette.*

baluster (balluster, ballister) A short pillar or colonnette, often turned with classical moldings and having a base, shaft, and cap. Balusters support the handrail and enclose the side of a staircase. A balustrade, a row of balusters surmounted by a railing that forms a low enclosure or parapet, was often found on terraces, balconies, roofs, staircases, altars, and magistrates' platforms. Although 18th-century English writers maintained that *baluster* was the proper term for this feature, the term was "corrupted" to *banister* by the time of English settlement in the Chesapeake. This latter term had far greater currency throughout the colonial and early national period than the more formal *baluster*. See also **banister.**

baluster
Christ Church, Lancaster County, Va.

1673 The area where the magistrates were to sit in a courthouse was "to be balistred in with turned balisters." Westmoreland Co., Va., Deeds and Patents Book 1665–1677.

1711 A courtroom was to have "Suitable railes and ballester round where the Grand and Pettit Jurys must stand." Talbot Co., Md., Land Records RF No. 12, MSA.

1750 A craftsman was paid for "turning 162 Balluster at 6d" at Marlborough in Stafford County, Virginia. Watkins, *Cultural History of Marlborough, Virginia.*

Banbury lock　An inexpensive, wood-cased stock lock constructed such that the ironworks are attached directly to the case and not to an independent iron plate. These locks were originally manufactured only in Banbury, Oxfordshire, but later the name was used synonymously for any cheap stock lock. See also **stock lock.**

1741 In Charleston, a notice offered "JUST IMPORTED . . . from London, and to be sold by Robert Wilson at his Store . . . banbury, plate and stock locks, stock and spring locs with knuts and screws, fine locks for parlour and chamber doors." *South Carolina Gazette.*

band　A flat face or square molding smaller than a fascia. See also **backband, fascia.**

1811 A workman fabricated several hundred feet of "Cock'd bead double Architrave fancy band." Riddell Accounts, Pleasants Papers, MHS.

banded architrave　A door or window architrave broken at intervals by a series of smooth, projecting blocks. This decorative device began to appear in southern architecture in the late colonial period, partly through the influence of English architect James Gibbs. Gibbs featured it in a number of his designs in *A Book of Architecture* (1728), a publication that circulated among a small but broad and influential audience. See also **architrave** (2).

bandelet (bandalet)　A narrow, flat molding slightly larger than a fillet but smaller than a fascia; a collar encircling a shaft. See also **annulet, taenia.**

banister (bannister)　A slender pillar or turned colonnette used to support a handrail and guard the side of a stair. Used in the plural form, the term referred to a balustrade. Although English writers maintained that *banister* was a corrupt or vulgar form of *baluster*, it was the preferred term in early America. See also **baluster.**

1678 On the magistrate's platform of a courthouse, the "first bannister [is to be] a foot from the floor and the second bannister on the assend." Westmoreland Co., Va., Court Order Book 1676–1689.

1745 A church gallery to be built "with four seats & rails and turned bannisters." Truro Parish, Fairfax Co., Va., Vestry Book.

1769 A craftsman was paid for "Turning 50 Seader Banisters for the Pulpit Staircase @ 3/6." St. Michael's Parish, Charleston, S.C., Vestry Book.

1793 "Old East" at the University of North Carolina was to have a stair with "pine handrails & square bannisters." University Archives, UNC, Chapel Hill.

banded architrave
Aquia Church, Stafford County, Va.

bank　A building housing an institution or establishment concerned with the lending, saving, and safeguarding of money and the regulation of monetary transactions. Buildings specifically erected to house such businesses appeared in the larger cities of the South in the late 18th and early 19th centuries. Most had a central room for the transaction of business as well as a counting room for accounts and a vault for the storage of notes, specie, bullion, and other valuable items.

1797 A house was advertised for sale "opposite the Bank of Baltimore." *Federal Gazette and Baltimore Daily Advertiser.*

1812 "The Directiors of the State Bank of North-Carolina have resolved to erect a Banking House in the City of Raleigh, the Foundation whereof will be of Rock, the Walls of Brick, and the Roof probably of Slate, or some other fire-proof material. The dimensions will be 33 feet by 53 feet, two stories high, with a Portico in front." *Raleigh Register.*

1815 In Raleigh, contractor Lewis Nicholson noted that "having built, completed and finished the State Bank building, I am as poor as a church mouse." He assured creditors that "if I was cashier instead of builder of the Bank, all of the above should be paid." *The Star.*

1816 "Committee to contract for the building of a BANK-HOUSE for the Branch Bank at Nashville, are ready to receive proposals for the building a brick house, forty-four by thirty-four, two stories high, . . . to be finished in a stile suitable for the accommodation of the Bank." *The Nashville Whig.*

bank barn A modern, originally English, term for a particular kind of *barn* of large dimensions, featuring multiple levels and built into the side of a hill or embankment. The lower level was served by an adjacent yard and usually fitted out for stables. A ramp leading up the hillside provided access to the upper level and its central threshing floor. Bank barns were confined to northern Delaware and southeastern Pennsylvania. They were built with increasing frequency beginning in the second quarter of the 19th century.

1828 A farm included "a stone barn, with frame oversett and stabling below." New Castle Co., Del., Orphans Court Valuations N.

banquet room A large formal room for receptions, entertaining, and dining.

1789 "The superb banqueting room" at Mount Vernon "has been finished since he returned home from the army." Morse, *American Geography.*

baptistery (baptistry) A room or space in a church in which the rite of baptism is performed. Most Anglican churches in colonial America had a font, and benches were sometimes set up around it near the west door for such services.

1747 "The space of the pews on the North side at the West end of the Church [is] to be set apart for a Baptistry with seats all round: A neat turn'd post erected in this Area with hansome mouldings round the Top, whereon to place the font or Bason, & a Desk adjoining . . . to lay the Book on." Albemarle Parish, Surry Co., Va., Vestry Book.

bar (barr) **1.** In general, a long, thin strip of material, especially iron, used for a variety of building purposes. In the very late 18th and throughout the 19th centuries iron bars were used sometimes instead of manteltrees for fireplace openings.

1810 The account of ironwork done for the Riddell House in Baltimore listed "6 Chimney Bars." Riddell Accounts, Pleasants Papers, MHS.

2. One of a series of wooden or iron strips inserted into the frame of an opening to prevent entry, often placed on the outside face of a glazed window. Many 17th-century dwellings had barred window openings in lieu of glazed casements. In the 18th and 19th centuries, barred apertures were frequently used for cellar and jail openings. See also **grate.**

1665 "Raymond Staplefort att night caused a Boy his servant called Humphrey Jones to enter att a window, wherof Two wooden Barrs had beene broken eyther by himselfe or by the said Boy, where the said Boy having entred, opened the Doore,

bar (2)
Coor-Gaston House, New Bern, N.C.

(which was fast shutt with a spring Lock) unto the said Staplefort." *Archives of Maryland* 49.

1773 Specifications for a prison in Edenton, North Carolina, noted that the window jambs were to be grooved to "receive the Iron bars and sashes, 2 Windows in the Debtors . . . Inch and a quarter Iron Bars set arris and let thro' flat bars." Hawks Papers, SHC.

1784 In Charleston, payment was made to "Stephen Shrewsbury for fixing Iron Bars to Treasury Windows." South Carolina Treasury Journal 1783–1791, SCA&H.

c. 1798 At John Dickinson's dwelling in Wilmington, Delaware, "the cellar windows [are] to be secured by iron barrs." Dickinson Plantation Research Files, Delaware Bureau of Museums.

3. A wooden horizontal member set into an ell-shaped bracket of iron known as a *bolt*, or one of wood, for the purpose of securing a door shut in place of a lock. See also **bolt**.

1753 A church was to have "a latch and bolt to the front door, a sufficient bar and bolt to the other doors." Wicomico Parish, Northumberland Co., Va., Vestry Book.

1788 William Anderson, joiner, was commissioned to install "2 pannel Doors ea door to be in 2 pieces holdfasts and staples to ea. a lock to be on one door, a bar to the other." Westmoreland Co., Va., Robert Carter Letterbooks, Duke.

1810 Ironwork fabricated for the Riddell House in Baltimore included "18 window Shutter Bars." Riddell Accounts, Pleasants Papers, MHS.

4. A railing or balustrade erected in a courtroom, council chamber, assembly hall, or other public space used to separate the general public from official members or those having business before an official body. The first bars appeared in southern courtrooms in the third quarter of the 17th century as court day procedures became more formalized and the need to separate the judges from the judged became imperative. In provincial assemblies, the bar symbolized the power of that body to protect its prerogatives by prohibiting unauthorized visitors from intruding upon their deliberations.

1671 "Whereas ye pressure of ye people is soe great a Disturbance to this Court whilst sitting to doe his maj^ties service for want of a Barr Itt is therefore ordered by ye Court that Col^l John Stringer agree with a workman to make a table and formes att ye Courthouse & sett up a Barr about ye Same for ye better accomodation of this court." Northampton Co., Va., Court Order Book 1664–1674.

1697 In the statehouse in Annapolis, rooms were to "be fitted up with all necessary and Convenient boxes, Shelves Desks and Tables to write on and att the door of every office a barr be made within which no person shall Come but the Clerk of such Office unless upon urgent and great occasion." *Archives of Maryland*, 19.

1742 The sheriff was required to "imploy some person to put a small ledg to the lawyers barr sufficient to hold their books." Amelia Co., Va., Court Order Book 1735–1746.

1798 A petition of lawyers from southside Virginia counties stated:
"May it please the worthy members of the Court
To lend attention to our sad report.
Confin'd within a compass three yards long,
We scarce can stand amidst the brawling throng,
Wedg'd in by shoulders, outstretch'd arms and knees,
Each poor Attorney scarce can fairly squeeze
His carcase to a seat within the bar,
Or stir his joints, so crouded is he there."
　　　　　Munford, *Poems and Compositions in Prose on Several Occasions*.

1828 Proposal for the Madison County, Virginia, courthouse noted that "the Barr to be elivated 6 inches each rize, and to finished with turned Balusters and proper seats with a small Desk or lid in front say 8 inches wide." Malcolm Crawford Papers, VSL.

5. (bar room) A small enclosed space in a tavern or inn where beverages are stored. Generally, bars adjoined the principal room of a tavern or stood in one corner and were enclosed by a lattice screen or a series of bars.

1747 A dwelling was to be sold in Charleston where "Mr. Samuel Davidson lately kept tavern; the house contains eleven rooms with sash'd windows and a very convenient bar." *South Carolina Gazette.*

1748 "In the Barr Room" of Ishmael Moody's tavern in Yorktown were "5 3 Qt. China Bowles . . . 2 Gallon Do . . . 1 large Case with 16 two Gallon Bottles . . . 1 less Do with 9 Gallon Bottles filled with Arrack . . . 2 smaller Do with 16 two Qt. Bottles . . . 10 earthen Bowls & 2 old waiters . . . 2 Bottle Sliders Candle Box and Tobo. Box . . . 1 pr large Money Scales 2 old Tables . . . 1 Tobo. Sive 2 Pewter Inkstands." York Co., Va., Will and Inventory Book 1745–1759.

1816 A tavern for rent at the courthouse in Person County, North Carolina, was "the most convenient and the best calculated of any in the Country for Public Entertainment. . . . The bar is in part of the body of the House with doors opening to the dining room and the public room—between the two latter there is no communication, except a window. The Bar windows open to the Piazzo, to the passage and to the Public Room." *Raleigh Register.*

bar iron   Wrought iron formed into bars for use by blacksmiths. For a more detailed description see **forge, wrought iron.**

1767 Charles Carroll of Mount Clare near Baltimore wrote to merchants in Bristol that "I shall Ship you in the first of your Ships that arrive here Bar and Pig Iron that will Amount in Value to about one hundred and thirty Pounds Sterling." Trostel, *Mount Clare.*

1777 At the ironwork of Mr. Hunter of Falmouth, Virginia, workmen made "(from Pig Iron) Bar Iron, Anchors, all Kinds of Blacksmith's Work, Small Arms, Pistols, Swords, Files, Fuller's Shears, & Nails." *VMHB,* 62.

bargeboard (varge board, verge board)   A board, often molded, carved, or otherwise ornamented, that runs at a sloping angle the length of the gable end of a building and covers the junction between the wall and end rafter pair.

1711 A courthouse roof was "to be well shingled with Cypress shingles shewing mundillions in the front barge boards at the ends; all the back eaves to be well boxt with good moulding." Talbot Co., Md., Land Records RF No. 12. MSA.

1726 A carpenter was paid "for putting up ye varge boards at 2/6" on a house in Caroline County, Virginia. Baylor Papers, CWF.

1773 A glebe house was constructed with "a plain cornish under the eaves and a barge board up the ends." Fairfax Parish, Fairfax Co., Va., Vestry Book.

bark   The outer protective layer of a tree, distinct and separate from the wood itself. Indians and white settlers peeled strips of bark to use as a covering for the roofs of their dwellings. *Barked* timber was that which had its bark removed in order for it to dry, or to prevent insect infestation.

c. 1609 At Jamestown, Virginia, "they have found the way to cover their houses now (as the Indians) with barks of trees, as durable and as a good proof against storms and winter weather as the best tile, defending likewise the piercing sunbeams of summer and keeping the inner lodgings cool enough." *Voyage to Virginia in 1609.*

1709 In North Carolina, a Tuscarora town had "Streets of Houses, built with Pine-Bark, not with round Tops, as they commonly use, but Ridge-Fashion, after the manner of most other *Indians.*" Lawson, *A New Voyage to Carolina.*

bark house   **1.** A building in which bark used for tanning is stored or prepared; a tan house. See also **tan house, tanyard.**

1757 "TO BE SOLD, A CONVENIENT TANYARD, lying in Annapolis, . . . with all the Appurtenances, thereunto belonging" including a "Bark-House, all covered with Shingles." *Maryland Gazette.*

1807 In southern Delaware, John Rowland operated a tanyard with "a bark house Currying shop." Sussex Co., Del. Orphans Court Valuations K.

2. A building or shelter constructed or covered with bark.

> **1674** In South Carolina, "the Indians [are] diligent in makeing two barke-covered Hutts, to shelter us from the injury of the weather." Salley, *Narratives of Early Carolina.*
> **1805** On the western frontier, "most of the houses were log cabins, covered with bark, straw or slabs." Bennett, *Memorials of Methodism in Virginia.*

bark mill A mill and the equipment for grinding bark used in tanning and dyeing processes. See also **tanyard.**

> **1786** On land rented to Abraham Smutes in western Virginia was "1 logg house 20 by 16 for dressing leather; bark mill with cover . . . 9 tan vats." *Jonathan Clark Notebook,* Filson Club.
> **1824** "A Tan Yard" on a farm in Delaware consisted "of thirty two laying Vatts, four limes, two bates, and one pool all in good repair, One bark house thirty six feet by eighteen in good repair, one bark Mill house twenty six feet by eighteen in bad repair, One Curring Shop thirty eight feet by eighteen in good repair." Sussex Co., Del. Orphans Court Valuations N.

barn A type of *outbuilding* used for a variety of agricultural purposes, such as crop or equipment storage. Less specialized than, for example, tobacco houses, barns served as generic, multi-purpose farm buildings throughout the South from the 17th century onward. They sometimes contained wooden threshing floors as well as shed additions often used as stables. See also **bank barn.**

> **1676** A division of property included half of a dwelling house, a dairy, kitchen, hen house, hog house, quartering house and "the norwest halfe part of the barn the one halfe of the sicty foot tobacco house." Blisland Parish, James City and New Kent Cos., Va., Vestry Book.
> **1730** It was decided "that a Barn be built at ye Glebe of Thirty Two foot long . . . [tw]enty foot wide Ten foot pitch underpined Three bricks high . . . to be Shingled wth good Cyprus Shingles . . . ye length & the whole breadth to be floored wth good white oake plank of Inch [and] half thick, the Studs Rafters Winbeams and braces to be Sawed & to be weather boarded with good Oake boads, one folding door & one single one opposite." Stratton Major Parish, King & Queen Co., Va., Vestry Book.

barn Plan and section, Retirement Barn, New Castle County, Del.

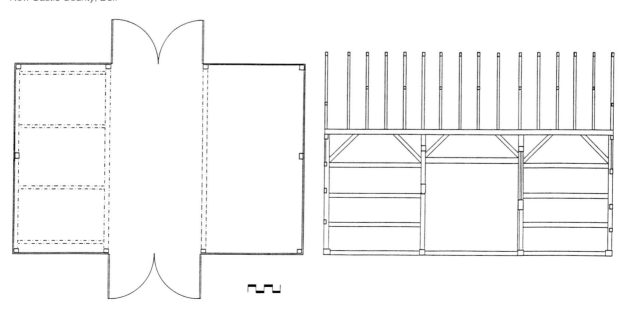

barrack, barracks 1. A building or group of buildings used to house soldiers. The most important early barracks in the South were built in Georgia during the first years of settlement and on the outskirts of Charleston.

> 1733 "We were all safely landed at the new fort where we found by Mr. Oglethorpes direction the barracks . . . clean'd out on purpose for our own refreshment." *The Journal of Peter Gordon.*
> 1746 At Frederica, Georgia, "there are Barracks . . . ninety feet Square, built of Tappy, covered with Cypress Shingles, and a handsome tower over the Gateway of twenty feet square." *London Magazine*, 16.
> 1763 In the back country of South Carolina, much effort went into "the compleat Rebuilding of Fort P. George, with intire New Barracks & Store Houses, a New Stone Well, one New Stone Magazine &c." *Papers of Henry Laurens*, 3.
> 1776 "A warrant to Samuel Spurr for £35.18.3 for brickwork to the barracks" was issued at Yorktown, Virginia. *Calendar of Virginia State Papers*, 8.

2. A lodging house.

> 1815 "I am now in a back Room of our Barracks which is an old brick building situate on the south side of the main street of the City of Williamsburg which is an old town of no considerable Size." *W&MQ*, 2d ser., 3.

3. An open walled structure used for the storage of hay, generally built with a pyramidal roof supported on earthfast corner posts. Barracks were sometimes associated with other farm buildings.

> 1776 On a farm in northern Delaware was "one Barrack with stabling under the same." New Castle Co., Del., Orphans Court Valuations E.
> 1827 There was a notation made of a "Hay-Barrack and stable wanting a roof." New Castle Co., Del., Orphans Court Valuations M.

base 1. In the most general sense, the bottom support of any object; the lowest part or division of an element; the lower part of a building. See also **plinth.**

> 1740 "The walls" of a courthouse were "to be three bricks thick from the foundation to the surface of the Earth from thence to the base two bricks." Lancaster Co., Va., Court Order Book 1729–1743.
> 1774 "If built of stone, the walls" of a church were "to be two feet thick . . . the Base to be of stone 2 1/2 feet thick." Shelburne Parish, Loudoun Co., Va., Vestry Book.

2. The lowest part of a column or pilaster composed of a series of moldings and resting on a plinth or pedestal. There is no base in the Greek Doric order, but other bases vary in profile according to their order. Most had some combination of torus and scotia moldings as their principal elements. Although Renaissance and English writers tried to codify the forms of each base according to ancient precedent, there was a significant variation of interpretations. In early America, concern for appropriate configurations increased in the second half of the 18th century, but great leeway was exercised by carpenters and builders throughout the period.

> 1711 A courthouse was to have "a hemsome Peddiment over the front doore supported with well turned Collums and bases of Cedar and Locust." Talbot Co., Md., Land Records Book No. 12.
> 1734 In columns designed on Roman precedent, "the Base is different in the different Orders. The Tuscan Base is the most simple of all Orders; consisting, according to some, only of a single Tore, besides the Plinth. The Doric Base has an Astragal more than the Tuscan, altho' that was introduced by the Moderns. The Ionic Base has a large Tore over two slender Scotia's, separated by two Astragals: But there are no Bases at all in the most antient Monuments of this Order . . . The Corinthian Base has two Tores, two Scotia's, and two Astragals. The Composite Base has an Astragal less than the Corinthian. The Attic Base, is so denominated,

Attick Bafe.
A:PALLADIO.

COLISÆUM.

VIGNOLE.

base

because it was first used by the Athenians. It has two Tores, and a Scotia, and is very proper for Ionic and Composite Columns." *Builder's Dictionary.*

1761 In Charleston, a cabinetmaker submitted a bill of work for "turning 4 large Attick Basses of Seader for the alter." Williams, *St. Michael's.*

1808 At Poplar Forest in Bedford County, Virginia, "we made the bricks for the bases and the capts of the columns as I thought it would make a better job than to have them in wood." Coolidge Collection, Massachusetts Historical Society.

3. A decorative molding, applied to the plinth board or integral to it, that runs along the floor at the base of a wainscotted or plastered wall. The most common names for this protective base were *mopboard, skirting board,* or *washboard* through the early 19th century. The term *baseboard* comes into prominence only after this time. See also **surbase, washboard.**

1774 A carpenter's bill for work at William Corbit's house in Odessa, Delaware, listed "35 ft 7 ins base & sr base at 9d." Sweeney, *Grandeur on the Appoquinimink.*

1805 The two rooms in a dwelling above a store in Wilmington, North Carolina, were to be fitted out with "base with mouldings and cornices." McKoy, *Early Wilmington.*

baseboard   See **base** (3), **washboard.**

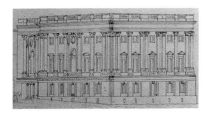

basement
B. H. Latrobe, U.S. Capitol
under construction

basement   The lowest story of a building or division of a column or pier. Unlike modern usage, the term rarely referred to a partially or fully submerged storage space under a building. Contemporaries described these areas as cellars. Until the middle of the 19th century, the term *basement* implied a location rather than a subservient functional space. See also **cellar.**

1783 At the Governor's House in New Bern, North Carolina, "the Basement story consists of apartments for the use of the Butler Housekeeper and Cellering &c., and is 7 f⁵ 6 In⁵ only in the clear." Hawks Letter, Miranda Papers, Academia Nacional de la Historia, Caracas.

1803 An estimate was made for "repairing the basements of the Columns" of a church. St. Michael's Parish, Charleston, S.C., Vestry Book.

1812 An English visitor to the Capitol in Washington noted that in the House of Representatives "the pillars stand upon a basement or on their own round bases and not upon plinths." Foster, *Jeffersonian America.*

1828 Specifications for the Madison County, Virginia, courthouse noted that the courtroom or "basement floor will be paved with tile." Malcolm Crawford Papers, VSL.

1851 Justices found "the basement story under the church now occupied as an office . . . as suitable . . . for holding their sessions." Northumberland Co., Va., Court Order Book 1844–1852.

basilica   In antiquity, a Roman hall of justice. The early Christian church used the Roman basilican form for many of its churches. It consisted of a long central nave flanked by colonnaded or arcaded side aisles and terminated at the east end by an apse. Although a few urban Anglican churches in the colonial South, such as St. Philip's and St. Michael's in Charleston, had many of the characteristics of this form, the term was rarely used in early America to describe such buildings. It was not until the early 19th century that the term began to be used with any frequency to refer to contemporary buildings constructed in this manner.

1817 "The general form of the interior" of St. Paul's Episcopal Church in Baltimore "is that of the ancient Basilica, a form adopted by the primitive Christians, and sanctified by long practice." *American and Commercial Daily Advertiser.*

basin (bason)   1. A partially enclosed, sheltered area along a river shore, often artificially created by dredging, used primarily for the anchorage of ships at a wharf or pier; a man-made body of water.

> 1785   A visitor to Alexandria, Virginia, advertised his services in improving the city's waterfront: "He professes also the capacity of building a complete pile-driver, one being sufficient for the whole place, and recommends the driving of large piles on the outside walls of every wharf, which is the custom in Baltimore even in the Bason." *Virginia Journal and Alexandria Advertiser.*

2. A reservoir of water built into pleasure grounds near a dwelling. The term was particularly used in South Carolina to describe such a feature. See also **artificial lake.**

> 1743   "As you draw nearer" to William Middleton's plantation Crowfield in South Carolina, "a spacious bason in the midst of a large green presents itself as you enter the gate that leads to the house." *Letterbook of Eliza Lucas Pinckney.*
> 1749   A plantation for sale on the Ashley River near Charleston contained "a very large garden both for pleasure and profit, with a variety of pleasant walks, mounts, basons, canals, and all sorts of fruit trees." *South Carolina Gazette.*

3. A circular container or bowl, wider than it is deep, used to hold water for baptisms.

> 1738   It was "Ordered that a Marble Font with Wooden Frame & Top with Pullys & Weights to Lift it off & on the Bason to be 18 Inches Deep & two feet Diameter be sent for the use of the Church in Annapolis." St. Anne's Parish, Anne Arundel Co., Md., Vestry Book.

bas relief   See **relief.**

bastard *(adj.)*   Having the appearance of a standard or familiar object, material, or construction method, but differing from it, and generally of an inferior quality. The most common use of the term appeared on the eastern shore of Maryland, where *bastard framing* was recognized as a distinctive type. Although the precise meaning of this phrase is uncertain, it appears that it probably referred to some form of earthfast construction, since it was easily recognized on a standing clapboarded building.

> 1730   Carpenters were ordered "to build one [vestry] house near ye Church Twenty feet Long with Bastard frame weatherboarded with Clap boards roof with Feather Edged Shingles." St. Luke's, Church Hill Parish, Queen Anne's Co., Md., Vestry Book.
> 1756   On the Jarmon plantation, appraisers found "a new 30 foot tobacco house by 20 covered and weather boarded with sapt clapboards, not finished wanting a length of boards on each side of the cover and half a length of boards on south side, the gable and northward wants several boards and a door, bastard frame and ordinary work the whole." Queen Anne's Co., Md., Deed Book E.
> 1787   A house was to be built containing "four stud partitions four doors bastard pannels." Charleston Co., S.C., Land Record Book 1787–1788.
> 1796   In developing the details for the "partition between Hall and Entry" at Monticello, Thomas Jefferson noted that there should be "no sash for the semicircle, and by confining the glass between a thick lining on each side it may be cut into polygons instead of portions of circles, the lower edge must rest in a bastard sash, to reduce the glass to 2 feet for convenience." Coolidge Collection, Massachusetts Historical Society.

bastion   A polygonal or round projection of a fortification or rampart that provides sweeping firepower support for flanking walls. Palisaded fortifications with bastions were used in the early plantation settlements of Virginia and continued to be an instrumental part of military engineering throughout the 18th century. Perhaps the most ambitious urban fortifications were Charleston's city walls, which contained a series of regularly spaced bastions.

> **1716** On the Meherrin River in the southside of Virginia, a fort was "built upon rising ground. It is inclosed on five sides, made only with palisadoes, and instead of five bastions, there are five houses, which defend the one the other." Fontaine, *Memoirs of a Huguenot Family.*
>
> **1741** Charleston was "fortified more for Beauty than Strength. It has six Bastions and a Line all round it." Oldmixon, *The British Empire in America.*

bat See **brickbat.**

bathing house A private or public building erected for hygienic and recreational bathing. Some 18th-century plantations and estates had small enclosures built over hot and cold springs or artificial water receptacles. Public bathing houses often contained dressing rooms, plunge baths, and other amenities and were operated in the late 18th and early 19th century as popular entertainments in cities. Saltwater bathing houses were erected in Charleston and other seacoast towns after the Revolution when the English custom for sea bathing became fashionable. At the same time, the first hot springs retreats in the Appalachian Mountains were being opened to visitors. See also **bagnio.**

> **1733** "A Plantation about two Miles above Goose-Creek Bridge" in South Carolina had "frames, Planks &c. ready to be fix'd in and about a Spring within 3 Stones throw of the House, intended for a Cold Bath, and a House over it." *South Carolina Gazette.*
>
> **1805** In Richmond was "ERECTED A BATHING HOUSE At the Falling Garden, CONTAINING four rooms: each has a Bath, and supplied with Hot and Cold Water. . . . The terms will be 2s 3d for a single Bathe." *Virginia Argus.*
>
> **1808** "The Hot Springs are in Bath county. . . . Here are three baths, one of vital heat, or 96 degrees of Farenheit's thermometer: one of 104, and it is said that the hottest is 112, and sufficiently hot to boil an egg. The patient, on coming out of the two latter, is wrapped up in blankets, and lies stewing in the swetting room adjoining the bath, until the perspiration has freely spent itself from every pore of the body." Caldwell, *A Tour Through Part of Virginia.*
>
> **1820** In Charleston, a proposal was put forth for a "SALT WATER BATHING HOUSE. . . . The building will be erected at the East end of Laurens street, at low water mark: the Foundation to be made of Palmetto Logs, 46 feet square, containing 14 private Baths, with a Bath in the centre of 20 feet diameter: the bottom of the baths to be floored: over the Dressing Room will be a Platform and Railing, over which there will be a Roof. There will be a Bridge leading from Laurens street to the Bathing House." *City Gazette and Commercial Daily Advertiser.*

Bath stove A cast-iron hob grate set in a fireplace opening. The stove consisted of a raised basket grate, a decorative front that radiated heat, and two side pieces with flat tops or hobs. Bath stoves initially appeared in England around the middle of the 18th century, but were not imported into America until the end of the century.

> **1773** A Williamsburg resident placed an order with an English merchant for "a bath Grate for one Chimney." *John Norton and Sons, Merchants of London and Virginia.*
>
> **1773** "MANSELL & CORBETT, . . . imported" into Charleston, "Bath stoves of different sizes, which always look clean, without much trouble to keep them so, and destroy but little coal." *South Carolina Gazette and Country Journal.*

batten
Tobacco House, Sudler's Conclusion, Somerset County, Md.

batten (battand) A plank or strip of wood or other material used to stiffen, seal, or secure a series of parallel boards by being nailed vertically or horizontally across their surface. Battens were applied most often to doors, shutters, and wall and partition sheathing. This construction was less complex than wainscotting or paneled doors or shutters and was often used for inferior spaces or structures. See also **ledge** (2).

> 1750   Glebe outbuildings were "to have battain doors." Southam Parish, Cumberland Co., Va., Vestry Book.
>
> 1755   A church interior was "done with popler plank in the nature of battons or instead of the plank being laid edge to edge to make a smooth neat wall the same is laid one upon another." St. George's Parish, Spotsylvania Co., Va., Vestry Book.
>
> 1774   An agreement between Macon Whitfield and carpenters Richard Gill and Benjamin Ward for a house in Windsor, North Carolina, called for "one pannel door . . . & the other doors to be Batten doors." Bertie Co., N.C., Land Papers 1736–1819, NCA&H.
>
> 1807   A kitchen for sale had "batten shutters." *Charleston Courier.*

batter   A slight inclination from perpendicular, particularly a wall whose face slopes inward as it rises.

> 1804   "When looking at a Collonade in profile, if the frieze which determines the place of the entablature be perpendicular to the diminished end of the Column, it must necessarily happen that the building will appear to batter or lean back." *The Correspondence and Miscellaneous Papers of Benjamin Henry Latrobe,* 1.

battery   A platform or fortification equipped with artillery. See also **bastion.**

> 1712   "Edward Powers, appointed overseer to the laborers on the Battery at Yorktown, made a claim to court . . . by account for his care and labor for 15 days." York Co., Va., Deed, Order, and Will Book 1711–1714.
>
> 1736   "The Commissioners appointed . . . for building and repairing the Fortifications within the Harbour of Charles-Town, do give this publick Notice, That it is Resolv'd forthwith to rebuild the Battery before Johnson's Fort, for which there will be wanted a large quantity of Bricks, Lime, Piles, Mud, Earth and Ballast Stones." *South Carolina Gazette.*

battlement   In fortification, a defensive parapet consisting of alternating raised sections known as merlons and lower open ones called crenels. By the time of American settlement, most battlements were purely decorative, sometimes used in a symbolic fashion to assert power or authority. The rear walls of the forecourt at the Governor's House in Williamsburg were capped with battlements.

> 1739   It was "Agreed with Mr. Michael Jeanes to Paint the Battlements of St. Philip's Church at the Rate of five Shillings per yard." St. Philip's Parish, Charleston, S.C., Vestry Book.

bay   **1.** In timber framing, the division of space between the principal framing timbers, such as posts. Also, the division of the facade of a building into discrete units based on the number of openings. Thus a dwelling with four windows and a door would be described as a five-bay building. Although the concept of bay in this sense was in English usage, it had little currency in southern building. See also **bay window.**

2. A division of a barn or other outbuilding into storage compartments. In English barns, the term was used to describe the space between the threshing floor and the end of the barn where grain and straw were stored.

bay window   A rectangular, polygonal, or semicircular window projecting outward from the facade of a building. For a more detailed description, see **bow window.**

1726 "Bay-window . . . is composed of an Arch of a Circle; and so by Consequence, such a one will stand without the Stress of the Building. By which Means Spectators may the better see what is acted in the Street." Neve, *City and Country Purchaser.*

beacon house   A lighthouse built on the coast or in the sea to warn ships and other vessels of danger. See also **lighthouse.**

1795 "PROPOSALS will be received . . . for building a BEACON HOUSE on Shell Castle, in Pamlico Sound, near Occacock Inlet, in North Carolina. . . . The form is to be octagon. The foundation is to be of stone. . . . The height of the wooden building . . . is to be fifty four feet and one half to the top. . . . The frame of the Pyramid is to be covered with boards of one inch and one half in thickness, over which is to be laid a good and complete covering of shingles. . . . The Beacon house is to have two windows in the east and three in the west. . . . A complete and sufficinet iron lantern in the Octagonal form is to rest thereon." *North Carolina Gazette.*

bead (beed)   A small, convex rounded molding, semicircular or greater in section. It differs from an astragal in that it was generally flush with the surrounding surface, rather than raised. One of the most common moldings in early America, a bead was the simplest method of finishing the edge or corner of exposed wooden elements such as framing members, exterior trim, weatherboarding, sheathing, doors, windows, architraves, chair boards, washboards, jambs, and chimney pieces. The fashion for beaded woodwork emerged in the late 17th century and was used in both plain buildings and more elaborate ones, where it was combined with other moldings. The use of decorative beads survived in some elements in many areas until the second quarter of the 19th century and beyond. Measuring from an eighth of an inch to nearly three quarters of an inch in width, decorative beads were applied to the edge of planed boards, planks, and strips with small bead planes. *Angle beads* or *corner beads* were beads applied at the juncture of two planes of woodwork or plaster work to mitigate the splitting or breaking inherent in a sharp corner. Similarly, a *return bead* was cut into the edge of a return and had nearly a three-quarters rounded profile and often served to disguise a joint. A *cock bead* was a molded or applied bead that projected beyond the surrounding surface. *Double beads* were two beads side by side sometimes found on the edge of shelves. A *flush bead* was one that was cut deeply so that the rounded edge was flush with the surrounding surface. A *parting bead* was a strip of wood, inserted vertically into the jamb of a sash frame to separate the upper and lower sash into two separate tracks. *Bead and butt* work consisted of a flat panel with beaded edges cut with the grain of the panel, that sat flush with the surrounding rails and stiles. This finish was often used on late 18th- and early 19th-century doors and window shutters. See also **astragal, parting strip, reed.**

1734 "BEAD a round Moulding, commonly made upon the Edge of a Piece of Stuff. . . . A Bead is usually one quarter of a Circle, and only differs from a Boultin in Size. . . . Sometimes a Bead-Plain is set on the Edge of each Fascia of an Architrave, and sometimes likewise an Astragal is thus carv'd: In both which these Carvings are called Reads. A Bead is often placed on the Lining-Board of a Door-Case, and on the upper Edges of Skirting-Boards." *Builder's Dictionary.*
1738 A church was to be "weather Boarded with feather edge Plank with a Bead." Bristol Parish, Prince George Co., Va., Vestry Book.
1748 In a glebe house, the ceiling "joists [are] to be Plained & a bead struck on Each Edge to be weather Boarded with Good Feather Edged Plank Beaded." Augusta Parish, Augusta Co., Va., Vestry Book.

1791 Courthouse window shutters were "to be made bead & flush." Amelia Co., Va., Deed Book 1789–1791.

1811 A carpenter's work on a dwelling in Baltimore listed "77 [feet] Angle Beads Double fillet . . . 81 [feet] Double beaded shelves . . . beaded Wash boards . . . 68 [feet] bead & butt framed back Lining . . . 100 [feet] Pannels in Shutters Cut bead & flush on Back." Riddell Accounts, Pleasants Papers, MHS.

1818 In a wooden courthouse, "the timbers that are exposed to view are to be plained and beaded if required." Northampton Co., N.C., Miscellaneous Court Records, NCA&H.

1820 Bill of work at Bremo in Orange County, Virginia, included in the southeast chamber "Corner beads." Cocke Papers, UVa.

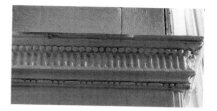

bead and reel
Henry Manigault House, Charleston, S.C.

bead and reel   A convex molding having the form of elongated beads alternating with short elliptical disks or reels. This form was often used as a decorative astragal, especially in architraves.

beam (beame)   A horizontal framing member bearing a load or acting as part of a truss. Sleepers, joists, girders, summers, ties, and collars, among others, are the most common beams found in early timber framing in the South. The word was almost invariably prefixed by the specific name of the horizontal member, such as collar beam. See also **collar beam, cross beam, tie beam.**

1674 At the statehouse in St. Mary's City, "every paire of Rafters to have two buttoned braced to the Collor beame." *Archives of Maryland, 2.*

1701 A workman was hired to build "a Church 25 feet long posts in the ground and held to the Collar beams." St. Paul's Parish, Chowan Co., N.C., Vestry Book.

1747 "The Walls & Roof" of a church were "to be strengthen'd with great Beams across in a number & size suitable." Albemarle Parish, Surry Co., Va., Vestry Book.

1754 Floor framing of a dwelling in Augusta County, Virginia, was to have "a Beam of a foot square under the middle of the sd Sleepers." Preston Papers, VHS.

beam filling   Brickwork, masonry, or some other material used to line the vacant space in the eaves between the upper side of the ceiling joists and the top of the wall plate.

1734 "BEAM-FILLING . . . is the Filling up the vacant Space between the Raison [plate] and Roof, whether Tiling, Thatching, or any other Roof, with Stones or Bricks laid between the Rafters on the Raison, and plaistered on with Loam." *Builder's Dictionary.*

beam house   A building at a tannery containing a large block or worktable upon which hides are scraped and shaved. See **tanyard.**

1757 Among the features of a tanyard in Annapolis were the ponds that were "constantly supplied, from a natural Spring, by a Drain under Ground, and are sunk in the Beam-House . . . The House is 40 Feet by 18, and framed with Poplar Scantling, and well covered." *Maryland Gazette.*

bearer   A small subsidiary horizontal timber; specifically, one of a series of short pieces used to support another member or element such as a gutter or the eaves.

1807 A bill of scantling for a stable in Nelson County, Virginia, listed "eve bareers." Massie Papers, Duke.

bed   1. *(n.)* A layer of mortar, cement, or other material in or on which bricks or stones are set. *(v.)* To fix or set something solidly into a prepared surface.

1796 A merchant advised his client to "be cautious in getting these chimney pieces set with much care" and to "bed the hearth slab in soft morter." Burwell Manuscripts, UVa.

1803 Specifications for a church in South Carolina noted that all the window glass should be "well bedded in putty." Johns Island Church Specifications, Library Society of Charleston.

1810 In Lexington, Kentucky, "the footways [are] neatly paved with brick, and the middle of the street with solid stone firmly bedded." *Virginia Argus.*

2. A level or smooth piece of ground in a garden, often slightly raised for the better cultivation of plants. The term appears by the middle of the 18th century. However, such a feature was also referred to as a square and was usually designed in geometric shapes. Beds were often separated by walkways and were usually two, three, or four times the width of the central garden walk.

1756 A contemporary South Carolina publication advised gardeners to "trim and dress your Asparagus-Bed." *The South-Carolina Almanack . . . with Directions for managing a Kitchen Garden.*

1768 Martha Logan advertised for sale in Charleston "flower shrubs and box for edging beds, now growing in her garden." *South Carolina Gazette.*

1792 An Annapolis gardener recorded in his diary that "this Day got a Root of Polianthus . . . and planted it on the Circul Bed." William Faris Diary, MHS.

bedchamber A room furnished and used primarily for sleeping but also used through-out the colonial period, as a place of reception and entertainment. The term emerges in the South in the late 17th and early 18th centuries to distinguish this space from the more generic term *chamber.* The synonymous term *bedroom* appears somewhat later in the second quarter of the 18th century and gradually supersedes *bedchamber* by the middle of the 19th century. The bedchamber was often one of the principal rooms on the ground floor of dwellings. This practice continued even in gentry houses through the early 19th century. In contrast, few manor houses in England retained a ground-floor bedchamber after the first quarter of the 18th century. See also **bedroom, chamber.**

1700 An indisposed governor bid members of the Virginia House of Burgesses to "his Bed Chamber That he may Communicate to you such things as are requisite." *Journals of the House of Burgesses,* 3.

1722 A Prince George's County, Maryland, inventory listed goods "in Mr. Levets bed chamber." Maryland Prerogative Court, Inventories, MSA.

1799 "On the third floor are two bed chambers" in a dwelling for sale in Richmond. *Virginia Gazette.*

bed molding The molding or group of moldings located beneath the corona of a cornice; any molding under a projection. See also **crown molding.**

bedroom A sleeping chamber. For a more detailed description, see **bedchamber.**

1741 An estate on the Santee River near Charleston contained a dwelling house with "two large rooms below, and above 18 by 18 two large bed rooms." *South Carolina Gazette.*

1764 On the Patuxent River in Maryland "a commodious well built wooden house" consisted of "one large wainscotted room 20 by 17, and two other small fire rooms; another Bed Room, and three closets, all below" on the ground floor. *Maryland Gazette.*

1783 The second story of the Governor's House in New Bern, North Carolina, was referred to as the "Bedroom floor" by its architect, John Hawks. Hawks Letter, Miranda Papers, Academia Nacional de la Historia, Caracas.

1826 A tavernkeeper boasted that "my Bed Rooms are good and clean enough for the President of the U. S. to sleep in." *The Intelligencer, and Petersburg Commercial Advertiser.*

bed sill   A sill laid on or in the ground to provide support for a superstructure. See also **mudsill, sill.**

> 1792   In Amherst County, Virginia, a "Bill of scantling for the House 18 feet by 22 feet, 2 stories" included "2 Side sills 22 feet 11 by 13 inches,...2 End sills 18 feet 11 by 13 inches,...2 Bed sills 22 feet 12 by 14 inches" is recorded. Hubard Papers, SHC.

bee house, bee shed   An apiary containing one or more hives.

> 1733   A carpenter in Williamsburg was paid for "plank & Work Done about the Beehouse." Jones Papers, LC.
> 1768   On the Blake farm in Queen Anne's County, Maryland, was "one bee shed 10 feet by 5." Queen Anne's Co., Md., Deed Book No. H.

belfry (bellfry, belfrey)   A bell tower or the room where the bells are placed. From the early 18th century onward, the term also referred to the open, paved area under a church tower where the bells where rung and the poor were sometimes seated.

> 1718   A belfry was constructed at an Anglican church and a workman was paid for "makeing & Setting the Vane of [the] said Belfry." St. Anne's Parish, Anne Arundel Co., Md., Vestry Book.
> 1767   Contract for a church in Somerset County, Maryland, included instructions to "Also Build a Belfry to the said Chapel Provided Two Workmen Can Compleat the Same in Twenty four Hours Otherwise be paid for the time over and Above in Proportion for the said Work." Touart, *Somerset.*
> 1769   Order was made "to erect a Bellfry at the Courthouse . . . wherein to hang a Bell Imported . . . for the use of the court." Loudoun Co., Va., Court Order Book 1767–1770.
> 1799   Estimates were to be made for "securing the bell & bellfry, & providing three ladders to reach the bellfry on the inside of the steeple." St. Anne's Parish, Anne Arundel Co., Md., Vestry Book.

bellflower   A stylized bell-shaped flower motif popular in the late 18th and early 19th centuries, especially when joined together as a string. The ornament was particularly popular as a decorative device in chimney pieces.

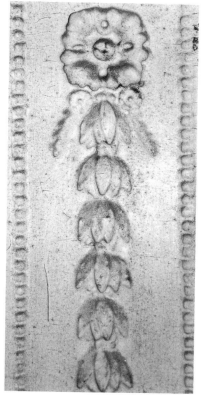

bellflower
54 Montague Street, Charleston, S.C.

bell hanger   An artisan engaged in the installation of housebells, often as a sideline to some other trade—upholstery, foundry, whitesmithing, and carpentry. Bell hangers' advertisements first began to appear in American newspapers about 1750. Judging from these ads, the popularity of bell systems grew significantly after the Revolution, especially in urban areas. Though the trade had been carried on in America since the mid-18th century, the designation *bell hanger* was rarely used before 1800. Occasionally the term described artisans who hung larger sorts of bells for ships, churches, and plantations.

> 1751   In Charleston, "Carpenter and Joyner" Dudley Inman, "lately arrived from London," proposed to "undertake all sorts of carpenters and joyners work," adding that he "hangs bell in the best, neatest and least expensive manner." *South Carolina Gazette.*
> 1801   John Tayloe's account book for construction of his elaborate house in Washington, D.C., included $150 "paid Bell hanger." Tayloe Papers, VHS.
> 1803   George Hedderly described himself as a "CHURCH BELL FOUNDER AND BELLHANGER," to which he added the following announcement: "Having been informed that a large Bell or Peal of Bells are about to be raised in Baltimore, proffers his services . . . having been brought up in the above line of business." *The Telegraph and Daily Advertiser.*
> 1809   Raleigh blacksmith Daniel Peck informed the public of his manifold services, adding, "HOUSE BELLS will be hung in town, or at a small distance in the country, and materials found for the purpose." *Raleigh Star.*

1819   In Savannah, S. A. Stephenson informed the public that he furnished "houses with Bells, in the most improved manner practiced in England . . . S.A.S. follows no other business than Bell-Hanging-nor is any person authorized to engage work in his name." *The Savannah Republican.*

bell roof   A curvilinear roof whose vertical profile is convex at the bottom and concave at the top as in the shape of a bell; an ogee roof. See also **ogee roof.**

1812   The Murfreesborough, Tennessee, courthouse cupola was to have "a bell roof." *Nashville Whig.*

belt course, belting   A projecting or flush horizontal band of wood or masonry extending across the face of a building. Through much of the 18th century, it was used to distinguish the approximate location of an upper floor level on two- and three-story structures. The term, like the synonymous *stringcourse,* may have come into use only in the 19th century.

belvedere (belvidere)   A cupola or room built on top of a roof, or a structure constructed on a hill or place of prominence from which to enjoy a view of a garden, town, or surrounding countryside.

1794   A visitor "took a walk . . . to the Belvidere, about two miles out of New York towards the Sound, an elegant tea drinking house, encircled with a gallery, at one story high, where company can walk round the building and enjoy at the fine prospect of New York harbour and shipping. You have a delightful sea view from thence." *Henry Wansley and His American Journal.*

bench   A long seat with or without a back. Benches were both moveable and fixed. See also **form.**

1663   Nicholas Emerson paid for a "table dores & benches in ye Court House." Norfolk Co., Va., Will and Deed Book 1656–1666.

1768   It was "Ordered that benches be made by Mr. Gilbert Leigh near the Court house table for the conveniency of the attorneys and grand and petit jurors." Chowan Co., N.C., Court Minute Book 1766–1772.

1828   The vestry agreed "that permanent benches be fixed on the west side of the Centre Cross aisle & in the recesses at the entrance of the North & South Long Aisles and in such parts of the Eastern Most Aisle as may not impede the entrance of the owners into their pews- By this Arrangement . . . all the Colored Communicant & elderly stated Worshippers at this Church will be accommodated with Seats as they are at present on the ground floor." St. Philip's Parish, Charleston, S.C., Vestry Book.

berth (birth)   A sleeping place in a ship or building, especially where a number of people shared a single space. Sometimes berths were further developed as shelves or boxes built along interior walls. Use of the term for built-in fittings in structures dates largely to the very end of the 18th century.

1749–50   While surveying in the Valley of Virginia, George Washington "lay down before the fire upon a Little Hay Straw Fodder or Bairskin whichever is to be had with Man Wife and Children like a Parcel of Dogs or Catts and happy's he that gets the Birth nearest the fire." *Writings of George Washington,* 1.

1798   It was "Ordered that the commissioners let the building of the following houses for the use of the poor of this county ... 8 logged cabins 16 by 12 in the clear with outside chimneys to cook and 3 births to lodge." Culpeper Co., Va., Court Order Book 1798–1802.

bettering house   A workhouse for the indigent. The largest and most prominent bettering house in late 18th-century America was erected

in Philadelphia in the late 1760s. For a more detailed description, see
poorhouse, workhouse.

> 1770 "Being informed that the people in the Bettering House had a desire to hear
> me, I went and preached in one of their work rooms . . . There are about three
> hundred persons in it, who are employed in some kind of work—the sick have
> proper attendance & the children are properly instructed. This is properly an House
> of Mercy, and is a credit to the City of Philadelphia." *Journal of Joseph Pilmore.*

between joints (betwixt joints)   The height of a wall from the sill to
the plate. The term rarely appears in the South, although it is found
in New England as early as the 17th century. The southern equivalent was *pitch*. See **pitch** (1).

> 1645 In Springfield, Massachusetts, "Thomas Cooper [is] to build a meetinghouse,
> length 40 foote, in breadth 25 foote, 9 foote betwixt joynt." Burt, *The First Century
> of the History of Springfield*, 1.
> 1836 The poorhouse was to be "thirty four feet Long and sixteen wide, ten feet
> between joints and a shed on the back side ten feet wide seven feet between joints."
> Wayne Co., N.C., Miscellaneous Court Records, NCA&H.

bevel   *(n.)* A surface or angle that does not form a right angle with
adjacent surfaces or faces; an obtuse angle.   *(v.)* To pare back or cut
away so as to form an obtuse angle. A bevel square is an adjustable
instrument used by woodworkers for laying out angles. See also
chamfer.

> 1729 An order read: "The window frames To be new Silled & bevelled off." Strat-
> ton Major Parish, King and Queen Co., Va., Vestry Book.

bill of lumber, bill of scantling   See **scantling.**

binding joist, binding beam   A horizontal framing member that supports a bridging joist above and the common joists of a ceiling below
in a double flooring system. The binding joists extend from wall plate
to wall plate or from girder to girder. On their lower sides, the ends
of smaller and shorter ceiling joists are let into a grooved channel or
tenoned into mortises. Bridging joists sit on the upper face or are
slightly notched over the tops of the binding joists. Floorboards are
laid over the bridging joists. This double flooring system sometimes
appeared in buildings with large room spans. In a more general sense,

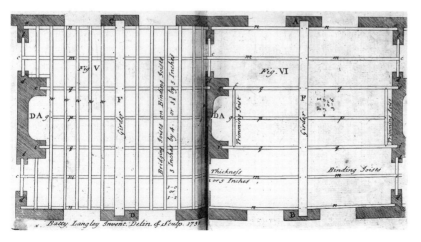

binding joist   Double floor frame

the term was occasionally used to refer to an interior girder. See also **bridging joist, girder.**

> 1755 "BINDING-JOISTS are those joists, in any floor, into which the Trimmers of Stair-Cases (or well-hole for the stairs) and Chimney-ways are framed; these Joists ought to be larger than common Joists." Salmon, *Palladio Londinensis.*
>
> 1806 Preparation for work on a dwelling in Berkeley County, Virginia, included "halling Rafters & binders & wall plates & coller beams." Gardiner Papers, Duke.

bit (bitt)   A metal blade fastened into the foot of a wooden brace or stock that is used to bore holes. Craftsmen employed a dowel bit to drill accurate holes to take the dowels that joined two pieces together.

blacksmith (smith)   A craftsman who forges iron. Southern blacksmiths principally did utilitarian work such as making and repairing inexpensive tools and hardware. The vast majority of fine smith work was imported. See also **smith shop, forge and wrought iron.**

> 1769 "JOHN DRAPER, Smith and Farrier, In the Main Street, *Williamsburg*, Has with Great Success made trial of a certain Medicine, very salutary in preserving from, or restoring those who have already catched the distemper, which now rages so generally." *Virginia Gazette.*
>
> 1771 "Francis Moss of the County of York . . . doth voluntarily and of his own free will and accord put himself apprentice to John Draper of the City of Williamsburg to learn his Art Trade and Mystery and after the Manner of an Apprentice to serve the said John Draper. . . . And the said Master shall use the utmost of his Endeavours to teach . . . the said Apprentice in the Trade or Mystery of a Blacksmith." York Co., Va., Deed Book 1769–1777.

black walnut   See **walnut.**

blank window   A false window set into a wall recess. It can neither be opened nor seen from the opposite side of the wall and is usually installed to preserve a sense of symmetry in a room or in the fenestration of a facade. See also **false** (2).

> 1738 Virginia planter John Carter wrote to his brother Charles that "as to the articles of Stone Work, I leave them to be fitted up by yourself. . . . The work is very nearly finished except the blank windows, which consisting of many small [pieces?] of stone make as I think a very indifferent figure." Carter-Plummer Letterbook, VHS.
>
> 1828 A courthouse to be built in Madison County, Virginia, included "Four Blank windows, finished on the outside as the other Frames are But no sash." Malcolm Crawford Papers, VSL.

blind   A protective screen or cover of cloth or wood used to shield an aperture from light and heat. On the inside of buildings, fabric blinds were rolled up, while louvered wooden ones were hinged. Cloth blinds appeared in the South at least by the first half of the 18th century, if not earlier. For exterior wooden screens, the terms *blind* and *shutter* were nearly synonymous if they had louvered slats. See also **shade, umbrella, shutter, Venetian blind.**

> 1736 Inventory of an estate in Williamsburg listed "2 pr Gingham window Curtains & blinds." York Co., Va., Will and Inventory Book 1732–1740.
>
> 1807 In church accounts there was a "payment for 10 yds green durant used for a sun blind, pulleys, rings and pins." This was followed three years later with "payment for green worsted blinds for heads of doors and windows." Congregational Church, Charleston, S.C., Record Book.
>
> 1819 In Georgetown, South Carolina, "a Carpenter from the North . . . will when at the North, make Window Blinds (traverse and standing) venetian Blinds, parlour Blinds . . . for any gentleman in this neighborhood who wish them, and bring them with him the ensuing fall at the New-York price." *Winyah Intelligencer.*

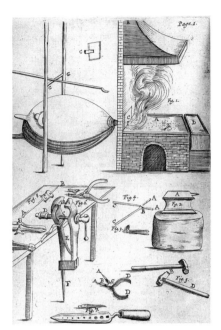

blacksmith   Smith's forge.
Fig. 1: (A) hearth, (B) hovel, (C) tewel, (D) trough, (E) bellows, (F) handle, (G) rockstaff.
Fig. 2: (A) anvil. *Figs. 3, 4:* tongs.
Fig. 5: hammers. *Fig. 6:* vises.
Fig. 7: screw plate.

1819 Thomas Jefferson instructed his carpenter that he should make "2 blinds of the North portico. These will need only half blinds, to wit, over the lower sash to prevent people seeing onto the rooms." Coolidge Collection, Massachusetts Historical Society.

blind nail To secure planks, boards, sheathing, wainscotting, and other woodwork to framing members by driving nails diagonally into their edges, so that the heads of the nails are concealed by the adjoining plank or board. Because of the added expense of such a method, the blind nailing of floors was often reserved for the most important spaces in a dwelling or public building. See also **secret nail.**

1790 A carpenter's bill for work done at Hampton near Baltimore included "12 sqr 1/4 flooring blind naild @ 45/ per sqr . . . £27.11.3." *MHM*, 33.

blind wall See **dead wall.**

block **1.** A log or short post placed on or in the ground beneath the sill, used to support the superstructure of a building. Such blocks of hard, durable woods provided a cheap substitute for masonry foundations and were more easily replaced than structural posts set in the ground. A sill-framed building resting on blocks was as impervious to damp as one raised on masonry foundations. See also **lightwood.**

1679 An agreement was made to frame a church "after the best manner as good workmen do laying locust blocks under the sd frame." Accomack Co., Va., Will, Deed, and Order Book 1678–1682.
1693 A dwelling was "to stand upon White oak Blocks." Essex Co., Va., Court Order Book 1692–1695.
1723 It was agreed to "build . . . a Courthouse of thirty feet in length eighteen feet in width with a fashionable over Jet framed Worke Standing on Cedar Blocks." *Higher-Court Records of North Carolina*, 5.
1771 "My Carpenters have been . . . repairing the sills of my Fork tobacco house, all rotten because never blockt up as they should have been." *Diary of Landon Carter*, 2.

2. A solid mass of stone, especially an unfinished one from a quarry.

1767 "The Pilasters are to be Joined in one, and as I Conceive Hewn out of the same Block or Blocks, that make up the Columns, and with the Columns . . . and those with the Pilasters Joined to them will be Composed of Different Blocks or Pieces of Stone." Trostel, *Mount Clare*.
1804 "In fixing the Subplinth or Base block on which the Colonnade is to stand, its width must be sufficient to receive the base and plinths of the Columns." *The Correspondence and Miscellaneous Papers of Benjamin Henry Latrobe*, 1.

3. A small piece of wood used behind a finished surface for support, such as a nailer for wainscotting; sometimes referred to as *plugs* or *plugging.*

4. A decorative corner piece in a door or window architrave. Often decorated with geometrical patterns, architrave corner blocks came into fashion in the South in the first decades of the 19th century and remained a popular decorative motif through the end of the century.

1811 Carpentry work at Montpelier in Orange County, Virginia, included "10 pair of architrave blocks." Cocke Papers, UVa.

blockhouse A detached fort blocking access to a river, pass, or other strategic area. Although the modern usage associates the term with a structure built of horizontal log walls, blockhouses in the early colonial period were built of various materials.

1622 A ship captain "made Tryall of those Bancks that lye out in James River neare Blunts-pointe and found that a Blockehowse or fforte might be erected upon them, wch would altogether forbidd the passage of shipps upp higher." *Records of the Virginia Company*, 2.

1715 At Germanna on the Rapidan River, settlers had built a palisade "with stakes stuck in the ground, and laid close the one to the other. . . . The place that is paled in is a pentagon, very regularly laid out; and in the very centre there is a block-house, made with five sides, which answer to the five sides of the great inclosure; there are loop-holes through it. . . . This was intended for a retreat for the people, in case they were not able to defend the palisadoes, if attacked by the Indians. They make use of this block-house for divine service." Fontaine, *Memoirs of a Huguenot Family*.

blocking course   A plain course of masonry surmounting the cornice at the top of a building.

1806 In the House of Representatives at the Capitol in Washington, "the 24 Corinthian columns which . . . support the dome, are 26 feet 8 inches in height, the entablature is 6 feet high, the blocking course 1 foot 6 inches, and the dome rises 12 feet 6 inches, in all 53 feet 8 inches." *The Correspondence and Miscellaneous Papers of Benjamin Henry Latrobe*, 2.

board   A piece of riven or sawn wood of a considerable length and measuring at least four inches wide and no more than two inches thick. Thinner pieces were known as strips and thicker ones were classified as planks. The most common use of boards were for interior and exterior sheathing and flooring. See also **clapboard, plank, weatherboard.**

boast   To pare stone with a broad chisel and mallet; to roughly cut around an ornament.

1806 Benjamin Henry Latrobe reported that work on the frieze carving for the Capitol in Washington was drawing to a close, "including the Eagle of which a considerable part is finished, one wing being nearly compleat, and the body and the other wing boasted." *The Correspondence and Miscellaneous Papers of Benjamin Henry Latrobe*, 2.

boghouse   A necessary house; privy. For a more detailed description, see **necessary house.**

1763 Property for sale in Annapolis included "a good Pump Well, Boghouse, and Garden Ground." *Maryland Gazette*.

bolection (belection, bilection, and bolexion)   A molding that projects beyond the face of an adjoining frame or panel. Such moldings are often used to decorate mantelpieces, and the joint between a panel and surrounding stiles and rails in doors and wainscotting.

1680 A Talbot County, Maryland, courthouse was to have "folding Wenscoatt dores where nessisary the lower Dores polectioned." Talbot Co., Md., Judgments 1675–1682.

1711 The largest room in a house was to be built with wainscotting "5 foot high with Large [b]olleccon with raised pannells." Rivoire, *Homeplaces*.

bollard   One of a series of posts made of stone, wood, or iron, used to protect footpaths from vehicular traffic. Also a short post used to secure vessels to docks and quays. The term did not come into use before the middle of the 19th century. Prior to this, bollards were simply referred to as *posts*.

1786 In Petersburg, "such persons as chose to put up Post before their houses or Lotts in Water and High Streets must place them at the exact distance of Eight feet from the line of the Street. . . . all such posts in the before mentioned Street to be five inches in diameter formed in an Octagon rounded at the top and four feet high,

bolection
Mantel architrave, 43 East Bay Street, Charleston, S.C.

they will be a great protection to the gutters which will run within and it would be proper to lay a small Fine upon persons riding on the inside of the Posts." Petersburg, Va., City Council Minute Book 1784–1811.

bolster   A short horizontal beam placed at the top of a post or pillar to provide greater bearing surface for a girder lying directly above. Bolsters were often used in buildings that required large, open internal spaces such as mills and warehouses.

bolt   **1.** An iron or brass locking mechanism used to secure shut the leaf of a door, shutter, or gate. A flat or round bar moves through staples fixed to a flat plate and rests in a mortise or staple in the adjoining jamb or sill. See also **spring bolt.**

> 1674   A dwelling converted to a courthouse in Charles County, Maryland, was to be fitted with "all necessary & convenient doores, locks, keyes, bolts, latches, hinges." *Archives of Maryland,* 60.
>
> 1725   A blacksmith was to be paid for "a large bolt 2 foot long & 3 staples." St. Anne's Parish, Anne Arundel Co., Md., Vestry Book.

2. One of a pair of iron, *L*-shaped brackets, or a bracket paired with a staple, in which a crossbar is dropped, securing a door shut. See also **crossbar.**

> 1756   A church was to have "a latch and bolt to the front door [and] a sufficient bar and bolt to the other doors." Wicomico Parish, Northumberland Co., Va., Vestry Book.

3. A threaded piece of iron on which a head is usually affixed at one end and secured by a nut on the other, used to fasten two pieces together.

> 1759   A tobacco prize at a warehouse was ordered repaired with "a bolt through the top of the posts as they are all split." Accomack Co., Va., Court Order Book 1753–1763.
>
> 1788   In constructing the roof of the Charleston County, South Carolina, courthouse, a blacksmith was sought for the "making of screwed bolts and nuts." *The City Gazette, or the Daily Advertiser.*

4. A pin used both to hinge a shutter strap at its fixed side and to secure the strap in place when the shutters are closed. See also **strap.**

> 1809   Specifications for the clerk's office at Henry County, Virginia, included "strong window shutters to each window, with iron straps and bolts across the same." Henry Co., Va., Order Book 1808–1811.

boltel   See **boultin.**

bolting house, bolting mill (boulting)   A building and its equipment, generally associated with a gristmill or bakehouse, where the meal of cereal grains is sifted through a fine cloth in an apparatus known as a bolting chest.

> 1735   An inventory of an estate near Edenton, North Carolina, listed items "in the millhouse [and] in the boulting house." Secretary of State Records, Inventories 1728–1741, NCA&H.
>
> 1753   "To be sold" in Frederick County, Maryland, was "a Merchant's Water Mill, double geered, with Geers for two Pair of Stones, with a good Bolting-Mill, the House 30 Feet long and 20 Feet wide." *Maryland Gazette.*

bond   The system of joining elements of masonry together in various patterns; specifically, the outer face pattern of brick courses. In brickwork, a *header* is a brick laid so that only its shorter side appears on the surface. A *stretcher* is the face of the longer side. Although there

bond
(a) header bond, St. Paul's Church, Edenton, N.C. (b) English bond, Eagle's Nest, Charles City County, Va. (c) Flemish bond, Blake Tenement, Charleston, S.C. (d) 1:5 bond, Pavilion 9, University of Virginia

a

b

c

d

were many variants, the most common bond patterns in the early South were *English bond, Flemish bond, header bond,* and *American* or *1:3, 1:5, 1:7 bond*. In English bond, masons alternated laying a course of stretchers with a course of headers. It was used throughout the 17th century and much of the 18th century and became a rare pattern of face decoration by the early 19th century. However, English bond continued to be used on the interior faces of many masonry buildings through the early national period. Bricklayers created Flemish bond by alternating stretcher and headers in each course so that a header would be flanked on both its sides and above and below by stretchers. Occasionally, bricklayers would break the header in half, so that it extended no further than four inches deep, a practice that made it simpler to maintain the face bond but provided a less secure tie with the inner mass of brickwork. Although less common than English bond, Flemish bond appeared in the Chesapeake in the early 17th century and became the predominant bond throughout the South in the late colonial period. It remained fashionable in many areas until the 1840s. In many buildings, bricklayers laid the foundation up to the water table in English bond, then switched to Flemish bond for the remainder of the wall. Less common than English or Flemish bond was a bond of all headers. It was used with some frequency in certain regions, including Annapolis and the eastern shore of Maryland, and for certain elements such as curved walls. American bond was a modified English bond in which a course of headers alternated with three, five, or seven courses of stretchers. This pattern came into fashion in the late colonial period in Delaware and Maryland, influenced by Philadelphia and Delaware Valley building practices. Because it was easier to lay, it was considered a cheaper bond than Flemish or English. However, it did not become common in the lower South until the beginning of the 19th century. In building contracts, it was relatively rare to specify the type of bonding to be used in a building. Occasionally, an agreement called for decorative patterns such as rubbed arches or glazed headers, but on the whole, the type of bonding was left to local custom. However, this did not mean that clients left their masons with entire freedom of choice. In some buildings, the front facade was laid in one bond, while the other sides were laid in a less costly and complicated bond. In the early 19th century, for example, Flemish bond was the preferred choice for the front of buildings, while the cheaper American bond was used on the back and side walls. See also **brick, closer, header** (1), **stretcher.**

1803 Bricks in a church designed by Robert Mills for an Episcopal congregation near Charleston were "to be sound and well burnt laid in flemish bond, no two Courses to be stretchers." Johns Island Church Specifications, Library Society of Charleston.

1807 "The Custom House to be erected at New Orleans" was to have the walls "faced with well burned Stretchers of an even color, laid in Flemish bond, all the headers to be whole bricks." *The Correspondence and Miscellaneous Papers of Benjamin Henry Latrobe,* 2.

1831 Specifications for a courthouse in Caswell County, North Carolina, noted that "the brick on the outside of the building to be laid in flemish bond jointed and penciled down . . . on inside English bond." Caswell Co., N.C., Court Minutes 1823–1831, NCA&H.

bond timber   Wooden timbers or planks inserted horizontally into masonry walls to strengthen and tie them together, as well as to serve as nailing surfaces for plaster laths, wainscotting, cornices, chair boards, and door and window architraves.

1791 An undertaker of a church was instructed "to put in the Walls as much Bond Timbers as the Vestry may Chuse." Trinity Parish, Charles Co., Md., Vestry Book.

1810 A bricklayer's account in Baltimore included "bedding & laying 640 ft. Bond Timber." Riddell Accounts, Pleasants Papers, MHS.

bonnet   A small, self-supporting protective hood or roof over an exterior doorway. The term enjoyed some currency in parts of colonial Virginia. See also **pent.**

1745 There were "to be bonnets . . . to each door" of a new church. Fredericksville Parish, Louisa Co., Va., Vestry Book.

1801 An order required "some person to build or fix bonnets over each of the doors of the courthouse." Goochland Co., Va., Court Order Book 1801–1803.

border   1. The edge of a surface that forms a boundary, often treated ornamentally with a decorative strip of woodwork, cloth, or some other material, or distinguished by gilding or a change in paint colors. Specifically, strips of wood that frame and separate the hearth from the floorboards.

1773 A visitor to Miles Brewton's house in Charleston thought it had "the grandest hall I ever beheld, azure blue stain window curtains, rich blue paper with gilt, mashee borders, most elegant pictures, excessive grand and costly looking glasses." *Proceedings of the Massachusetts Historical Society,* 49.

1774 The work at William Corbit's house in Odessa, Delaware, included a "Bordr round hearth 3/." Sweeney, *Grandeur on the Appoquinimink.*

1777 A workman was paid for "putting new Wash Boards in Council office new Borders &c. round the Harth" in the capitol in Williamsburg. State Auditor's Papers, Vouchers 1777–1778, VSL.

1811 A carpenter installed in a Baltimore dwelling "3 fire borders returned." Riddell Accounts, Pleasants Papers, MHS.

1817 "The canopy" of the pulpit in an Episcopal church in Baltimore "is wholly of stucco, and is semi circular . . . the top semispherical, ornamented with Palm leaves, and terminated with a crown of foliage, a border of foliage continued round on the top of the cornice." *American and Commercial Daily Advertiser.*

2. A side edge, or part of a garden or pleasure grounds lying along its boundary or outline; a bank raised at the side of a garden for the cultivation of flowers or plants.

1785 At Mount Vernon, George Washington "planted border of Ivy under the No. side of the Garden wall" and later "moved the Apricots and Peach Trees which stood in the borders of the grass plats." *Diaries of George Washington, 2.*

1792 A gardener in Annapolis "sowed a border next the Dining Room with Radish & Large Winter Cabbage." William Faris Diary, MHS.

botanical garden A public or private garden or part of one, where a variety of plants were grown either outdoors or indoors and displayed for purposes of science, status, and art. Such gardens begin to appear in the South in the late 18th century. See also **garden.**

1785 Over the course of a summer and fall at Mount Vernon, George Washington noted that he "sowed one half the Chinese Seed given me by Mr. Porter . . . in three rows . . . in my Botanical garden. . . . The Guinea Grass in my Botanical Garden was much injured by the frosts. . . . Covered my exotic plants in . . . my Botanical Garden." *The Diaries of George Washington, 2.*

1805 Opened in Norfolk, Virginia, was a "Museum Naturae [or] Botanical Garden, containing specimens of all the vegetable productions of this country, and furnished with green-houses, for all such exotick and rare plants, as may be procured from abroad." *Norfolk Gazette and Public Ledger.*

1807 The "Botanick Garden of South Carolina" in Charleston contained "as large a collection of plants, as any garden in the United States, and it is peculiarly rich in rare and valuable exoticks . . . Lovers of science . . . acquire a knowledge of the most beautiful and interesting of the works of nature. The Florist may be gratified with viewing the productions of the remotest clime, and the Medical Botanist with the objects of his study . . . affords an agreeable recreation both to those who visit it merely for amusement, and who seek . . . information." *Charleston Courier.*

boultin (boltel) An English name for a quarter round molding; an ovolo. The term was rarely used in the southern colonies and states. For a more detailed description see **quarter round.**

bounds The limits, confines, or boundary of an area or piece of land. The term was used specifically to refer to a demarcated area around a prison, usually ten acres. Here prisoners such as debtors and petty offenders were freely allowed to walk about so that they could enjoy the fresh air and preserve their health against contagious diseases that threatened them in the cramped confines of prison rooms. In some instances, prisoners were also allowed to live outside the prison but within the bounds. The term was synonymous with *rules.*

1661 The Virginia General Assembly passed an act concerning "Persons dwelling in the rules of the prison." It stated that "noe person dwelling within the rules of any prison shall have the benefitt of walking in the rules or lodging in his owne house but shall be confined to close imprisonment and if the sheriffe shall permit any person soe dwelling within the rules as aforesaid to goe abroad out of prison though with a keeper he shall be liable to pay the debt as in case of escapes." Hening, *Statutes at Large, 2.*

1685 "Justices requested and desired . . . to measure out and ascertain bounds of

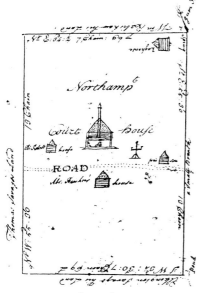

bounds
Prison bounds, Northampton County, Va., 1724

liberty (for prisoners to walk and refresh themselves in) about ye County Prison." Henrico Co., Va., Court Order Book 1678–1693.

1789 It was "Ordered that the prison bounds for the county be the same as those for the District Goal to wit an area of ten acres the Court house the centre the sides of the area parallel to the sides and ends of the Court house to be laid off in a square but every house within the said bounds where a billiard Table is kept to be considered as without the bounds." Accomack Co., Va., Court Order Book 1787–1790.

bower A shelter or covered place in a pleasure ground or garden, usually made with boughs of trees bent and twined together for shade from the sun; a crude dwelling made from sticks, bark, and other natural, unworked materials. See also **arbor (1)**, **summerhouse**.

1728 On the Virginia–North Carolina border, "not far from the Inlet, dwelt a Marooner, that Modestly call'd himself a Hermit, tho' he forfeited that Name by Suffering a wanton Female to cohabit with Him. His Habitation was a Bower, cover'd with Bark after the Indian Fashion, which in that mild Situation protected him pretty well from the Weather." Byrd, *History of the Dividing Line*.

1809 "In the centre of the Garden" of a tavern keeper in Salisbury, North Carolina, "was a handsome bower, neatly built, & adorned with English Honey Suckle, Wood-bine & a few Jessamine." *Journal of William D. Martin*.

1819 An English visitor in Charleston "called on the venerable Nathaniel Russell, Esq., residing in a splendid mansion, surrounded by a wilderness of flowers and bowers of myrtles, oranges and lemons, smothered with fruit and flowers." Faux, *Memorable Days in America*.

1827 A visitor to one of the gardens in the Moravian town of Salem, North Carolina, "saw what I conceived to be a curiosity and itself extremely beautiful. It was a large summer house formed of eight cedar trees planted in a circle, the tops whilst young were chained together in the center forming a cone. The immense branches were all cut, so that there was not a leaf, the outside is beautifully trimmed perfectly even and very thick, within were seats placed around and doors or openings were cut through the branches, it had been planted 40 years." *Juliana Conner Diary*, SHC.

bowling green A smooth, level lawn or green often used for playing bowls upon, usually measuring one hundred by two hundred feet and sunken below the general level of the ground surrounding it. Sometimes called a square in the late 18th and early 19th centuries, the bowling green offered beauty and ornament as well as recreation. Public and private bowling greens, often associated with taverns and race courses, appeared throughout the colonies from the middle of the 17th century onward.

1743 At Crow-Field near Charleston, "opposite on the left hand is a large square boleing green sunk a little below the level of the rest of the garden with a walk quite round composed of a double row of fine large flowering Laurel and Catalpas which form both shad and beauty." *Letterbook of Eliza Lucas Pinckney*.

1773 At Nomini Hall in Westmoreland County, Virginia, "the area of the Triangle made by the Wash-house, Stable, & School-House is perfectly level, and designed for a Bowling-Green." *Journal & Letters of Philip Vickers Fithian*.

1785 George Washington "finished levelling and Sowing the lawn in front of the Ho. intended for a Bolling Green." *The Diaries of George Washington*, 2.

bow window A bay window of rectangular, polygonal, or semicircular form projecting outward from the facade of a building. Such windows appeared by the third quarter of the 18th century, most often on shop fronts. Contemporaries in the colonial and early national period apparently did not follow the modern convention of distinguishing polygonally shaped windows as *bay windows* and curvilinear ones as *bow windows*.

1775 For sale in Williamsburg was "a large BOW-WINDOW, with bars and shutters." *Virginia Gazette*.

bow window
Post office, New Castle, Del.

1784 While "looking thro my large Bow window," planter Richard Henry Lee observed "there were openings in the ice, one upon the River Shore directly opposite to the great walk in my Garden." *Richard Henry Lee Memorandum Book 1776–1794*, Huntington Library.

1788 At Belvedere near Baltimore, "the perfections of the landscape, its near and distant scenery, were united in the view from the bow-window of the noble room in which breakfast was prepared." Twining, *Travels in America 100 Years Ago*.

1797 In Charleston, an advertisement read: "to be sold Cheap, A BOW WINDOW with SHUTTERS &c. complete; Lights 18 by 12." *City Gazette and Daily Advertiser*.

1799 A house in Norfolk, Virginia, was so poorly constructed that "no two sides of the bow window were equal, or set out from the same center." *The Correspondence and Miscellaneous Papers of Benjamin Henry Latrobe*, 1.

box **1.** A container, case, or receptacle with a lid or door.

> **1676** The inventory of an estate listed "in the closett in the Lodging chamber . . . 1 desk with drawers and box with drawers." *Maryland Prerogative Court Inventories and Accounts 2*, MSA.
> **1751** For the better storage of papers and books, a court ordered "a workman to make a Box to the Lawyers Barr." *Frederick Co., Va., Court Order Book 1748–1751*.

2. A small dwelling in the countryside serving as a rural refuge.

> **1747** Charles Pinckney advertised for sale near Charleston "a pleasant Hill on which to fix a little Box for the Summer's Retreat." *South Carolina Gazette*.

3. A small structure providing shelter for individuals such as watchmen and sentinels involved in various civic and military duties. See also **sentinel box, watch box.**

4. An enclosure with benches or seats in a courtroom for public officials and members of grand or petit juries. Enclosed by wainscotting or balustrades, sheriffs' boxes stood on a raised platform on or near the magistrates' bench in early Virginia courtrooms. They were occupied by county sheriffs, one of their deputies, or court criers. Occasionally arranged on platformed tiers, jury boxes appeared in colonial courtrooms throughout many colonies in the early 18th century to provide jurymen with a seat or bench within the bar. The term *jury box* does not appear in Virginia until the early 19th century.

> **1744** A courthouse undertaker was ordered "to build a Box For the Use of the Sheriff as is Usuall in Court Houses." *Spotsylvania Co., Va., Court Order Book 1738–1749*.
> **1801** Repairs in a courtroom included placing "three benches of seats where the present Jury Boxes are. The first one Eighteen inches high, the others to be raised Eighteen inches above each other, with Bannisters." *Caroline Co., Md., Court Minute Book No. 7*.

5. A compartment or section in a theater enclosed by panelling or railing for the accommodation of a small number of people. Boxes were the choice seats in a building, arranged at various levels along the front and side of the stage in the theater. Box seats were more expensive and exclusive than those in the pit. See also **pit (1), theater.**

> **1786** In Charleston, "a building called HARMONY HALL" was erected "for the Purpose of Music Meetings, Dancing, and Theatrical Amusements . . . The boxes are 22 in number with a key to each Box—The Pit is very large, and Theatrum and Orchestra elegant and commodious." *Maryland Journal and Baltimore Advertiser*.
> **1797** A full bill at the theater in Petersburg, Virginia, included "the Comic Song of *The Learned Pig* . . . to which will be added the Comic Opera of *Peeping Tom of Coventry*. Tickets . . . Boxes 6d, Pitt 4s 6d." *Virginia Gazette and Petersburg Intelligencer*.
> **1819** In "the new Richmond Theatre. . . . The whole range of boxes above and

box (5)
Charles Fraser, Tightrope Walker,
Charleston, S.C., c. 1796.

below is interspersed with painted pannels, each of which is different and all have some classic allusion . . . The designs are said to be somewhat similar to those of Drury Lane." *Norfolk Herald.*

6. An open-air table enclosed by boards on three sides found in some public pleasure gardens. Often additional seating within the box was available on banquettes attached to the walls, and privacy could be obtained by closing curtains across the fronts of the boxes. These features were often painted green or whitewashed. In the evening, oil lamps mounted on stanchions or suspended from branches provided light. Awnings were occasionally erected over boxes for shade and protection from inclement weather.

1797 In the Apollo Garden in New York, "the Garden is elegantly set up with a quantity of boxes lighted with lamps in a fine & new stile." *New York Daily Advertiser.*

7. Wooden formwork used to prepare tabby. Sand, lime, oyster shells, and water were mixed together and poured into the box until it settled and hardened. See also **tabby.**

1802 Payment was to be made to the builder of a "parsonage house so soon as the first box of tabbey is made." St. Helena's Parish, S.C., Vestry Book.

boxed, boxing **1.** The recessed casing on each side of a window jamb into which shutters can be folded back.

1762 "The frames of the windows" in a church were "to be boxed." Frederick Parish, Frederick Co., Va., Vestry Book.
1803 An Episcopal church in South Carolina was to have "box'd Sash frames to all the lower Windows." Johns Island Church Specifications, Library Society of Charleston.

2. An enclosed eaves with boards nailed to form a fascia and soffit, occasionally enriched by moldings. Also, an encasement for the corner notching of a log building with boards in order to protect it from deterioration. See also **cornice** (1).

1795 Repairs were ordered to "a Barn of sawed Logs, the said Barn to be underpinned with stone . . . and the East end and each side to the doors to be weather boarded with Boards and the other corner to be box'd." New Castle Co., Del., Orphans Court Valuations H.
1802 Repairs to the Lockerman dwelling in Kent County, Delaware, included "The corners and eves boxed." Kent Co., Del., Orphans Court Valuations H.
1813 "The Eves" of a jail were "to be plainly & strongly Boxed with 1 1/2 inch plank." Wayne Co., N.C., Miscellaneous Court Records, NCA&H.

box lock An iron lock with a wood case. See also **stock lock.**

1726 The vestry paid "for one large double Spring box Lock." St. Anne's Parish, Anne Arundel County, Md., Vestry Book.

box rule A measuring instrument used by craftsmen and others, constructed of boxwood, divided into sections, and connected by brass hinges.

brace **1.** A wooden or metal member used to stiffen or support another member or an assemblage of roof or wall framing. Specifically, in traditional Anglo-American frame construction, angled braces frequently ran from corner and doorposts to the sill, or from a principal post to the plate or tie beam. The terms were not used with any frequency, if at all, in the early South. The former is now called a *downbrace,* and the latter, an *upbrace.* The angled strut supports that

brace

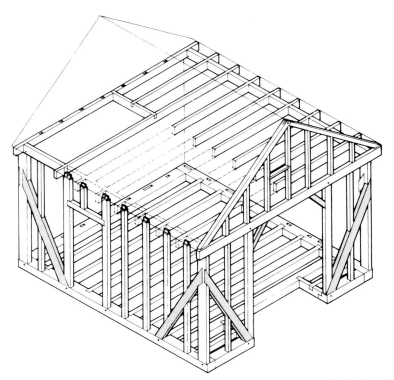

bracket
Above: jetty bracket, Cupola House, Edenton, N.C.
Below: stair bracket, Miles Brewton House, Charleston, S.C.

run from the base of a king post roof truss to the principal rafters were also known as braces.

> 1652   An order was issued to build a house "& brace it with 4 braces to the Ground-sell." Surry Co., Va., Deed Book 1652–1672.
>
> 1691   A post-in-the-ground courthouse was to "be well Braced Above & below studded." Middlesex Co., Va., Deed Book, 1687–1750.
>
> 1726   "BRACE. In a Building, is a piece of Timber, which is framed in with bevel Joints. Its use is to keep the Building from swerving, either this, or that way; they are sometimes call'd Strutts, viz. When they are fram'd in the King-Piece, and principal Rafters." Neve, *City and Country Purchaser.*
>
> 1750   A glebe house roof was to have "3 pair of principal Rafters and Purlins and braces of 6 by 4 inches." Newport Parish, Isle of Wight Co., Va. Vestry Book.
>
> 1793   In a courtroom, "the attornies bar is slight and requires braces to strengthen it." Nottoway County, Va., Court Order Book 1793–1797.

2. A wooden tool used for boring holes. A brace consists of a head that is held in one hand, a central curved crank that is rotated by the other hand, and a foot that holds a metallic bit that bores through the material. See also **stock.**

bracket   **1.** In general, a support that helps carry the weight of an overhanging or projecting object or members, such as jetties, shelves, benches, pediments, and cornices. See also **ancone, console, modillion.**

> 1741   The vestry paid a workman "for the Seats and Brackets in the pews." St. Anne's Parish, Anne Arundel Co., Md., Vestry Book.
>
> 1777   Repairs in the capitol in Williamsburg, Virginia, included "putting new seat & Bracket in Burgess's Room." State Auditor's Papers, VSL.

2. A decorative element applied to the string of a stair beneath the projecting nosing of the treads.

> 1772   A glebe house was to have "a genteel pair of stairs with scroll brackets in the passage." St. Mark's Parish, Culpeper Co., Va., Vestry Book.

brad A thin, flattish nail with a slight projecting lip rather than a broad head, as is typical of most nails; a headless nail. Fabricated in various sizes, brads were used for a number of purposes, especially for finish work such as flooring, wainscotting, and trim. Because they lacked heads, brads were often driven below the surface of the wood with nail punches and the holes filled with putty to mitigate the effect of nailing. See also **nail.**

1726 "Brads- Are a sort of Nails without Heads, some Iron-mongers distinguish them by six Names, as followeth, viz. Joyners Plain for hard Wood wainscot, from 1 Inch to 2 1/4 in Length. Batten for soft Wood wainscot. . . . Flooring Plain for softwood, joysts. . . . Flooring strong fit for hard Joysts. . . . Quarter heads for soft Wood. . . . Quarter heads strong for hard Wood joysts. . . . All Bill-brads, alias Quarter heads, are very fit for shallow joysts that are subject to warp, or for Floors laid in Haste, or by unskillful persons, because the Bill to head will hinder the Boards from starting from the Joysts, but doth not make so smoothe Work as the plain Brads." Neve, *City and Country Purchaser.*

1738 It was ordered that the interior sheathing of a church be "naild on with 8d nailes or Brads." Bristol Parish, Prince George Co., Va., Vestry Book.

1805 To be sold at "McCall's Nail Manufactory" in Richmond were "24d, 20d, & 12d Cut nails & Brads, 11 Cts. per lb." *The Enquirer.*

1810 Imported into Baltimore from Liverpool were "a few casks 20d wrought Flooring BRADS." *American and Commercial Daily Advertiser.*

brad awl See **awl.**

brandy house A building used for distilling brandy and other liqueurs. The term was used mainly in Delaware in the late 18th and 19th centuries. See also **still house.**

1790 A farmstead contained a "Brandy house." Sussex Co., Del., Orphans Court Valuations E.

1822 In southern Delaware, an orphan's estate had "one Brandy house Sixteen by twelve feet in bad repair" along with an orchard containing 150 apple trees and 15 peach trees. Sussex Co., Del., Orphans Court Valuations M.

brass A metallic alloy composed of copper and zinc in varying proportions. Brass ornaments and implements appeared in the southern colonies in the 17th century; however, the metal did not become important in architectural decoration until the next century. By the middle of the 18th century, merchants imported brass nails for hanging pictures, flashing, and coffins; brass hinges for case furniture and doors of public rooms; and brass locks and door knobs. In some of the affluent households, servants were called by brass house bells. Because it was a costly material that conveyed a certain cachet, early Americans also purchased brass fireplace furnishings, chandeliers, and sconces.

1735 "Just imported" into Charleston "most sorts of brass and japanned Locks." *South Carolina Gazette.*

1749 A Yorktown, Virginia, merchant sold "1500 brass nails . . . 1 brass padlock . . . 6 pr brass hinges." Journal of Francis Jerdone 1749–1755, VSL.

1749 In Daniel Rawlings's hall stood a "corner Cupboard neatly Painted with Brass Lock Hinges and Bolts." Calvert Co., Md., Prerogative Court Records, 40, MSA.

1760 There were imported into Annapolis "from Glasgow . . . Stock locks, plated and pull back, Closet Ditto with Brass Knobs, all Brass Chamber Ditto." *Maryland Gazette.*

1771 Court paid a workman for installing in the clerk's office "1 Brass knob lock £0.14.0." Chowan Co., N.C., Miscellaneous Court Accounts, NCA&H.

1777 To be sold at shop in Sussex County, Virginia, was "a new Pair large Brass Hinges, fit for large Doors." *Virginia Gazette.*

1805 A dwelling in Wilmington, North Carolina, was to be built with "the Room doors of the second Story with Iron Locks with Brass knobs." McCoy, *Early Wilmington.*

braze (braize)   To solder with a metallic alloy. See also **solder.**

> 1810   In a discussion about the best way to join pieces of gutters, it was written that "in your calculation you make no allowance for lapping your joints it may be that you suppose it would answer to solder or Braize them edge to edge." Carter Collection, MHS.

break (brake)   *(n.)* A projection or recess in an element, piece, or molding beyond the existing surface or face.   *(v.)* To create a return or change directions. To break joint is to stagger the ends of two adjoining pieces or elements such as bricks or weatherboards from one course to another, so that they do not form a continuous vertical line or a straight joint over several courses.

> 1751   An order stated that public wells were to be "well done with Brick and to have a Curb made with . . . plank, and to be covered with . . . plank, so that the same break the joints thereof." Norfolk, Va., Common Hall Order Book 1736–1798.
> 1769   A churchyard fence was to be built with a series of posts enclosed with planks with "the Joint of each plank to be broke." Chester Parish, Kent Co., Md., Vestry Book.
> 1792   The North Carolina legislature sought an alteration to the plan of the statehouse for the new capital in Raleigh. They suggested that it should "have a brake in the center of the East and West front walls projecting two feet by twenty four feet in length, so as to have a Frontispiece East and West, something similar to the front of the public buildings of New Bern." Legislative Papers, NCA&H.
> 1797   In Lexington, Kentucky, carpenters charged $3.50 per square of "broken joint flooring" and $3.00 for "Straight" joint flooring. *Kentucky Gazette.*

breakfast room   A room used to serve breakfast and informal meals. Although many large dwelling houses had two dining rooms in the late colonial period, the distinctive term *breakfast room*, to distinguish the smaller of these eating rooms, appears only in the very late 18th and early 19th centuries.

> 1811   A carpenter installed a "chimney piece in [the] Breakfast Room" of a Baltimore dwelling. Riddell Accounts, Pleasants Papers, MHS.
> 1812   Estimates were made for plastering the "Breakfast room" at Fairntosh in Orange County, North Carolina. Cameron Papers, SHC.

breast (breastwork, brest)   **1.** The part of the chimney projecting into a room, specifically the area above the fireplace opening.

> 1746   Glebe building repairs included "the breast of the chamber chimney to be plaister'd." Christ Church Parish, Lancaster Co., Va., Vestry Book.
> 1793   "Old East" at the University of North Carolina was to have "eight rooms on a floor with a chimney in each Room. The breast or front of the chimney six feet in width three feet nine inches in the opening & eighteen inches deep." University Archives, UNC, Chapel Hill.

2. A decorative parapet or front of a gallery.

> 1747   Construction on a church was to include "A gallery in the West end of the Church of Pitch, Dimension & Form according to the plan with a proper stair case & close Breast or Front of Wainscot quartered round." Albemarle Parish, Surry Co., Va., Vestry Book.
> 1770   "The Breast work of the said Gallery" in a church was "to be Three pannelled work." St. David's Parish, Craven Co., S.C., Vestry Book.
> 1812   A workman was to "have the breast work of the inn or West Gallery secured to the wall, and a seat erected against the said breast work." William and Mary Parish, St. Mary's Co., Md., Vestry Book.

3. The section of a wall beneath a window sill.

> 1674   Statehouse brickwork to be "Ninteene Inches thick upp to the wale plate and soe from the wall plate to the brest of the windows of the Garrett att the Gable Ends and from the brest of the said windows upp to the point of the Gable Ends fourteen Inches thick." *Archives of Maryland,* 2.

breastsummer, bressummer (brestsummer) A beam spanning over a large opening, especially one that supports the second floor over a shop front. The term was used broadly in the early period to describe large, horizontal, exterior framing timbers located between the lower sills and the upper plates and tie beams.

> 1740 Following a devastating fire in Charleston, a law was passed requiring "buildings hereafter to be erected . . . be henceforth made of Brick or Stone . . . and be covered with tile, slate, stone, or Bricks, except Doors, Door Cases, and Window Frames and Window Shutters, the Brest Summers and other Parts of the first Story to the Front between the Piers." *South Carolina Gazette.*
> 1806 Specifications for the renovation of St. Paul's Church in Edenton, North Carolina, by Williams Nichols called for "the joists of the side Galleries to be framed raking into Brissumers level with that of the end Gallery." St. Paul's Parish, Chowan Co., N.C., Loose Papers.

breastwork A defensive work, usually temporary in nature. Also a parapet or retaining wall. See also **breast** (2).

> 1781 After the battle of Yorktown, assessment was made of the "damage done . . . by throwing up intrenchments & Breast Works." York Co., Va., Claims for Losses.
> 1811 "The abutment of the wharf should extend up the street to the plank that forms the breast work across the street." Elizabeth City Co., Va., Deed and Will Book 1809–1818.

brewery, brewhouse A building or group of buildings where beer, ale, and other spirituous beverages are produced by steeping, boiling, and fermenting malt, barley, and hops in large vats. The terms were used for commercial ventures as well as for those operated for domestic consumption. See also **distillery, still house.**

> 1755 "To be sold . . . a large brew and still house, in the city of Annapolis, . . . whereon is erected a good Copper and Still, a good Malt Kiln, and several Brewing Utensils." *Maryland Gazette.*
> 1769 "BREW-HOUSE. ALE, Table and Ship BEER, delivered to any Part of the Town, in any Quantity not under five Gallons." *South Carolina Gazette and Country Journal.*
> 1819 A notation appeared concerning Caleb Sheward's "one large stone Brewery ninety nine feet long by fifty wide" in the borough of Wilmington. New Castle Co., Del., Orphans Court Valuations K.

brick A rectangularly shaped building material composed of clay, sand, and water that has been hardened by firing in a kiln. Laid one on top of another in a regular series of horizontal rows or courses, bricks were bonded together by mortar or putty and were used to build walls, foundations, piers, columns, and chimneys. They were laid without mortar or *dry laid* in some instances, especially when they were used to pave floors and walks. In general, bricks measured about 2 1/2 to 3 inches high, 4 to 4 1/2 inches wide, and from 8 to 9 inches long. Differences in size varied from place to place rather than over time. Although some bricks were imported into the colonies from England in the 18th century and shipped from Philadelphia and Baltimore to ports farther south, their numbers were insignificant compared to the vast majority made on or near the building site. Brickmakers were active in the southern colonies from the time of first settlement. Southern brickwork developed distinctive patterns, which changed over time with the introduction of classical detailing and new aesthetic preferences. Bricks were sometimes rubbed with a brush or some other abrasive to produce a uniform color. Laid in thin putty or mortar joints, these *rubbed* bricks often served to highlight arches, frontispieces, and aperture openings. Throughout much of the 18th century, the fashion for decorative glazed brickwork was expressed in walls that had all their exposed headers picked out with a greenish-gray glaze. Glazing was a result of the uneven heating conditions present in the kiln. Besides fluctuations in color, the durability of bricks varied enormously as a result of uneven firing temperatures in the kiln. Some were brittle, overfired *clinkers*, while others were underfired *salmon* bricks. Many were tossed out but some, especially salmon bricks, were used on the inside of walls, where they were least affected by moisture penetration. Inferior or salmon bricks, which may have been tempered poorly or combined with many foreign inclusions such as pebbles, twigs, and dirt, were also known as *place* bricks or *common* bricks. The better sort of bricks, generally used on the exterior face of a building, particularly the front facade, were sometimes known as *stock* bricks. Imported from England and perhaps made domestically, *Dutch bricks* were hard yellow bricks used to pave floors and hearths. *Fire* brick was a very durable brick used to line the hearths of fireplaces. Specially molded bricks were made in great numbers and patterns, and served a variety of purposes. *Well* bricks were wedge shaped and used to line wells. Like a well brick, a *gauged* brick was also wedge shaped, usually in thickness rather than in width. It was used to face the outside of an arch or a flat-arched opening. Specially molded bricks were used to create curved profiles of water tables, cornices, pilasters, and pediments. See also **bond, brickbat, brickmaker, clinker, rubbed.**

1643 A tenant leased land and agreed to build "one good and sufficient framed dwelling house conteyning forty five foot in length and twenty foot in breadth with two chimneys and glass windows . . . and a cellar adjoining to it . . . the said house to be groundselled & underpinned with brick." Surry County, Va., Deed and Will Book 1652–1672.

1687 "Thomas Brown of Talbot County . . . bricklayer" was to make "Sixty three thousand of good & substantiall well made and well burnt bricks to contain in length nine inches, in breadth four inches, in thickness two inches and a halfe." Talbot Co., Md., Land Records.

1721 A notation stated: "Agreed with Benjamin Brown to underpin the church a brick & a half wall & ye vestry house with a brick & to make a back and harth & to plaster the chimney of ye vestry house he is to levell ye church & do itt with well burnt bricks no samon bricks to be made use of." St. George's Parish, Harford Co., Md., Vestry Book.

1764 A plantation for sale on the Patuxent River had "a large Stable of Fraim'd work, paved with Dutch Bricks." *Maryland Gazette.*

1764 Work to be let in Norfolk, Virginia, included "the digging and bricking with proper well bricks, a well of ten feet diameter." Norfolk, Va., Common Hall Order Book 1736–1798.

1766 "The Walls" of a church were "to be built of good bricks well burnt, of the ordinary size, that is nine Inches long, four and an half Inches broad, and three Inches thick the outside bricks to be laid with mortar, two thirds lime and one third Sand, the inside Bricks to be laid with mortar half lime and half sand. The Corners of the house, the windows & Doors, to be of rubbed brick. The Arches and Pediment heads of the Doors & Windows to be of bricks rubbed, gauged and set in Putty." Truro Parish, Fairfax Co., Va., Vestry Book.

1771 Accounts for construction of the Chase-Lloyd House in Annapolis listed "16,500 stock bricks . . . 346 M place bricks at 30/ per M." *MHM*, 33.

1819 At the University of Virginia in Charlottesville, "it is proposed to lay about a million of bricks this season in buildings so far distinct that the undertaking may be in one or more proportion of about an hundred thousand bricks each, the undertakers finding materials as well as work, the front walls are to be faced with oil stock

bricks, the others with sand stocks, the interior mass to be of plane bricks, all to be laid with good bond to be clinkers, and not a single sammell brick to be used in any part of the work under a penalty of 5 cents for every such brick, nor more than 2 bats to 9 whole bricks." *Lynchburg Press and Public Advertiser.*
1820 An act passed by the city of Washington, D.C., regulated the size of "all bricks made in the City." They were to "be made in moulds of the following size and dimensions . . . nine inches and one quarter long in the clear, four inches and five eights wide in the clear, in moulds two inches and five eights deep in the clear." *City of Washington Gazette.*

brickbat (bat)   A fragment of a brick, usually about half the size with one unbroken end. Brickbats were occasionally inserted into walls as closers or as makeups, but were more often used as paving for walks and floors.

1723 A workman contracted "to clear all the brick batch and loose durt that is faceing the New Church." Petsworth Parish, Gloucester Co., Va., Vestry Book.

brickmaker, bricklayer   A craftsman engaged in the manufacture of bricks or one whose chief responsibility is the laying of brickwork. The term *brickmason* was seldom used in the early South. As in other crafts, many brickmakers were also bricklayers, laying the bricks that they had made at their kiln. Bricklayers often took on the responsibilities of plastering as well. Immigrants to the early South practiced a brickmaking tradition that had scarcely changed in several hundred years. Although a number of 18th- and early 19th-century towns had permanent *brickyards* established on their outskirts and maintained a constant supply of materials for a local market, the bricks made for most projects were fabricated on or near the building site. The first step of a brickmaker was to select a place to dig clay. After the clay had been dug, it was crushed to break up large chunks and remove intrusive material such as small stones. The excavated clay was either tread upon or left exposed over the winter months so that the frost could break it up to make it more workable. The clay was then *tempered* with sand and water to form a homogeneous and malleable material that could be shaped properly. It was then placed into wooden or iron molds, which were often sanded or oiled to alleviate the sticking. Laborers then removed the green molded bricks to an open, sanded bed or a storage shed called a *hack*, where they were left to dry for a few weeks. Afterward, the bricks were placed in a kiln to burn at a high temperature for several days. The bricks were then removed from the kiln and separated out into usable ones and wasters. Considerable skill and luck were involved throughout the process and the best brickmaker understood well the properties of the materials that he worked with and prayed often for good weather and a well-burning kiln. See also **clamp, kiln, temper.**

1651 "William Eale bricklayer . . . shall well & substantially plaister, White lyme & wash over the dyninge roome, the yellowe roome & kitching, & chamber over the kitching, and . . . to mend & repair all the Bricke worke about the dwelling house at Keycoutan without dores & to ruff cast the same with lyme & gravell." Norfolk Co., Va., Will and Deed Book 1646–1651.
1662 An act to stimulate the construction of a town stipulated the price of workmanship and labor of a number of trades: "Brickmakers haveing theire diett and sizable labourers to helpe them, provided at his or their charge that employ them, and wood sufficient brought in place for each thousand bricks moulded and burned, fortie pounds of tobacco." Hening, *Statutes at Large, 2.*

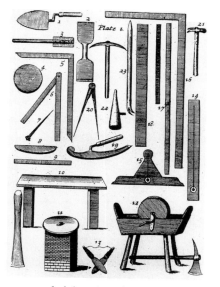

brickmaker, layer
Bricklayer's tools: (1) brick trowel, (2) brick ax, (3) saw, (4) rubstone, (5) small square, (6) bevel, (7) iron treenail, (8) float stone, (9) ruler, (10) banker, (11) brick pier in which to lay rubbing stone, (12) grind stone, (13) line pins, (14) plumb rule, (15) level, (16) large square, (17) ten- and five-foot rods, (18) jointing rule, (19) jointer, (20) compass, (21) hammer, (22) rammer, (23) crow

1682 "William Wood an Orphan of the County appeared at this Court and declared his consent to be bound to John Linham to the trade of Bricklayer for eight years." Westmoreland Co., Va., Court Order Book 1676–1689.

1702 The Churchwarden was to send for "Thomas Becket and Zackery Ellis or any other Bricklayers to Come and view the Bricks made by Thomas Hackson for the building a brick Church in this parish whither they are good and well burnt, fitt for building." St. Peter's Parish, New Kent Co., Va., Vestry Book.

1748 A notice appeared for a plantation to be sold on the Wando River with "a good Brick-Yard (with two large Houses, near 100 Feet in length, and about 30 in Breadth each) and a good Brick Case for burning them, about 45 Feet in Length near 20 in Breadth, and 9 in Height, with 12 Arches and a Division in the Middle, a large quantity of wood near at Hand." *South Carolina Gazette.*

1757 "WILLIAM VENNELL, BRICK-MAKER, Living near ANNAPOLIS . . . will Make BRICKS, and Burn them, and stand to the Lots, at 2/6 per Thousand, the Employer finding him Provisions and Hands; the Hands to consist of Two Men and Three Boys." *Maryland Gazette.*

1797 At the penitentiary in Richmond, "the bricks which have been burned in the only kiln which is now ready for delivery are so very rough and tender, that the Gateway arch cannot possibly be turned in them. It is intended to burn some thousand better and cleaner moulded bricks, for this purpose, in the second kiln . . . I have small hopes of their proving very good. The earth has never been well tempered and is not of the best sort. The Brick maker is not much in fault. . . . Many days, I have seen all the Bricklayers and laborers idle for one third of their time for want of bricks, and this morning the bricklayer has been obliged to employ his Laborers to bring bricks from the Kiln to the Wall upon their Heads." *The Correspondence and Miscellaneous Papers of Benjamin Henry Latrobe,* 1.

bridewell Originally St. Bride's Well in London, later a hospital on the site converted in the late 16th century into a house of correction. By the beginning of the 17th century, the term denoted any prison or jail for the confinement of felons and debtors, but was rarely used in colonial America.

1677 It was "Ordered that John Cross be committed to Bridwell for a year and a day to whips and work." Accomack Co., Va., Court Order Book 1666–1676.

bridge A structure spanning and providing passage over a river, creek, gully, and the like. Through the early 19th century and beyond, many sections of the South were isolated from one another for lack of bridges to span the broad rivers that bisected the coastal plain and piedmont. Except for parts of western Maryland and Virginia, almost all bridges constructed in the early South were wooden structures that stood on heavy timber posts sunk into river beds. Such bridges were always being damaged or destroyed in heavy floods or freshets. Traffic across many bridges was obliged to pay tolls. See also **abutment, mud sill, pier, pile.**

1667 Edward Rogers was engaged to build "a bridge over Pasbitansy Creek." The timber for the bridge was to be taken from the land of Mr. Traverse. Stafford Co., Va., Court Order Book 1664–1678.

1740 "William Walker undertaker and Arthiteck" agreed to build "bridges over the creeks called Rappahannock and Totusky." Each bridge "to be twelve feet wide in the clear at the top with such easy ascent that all coaches and carts may conveniently pass from the usual high water mark on both sides of the said creeks at the place where the Ferry's over the said creeks are usually kept. The said Bridges to be of such proper higth from the usual high water . . . as not to interrupt the Navigation of all Boats and flats without masts erect and these bridges to be well and substantially railed at the top from one side to the other to prevent any danger that might otherwise happen to persons travelling over the same. The sd Walker . . . building a convenient dwelling house of twelve feet square at some proper place near each of the said bridges and a good and substantial gate to be hung and fitted with substantial locks on . . . each bridge." Richmond Co., Va., Account Book 1724–1783.

1770 Planter Landon Carter of Richmond County, Virginia, "rode out on Saturday as far as the Rappahannock bridge to view it and receive it for the Country from John Redman, the undertaker. . . . The plan was my own taken from Vitruvius's bridge over the Rhine in Julius Caesar's days. Two stout freshes have gone over the bridge since finished above 3 feet but as it was part of a sphere the water rising not possessing the whole length had very little effect upon it." *Diary of Landon Carter*, 1.

1809 "POTOMAC BRIDGE. . . . The Washington Bridge was opened for the accommodation of the public. . . . The Washington Bridge is the longest in the United States, and, we believe, in the world. Its length is upwards of 5000 feet, and with the abutments, is a mile. It is 39 feet wide 29 of which is appropriated for a carriage way, and a foot way on each side of 4 1/2 for foot passengers, separated from the carriage way by a light railing. The bridge is supported by 201 piers, 25 feet opening. Each pier is composed of 5 piles on the flats, 6 in the channel, and 7 at the draw." *American and Commercial Daily Advertiser.*

bridging joist, bridging beam In a double flooring system, a joist that rests on and is carried by a binding joist or girder below and supports floorboards above. On an upper story, floorboards are notched or laid flat over the top of bridging joists. In attic framing, bridging joists were occasionally used to support the lower end of king and queen posts. See also **binding joist, galloping joist, girder.**

> **1790** A carpenter's work at Hampton in Baltimore County, Maryland, included "11 sqr joists bridgd . . . 1 sqr 10 feet fraiming with bridging joice." *MHM*, 33.
> **1806** "The Joists of the said Galleries [are] to be framed raking into Brissummers level with that of the end Gallery— Bridgings to be raised for the back Pews and Passages." St. Paul's Parish, Edenton, N.C., Miscellaneous Vestry Papers.
> **1811** At Montpelier in Orange County, Virginia, building accounts listed "7 1/3 square of floor & Bridging joist on sheet iron." Cocke Papers, UVa.

Bristol stone An American term for any creamy white limestone quarried in the limestone belt southeast of Bristol. The stone was exported through the port of Bristol and used in the Chesapeake and the Carolina lowcountry primarily as paving for public buildings and a few dwellings.

> **1733** It was specified that the church "Isle . . . be laid with white Bristol Stones." Blisland Parish, James City and New Kent Cos., Va., Vestry Book.
> **1767** In requesting white stone for the portico addition to his dwelling at Mount Clare in Baltimore County, Maryland, Charles Carroll wrote to a merchant in Bristol that he intended to purchase "Round columns and those to which the Pilasters Join. The Stone, and marble mentioned in it I do not Know the Cost of such mentioned but I suppose the stone must come Cheaper from the Quarries near Bath than Else where as it is Easily Hewn and the water Carriage to Bristol Convenient." Trostel, *Mount Clare.*

Bristol stone
Christ Church, Lancaster County, Va.

broken joint See **break.**

bucranium In classical architecture, a sculptured representation of the head or skull of an ox, frequently used to decorate metopes in the Doric order or combined with festoons in Ionic and Corinthian friezes.

> **1823** Craftsman William Coffee wrote to Thomas Jefferson about the installation of a decorative entablature at Poplar Forest in Bedford County, Virginia: "The human masks and ox sculls should be put up with white lead as stiff as Bookbinders paste." Jefferson Papers, UVa.

buffet (bowfat, beaufet) A closet or cupboard for the storage of tablewares. These were often built-in, though freestanding buffets were also common. Most often found in public rooms, these highly orna-

buffet
Branford-Horry House, Charleston, S.C.

mental features were made for display, with glazed doors and/or shelving fashioned in decorative shapes. Buffets were rare before the 1740s, but the unprecedented prosperity of subsequent decades led to dramatic improvements in gentry housing and to continuing elaboration of table equipage. Both trends contributed to the popularity of buffets as a means of displaying these wares. See also **sideboard.**

> 1742 A house advertised for sale in Dorchester, South Carolina, was "conveniently fitted up with Beaufaits, Closets, &c." *South Carolina Gazette.*
> 1745 In Major Henry Tripp's dwelling in Dorchester County, Maryland, were "Hall Buffats" containing silver, flatware, and hollowware. Maryland Prerogative Court Inventories 1745, MSA.
> 1764 In Charleston, James Reid's dwelling contained thirteen rooms, "most of them large and well finished, with beaufets, closets, and every other requisite." *South Carolina Gazette.*
> 1791 Large quantities of silver, glassware, china, and a miscellaneous collection of containers were listed among the contents of the "Bow-Fett" in Benjamin Harrison's "Great Room" at Berkeley in Charles City County, Virginia. Harrison Papers, VHS.

builder 1. A person who undertakes the fabrication of a structure, including the organization and management of the various trades and labor force involved in the project. The responsibility of the builder was to organize and complete the construction of a building according to the specifications set out in a contract or instructions given by a client or committee. The term was synonymous with the more common *undertaker* during the colonial and early national period and comes into limited use in the early 18th century. Its use was generally restricted to the upper South, rarely appearing in the coastal regions of North and South Carolina and Georgia before the 19th century. See also **contractor, undertaker.**

> 1710 Window placement in a courthouse was to be left to "the discretion of the builder." Baltimore Co., Md., Land Records IS No. B.
> 1752 The court "agreed with Charles Curtis, Gentleman the builder of the Court House . . . to receive the said Court House of him . . . as a full reward for building the same." Orange Co., Va., Court Order Book 1747–1754.
> 1767 A notice read: "To be let to the lowest undertaker . . . at Edenton, in North Carolina, THE building a brick Court-House . . . The builder will be furnished with bricks and lime, and may depend on punctual payments." *Virginia Gazette.*

2. A master artisan who undertakes the construction of buildings and structures as a profession. In this sense, the term *builder* identified those few men who moved from the craft ranks into the entrepreneurial role of organizer and overseer of building projects. A professional builder generally had years of practical experience in either the trowel or woodworking trades, gained the respect of merchants and planters willing to support him financially through the posting of performance bonds, and had some knowledge of contemporary design ideas. At the head of the profession was the master builder, an undertaker of many building projects across a broad region and the supervisor of a large labor force of craftsmen and unskilled laborers. With the growing architectural ambitions of planters and merchants throughout much of the South in the early 18th century, a few men rose to this recognized pinnacle of the building trades.

> 1740 It was "Agreed with Mr. William Walker of the Parish of St. Paul, in the County of Stafford, Builder, to Erect & Build a Steeple & Vestry Room according to a Plan delivered into the Vestry drawn by the said Walker." St. Peter's Parish, New Kent Co., Va., Vestry Book.
> 1741 "Mr. William Walker, a Master Builder, by his proposal to this Court set forth that he would at his own proper cost & charges . . . build and erect . . . a bridge." Richmond Co., Va., Court Order Book 1739–1746.

bulkhead **1.** A framed, boxlike structure rising above a roof or a floor, providing either light or cover for a stairwell opening; a hatch.

> **1790** Accounts at Hampton in Baltimore County, Maryland, listed "work in garrot: to fraiming Railing and Laying 4 flat forms to go up the Bolk heads on Roof." *MHM*, 33.

2. An enclosed outside entrance with sloping doors leading into a cellar. In this sense, the term only appeared in the mid-19th century, chiefly in New England. See also **cellar cap.**

3. A retaining wall or structure built of timber or masonry used for the protection of the shoreline of a harbor or the superstructure of a bridge.

> **1758** An agreement was made with a workman to build a bridge "and make or raise Bulkheads to the same." Spotsylvania Co., Va., Will Book 1749–1759.

bull's-eye window A round or oval window often found in gable ends, pediments, and above doors in public buildings. See also **oval, oxeye window.**

> **1797** Parsonage house to have "A Bulls Eye Window & frame in the pediment wt. Glass." St. Michael's Parish, Charleston, S.C., Vestry Book.
>
> **1815** New church "with a Roof to be hip at one end & pitch at the other with a Sash (called the Bulls Eye) in the Center." St. John's Parish, Colleton Co., S.C., Vestry Book.

burial ground, burying ground A place of interment of the dead; a graveyard. Such grounds were laid out on family farms, on lands on the outskirts of towns, on public lots in cities, and next to churches and meetinghouses. See also **graveyard.**

> **1686** A grand jury presented "Jonathan Baily for fencing in the burying place for his owne use and benefit." *Records of the Courts of Sussex County Delaware 1677–1710*, 1.
>
> **1748** An Anglican minister in Kent County, Delaware, explained to the Society for the Propagation of the Gospel in London that there were "many that are Buryed in the church yard, in proportion to those who are Buried elsewhere, some burying in their own Burrying Ground, & the Quakers and the Roman Catholicks at their own Plantations." Perry, *American Colonial Church*, 5.
>
> **1773** At St. Michael's Church in Charleston, Richard Downes requested "permission to erect a Tomb Stone, now Imported over the Grave of his Brother in Law Mr. Lejean, That upon debating the matter, and considering the small space alotted as a Burial Ground to the Church, with the several Inconveniences, that would attend a permission of the kind, it was unanimously refus'd, and agree'd that none such should be put up in Future- only with this proviso, that the same be put up endways at the Head of the Graves." St. Michael's Parish, Charleston, S.C., Vestry Book.
>
> **1800** The will of George Nixon requested his executors to lay out "one quarter of an acre of Land on my plantation, where I have buried part of my family and am to be buried myself that they keep the same inclosed with a post and rail fence . . . until my son John comes into the possession of the plantation after which time he shall keep the said burial Ground in Good repair and Except the same out of any Deed he may Execute if he should ever sell the said Plantation." Loudoun Co., Va., Will Book 1797–1802.
>
> **1810** "At a meeting of the Wardens of Christ Church, Newbern, RESOLVED, that the old Church-yard and New Burying Ground, be repaired as soon as possible." *Newbern Herald.*
>
> **1818** The "worshippers in the Baptist Church of Charleston feels that there should be set aside a permanent and separate parcel of ground apart from and independent of the common burial ground provided by the district." Charleston Co., S.C., Land Records Book B9.
>
> **1830** In Portsmouth, a committee appointed by the city "to ascertain the best method of enclosing the new burying ground, the probable cost of such inclosure and to ascertain what some may probably be obtained by the sale of family burying lots." Portsmouth, Va., Town Minute Book 1822–1843.

burnt post The practice of charring the ends of fence and building posts before they were set into the ground. A similar practice was tarring the ends of wooden members that were to be placed directly into the ground. Both methods grew out a belief that this would make the wood more resistant to rot and insects.

> 1754 "The posts" of a garden fence were "to be of good Saw'd white oak 6 inches square and burnt as usual as far as they go into the ground which must be 30 inches." Suffolk Parish, Nansemond Co., Va., Vestry Book.
> 1774 The churchyard was to "be inclosed with a Post and Rail Fence . . . with sawed Cedar Posts to go two feet and a half in the ground, to be first burnt." Truro Parish, Fairfax Co., Va., Vestry Book.

butler's room (butler's pantry) A service room near the kitchen and dining room specially equipped with counters and shelves for the serving of meals and wine and for the storage of plate, silver, and other items. See also **pantry.**

> 1783 At the Governor's House in New Bern, North Carolina, "the room at the N.W. angle 22 by 14 feet (on the right hand of the Hall at entrance) for the Steward or Butler." Hawks Letter, Miranda Papers, Academia Nacional de la Historia, Caracas.
> 1812 An estate for sale near Baltimore featured "a hall or saloon . . . two parlors, a library, butler's room." *Federal Gazette and Baltimore Daily Advertiser.*

butt 1. The end or back of any member or piece, especially the thick end of a shingle.

> 1723 The church was "to be shingled with Poplar three quarters of an Inch thick at the butt." St. George's Parish, Harford Co., Md., Vestry Book.
> 1768 Fence planks were "to be nail'd with 20d nails 3 nails in each butt & middle." Chester Parish, Kent Co., Md., Vestry Book.

2. *(v.)* To join squarely at the ends of two members or pieces, used especially in carpentry. *(n.)* The joint formed by the meeting of the ends of two members or pieces.

buttery A service room for the storage of household provisions such as beer, liquors, and foodstuffs, as well as implements for food preparation. Butteries, along with dairies, appeared in 17th-century estate inventories as unheated rooms near the kitchen or hall in a dwelling. Few room-by-room inventories mention the presence of both service rooms, which suggests that their distinct functions had merged into one or the other. By the early 18th century, the term all but disappears, perhaps in response to the removal of cooking to a detached kitchen and the increasing use of cellars for the storage of provisions.

> 1635 Construction on a 40-by-18-foot parsonage house included "a chimney at each end of the house, and upon each side of the chimneys a rome, the one for a study, the other for a buttery, alsoe a pertition neer the midest of the house with an entry and two doures the one to goe into the kitchinge the other into the chamber." *County Court Records of Accomack-Northampton, Virginia 1632–1640.*
> 1655 In the Albemarle area of North Carolina, a dwelling house was built "20 foote square, wth a lodging chamber, and a Buttery, and a chimney." Norfolk Co., Va., Will and Deed Book 1651–1656.
> 1667 "In the Buttery" of Mathew Huberd's house were "Three Iron pestells, One Stone Mortar & wodden pestle, One old Iron kettle, two pye peeles, One old Churne, One old earthen pott, two good & two Crackt Milktrayes." York County, Va., Deed, Order, and Will Book 1665–1672.
> 1755 Property for sale in Charleston included a "large kitchen and buttery." *South Carolina Gazette.*

butt hinge A hinge consisting of two flat plates or leaves connected in the center by a pin, one of which is secured to the narrow edge or butt of a door, sash, or other swinging member and the other anchored to the face of the jamb. When closed the two leaves fold back against one another. Because no part of the hinge is secured to the face of the swinging element, their advantage lies in their inconspicuousness when in a closed position. Small butt hinges where used throughout the colonial period for cabinets, closets, and other modest openings. Early butt hinges were made of wrought iron, later ones were made of cast iron. By the late 18th century, some larger butt hinges had appeared on doors and shutters but did not displace side and strap hinges as the most common form until the second quarter of the 19th century. See also **hinge.**

1727 In the inventory of a joiner in Chowan County, North Carolina, was "One pair of but hinges." Secretary of State Records, Wills 1722–1735, NCA&H.
1788 The door in "the partition between the Gaolers Rooms to be a good 6 panel door with common HL or butt hinges & an iron lock with brass knobs." Prince William Co., Va., Deed Book 1787–1791.

button
Prestwould, Mecklenburg County, Va.

button A small wooden or metallic knob, secured through the center by a pin so that it can swivel back and forth, used to keep doors, windows, and shutters closed. Often found on cabinet, closet, and pew doors, buttons were secured to the jamb and turned across the plane of the swing to keep the door fastened. See also **bolt.**

1742 Doors in a glebe house were to be "fastened with wooden bolts or buttons." Bristol Parish, Prince George Co., Va., Vestry Book.
1762 It was required that the church have "a wainscoted Door to each Pew with Proper Hinges to Hang them upon and a button or bolt on the inside of each Pew." Frederick Parish, Frederick Co., Va., Vestry Book.
1768 A workman was paid for "nailing buttons to the window shutters." Cumberland Parish, Lunenburg Co., Va., Vestry Book.

cabin (cabbin) **1.** A small building of simple or crude construction, usually intended for domestic use. In the 17th century, the term was often applied to Native American structures, as well as the earliest shelters built by English colonists. Additional associations with slave dwellings and log construction developed in the 18th century, though not all cabins were built of logs, nor were they occupied exclusively by slaves.

1608 The Jamestown colonists had "no houses to cover us, our Tents were rotten, and our cabbins worse than naught." *Complete Works of Captain John Smith,* 1.
1707 "Some of their [the Maherine Indians] straglers planted corne and built Cabbins on the Chowanacke old fields." *Colonial Records of North Carolina,* 1.
1756 An Anglican minister in the backcountry of South Carolina opined that there was "not a House to be hir'd- nor even a single Room on all this River to be rented— The People all new settlers, extremely poor-Live in Logg Cabbins like Hoggs." Woodmason, *The Carolina Backcountry.*
1762 Description of tract of land includes "1 logg house, 16 feet square, 1 cabbin covered with puncheons 12 feet by 10." Frederick Co., Md., Patents, MSA.
1793 Carpenters were instructed to "remov[e] the larger kind of the Negro quarters (the smaller ones or cabbins, I presume the people with a little assistance of Carts can do themselves) to the ground marked out for them opposite to Crow's New house." Conway, *MLIHS,* 4.
1803 On the western frontier of the Alleghany Mountains, a traveler observed that "the temporary building of the first settlers in the wilds are called Cabins. They are built with unhewn logs, the interstices between which are stopped with rails, calked with moss or straw, and daubed with mud. The roof is covered with a sort of thin staves split out of oak or ash, about four feet long and five inches wide, fastened on

by heavy poles being laid upon them. . . . If the logs be hewed; if the interstices be stopped with stone, and neatly plastered; and the roof composed of shingles nicely laid on, it is called a log house." Harris, *Journal of a Tour into the Territory Northwest of the Alleghany Mountains.*

2. A built-in, bench-like structure observed inside certain Native American buildings.

1791 "All around the inside of the building, betwixt the second range of pillars and the wall, is a range of cabins or sophas . . . the aged chiefs and warriors are seated on their cabbins or sophas." Bartram, *Travels.*

cabinet joiner A joiner skilled in cabinetwork. The distinction between this term and *cabinetmaker* is slight, the former appearing at the time when the latter was just emerging as a distinctive trade in the first half of the 18th century.

1745 An orphan was bound apprentice "to Ebenezer Stevens . . . he to teach the said Orphan to read & write & the trade of a house & Cabinet joyner." Princess Anne Co., Va., Court Minute Book 1744–1753.

cabinetmaker A craftsman specializing in fine joinery with the skills, materials, and tools necessary to make furniture and other intricate pieces of woodwork. The trade grew out of the work traditionally practiced by joiners and became a distinctive craft in the South as well as other parts of the American colonies by the second quarter of the 18th century. The best cabinetmakers distinguished themselves from joiners and carpenters by their carving skills and their concern for accurate fitting and smooth-surfaced finishes on pieces often fabricated with costly woods. Except for the most slapdash, all the products of a cabinetmaker involved a labor-intensive process of cutting, carving, sanding, polishing, and assembly. The bookpresses, cabinets, and tables that came from their shops responded to the changing tastes of fashionable members of early southern society. Many terms associated with classical architecture first appear in cabinetmakers' accounts, perhaps indicative of their keen awareness of stylistic nuances.

1736 Ebenezer Stevens described himself as a "Cabt. maker." Norfolk Co., Va., Deed Book 1733–1739.

1740 In Charleston, "Notice is hereby given, that all Persons may be supplied with all sorts of Joyner's and Cabinet-Maker's Work, as Desk and Book Cases, with arch'd, Pediment, or O G Heads, common Desks of all sorts, Chests of Drawers of all Fashions, fluited or plain; all sorts of Tea Tables, Side-Boards and Waiters, Rule joint Skeleton Tables, Frames for Marble Tables, all after the newest and Best Fashions, and with the greatest Neatness and Accuracy by Joseph Claypoole from Philadelphia." *South Carolina Gazette.*

1763 It was "Order'd . . . that directions be given by the Church Wardens to Elfe & Hutchinson Cabinet makers, to make a Mahogany Communion Table of such Demensions as will fit the Velvet Covering to be ready against Easter Sunday." St. Michael's Parish, Charleston, S.C., Vestry Book.

1776 "B. Bucktrout, cabinet maker, from London, on the Main Street near the Capitol in Williamsburg, makes all sorts of cabinet work, either plain or ornamental, in the neatest and newest fashions." *Virginia Gazette.*

1803 "For any slave to exercise the trade of a Cabinet-maker" in Savannah, his slaveowner was required to pay the yearly sum of eight dollars. *Columbian Museum and Savannah Advertiser.*

cabin roof
Sink Farm, Davidson County, N.C.

cabin roof A roofing system wherein a series of logs are stacked upon gable-end logs of decreasing length, until they reach the apex of the roof. The area between the log purlins was often filled with board slabs, shingles, moss, straw, and other impermanent materials. This simplified method required little carpentry and was often the expedient method on the frontier and in the backwoods for covering dwellings, outbuildings, and other structures.

> 1786 The improvements on the land in western Virginia claimed by Henry Redenhour consisted of a "log dwelling house 20 by 16, cabbin roof, loose plank floor above and a very bad floor below, inside wood chimney; log barn 42 by 24, cabbin roof no doors." Jonathan Clark Notebook, Filson Club.
> 1792 At the Sweet Springs in western Virginia, the guest "Hutts are . . . built of round loggs of wood about the Bigness of a man's legg, the loggs are upt one on the Top of the other like a pen untill they are about seven feet high, then they draw the loggs in and form a Roof, then they cover it with slabs or boards & lay loggs on them to keep the slabs down." *VMHB*, 41.

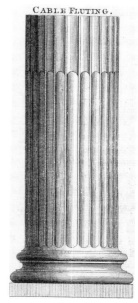

CABLE FLUTING.

cable, cabling

cable, cabling A molding with a convex, circular profile in the flutes of some classical columns and pilasters. Also, a molding with a spiraling treatment resembling a rope or cable, applied variously along borders of woodwork. See also **flute.**

cage A place of temporary confinement for petty offenders, often with some iron bars to allow for the circulation of air and light; a lockup. In towns, cages were often erected on a public square near the market house.

> 1699 The court ordered the construction of "a Cage of Twelve ffoot square sufficient & strong to secure Prisoners In." Charles Co., Md., Court Proceedings No. 10, MSA.
> 1803 "The Court recommends . . . to build a Cage in the Borough, the prison being so crouded at times as to require another room, for want thereof it may become infectious and spread diseases among the Inhabitants." Norfolk, Va., Hustings Court Order Book 1802–1804.
> 1826 A "committee [was] appointed to enquire into the best mode of erecting a cage for the confinement of disorderly and suspicious persons." Fredericksburg, Va., City Council Minute Book 1801–1829.

caisson A sunken panel in a flat or vaulted ceiling; a coffer.

> 1806 In a design detail for the Capitol in Washington, architect Benjamin Henry Latrobe noted that "the whole arrangement . . . I must see at large, before we determine how we shall place the odd block, and square (Caisson)." *The Correspondence and Miscellaneous Papers of Benjamin Henry Latrobe*, 2.

camber A slight upward curve or arch in a horizontal member or structure, with its center higher than its two ends, so that the tendency to sag is diminished.

> 1811 The construction of a dwelling house had the "joist framed in Small Girders Cambered & Doubled Stayed." Riddell Accounts, Pleasants Papers, MHS.
> 1831 A brick courthouse was to have "all apertures . . . gaged arches on centers on the outside & ruff camber arches on the inside." Caswell Co., N.C., Court Minute Book 1823–1831, NCA&H.

came A small, slender rod of cast lead, which when drawn through a glazier's vise becomes flattened and grooved to receive and secure pieces of glass in a window frame. It is then properly called *turned lead*, but occasionally in England retained its original, preprocessed name.

canal An artificial waterway used for navigation, irrigation, and decoration. Serious efforts to build navigational canals, which would promote trade with hinterlands and isolated regions in the South, began in the late 18th century. These efforts culminated early in the next century with the construction of the Chesapeake and Ohio Canal along the Potomac, the James River Canal in Virginia, the Chesapeake and Delaware Canal linking those two bays, the Dismal Swamp Canal in southern Virginia and the Albemarle Region of North Carolina, and the Santee Canal in South Carolina. On a domestic scale, canals were sometimes built in the 18th century as ornaments in pleasure grounds, providing a source of interest and decoration as well as fish, irrigation, and ice. The term was occasionally used to refer to the race of a watermill.

> 1722 "The Palace or Governor's House" in Williamsburg was "finished and beautified with Gates, fine Gardens, Offices, Walks, a fine Canal, Orchards." Jones, *Present State of Virginia.*
>
> 1749 At the end of "a very large garden" in Charleston was "a canal supplied with fresh springs of water, about 300 feet long, with fish." *South Carolina Gazette.*
>
> 1776 An individual was given liberty to use "the canal or race which he hath already dug to carry and divert the water of Backlick to the said . . . Mill with free liberty of Souring cleaning or deepening the said race or Canal as often as necessary." Fairfax Co., Va., Deed Book 1774–1777.
>
> 1777 Near Falmouth, Virginia, Mr. Hunter's ironworks had "a Canal, 3/4 of a Mile in Length by which the Water is conveyed (Part of the Way through Rocks) from the River to his Mills." *VMHB,* 62.

canopy A fabric covering or wooden superstructure suspended over a seat or place of honor such as a pulpit or chief magistrate's chair. For a more detailed description, see **sounding board** (1). See also **type.**

> 1715 The vestry of Bruton Parish in James City County, Virginia, paid a craftsman for "the Pulpit and Canopy £1.10.0." Jones Papers, LC.
>
> 1755 Payment was made for "Carv'd Work about ye Canopy." Trinity Parish, Charles Co., Md., Vestry Book.
>
> 1777 In the Anglican parish church in Williamsburg, "the Govrs. Pew is elegant, & elevated above the rest: a silk Curtain hangs on each Side & in Front of it from a Canopy supported by two fluted, gilt Pillars." *VMHB,* 62.
>
> 1793 In a courthouse, the judge's seat was to have "a Well Constructed Canopy Over head." Henry Co., Va., Court Loose Papers.

cantilever A bracket or horizontal beam whose length is greater than its breadth and that projects out beyond the wall to support a balcony, pediment, or entablature. In structural terms, a cantilever is any rigid construction whose horizontal projection extends far beyond its vertical support. The cantilever is supported by a downward force behind the fulcrum point.

canvas (canvass) A strong and closely woven fabric made of hemp, flax, or linen and used mainly for sails, screens, mattresses, tents, and by painters for oil paintings. In an architectural setting, painted canvas floor cloths appeared in a number of homes. Canvas also was used occasionally as a backing to hang decorative paper on walls.

> 1723 John Custis, a noted Williamsburg horticulturalist, requested a painting be made "of some good flowers in potts of various kinds . . . done on canvas" to be put over his fireplace. John Custis Letterbook 1717–1741, LC.
>
> 1736 An estate inventory noted "In the Entry . . . A Flor Cloth of Painted canvas . . . £0.7.6." Westmoreland Co., Va., Records and Inventories 1723–1746.
>
> 1805 In Norfolk, a dwelling contained "a canvas passage Carpet." Norfolk, Va., Will Book 1772–1788.

cap **1.** The uppermost finishing or crowning feature of a vertical member. Specifically, a capital of a column, pier, or the surbase of a dado or pedestal; coping of a wall; a door lintel; a handrail of a balustrade; an overdoor; the shelf of a chimney piece; or the top projecting courses of a chimney stack.

1747 The wainscotted pews of a church "to be neatly cap'd." Albemarle Parish, Surry Co., Va., Vestry Book.

1766 A cabinetmaker submitted his bill for constructing a pulpit staircase including "one Newill and one cap" and for "turning 4 Cullums with their Bases and Caps for the alter of Seader." St. Michael's Church, Charleston, S.C., Vestry Book.

1783 In the council chamber in the Governor's House in New Bern, North Carolina, "over the doors are flat Caps with contracted swelling Friezes . . . the Chimney Cap or shelf is of statuary marble fully inriched and supported by two Ionick Columns of Siana marble." Hawks Letter, Miranda Papers, Academia Nacional de la Historia, Caracas.

1808 "Proposals are requested . . . to construct Four New Gates, for St. Philip's Church . . . they are to be of the same form and structure as the present, to be made of cypress capped with lead." *Charleston Courier.*

1810 In Baltimore, payment was made for "3 Chimney Capps." Riddell Accounts, Pleasants Papers, MHS.

2. A protective covering for various things. See also **cellar cap.**

1751 "There is to be one Pump in each Well made of old Pine with Spout and Caps to Each Well." Norfolk, Va., Common Hall Order Book 1736–1798.

capital (capitol) The upper part of a column or pilaster that supports the entablature. See also **Composite order, Corinthian order, Doric order, Ionic order, Tuscan order, order.**

1734 "CAPITAL . . . is the uppermost Part of a Column or Pilaster, serving as the Head or Crowning thereof, placed immediately over the Shaft, and under the Entablature. . . . The *Capital* is the principal and essential Part of an Order of Column, or Pilaster: It is of a different Form in the different Orders; and is that which chiefly distinguishes and characterizes the Orders. Such of these as have no Ornaments, as the *Tuscan* and *Doric*, are called Capitals with Mouldings, and the rest which have Leaves and other Ornaments, Capitals with Sculptures." *Builder's Dictionary.*

1754 "Vestry agree to take of the said Mr. Ariss Seven Capital of the Corinthian order at four Pistoles pr Capital." Trinity Parish, Charles Co., Md., Vestry Book.

capital

1760 Construction of a church required "five Pillars of Cypress on each side for the support of the Roof, the Columns to be 15 inches Diameter at the bottom of the Shaft, to be Fluted & the Capitols of the Dorick Order." Stratton Major Parish, King and Queen Co., Va., Vestry Book.

1819 "Specifications of the Corinthian & Ionic capitals wanting for the University" of Virginia called for "4 Corinthian capitels for columns . . . to be copied exactly from the Corinthian capitel of Palladio, as given in his 1st Book wherein he treats of the orders in general and it's 17th chapter in which he describes the Corinthian capitel particularly, the drawing of which is in plate XXVI Leoni's edition publd. in London 1721." Lambeth and Manning, *Thomas Jefferson as an Architect.*

capitol (capitoll, capital)   A building where provincial, state, and national legislative and judicial bodies convened; a statehouse. The term was first applied to the building constructed between 1701 and 1705 in Williamsburg to house the General Court, provincial council, and House of Burgesses of the royal colony of Virginia. A classical reference, the name derived from its association with the ancient Roman temple dedicated to Jupiter located on the Capitoline Hill, the center of power and prestige in ancient Rome. Despite its classical allusion, the first capitol in Williamsburg showed little architectural affinity with its ancient predecessor. Built of brick, H-shaped in plan with two apses at one end, and a semicircular entrance porch on the main west facade, the building burned in 1747 and was replaced by a structure, similar in plan but with a two-story, pedimented portico on the west facade. In the 1780s, Thomas Jefferson's prostylar temple design for the new capitol in Richmond was the first building that clearly articulated the association of republican virtues with the language of classical architecture. Jefferson patterned his capitol design after a Roman temple, the Maison Carrée, in Nîmes, France. Although accepted in Virginia from its inception, the term *capitol* failed to gain many adherents in other colonies and states until the last decade of the 18th century when construction began on a national capitol in Washington, D.C. Clothed in a classical design replete with a dome, the nation's Capitol gradually exerted a strong influence on statehouse design throughout America. Along with the domed temple form came the new name of *capitol*, replacing the once ubiquitous *statehouse.*

1699 "Whereas the state house of this his majesties colony and dominion in which the generall assemblyes and general courts have been kept and held hath been unhappily destroyed and burnt downe, and it being absolutely necessary that a capitoll should be built with all expedition, and for as much as a more suitable expedient cannot be found for avoiding the laying a levy upon the poll for the building the same than by laying an imposition upon servants and slaves imported into this his majesties colony and dominion." Hening, *Statutes at Large*, 3.

1789 In Richmond, "a large and elegant state-house or capitol, has lately been erected on the hill." Morse, *American Geography.*

1803 "In considering the general plan of the Capitol the first remark that occurs is; that by the mode in which the exterior appearance has been connected with the internal arrangement, a radical and incurable fault has been grafted upon the work, and made an essential part of it. The building has the appearance of a principal floor elevated upon a basement story. (A magnificent flight of steps leads up to the Portico on the West front, and that towards the East, though placed upon an arcade has the effect of belonging to that floor.) But in the interior all this expectation is disappointed. The Porticoes lead only to the Galleries and committee rooms." *The Correspondence and Miscellaneous Papers of Benjamin Henry Latrobe*, 1.

1809 In Richmond, "on first view, the capitol attracts the most particular attention. It is a large, massy building, with a portico extending the full width of the end in front, supported by Six majestic pillars, very much resembling marble. Its enormous size, & elevated situation, together with the architectural genius it possesses is of great importance to the beauty of the City." *Journal of William D. Martin.*

capitol

Above: First capitol, Williamsburg, Va.
Center: Virginia State capitol, Richmond.
Below: West elevation of the Capitol, Washington, D.C.

1820 "PROPOSALS are desired for covering the Roof and Dome . . . of the Capitol of North Carolina." *The Star, and North Carolina State Gazette.*

capstone A crowning stone, the topmost stone of an object; specifically, a staddle stone at the top of a foundation pillar that extends outward beyond the face of the pillar to prevent rodents from crawling up into the superstructure. See also **cap.**

1764 In Richmond County, Virginia, "Col. Tayloe's Ralph [was] sent back here to cut my dishing capstones for my Pigeonhouse posts to keep down the rats." *Diary of Landon Carter*, 1.

carcass (carcase) The frame of a building before it is enclosed by exterior sheathing and roofing or finished on the inside with sheathing or plastering. Also the main framing members that carry boards and other sheathing. See also **framing, hull.**

1703 The "carcase, is (as it were) the Skelleton of a House, before it is Lath'd and Plastered." Moxon, *Mechanick Exercises.*

carpenter A craftsmen skilled in the transformation of timber into building materials and the framing and enclosing of structures. Many carpenters were also trained in and practiced the handicraft of a joiner by executing finish work such as doors, windows, stairs, and chimney pieces. In parts of the Chesapeake, those woodworkers who specialized in the rough framing of houses were known as *clapboard carpenters.* For a more detailed description, see **joiner.**

1726 "The several kinds of Work done by Carpenters, (in relation to Building)" included "Framing, Flooring, Roofing, &c. . . . If the Carpenter does not work by the Day, then he writes: For so many Square of Roofing (at what Price they agreed upon per Square) so much Money. Likewise for so many square of Flooring, at so much per Square, so much Money. Also for so many Square of Partitioning, at so much per Square, so much Money. And so for so many Square of Ceiling Joysts, &c. The Windows they set down either at so much per Light, or so much per Window. The Door-cases at so much a piece, either with, or without Doors. The Mantle-trees, Tassels, &c. at so much a piece. The Lintelling, Guttering, Cornish, Winder-boards, &c. at so much per Foot. Stairs, at so much per Step, or so much a Pair, &c." Neve, *The City and Country Purchaser.*

carriage house A building or part of a building used for the storage of wheeled vehicles. Many carriage houses were accompanied by a stable arranged under the same roof. The term comes into use in the South in the late 18th century, and in the first decades of the 19th century gradually displaces *chair house* and *chaise house* to define such structures. See also **chair house, chaise house, coach house.**

1781 Destroyed in the siege of Yorktown was "a cow room, carriage house and cow shelter" valued at £100. York Co., Va., Claims for Losses.

1797 An orphan's estate in Maryland included a "carriage house 16 feet by 11 feet with a shed 8 feet wide and the length of the carriage house." Queen Anne's Co., Md., Guardian Bonds and Valuations SC.

1823 A vestry in Charleston decided to build a new two-story "carriage house and stable" with "two good rooms for servants" on the second floor. St. Philip's Parish, Charleston S.C., Vestry Book.

cart house A building or shed used for storing a two-wheeled farm vehicle.

1759 On the Baynard farm on the Eastern Shore of Maryland was "a cart house posts in the ground covered with boards." Queen Anne's Co., Md., Deed Book F.

1773 Outbuildings on a plantation included "one cart house of round logs 8 by 10." Queen Anne's Co., Md., Deed Book K.

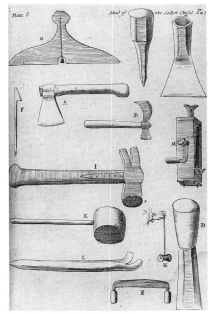

carpenter

Carpenter's tools: (A) ax, (B) adz, (C) socket chisel, (D) ripping chisel, (E) drawing knife, (F) hookpin, (G) level, (H) plumb line, (I) hammer, (K) commander, (L) crow

cartouche
Bray Monument, Bruton Parish
Churchyard, Williamsburg, Va.

cartouche A rounded, convex surface surrounded by carved scroll-work, often ornamented in the center with a low relief decoration such as armorial bearings, a cipher, or an inscription.

carver A craftsman skilled in the ornamental engraving and cutting of wood or stone in relief with chisels and other tools. In building, carvers applied their skills to the enrichment of moldings, capitals, chimney pieces, altarpieces, finials, stair brackets, and decorative frieze and spandrel ornaments. Many carvers worked as cabinetmakers or in cabinetmakers' shops. Stone carvers worked on funerary monuments as well as exterior moldings and capitals. See also **cabinetmaker, joiner, stonecutter.**

> 1739 In Charleston, "STONE and Wood Carving and Carpenters and Joyners Work, done by Richard Bayliss, from London." *South Carolina Gazette.*
> 1760 Henry Burnett's bill for work on the pulpit for St. Michael's Church in Charleston listed "24 feet of Ogee Carved . . . 22 feet Large Ogee fully Enriched; 22 feet 3/4 Ogee Carved . . . Carving a Swelling Torus cut with Foliage Flowers & cut through & Relieved on the Backside . . . 6 Brackets or Supports under the pulpit; 2 Corinthian Capitals for the Columns that Support the Type of the pulpit." Williams, *St. Michael's.*
> 1768 At the statehouse in Charleston, payment was made "to Thomas Woodlin for carving 16 Corinthian Capitals for the Council Chamber £471.18.0." Journal of the Commons House of Assembly No. 37, SCA&H.
> 1771 The account of workmanship for the Chase-Lloyd House in Annapolis listed the "Carver for 161 Modillions (to be finished by S. Chase) . . . £20.2.6." *MHM,* 33.
> 1771 Builder William Buckland wrote to planter Robert Carter III that "I have lately heard You had some Notion of Makeing Nomony Your Sumers Residence, I have Now Some of the Best Workmen in Virginia among whom is a London Carver [and] Masterly Hand, it is Probable you will before You Leave these Parts be within Sight of My Shop Should Yr Fondness for Work of that Kind, & Drawings Induce Your to Call in I shall ever Remember the Honr done Mee." Carter Papers, VHS.
> 1774 In Williamsburg, "GEORGE HAMILTON, CARVER and GILDER, just from Britain . . . intends carrying on this Business in all its Branches, viz. Looking-Glass Frames in Burnish or Oil Gilding Girandoles, Ornaments and Decorations for Gentlemens Houses, Chimney Pieces, Door and Window Cornices, Mouldings and Enrichments, Hall and Staircase Lanthorns, Picture Frames black and gilded, Ladies Toilet and Dressing Glasses; all the above after the new Palmyrian Taste. Any Gentleman wanting Designs of the above Articles may be furnished either at their respective House in Town or Country, or at Mr. Edmund Dickinson's, Cabinet Maker." *Virginia Gazette.*

caryatid A sculptured female figure used as a support for an entablature instead of a column or pilaster.

cascade In a garden setting, an artificial waterfall that noisily breaks the water as it flows over stone steps. They were often designed so that water splashed over evenly stepped stone breaks with a slight lip on the top of each course.

> 1752 "To Gentlemen . . . as have a taste in pleasure . . . gardens . . . may depend on having them laid out, leveled, and drained in the most compleat manner, and politest taste, by the subscriber; who perfectly understands . . . erecting water works . . . fountains, cascades, grottos." *South Carolina Gazette.*

case, casing 1. *(v.)* To cover or line the surface of an area with another material. *(n.)* The outer covering or surface of a building or part of a building.

> 1770 Nathaniel Hanson's barn "The Barn to be cased at the end to preserve the Duftales." New Castle Co., Del., Orphans Court Valuations D.

1786 On Nicholas Strayer's farm in western Virginia was an "old fraimed barn 40 by 24, covered with straw . . . the body cas'd with clap boards," while on a neighboring farm was an "old log dairy 12 by 8 cased and covered with clap boards." Jonathan Clark Notebook, Filson Club.

1803 A list of options for finishing work at the Capitol in Washington included "the columns may be either of Timber, cased with plank glued up; of timber frames, lathed and plaistered or stuccoed; of bricks stuccoed; of freestone plain or fluted; or of Pennsylvania marble." *The Correspondence and Miscellaneous Papers of Benjamin Henry Latrobe*, 1.

1809 The walls on the second floor of a jail in Randolph County, Georgia were "to be formed of foot square timber and cased with 2 inch oak boards put on with 8 inch spikes at every 4 inches distance." *Georgia Express.*

2. The surrounding framework of a door or window; the exposed framing, molding, and lining around a door or window. A doorcase consists of two side pieces or jambs, which are framed or nailed to a lintel or headpiece. The door is hung on hinges from one of the jambs and stopped by a rabbet cut into the other one. These pieces were sometimes finished with decorative architraves and beads. A *doorcase* was also called a *doorframe.*

1711 An agreement was made with an undertaker to build a church with "5 Windows, 2 Doors & Cases." St. Paul's Parish, Kent Co., Md., Vestry Book.

1726 A carpenter's account for building a dwelling in Caroline County, Virginia, listed "making one frunt door to ye little dining roome & caseing ye same." John Baylor Papers, CWF.

1746 In calculating the joiner's work for his dwelling house in Charleston, Charles Pinckney estimated that he would need "7 cases or door frames for Inner doors to be lined." Huger Smith, *The Dwelling Houses of Charleston.*

1755 An account of work done in building a house listed "casing 5 doors and 5 windows." Bertie Co., N.C., New Court Actions, NCA&H.

1790 In Columbia County, Georgia, carpenter John White charged Thomas Carr for "caseing three Doors all round @ 12/6 Each £1.17.6; to Caseing two Doors in Side @ 3/ Each £0.6.0; to Caseing nine windows in Side @ 3/ Each £1.7.0." Thomas Carr Accounts, UGa.

1805 In a church near Charleston, "the inside casing of the doors and windows [are] to be single architraves." *City Gazette.*

3. An enclosure, box, or receptacle.

1763 The vestry of a church ordered an "Organ Case which will best suite Our Church" from a London merchant. St. Michael's Parish, Charleston, S.C., Vestry Book.

1809 A clerk's office in King George County, Virginia, was to have "an inside chimney, each side of whereof to be cased for reception of record books, papers, &c. A similar division in the upper story is to be made with like cases by the chimney." *Virginia Herald.*

casement A window hinged or pivoted on one of its sides to open and shut. Throughout the 17th century and through the early decades of the 18th, most windows in colonial America were of this type, usually with wooden or iron frames containing panes of glass set in lead. With the introduction of sliding sash windows with large lights and wood muntins in the last decade of the 17th century, the use of casement windows decreased. In the 1730s and 1740s there was a wholesale replacement of older casement windows with new-fashioned sash ones in older public buildings and fashionable residences throughout much of the South. However, casements did not disappear entirely as they became relegated to subsidiary apertures in dormers and outbuildings. See also **sash.**

1674 In the statehouse at St. Mary's City, there were "two iron Casements to every window in the sad house the frames and Casements to be well laid in Lynseede Oyle . . . and glased with good Cleer square glasse." *Archives of Maryland*, 2.

casement
Iron casement from Corotoman, the house of Robert "King" Carter, Lancaster County, Va., c. 1725

1686 A courthouse in Dorchester County, Maryland was to have "four large windows below, and one small Casement Window, with two large casements to each window, and two large transom windows above one at each end." Dorchester County, Md., Land Records Book 1669–1683.

1719 Imported from England was a "case or chest of window Glass Containing one hundred foot Square Iron Latches hasps and Doftails hinges for Casements." All Faiths Parish, St. Mary's Co., Md., Vestry Book.

1724 A workman was hired "to make five sash windows to the chappell the said windows to be made up with sash glass the same to be the breadth of the old windows and about one foot or more longer & . . . to make a casement to the little window next to the pulpett." Bristol Parish, Prince George Co., Va., Vestry Book.

1734 A Williamsburg carpenter was paid for "mending a Light in an Iron Casement." Jones Papers, LC.

case step One of a series of steps framed as a stairway; a staircase.

1726 Specifications are noted for "case steps and stairs to go into" a courthouse. Norfolk Co., Va., Court Order and Will Book 1723–1734.

cast iron Decorative or structural members of iron formed in a mold when molten. Although this technology was rarely used during the colonial period, cast-iron material became common in the early 19th century.

1793 Items stolen from a Richmond theater included "one pair of cast-iron kitchen dogs." *The Virginia Gazette, and General Advertiser.*

1807 Thomas Jefferson requested that "some cast iron semicircular sashes [be put] in the windows of the covered ways" at Poplar Forest. Coolidge Collection, Massachusetts Historical Society.

cat and clay chimney A rare term for a variety of wooden chimney. *Cat* refers to the small pieces of wood sometimes secured to a ground-set frame and daubed with a mixture of clay and straw to form the walls of the chimney. For a more detailed description, see **chimney**.

1786 On a Frederick County, Virginia, farm was "one scalp'd log cabin 30 by 18 cat and clay chimney." Jonathan Clark Letterbook, Filson Club.

catch (ketch) **1.** A clasp or box that secures the bar or bolt of a lock or latch, holding a door or other hinged element in place; a keeper.

1664 "The defects of the said Catch may be sufficiently repair'd by two able Carpenters." *Archives of Maryland*, 49.

1732 A carpenter was paid for "materials and workmanship about Building a Catch att the Doore." Jones Papers, LC.

1769 It was required that a "gate . . . be hung to good locust posts with good iron hinges with an iron latch and ketch." Chester Parish, Kent Co., Md., Vestry Book.

2. A hook for a shutter. See also **hook**.

1769 The vestry ordered the chapel to have "shutters to the windows with bolts within to keep them close when shut, and catches without to keep them back when open." Frederick Parish, Frederick Co., Va., Vestry Book.

1800 "New window shutters [are] to be made with bolts and ketches." Gates Co., N.C., Miscellaneous Court Accounts, NCA&H.

catery closet A space for the storage and distribution of household goods, taking its name from the office traditionally charged with provisioning the royal household. The term was used here in the broadest sense, embracing all aspects of domestic supply. In this regard, it resembled the storeroom maintained by many planters and merchants. See also **closet** (3), **storeroom**.

1776 An inventory of Dr. Nicholas Flood's estate mentions a "Catery Closet" where appraisers found large quantities of cloth, assorted domestic implements, ceramics, and items of horse gear as well as coffee and sugar. Richmond County, Va., Will Book 1767–1787.

caulicole   The volutes of stylized acanthus stalks in a Corinthian or Composite capital. Also called a *helix* or *urella*. See also **acanthus.**

> 1819   In ordering the marble capitals for the pavilions at the University of Virginia, Thomas Jefferson noted that he would "have only the ovolo of the abacus carved and it's cavetto plain, as may be seen in Scamozz[i] . . . nor would I require it's volutes or caulicoles to be so much carved, as those of Diocletian's Baths, finding the simplicity of those in Palladio preferable." Lambeth and Manning, *Thomas Jefferson as an Architect.*

caulk   To render a joint tight against the elements by means of filling the seam with a malleable substance such as tar, lead, oakum, putty, and the like.

caulk (Variant spelling for cock)   See **cock.**

cavetto   A concave molding containing a quadrant of a circle used in entablatures, surbases, and bases. A deeper hollow molding with a greater segmental curve is known as a *scotia*.

> 1823   "In the Corinthian capitels" on the pedimented Rotunda at the University of Virginia, Thomas Jefferson observed that "there is a want of the cavetto and listel of the astragal." Lambeth and Manning, *Thomas Jefferson as an Architect.*

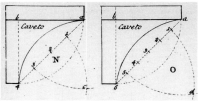

cavetto

cedar (ceder, sedar, seadar)   Despite its name, the Eastern red cedar is not a cedar but a juniper (*Juniperus virginiana*). A durable softwood, its natural habitat is in drier inland areas. It was used in building for fence posts, blocks, framing members, and some interior woodwork such as pews, doors, and wainscot. Although it was a resistant wood, red cedar proved to be too knotty for splitting into shingles. Neither a cedar nor a juniper, the coniferous Atlantic white cedar thrived in coastal swamps and was ideally suited for shingles.

> 1677   Payment was made for "33 Cedar posts." Petsworth Parish, Gloucester Co., Va., Vestry Book.
>
> 1701   In Williamsburg, it was required that "the porches of the . . . Capitoll be built circular fifteen foot in breadth . . . and that they stand upon cedar columns (if to be had) if not the same be sett upon other good, lasting wood." Hening, *Statutes at Large*, 3.
>
> 1709   "The red sort of Cedar is an Ever-green, of which *Carolina* afford Plenty. That on the Salts, grows generally on the Sandbanks; and that in the Freshes is found in the Swamps. Of this Wood, Tables, Wainscot, and other Necessaries, are made, and esteemed for its sweet Smell. It is as durable a Wood as any we have, therefore much used in Posts for Houses and Sills. . . . Of this Cedar, Ship-loads may be exported. It has been heretofore so plentiful in this Settlement, that they have fenced in Plantations with it, and the Coffins of the Dead are generally made thereof." Lawson, *A New Voyage to Carolina.*
>
> 1723   The frame of the Currituck County, North Carolina, courthouse was to stand "on Cedar Blocks." *Higher-Court Records of North Carolina*, 5.
>
> 1723   A church in St. John's Parish, South Carolina, "is finish'd & pew'd with cedar." SPG Letterbook B, SPGFP.
>
> 1764   Henry Laurens of Charleston wrote to an English merchant in Liverpool that he would "send you little or no Cedar or Red Bay. The former is become very scarce & dear in this Country, almost as dear as Mahogany. . . . Cedar is brittle, splintery, & without an excess of rubbing & waxing fades and loses its colour in a very few years." *Papers of Henry Laurens*, 4.
>
> 1794   A barn to be built in Delaware was "to be covered with the best Cedar three feet shingles." Dickinson Papers, Del. Hall of Records.

ceiling   The overhead surface of a room, often specifically a lath and plaster finish applied to and concealing the floor joists of the room above. See also **seal, plaster.**

1677 "Ye inside worke of ye Church now in Buildinge at poplare Springe bee done in manner as followeth vizt: the walls and ceilinge over head to be substantially lathed, daubed & plastered." Petsworth Parish, Gloucester Co., Va., Vestry Book.

1734 "CEILING, the upper Part or Roof of a lower Room, or a Lay or Covering of Plaister over Laths nail'd on the Bottom of the Joists, which bear the Floor of the upper Room, or on Joists put up for that purpose, and called Ceiling-Joists, if it be in a Garret. These Plaister'd Ceilings are much used in England, more than in any other Country, nor are they without their Advantages, they making the Rooms lightsome, are excellent in Case of Fire, stop the Passage of the Dust, and lessen the Noise over Head, and in the Summer-Time, make the Air of the Rooms cooler." *Builder's Dictionary.*

cellar (celler, sellar, seller) A space, whether above, partly submerged, or entirely below ground, used for storage. While most cellars were part of a building, some were constructed as detached storage areas sheltered by roofs and these were known as cellar houses. See also **storehouse, storeroom.**

1643 There was a contract to build a "framed house conteyning forty five foot in length and twenty foot in breadth with two chimneys . . . and a cellar adjoining to it also of fifteen foot square." Surry Co. Va., Deeds, Wills, etc. 1652–1672.

1694 Advertisement: "English framed dwelling house with a good cellar under it." York Co., Va., Deed, Order, and Will Book 1694–1698.

1713 Construction was ordered for a glebe house "Fourty two feet in Length, Twenty feet wide, A seller three feet in the ground and three feet above." St. Peter's Parish, New Kent Co., Va., Vestry Book.

1718 A description of a plantation noted the presence of "a celler with a good roof over it." Richmond County, Va., Miscellaneous Court Record Book.

1804 A plantation had "one old Celler House with Brick Celler twelve feet by ten in bad repair." Sussex Co., Del., Orphans Court Valuations IJ.

cellar cap An enclosed outside entrance with sloping doors leading into a cellar. In 19th century terminology, a *bulkhead*. See also **cap (2).**

1764 An agreement was made to "put and build a Cellar Cap to the East end . . . and a Cellar Cap in Front" of a dwelling in Williamsburg. York Co., Va., Deed Book 1763–1769.

cement Any soft, gelatinous, or pasty substance that acts as a binding agent when it hardens or sets. Specifically, a finely ground powder composed of various calcined mixtures of clay and limestone used to bond masonry. It is known as *hydraulic cement* since it reacts with water to form a hard, stonelike material that is resistant to deterioration in water. It does not contain an aggregate but is composed of various proportions of chalk, limestone, shells, and clay. When combined with sand, it is called *mortar*. A *natural cement* was prepared directly from one of the naturally occurring forms of impure limestone. In contrast, *artificial cement* required the mixing of limestone, chalk, or shells in certain proportions of clay. *Roman cement* was one such artificial cement that set rapidly and was relatively impervious to water. In the early 19th century, it became a valuable ingredient in exterior stucco work. With the growth in engineering projects such as canals, bridges, and sewer systems, a concerted effort was made to develop a more durable form of hydraulic cement, one that would set rapidly underwater. Developed in England in the first half of the 19th century, *Portland cement* proved to be a very effective artificial cement. By the very late 19th and early 20th centuries, it had gradually supplanted earlier types in America. See also **mortar, plaster, puzzolana, tabby.**

1745 Payment was made to a workman for "118 foot of old Glass new leaded & Cemented." St. Anne's Parish, Anne Arundel Co., Md., Vestry Book.
1746 Frederica, Georgia, "has several Streets, in every one of which are many good Houses, some of Brick, some of Tappy (which is a Cement of Lime and Oyster Shells)." *London Magazine*, 16.
1747 "One of the finest" marble slabs imported into Charleston "had been broken in England and Cemented together." *The Papers of Henry Laurens*, 1.
1767 Charles Carroll of Baltimore County, Maryland, wrote to an English merchant that "Putty or Cement for Joining" various blocks of limestone columns and pilasters "must be sent in with them or Instructions How to make it." Trostel, *Mount Clare*.
1796 A visitor to Norfolk noted that "the ruins of the old houses in this town (which was burnt down in 1776) are almost as numerous as the inhabited houses. [They] are intermixed in every street, and the former give way very [slow]ly to the latter. One cause of this is the difficulty found in pulling down the old walls, cemented together by Shell lime . . . a strong mortar." *The Correspondence and Miscellaneous Papers of Benjamin Henry Latrobe*, 1.
1822 The front facade of a library to be built in Charleston was "to be covered with Roman Cement, & the sides either with Roman Cement, or Rough Cast." St. Michael's Parish, Charleston, S.C., Vestry Book.

cemetery   A burial ground around a church; land set aside for the interment of the dead. The term was little used until the late 18th century. *Graveyard, churchyard,* and *burial ground* were the more common names given to this space.

1741 An act established that Charleston was to "be a distinct Parish, by the Name of St. Philip's in Charles-Town: And the Church and Cemetery of this Town were enacted to be the Parish Church and Church-yard of St. Philip's in Charles-Town." Oldmixon, *The British Empire in America.*
1789 In Savannah, plans were made "for enlarging the present Cemetery or Public Burial Ground." Christ Church Parish, Savannah, Ga., Church Records, GHS.
1823 At a meeting of the vestry of St. Philip's Church in Charleston, "a letter from E.S. Garden & B. Bamfield (persons of Colour) was presented . . . wishing to know whether the Vestry would permit their remains to be interred in the Cemetery of the Church at some future day." St. Philip's Parish, Charleston, S.C., Vestry Book.

centering   Temporary wood framing prepared to serve as a form and support for the construction of a masonry arch. Once the masonry work had set, the centering could be removed and the arch was self-supporting. Most commonly used in the South for relieving arches in chimney bases and for segmentally arched door and window openings, centering was also used for vaulted cellars, arcades, and in public buildings for more complex masonry arches. In a large arch or vault, premature removal of the centering could be disastrous.

1802 A carpenter's accounts for construction of the Tayloe house in Washington, D.C., included "Centring to vaults" and "centring to arches." Tayloe Papers, VHS.
1808 In a letter to the *National Intelligencer*, architect of the Capitol Benjamin Henry Latrobe reported on the death of John Lenthall: "Yesterday the Vault of the Court Room in the North Wing of the Capitol fell down. Several workmen, under the direction of Mr. John Lenthall, the clerk of the works, were under the vault, lowering down that part of the centre which still stood under it, just before it fell. A loud crack gave notice of their danger, and all of them escaped out of the windows, or under the adjoining vaults excepting Mr. Lenthall . . . being under that part of the arch, the centre of which had been removed on Friday; he was suddenly buried under many tons of bricks." *The Correspondence and Miscellaneous Papers of Benjamin Henry Latrobe*, 2.

center to center (centre to centre)   A lineal measurement from the middle of one piece to the middle of the next and so on. The term was used to describe the spacing of a series of repetitive members such as sleepers, joists, or studs.

1768 A churchyard was to be enclosed with a fence of "good and Sufficient Locust Post or Cedar, to be placed eight foot from Center to Center, 2 1/2 foot in the Ground." Chester Parish, Kent Co., Md., Vestry Book.
1804 "I cannot send any of the sheet iron for the roofs until I know what is the distance of the rafters from center to center." *The Correspondence and Miscellaneous Papers of Benjamin Henry Latrobe*, 1.
1806 In Fayette County, Kentucky, a brick meetinghouse was to have "sleepers 3 by 14, the sleepers put 18 inches from centre to centre." *Kentucky Gazette and General Advertiser.*

chaff house A building used for the storage of cornhusks and other fodder. See also **fodder house.**

> **1789** An estate survey in northern Delaware listed "one chaff and corn house next the barn of loggs in good repair." New Castle Co., Del., Orphans Court Valuations F.

chain house A building used for the storage of surveying equipment. Among the items housed in such a structure would be a Gunter's or surveyor's chain, which measured 66 feet in length. Besides being used for land surveys, such chains were also used to lay out gardens.

> **1793** On James Buchanan's estate in southern Delaware was "an old chain house." Sussex Co., Del., Orphans Court Valuations E.

chair board (chear board) A horizontal board fixed on a wall at the level of the back of a chair. It is the uppermost element of the dado and is often molded with beaded edges. The surbase is the molded part of the chair board. See also **surbase.**

> **1750** Ground floor rooms of a dwelling were to have "skirting & Chair boards." Newport Parish, Isle of Wight Co., Va., Vestry Book.
> **1774** Repairs to a glebe house included "new Chair boards in the Hall and passage to be put on & placed lower than the former with a moulding on them." St. Patrick's Parish, Prince Edward Co., Va., Vestry Book.
> **1816** An academy building in Sparta, Georgia, was to have "plain dado—chairboard high, including chairboard and wash-board." *The News.*

chair board
Chair board and molded surbase,
54 Montague Street, Charleston, S.C.

chair house A building for the storage of a light-weight, two-wheeled, horsedrawn vehicle, often constructed with an adjoining stable area. The term appeared in the South in the mid-18th century but gradually gave way in the early 19th century to the more common *carriage house* to describe a shelter for wheeled vehicles. See also **chaise house, carriage house, coach house.**

> **1752** On the lot of a dwelling house for sale in Charleston was "a brick chair house and stable." *South Carolina Gazette.*
> **1771** A stable was to be built on a glebe "24 feet long and 16 feet wide . . . to have stalls, maingers, and wrecks for four horses, with a partition at one end 8 feet for a chair house." Elizabeth City Parish, Elizabeth City Co., Va., Vestry Book.
> **1772** An estate on the Eastern Shore of Maryland contained a "chair house 8 feet by 14." Queen Anne's Co., Md., Deed Book K.
> **1790** It was "agreed that a building should be erected in the Parsonage Yard, to serve as a Chair House and Horse Stable with a loft to it." St. John's Lutheran Church, Charleston, S.C., Church Minute Book.

chair rail See **chair board, surbase.**

chaise house (shay) A building used to shelter light, open carriages, standing either separately or constructed as part of a stable. The distinction between *chaise house* and *chair house* is a subtle one; the former term appears slightly earlier in the 18th century and may have been used to distinguish the storage building of a larger vehicle. Both terms gradually gave way in the early 19th century to *carriage house* to refer to buildings for the storage of wheeled vehicles. See also **carriage house, chair house, coach house.**

> **1734** A plantation to be sold near Dorchester, South Carolina, contained a "stable and Chaise house with a Dutch Roof." *South Carolina Gazette.*
>
> **1772** The plantation known as Lord's Gift had "one chaise house about 16 by 12" feet. Queen Anne's Co., Md., Deed Book K.
>
> **1784** On the Gordon estate in Delaware was "one frame Stable and Shay house 18 feet by 16 feet Weatherboarded with Oak Clapboards the Ruff Oak shingles the doore of the Shay house and some the Weatherboardding wanting Otherwise in good repair." Kent Co., Del., Orphans Court Valuations.

chalk A soft, white limestone composed primarily of fossil shells of *foraminifera*. Although chalk was used in the manufacture of paint pigments and cements in Great Britain, its primary use in the early South was in the woodworking trades, where craftsmen used a chalk line to set out straight lines on timber. The chalk line consisted of a length of twine, usually kept on a wooden spool or reel, which was rubbed over a lump of chalk. Once the chalked line was pulled tightly over a timber, it was snapped, leaving a mark. Craftsmen then sawed or hewed to the line when shaping their framing timbers, planks, and boards.

> **1736** A notice read: "House, Sign, and Ship-painting and Glazing Work done after the best manner, imitation of Marble, Walnut, Cedar, &c. at five Shillings a yard, also plain painting, as cheap as any one shall without using of Chalk which is practic'd very much in Carolina." *South Carolina Gazette.*

chamber **1.** In a house of two or more rooms, the principal ground-floor sleeping space, often referred to in early records as the *inner room* or *parlor*. Early in the 18th century these terms were dropped in favor of *chamber*. Initially the space served not only for sleeping, but also as a place to socialize on more intimate terms than was possible in the *outer room* or *hall*. Though sleeping arrangements varied greatly, the mistress often occupied the chamber while her husband slept in the hall. As a result, the chamber acquired a feminine association that informed its use by women and children throughout the 18th century, even though husbands often cohabited there. In the last half of the 18th century, the creation of additional domestic spaces made it possible to draw some social functions out of the chamber. The narrowed role of the chamber was reflected in the growing use of the terms *bed chamber* and *bedroom*. By 1800 a desire for greater privacy led to the removal of all sleeping spaces from the ground floor, especially in urban situations.

> **1635** A new glebe in Accomack County, Virginia, was to have a "pertition in the midest . . . with an entry and two doures the one to goe to the kitchinge the other into the chamber." *County Court Records of Accomack-Northampton, Virginia 1632–1640.*
>
> **1657** In a deposition, Ann Stanly of Kent County, Maryland, described a domestic dispute between her master and his wife: "Your deponent standing theare my maister comming forth of his owne chamber hearing some disturbance in the Hall." *Archives of Maryland,* 54.
>
> **1781** "In the Chamber" of Rawleigh Downman's house was a single bed and bedstead, a dressing table and glass, a small desk, 12 walnut chairs, a chest of drawers, 2 tin sugar boxes, a coffee mill, a marble tea canister, together with other household items. Lancaster Co., Va., Will and Deed Book, 1770–1783.

2. A general term referring to any sleeping space. In this case a modifying adjective often accompanies the term, describing the color, occupant, or location of the room relative to certain ground-floor spaces. In the latter case, *hall chamber* referred to the chamber situated over the hall; *hall back chamber* referred to that behind the hall. By this convention, the *chamber chamber* was the room situated over the chamber.

> **1679** Among the upper rooms of Colonel Southy Littleton's house were the "back Roome Chambr . . . Parler Chamber . . . Porch Chamber" and "Hall Chamber." Accomack Co., Va., Will and Deed Book 1676–1690.
> **1712** After Robert Wallis's death in 1712, appraisers listed belongings in two upstairs rooms called the "inner chamber" and "outward Chamber." Pasquotank Co., N.C., Will Book 1712–1722.
> **1718** Appraisers of John Ingram's estate listed belongings in the "Hall Chamber . . . Porch Chamber" and "Parlour Chamber." Anne Arundel Co., Md., Prerogative Court Records, Inventory Book, 1718.
> **1724** In Charleston, the estate inventory of Joseph Morton listed, among other things, "Furniture in the best chamber, valued at £195." Charleston Co., S.C., Will Book, 1724–1725.
> **1747** The inventory of John Tayloe's estate lists a "Great Chamber" and "Mr. Fauntleroys Chamber" among the second-floor rooms. Richmond Co., Va., Will Book 1725–1753.
> **1774** The inventory of George William Fairfax mentions a "Yellow Chamber . . . Chintz Chamber . . . Red Chamber" and "Dresing Chamber" on the upper floor of his house, Belvoir. Fairfax Papers, VHS.

3. Any room between the ground floor and the loft or garret. This usage is illustrated in the occasional designation of an upper story as the *chamber floor*.

> **1734** "Chamber, in a House, or Building, is any Room situate between the lowermost (excepting Cellars,) and the uppermost Rooms. So that there are in some Houses two, or in others three or more stories of Chambers." *Builder's Dictionary*.
> **1760** A period plan for an unidentified house identifies the lower story as the parlor floor, the upper level as the "chamber floor." Armistead-Cocke Papers, W&M.
> **1783** In a related usage John Hawks of New Bern, North Carolina, referred to the upper floor of Governor Tryon's house as the "one pair of stairs or Bedroom floor." Hawks Letter, Miranda Papers, Academia Nacional de la Historia, Caracas.

4. A room or building in which to convene a governing body. These spaces were often used by the community on social or public occasions.

> **1702** In Williamsburg, Virginia, the Council directed "Mr. Auditor Byrd to send to England for . . . wax, wafers, Quills and Ink for the use of the Council Chamber." *Executive Journals of the Council of Colonial Virginia*, 2.
> **1732** In Charleston, "his Excellency (our Governour) met the Gentlemen, Merchants, and Captains of Ships . . . at the Council Chamber." *South Carolina Gazette*.
> **1769** William Eddis's description of Annapolis included the following observation: "The council chamber is a detached building, adjacent to the [courthouse], on a very humble scale. It contains one tolerable room for reception of the governor and his council, who meet here during the sitting of the assembly." Eddis, *Letters from America*.
> **1776** On Thomas Jefferson's plan for a new Capitol, the original designation, "Burgesses' Chamber," was changed to "Delegates Chamber" after passage of a new constitution. Jefferson Papers, Huntington Library.

5. A synonym for *room*, often used with an identifying adjective.

> **1704** In Middlesex County, Virginia, the courthouse was to have a "Close staircase and door for a jury chamber." Middlesex Co., Va., Order Book, 1694–1705.
> **1764** Accounts for maintaining and operating the State House mention £23 paid out for "A Glass for the Speaker's Chamber." South Carolina General Tax Receipts and Payments 1761–1769, SCA&H.
> **1800** Discussing his proposals for Washington's mausoleum, Benjamin Latrobe wrote:

"The building is a Pyramid, upon a base of 13 steps, of 100 feet side and height. It contains one chamber, 30 feet square." *The Correspondence and Miscellaneous Papers of Benjamin Henry Latrobe*, 1.

chamfer   A bevel or oblique surface formed by cutting off a square edge. If the chamfer does not continue the full length of the edge but is terminated, it is called a *chamfer stop*. In the early South, the sharp edges of exposed framing members such as posts, joists, and girders were often chamfered. Following traditional English custom, early colonial carpenters often carved elaborate stops, a practice that gradually gave way in the 18th century to ones of simple shape. See also **bevel**.

> 1796   An English immigrant architect described Mount Vernon in Fairfax County, Virginia, as "a wooden building, painted to represent champhered rustic and sanded." *The Virginia Journals of Benjamin Henry Latrobe*, 1.
> 1811   At Montpelier in Orange County, Virginia, a building account listed "21 ft rung of girder plained & chamfered." Cocke Papers, UVa.

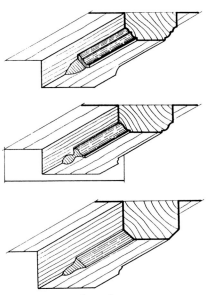

chamfer
Above: Criss Cross,
New Kent County, Va., c. 1700.
Center: Bacon's Castle,
Surry County, Va., 1665.
Below: Belle Aire,
Charles City County, Va., c. 1725.

chancel (chancell, chancil)   That part of an Anglican and Roman Catholic church containing the altar. Following English precedent, chancels in some 17th- and early 18th-century Anglican churches in the South were set apart from the rest of the body by a screen or railing. Because of their proximity to the altar and pulpit, pews in the chancel were symbols of prestige for their occupants. However, their status gradually diminished in the second half of the 18th century.

> 1677   "The Chancell" at Poplar Spring church in Gloucester County, Virginia, was "to be 15 foote and a Scrime to be runn a Crosse ye Church wth ballisters." Petsworth Parish, Gloucester Co., Va., Vestry Book.
> 1704   In the new capital of Williamsburg, it was recommended that "ye south side of ye chancel of ye church . . . be fitted up as a pew for ye Governour & Council." *Records of Bruton Parish.*
> 1730   For burials in a church, a South Carolina vestry charged £25 "for breaking ground in the chancel and every person that shall have ground broke in any part of the said church for the future shall pay fifty pounds." St. Helena's Parish, S.C., Vestry Book.
> 1766   The vestry noted that the pew in "the Chancel is appropriated by us for the poor at the workhouse" and directed the churchwarden "not to suffer any other persons to sit there." St. Philip's Parish, Charleston, S.C., Vestry Book.
> 1767   An Anglican Church in Somerset County, Maryland, was "To be Sixty feet In Length and Forty feet in Wedth in the clear: Exclusive of an Arch or Simey Circle for the Communion Table or Chancel." Touart, *Somerset.*

channel   A decorative groove or furrow. In the Greek Doric order, channels appeared in triglyphs in the entablature and the unfilleted flutes of columns.

chapel (chappel, chappell, chaple, chapple)   A place of Christian worship; a room or space within a building for prayers and worship services. The term was used in the early South primarily to describe a small secondary church in an Anglican parish or a Roman Catholic church. Only very rarely was the term used to denote the place of worship of dissenting congregations such as Presbyterians, Baptists, and Methodists. A *chapel of ease* was a building constructed some distance from the main Anglican parish church for the convenience of parishioners living in the region, as Anglican parishes in many parts of Virginia, North Carolina, Maryland, and South Carolina were ex-

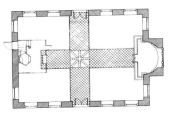

chapel
Exterior, interior, and plan,
Pompion Hill Chapel,
Berkeley County, S.C., 1765

tremely large, occasionally encompassing several hundred square miles. In the older, more settled regions along the coast, the more fortunate and richer parishes managed to erect one or more chapels of ease for their members. However, even the best parishes suffered from the paucity of clergymen capable of performing divine services every week. Many had lay readers or clerks, while others followed a more irregular schedule of services. While chapels varied in architectural elaboration from large brick structures with well-appointed furnishings to small, earthfast buildings with dirt floors and wooden benches, most were of a modest scale, built of wood, and simply furnished.

1673 It was ordered that "Mr. Nicholas Cock be paid . . . for shingling ye uper Chappell." Christ Church Parish, Middlesex Co., Va., Vestry Book.

1698 In St. Mary's County, Maryland, the "Roman Catholics [had] 1 brick chapel at St. Mary's; 1 wooden chapel at Mr. Gewlick's Plantation; 1 wooden chapel at Clement's Town; 1 wooden Chapel beyond Petuxant Road, near Mr. Haywards." Perry, *American Colonial Church*, 4.

1717 On White Clay Creek in New Castle, County, Delaware, "the frame" of St. James Church "was raised the 4th of December 1716, lies 10 or 11 miles distance from the town of Newcastle, and serves at present, for a Chapel of Ease to Emanuel Church there. 'Tis made of wood, in length 32 foot and breadth 22. . . . When thoroughly finished [it] will make, we think as fair and compleat an oratory, as any not made of Brick within this Govt." Perry, *American Colonial Church*, 2.

1729 Thomas Merritt, the minister of Winyah Parish in South Carolina, noted that there were "700 white inhabitants, near as many Negros. The parish is of great extent near 130 miles in breadth along ye coast & settled within land upwards of 80 miles." There was a "chappel of ease about 14 miles from ye parish church for the conveniency of about 15 families. . . . The church is a Wooden fabric but very decently rais'd 45 foot long and 25 wide and is very commodiously situated on ye side of a river where it branches and makes it convenient for about 120 Families which are not above 12 or 14 miles at farthest distance from ye church where most can and do come by water." SPG Letterbook B, SPGFP.

1760 John McDonald, an Anglican minister in Brunswick County, North Carolina, observed that in Virginia and South Carolina "every thing [was] quite comfortable and easy to ministers, they having for the most part only two or three places to attend and these not more than 10 or 12 miles from the Parsonage and good churches or decent Chapels to officiate in—But here our Chapels or rather People's house, where we are obliged to attend, are more than 30 some of them 40 miles distant from the center of the Parish." SPG Letterbook B, SPGFP.

1765 The Reverend Alexander Garden of St. Thomas Parish in South Carolina wrote that "my chapel of ease at Pompion hill is now almost finish'd in a very commodious & decent manner. . . . The Assembly granted the sum of £200 sterling . . . which it is thought will enable the Church Wardens and Vestry not only to compleat and adorn the Inside of the Church, but also to build a new & genteel Pulpit of Cedar. . . . When the whole is finished I think it will be one of the best country churches in Carolina." SPG Letterbook B, SPGFP.

1794 In Hagerstown, Maryland, "PROPOSALS will be received . . . for Building a stone chapel . . . for the use of the Roman Catholic congregation . . . the walls to measure on the outside 50 feet in length, and 35 feet in breadth, and to be 19 feet high from the ground." *Washington Spy*.

checker Flemish bond brickwork with all glazed headers forming a decorative pattern of alternating colors. The term was seldom used in the South to describe such glazed brickwork. It may have been employed there and elsewhere to refer to similar patterns of decoration on other materials.

1704 Sarah Knight of Boston noticed in New York that "the bricks in some of the houses are of diverse colours laid in checkers; being glazed, look very agreeable." Peckham, *Narratives of Colonial America*.

cheek A narrow vertical face forming the end or side of a structural element, usually forming one of a pair of corresponding faces such as a chimney breast or the side of a dormer window or cellar entrance. See also **chimney.**

> 1779   It was ordered that the guardian of an orphan "make new cheeks and door to the cellar." New Castle Co., Del., Orphans Court Valuations F.
> 1811   A workman was paid for "lath[ing] & Shingling Cheeks & Top of Dormands" in a house in Baltimore. Riddell Accounts, Pleasants Papers, MHS.

chestnut (chesnut)   A hardwood of the beech family of moderate hardness and durability. It was used in building for fence posts and rails, shingles, and some framing members.

> 1653   Thomas Hawkins was to set up "150 pannell of posts and rails . . . sufficient to keepe out hoggs and Cattle." The posts were "to be of Locust or Chestnutt." Westmoreland Co., Va., Deed, Will, and Patent Book 1653–1657.
> 1709   "The Chesnut-Tree of *Carolina*, grows up towards the hilly Part thereof, is a very large and durable Wood, and fit for House-Frames, Palisado's, Sills, and many other Uses." Lawson, *A New Voyage to Carolina.*
> 1744   The prize house at Morattico in Lancaster County, Virginia, was to be repaired with "stout End cills of white oak or Chestnut." Joseph Ball Letterbook, LC.
> 1753   The kitchen on the Stephens farm in Maryland was made of "chestnut logs hewed and dovetailed." Queen Anne's Co., Md., Deed Book D.
> 1820   Thomas Jefferson wanted "500 or 1000 chestnut shingles got and ready drawn for" repairing the roof of Poplar Forest. Coolidge Collection, Massachusetts Historical Society.

cheval-de-frise (cheval-de-frize)   A military barricade composed of a large timber or beam from each side of which project numerous wooden poles or spears. The ends of the poles are sharpened or pointed with iron. Such structures are used in quantity, joined end to end, and called *chevaux-de-frise*, the most common form of the term. The name *horse of Friseland* derives from the first use of the structure in that province of the Netherlands in the 17th century.

> 1777   "The Magazine in Williamsburg [Virginia] . . . is a small, circular Brick Building; it is at present surrounded with Chevaux de Frize, made by Col. Bullit." *VMHB*, 62.

chicken coop   See **coop.**

chicken house   A henhouse. The term was little used until the 19th century. For a more detailed description see **henhouse, poultry house.**

> 1821   On a Delaware farmstead stood a "chicken House twelve by twelve feet." Sussex Co., Del., Orphans Court Valuations M.

chimney (chimbly, chemney)   A structure containing the hearth and vertical mass that carries the flue by which smoke and gases are vented from a building. The term was sometimes used to refer just to the hearth. Chimneys were composed of several different elements, each with a specific name and function. The entire mass of masonry or wood was the *stack*. The floor-level opening in a room where the fire was made was the *fireplace* or *hearth*. By the early 18th century, the masonry flooring in front of this firebox was also known as the *hearth*. The side walls of the fireplace were the *cheeks* and the rear wall, the *back*. Supporting the masonry over the opening was a wooden *mantel-tree* or *lintel*. By the end of the 18th century, iron bars were being used as a substitute for the manteltree. *Chimney pieces* or *mantels* formed the decorative surround of the fireplace opening. If the chimney were constructed within the walls of a building, it was known as an *inside chimney*, and the mass of masonry projecting into the room was the

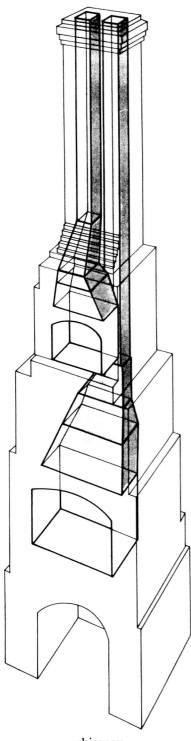

chimney
View of a chimney with its flues rising
through the stack

breast. Chimneys whose stacks rose on the exterior of buildings were *outside chimneys*. Those that served two rooms from one stack and stood at the intersection of two walls were known as *corner chimneys* or *angle chimneys*. The top of the firebox narrowed to a *throat*, which regulated the draft through the *flue*. The narrow channel or *flue*, which extended up through the chimney mass to the top or *cap*, was also known as a *funnel*. A *double chimney* had two fireplace openings back to back, serving two different rooms with two or more flues running up the stack. As with most elements in a building, the quality and construction of chimneys varied widely. The biggest difference was in the type of materials used in their construction. Wooden chimneys were a common feature of the southern landscape from the 17th through the 19th centuries. They heated the homes of small planters, backwoods settlers, slaves, and poor tenants. In the 17th and much of the 18th centuries, they were perhaps the most common type in many areas of the South. Some were built with logs or splints stacked horizontally; others were fabricated with corner posts and had wattled infill. Both were usually daubed on the inside to provide a protective coating. In many towns in the 18th and 19th centuries, laws were passed to eliminate wooden chimneys, considered a danger. Besides being less of a fire hazard, a brick chimney was a status symbol, a sign of permanence and prestige. In the second half of the 17th century, more and more successful planters chose to build brick chimneys. It was during this period that chimney placement became standardized. Prior to this time, settlers in the Chesapeake and Carolinas built dwellings with chimneys located along interior wall partitions as well as on gable-end walls. These patterns followed traditional English ones. Interior chimneys often stood at the point where exterior doorways opened into the house, creating a lobby entrance from the outside. However, environmental and social circumstances worked against the retention of interior chimneys. For the most part they were given up in favor of exterior, gable-end chimneys. From the late 17th through the 19th centuries, the gable end became the predominant position of chimneys in southern buildings. Only in a few particular circumstances, such as in the cramped urban sites in Charleston and in some double-pile dwellings, was this gable-end preference eschewed. Interior chimneys returned in the early and mid-19th century, with stacks built on the partition walls between front and back rooms being especially popular. See also **breast, cat and clay chimney, cheek, chimney back, chimney piece, dirt chimney, fireplace, flue, funnel, hearth, mantel, plastered chimney, stack, stick and clay chimney, Welsh chimney, wooden chimney.**

1635 A parsonage house was to be built on glebe land "forty foot long and eygteene foot wyde . . . a chimney at each end of the house, and upon each side of the chimneys a rome." *County Court Records of Accomack-Northampton, Virginia 1632–1640.*
1653 Carpenter Thomas Felton was engaged "to build Mr. John Holmwood a dwelling house, fiftye foote long, twentye foote wide with a shedd all along the side, and a shedd at one end, a chimney at the inside at one end, and at the other end a chimney without, and a chimney at the side of the house on the outside, to partition the house into three roomes." Surry Co., Va., Deed and Will Book 1652–1672.
1728 William Byrd of Westover caustically remarked that in Edenton, North Carolina, "a Citizen is considered Extravagant, if he has Ambition enough to aspire to a Brick-chimney." Byrd, *History of the Dividing Line.*

1732 A visitor to Virginia observed that travelers could expect entertainment "where two brick Chimbles shew there is a spare bed and lodging and Welcome." *VMHB,* 85.

1736 In Wilmington, North Carolina, a grand jury presented "a certain Chimney of a house . . . inhabited by John Ingram Twanbrook (near adjoyning the house inhabited by Nicholas Brewer) [as a] Nuisance to the Inhabitants of the said Town it being built with pine boards and thereby very lyable to take fire which may occasion the destruction of Several other houses in the said Town." Colonial Court Records, Criminal Papers. NCA&H.

1777 For sale: "In the town of York, A Dwelling-House twenty four feet by sixteen, with a shed the full length of the house, eight feet wide, and an angle chimney that serves both rooms." *Virginia Gazette.*

1799 Plan for a double-pile, side-passage dwelling in Rowan County, North Carolina, caused concern by one of the building's overseers. He wrote to John Steele, his client, that "if the building was mine I would make two outside Chimneys, it would make your parlours more roomy, and the House as to the outward appearance would look better to my notion; However dont let my opinion operate against your own Inclination; for in our free Country every man ought to please himself in the Construction of his house." John Steele Papers, SHC.

1821 It was ordered that cabins for the poor to have "outside chimneys, not to smoke, with backs to be well made and sufficiently large to guard against fire, of good and well tempered mortar . . . no log to be put in the frame or chimneys of the houses whose diameter at the small end shall be less than five inches, the spaces between the logs to be well chinked and daubed." King George Co., Va., Court Order Book 1817–1822.

chimney back (back, iron back) The back of the fireplace against which the fire is built. Specifically, a moveable and sometimes decorative cast-iron plate placed against the back of the fireplace to help reflect heat and protect the clay, stone, or brick of the chimney base. Iron chimney backs were imported into America from the beginning of settlement. By the middle of the 18th century, a number of regional furnaces cast their own decorative pieces. Brick was used in a similar fashion in wooden chimneys, where it was inserted at the back of the hearth to protect the daubing.

> **1721** An order was given "to make a back and harth & to plaster the chimney of ye vestry house." St. George's Parish, Harford Co., Md., Vestry Book.
>
> **1748** "Just imported" into Charleston were "Sash Weights for Windows, Iron Chimney Backs." *South Carolina Gazette.*
>
> **1771** A Virginia planter wrote to the proprietor of the Baltimore Furnace: "Send me the castings enumerated . . . 2 large Chimney backs, for a Kitchen & Laundry, 6 small Chimney backs." Robert Carter Collection, MHS.
>
> **1820** Among the items manufactured at an iron furnace in Jackson County, Georgia, were "Backs for Chimneys." 1820 U.S. Census of Manufacturing, Georgia.

chimney back
Chimney back manufactured at the Zane Marlboro Furnace near Winchester, Va., 1770. The coat of arms is that of the Fairfax family.

chimney piece The decorative elements covering the jambs and manteltree of a fireplace opening, including the architrave, columns, pilasters, cornice, shelf, and superstructure or overmantel above the shelf. Although the term is practically synonymous with the less common *mantelpiece* in contemporary usage, occasionally some distinction may have been made between the two terms. The use of the term *chimney piece* may have applied to all the decorative elements of a fireplace surround including the shelf and decorative superstructure, while *mantelpiece* may have been more limiting, used to describe the area up to the shelf. See also **mantelpiece.**

> **1680** Courthouse to be built "with two chimney pieces for the lower roomes." Talbot Co., Md., Court Judgments 1675–1682.
>
> **1711** The largest room in a dwelling in Charles County, Maryland was to be fitted up with a "Chimney peace with very good Stone mouldings and a large Landscipp pannell." Rivoire, *Homeplaces.*

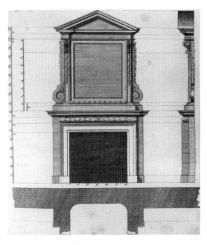

chimney piece

Chinese
Chinese style balustrude, Battersea,
Petersburg, Va.

1738 A Charleston merchant offered for a sale "A Marble Chimney Piece compleat." *South Carolina Gazette.*

1750 Specifications called for "a plain Chimney piece in each room to be Painted of a Marble Colour." Newport Parish, Isle of Wight Co., Va., Vestry Book.

1751 Imported into Annapolis were "painted Dutch tiles for Chimneypieces." *Maryland Gazette.*

1755 "Chimney-Pieces, certain Mouldings of Wood, or Stone, standing on the foreside of the Jaumbs, and coming over the Mantle-Tree." Salmon, *Palladio Londinensis.*

1777 A cabinetmaker advertised that he would fabricate "Pediment & plain Tabernacle chimney pieces." *Virginia Gazette.*

1803 For sale in Alexandria, Virginia, were "a few handsome Italian Marble chimney pieces with Janis and Alabaster chimney ornaments." *Alexandria Advertiser and Commercial Intelligencer.*

chimney sweep   See **sweep** (2).

chimney tile   See **tile.**

Chinese (Chineas)   A decorative fashion inspired by Oriental motifs. Although the European passion for Chinese porcelain introduced a number of eastern design motifs into the West, it was not until the second quarter of the 18th century that the fascination with nonclassical design elements, characterized by the rising wave of Rococo asymmetry, spread to other forms of the decorative arts and, in a limited fashion, to architecture. In England, craftsmen used Chinese motifs featuring pagodas, landscapes with dragons, and oriental figures carrying parasols or wearing drooping mustaches in silver designs, paperhangings, engravings, and carved chimney pieces, often combined with Rococo elements. In furniture, fretwork composed of rectangular and diagonal slats and lattices appeared in a number of the designs published by Thomas Chippendale in *The Gentleman and Cabinet Maker's Director* (1754, 1755, 1762), which enjoyed considerable popularity in the American colonies. Some architects also employed the diagonal slatted fretwork and lattice motifs for garden gates, fences, balustrades, bridges, and staircases. More enthusiastic interpretation of the Chinese motif appeared in William and John Halfpenny's *Rural Architecture in the Chinese Taste* (1750, 1752), followed by *Chinese and Gothic Architecture Properly Ornamented* (1752), which featured several plates of temples, triumphal arches, garden seats, palings, and bridges. The Chinese mania was tempered considerably in the new world, where architectural expression of oriental forms was, with a few exceptions, almost entirely limited to balustraded railings. In the late 1750s, the English builder William Buckland designed scalloped window cornices and pagoda-shaped hoods over the doors in the dining room at Gunston Hall in Fairfax County, Virginia. Early in his thinking about the design of Monticello, Thomas Jefferson toyed with the idea of building Chinese temples at the juncture of the turning of the two wings of the house. Whatever the architectural taste for the Chinese, it had all but disappeared by the second quarter of the 19th century. The introduction of the French word *chinois* into English to describe the *Chinese* taste or *chinoiserie* did not occur until the rise of art historical scholarship in the late 19th and early 20th centuries.

1756 In Charleston, James Reid's dwelling "is new built, strong, and madith after the Chinese taste, which spreads 60 feet square, including the balconies." *South Carolina Gazette.*

1773 In Williamsburg, "there is but two private buildings of note, the Governor's and the Att'y General's. The first is not remarkable: the other is in the Chinese taste, and it the handsomest of the two." *Proceedings of the Massachusetts Historical Society*, 49.

1777 Mardun Evington, a builder and cabinetmaker working in Virginia, advertised his skills, noting that "he understand the various branches of the cabinet business, Chinese and Gothick work, carving and turning, and is adept in the several branches of architecture, both ancient and modern." *Virginia Gazette*.

1808 At Monticello, workmen were "engaged at the Chinese railing." Coolidge Collection, Massachusetts Historical Society.

chink, chinking *(v.)* To stop or fill in a crack in a wall or the spaces between logs. *(n.)* Material used to fill in crack or spaces between logs in a wall. In log construction, such materials ranged from sticks, chips, boards, bricks, and brickbats, to rags, newspapers, and moss. The chinking was often daubed over with mud or mortar to fill in the gaps and prevent it from falling out. See also **daub.**

1821 The log cabins to be built for relief of the poor were to have "the spaces between the logs to be well chinked and daubed." King George Co., Va., Court Order Book 1817–1822.

chinquapin A shrubby chestnut hardwood, of the beech family, native to the Southeast. The chinquapin was little used in building, but did occasionally serve as fence posts.

1709 "*Chinkapin* is a sort of Chesnut. . . . The Wood is much of the Nature of Chesnut, having Leaf and Grain almost like it. It is used to timber Boats, Shallops, &c. and makes any thing that is to endure the Weather." Lawson, *A New Voyage to Carolina*.

1810 "The new Burying Ground Fence" for Christ Church in New Bern, North Carolina, was "to be done in the same manner it formerly was, the posts . . . to be of the best lightwood, Chinquepin or Cedar." *Newbern Herald*.

chisel (chissel, chizell, chizzel) A cutting tool of steel or iron with a flat rectangular blade beveled at one end and usually fitted with a wooden handle at the other end. All the woodworking trades used a variety of chisels for many purposes. Along with the curved bladed gouge, chisels were an essential tool for cutting and shaping. The most common types were *firmer* or *former chisels* used for general shaping. These were the largest bladed chisels and were struck with a wooden mallet. A thinner and lighter type often with bevel edges on three sides of the blade were known as *paring chisels*. They were used without a mallet by cabinetmakers, carvers, and joiners for detailed work. The third general class of chisels were *mortise chisels*, used by carpenters and joiners to fabricate mortises. These were narrow but thick bladed tools.

1703 "*Formers* . . . are used before the *paring Chissel*. . . . The *Stuff* you are to work upon being first scribed . . . you must set the edge of the *Former*, a little without the scribed Stroak with its *Basil* outwards, that it may break, and shoulder off the Chips from your Work, as the Edge cuts it. . . . you make several Cuttings, to cut it straight down by little and little, till your Work is made ready for the *paring Chissel*. . . . The *Paring-Chissel* . . . must have a very fine and smooth edge: Its Office is to follow the *Former*, and to *pare* off, and *smoothen*, the Irregularities the *Former* made. It is not knockt upon with the *Mallet*, but the Blade is clasped upon the out-side of the hindermost Joints of the fore and little Fingers. . . . The *Mortess Chissel* . . . is a narrow *Chissel*, but hath its *Blade* much thicker, and consequently stronger (that it may endure the heavier blows with the *Mallet*) than other *Chissels* have. . . . Its Office is to cut deep square holes, called *Mortesses*, in a piece of Wood. Joiners use them of several Breadths according as the Breadths of their *Mortesses* may require. . . . Though Carpenters for their finer Work use all the sorts of

chink, chinking
O'Quinn House, Moore County, N.C.

[the above] *Chissels* . . . they also use a stronger sort of *Chissels*; and distinguished by the name of *Socket-Chissels:* For whereas those *Chissels* Joiners use have their wooden Heads made hollow to receive the Iron Sprig above the Shoulder of the Shank, Carpenters have their Shank made with a *hollow Socket* at it Top, to receive a strong wooden Sprig made to fit into the *Socket*, with a square Shoulder above it . . . which makes it much more strong, and able to endure the heavy blows of the *Mallet.*" Moxon, *Mechanick Exercises.*

chocolate color   A dark brown paint composed of *Spanish brown* and *lampblack* mixed in oil. It was most often used for interior work.

> 1750   The interior of a glebe house was to "be painted of a Lead Colour & the lower one of a Chocolate Colour." Newport Parish, Isle of Wight Co., Va., Vestry Book.
> 1798   In Williamsburg, an agreement between Jeremiah Satterwhite and St. George Tucker directed Satterwhite to paint "the outer doors a . . . chocolate colour" and the foundation "dark brick colour, nearly approaching to a chocolate color." Tucker Papers, W&M.

choir   In larger cruciform Anglican churches in Great Britain and Roman Catholic churches throughout Europe, that part of the church east of the crossing intersection of the *transepts*. It was the part of the church in which the singers were accommodated. Beyond the choir stood the *chancel*, where communion was celebrated. As a reference to a part of a church, the term was scarcely used in the colonial period. Singers were often accommodated in galleries in the west end of a church or in a specially reserved pew near the pulpit. It was not until the early 19th century when much larger and more pretentious churches were constructed that *choir* was used to refer to a place in the church.

> 1805   Writing of his proposed plans for a Roman Catholic Cathedral in Baltimore, architect Benjamin Henry Latrobe observed that "a Cathedral of the Latin Church, has a prescribed form. . . . This form is that of a cross, the style of which is longer than the head, or either of the arms. The head of the cross is also necessarily the Choir. . . . The Choir being that part of the Church which is devoted to divine Service, must be of a size to admit of the commodious arrangement, and movements of the Clergy engaged in its performance. If it be ascertained, what is the smallest space, in which the ceremonial of the high festivals of the Church can be decently, that is commodiously, exhibited (for embarrassment arising from a croud, destroys solemnity) the smallest possible size of the Choir of a Cathedral would be determined. The Choir, governs the dimensions of the remaining parts of the Church." *The Correspondence and Miscellaneous Papers of Benjamin Henry Latrobe, 2.*

church   A building in which to conduct Christian worship. As an arm of the state, Anglicans were the dominant sect in many of the southern colonies, especially Virginia, parts of Maryland, and the low country of South Carolina. Elsewhere, dissenting groups such as Quakers and Presbyterians were an important presence. In Maryland, Catholics made up a large proportion of the 17th-century population and remained an influence well into the next century. After 1750, Baptists, Methodists, and Presbyterians challenged Anglican authority, reshaping religious life throughout the region. In most cases, these dissenting sects avoided the term *church* in favor of *meetinghouse*. Anglican churches were elongated in plan, with the principal door at the west end with a cross-axial entrance along either one or both of the longer north and south walls. Following liturgical requirements, the altar stood in the chancel altar at the east end. In the southern colonies there was little to distinguish the earliest churches from other buildings, these being earthfast structures of wood with little in the way of fixed furniture. By the end of the 17th century, substantial churches with specialized fittings—pews, pulpits, reading desks, communion rails, etc.—were beginning to appear in the more settled parts of Virginia. By 1730 brick churches with classical detailing and painted interiors were a common sight in these areas as well as Maryland and the parishes surrounding Charleston, South Carolina. Before the Revolution these rectangular churches generally had a single aisle, flanked with square or rectangular pews in which worshipers were seated on benches lining the paneled partitions. However, not all churches were entirely pewed. Many smaller ones and those constructed by poorer parishes contained only benches or forms. Pulpits generally stood near the center of the church on one of the long walls or near the east end of the building near the chancel. Beginning in the second quarter of the 19th century, a reorientation occurred in ecclesiastical architecture throughout America. A growing numbers of churches of all denominations were equipped with slip seats so that all worshipers faced the pulpit. The seating was now divided by one or two aisles, terminating at one or more pair of doors at the west front. See also **basilica, chapel, meetinghouse.**

1619 Officials of the Virginia Company noted "divers Presents of Church plate, and other ornaments - 200li already given towards buildinge a Church." *Records of the Virginia Company*, 1.

1677 The vestry of Petsworth Parish directed "that ye: inside worke of ye: Church now in Buildinge at poplare Springe, bee done in manner as followeth vizt: the walls and ceiling over head to be substantially lathed, daubed & plaistered; the Chancell to be 15 foote and a Scrime to be runn a Crosse ye: Church wth: ballisters; a Communione table 6 foote & 1/2 to be inclosed on 3 sides at 3 foote distance, to be done wth. ballisters, 2 wainscoate double pews one each side of ye. Chancell, Joyninge to ye Scrime with ballisters suitable to ye: said Scrime. 1: double pew above ye: pulpitt & deske Joyninge to ye Scrime, all ye: rest of ye: pews of both sides of ye: said church to be double, and all to be done wth: wainscoate Backs, the pulpit to be of wainscoate 4 foote diameter, & made with 7 sides, 6 foot allowed for ye: reading desks & passage into ye: pulpitt ye: ministers pew to be under ye: pulpitt, & raised 18 Inches and ye: readers deske under it, the two uppermost pews in ye: Body of ye: Church & ye: two pews in ye: Chancell to have doores. Petsworth Parish, Gloucester Co., Va., Vestry Book.

church Christ Church, Lancaster County, Va., c. 1732

1693 In All Faith Parish, the vestry agreed to "post the Church with Seader post to recover the roof with clapboards with three large window frames and . . . a decent pulpit with a canopy over head with a deske for Clark and to lay the flowors of the church with planks, to raise and Banister for a communion Table . . . and to cover the Church over head and to batten . . . with plank." All Faith Parish, St. Mary's City Co., Md., Vestry Book.

1701 In Edenton, North Carolina, the vestry authorized "building a Church 25 feet long posts in the ground and held to the Collar beams." St. Paul's Parish, Chowan Co., N.C., Vestry Book.

1737 The Georgia trustees directed that a church be made "80 feet long, & 40 feet broad in the clear, with a Square tower 40 feet high, and 20 feet square from out to out. The walls to be 3 feet thick, 10 feet high, and 2 brick & half upwards, all to be render'd and white wash'd on the Inside. No windows from 10 feet high to the ground, but loop holes for muskets on occasion. A pulpit, reading desk, communion rail and table, & no pews, but benches, as at Tunbridge." *Journal of the Earl of Egmont.*

churchyard See **yard** (1).

cincture A fillet at either end of a shaft of a column, pilaster, or pillar, especially one at the lower end; the uppermost member of the base of a column.

cipher (cypher, sipher) **1.** To join two boards or planks together by lapping the end of one piece over the other with a bevelled edge, so that the surface of both pieces are in the same plane.

1738 A church interior was to be "ceald with 3/4 plank Cyphered the Height of the Pews, Naild on with 8d nailes or Brads." Bristol Parish, Prince George Co., Va., Vestry Book.

1747 A prison roof was to be "planked with pine Plank siferd & Shingled." Northumberland Co., Va., Court Record Book 1743–1749.

1766 "The open part" of a church steeple was to "be closed up with cyphered plank." Elizabeth City Parish, Elizabeth City Co., Va., Vestry Book.

2. Letters combined in a design; a monogram.

1769 Painters advertised: "GILDING, and CIPHERS put on carriages." *Virginia Gazette.*

circular stair See **stair.**

cistern A wooden or masonry receptacle for the storage of water and other liquids. Rainwater channeled into eaves and ground-level gutters fed underground masonry cisterns, which were often vaulted and lined with cement to prevent stagnation and contamination.

1749 A prison was to have a "cistern . . . lin'd with Lead." Westmoreland Co., Va., Court Order Book 1747–1750.

1797 Construction plans for a market house in Charleston included a "foundation . . . sufficiently thick and compact to admit a Cistern under the whole." *City Gazette and Daily Advertiser.*

1804 A leaking roof at the President's House in Washington "arose from two principal causes: the very injudicious manner in which the gutters, and the troughs conveying the water to the Cistern were constructed, and the badness of the Slating." *The Correspondence and Miscellaneous Papers of Benjamin Henry Latrobe*, 1.

city hall A public building housing the offices and meeting spaces of a civic corporation; a town hall. See also **town hall.**

clamp **1.** A brace, clasp, or band of iron or other material used to strengthen, support, or fasten two or more pieces or elements together.

1767 In order to strengthen the roof of a church, a vestry hired a workman to install "King Posts . . . with sufficient Heads thereto & to be strap'd with Clamps of Iron round the Coller Beams & up the said King Posts Twenty Inches on each side . . . the said Clamps of Iron to be 2 1/2 Inches Broad & 1/2 Inch thick each Clamp." Chester Parish, Kent Co., Md., Vestry Book.

1796 In the installation of a stone chimney piece, a merchant advised his client to "let the Man who fixes them cut the holes in the wall for the clamps before he attempts to sett the Jambs." Burwell Manuscripts, UVa.

2. A brick kiln. The term appears to have been synonymous with *kiln* during the colonial period. However, it was rarely used. See also **kiln.**

1668 "In every Clampe or Brick Keele . . . there are three degrees of Brick in goodness." Leybourn, *Platform Guide Mate for Purchasers, Builders, Measurers.*

clapboard (clabboard)   **1.** A small, thin board split from oak and other species, used to make barrels and casks. The meaning of the term in this sense disappears after initial settlement of Virginia in the first half of the 17th century.

1612 In an attempt to provide exportable commodities, a number of the settlers at Jamestown, Virginia, "made clapboard, wainscot, and cut downe trees against the ships comming." *Complete Works of Captain John Smith*, 1.

2. A thin, riven board, often tapered along one side and generally measuring four or five feet in length, used to cover roofs, walls, and floors. Laid horizontally over one another with the thicker edged lapped over the thin edge of the board underneath, riven clapboarding was a relatively cheap means of enclosing a space compared to the more labor intensive effort needed to saw, joint edges, plane, and finish the much longer and thicker exterior sheathing board known as a *weatherboard.* The use of the term *clapboard* in this sense comes into prominence in the middle third of the 17th century when, among other things, the high cost of skilled labor compelled settlers in the Chesapeake to construct simple frame dwellings. Riven clapboards proved to be an ideal material to provide the structural rigidity to the flimsy framing system known as the *Virginia house* that emerged as the primary housing form. In the 18th and early 19th centuries, clapboards continued to be used on poorer housing and outbuildings. Specifications often called for buildings to be *weatherboarded* with *clapboards*, which meant covering their exteriors with riven boards. Although the two terms appear nearly synonymous, early southerners carefully distinguished between the two. *Weatherboarding* was a more generic term for any exterior board covering, including long, sawn boards, whereas *clapboarding* referred to any roughly worked lapped sheathing nailed either on the inside or outside of a building.

1666 Workman agreed to "new Cover the Barne with Clapboard." Northampton Co., Va., Deed and Will Book 1655–1668.

1671 John Anderson, sawyer, was bound to John West of Somerset County, Maryland, for "fifteene hundred good sufficient well rived Claboards & also to Deliver ye said West as aforesaid his shalops full load of good Cypress quarters fitt to make good covering Claboard of five foot four inches long." Touart, *Somerset.*

1684 A craftsman agreed to build "A Chimny, A Clap board loft and partition." *Records of the Courts of Sussex County Delaware 1677–1710*, 1.

1692 A courtroom was "to be ceiled and arched with good thin clapboards, the other room to be lofted with good thick clapboards." Princess Anne Co., Va., Court Order Book 1691–1709.

1702 A courthouse was "to be well covered with Good Red oake clapboards Five Foot long and to be well shingled upon them with Cyprus shingles" with the body of the building "to be weather boarded with Pine Plank." Essex Co., Va., Will and Deed Book No. 10.

clapboard
Tobacco house, Carter's Grove,
James City County, Va.

1733 "The first house" in Savannah "was framed, and raised . . . Before this we had proceeded in a very unsettled manner, having been imployed in severall different things such as cutting down trees, and cross cutting them to proper lengths for clapp boards. And afterwards splitting them into clapp boards, in order to build us clapp board houses." *The Journal of Peter Gordon, 1732–1735.*

1737 To be built on a glebe "a dairy twelve foot square . . . to be well framed & covered and weatherboarded with good four foot clapboards." Truro Parish, Fairfax Co., Va., Vestry Book.

1776 On the Stockley farm in southern Delaware was a "log'd house Twelve by Sixteen feet . . . with a Chimney made of Wood, and a Cipries Clabboard rough." Sussex Co., Del., Orphans Court Valuations A.

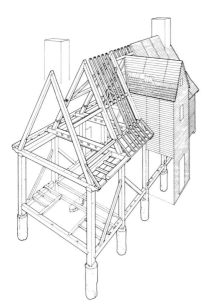

clapboard house, work
Frame and clapboard covering,
Cedar Park, Anne Arundel, Md.

clapboard house, clapboard work A shorthand reference to a simplified framing system developed in the Chesapeake by the third quarter of the 17th century that eliminated much of the complicated joinery and preparation of materials inherent in traditional English construction. This type of construction was also known as a *Virginia house*. One of the hallmarks of this system was the covering of four- or five-foot-long riven clapboards, which provided the structural rigidity necessary to secure the principal wall-framing members and roof trusses. With the reduction in the cost of preparation and skilled labor, *clapboard work* sacrificed permanency and refinement of detail. However, the *clapboard house* was an important element in the southern landscape for more than two hundred years, providing housing for the pioneer, the poor, and the unfree, as well as sheltering a variety of domestic and agricultural functions. See also **Virginia house.**

1698 In Talbot County, Maryland, the Catholics had constructed a "clapboard house at Doncaster Town; Quakers- a small meeting house at Ralph Fishbourne's, another at Howell Powsby, another between King's Creek & Tuckahoe, these are Clapboard houses about 20 feet long. Another framed house at the head of Third Haven Creek, about 50 feet long." Perry, *American Colonial Church*, 4.

1727 Justices were to "agree with a workman to build a house to hold court in, of common clapboard work thirty foot long and twenty foot wide." Essex Co., Va., Court Order Book 1726–1729.

1733 In the new town of Savannah, "we were taken of[f] from the palisadoes and sett about sawing and splitting boards eight feet long in order to build clapp board houses, to get us under better cover till our framed houses could be built." *The Journal of Peter Gordon, 1732–1735.*

1751 At the expiration of his apprenticeship, a young carpenter was to receive "as many tools as shall be thought sufficient to build a clapboard house." York Co., Va., Deed Book 1741–1754.

1761 A master "agreed to instruct his apprentice in the art and science of a clap board carpenter." Spotsylvania Co., Va., Will Book 1749–1759.

clasp head nail See **wrought nail.**

clear in height See **in the clear.**

clear length See **in the clear.**

clear of ground The height of an object or part of a building above ground level.

1754 Courthouse to "be underpinned three feet clear of ground." Prince Edward Co., Va., Court Order Book 1754–1758.

clear of sap The inner heartwood of a timber, which is more durable than the softer sapwood. See also **sapped.**

1739 Church pews were to be made with "good Substantial Pine plank Clear of Sapp." St. Anne's Parish, Anne Arundel Co., Md., Vestry Book.

cleave To part, split, or divide a material such as wood or slate along the grain by cutting, hewing, or riving it with a bladed instrument. See also **rive, split.**

> **1726** In English roofing materials, "Shingles are to be prefer'd before thatch; and if they are made of good Oak, and cleft out (not saw'd) and then well season'd in the Water and Sun, they become a sure light, and durable Covering." Neve, *City and Country Purchaser.*
> **1789** On "Zachary Weaver's Tenement" in Westmoreland County, Virginia, a "new Corn House [is] to be built thereon 12 feet square 5 1/2 feet Pitch of sawn Logs and Dovetailed, and to be covered with Cleave Boards." Carter Papers, UVa

clerestory (cleerstory) **1.** A large, unobstructed window that is not divided into two or more tiers of lights by a transom or cross bar.

2. The upper part or upper stories of a building containing a series of windows admitting light into the central part of the structure.

> **1680** It was ordered that a three-story courthouse have "twelve Archytryve Windowes in the two Cleere storyes." Talbot Co., Md., Judgements Book 1675–1682.

clinker A very hard, pale brick whose surface has become vitrified by overheating in the kiln.

> **1757** An agreement was reached "to make as many Clinkers and Stock bricks as will be Sufficient to lay the Foundation and Carry up the Front of the Church . . . the Clinkers to be laid in the Foundation and as high up the wall as the Water Table." St. George's Parish, Harford Co., Md., Vestry Book.

cloacina temple A structure housing a close stool; a privy. Classical wags christened these structures *cloacina temples,* a name derived from the principal sewer of Rome. For a more detailed description, see **necessary house, temple.**

> **c. 1775** A memorandum concerning the outbuildings at Monticello specified 4 walnut sash for the "cloacinae." Coolidge Collection, Massachusetts Historical Society.
> **1783** A visitor sketched a plan of Westover in Charles City County, Virginia, including the location of the "Temples of Cloacina." Shippen, *Westover Described.*
> **1806** The index in a court order book for Lancaster County, Virginia, listed a "cloacina temple to be erected," referring to an order "to build a necessary for public use on the Courthouse bounds." Lancaster Co., Va., Court Order Book 1805–1808.

cloak rail A horizontal strip of wood with a series of pegs used for hanging garments and other household items.

> **1774** Carpenter's work done for William Corbit in Odessa, Delaware, listed "44 ft rabt strips & Cloke rail at 3d." Sweeney, *Grandeur on the Appoquinimink.*
> **1802** Carpenter Andrew McDonald's bill for work on the Tayloe house in Washington, D.C., included entry for "17 [feet] Cloak pin Rail & holes [at] 1/." Tayloe Papers, VHS.

closer
Blandfield, Essex County, Va.

closer Part of a brick, usually smaller than a header, inserted into the wall surface to finish a course, usually near the end of a wall or around an aperture. See also **bond.**

close stool See **necessary house.**

closet **1.** A small withdrawing room, office, or space for study, writing, privacy, or retirement. Seldom used in this context in America after the mid-18th century.

> **1687** There was "A fair closett or office for the clerk" in the courthouse. Charles City Co., Va., Court Order Book 1687–1695.

1691 "The little closett [in the courthouse is to] be fitted up with a bench or table to write upon with some shelves to lay books and papers on." Westmoreland Co., Va., Court Order Book 1690–1698.

1701 Ralph Wormeley's estate inventory listed "Madam Wormeley's Closet," filled with many books. Middlesex Co., Va., Court Records.

2. A stair wellhead with a small enclosed space containing the stair, a meaning that had evolved in the Chesapeake in the early 18th century.

1708 "A pair of Stairs [is] to go up in the Clossett in the Hall." St. Peter's Parish, New Kent Co., Va., Vestry Records.

3. A small enclosed space for storage, a meaning that came into common use in the 18th century. See also **catery closet, cuddy, hot closet, sideboard.**

1739 "Closets or cup boards" were to be added to a glebe house where space permitted. Truro Parish, Fairfax Co., Va., Vestry Book.

1746 Upper chambers in a house were to have "Shelving in two closets." Huger Smith, *The Dwelling Houses of Charleston.*

1784 A log dwelling house was to have the "Brick Chimney and Brest Work and Closets finished off." Kent Co., Del., Orphans Court Valuations.

clubhouse, clubroom   A building or room used for social or recreational activities.

1782 In Baltimore, "THOSE who consider themselves members of the SMOAKING SOCIETY, are requested to meet at the Club Room . . . on business of the greatest importance." *Maryland Journal, and Baltimore Advertiser.*

1797 "THE Anniversary of the South-Carolina Golf Club, will be held . . . at the Club House." *City Gazette and Daily Advertiser.*

clump   A cluster of trees or shrubs intentionally planted on the pleasure grounds of a dwelling house to relieve the monotony of open ground.

1789 Mount Vernon was "laid out somewhat in the form of English gardens, in meadows and grass grounds, ornamented with little copies, circular clumps and single trees." Morse, *American Geography.*

1804 At Monticello, Thomas Jefferson noted that a patch of ground "must be broken by clumps of thicket, as the open grounds of the English are broken by clumps of trees." Coolidge Collection, Massachusetts Historical Society.

coach house   A building or part of a building, often combined with a stable, used for the storage of a coach or carriage. See also **carriage house, chair house,** and **chaise house.**

1724 Daniel McCarty stored many of the imported goods that he sold to his neighbors in Westmoreland County, Virginia, in his "coach house." Westmoreland Co., Va., Court Records.

1770 A traveler noted that "all my Harness has been stole out of a Coach House in Baltimore." *VMHB,* 45.

1798 At the Carroll Mansion in Annapolis was a "brick coach house 20 by 60" feet. 1798 US Direct Tax, MSA.

1799 A dwelling for sale in Richmond advertised a "coach house to hold two carriages." *Virginia Gazette.*

coach steps   Freestanding steps or a small block or platform at the curb of a street to facilitate entry to a carriage or coach. See also **horse block, upping block.**

1802 The stonecutters' accounts for John Tayloe's elegant Washington, D.C., residence included a charge for "Coach Steps Moulded...11.7.6." Tayloe Papers, VHS.

Coade stone   An artificial cast stone manufactured in England in the late 18th and early 19th centuries. This durable ceramic stoneware

Coade stone   Drawing room chimney piece, Octagon, Washington, D.C.

was used for decorative work including capitals, bases, keystones, quoins, and chimney pieces. The material had a limited circulation in the South. In 1801 John Tayloe purchased two Coade stone chimney pieces and Ionic capitals for the Octagon, his dwelling in Washington, D.C. See also **composition ornament.**

> **1799**   In correspondence with the London firm of Bird, Savage, and Bird, Gabriel Manigault of Charleston noted: "There was lately a manufactory, the property of a person of the name of Coade, at or near Lambeth, for working ornamented composition in imitation of Stone, to be used in Buildings instead of Stone. I shall be much obliged by your having inquiry made whether he has any printed description or plates of the articles made or list of their prices & if he has, by our sending them to me." Manigault Papers, South Caroliniana Library.
>
> **1801**   John Tayloe wrote to London merchants declaring that "Mr. Coade—*ought to be Mr. Shark.* . . . Astonishing as it will appear to you 'tis no less true, that the mantle of the drawing room Chimney piece (as P the Sketch you sent me) has in the packing been omitted, for 'tis in neither of the three packages sent, and my room without it cannot be finished, you will therefore please send it me immediately. . . . The Portico Pieces, as ordered—if not already forwarded, I wish not now to be sent, for the Buildings can't wait for them." Ridout, *Building the Octagon.*

coal hole   A storage place for coal; a cellar or part of one where coal is stored.

> **1746**   "TO BE LET . . . a Brick Tenement two Story high two Rooms on a Floor, and a Loft over all, with a good Coal Hole that may hold about eight Tuns of Coal." *South Carolina Gazette.*
>
> **1802**   Washington, D.C., stonecutters Shaw & Birth charged John Tayloe to "Cover Stone Coal Hole 26/#Iron Ring Do 3/," referring to a large masonry vault accessible from the area way behind the Tayloe residence. Tayloe Papers, VHS.

coal house   A building for the storage of coal, often associated with blacksmiths' shops.

> **1755**   A dwelling for sale in Charleston included "many conveniences such as a new store, a coal-house, mill-house." *South Carolina Gazette.*
>
> **1766**   Property in Frederick County, Maryland, contained "a good new Smith's Shop 24 Feet by 16, with a Coal House adjoining, 24 Feet by 8, both under a good Shingle Roof." *Maryland Gazette.*
>
> **1823**   In operation in southern Delaware was a "Forge 32 by 35 Newly rebuilt one house Called the Iron house 9 by 15 in Good repair, one Coal House 25 by 54 in Tolerable repair." Sussex Co., Del., Orphans Court Valuations N.

coat A layer of a liquid or semiliquid substance such as paint, tar, plaster, and stucco applied to the walls, floors, and roofs of buildings.

> **1720** A dwelling was to have its clapboards and shingles "covered [with] a good coat of tar." Northampton Co., Va., Loose Court Papers.
>
> **1742** The vestry discussed "the necessity of painting the Inside of the Chapel of Ease . . . also coating the Outside thereof with Tar and Red paint . . . for its Security and Preservation." St. Anne's Parish, Anne Arundel Co., Md., Vestry Book.
>
> **1798** In Washington, the President's House "is roofed and boarded, ready to receive the slate; the boarding is covered with a coat of composition to protect the roof and inside work from the weather." *The Observatory.*
>
> **c. 1798** In John Dickinson's dwelling in Wilmington, Delaware, "none of the inside woodwork, not even the laying of the floors, is to be done until the first coat of plastering is finished and dryed, so that no vacancies may be caused by shrinking." Dickinson Plantation File, Delaware Bureau of Museums.
>
> **1809** In Augusta, Georgia, proposals were accepted "for Plaistering the said Church, three Coats, per yard, including everything but lime." *Augusta Chronicle.*

cobblestone A water-worn, rounded stone, measuring from a few inches to a little less than a foot in diameter. In the late 18th and early 19th centuries, cobbles were used in paving streets of major cities. They were also used in foundations, generally as a lower level on top of which bricks were laid. A building at Causey's Care, a 1620s settlement site in Charles City County, Virginia, had foundation walls composed of cobbles.

cock **1.** (caulk) To let the end of a beam into the side of another beam by means of series of notches or dovetails. The cock tenon was often used to firmly secure the ends of tie beams and girders to wall plates.

> **1760** A prison was to be framed with "cock tenants." Prince Edward Co., Va., Will Book 1754–1784.
>
> **1771** The plates and joists of a St. John's Church in Granville County, North Carolina was to have "cock Tennants." Francis Hawks Collection, Church Historical Society, Austin.
>
> **1803** The joists of a church in South Carolina were "to be caulk'd and notch'd down." Johns Island Church Specifications, Charleston Library Society.

2. A mechanical device for controlling the flow of liquids at the end of a pipe.

> **1773** A firm of tin plate workers in Charleston offered for sale "Brass Cocks." *South Carolina Gazette and Country Journal.*

cockloft A small, unfinished attic space or loft above the garret and immediately beneath the ridge of the roof, usually accessible by a ladder.

> **1699** A tenant agreed to undertake the "Laying the Cock loft of the . . . house and making 2 Windows in the Cellar." *Records of the Courts of Sussex County Delaware 1677–1710*, 2.
>
> **1774** A dwelling for sale in Charleston contained "a Cockloft over the whole House." *South Carolina Gazette and Country Journal.*

cockpit An enclosed arena or pit specially built in which gamecocks are set against one another for sport. Because the sport required little more than an open area, or a fenced-in ring and benches at best, purpose-built cockpits were relatively rare, generally appearing in towns. Although railed against by the sober-minded for its violence and the associated gambling and carousing, cockfighting drew rich and poor men together in a festive and competitive atmosphere matched only by horse racing in popularity.

1804 Over a period of three days, "A MAIN OF COCKS, WILL be fought" in Raleigh "in Peter Casso's inclosure, for one hundred dollars, and a purse of fifty dollars, raised at the Cock Pitt Door." *Raleigh Register*.

1809 At the "WIG-WAM GARDENS" in Norfolk, "the Proprietor has erected A COCK-PIT, of the purpose of fighting every Saturday throughout the season." *Norfolk Gazette and Publick Ledger*.

coffeehouse A public place of entertainment where coffee, chocolate, and other refreshments were served. Some establishments also provided lodging and meals. In England and colonial America in the late 17th and 18th centuries, most towns had such an establishment where people would gather to discuss politics and business, dine, read newspapers, and play cards. In many respects, coffeehouses differed little from taverns and inns. See also **tavern**.

1710 In Williamsburg, William Byrd "went to the coffeehouse where after we had settled some accounts of the naval officers we played at cards till 11 o'clock." *Secret Diary of William Byrd of Westover*.

1753 In Charleston, "the Exchange Coffee-House. Will be opened To-Morrow at ALEXANDER CHISOLM on the Bay; where Gentlemen will have the Entertainment and Attendance usual in Coffee-Houses a broad. Lodgings may be had [at the] said COFFEE-HOUSE." *South Carolina Gazette*.

1756 "JOHN CRANMER . . . intends to keep a COFFEE HOUSE up one pair of stairs, having the English, Carolina, and other NEWSPAPERS." *South Carolina Gazette*.

1785 "The Alexandria Inn and Coffee-House, Is now open, and ready for the Reception of TRAVELLERS and others: The house is large, and well calculated for the above purpose. . . . I have in this house several very convenient private rooms, with fire-places, where gentlemen may be most comfortably accommodated. It will continue to be furnished with most kinds of liquors of the best quality, and such rarities of the seasons as our maker will afford. . . . HENRY LYLES." *Virginia Journal and Alexandria Advertiser*.

1797 "SUMMER COFFEE-HOUSE, Near the Landing, Sullivan's Island. . . . The above Coffee-House is open, and ready for the reception of genteel company. He has two large Halls added to the House, elegantly paperd, capable of accommodating 100 persons. There will be Dinner, and the best Liquors, provided every day, and the best attendance, for Cash only; as no Credit will be given on any account." *City Gazette and Daily Advertiser*.

collar beam A horizontal cross beam in a roof truss that ties a pair of rafters together at a level above the wall plate. See also **windbeam**.

1674 Specifications for the roof of a statehouse at St. Mary's City called for "every pair of Rafters to have two button braces to the Collor beame." *Archives of Maryland*, 2.

1763 Changes in specifications for a church noted that "the coller Beames be [of pine] 12 deep by 8 inches, and that the ruff be framed after the New England manner." St. George's Parish, Accomack Co., Va., Vestry Book.

1818 "The collar beams [are] to be about half way the rafters" in the roof of a new courthouse. Northampton Co., N.C., Miscellaneous Court Records, NCA&H.

colonnade (colonade) A series of regularly spaced columns supporting an entablature and usually one side of a roof. In the language of classical architecture, when a *colonnade* stands in front of a building and serves as an entrance porch, it is known as a *portico*. If a colonnade extends around the outside of a building on three or four sides, it is called a *peristyle*. Colonnades could also be freestanding structures that linked two or more buildings or parts of a building together and were sometimes known as *covered ways* or *covered passages*. See also **arcade, covered way, portico**.

1758 A proposal was made to build a house at Tower Hill for the governor of North Carolina with a "Kitchen . . . placed at Thirty Feet Distance from one Corner of

colonnade
West Lawn, University of Virginia

column
St. James, Santee, Charleston County, S.C.

the Front of the said Dwelling-House, and the Stable at the same Distance from the other Corner of the Front of the said House; and a Colonade of Eight Feet wide from Outside to Outside, from each of the said Corners to the said Buildings respectively." *State Records of North Carolina*, 25.

1767 At Mount Clare in Baltimore County, Maryland, Charles Carroll proposed to build a "Portico or Colonade to be Joined to the Front of a House and project Eight feet from it, An Arch at Both Ends, for a Passage through it." Trostel, *Mount Clare.*

1783 For the Governor's House in New Bern, architect John Hawks designed "an Ionick portico Frontispiece to the North front and a range of Iron palisadoes from this to each Circular Colonade" that led to the kitchen and stable blocks. Hawks Letter, Miranda Papers, Academia Nacional de la Historia, Caracas.

1828 On a farm in southern Delaware, a kitchen was "connected with the mansion by a colonade eight by twenty feet." Sussex Co., Del., Orphans Court Valuations O.

column (collum)   A long, generally round, vertical support that carries the weight of an entablature or other structural elements. In classical architecture, a column consisted of a short base, the long shaft, and a decorative capital or cap. The term was sometimes used interchangeably with *post* and *pillar.* See also **Composite order, Corinthian order, Doric order, flute, Ionic order, pillar, post, Tuscan order.**

1701 "The porches of the . . . Capitoll" in Williamsburg were to "be built circular fifteen foot in breadth from outside to outside, and that they stand upon cedar columns." Hening, *Statutes at Large*, 3.

1711 The courthouse was to have "a hemsome Peddiment over the front doore supported with well turned Collums and bases of Cedar and Locust." Talbot Co., Md., Land Records Book No. 12.

1752 "The Galleries of the Church [are] to be Supported with four Turned and Fluted Columns to be twelve Feet high or higher." Trinity Parish, Charles Co., Md., Vestry Book.

1760 Henry Burnett paid for "2 Corinthian Capitals for the Columns that Support the Type of the pulpit." Williams, *St. Michael's.*

1808 A brick courthouse in Columbia, Tennessee, was "to have a porch and portico on each side 12 by 20 feet of the same pitch, of open work, supported by brick columns at least 3 feet in diameter of an octagon shape, or to have six equal squares and arched above." *The Impartial Review and Cumberland Repository.*

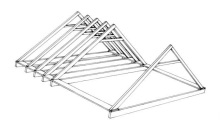

common rafter

common rafter (small rafter)   One of a series of rafters of a uniform size spaced evenly along the length of a roof, used to support lath or sheathing. In a *principal roof*, the common rafters are set between principal rafter trusses. In such roofs, the common rafters either extended over the tops of purlins or were divided into sections and mortised into the purlins in the same plane. A *common rafter roof* consisted entirely of smaller rafter pairs. Unlike a principal roof, it required a layer of sheathing in order for it to be structurally rigid. With the feet of the rafters resting on a false plate, the common rafter roof could be made independent of the wall-framing system and thus much simpler to construct. Because of the reduction in labor and joinery associated with a principal roof, the common rafter roof became one of the most widespread systems used in the early South for smaller spans. See also **principal rafter, rafter.**

compartment   A small space within a larger enclosed area, often separated by partitions.

1812 A visitor to Monticello observed that "on the ground floor were four sitting rooms, two bed rooms and the library, which contained several thousand volumes classed according to subject and language. It was divided into three compartments, in one of which the President had his bed placed in a doorway." Foster, *Jeffersonian America.*

compass (compass head, compast, cumpas) **1.** An architectural element having in part a curved or semicircular section or shape: a compass window or door has a semicircular head; a compass roof or ceiling has a curved inner surface. These were typically found in churches and chapels. The term was also used in the 18th century to describe an apse or curved end of a church or courthouse. See also **arch, cove.**

> **1730** "All ye Doors & Windows" in a church were "to be Compast Roofe." St. Luke's Parish, Church Hill, Queen Anne's Co., Md., Vestry Book.
> **1734** A church was to be built "with Compass Sealing and Compass Windows." Bristol Parish, Prince George Co., Va., Vestry Book.
> **1740** Magistrates ordered the construction of "a Brick Courthouse: Thirty eight foot in length and 25 foot bredth from out to out . . . one compas end." Lancaster Co., Va., Court Order Book 1729–1743.
> **1751** For a new church, the vestry decided that "instead of Square Arches to the windows they have compass heads." Upper Parish, Nansemond Co., Va., Vestry Book.
> **1767** Examination of the work on a parsonage house noted that "the windows on the Stairs want the Compass Heads agreed for." St. Michael's Parish, Charleston, S.C., Vestry Book.
> **1770** It was ordered that the church "doors and windows . . . be with Compass Roofs." St. John's Parish, Queen Anne's Co., Md., Vestry Book.
> **1784** Construction of a prison required "the roof to be of morter arched as by Compass." Charlotte Co., Va., Court Order Book 1780–1784.

2. An instrument used in drawing and the building trades for laying off measurements and for describing circles and arches.

> **1734** "A Pair of COMPASSES is a Mathematical Instrument used for the describing of Circles, measuring the Distances of Points, Lines &c. The common Compasses consist of two Branches or Legs of Iron, Brass, or other Metal, pointed at Bottom, and at the Top joined by a Rivet, whereon they move as on a Centre." *Builder's Dictionary.*

compass (1)
Bruton Parish Church, Williamsburg, Va.

Composite order The most elaborate of the five orders of classical antiquity, whose details and proportions were recognized and codified by Renaissance writers in the 15th and 16th centuries. Its origins probably date from the period of the Roman empire rather than the republic and was thus the last of the ancient orders to emerge. As described by Serlio and later scholars of classical architecture, the chief feature of the *Composite order* was the capital, which combined the circle of acanthus leaves of the lower part of the bell of the *Corinthian* capital with the volutes and ovolo of the *Ionic* capital. Because of its rich detailing, the *Composite order* was rarely used in the colonial South. Only in the early 19th century did it become an integral part of the southern design vocabulary. See also **order.**

> **1734** "COMPOSITE Order . . . is the last of the five Orders of Columns, so called, because its Capital is composed out of those of the other Columns. It borrows a Quarter-Round from the *Tuscan* and *Doric*; a Row of Leaves from the *Corinthian*; and Volutes from the *Ionic*. Its Cornice has simple Modillions or Dentils. The *Composite* is also called the *Roman*, or *Italick Order*, as having been invented by the *Romans*. . . . This by most Authors is ranked after the *Corinthian*, either as being the richest, or the last that was invented. . . . In Fact, it was *Serlio*, who first added the *Composite* Order to the Four of *Vitruvius*. . . . Till that Time, this Order was esteem'd a Species of the *Corinthian*, only differing in its Capital. This Order being thus left undetermin'd by the Antients, the Moderns have a kind of a Right to differ about its Proportions, &c." *Builder's Dictionary.*
> **1808** Thomas Jefferson's house, Monticello, "contains specimens of all the different orders, except the composite, which is not introduced." Caldwell, *A Tour Through Part of Virginia.*

composition ornament The name given in the late 18th and early 19th centuries to a material used for decorative moldings and orna-

Composite order

ments. It consisted of resin, linseed oil, glue, and whiting combined into a stiff paste. After it had been steamed, this paste was pressed into either wooden or metal molds. Composition ornament first appeared in the South in the last decade of the 18th century and was used for cornices, chimney pieces, bases, surbases, and ceiling ornaments. Most of these items were imported from England or from one of a few northern manufacturers in New York, Boston, and Philadelphia.

1796 Gabriel Manigault of Charleston ordered from the firm of Bird, Savage, and Bird in London "the following compositions ornaments, vizt. 100 feet of Composition for the Frieze of a room, of a simple pattern & such as will be easily put up, the Frieze is 7 1/2 inches wide. . . . You sent me some last spring wch was bought of John Jaques, & cost 2 1/2 per foot; 25 to of the best glue for fixing the composition. It frequently drops off here owing to bad glue." Manigault Papers, South Caroliniana Library.

1797 Advertised for sale in Baltimore: "A PLEASING variety of elegant (American manufactured) Composition Ornaments for Chimney Pieces, Frontispieces, Pillasters, &c. among which are the following articles- viz. Landscape tablets, with rich flower festoons, Vase tables, with wheat festoons, Eagle do. with vine and ivy festoons, Flora do. and festoons, Figures of Apollo and Flora with pedestals, Do. of Flora and Pomona, with frames—Also a great variety of mouldings, patras, beads, husks, pine apple, war trophe, wheat trophe, music trophe, liberty cap, fruit baskets, &c. The above are far superior to any imported and much cheaper." *Federal Gazette and Baltimore Daily Advertiser.*

1823 At Poplar Forest in Bedford County, Virginia, workman William Coffee wrote to Thomas Jefferson that "the composition ornaments are not of the nature of Potters ware. Still they have been hardened by fire. . . . Any kind of ornaments for inside or outside to stand any climate equal to marble can be made in this composition adjusting the composition to the situation. Caps of all kind be done in it from those can be cut in stone of any kind and as to the adhesion to wood, stone, or brick, nothing is so sure. The only thing is care and attention. No other composition can secure so delicate work and at a less price than any other material. One half less than lead or stone." Jefferson Papers, LC.

compting house   See **countinghouse.**

compting room   See **counting room.**

conductor   See **electrical conductor.**

conduit   An open or closed channel or pipe for conveying water and other fluids. See also **drain.**

congé   A concave, quarter-round molding that begins tangent to a vertical surface and is terminated by a fillet parallel to that surface. The difference between a *congé* and a *cavetto* is that the latter is set off by two fillets.

console
Edward Barradall Tomb,
Bruton Parish Churchyard,
Williamsburg, Va.

console   A decorative bracket in the form of a vertical scroll, used to support a cornice and other projecting elements. The term was little used in the early South. See also **bracket.**

contractor   A person who enters into an agreement or contract to supply various materials or perform certain work such as the construction of part or all of a building or structure. The term appears infrequently in the colonial period, only coming into general use in the 1790s. Before that time and through the 1820s, the most common name for such a person was *undertaker*. See also **builder, undertaker.**

1760 Francis Smith of Hanover County, Virginia, and two men posting his security bond became "Contractors for Building a Church." Augusta Parish, Augusta Co., Va., Vestry Book.

1804 "The Commissioners for building a Jail . . . have had frequent communications with contractors and have uniformly found that no bargain can be made until they have Money in hand." York Co., Va., Court Judgments and Order Book 1803–1814.

1809 In Brunswick County, North Carolina, "ANY PERSONS willing to contract for building a Court-House at Smithville" were told that "materials all of the best kind, to be found by the Contractor." *The True Republican or American Whig.*

1828 A letter of recommendation for a builder noted that if "Mr. Phillips became the undertaker I should not deem it necessary for me to see the work during its progress such is my confidence in Mr. Phillips as a workman, again if Mr. Phillips becomes the contractor, you may rely not only on the faithfullness with which the work will be executed, but it will be done with dispatch and without trouble to the commissioners." Malcolm Crawford Papers, VSL.

cookhouse, cookroom A building or part of a building where food is prepared; a kitchen. The term appeared frequently in Delaware in the 18th and early 19th centuries but in few other places in the South. It may have been used as a synonym for *kitchen* or referred to a secondary space where cooking occurred. A number of the cookhouses listed in orphans court valuations were located next to the dwelling, which suggests that they may have been used as winter kitchens. The large size of a number of them also argues that they served some other domestic function.

1776 On the Smith farm stood "One Mention house, One New Kuch House Not Quite Finished and One Old Kuck House." Sussex Co., Del., Orphans Court Valuations A.

1797 The Hooper estate contained "one Brick Dwelling House 34 feet by 18 feet . . .one Porch Milk & Cook Houses all adjoining the Dwelling House and a Brick Chimney in the Cook House 27 feet by 18 . . . one Hue'd log Kitchen with Brick Chimney 16 feet by 16." Sussex Co., Del., Orphans Court Valuations G.

1811 On the Countess farm stood a "log dwelling house 25 feet by 18 . . . with two rooms on each floor, the rooms on the lower floor divided by a plank partition, and that on the upper floor by a clabboard partition, in each room there are good fire places. . . . there is under the whole house a cellar which is used for a Cook room." Kent Co., Del., Orphans Court Valuations.

1815 Noted: "One dwelling House and Cook House adjoining, one Story high framed 16 by 32 feet . . . One old loged Kitchen 12 by 14." Sussex Co., Orphans Court Valuations L.

coop A woven enclosure, cage, or pen used to confine fowls and other small animals for fattening or transportation.

1789 The "Chicken coop [is] finished." Robert Carter Papers, LC.

1818 A carpenter "has erected on the lawn a handsome Cage for the Hawk Pen, he has also made for us a chicken, a duck, a Turkey, and a goose Coop." *The Diaries of Martha Ogle Forman.*

cooper A person who makes wooden staved containers. The cooper used three basic parts for his containers: staves, heads, and hoops. The wide variety of containers included hogsheads, barrels, buckets, tubs, kegs, and pails. Coopers were common rural tradesmen in the Chesapeake region, as their containers were used for many everyday functions from shipping to storage to temporary transport.

1661 "Thomas Horne hath put himselfe apprentiss to Bartholomew Engelbretson a Cooper." Norfolk Co., Va., Wills and Deeds Book D.

1694 "Samuel Demonville . . . pretending himselfe to be a tite cooper or a cooper able to make & set up tite cask did undertake . . . to sett up & make 3 tun of tite syder cask . . . but all were so farr from being tite & workmanlike done that they were very faulty & leaky." Westmoreland Co., Va., Order Book 1690–1698.

coping (1)
Churchyard wall,
Bruton Parish Churchyard,
Williamsburg, Va.

Corinthian order

cope, coping 1. A protective cap placed at a sloping angle over a wall, pier, chimney, or other exposed element to prevent water from penetrating below.

> 1719 A wall around a churchyard was to have "a handsum Coopin Brick upon the Top." St. Peter's Parish, New Kent Co., Va., Vestry Book.
> 1746 It was ordered that a glebe house have "the copings of the chimney mended." Christ Church Parish, Lancaster Co., Va., Vestry Book.
> 1798 Report of work at the penitentiary in Richmond noted that "in about a fortnight the Gate will be compleated, and the front Wall coped." *The Correspondence and Miscellaneous Papers of Benjamin Henry Latrobe*, 1.

2. To join two pieces together by undercutting the end of one so that it will match the contour of the adjoining member. Moldings meeting at a perpendicular angle, such as an interior cornice, were often cut to form a coped joint.

copper A large, fixed vessel of copper, used for heating water in kitchens, laundries, brewhouses, and other service spaces.

> 1739 In Charleston John Fenwicke advertised a house to let, "having all necessary Conveniences, &c. besides a Copper, Stoves, Oven &c. in the Wash House and Kitchen. *South Carolina Gazette*.
> 1767 In Annapolis accounts for work on the Annapolis kitchen of James Brice included charges for a "Copper . . . Fixing it . . . leading and soldering it." James Brice Ledger, 1767–1801, MSA.

copse (coppice) A thicket of small trees or dense undergrowth, often placed in a pleasure ground near a dwelling to add variety to the scene.

> 1789 Mount Vernon was "laid out somewhat in the form of English gardens, in meadows and grass grounds, ornamented with little copies, circular clumps and single trees." Morse, *American Geography*.

corbel 1. A small bracket, sometimes used to support the spring of an arch.

> 1798 Extra work on the penitentiary in Richmond included "Stone Pillars to support the Groins of 6 rooms, stone imposts to all the external Arches, stone Corbels in the Spandrils of the Arches, and Keystones to the large Groins." *The Correspondence and Miscellaneous Paper of Benjamin Henry Latrobe*, 1.

2. The projection of masonry courses in a stepped series so that each course of bricks or stones extends further forward than the one below. Corbelling appeared in parapets, chimney shoulders, chimney caps, and masonry cornices. The fashion for the latter appeared in the late 18th century and continued through the antebellum period.

cord A braided linen or cotton rope attached to the sash of a window at one end and a counterweight at the other. The cord is threaded through a pulley, allowing the free movement of the cord. See also **pulley, weight, sash.**

> 1774 An account for building William Corbit's dwelling in Delaware listed "lead for Window Cord £6.9.11 1/2." Sweeney, *Grandeur on the Appoquinimink*.
> 1808 Writing to Thomas Jefferson about work at Poplar Forest, James Dinsmore noted that "we have three twists of sash cord to spare from here which will be sufficient for twelve windows and will nearly do all the weights." Coolidge Collection, Massachusetts Historical Society.

Corinthian order One of the five orders of classical antiquity, it was the last and most ornate to develop in ancient Greece. The form with its capital, composed of two rows of carved acanthus leaves between which arise a series of stalks or caulicoles, was adopted by the Romans and was spread throughout their empire. The Italian theorists and architects used the Roman prototype to codify the rules about the proportions and detailing of its base, shaft, capital, and entablature. In the late 17th and 18th centuries, these treatises became the source of authority for English writers, whose books were imported into the American colonies and informed the ideas of gentleman clients and sophisticated builders. Elements of the Corinthian order appeared in southern architecture by the second quarter of the 18th century, if not slightly earlier. See also **order.**

1754   The roof of an Anglican church designed by John Ariss was supported by a "Capital of the Corinthian order." Trinity Parish, Charles Co., Md., Vestry Book.

1756   "The base of the *Corinthian* column consists of a torus set upon a plinth, a scotia, two astragals, another scotia, and then an upper torus. The column has nine diameters and an half in height, the capital is composed of leaves and stalks of the acanthus, which last, turning in spires under the abacus, makes a number of small volutes. The architrave consists of three faces, the freeze is usually decorated with sculptures, and the cornice has modillions, and is in most places beautifully decorated with sculpture." Ware, *A Complete Body of Architecture.*

1768   In finishing the interior of the statehouse in Charleston, payment was made "to Thomas Woodlin for carving 16 Corinthian Capitals for the Council Chamber £471.18.0." Journal of the Commons House of Assembly No. 37, SCA&H.

1783   The tabernacle frame of the chimney piece in the council chamber in the Governor's House in New Bern consisted of "Corinthian Columns and pillasters fluited with the proper Entablature fully inric[hed] and an open pediment." Hawks Letter, Miranda Papers, Academia Nacional de la Historia, Caracas.

1804   In selecting the appropriate elements for the design of the Capitol in Washington, architect Benjamin Henry Latrobe wrote to President Jefferson that "the Athenian capital I allude to, is of the best Age of Athenian architecture, as it is to be found in the 1st. or 2d Volume of Stuart's *Athens.* The exterior decoration of the house furnishes a very good specimen of Corinthian Architecture. Should you however prefer the same order for the Hall of Representatives I will immediately proceed to make the necessary drawing, and take the steps to have the Capitals executed during the present season." *The Correspondence and Miscellaneous Papers of Benjamin Henry Latrobe,* 1.

corncrib   See **crib, cornhouse** (1).

corner board   A vertical board at the corner of a wooden structure used as decorative trim, against which the ends of weatherboards are fitted.

1769   Construction of a dwelling in Louisa County, Virginia, included making "barge & Corner boards 7/6." Garrett Minor Papers, CWF.

corner board
Eagle Tavern, Halifax County, N.C.

corner post   A timber post at the angle of two exterior frame walls and one of the most substantial framing members in a wooden building. In earthfast construction, it sat directly upon the ground or was embedded three or four feet below the surface and secured at the top into the wall plate. In more substantial framing systems, the plate was tenoned into a sill at the bottom and a plate or girder at the top. Angled braces often extended from the corner post to the tie beam, plate, or sill to provide additional structural support for the frame. In order to diminish the visibility of these posts in finished rooms, builders in the late 18th and throughout the early 19th centuries often cut out the inside edge of the post, creating an L-shaped configuration. See also **gutter** (2).

1742   A church was to have "corner posts 14 inches by 6 . . . the other posts 8 by 6 inches." Albemarle Parish, Surry Co., Va., Vestry Book.

1759 A bill of scantling for a prison noted that "the sills to be 12 by 10 inches, plates, corner posts and braces 10 by 6 inches." Fauquier Co., Va., Court Records.
1771 "The Corner posts" of St. John's Church in Granville County, North Carolina, were to "be got fourteen Inches one way & twenty-two Inches the other to be Rabited out so as to make flush walls with the other framing Six inches." Francis Hawks Collection, Church Historical Society.

cornerstone   **1.** A ceremony at the beginning of the construction of an important structure was celebrated by the laying of stones and bricks by prominent officials, builders, and clients. From the early 18th century onward, these festive ceremonies also included official and masonic processions, sermons, grand dinners, and toasts**.** By the early 19th century many buildings had a specially prepared stone or brick with the date and occasionally the name of the architect, builder, and client placed in a prominent location at the corner or near the corner of a wall or foundation.

1751 During the rebuilding of the capitol in Williamsburg, John Blair, a member of the colonial council of Virginia, noted that he "had laid a foundation brick at the first building of the capitol above 50 year ago [c. 1701], and another foundation brick in April last." *W&MQ*, 1 ser., 7.
1753 "On Thursday the 22d of June . . . the CORNER STONE of our STATE HOUSE, was laid, by His Excellency the Governor, and a sum of Money thereon: After him, the several Members of His Majesty's Council and Assembly, the Commissioners, and other Gentlemen. . . laid a Brick in the proper manner; and then they all proceeded to Mr. Gordon's [tavern], where, after Dinner, Toasts suitable to the Day and Occasion were drank." *South Carolina Gazette.*
1774 Members of the Masonic Lodge in Williamsburg met "to lay the Foundation Stone of the Stone Bridge to be built at the Capitol Landing—The Lodge accordingly Repaired thereto and after the Usual Libations and having placed a medal under the corner stone and laid the same in due form." Williamsburg Masonic Lodge Minute Book 1773–1779.
1826 "The corner stone of Goochland Courthouse was laid by the Masonic society at that place . . . the stone . . . [is] inscribed on one side- Dedicated to Justice & Masonry. On one other side- Sep 23^d A.L. 5826 A.D. 1826– On one other side D. Cosby & V. Parrish architects & on the fourth side-Goochland Lodge N 115, Fecit Wm. Mountjoy Richmond." Goochland Co., Va., Court Order Book 1825–1831.

2. A boundary marker, often deliberately placed to denote the corner of a piece of property.

1722 A parcel of land was described as "beginning at a corner stone standing 10' to the westward of the Church Yard." Norfolk Co., Va., Deed and Will Book 1721–1725.

cornhouse (corn loft)   **1.** A storage building for shelled corn or for ears of corn. In the 17th and early 18th centuries, planters sometimes stored barrels of corn in the lofts of their dwellings and other outbuildings. However, by the early 18th century separate structures were built to house the crop. It appears that some Southerners used the terms *cornhouse* and *corncrib* very loosely to describe any type of building where corn was stored, whether shelled and intended for human consumption or on the cob and provender for livestock. Although many cornhouses were solid structures, others may have been built like cribs with spaced openings in the walls to provide for air circulation. See also **crib.**

1640 A carpenter was paid for "5 daies work in laying the floore makeing doore and staires of the corn loft." Maryland Patents Certificates and Warrants 1637–1650, MSA.
1670 In Charles County, Maryland, a servant named "John Decreveire being intrusted by the . . . master with the key of the Corne Loafte gave it to Melliky Kirkman to fetch corne with which said key the said Kirkman did opened a Doore where was a Quantity of Wines laid." *Archives of Maryland*, 60.

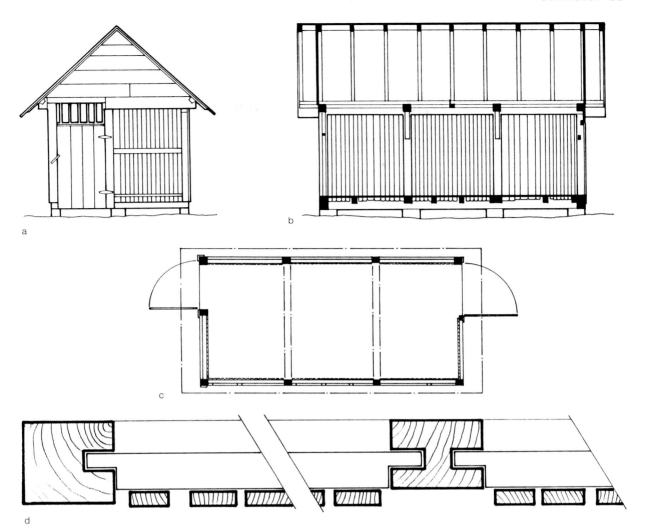

cornhouse Chaney Farm, Anne Arundel County, Md. (a) elevation, (b) section, (c) plan, (d) detail of wall framing

1714 On the Baxter plantation in Queen Anne's County, Maryland, was "one corn house." Queen Anne's Co., Md., Deed Book A.

1751 Churchwardens were to "agree with a workman to build a corn-house on the glebe twenty four foot long and twelve foot wide framed." Stratton Major Parish, King and Queen Co., Va., Vestry Book.

1769 On a farm near Augusta, Georgia, were "three new corn-houses made of four-inch plank, capable of containing 1000 bushells each." *South Carolina and American General Gazette.*

1774 Planter Robert Wormeley Carter of Richmond County, Virginia, "agreed with John Reynolds junr to overlook Hiccory Thicket; gave him the Key of my Corn House where I had lofted 15 hhds Corn; directed him to give out 7 bush. 1 peck p week & he was to shell out a hhd to see what it produced in shelld corn." Diary of Robert Wormeley Carter, American Antiquarian Society.

1789 On a farm in southern Delaware was "a log corn house eight by sixteen" feet. Sussex Co., Del., Orphans Court Valuations E.

2. A building for the storage of any threshed grain; a granary. The term was used in the English sense of *corn* as a cereal, such as barley, rye, or wheat. By the late 17th century, it had been largely superseded by the first meaning. See also **granary.**

1654 Edward Wilder agreed to build for planter John Godfrey "one sufficient Cornehouse, thirty foote long & twenty foote wide, with Loft & dores." Norfolk Co., Va., Will and Deed Book 1651–1656.

cornice (cornish) **1.** A horizontal molded projection crowning the ceiling or roof and wall or some part of a building such as a dado or window. Beginning in the late 17th century, classically inspired cornices, enclosing the juncture of the wall and roof framing at the eaves, generally consisted of a bed molding, soffit, fascia, and crown molding. Many early exterior cornices did not have a return at the end but were terminated by a curved end board that mirrored the profile of the cornice. Contemporaries sometimes distinguished types of cornices. A *modillion cornice* was the most decorative interior and eaves cornice constructed during the colonial period; a *block cornice* was a simplified modillion cornice, the block modillions being as wide as they were deep and spaced much closer together than in a regular modillion cornice; and a plain cornice had no such elaboration. A *box cornice* was a hollow cornice with the boxing, the fascia and soffit boards, and moldings, nailed over the ends of rafters and short braces. See also **eaves.**

1680   A courthouse was to have "Cornishes over the heads of the Windowes." Talbot Co., Md., Court Judgments 1675–1682.
1707   A building was to be "jettied nine inches on a side and cornish'd and mundillion'd round." Westmoreland Co., Va., Court Order Book 1705–1721.
1737   A workman was selected to determine "the difference between a plain cornice and [a] mundillion" one. Bristol Parish, Prince George Co., Va., Vestry Book.
1757   Payment was made "to William Waite for a plaister cornice." Dettingen Parish, Prince William Co., Va., Vestry Book.
1766   A church was to be built with "a block Cornish." All Faiths Parish, St. Mary's Co., Md., Vestry Book.
1791   A workman undertook "To Cover the Church on both sides under the Eves with a plane but Neat Cornice, to set on barges on the End." Trinity Parish, Charles Co., Md., Vestry Book.
1797   An account for work included "34 feet Raking Modillion cornice to the pediment." St. Michael's Parish, Charleston, S.C., Vestry Book.
1804   The Savannah exchange was to have "a large stoco cornice in the front room & a small one in the two back rooms." *Columbian Museum and Savannah Advertiser.*

2. The crowning member of a three-part classical entablature, resting on the frieze.

1760   A cabinetmaker was paid for "61 1/2 Doz. of drops for the Dorrick order in the Cornish Round the outside of the Church @ 7/6." St. Michael's Parish, Charleston, S.C., Vestry Book.
1820   A bill of work executed by a carpenter at Bremo in Fluvanna County, Virginia, listed a "Tuscan entablature cornice . . . Arch: & frieze." Cocke Papers, UVa.

corona A large, projecting, upper vertical face of a cornice, supported by a bed molding below and the crown molding or cymatium above. The soffit of the corona is slightly recessed to create a drip, which deflects water away from the building.

1756   "CORONA or CORONIS—These terms are sometimes used to signify any crowning or finishing of a work, at the top, of whatever kind that be, as pediment, or the like. Corona is also sometimes used to express particularly that flat square and massy member of a cornice which is more usually and distinctively called the drip, or Larmier. This is placed between the cymatium and the ovolo, and its use is to carry off the water drop by drop from the building." Ware, *A Complete Body of Architecture.*
1803   Specifications for a Episcopal church near Charleston called for the "entablature to the Top of Corona 3 Ft. 8 ins." Johns Island Church Specifications, Library Society of Charleston.

coronet See **overdoor.**

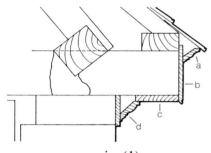

cornice (1)
Section of cornice, Mason House, Accomack County, Va. (a) cymatium or crown molding, (b) corona or fascia, (c) soffit, (d) bed molding

corpse house A small, often subterranean, structure constructed near a church where bodies of those who died during the winter were placed to await burial when the ground was sufficiently thawed.

corridor A passageway in a building into which several rooms or apartments open.

> 1804 A design for the Capitol in Washington noted that "through the Center of the building from East to West, a wide Corridor borrows light from the two Common antichambers to the Committee rooms." *The Correspondence and Miscellaneous Papers of Benjamin Henry Latrobe*, 1.
> 1809 Margaret Izard Manigault described a ball given by Mrs. Radcliffe in her Charleston dwelling: "After one dance, the elder part of the assembly had their time of pleasurable surprise. Gen. Wilkinson's band charmed us with some well executed military pieces during which we paced up & down the spacious corridor which was brilliantly illuminated, and into her handsome bedroom, which was likewise lighted." Izard Papers, LC.

cottage A small dwelling. The term was seldom used in the early South. However when it was, it generally referred to a house of modest proportions and simple construction.

> 1714 The splenetic Reverend John Urmston wrote to London that "we expect to hear that famous city of Bath [North Carolina] consisting of 9 houses rather cottages once stiled the Metropolis and seat of Government will be totally deserted." *Colonial Records of North Carolina*, 2.
> 1766 On a summer's evening in Prince George County, Virginia, "a very gloomy cloud suddenly arose, and violent lightning and thunder ensued. It passed over several large houses with brick chimnies (belonging to Mr. James French, a merchant . . .) without affecting any thing; and a small house (the residence of James Smith a taylor) on lower ground, at 30 or 40 yards distance, with a wooden chimney at the further end, was struck by lightning. The lightning entered at the upper shingle on the end of this cottage, next to Mr. French's houses." *Virginia Gazette*.

counter A table or built-in case in a store or shop for the display of goods and transaction of business. See also **store.**

> 1756 On a plantation on the eastern shore of Maryland was a "store house 16 feet square with . . . a planked floor, counter and shelves." Queen Anne's Co., Md., Deed Book E.
> 1770 "Account of work done by William Bales at the Stone House Plantation for Israel Christian" included "making a Counter & Shelves in the Store." Bedford Co., Va., Loose Court Papers, VSL.
> 1773 In Charleston, there was "to be let . . . the large and commodious HOUSE in Broad Street . . . well situated for Business, both back and front Stores compleatly fitted up with Shelves, Glass Cases, and Counters, a Compting-House, Kitchen, and good Cellars." *South Carolina Gazette and Country Journal.*
> 1785 "There is one framed Shed Adjoining the West End of [the] House 22 by 16 feet . . . with Counter and Shelves inside for selling Goods with a brick Chimney and plaistered in good repair." Kent Co., Del., Orphans Court Valuations.

counterfloor A rough, plain floor laid beneath a finished surface; a subfloor. The practice was rare until the early 19th century and then only used in better buildings. The term may have also been used to refer to *counter sealing*. See also **counter seal, subfloor.**

> 1802 The carpenter's bill for work on the Octagon, John Tayloe's Washington residence, included "6288 [feet] Flooring Straight Joint secret nail'd p[er] 100 ft 50/ ...5988 [feet] Counter flooring [at] 12/6." Tayloe Papers, VHS.
> 1805 Recommendation made "that your Crypt" at the Roman Catholic Cathedral in Baltimore "should be vaulted, and I made a calculation which provided that it would cost little or nothing more than a good strong floor of joist and boards counterfloored or lathed and plaistered underneath." *The Correspondence and Miscellaneous Papers of Benjamin Henry Latrobe*, 2.

1811 In the southwest wing of Montpelier in Orange County, Virginia, carpenters charged for "6 square 58 ft clean laid flor @ 30/ £9.17.4; 6 square 58 ft counter flooring @ 9/ £2.19.3." Cocke Papers, UVa.

1820 At the President's House in Washington, "the garret and second story floors have been laid of best 5/4 heart pine, and the whole of these stories counter-floored and pugged to guard against fire." *Daily National Intelligencer.*

counter seal To enclose the space beneath floor joists with a covering of boards or plaster for fireproofing or soundproofing. See also **pug.**

1812 In a discussion about fireproofing, Thomas Jefferson observed that he knew of three methods of construction: "The first is by planking strips of lath on the inside of every joist at bottom, laying short planks closely on these and filling the interval between them and the floors with brick and mortar. This is usual to the northward under the name of counter sealing and is used in my own house, and has once saved my house by the floor resisting the taking fire from a coat of sawdust spaced over it and burning on it a whole night." Jefferson Papers, LC.

countinghouse (compting house) An office, building, or part of a building appropriated for the keeping of accounts.

1763 In Charleston, a merchant "question'd the Young Man in my Counting House." *Papers of Henry Laurens*, 3.

1811 In Albemarle County, Virginia, a payment was to be lodged in a "counting house." Jefferson Papers, UVa.

counting room (compting room) A chamber or room in a building where accounts were kept. The archaic form of the term, *compting room*, continued in use along with *counting room* through the early 19th century.

1703 An estate inventory of a merchant in St. Mary's County, Maryland, listed a "compting room." Maryland Provincial Court Records, MSA.

1765 The back part of a large brick warehouse on the bay in Charleston had a heated "Compting room, lathed and plaister'd." *South Carolina Gazette.*

1766 Advertised for sale in Smithfield, Virginia, was "a store house and counting room under the same roof." *Virginia Gazette.*

1784 For sale in Charlotte County, Virginia, was "a commodious and well built storehouse 36 by 18 feet, the store room properly shelved and finished, the compting room plaistered and a good brick chimney with one fireplace." *Virginia Gazette.*

couple In carpentry, a pair of opposite rafters joined together at their apex and usually connected by a tie beam or collar beam; sometimes referred to as *coupling.*

1688 Specifications for a house in Somerset County, Maryland, called for "Rafters eighteen foot & halfe Longe the Couplings for every rafter nine foot long three & four inches thick on the flatt sides." Touart, *Somerset.*

1693 An agreement was reached to build "a good firme Substantiall dwelling house to be twenty eight foot long and twenty foot wide of four foot lengths framed on sells the Rafters Coupled." Surry Co., Va., Court Order Book 1691–1713.

1794 In Orange County, Virginia, "C. Leathers finished getting Rafters, had them brought in and he began to couple them." Francis Taylor Diary, CWF.

course A single continuous row or layer of materials such as bricks, stone, or shingles laid at the same height or level in a wall or roof. See also **bond.**

1712 It was "Ordered that Alexander Graves build the Church walls five courses higher all round then already ordered." Christ Church Parish, Middlesex Co., Va., Vestry Book.

1719 The "Church [is] to be repaired with Shingles wherever there is any wanting, And to Lay two Course of Shingles on each side to enclose the Rough." St. Peter's Parish, New Kent Co., Va., Vestry Book.

1753 "Mr. John Ariss is to raise the Walls of the Church now building Six courses of brick higher than they are at present." Trinity Parish, Charles Co., Md., Vestry Book.

1788 The stonework of the jail walls in Dumfries, Virginia, "to be laid in Regular courses on the outside." Prince William Co., Va., Deed Book 1787–1791.

1794 Specifications for a clerk's office included "the foundation . . . [composed of] five courses of brick below the surface of the Ground." Accomack Co., Va., Court Order Book 1793–1796.

courthouse   A building containing courts of law, offices, and jury rooms; a building housing the judicial and administrative branches of local government. As in many towns in Stuart England, the early law courts in Virginia and Maryland were held in private dwellings and taverns. Although the colony of Virginia established local courts in the 1620s, it was not until the 1650s that the first purpose-built courthouses were erected.   Most stood isolated in the geographic center of a county, coming to life one or two days each month during court sessions. For the next 75 years, the form of these framed structures could scarcely be distinguished from neighboring farmhouses. There was nothing in their scale or exterior appearance that indicated their special function. In plan, they contained a large room for the court and one or two smaller rooms given over occasionally to deliberations of juries and magistrates, and used as process rooms for clerks to arrange the court's docket and store official papers. In Maryland, a number of courthouses were multistoried, often with rooms set aside for lodging of magistrates and others. In the early 18th century the domestic appearance of the county courthouse gradually gave way to one with a more dignified public image. In their desire to create a more durable and imposing structure, magistrates in the Chesapeake incorporated architectural elements and images from neighboring churches, English town halls and market houses, and the arcaded and apsidal General Court in the capitol in Williamsburg. By the 1750s brick arcades, compass-headed windows, and apsidal magistrates' benches became the hallmarks of public building in counties across Virginia as well as in parts of Maryland and North Carolina. In the courtroom, the chief feature was the railed magistrates' platform: here the four or more justices of the peace sat raised above their fellow citizens on a bench that curved around one end of the courtroom. Below them, were seats, benches, and boxes arranged for the jury, clerks, sheriffs, constables, and lawyers. For the most part, the public stood behind a railed bar. Following the Revolution, a new image transformed public building. Like the first capitol in Williamsburg, Thomas Jefferson's Roman temple design for the new capitol in Richmond had a profound influence on subsequent courthouse design, not only in Virginia but throughout the rest of the South and much of the new nation. Temples of republican justice arose on many courthouse grounds throughout the Old Dominion and neighboring states in the first three decades of the 19th century. Robert Mills's monopoly of public building designs in South Carolina ensured that his essay on the temple form spread across that state in the 1820s. Despite the changes in the outer shell, the courtroom plan itself underwent few alterations until after the Civil War, when new state constitutions transformed the institutions of local government.

courthouse Exterior and plan, Chowan
County Courthouse, Edenton, N.C., 1767.

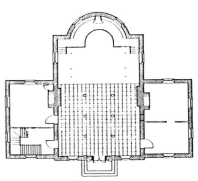

1655 "Major John Carter has undertaken to build the Courthouse at Corotoman. Mr. William Underwood to build the like on land adjacent to his house." Lancaster Co., Va., Court Order Book 1652–1655.

1686 An agreement was made with Anthony Dawson to build a "court house . . . fourty foott in length and twenty four foot in Breadth the two floors above and below to be laid with Plank and four large windows below, and one small Casement Window, with two large casements to each window. . . . the chambers to be sealed with rived Boards one large pair of Stairs with Rails and Banisters. . . . One large table Inclosed with rails and Banisters, and seats inclosed, likewise, Seats for the Justices with a Judges Chair Going up two or three steps with rails and Banisters before. . . . a large Porch att the end of the house." Dorchester Co., Md., Land Records Book 1669–1683.

1732 In Yorktown, Virginia, "they are just finishing a Court house or Town hall of Brick with a Piazza before it (which is) very handsome and Convenient." *VMHB,* 22.

1766 A frame "courthouse [is to] be built . . . twenty four by thirty six feet 12 foot Pitch, two 12 feet Square Rooms with a Brick Chimney with a fire Place in each Room. Wainscot 4 feet High & Plaistered above. . . . The House to be under pin'd with brick one foot & a half from the Ground. The Bench to be Built in a Quarter Circle with a Bar & two Sheriffs Desks a Clerks Table & that the flour from the Barr to the Bench be Raised & layd with Plank & the other to be Laid with Brick or Tyle." Bedford Co., Va., Court Order Book 1763–1771.

1767 "To be let to the lowest undertaker . . . at Edenton, in North Carolina, THE building a brick Court-House, 68 feet by 45." *Virginia Gazette.*

1820 In South Carolina, "the Board of Public Works have adopted a general plan for the Court-Houses in the State, varying little in size, in proportion to the difference of the Districts in which they are erected. In this plan, durability, strength, convenience, neatness and economy have been consulted. . . . it will be in height two stories, and its first floor will contain a large lobby for the stairs, through which you enter . . . a spacious court room and two offices. The arrangement of the court room is remarkable for it convenience, affording accommodation to the Judges and other officers, the Lawyers, Jurors and such of the community as attend either upon business or as spectators. . . . In the court room there is also a gallery of considerable width, ornamented with neat columns, extending the whole length of the building, in front of the judges bench. . . . On the second floor there will be five offices with a large passage into which they will open. The walls of the building will be of brick with stone sills to the doors and windows. . . . the whole will be of a superior character, the finish will be particularly neat, entirely devoid of that coarseness which disgraces so many of our public buildings. In the exterior appearance there are no expensive ornaments, but it possesses a simple neatness very appropriate to a building intended for its use. Buildings of this kind excite a respect for and add dignity to our institutions." *Camden Gazette and Mercantile Advertiser.*

courtyard See **yard** (1).

cove, coving A molding or part of a building with a concave profile, especially the arch of a ceiling. The segmental arch between the ceiling of a room and its cornice. A few exterior cornices were constructed with a coved profile, a form that had some currency in the 18th century in dwellings in parts of the Chesapeake and especially in dairies and milk houses throughout the region. See also **cavetto, compass.**

cove, coving
Drawing room, William Gibbes House,
Charleston, S.C.

1738 A workman was to be hired to "paint coving within the church that has bent spoilt by means of leacage of the roofe of the church angles." Petsworth Parish, Gloucester County, Va., Vestry Book.

1746 In planning his dwelling, Charles Pinckney of Charleston called for "the dining room ceiling to be coved into the roof, so as to make this room at least 14 foot high in the clear." Huger Smith, *Dwelling Houses of Charleston.*

1771 "There shall be no Joists but end Joists except such short Joists as are Necessary According to the Rules of Architecture in framing a Cove Arch or Concave Roof" in a North Carolina church. Francis Hawks Collection, Church Historical Society.

cover To enclose the frame and roof of a building with a protective material. Although the term was occasionally used to refer to wall cladding, for the most part it referred to sheathing a roof with a layer of laths or boards and/or an outer layer of shingles, clapboards, slabs, tiles, or some other material.

1623 Dwellings in Virginia "stande scattered one from another, and are onlie made of wood, few or none of them being framed houses but punches sett into the Ground and Covered with Boarde so as a firebrand is sufficient to consume them all." *Records of the Virginia Company,* 4.

1683 Repairs to a church required that the "shingles be all taken off, and the lathes also ript off, and every shingle now nailed on, with one good naile upon the Covering." Christ Church Parish, Middlesex Co., Va., Vestry Book.

1707 A workman was to "undertake to Cover the Church wth four foot wd Oke boards with the Sapp taken off." All Faiths Parish, St. Mary's Co., Md., Vestry Book.

1728 On the North Carolina-Virginia border, "most of the Houses . . . are Loghouses, covered with Pine or Cypress Shingles, 3 feet long, and one broad. They are hung upon Laths with Peggs." Byrd, *History of the Dividing Line.*

1765 A dwelling was "to be covered with lap shingles, clear of sap, and fourteen inches to the weather." Augusta Co., Va., Court Judgments.

1778 The roof of a dwelling in Berkeley County, Virginia, was to be built "of plank laid long wall from the Ridge to the Eves & double cover every joint to keep out rain." Charles Yates Letterbook, UVa.

covered way (covered passage) **1.** A sheltered walk or passage, sometimes with balustraded or partially enclosed sides, connecting two parts of a building or two separate buildings. Jefferson used *covered way* to describe the colonnade and arcade linking the pavilions at the University of Virginia. See also **arcade, colonnade, passage** (2), **piazza** (3).

1772 An assembly room was to have "a covered WAY and elegant PORTICO next the Street; thereby to enable Ladies and Gentlemen always to go to the New Suit of Rooms without being incommoded by the Weather." *South Carolina Gazette.*

1808 On a Delaware farm was a "Coverway from the Dwelling House to the kitchen Ten feet long and Sixteen feet wide." Sussex Co., Del., Orphans Court Valuations K.

1819 "The Covered way in front of the whole range of buildings" at the University of Virginia "is to be Tuscan with columns of brick roughcast . . . but in front of the Pavilions to be arches, in order to support the Columns of the Portico above more solidly." Lambeth and Manning, *Thomas Jefferson as an Architect.*

1820 A tavern for sale at Culpeper County, Virginia, courthouse included "a good kitchen under the house, with a covered way to the dining room." *The Virginia Herald.*

2. An enclosed outside entrance, usually with a sloping door, leading into a cellar. See also **cellar cap.**

> **1742** A glebe house was to have a "covered way without into the seller." Bristol Parish, Prince George, Co., Va., Vestry Book.
> **1770** Changes to a glebe house in Prince George County, Virginia, called for "the covered way into the cellar to be altered." *Virginia Gazette.*

cowhouse A structure where cattle are sheltered.

> **1764** Outbuildings on a farm in Charles County, Maryland, included "a Brick Dairy, Stable, Corn House, Tobacco and Cow Houses." *Maryland Gazette.*
> **1784** A Virginia planter "counted the Sheep carefully & their were 32 head including the sick one in the Cow house." Richard Henry Lee Memorandum Book, Huntington Library.
> **1823** Among the outbuildings on a farm in southern Delaware was "one Cow house 11 by 40 in bad repair." Sussex Co., Del., Orphans Court Valuations N.

cowshed A cowhouse. See **shed** (2).

cram To pack or fill a space or cavity with clay or some other material. The term is generally used to refer to the packing of an earthen floor or the filling of the interstices of a log wall. See also **daub, ram.**

> **1778** "The Loggs [are] to be well heart Crammed & hewed on the outside after they are put up." Yates Letterbook, UVa.
> **1787** "Got some Clay drawn up by the Cart to cram the Kitchen." Francis Taylor Diary, CWF.

cramp **1.** An iron staple used to hold two adjoining pieces of masonry together to prevent them from slipping. An iron bar with its two ends turned at right angles, a cramp is generally set in a bed of mortar or lead into holes cut into the stone. They were used in stone cornices, chimney pieces, wall coping, and steps.
2. A wooden or metal device used for holding pieces of work together during assembly or when being glued. Cramps were portable implements with one or two adjustable jaws or heads that were tightened by a screw. See also **holdfast** (2), **vice.**

> **1778** A woodworker in York County, Virginia, owned at his death "2 iron holdfasts 30/, 1 large cramp 40/, 1 small do 4.10.0, 1 bench vice." York Co., Va., Will and Inventory Book 1771–1782.
> **1802** Washington blacksmith James Worrell charged John Tayloe for "Altering 6 Cramps for stone work 0.0.9." Tayloe Papers, VHS.

crane A wrought-iron mechanism on which pots and kettles were suspended over a fire. It was constructed with a vertical post which pivoted in a pair of eye joints set into the fireplace jamb and sometimes the hearth as well. A horizontal bar, on which the pots hung, was joined and braced to the vertical member.

> **1801** James Worrell's bill for smith's work on John Tayloe's Washington residence included "2 Cranes & 4 eyes to a Kitchen fire place 72 lb 1/2 at 1/3." Tayloe Papers, VHS.
> **1816** Two dwellings for sale at the courthouse in Person County, North Carolina, contained "twelve fire places, two of which are appropriated for Cooking, fixed with Cranes." *Raleigh Register.*

crazy Unsound, full of cracks, likely to break or fall apart.

> **1808** On the Howell farm were "2 Corn houses and a Stable all old and crazy." Kent Co., Del., Orphans Court Valuations.

cramp (1)
Iron cramps reset in mortar,
Palmer House, Williamsburg, Va.

cream color A yellowish white paint color. Cream color was made up of the same ingredients as straw color, only in different proportions to produce a lighter hue. It was generally used for interior work.

> **1727** At the Governor's House in Williamsburg, it was noted that "the great Dining room and Parlor thereto adjoining be new painted, the one of pearl colour the other of cream colour." *Executive Journals of the Council of Virginia*, 4.
> **1771** Vestrymen of St. John's Church, Granville County, North Carolina, directed that "the Pews Desks Pulpit Banisters Cornish & every part of the wooden work exposed to view be well painted of a Cream Collour." Francis Lister Hawks Collection, Church Historical Society.
> **1812** "Cream Colour" required two coats of white, finished with a third coat composed as follows: "Add to white in the proportion of one pound to thirty pounds Spruce Yellow or English Ochre, well ground. The yellow tinge may be varied at pleasure." Reynolds, *Directions for House and Ship Painting.*

crib (corn crib, cribb) A log or frame structure well ventilated with generously spaced openings in the walls, used for the storage of fodder, grain, and corn. The term appeared in the second quarter of the 18th century to describe such a structure. However, the nearly synonymous *cornhouse* came into use slightly earlier. See also **cornhouse** (1).

> **1739** It was "Resolved that a good cribb of twelve foot long be built on the gleeb land to be made with good mauld popler peices." Lynnhaven Parish, Princess Anne Co., Va., Vestry Book.
> **1756** "A corn crib eight feet by fourteen" was to be built on a glebe. Bristol Parish, Prince George Co., Va., Vestry Book.
> **1781** At David Jameson's "Farm near York," Virginia, were "about 25 barrels of old Corn in the Crib." York Co., Va., Claims for Losses, CWF.
> **1798** Standing on Arthur Chinowith's farm in Soldiers Delight Hundred, Baltimore County, Maryland, was a "log corn crib, 1 story, 14 by 8." U.S. Direct Tax, MSA.

cricket A footstool.

> **1771** St. John's Church in Granville County, North Carolina, was to have "a Cricket & Seat" in the pulpit and in the desks reserved for the minister and clerk. Francis Hawks Collection, Church Historical Society.

cripple Any member shorter than most of the others in a structure such as a rafter butting into a chimney stack or a stud beneath a window. See also **jack rafter.**

> **1771** An arched roof in St. John's Church in Granville County, North Carolina, was to have "each Principal Rafter with Collar Beams Struts King Posts & Braces . . . with substantial purlins suitable Braces criple Rafters." Francis Hawks Collection, Church Historical Society.

crossbar **1.** A horizontal bar used to keep a door closed. A wooden board or plank placed in two staples on each side of the inside of a doorway to prevent the door from being pushed open.

> **1714** The vestry was to find a workman "to fit the two Doors" of a church "with a Lock to one, & a Cross Bar on the Inside of the other." St. Paul's Parish, Kent Co., Md., Vestry Book.

2. One of a series of horizontal iron bars that formed a grate, used to cover windows, especially ones in prisons. See **grate** (1).

> **1706** A prison was to have "one window with cross iron barrs." Northumberland Co., Va., Court Order Book 1699–1713.
> **1788** The windows of a prison were "to be in size sufficient to contain 15 pains of 9 by 7 inch glass & each to have an iron grating of 6 inches wide of iron 2 1/4 inch broad & 5/8 thick for the cross barrs And the upright barrs of 1 inch square to be let through the cross barrs." Prince William Co., Va., Deed Book 1787–1791.

crossette
Coor-Gaston House, New Bern, N.C.

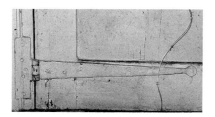

cross garnet
Strawberry Hill Chapel,
Berkeley County, S.C.

cross beam (crosse beame, x beam) **1.** The principal transverse framing member connecting the tops of walls at the front and rear wall plates. These tie beams sometimes formed the bottom chord of principal rafter trusses, restraining their outward thrust against the wall. Until the second quarter of the 19th century, when the term *tie beam* became prevalent, the name given to this member varied; it was sometimes called a *girder, cross beam,* or simply *beam.* See **girder, tie beam.**

> **1742** A chapel was to be repaired by "placing & putting in two strong & substantial cross beams in the sd chapel for better supporting & strengthening the Roof." Albemarle Parish, Surry Co., Va., Vestry Book.
> **1757** It was "Ordered that the Westernmost x beam in the church be immediately secured, it appearing to be very rotton and Dangerous." St. Helena's Parish, S.C., Vestry Book.

2. Another name for a collar or windbeam connecting rafter pairs at a level above their feet. See also **collar beam, windbeam.**

> **1677** It was "Ordered that Sam. Duninge put crosse beames to every small rafter." Petsworth Parish, Gloucester Co., Va., Vestry Book.

crossette (crosete) A lateral projection of an architrave molding at the end of the head or lintel used in classical design, found most commonly in door and window surrounds and chimneypieces. The projection is also known as an ear.

cross garnet (cross garnish, x garnet) A T-shaped hinge with a stationary vertical member fastened to the doorcase and the moveable, horizontal tailpiece connected to the door.

> **1640** A craftsman's bill included "14 pair of cross-garnish for the doors." Maryland Patents Certificates and Warrants 1637–1650, MSA.
> **1702** Courthouse doors were to be "hung with good and strong hookes and hinges or Cross Garnets." Essex Co., Va., Will and Deed Book No. 10.
> **1716** A North Carolina planter ordered from Boston "12 pair of cross garnett hinges, I would like to have them good being for inner room dores for my own house." Pollock Letterbook, NCA&H.

crowbar (crow) A long iron tool slightly curved at one end, used for prying and levering.

> **1775** In the list of tools owned by bricklayer Matthew Tuell was an "iron crow." York Co., Va., Will and Inventory Book 1771–1782.

crown glass A type of blown window glass produced in England from the late 17th through the early 19th centuries that, because of the relative clarity and strength of the material, became the preferred window glass in the American colonies and early republic. Unlike the much more brittle and inferior *cylinder glass,* also referred to as *broad* or *sheet glass, crown glass* was more durable and had fewer streaks and waves. It was made by blowing a large bubble and attaching a rod opposite the blowpipe. The glass was then reheated and rotated to form a large disc or table. After it had cooled, the table was cut into various-sized panes. Crown glass production in England centered around London, followed by Bristol and Newcastle as important regional centers. As with paint, nails, and other English-produced goods, southern builders purchased cases of crown glass from merchants in cities like Charleston, Williamsburg, and Annapolis as well as in smaller ports. Following the Revolution, a number of American manufacturers of crown glass appeared, some even in the South. The most prominent center of glass production to emerge in the first decades of the 19th century was in New England, especially around Boston. See also **glass, sheet glass.**

> **1728** Vestry noted that "Four duz: panes of London duble crond glass of about 11 & 12: size [are] to be sent for by the rev Emanuel Jones." Petsworth Parish, Gloucester Co., Va., Vestry Book.
> **1736** Courthouse windows were "to be Done with Crown Glass from London." Spotsylvania Co., Va., Will Book 1722–1749.
> **1753** "To be Sold by the Subscriber in ANNAPOLIS BEST London Crown Glass, 8 by 12, 10 by 12, and 6 by 4. . . . Beale Bordley." *Maryland Gazette.*
> **1756** Henry Laurens of Charleston wrote to a merchant in Bristol that "our Glaziers assure us that the glass which has been usually ship'd by Mr. Cowles at something less than 4d per foot will yield them as much money as the London Crown which costs double the price." *Papers of Henry Laurens, 2.*
> **1795** Gabriel Manigault of Charleston ordered from London "700 Panes best London crown Glass as straight as possible, & in size exactly 17 inches by 11." Manigault Papers, South Caroliniana Library.
> **1817** "The Richmond Crown Glass Manufactory is in operation; carriage sheet & box glass, can be furnished at short notice." *Richmond Enquirer.*
> **1820** The sashes of the President's House in Washington "have been glazed with best Boston crown glass." *Daily National Intelligencer.*

crypt A subterranean chamber or vault beneath the floor of a church, used as a place for burial.

> **1806** In his design for the Roman Catholic Cathedral in Baltimore, Benjamin Henry Latrobe noted that "your Crypt (for I hate to talk about a Church cellar) should be vaulted." *The Correspondence and Miscellaneous Papers of Benjamin Henry Latrobe, 2.*

cuddy A small closet or cupboard for the storage of miscellaneous goods.

> **1694** "In the Cuddy in the Outward Room" of William Nickles dwelling were "1 old . . . feather bed and two old blanketts, 1 pr Stillyards." Norfolk Co., Va., Deed Book 1686–1695.
> **1698** Appraisers listed an assortment of tools in "Chamber Cuddy" of Richard Church's house. Norfolk Co., Va., Deed Book, 1695–1703.
> **1756** A "Cuddie under the Stairs" was among the spaces inventoried by appraisers of Chanderler Awbrey's estate. Westmoreland Co., Va., Inventory Book 1752–1756.
> **1793** The sense of cuddy as a tiny space quickened Thomas Jefferson's sarcasm about rented quarters in Philadelphia: "we must give him four to six or eight dollars a week for cuddies without a bed." *The Writings of Thomas Jefferson, 4.*

cupboard Most often used to identify a free-standing item of furniture, this term occasionally applied to a built-in closet or some other fixed, upright receptacle for miscellaneous storage. Such features were rare before 1750. See **buffet.**

> **1739** Vestry authorized an addition to the glebe house, wherein Dr. Charles Green was directed to "erect closets or cup boards." Truro Parish, Fairfax Co., Va., Vestry Book.
> **1762** Appraisers in Lancaster County, Virginia, listed "1 Sugar Box and Lumber in the Cupboard" of Captain John Bailey's house. Lancaster Co., Va., Deed and Will Book 1758–1763.

cupola (cupilo, cupalo, cupolo) A domical roof resting on a small circular or polygonal projection at the ridge of a roof, used for observation, a belfry, or as an eyecatching terminus on a pretentious dwelling or public structure. The drums of the cupolas on important dwellings such as the Cupola House in Edenton, North Carolina (1758) were often glazed and provided a place to observe the topography of

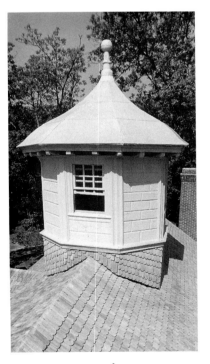

cupola
Cupola House, Edenton, N.C., 1758.

the surrounding area, a place of entertainment, and a ventilation shaft for cool breezes. Public buildings with cupolas often contained bells and clocks on the cupola superstructure. See also **belfry, dome, turret.**

> **1704** The committee charged with building the capitol in Williamsburg decided that "the Dyal plates for the Clock to be drawn on the Square of the Cupolo." *Journals of the House of Burgesses,* 4.
>
> **1718** It was "Ordered that a convenient cupolo be forthwith built at the west end of the mother church, to hang the said bell in." Christ Church Parish, Middlesex Co., Va., Vestry Book.
>
> **1736** A plantation for sale north of Charleston contained a dwelling with "a cupola 9 feet square, neatly wrought, and commands the prospect of Goose Creek and the low lands for several miles round." *South Carolina Gazette.*
>
> **1789** A building committee decided that "a cupalo would be an ornamental addition" to the courthouse in Norfolk. Norfolk Co., Va., Court Order Book 1788–1790.
>
> **1797** "From the cupola" of Ralph Izard's dwelling on White Point in Charleston, "there is an extensive prospect of the City, and a very pleasing view of the Sea from Long Island to the Light House, by which means every Vessel going out or coming in at the different Bars or Channels, may readily be seen in clear weather." *City Gazette and Daily Advertiser.*
>
> **1817** At the First Presbyterian Meetinghouse in Lexington, Kentucky, "lightning struck the spire of the church, passed over the ball, and entered the cupola near the top, splintered one of the posts of the belfry, passed the roof and rund down the iron rod, in the centre of the building, by which the Chandelier was suspended, and killed 2 ladies." *Richmond Commercial Compiler.*

curb (kerb, kirb)   A low, solid barrier used to enclose, strengthen, or restrain parts of buildings and other structures, especially between different levels. The term was applied almost exclusively to the edging around wells during the 18th century, but later denoted the edge of a portico base and an important element of street paving. See **curbstone.**

> **1709** New construction on a glebe included "a Curb and Windless for the well, and a Shed over the Well." St. Peter's Parish, New Kent Co., Va. Vestry Book.
>
> **1751** "The said Wells are to [be] Twelve feet deep and well done with Brick and to have a Curb to Each made with two inch oak or pine plank, so that the same break the joints thereof, and that there be a Cross piece for the Pumps to rest on." Norfolk, Va., Order Book of the Common Hall 1736–1798.
>
> **1802** Stonecutters' bill for work on John Tayloe's Washington, D.C., residence included "509 [feet] 8 [inches] Strong Kirb to area walls & windows [at] 5/9...146.10.7." Painter Lewis Clipham charged Tayloe for "21 yards 1 Coat on Stone at area Kirbs...17.6." Tayloe Papers, VHS.
>
> **1812** Proposals sought for street paving "with side or curb stones of falls stone, at least 15 inches in depth, well jointed and the whole of these and the pavement to be placed upon a good bed of sand." *Alexandria Daily Gazette, Commercial and Political.*

curb roof   A gable roof divided into two sections of unequal slope. This term was used by the English in the 18th-century to describe what contemporary southern Americans called a *Dutch roof* and what is today known in America as a *gambrel roof.* See **Dutch roof.**

> **1796** An English immigrant described the houses in Norfolk as "chiefly framed and weatherboarded, and the sort of double roof, called by the french un Mansard . . . and by the English Carpenters, a Curbroof, are very common. I suspect that they may have been introduced by German builders, after the fashion of Saxony, and most other parts of Germany." *The Virginia Journals of Benjamin Henry Latrobe,* 1.

curbstone   One of a series of stones or other components used to construct curbs for areas of paving.

1815 A city ordinance called for "filling up footways, setting curb stones on West Washington street and charging the expense to the lot owners." *Maryland Herald & Hagers-Town Weekly Advertiser.*

1835 "Resolved that the building committee be authorized to contract for grading & paving the market house with hard Baltimore or Alexandria bricks (curb stone for the same 4 inches thick and 16 deep) for $526 or less." Portsmouth, Va., Town Minute Book 1822–1843.

curtail step The lower step or steps of a stair having one or both ends of the tread terminating in the form of a scroll, usually with the railing and balustrade scrolled in the same fashion.

1811 Construction of a stair included "one mahogany Scroll & Curtail Step." Riddell Accounts, Pleasants Papers, MHS.

curtilage A courtyard or piece of ground and outbuildings adjacent to a dwelling house forming part of an enclosure. The term was used in a legal sense to describe a residence and its immediate surroundings. See also **messuage.**

1813 On one of Thomas Jefferson's properties, the former president had "engaged a workman to build office, have laid off a handsome curtilage connecting the house with the Tomahawk, [and have] divided into suitable appendages to a Dwelling house." *Huntington Library Quarterly,* 6.

cushion board A shelf in a church pulpit covered with velvet, damask, or some other textile to protect the Bible placed there.

1762 Pulpit in a church to be constructed with "a cushion board." Frederick Parish, Frederick Co., Va., Vestry Book.

custom house A building or office used to collect duties on imported goods, generally located in a port. Although some custom houses may have been no more than a small office, others had warehouse storage.

1728 "The Incorporate Body Politick of . . . Annapolis were Authorized by an act of Assembly . . . to appropriate part of the land laid out in the city of Annapolis for the Building A Custom House on." Anne Arundel Co., Md., Land Records Book 1729–1730.

1767 In Charleston, money was appropriated "for the building an Exchange and Custom House. . . . The old watch house is to be pulled down, and the exchange and custom-house erected in its stead, according to a plan . . . extending on the Bay from north to south 92 feet, and from east to west 72, and to contain (besides several cellars to lett) the collector's and naval offices, and a large room for the meeting of the inhabitants." *South Carolina Gazette.*

1820 A fire destroyed much of Savannah. "The Branch Bank and the New Custom-House with Stores not occupied, are burnt." *American Beacon and Norfolk and Portsmouth Daily Advertiser.*

cut nail A pointed metal fastener driven by a hammer and used to joint one piece to another. A *cut nail* differs from a *wrought nail* in the manner of its manufacture. Cut nails were produced by a machine that cut each shaft from a sheet of iron or steel and thus tapered along its length on only two, instead of all four, sides. Cut nails were produced in a variety of sizes and shapes. Although cut-nail machinery was invented in the 1780s, nails produced by these machines did not become widely available until the beginning of the 19th century in the South. From the 1790s through the early 1820s, the most common form of cut nails consisted of brads and nails whose heads were hand

curtail step
Kenmore, Fredericksburg, Va.

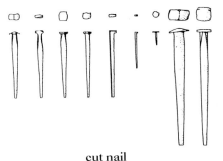

cut nail
Types of machine-cut nails
(*left to right*): cut shaft with double-struck wrought head, cut shaft with a clasp-wrought head, early machine-cut head, "mature" machine-cut head, brad, sprig, tack, wrought-head spike, machine-cut head spike.

forged. Around 1815, machines capable of heading nails were introduced and hand-heading soon disappeared. Cut nails were initially used for framing, or when made into brads, for trim work. Because they were not as pliable as wrought nails, the latter continued to be used when clinching was required, as well as for the installation of hardware, well into the second quarter of the 19th century. See also **brad, nail, sprig, wrought nail.**

> **1796** In Fayetteville, there was "for sale . . . WHOLESALE and RETAIL, A quantity of all kinds of wrought, and some cut NAILS." *North Carolina Minerva and Fayetteville Advertiser.*
>
> **1805** Davis and Southwick of Fredericksburg, "have lately established a Cut Nail Manufactory IN the house lately occupied by Mr. Mordecai Barbour, where they will sell Cut and wrought Nails, Brads, Sprigs, Sadlers' Tacks of all sizes on the lowest terms. . . . Also, Machines will be made to carry on the Cut-Nail business." *Virginia Herald.*
>
> **1817** "Cut Nail Factory. The subscriber at his old stand, two miles above the Trap, on the road to Harper's Ferry, where he has carried on the nailing business for the last 20 years . . . has commenced the manufacture of cut nails and will constantly keep on hand a general assortment of both Wrought and Cut Nails, Sprigs, Brads and Spikes. . . . Jacob Easterday." *Frederick Town Herald.*

cutting box   A U-shaped box with saw kerfs cut at various angles in the two sides, used for holding large pieces of molding when sawing miters and other angled joints; a miter box.

> **1802** Among the tools listed in builder John Ariss's estate inventory were "1 cutting box $3.00, 1 tenon saw $1.66." Berkeley Co., Va., Will Book 1796–1805.

cylinder glass   See **sheet glass.**

cyma

cyma (cima)   A double curved molding with an S-shaped profile. The term was rarely used in America but was popular among English architectural writers. Workmen in the colonial and early national periods referred to this molding as an *ogee.* When the concave section of the molding was above and the convex below, it was known as a *cyma recta.* When the convex section was above and the concave below, it was called a *cyma reversa.* See also **ogee.**

cymatium   The top member of a classical molding, especially the crown molding of a cornice. Although it refers to a feature rather than to a profile, the most common form is a cyma recta.

cypress (cipress, cyprus, siprus)   A nonresinous softwood that grows in swampy lowlands of the southeast. The Pennsylvania border is the northern limit of its growth area.   The tree was prized by early builders for its durability and was especially favored for shingles and weatherboards in the upper South. In the lowcountry of South Carolina and Georgia where cypress was much more prevalent, the wood was used not only for shingles and boards, but for framing members and some interior woodwork.

> **1685** A courthouse "roofe [is] to be Covered wth good cypress shingles." Middlesex Co., Va., Court Order Book 1680–1694.
>
> **1701** An agreement was made with Henry Wyatt "to get 20,000 good sound sipres shingles for covering for the brick church and each and every shingle to be 18 inches in length, and none to be more than 5 inches in breadth, or none under three inches, and not to be less than 1/2 an inch or more than 3/4 of an inch thick, and all to be well rounded and bundled up fit to be layed into a cart." St. Peter's Parish, New Kent Co., Va., Vestry Book.

1709 "Cypress in not an Ever-green with us, and is therefore call'd the bald Cypress, because the Leaves, during the Winter-Season, turn red, not recovering the Verdure till the Spring. These Trees are the largest for Height and Thickness, that we have in this Part of the World. . . . This Wood is very lasting, and free from the Rot. A Canoe of it will outlast four Boats, and seldom wants Repair." Lawson, *A New Voyage to Carolina*.

1753 A dwelling for sale in Charleston was described as having "the frame of the house all heart of cypress." *South Carolina Gazette*.

1764 Henry Laurens of Charleston wrote to a Liverpool merchant that "Cypress is the best & Cheapest Wood with us for Wainscot, but your Oak is in my judgment infinitely preferable." *Papers of Henry Laurens*, 4.

1815 In Cecil County, Maryland, a diarist noted that "my husband planted two bald cypress (or Crupressus Disticha) trees, one in the big Valley going to the quarter, the other the head of the east Valley, about one inch diameter each. These trees he brought from the great Dragon swamp in the South of Virginia." *The Diaries of Martha Ogle Forman*.

dado 1. In classical architecture, the middle portion or flat face of a pedestal between the base and cap. It is also called a *die*. By extension it is the center section of any ornamental decoration covering the lower part of a wall. The dado of this continuous pedestal is crowned at the top by a molded surbase and at the bottom by a base. Dado finishes consisted of wainscotting with raised or flat panels, flush board sheathing, or plaster. See also **pedestal, surbase, wainscot.**

1774 Carpentry work for William Corbit's house in Odessa, Delaware, included fabrication of "15 yds 5 ft 3 ins Dado at 4/6, 76 ft 6 ins Base & sr base a fret in each at 2/6 £1.3.10." Sweeney, *Grandeur on the Appoquinimink*.

1783 The library at the Governor's House in New Bern was finished with "pedistals on the dado to receive the Window architraves." Hawks Letter, Miranda Papers, Academia Nacional de la Historia, Caracas.

1805 The inside of a church near the Santee Canal in South Carolina was "to be plain dedo, and above that to be plaistered." *City Gazette*.

1816 The interior of an academy to be built in Sparta, Georgia, was to be divided by "framed partitions, plain dado, chairboard high, including chairboard and washboard above and below." *The News*.

2. A rectangular groove cut into a piece so as to receive the end of another member.

dairy (dary, dayry) A ventilated room or building where milk, butter, and cheese were stored. Chesapeake residents gradually broke with the English practice of having a service room for this function within the house, so that by the third quarter of the 17th century, separate, detached dairies or milk houses were being constructed. By the early 18th century *dairy* supplanted *milk house* as the name for such structures in Virginia and parts of the lower South, while in the northern Chesapeake the term *milk house* remained predominant. Most dairies were 10- or 12-foot square structures with latticed windows, plastered walls, shelves, deep eaves, and paved floors. A number had double walls insulated with sawdust or some other filling. Some very small dairies stood on posts raised off the ground. See also **milk house.**

1677 "A dary or milkhouse" was to be built on glebe land. Blisland Parish, James City and New Kent Cos., Va., Vestry Book.

1750 A carpenter was hired to build "a dary twelve foot square nine foot pitch Bricked underneath . . . & covered & weather boarded . . . two sides of the house [to be] lattised eighteen inches Deep the Jetts to be two foot the same to be plaistered & white washed . . . with convenient shelves & dressers round the House & the floors to be paved." Southam Parish, Cumberland Co., Va., Vestry Book.

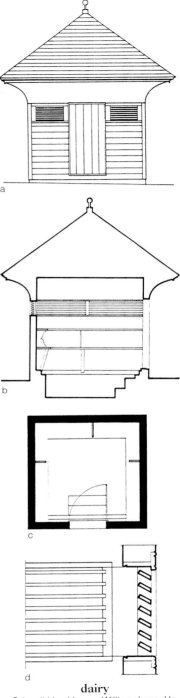

a

b

c

d

dairy
Grissell Hay House, Williamsburg, Va.
(a) elevation, (b) section, (c) plan,
(d) detail of lower window

damper A movable metal plate at the narrowing of a stove or chimney flue that regulates the flow of air into the firebox.

> 1801 In Washington, blacksmith James Worrell charged John Tayloe for "Mending a plate to a stove and a new Damper including taking to pieces & putting together 2.12.6." Tayloe Papers, VHS.

daub (dawb) *(n.)* A rough coat of plaster, mortar, clay, mud and straw, or a combination of such materials applied over the face of a wall, wattle, or in the interstices between logs. *(v.)* To apply a coat of various ingredients over wattles, against the face of a wall, or between the spaces of log buildings as a means of weatherproofing and insulating a structure. See also **chink, chinking, fill, roughcast.**

> 1656 The dwellings of the Chesapeake were glowingly described as "built of wood, yet contrived so delightfull, that your ordinary houses in England are not so handsome, for usually the rooms are large, daubed and whitelimed." Hammond, *Leah and Rachel.*
>
> 1674 "The upper roome" of the courthouse in Charles County, Maryland, was "to be well daubed & sealed with morter white limed & sized." *Archives of Maryland,* 60.
>
> 1765 "The vacancies between the logs [are] to be daubed or filled with good mortar in bothe sides." Augusta Co., Va., Court Judgments.
>
> 1821 Cabins to be built for the poor "are to be skinned pine and no log to be put in the frame or chimneys of the houses whose diameter at the small end shall be less than five inches, the spaces between the logs to be well chinked and daubed." King George Co., Va., Court Order Book 1817–1821.

deadlight An opaque infilling, such as wood or tin, of a glazed opening.

> 1769 Payment "to George Pitman for putting in 13 dead lights in ye windows" of a church. Wicomico Parish, Northumberland Co., Va., Vestry Book.
>
> 1777 A carpenter was paid for "putting 67 dead lights in the Windows" of the capitol in Williamsburg. Va., State Auditor's Papers, VSL.

dead wall A solid-faced wall unbroken by any apertures; a blind wall.

> 1803 "As to the redundant 16 inches" at the Capitol in Washington, "it must be lost either in throwing the return a little out of square, or my making the South dead wall, which Thornton stole from Hatfield, 16 inches wider than the North. This difference no one will perceive." *The Correspondence and Miscellaneous Papers of Benjamin Henry Latrobe,* 1.
>
> 1806 An objection was made by the undertaker of a jail in Charles Town, Virginia, that "the site selected was too small and would preclude building a dead wall surrounding the criminals apartment without enclosing almost the whole building." Jefferson Co., Va., Court Minute Book 1803–1807.

deck A floor or platform, usually open to the weather.

deer park A large enclosed area of wood and field where deer were kept. Following English fashion, a few members of the southern gentry class maintained deer parks as integral parts of pleasure grounds.

> 1727 A new governor of Virginia noted that his house in Williamsburg contained "an handsome garden, an orchard full of fruit, and a very large Park." He intended to turn the park "to better use I think than Deer, which is feeding off of all sorts of Cattle." Gooch Transcripts, VSL.
>
> 1789 At Mount Vernon, there was "a small part on the margin of the river, where the English fallow-deer, and American wild-deer are seen through the thickets." Morse, *American Geography.*

dentil (dental, dentile, dentle) A small, rectangular block closely set in a row and generally used between two moldings, especially beneath the corona of Ionic, Corinthian, and Composite cornices. From the mid-18th to the early 19th century, dentils became an especially popular decorative motif for wall, overdoor, and chimney piece cornices. See also **modillion.**

1734 "Vitruvius prescribes the Breadth of each Dentil, or Tooth, to be its Height; and the Indenture or Interval between each two, he directs to be two Thirds of the Breadth of the Dentil." *Builder's Dictionary.*

1766 It was specified that "The Cornish" of a church "be in Proportion to the hight of the Walls. . . .with Dentile Blocks." Truro Parish, Fairfax Co., Va., Vestry Book.

1766 In a church "the front of the Gallery is to be wainscotted, and Dental Cornice for the Same" with "the other two Cielings to be flat a Dental Cornice to go round them." All Faiths Parish, St. Mary's Co., Md., Vestry Book.

1783 The dining room of the Governor's House in New Bern contained "a double cornice with a dentil Bedmould to the Cieling." Hawks Letter, Miranda Papers, Academia Nacional de la Historia, Caracas.

dentil
Pavilion 6, University of Virginia.

design 1. A plan or scheme to be carried into effect.

1727 "When you write your next I expect you will let me know what is done at your new design. If I remember right I ordered your quarter and overseers house to be lofted. It is very necessary not only for the warmth of the house but to lay the peoples corn up in." Carter Papers, UVa.

1728 A petition was made to enlarge the gallery in a church "by Makeing it to Extend from near the Pulpit, all over the Assembly Pews & over the Chancell & untill it should reach near the Governours pew; a Designe Very much wished for." St. Anne's Parish, Anne Arundel Co., Md., Vestry Book.

2. *(v.)* To plan and prepare a preliminary sketch for a building. *(n.)* A drawing or set of drawings, specifications, proposals, etc., for a structure or building. By the end of the 18th century, the term was frequently used to describe the art and practice of arranging forms and devising elements and buildings in a manner agreeable to the rules of architecture and individual taste.

1755 "*Draught*, or *Design*, is the Picture of an intended Building, described on Paper, wherein is laid down (by Scale and compass) the devised Division and Partitions of every Room, in its due Proportions to the whole Building." Salmon, *Palladio Londinensis.*

1786 Two house builders in Annapolis advertised their services, noting that they also "design, estimate, measure and survey any building, and make out bills of scantling." *Maryland Gazette.*

1790 The building of warehouses in Dumfries, Virginia, were to be let "agreeable to a plan which may be seen by application to Mr. Lithgow. The design is three sides of a square built up, with an enclosure to the south." *Virginia Herald and Fredericksburg Advertiser.*

1798 Benjamin Latrobe made note of a "Design of the House of Captain William Pennock. . . . This design was made in consequence of a trifling Wager laid against me by Captn. Pennock that I could not design a house which should be approved by Mr. Luke Wheeler; which should have only 41 feet front; which should contain on the Ground floor, 2 Rooms, a principal Staircase and backstairs; and, which was the essential requisite, the front door of which should be in the center." *The Correspondence and Miscellaneous Papers of Benjamin Henry Latrobe*, 1.

1806 Benjamin Latrobe wrote to his former pupil Robert Mills that "it is . . . with sincere regret that I have observed your talents and information thrown into a sort of scramble between the two parties, in the designs of the churches you have given to the congregations [of] Charleston." *The Correspondence and Miscellaneous Papers of Benjamin Henry Latrobe*, 2.

dial (dyal, sun dial) A graduated surface such as a plate or disk on which the hours of the day are marked out and calibrated to the movement of a shadow over a protruding rod; the face of a clock. Sun dials were sometimes placed on the face of public buildings and other structures or set on a pedestal in a garden or public square.

1705 It was ordered "that there be Six Large Sundialls painted upon the Cupulo" of the capitol in Williamsburg. *Journals of the House of Burgesses,* 4.

1744 A London merchant was requested to supply "a good plain Substantial Church Clock Compleatly fitted for the Steeple of St. Philips, to go eight dayes to be made for four . . . dial plates and mind that due regard be had to the heat of ye climate." St. Philip's Parish, Charleston, S.C., Vestry Book.

1764 It was "Ordered that two dials [be] presented to the parish by the Revd John Dixon be fixed up on substantial and neat posts of cedar locust or mulberry." Kingston Parish, Gloucester County, Va., Vestry Book.

1772 Churchwardens were to "send for three dials for the latitude 37 degrees one of each to be fix't at the Church, one at the Eastern Shore Chapel, and one at Pungo Chapel." Lynnhaven Parish, Princess Anne Co., Va., Vestry Book.

1806 A contract was offered "for making and fixing on the front of the Court-House in this City, a complete South Vertical SUN DIAL, to be made of white Marble—Diameter three feet, and of a thickness not less than three inches, with suitable mouldings; the Engraving to be of a durable black colour." *Charleston Courier.*

diamond (3)
Wilson Tobacco House,
Calvert County, Md.

diamond **1.** A lozenge- or rhombus-shaped piece of glass set in lead cames in casement windows; a quarrel. Manufactured in England, diamond panes were imported into the southern colonies until the middle of the 18th century, when they were replaced by larger and more fashionable rectangular panes used in sash windows. See **quarrel.**

1668 "To cut a Case" of glass "into Quarries Diamond-fashion (with halves, quarters, and three quarters of Quarries, as the Glass falls out) it is worth about 6 or 7s. . . . Of these Quarries there are several forms, some bigger, some lesser; but the most generall size is six inches from angle to angle one way, and 4 inches the other." Leybourn, *Platform Guide Mate for Purchasers, Builders, Measurers.*

1698 Shipped to Virginia was "a box of glass in quarries with lead answerable in Diamond Cut containing about 80 or 100 feet." *William Fitzhugh and His Chesapeake World.*

1732 An account of work of a Williamsburg carpenter included "18 1/2 feet of old Glass sett in New Lead at 6d . . . putting in 49 Diamond panes of Glass at 2d . . . mending a Light in an Iron Casement . . . 6 square panes of glass . . . a bottom Raill to a Sash." James Wray Accounts, Jones Papers, LC.

2. A tool for cutting glass consisting of a diamond set in a handle.

3. The form of a log notch used in constructing fence rails and log buildings.

1758 Fence "rails [are] to be Five Inches Square & split to show a Diamond." Trinity Parish, Charles Co., Md., Vestry Book.

1778 "The kind of House or Cabin I would propose" to be built at Berkeley Springs resort in western Virginia "is to have it of Loggs or Poles 18 feet Long & 12 Wide . . . the Loggs to be well heart Crammed & hewed on the outside after they are put up the Ends to be notched in Diamond way as is the method over the ridge." Yates Letterbook, UVa.

diastyle See **intercolumniation.**

die A dado. For a more detailed description, see **dado** (1).

dining room This term first appeared in Chesapeake records by the 1650s, being synonymous with *hall* in referring to a planter's principal living space. Not until the late 1720s did the term appear frequently, and only then did it refer to a separate space wholly or mostly dedicated to meals. One or more beds often appeared among the furnishing of these spaces, set aside for informal meals. Beginning in the second quarter of the 18th century, beds gradually disappeared from the dining room as it evolved into a formal setting for public entertainment. After 1750, the escalating importance of the meal led to further expansion and elaboration of the dining space until, in a handful of larger dwellings, it became the largest and best room in the house. In the more opulent houses, a second, informal dining space was sometimes provided for private meals, variously referred to as the *small dining room, wainscotted dining room, back parlor,* or *breakfast room.* See also **breakfast room.**

1651 A workman was hired to "substantially plaister, White lyme & wash over the dyninge roome, the yellowe roome & kitchinge, & chamber over the kitchinge." Norfolk County Will and Deed Book 1646–1651.

1665 "In the Dineinge Roome" of Thomas Keeling's house were "two ffetherbeds one boulster two pillowes two Blanketts and Greene Rugg greene Curtaines . . . one livery cubbard Cloth and cushion, one Table forme and one old chest, four lether chares, three Turkie worke Chares . . . one Couch two Couch bedds one Coverlet and one small carpet . . . one Lookinge glass, plate . . . one paire of Andirons . . . one small Trunke." Norfolk Co. Va., Will Book 1666–1675.

1742 Among the items in Sarah Ball's "Dining Room" were "1 dozen leather Chairs, 1 cloaths press, 1 large oval Table, 1 small Do, 1 pr Andirons . . . 1 Dressing Glass, 1 Bed & furniture." Lancaster Co., Va., Deed Book 1736–1743.

1746 In planning his dwelling in Charleston, Charles Pinckney specified that "the dining room ceiling to be coved into the roof, so as to make this room at least 14 foot high in the clear. N.B. This room is intended to be wainscotted and finished as Mr. Graeme's is." Huger Smith, *The Dwelling Houses of Charleston.*

1758 An inventory of the estate of Major Moore Fauntleroy listed goods "in the Wainscoated dining Room" along with those "in the room called the small dining room." Richmond Co., Va., Will Book 1753–1767.

1764 Henry Laurens of Charleston wrote to an English business partner that "the looking Glasses which you sent me . . . were truly elegant & worthy a place in my dining Room occupied by a Merchant." *The Papers of Henry Laurens,* 4.

1783 "The dining room" of the Governor's House in New Bern "in the S.W. angle is 28 by 22 feet and wainscoted with a plain molding and flat pannel, Architraves and Caps to the doors and windows . . . and double cornice with a dentil Bedmould to the Cieling, the Chimney piece of black and white Vein'd marble over which is a frame with an Ogee scrole pediment." Hawks Letter, Miranda Papers, Academia Nacional de la Historia, Caracas.

dining room
Peter Manigault and friends, 1760, Goose Creek, S.C.

dipteral In classical architecture, a building flanked on each of its sides by a double row of columns.

dirt chimney, dirt and stick chimney Comparatively rare names for a wooden chimney, used in the upper South during the 18th and early 19th centuries. For a more complete account, see **chimney.**

1786 On a Frederick County, Virginia, tenant farm was "an old log house 20 by 16 with a plank floor below, a dirt and stick chimney." Jonathan Clark Notebook, Filson Club.

1791 Between Petersburg and Halifax, Virginia, the houses "are altogether of Wood and chiefly of logs - some indd. have brick chimneys but generally the chimneys are of split sticks filled with dirt between them." *The Diaries of George Washington,* 6.

distemper A water-based paint in which size (animal glue or melted parchment) served as the binder. Used with a wide variety of colors, this finish was sometimes protected with a coating of varnish. In still other applications, a coat of size and whiting was sometimes followed by a single coat of oil-based color.

1774 In Annapolis, self-styled architect Joseph Horatio Anderson advertised his readiness to carry on "house-painting in distemper." *Maryland Gazette.*

1805 Benjamin Latrobe wrote to Samuel Fox that "If the plaistering is not moist . . . I do not believe that the Distemper colors will run." *The Correspondence and Miscellaneous Papers of Benjamin Henry Latrobe,* 2.

distillery   A commercial establishment where the distilling of spirits takes place, generally consisting of several covered sheds or more substantial buildings housing vats and stills. See also **still house.**

> 1759   "To be SOLD . . . A DISTILLERY, with its Appurtenances, in CHARLESTOWN, MARYLAND. . . . The Still-House is built of Cedar 39 1/2 by 26 1/2 Feet clear: In it are two Stills fix'd, the largest containing between 1400 and 1500 Gallons, and the other about 300 Gallons, with Cooler and Worms, sixteen Cisterns, two Returns, one Low-Wine Cistern, Pumps, &c." *Maryland Gazette.*
>
> 1784   On General Charles Lee's land in Berkeley County, Virginia, was "a distillery that works six stills . . . a malstery." *Alexandria Gazette.*
>
> 1793   For sale in Murfreesboro, North Carolina, was "an Extensive Rum and Whiskey DISTILLERY: Together with a Malt-House, Malt-Kiln, Mill, and every necessary Utensil for carrying on distilling on the most easy plan." *North Carolina Journal.*

ditch   A long, narrow cut or trench facilitating the drainage or irrigation of land and often used with fences or alone to define or enclose property boundaries, areas of cultivation, and environs of public buildings.

> 1698   "The Church wardens of this parish are ordered forthwith to Caus the Lower Church yard to bee fenced in with a Good Ditch." St. Peter's Parish, New Kent Co., Va., Vestry Book.
>
> 1705   One type of legally endorsed fence in Virginia was "an hedge two foot high, upon a ditch of three foot deep, and three foot broad, or instead of such hedge, a rail fence of two foot and half high." Hening, *Statutes at Large,* 3.
>
> 1736   In Savannah, Georgia, it was recommended "that the Church Yard should be inclosed with a Pallisade and a Ditch." *Colonial Records of the State of Georgia,* 29.
>
> 1770   At a Richmond County, Virginia, plantation "the jobbers are scoureing the wormditch [a ditch and worm fence] round by Lawson's house in order to fence in the new Corn Field." *Diary of Landon Carter,* 1.

divider   A small compass. See **compass** (2).

> 1703   "You may in small Quadrants divide truer and with less trouble with Steel Dividers, (which open or close with a Screw for that purpose), then you can with Compasses." Moxon, *Mechanick Exercises.*

division   A wall or fence that separates or marks off into discrete units, rooms, areas, or sections. See also **partition.**

> 1767   A 24-by-16 foot prison was to be built with "a Division in the first and second story to be two feet thick . . . and a fireplace in each side of the Division of the sd rooms." Loudoun Co., Va., Court Order Book 1765–1767.
>
> 1778   In Berkeley County, Virginia, an 18-by-12 foot log cabin was to have "a division in the House to make a Room 12 feet square & a Passage 6 feet." Yates Letterbook, UVa.
>
> 1781   A plantation was noted with "indifferent fencing having on it a division fence." Queen Anne's Co., Md., Guardians Bonds and Valuations SC.

dog, dog iron (iron dog)   An andiron. See **andiron.**

> 1746   To be purchased were "Iron plates & dogs for the Chimney in the Courthouse." Frederick Co., Va., Court Order Book 1745–1748.
>
> 1802   The jailor was to "procure four pair of dog irons for the new jail." Shenandoah Co., Va., Court Order Book 1802–1805.

dog-leg stair   See **stair.**

dog nail   See **wrought nail.**

dome (doom)   A hemispherical vault forming the roof or part of the roof of a building, having a circular or polygonal base. One of the most prominent domes erected in the South in the 18th century was the multistoried one constructed in several stages in the 1780s atop the slightly earlier statehouse in Annapolis. In the early 19th century, the Capitol in Washington, the Catholic Cathedral in Baltimore, and the Rotunda at the University of Virginia became powerful manifestations of the classical influence on public building in the age of Jefferson. See also **cupola.**

> 1781 "The State House, in the center of the city [of Annapolis], is a most splendid and magnificent piece of architecture; it is topped with a handsome dome." Thatcher, *A Military Journal During the Revolutionary War.*
>
> 1787 At the Governor's House in New Bern, "the grand Staircase [was] lighted from the Sky by a low Dome, which being glazed kept out the Weather." Attmore, *Journal of a Tour to North Carolina.*
>
> 1790 At Hampton in Baltimore County, Maryland, "Mr. Richardson in the Spring has promised . . . to make my Doom." *MHM,* 33.
>
> 1798 The plan of the Capitol in Washington called for "a main body and two wings; the main body is composed of two parts—a grand circular vestibule to the east, of 112 feet elevation . . . covered with a dome." *Norfolk Herald.*

dome
B. H. Latrobe, Dome over Central Crossing, Roman Catholic Cathedral, Baltimore.

door cap   See **cap, overdoor.**

doorcase   The finished frame around a door. For a more detailed description, see **case** (2).

doorframe   **1.** The structure of a door opening, either assembled as a prefabricated unit and set into a frame or masonry wall, or joined as an integral part of a frame wall.

2. The exposed, often molded casing of a doorway. From the 17th through the early 19th centuries, such finish was commonly applied directly to the framing members or cut directly into their surface.

doorpost   A large post framing one side of a doorway. In many instances, doors were hinged directly on the doorpost. However, many were cased. See **post.**

door puncheon   A doorpost. Use of the term was rare in America.

doorsill   See **sill.**

doorway   The entrance into a building or room.

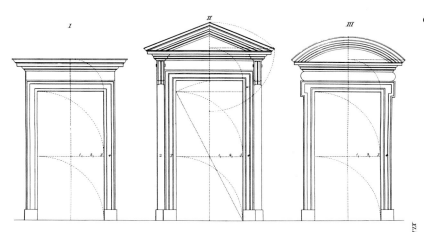

doorcase

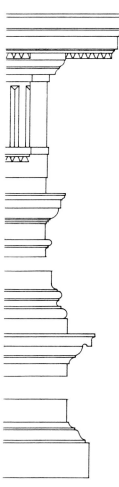

Doric order

Doric order (Dorick)   One of the earliest and simplest of the five orders of classical architecture recognized by Renaissance writers in the 16th and 17th centuries. As with the other elements of classical design, the Italian writers Serlio and Vignola along with French and English authors codified the form, proportions, and details of the Doric order, subdividing it into two distinctive types, the Greek Doric and Roman Doric. The principal distinguishing feature between the two is the absence of a base in the former. The Roman Doric base consists of a plinth, torus, and fillet. The most decorative feature of this otherwise relatively plain order is the frieze with its regularly spaced series of triglyphs and metopes. See also **order.**

> **1734**   "The Characters of the *Doric* Order, as they are now manag'd, are the Height of its Column, which is now eight Diameters; the Frize, which is adorn'd with Triglyphs, Drops, and Metopes; its Capital, which is without Volutes; and its admitting of Cymatiums. . . . The *Doric* is used by the Moderns on Account of its Solidity in large strong Buildings, as in the Gates of Cities and Citadels, the Outsides of Churches, and other massy Works, in which Delicacy of Ornaments would be unsuitable. . . . *Vignola* adjusts the Proportions of the *Doric* Order, as follows: He divides the whole Height of the Order, without the Pedestal, into twenty Parts, or Modules; one of which he allows to the Base, fourteen to the Shaft or Fust, one to the Capital, and four to the Entablature." *Builder's Dictionary.*
>
> **1760**   A church was to be built with "five Pillars of Cypress on each side for the support of the Roof, the Columns to be 15 inches Diameter at the bottom of the Shaft, to be Fluted & the Capitols of the Dorick Order." Stratton Major Parish, King and Queen Co., Va., Vestry Book.
>
> **1767**   In ordering stone from an English merchant, Charles Carroll of Mount Clare in Baltimore County, Maryland, noted that "the Columns must be Round of the Plain Doric order and the Proportions Exact according to the scale and Plans in Length and Diameter." Trostel, *Mount Clare.*
>
> **1822**   Thomas Jefferson wrote to one of his workmen that "when in Bedford" at Poplar Forest, "I examined the Doric entablature for which I should want ornaments, on the model of that of the Thermae of Dioclesian of which you took a note. My room will require 16 of the human busts, 20 ox sculls entire, and 4 other ox sculls cut in halves and mitered for the 4 corners, to be of composition. The spaces for the metopes are 15. I high and 14. I wide." Coolidge Collection, Massachusetts Historical Society.

dormant tree   A summer beam or large sleeper. This archaic term was rarely used in the South. See also **summer.**

dormer window (dorman[t], dormen[t], dormon[t])   Originally the window of a dormitory or sleeping chamber. The term was used in the South to describe a vertical window housed in a frame that rests on a sloping roof. Dormers were not integral parts of the roof structure but were framed separately. The side walls of the dormer were fixed to the upper surface of two rafters, over which board sheathing was attached. Gabled, pedimented, and hipped were the most common forms of dormer roof types. See also **lucarne.**

> **1678**   A courthouse was ordered to be built with five transom windows below "and 3 dorment above." Westmoreland Co., Va., Court Order Book 1676–1689.
>
> **1710**   The upper floor of a courthouse was to have "four Dormant Windows Two on each side five foot high and four foot wide." Baltimore Co., Md., Court Record Book IS.
>
> **1713**   The glebe house contained "two three light Dormant Windows in each Room above stairs." St. Peter's Parish, New Kent Co., Va., Vestry Book.
>
> **1790**   At Hampton in Baltimore County, Maryland, a workman charged his client for fabricating "8 arched dormont windows shingled at sides @ 80s. . . .£32." *MHM,* 33.

dormitory   A room containing a number of beds and used as a sleeping chamber in an institution such as a hospital or school.

> 1798   The penitentiary in Richmond contained a number of "dormitories" for the male and female inmates. *The Correspondence and Miscellaneous Papers of Benjamin Henry Latrobe*, 1.

double door   **1.** A large door consisting of two sections or leaves hung on opposite jambs whose edges meet when closed together. For a more detailed description see **folding door.**

> 1711   The front door of a courthouse was "to be handome Double Doore." Talbot Co., Md., Land Records Book No. 12.
>
> 1714   A craftsman was paid "for a Double Door" to a church. St. Peter's Parish, New Kent Co., Va., Vestry Book.

2. A door generally lined with two thicknesses of boards or planks, or boards and a sheathing, or ironwork. Most such doors were constructed for prisons to ensure security.

> 1736   Specifications for a prison in Beaufort, North Carolina, included "one Strong Double Door on the out side not less than three Inches thick." Carteret Co., N.C., Court of Pleas and Quarter Session Minute Book, NCA&H.
>
> 1819   A prison was to have a "double door at the entrance and outer and inner door both to be made double of 2 inch white oak plank." Lancaster Co., Va., Deed Book 1812–1823.

3. An opening that is closed by two doors hung from the same jamb. The most common appearance of such doors was in prisons as a security measure.

> 1778   "The outside Door" of a prison was "to be Doubled, that is one to open inside and one outside, with strong hinges to lock with two large hasps and staples to the inside Door to be inclosed by the outside Door and two large hasps and staples to the outside door with a good lock." Princess Anne Co., Va., Loose Court Papers.
>
> 1813   The outside doors of a jail were "to be double that is to say the inside door to be made of Iron Bar 1/2 inch thick and 2 Inches wide and the Barrs to cross so as to form Squares 6 Inches the other to be of hart pine or Oak 1 1/2 inches thick." Wayne Co., N.C., Miscellaneous Court Records, NCA&H.

double hung   An term applied to any window having two movable, counterweighted sash. This arrangement required two sets of pulleys for the sash lines and weights, and also *parting strips*, vertical strips that separated the upper and lower sash as they moved by one another. Instances of double hung sash were rare before the Revolution, and the terminology does not appear in southern records until the early 19th century. See also **sash, single hung.**

> 1811   In Baltimore, John Donaldson was paid for "9 pair of sashes double hung & sash Locks put on." Riddell Accounts, Pleasants Papers, MHS.

double studded   See **stud.**

double work   See **work.**

dovecote (dovecot)   A structure housing doves or pigeons with multiple entrances and internal niches or boxes for roosting and nesting. The term is gradually displaced by *pigeon house* over the course of the 18th century. For a more detailed description, see **pigeon house.**

> 1686   Among the outbuildings on a plantation in Stafford County, Virginia, was a "Dovecote." *William Fitzhugh and His Chesapeake World*.
>
> 1736   A plantation to be sold near Goose Creek, South Carolina, contained "a necessary-house neatly built, and above it a dove-house with nests for 50 pair of pigeons." *South Carolina Gazette*.

dovetail
John Stone House, Vance County, N.C.

dovetail (dufftail) One of the most basic of woodworking joints, consisting of a piece of timber whose end has two flaring wedge-shaped sides or edges in the shape of a dove's tail and fits into a correspondingly shaped mortise or recess. Half dovetail joints have only one flaring edge, the other being a straight edge. A dovetail joint provides tensile strength, restraining two pieces from pulling apart under opposing thrusts. Because of the strength and precision of the joint, cabinetmakers and joiners used the dovetail widely. In building, collar beams frequently had lapped dovetail joints to prevent the rafter pairs from spreading. The feet of the rafters might be dovetailed into the plate for the same structural reasons. In the frame of the building, members that tied parts together, such as cross or tie beams and joists, were often given dovetail joints. In log construction, dovetail joints at the corners were one of the most secure joints that could be employed and often appeared in specifications for the construction of prisons and other buildings where strength and security were of great necessity. They were especially common in sawn or hewn plank buildings.

> 1681 In a roof, "the wind beams [are] to be dovetayled." Northumberland Co., Va., Court Order Book 1678–1698.
> 1736 "The Walls of sd Prison [are] to be Saw'd Loggs not less than Foure Inches Thick and Duftailed at the Corners." Carteret Co., N.C., Court of Pleas and Quarter Sessions Book, NCA&H.
> 1748 A prison was "so poorly dufftailed at the corners so that [it] would be a very easy matter to pull it all down." Augusta Co., Va., Court Order Book 1748–1751.
> 1784 On Robert Lacy's land in Delaware was a "dwelling house twenty feet by sixteen built of huged logs doftailed, hip-roughed, covered with Pine Boards." Sussex Co., Del., Orphans Court Valuations E.

dovetail hinge A hinge consisting of two flaring, wedge-shaped leaves pinned together at the center pivot. Such hinges were generally used in cabinetwork and for small boxes. In buildings, dovetail hinges appeared on trap doors, casement windows, closets, and furnishings such as buffet doors. *Butterfly hinge* is a modern term for this type.

> 1719 A vestry ordered "Doftail hinges for Casements" from England. All Faiths Parish, St. Mary's Co., Md., Vestry Book.
> 1758 A merchant in Savannah ordered from Liverpool "2 doz. dove tail Hinges at 2/6 per doz." *Collections of the Georgia Historical Society*, 13.

dowel (dowl, dowell) *(n.)* A small pin inserted into two abutting pieces of wood, stone, etc., to prevent movement or slippage. To prevent lateral racking, many plank buildings had dowels inserted into each plank edge as they were laid on top of each other. *(v.)* To cut a small hole into two members in order to insert a pin. See also **treenail**.

> 1749 A prison "wall all round the outside [is] to be close and neatly done with inch poplar plank plained, beaded, and to be dovetailed at the corners and dowel'd in two parts at an end." Westmoreland Co., Va., Court Order Book 1747–1750.
> 1773 "The body" of a stable was "to be sawed logs four inches thick, to be dowld and dovetailed." Fairfax Parish, Fairfax Co., Va., Vestry Book.
> 1809 "The second Story walls" of a jail were to be "Logs Nine Inches Thick Dovetailed & Dowelld with 1 1/2 Inches Dowels." Pasquotank Co., N.C., Accounts, NCA&H.

dowel bit See **bit.**

down brace See **brace** (1).

draft (draught) *(n.)* A drawing or sketch of a building or parts of a building. The term was used almost synonymously with *plat* in the late 17th century to denote the graphic representation of a design. It was supplanted by the term *plan* by the 1730s. *(v.)* To devise a scheme or drawing of a building. See also **plan, plat.**

1700 The vestry requested a carpenter "to draw a Draft" of a church, in which he complied by producing "Sevrall Draffts." St. Peter's Parish, New Kent Co., Va., Vestry Book.

1711 The vestry received "a platt or draught of a church" from Governor Alexander Spotswood. Bruton Parish, Williamsburg, Va., Church Records.

1734 "Draught, Draft, in Architecture, is the Figure of an intended Building described on Paper; in which is laid down, by Scale and Compasses, the Several Divisions and Partitions of the Apartments, Rooms, Doors, Passages, Conveniencies &c. in their Due Proportion to the whole Building." *Builder's Dictionary.*

1734 "Samuel Holmes of Charlestown Bricklayer undertakes and performes in workmanlike manner all sorts of Brickwork and Plaistering at reasonable Rates. He likewise if required draws Draughts of Houses, and measures and values all sorts of Workmanship in Houses or Buildings." *South Carolina Gazette.*

1775 Magistrates were to "plan and lay off a Draugh for a new prison." Accomack Co., Va., Order Book 1774–1777.

dragon beam In English carpentry, a diagonal girder projecting out over the corner of a building to support a post and overhang where a building jetties on two sides. In southern buildings, dragon beams supported the feet of hip rafters at the intersection of two wall plates.

drain A channel, conduit, or pipe used to remove rain, wastewater, or sewage. Many early buildings had such features constructed of masonry to carry off water from cellars and from low-lying areas. Sir William Berkeley's Green Spring, one of the largest dwellings built in 17th-century Virginia, contained a number of brick drains covered by stone running several hundred feet from the main structure. Although lack of an efficient system for the removal of sewage and wastewater plagued most southern cities until the late 19th century, Charleston-

dragon beam
Edenton Courthouse, Edenton, N.C.

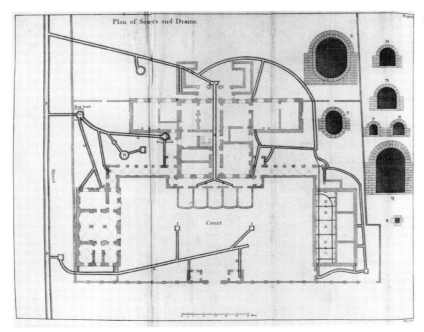

drain

ians in the late colonial period constructed a series of drains leading from private lots into a common sewer which ran beneath a number of its streets. See also **conduit, sewer.**

> 1744 "To be Sold . . . a large brick three Story House . . . situate on the Bay of Charles Town . . . well seated for Trade, and hath the Convenience of good Stores, with Cellars underneath and Drains in them." *South Carolina Gazette.*
>
> 1768 Payment was made to Peter and John Horlbeck for "carting earth to and levelling the Yard" of the statehouse in Charleston, and for "sinking a Drain therefrom to the Common Sewer, laying a kerb, Grate." Journal of the Commons House of Assembly No. 37, SCA&H.
>
> 1772 In Charleston, "ANY Persons willing to undertake the SINKING OF A DRAIN, to be Two Feet and a half Wide, Three Feet and a half high in the Clear, and to be [fabricated] with Two Inch Cypress Plank, and deep enough to commit of Cellars Six Feet deep, in Old Church-street, from the Corner of the Alley leading to King-street into Ashley River, are desired to send in their Proposals." *South Carolina and American General Gazette.*
>
> 1783 The Governor's House in New Bern was equipped with "a Lead Gutter to receive the water from the In and outside of the roof . . . with 6 stacks of Lead pipes to convey the water into drains which lead to Reservoirs." Hawks Letter, Miranda Papers, Academia Nacional de la Historia, Caracas.

draw 1. *(v.)* To shape and work a piece of material by cutting off thin slices. The term was generally used to describe the riving and finishing of boards. *(n.)* Riven or split boards; clapboards. See also **dub, rive.**

> 1653 Carpenter Thomas Felton agreed to build a frame house and to "rive, dubb, and draw all the boards." Surry Co., Va., Deed and Will Book 1652–1672.
>
> 1706 A prison was "to be Double Raftered and Covered with Drawn Boards." Kent Co., Del., Court Record Book 1703–1718.
>
> 1725 Obadiah Pritchard was hired to cover a vestry house with "good drawn Boards of red Oak, well lapp'd & well done, he the said Obadiah to draw the Boards down." St. George's Parish, Harford Co., Md., Vestry Book.

2. A sliding compartment in a piece of furniture; a drawer.

> 1773 A "Table [was to] be made for the use of the Clerk with a large Draw & good lock." Goochland Co., Va., Court Order Book 1772–1778.
>
> 1822 The commonwealth's attorney was to have "an Arm Chair with a Draw." Essex Co., Va., Court Order Book 1821–1823.

3. (drawing) *(v.)* To render a sketch of a design showing the arrangement of various parts of a building. *(n.)* A sketch showing the plan, elevation, section, or details of a structure. Such drawings were generally executed in ink or graphite. Some were carefully rendered to a given scale such as a quarter inch to the foot, while others were hasty efforts, sometimes sketched on the back of a piece of material at the job site. By the late colonial period, full-scale working drawings depicting the arrangement and shape of many details were an integral part of the building process on complex or unusual buildings. See also **draft, elevation, plan** (1), **plat, section.**

> 1760 Lewis Delony paid "twenty five shilling current money for drawing a plan of a church." St. Andrew's Parish, Brunswick Co., Va., Vestry Book.
>
> 1769 In Charleston, "EZRA WAITE, Civil Architect, House-builder in general and Carver . . . calculated, adjusted, and draw'd at large for to work by, the Ionick entablature, and carved the same in the front and round the eaves of MILES BREWTON, Esquire's House." *South Carolina Gazette and Country Journal.*
>
> 1773 A set of specifications for a prison in Edenton, North Carolina written by John Hawks was accompanied by a plan and elevation. He noted that "the Dimensions of the several Rooms and height of the Story's are figured in the Drawing." Hawks Papers, SHC.

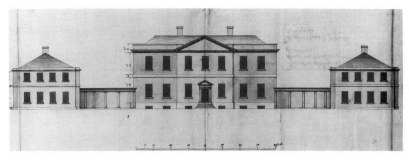

a

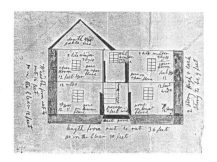

c

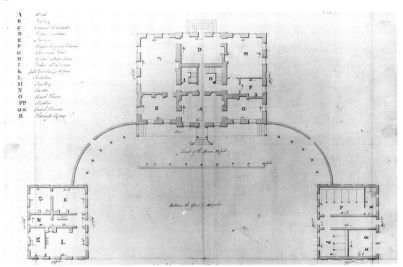

b

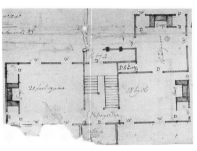

d

draw (3) (a-b) John Hawks, elevation and plan of the Governor's House, New Bern, N.C., 1767; (c) elevation overlaid on a plan for a jail, Westmoreland County, Va., 1826; (d) plan of a house to be built for William Cabell of Nelson County, Va., 1784.

1798 Proposals were received for work on the penitentiary in Richmond, noting that the "framing [of the] principal roofs [would be] according to directions and drawings to be given by the Architect." *The Correspondence and Miscellaneous Papers of Benjamin Henry Latrobe*, 1.

drawing instruments Architects and builders often produced design and full-scale working drawings for building projects. Although many of these drawings were no more than hasty sketches, others were carefully executed in pencil or ink and drawn to scale. For these purposes, draftsmen used compasses with shifting pencil and pen legs, scales, protractors, dividers, parallel rules, and squares set at various angles. The T square provided a means of drawing parallel lines and provided support for squares set at various angles.

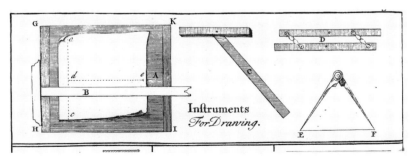

drawing instruments (A) board, (B) T-square, (C) bevel, (D) parallel ruler, (E-F) compass

drawing knife (draw knife) A woodworking tool in the form of a curved blade from 8 to 20 inches long that tapers and bends at right angles to the cutting edge at both ends, each of which is fitted with wooden handles. The drawing knife was an all-purpose implement used for the removal of surplus wood and rounding edges. Craftsmen shaped shingles and other small items by placing their objects in bench vices, shaving horses, or other clamps and pulling the sharp edge of the drawing knife toward them. Because of its versatility, farmers as well as craftsmen frequently kept one in their possession.

drawing room A large, formal entertaining space; a reception room. Replicating English fashion, the term comes into use in the South in the third quarter of the 18th century to describe a room in which polite company was entertained. In terms of function, *drawing room* is nearly synonymous with *saloon*. However, rooms described as saloons generally were found in the center of a dwelling behind the *hall* or *entry*, whereas drawing rooms could be situated in a number of prominent locations in a dwelling. Many were located next to dining rooms and served as places to retire after dinner. See also **hall, parlor, saloon.**

> **1777** The inventory of the estate of Sir John Colleton of Charleston, South Carolina, listed furnishings in the "Drawing Room." Charleston Co., S.C., Will Book 1776–1778.
> **1783** Next to the dining room and opposite the north entrance hall, "in the center of the South front" of the Governor's House in New Bern "is the drawing room 26 by 18 feet" with "the cieling Coved, this is alowed the most light and Airy finished room in the House." Hawks Letter, Miranda Papers, Academia Nacional de las Historia, Caracas.
> **1809** A visitor to Baltimore met an acquaintance "at a friend's house that evening. . . . I . . . found her at Mr. McCortland, who conducted us to a neat drawing room, where were several gentlemen & ladies. . . . After tea we attended the Company to the Theatre." *Journal of William D. Martin.*
> **1813** The President's House in Washington had "on the side opposite to the entrance . . . doors opening to four rooms. The corner is the dining room and is very spacious. . . . This room opens by a single door into Mrs. Madison's sitting room which is half as large. . . . This room, in the same way, enters into the drawing-room, which is an immense and magnificent room, in an oval form. . . . A door opens at each end, one into the hall, and opposite, one into the terrace. . . . The windows are nearly the height of the room, and have superb red silk velvet curtains. . . .The chairs are wood painted, with worked bottoms and each has a red velvet large cushion. They are arranged on the side, and are divided into four divisions by sofas. These three rooms are all open levee nights." *Diary of Elbridge Gerry, Jr.*
> **1819** The second-floor "drawing room" in bank president James McKinlay's dwelling in New Bern was furnished with two sofas, 12 chairs, 3 tea tables, carpet, fireplace equipment, eight prints, and window curtains. Craven Co., N.C., Estate Papers, NCA&H.

dress To prepare, shape, or finish a smooth or even surface by rubbing or cutting. Dressed lumber has been planed smooth on one or more faces. Stone is dressed by chipping away the irregularities of the face side.

> **1745** A church was to be weatherboarded "with feather edged plank dress'd and beaded." Fredericksville Parish, Louisa Co., Va., Vestry Book.
> **1766** A church roof was to be "covered with good Eighteen Inch Cypruss Shingles well Dressed." Chester Parish, Kent Co., Md., Vestry Book.
> **1800** Work on an academy in Edenton, North Carolina, included "Old Welcome laying foundation & dressing Stones. Joe Welcome dressing Stone. Jeffrey, Andrew dressing stone, digging foundation. Lewis dressing Shingles." Cupola House Papers, SHC.

dresser A piece of furniture, usually built-in, that facilitated food preparation and other domestic activity. While the term appears only occasionally in documentary sources, most often in kitchens, pantries, or similar domestic spaces, examples of these simple, utilitarian furnishings are relatively common.

1730 A workman was hired to install "Dresser and Shelves" in a kitchen. Prince Frederick, Winyah Parish, S.C., Vestry Book.

1770 Property to be let in Charleston contained "a two story kitchen with four rooms, lathed and plaistered, a good oven, dressers, and shelves." *South Carolina Gazette and Country Journal.*

1802 A carpenter's accounts for John Tayloe's house in Washington, D.C., include "Framing to dresser . . . dovetail'd drawers" and "Columns to dresser 1/6 legs to sink." Tayloe Papers, VHS.

dressing room In larger dwellings, a space located next to a bedchamber, used for dressing. Among the fashionable upper classes, the morning toilet was a social occasion where intimates came to a dressing room to discuss news and gossip. The term came into fashion in England in the second half of the 17th century and in the American colonies in the middle of the 18th century. The term *closet* was sometimes used earlier to describe the function of this space. The term was also used to describe a room in a theater where actors changed costumes. See also **closet** (1).

1758 At Stratford in Westmoreland County, Virginia, "a large walnut linnen press wth draws [and] Chest Draws" were located "in the Dressing Room." Westmoreland Co., Va., Record Book 1756–1767.

1767 In John Hawks's second-floor plan of Governor Tryon's dwelling in New Bern, the room next to "His Excellencys Bed room" was marked "Mrs. Tryons Dressing Room and Closet." Hawks Papers, NYHS.

1796 A "proposal for Building a Theatre" in Petersburg, Virginia, noted that "the building to Consist of a Stage upper and under Boxes, a Pitt, & proper Offices, together with two Dressing rooms under the Stage." Petersburg, Va., Hustings Court Minute Book 1791–1797.

drip The projecting edge of a molding or any other protruding piece that is channeled beneath to prevent water from running back against the surface of a wall.

1756 The corona of a cornice "is more usually and distinctively called the *drip*, or *Larmier*. This is placed between the cymatium and the ovolo, and its use is to carry off the water drop by drop from the building." Ware, *A Complete Body of Architecture.*

1803 The lead gutters of the Capitol in Washington needed to be "cut and groved together, with a good drip" to prevent further leaks. *The Correspondence and Miscellaneous Papers of Benjamin Henry Latrobe*, 1.

drop An ornament in the form of a cone attached to the underside of mutules or beneath triglyphs in a Doric entablature; a gutta. See also **gutta.**

1760 The work of the carvers Elfe and Hutchinson at St. Michael's Church in Charleston included the fabrication of "61 1/2 Doz of drops for the Dorrick order in the Cornish Round the outside of the Church." Williams, *St. Michael's.*

dry *(adj.)* Masonry laid without mortar or other cementitious material.

1793 Specifications for "Old East" at the University of North Carolina noted that "the whole of the brick work to be laid mortar made of lime & sand. The stone work underground a dry wall." University Archives, UNC, Chapel Hill.

dub (dubb)   To trim, smooth, and make level with an adz.

> 1628   A deposition noted that "several parcells of dubd board Ly at the Church at Hogg Iland." *VMHB*, 30.
> 1653   In building a house, a carpenter was to "rive, dubb, and draw all the boards." Surry Co., Va., Deed and Will Book 1652–1672.
> 1681   Rafters for a courthouse were "to be soe dubd that they may have a square shoulder to come upon the plate." Northumberland Co., Va., Court Order Book 1678–1698.
> 1737   "It is much better to Weatherboard with 3/4 boards and where ye Boards ly against ye Studs to dub it thin like ye feather edge." Thomas Pollock Letterbook, NCA&H.

ducking stool (cooking)   An instrument of punishment for nags, gossips, witches, and difficult individuals. Primarily intended for women, ducking stools were erected in every county at some convenient place, sometimes at a creek, a wharf, or at a specially constructed pit near the courthouse grounds. The stool varied in construction; it was sometimes no more than a chair suspended from a sweeplike pole. Others were fashioned with a frame carriage supported on wheels, which enabled the guilty party to be strapped into a seat and rolled and fully immersed in the water. Like many public punishments, the shame associated with ducking may have been far more painful than the actual experience. Although Virginia and other colonies and states required each county to have a ducking stool at hand, it is evident by the conspicuous absence of orders for duckings in court and parish records books in the Old Dominion that the instrument was seldom used. Ducking stools continued to be erected through the early 19th century.

> 1654   "For speciall reasons & considerations manifested to this Court It is ordered that Wm. Hattersley build sufficiently one duckinge or cookinge stoole in some convenient place in the little Creek in the parish of Lynhaven." Norfolk Co., Va., Will and Deed Book 1651–1656.
> 1716   It was declared that "Alexander Gwin [is] to Erect a Ducking Stoole at the uper End of the Town and at the End of Majr. Samuel Boush's wharff good and Substantiale." Norfolk Co., Va., Deed Book No. 9A.
> 1717   "John King undertakes to build a paire of Stocks, Pillory, & whipping post according to the pattern of them at Williamsburgh he finding iron worke and what else convenient and to build a ducking stoole to goe upon three wheels three foot high." Elizabeth City Co., Va., Deed, Will, and Order Book 1715–1721.
> 1822   John Ferneyhough was to be paid "for a Ducking Stool the sum of $30." Fredericksburg, Va., City Council Minute Book 1801–1829.

dumbwaiter   A mechanical conveyance for moving food, drink, and related articles between dining and service areas on different floors. Dumbwaiters were rare in 18th-century America, the earliest instance in the region being Thomas Jefferson's dining room installation at Monticello. Used in concert with subterranean service rooms, a house bell system, a rotating door of shelves and special serving tables, Jefferson's dumbwaiter served to limit the visibility of servants. In the 19th century, systems of this kind became more common in houses of the well-to-do.

> 1770   Thomas Jefferson's floor plan for Monticello shows voids in the sides of the chimney for the existing dumbwaiter installation. Coolidge Collection, Massachusetts Historical Society.
> 1820   Accounts for work performed at Bremo, Fluvanna County, Virginia, included a charge for a "D waiter." Cocke Papers, UVa.

dungeon A prison cell used to house those charged with felonious offenses or those of a desperate or disagreeable character. Although many prisons built in the colonial and early national period made little or no architectural distinction in the housing of criminal offenders and debtors, a few were concerned with securely confining the former. The walls, floors, and ceilings of the dungeons of county prisons were generally made with the strongest materials and constructed in the most secure manner possible. Most were small rooms with double or triple lining and, perhaps, one or two heavily barred openings. See also **prison.**

1697 "Richard Lewis one of the Carpinters . . . imployed ab[t] the State House worke has made great neglect of his time and is usually drunck every day. . . . ordered that if in Case the s[d] Lewis do not for the ffuture mind his work . . . the Sheriff of Ann Arundell County do . . . commit him to the Prison Dungeon there to remain . . . untill he shall better behave himself." *Archives of Maryland*, 23.

1745 Hugh Campbell paid "for digging the Dungeon of the prison." Frederick Co., Va., Court Order Book 1743–1745.

1813 Jail in Wayne County, North Carolina, was "to be built out of Sawed Timber. . . . The underpinning of all the House except the dungeon to be of Good brick or hewn Stone. . . . that part of the House called the dungeon the Joists to be placed within 4 inches of each other." Wayne Co., N.C., Miscellaneous Court Records, NCA&H.

Dutch brick See **brick.**

Dutch roof A curbed gable roof divided into two sections of unequal slope. The term appears in the early 18th century to describe what is now commonly referred to as a *gambrel roof.* This latter term, while in circulation in the North, did not appear in the South until after the first quarter of the 19th century. The origins of the term *Dutch roof* are obscure. Roofs of this type began to appear in eastern England and London in the 17th century, perhaps as a result of the strong architectural influence of the low countries of Europe and the concomitant desire for more habitable space in garrets. However, contemporary French and some English sources referred to such roofs as *Mansard roofs,* eponymously named for the 17th-century French architect Francois Mansart.

Dutch roof
Dutch roof truss, Nicolson House,
Williamsburg, Va.

1734 In Charleston, construction was underway on "a Pine Frame of a Dutch roof'd House, four rooms on a floor." *South Carolina Gazette.*

1761 A glebe house was to be built 50-by-18 feet "with a Dutch roof." Cumberland Parish, Lunenburg Co., Va., Vestry Book.

1774 A barn was to be built on a Norfolk County, Virginia, glebe 26-by-15 feet "with a Dutch roof." *Virginia Gazette or Norfolk Intelligencer.*

1804 On a farm was "one Dwelling house, eighteen by twenty feet, one Story high Dutch roof." Sussex Co., Del., Orphans Court Valuations IJ.

Dutch tile See **tile.**

dwelling house A term distinguishing the planter's residence from other houses—wash house, meat house, milk house, meal house, coach house—that often surrounded it. See also **house.**

dwelling plantation A term used in Maryland to designate a tract of cultivated land incorporating the landowner's residence. See also **home farm, home house, home plantation.**

1745 An estate account listed the buildings "on the dwelling plantation" and those "belonging to the home plantation." Queen Anne's Co., Md., Deed Book C.

D window
Pavilion 2, University of Virginia

D window   A semicircular window so named because of its resemblance to the letter "D" turned on its back. D windows gained popularity in the late 18th and early 19th centuries, when they were installed over entrance doors and in the tympanum of pediments. See also **transom window**.

> **1797**   A parsonage house was constructed with "a D window over the front door with Glass & Glazing." St. Michael's Parish, Charleston, S.C., Vestry Book.
> **1828**   Madison County, Virginia, courthouse specifications called for "the front pediment to be of plank with a D window in it." Malcolm Crawford Papers, VSL.

earthen floor   The name given by contemporaries to hard, packed, clay floors found in many dwellings, outbuildings, and some public structures throughout the South from the 17th through the early 19th centuries. Clay, loam, straw, lime, and other materials were often combined to produce a more durable surface. Many early structures in the Chesapeake had earthen floors, which eliminated the need for sawn floor boards, sleepers, and sometimes groundsills. Such floors continued to be used for outbuildings, slave houses, and among the poorer settlers on the frontier and in the backwoods.

> **1714**   Magistrates in Norfolk County, Virginia, granted leave to an individual "to build a little house or barbors shop between the Court House and prison . . . [with] a brick chimney and making one Earthen floor to the same." Norfolk Co., Va., Court Order Book 1710–1717.
> **1715**   A frame courthouse was to be built with "an earthen flower except where the justices is to sitt." Northampton Co., Va., Court Order Book 1710–1716.
> **1768**   A new glebe kitchen was to be built "28 by 16 feet 9 feet pitch with an inside brick chimney with a partition a cross the house . . . to be a good sawed Frame weather boarded with plank and cover'd with good chestnut shingles good earthen Floor." Fredericksville Parish, Louisa Co., Va., Vestry Book.
> **1798**   Standing in Queen Anne's County, Maryland, was "one frame dwelling house 32 feet by 16, one brick chimney earthen floor below divided into two rooms by a clapboard partition." Queen Anne's Co., Md., Guardian Bonds and Valuations SC.

earthfast   A modern name given to a variety of impermanent construction techniques that flourished in the southern colonies from the early 17th century through the Civil War. The term *earthfast* describes buildings whose lower framing members are not supported by masonry foundations but stand or lie directly on the ground or are sunk into postholes. Contemporaries often used the term *post in the ground* or, more obliquely, *Virginia house* to refer to this type of construction. For a more detailed description, see **Virginia house**.

ease   To form a curve at the junction of two members to prevent an awkward angle.

> **1764**   The steps of a step ladder were "to be eased at the bottom." Cumberland Parish, Lunenburg Co., Va., Vestry Book.

eating house, eating room (eat house, room)   A public or private building or room where meals are served; a dining room. See also **dining room**.

> **1741**   At Jamestown, Virginia, "there are several . . . Taverns and Eating Houses, for the Convenience of Voyagers and Travellers." Oldmixon, *The British Empire in America*, 1.
> **1798**   Among the buildings ordered constructed for the poor were "a kitchen for all a general cooking and eat house 30 by 16 feet with two fireplaces." Culpeper Co., Va., Court Order Book 1798–1802.
> **1799**   "For sale: A house on Shockoe Hill near the Capitol in Richmond. The house consists of an eating room 28 by 22 feet with a bow window." *Virginia Gazette*.

eaves (eave, eves) The lower part of a sloping roof projecting beyond the wall and forming a protective overhang. See also **cornice.**

> 1699 Specifications for "Ye Courthouse to have mondelion Eaves." Lancaster Co., Va., Court Order Book 1699–1702.
> 1711 The cornice of a courthouse to have "mundillions in the front, barge boards at the ends, all the back eaves to be well boxt with good moulding." Talbot Co., Md., Land Records RF 12.
> 1797 A market house roof in Charleston was "to be supported by Arched Pillars . . . to be covered with glazed Pan Tiles, and the eves to project 7 feet over the Pillars on every side." *City Gazette and Daily Advertiser.*

echinus

echinus A convex molding on a Doric capital located between the abacus above and the necking or top of the shaft below. Because of its near quarter-round profile, the elliptically shaped echinus was often associated with the similar form of the Roman ovolo in 18th-century English architectural publications. The echinus was embellished often with an egg and dart ornament, especially on the Ionic capital.

edge to edge Two surfaces butting against one another but not overlapping.

> 1755 A complaint about the wood sheathing inside a church stated that "instead of the plank being laid edge to edge to make a smooth neat wall the same is laid one upon another." St. George's Parish, Spotsylvania Co., Va., Vestry Book.
> 1810 The planks of the outer walls of a jail were to "stand perpendicular edge to edge." Randolph Co., N.C., Court Accounts, NCA&H.

edge tool Any tool with a sharp cutting edge or blade. In the woodworking trades, edge tools used by carpenters, joiners, and cabinetmakers include adzes, axes, chisels, draw knives, froes, gouges, hatchets, and planes. Throughout the colonial period, most such tools were imported from Great Britain.

edgewise (edgeways) An object with the narrow rather than the broad side positioned upward or forward to view.

> 1756 "Place bricks are used in paving dry, or laid in mortar, and they are put down flat or edgewise, if they are laid flat, thirty-two of them pave a yard square; but if they be placed edgewise it takes twice that number." Ware, *A Complete Body of Architecture.*
> 1771 In a church the "alleys [are] to be laid with tile or Brick edgways." St. George's Parish, Harford Co., Md., Vestry Book.
> 1808 The floor in the courthouse in Columbia, Tennessee should "be laid of brick edge-ways, or, 4 inch tile." *The Impartial Review and Cumberland Repository.*
> 1829 In the courtroom in Madison County, Virginia, "the floor [is] to be brick or tile, if of brick to be laid edge wise." Malcolm Crawford Papers, VSL.

edging A border of plants or shrubs surrounding a bed of flowers and the like.

> 1768 A Charleston woman advertised for sale "Flowering shrubs and box for edging beds, now growing in her garden." *South Carolina Gazette.*
> 1804 "January. Edgings for borders may be planted this month." Gardiner and Hepburn, *The American Gardener.*

edifice A fabric, structure, or building, especially one of large or comely proportions.

> 1722 At St. James, Goose Creek, South Carolina, "the Church, a beautiful Brick Edifice, was erected at ye Expence of ye Parishioners." SPG Letterbook B, SPGFP.
> 1751 "If any Gentlemen should want Plans, Bills of Scantling, or Bills of Charges, for any Fabric, or Public Edifice, [he] may have them by applying to the Subscriber . . . JOHN ARISS." *Maryland Gazette.*

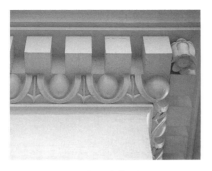

egg and dart
Pavilion 6, University of Virginia

1766 In New Bern, "the schoolhouse is at length inclosed & . . . is a large & decent Edifice for such a young country." SPG Letterbook B, SPGFP.

1810 In response to a questionnaire about architecture in various North Carolina localities, one correspondent noted that "the first Inhabitants of Duplin and Sampson Counties built and lived in log Cabbins, and as they became more Wealthy, some of them Built framed Clapboard Houses with Clay Chimneys; at present there are many good Houses, well Constructed, with Brick Chimneys, and glass lights; there are no Stone or Brick Walled houses, nor any that can be called Edifices." Thomas Henderson Letterbook, NCA&H.

egg and dart (egg and anchor) A classical molding consisting of convex egg shapes alternating with narrow vertical bands called darts or anchors. The ornament became a popular motif in the 18th century as an enrichment of ovolo moldings and was frequently used as the echinus on Ionic capitals.

elbow A sharp angular change in direction in a wall such as the recess for a window. In joinery, the vertical lining of a window recess between the floor and the boxing of the window shutter.

1750 An order required "the window seats to be 18 inches high with backs and Elbows to be painted as the inside Work." Newport Parish, Isle of Wight Co., Va., Vestry Book.

1766 Church records contain an "Account for Altering the Doors and Elbows of the old Pews." St. Michael's Parish, Charleston, S.C., Vestry Book.

1811 Construction of a Baltimore house included "Splayed Elbows [with] fancy mitered moulding." Riddell Accounts, Pleasants Papers, MHS.

electrical conductor, electrical rod, lightning rod A strip, bar, or piece of metal attached to a chimney, steeple, cupola, or apex of a roof and connected to the ground by a series of long rods that prevent lightning from striking a building by providing a direct path to the ground. Such devices came into common use in the third quarter of the 18th century and were called by various names, including *conductor*, *electrical rod*, *lightning rod*, *points*, and *Franklin*. By the end of the century, most public buildings and some dwellings had one or two electrical conductors perched upon their rooftops to divert the destructive force of lightning. See also **Franklin** (1).

1753 It was "Agreed that John Scott Gunsmith be employ'd to erect proper points at the steeple of this church to preserve the Building from Lightning." St. Philip's Parish, Charleston, S.C., Vestry Book.

1770 After a storm struck Charleston, "the Electrical Rod" at St. Michael's Church was "examined & found to have no deficiency, wch the Vestry were apprehensive of but the Joints being slack Messrs. Gilbert & Worthington were desir'd to tighten them, and . . . the Vestry were of opinion it would be better to have the Rod taken down & placed on the outside, from the highest Gallery & have screw joints instead of being hook'd as they are at present." St. Michael's Parish, Charleston, S.C., Vestry Book.

1795 A lighthouse on the Pamlico Sound in North Carolina was "to be furnished with two complete electrical conductors or rods with points." *North Carolina Gazette*.

1819 "Electrical rods- As soon as the season of Thunder and Lightning is approaching, it may be useful to know that if the points are not clean and sharp, they are of little use—if they are of Gold or Platina, they will not rust for a long time—but if of Steel or Iron, they will rust in the course of a year at least. The points may also be rendered, in a great measure useless, by being melted and blunted in the transmission of large quantities of the electric Fluid." *Star of Federalism*.

elegant Tastefully refined and luxurious. The term came into fashion in the South in the early 18th century to describe modes of social behavior. By mid-century, it was being used along with *genteel* to describe objects, buildings, and landscapes that presented a pleasing aspect through regularity of form, elaboration of design, and intricacy and skill of execution. See also **fashionable, genteel, taste.**

> 1747 After a fire destroyed the capitol in Williamsburg, the governor urged the General Assembly "to apply the most effectual Means for restoring that Royal Fabric to its former Beauty and Magnificence, with the like elegant and capacious Apartments, so well adapted to all the weighty Purposes of Government." *Journals of the House of Burgesses*, 7.
>
> 1767 A dwelling in Kent County, Maryland, contained "eight genteel Rooms, Six of which are papered with most elegant Paper, five of which are genteel Lodging-Rooms." *Maryland Gazette.*
>
> 1770 In Annapolis "during the winter there are assemblies every fortnight; the room for dancing is large; the construction elegant." Eddis, *Letters from America.*
>
> 1774 A visitor to Mount Airy in Richmond County, Virginia, observed that "here is an elegant Seat! The House is . . . built of Stone, & finished curiously, & ornamented with various paintings." *Journal and Letters of Philip Vickers Fithian.*
>
> 1777 "MARDUN V. EVINGTON . . . would be glad to be employed as a master workman in the various branches of architecture, either publick or private buildings, from the most elegant and superb, down to the gentleman's plain country seat." *Virginia Gazette.*
>
> 1798 For sale in Charleston: "A FEW ELEGANT Marble Chimney Pieces." *City Gazette and Daily Advertiser.*
>
> 1818 A dwelling in Fayetteville, North Carolina, was to be "finished in the first

elevation 1. A geometrical drawing depicting the vertical plane of a building, part of a building, or an object. Although elevations appear in the late colonial period, there is little evidence that they were used on any regular basis in the 17th or early 18th century. As with plans, elevational drawings for the most part were used to develop design ideas or convey those ideas to clients and were not intended as working drawings for craftsmen. Architects, craftsmen, and other designers most often devised elevations for buildings that had unusual structural requirements or design features outside the local building tradition. Following European and English graphic conventions, some elevational features in early American drawings were overlaid on ground plans.

elevation (1)
John Izard Middleton, elevation for a dwelling, South Carolina, 1811

> 1734 In Charleston, "Mr. Peter Chassereau, newly come from London, surveys lands and makes neat maps thereof, draws plans and elevations of all kinds of buildings, whatsoever." *South Carolina Gazette.*
>
> 1755 An elevation "shews the Stories, their Heights and outward Appearances of the whole Building." Salmon, *Palladio Londinensis.*
>
> 1774 A courthouse was to be built in Caroline County, Maryland, "agreeable to plans and elevations" produced by architect William Buckland. *Maryland Gazette.*
>
> 1788 A jail was to be built "agreeable to a plan of the floor and elevation made out by Edwd Vieller." Prince William Co., Va., Deed Book 1787–1791.

2. The height of vertical plane of a building; the wall height.

> 1800 A Culpeper County, Virginia, clerk's office was to be "44 feet long and 21 feet wide, the elevation 19 feet." *Virginia Herald.*

ell A rear addition or wing constructed at a right angle to the main structure. The term was rarely used in the early South.

> 1744 A minister was to "febrecate erect and build to the gleeb house . . . a roome twenty foot long and twenty six foot wide in the form of an ell." St. Mark's Parish, Culpeper Co., Va., Vestry Book.

embankment A raised earthen bank or mound constructed to hold a river or stream in a confined course.

emboss
Composition ornament applied to
chimney piece, 60 Montague Street,
Charleston, S.C.

emboss To carve or mold in relief; to decorate a surface with raised ornament. See also **relief.**

> 1734 "EMBOSSING . . . is the forming, or fashioning of Works in Relievo, whether cut with a Chissel, or otherwise; it is a kind of Sculpture or Engraving, wherein the Figures stick out from the Plane whereon it is engraven, and according as they are more or less protuberant. It is called by the *Italians*, Basso, Mezzo, or Alto Relievo, and by the *English*, Bass-Relief, Mean Relief, or High Relief." *Builder's Dictionary.*

embrasure 1. In civil architecture, a splayed opening toward the inner face of a window or door. See also **splay.**

2. In military architecture, the openings between merlons in a battlement; a crenel. See also **battlement.**

> 1716 "The place where" Jamestown, Virginia, "is built is on an island, it was fortified with a small rampart with embrasures, but now all is gone to ruin." Maury, *Memoirs of a Huguenot Family.*
> 1777 "A little above" the decayed village of Jamestown, "is a small Battery with Embrasures for six Guns, but only two are mounted." *VMHB*, 62.

encarpus A carved festoon of fruit and flowers, used to decorate a frieze. See also **festoon.**

end board A shaped, wooden board at the eaves that terminates and encloses the end of a classical cornice when there is no return.

engine house A building or space within a building where fire engines and other fire-fighting equipment are stored. Because of the constant threat of fire, corporations constructed engine houses in the major towns of the South in the second half of the 18th century and equipped them with small, hand-powered, water-pumping engines that could be pulled around town by volunteers. In some of the smaller towns, the engine house was located on the public lots, sometimes standing separately or incorporated into a shed or wing of a market house. Despite the effort to maintain these engines in good working order, many, such as the ones owned by the corporation of Williamsburg, were in constant disrepair and did little to contain serious fires. As a result, towns such as Charleston suffered from a plague of serious fires that destroyed several blocks of buildings well into the 19th century.

> 1783 "On application of the Fire Masters in Charlestown for leave to erect an Engine house on the lot belonging the Church, leave was granted." Congregational Church, Charleston, S.C., Church Record Book.
> 1788 Payment was made for placing "sand in the engine house." Fredericksburg, Va., City Council Minute Book 1782–1801.
> 1807 A newspaper notice read: "Fire Masters' Department, WANTED to be built immediately, on the north side of the Poor House Lot, an ENGINE HOUSE, of brick, to be 24 feet wide, 18 feet deep, and 8 feet story, with a paved floor, tiled roof, and partition wall." *Charleston Times.*

English bond See **bond.**

English frame, English house 1. The name given by 17th- and early 18th-century Chesapeake residents to well-constructed frame buildings, in contrast to the earthfast clapboard work of the *Virginia house.* The term was used to distinguish a quality of construction associated with the more durable techniques of traditional English box framing. In contrast to small riven framing members, lap joints, and earthfast construction, Chesapeake builders thought of an English house as one with a tightly fitting sawn frame secured with mortise and tenon joints. An English frame also had a number of additional intermediary stiffeners, such as summers and girders along with groundsills. Roof framing often consisted of a series of principal rafters that were tied together by girders or cross beams. On each slope, one or two purlins were mortised into the principals. Despite the name, many of the joinery techniques employed in fabricating an English house in the Chesapeake were far simpler than those practiced in England and New England. At Bacon's Castle (1665) in Surry County, Virginia, the principal rafter roof would have been considered by contemporaries as a solid English frame, yet the collars are lapped into the rafters, a practice that was common to clapboard carpentry in the Chesapeake but unusual in England in the 17th century.

1680   In Virginia, an act was passed to build a "twenty foot Square house English frame under pinned with brick, flowr'd with Sawen boards, fil'd on ye inside & Sealed and double covered." *Journals of the House of Burgesses, 2.*

1686   A planter in Stafford County, Virginia, advised an English friend contemplating settlement that he should "not build either a great, or English framed house, for labour is so intolerably dear, & workmen so idle & negligent that the building of a good house, to you there will seem insupportable, for this I can assure you when I built my own house, & agreed as cheap as I could with workmen, & as carefully & as diligently took care that they followed their work notwithstanding . . . the frame of my house stood me in more money . . . than a frame of the same Dimensions would cost in London, by a third. . . . Your brother Joseph's building that Shell of a house without Chimneys or partition, & not one tittle of workmanship about it more than a Tobacco house work." *William Fitzhugh and his Chesapeake World.*

1704   A courthouse was to be built with "a good English frame, to stand upon locust or cedar blocks. The frame to be all sawed, to be double raftered." Middlesex Co., Va., Court Order Book 1694–1705.

1707   An undertaker was engaged to build "a good substantiall English fram'd house with summers, girders and half joists." Westmoreland Co., Va., Court Order Book 1705–1721.

1737   The vestry agreed with a workman to build a glebe house with "the frame to be well sawed, and neatly & well set together, after the manner of English building." Truro Parish, Fairfax Co., Va., Vestry Book.

2. A building constructed by the English settlers of the Chesapeake to distinguish it from structures erected by the natives.

1654   Francis Yeardley of Virginia agreed "to build the King" of the Indians near Roanoke Island, North Carolina, "an English house." Salley, *Narratives of Early Carolina.*

1662   A "complaint [was made by] the king of the mattapony Indians concerning the burning of his English house" by a white settler. Hening, *Statutes at Large, 2.*

English garden   A carefully cultivated landscape of informality with open vistas punctuated by clumps of trees, irregular lakes, and large grassy areas unencumbered by walls and geometric plantings. The dominant figure in the English garden movement, which swept away the formality of an earlier style and transformed many of the great estates of Britain during the middle of the 18th century, was Capability Brown, whose influence and ideas were eventually felt in America by the end of the century. Although few southern planters could rival the grand scale that characterized this gardening form, a number sought to introduce the spirit of an improved *natural* landscape to their estates through the use of ditch fencing, clumped plantings, and an occasional temple to create interesting vistas.

1782 Thomas Jones's plantation on the Pamunkey River in Virginia was "embellished with a garden laid out in the English style. It is even said that this kind of a park, which is bounded in part by the river, yields not in beauty to those English models which we are now imitating with much success." Chastellux, *Travels in North America*, 2.

1788 At Mount Vernon, George Washington was "laying out his grounds with great taste in the English fashion. If Brown was alive and here would certainly say this spot had great Capabilities but he could never call it good soil." *The American Journals of Lt. John Enys.*

1789 The grounds at Mount Vernon were "laid out somewhat in the form of English gardens, in meadows and grass grounds, ornamented with little copies, circular clumps and single trees. A small part on the margin of the river, where the English fallow-deer, and American wild-deer are seen through the thickets." Morse, *American Geography.*

1794 Governor John Howard's estate near Baltimore "was upon the plan and possessed all the elegance of an English villa. Situated upon the verge of the descent upon which Baltimore stands, its grounds formed a beautiful slant toward the Chesapeake. From the taste with which they were laid out, it would seem that America already possessed a Haverfield or a Repton." Twining, *Travels in America 100 Years Ago.*

1801 "The Gardens" at the Hermitage near Wilmington, North Carolina, "were large, and laid out in the English style." *Autobiography and Diary of Mrs. Eliza Clitherall.*

enrich
Parlor chimney piece, Shirley, Charles City County, Va.

enrich To enhance with decoration. The term was often used to describe moldings or other elements that contained carved ornaments, or applied to composition elements.

1760 A cabinetmaker's account for fabricating the pulpit at a Charleston church included "22 feet Large Ogee fully Enriched." Williams, *St. Michael's.*

1783 The walls of the council room in the Governor's House in New Bern "are covered with modern wainscot with a Carved enrichment in the Base and Sur Base." Hawks Letter, Miranda Papers, Academia Nacional de la Historia, Caracas.

1802 The construction accounts for the Tayloe house in Washington, D.C., include entries for "Composition; bed mould . . . Cornice and bed mould . . . Moulded architrave & Enrichment . . . ornamental Pilaster, Base & Cap . . . Plain moulded cornice." Tayloe Papers, VHS.

1805 "The principal sculpture required" at the Capitol in Washington "will be of 24 Corinthian capitals . . . and of an enriched entablature of 147 feet. . . . There are besides 5 pannels . . . enriched with foliage, and an Eagle of colossal size in the frieze." *The Correspondence and Miscellaneous Papers of Benjamin Henry Latrobe*, 2.

entablature (entabliture) The whole of the horizontal part of a classic order above the columns, generally consisting of three parts. The lowest part, the *architrave*, rests upon the abaci of the columns; the center part, the *frieze*, sits atop the architrave; and the uppermost part is the *cornice*. The entablature of the different classical orders is subdivided into a variety of smaller and distinctive parts. Colonial builders freely adapted the prescriptive rules governing arrangement and proportion of entablatures set out in English architectural books to devise ones that ranged from the utmost simplicity to the highly imaginative.

1778 Robert Carter of Nomini Hall in Westmoreland County, Virginia, wrote to a joiner that "the present Cornice of my dwelling House here, is to Stand as it now is. The Entabliture of all the Columns which are to be erected is to correspond with the Cornice mentioned above." Robert Carter Letterbook, Duke.

1783 "The ornaments over the marble Chimney Commonly called Tabernacle Frame" in the council chamber of the Governor's House in New Bern "consists of Corinthian Columns and pillasters fluited with the proper Entablature fully inric[hed] and an open pediment." Hawks Letter, Miranda Papers, Academia Nacional de la Historia, Caracas.

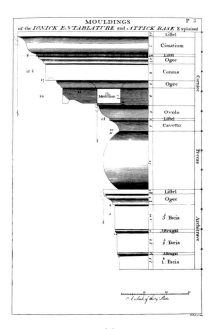

MOULDINGS P 3
of the *IONICK ENTABLATURE* and *ATTICK BASE* Explained

entablature

1828 In Madison County, Virginia, a builder noted that "the Cost of your Court House Embraces the following. . . . A Tuscan Cornice with a full entabliture, Drawn in proportion to its Hight." Malcolm Crawford Papers, VSL.

entasis The slight swelling intentionally given to a column or pilaster to correct an optical illusion of concavity present in straight-sided ones. See also **swelling** (1).

entresol (entersole) A low story located between the ground floor and the primary upper floor, sometimes treated architecturally as part of the ground floor; a mezzanine story. English writers sometimes defined it as a smaller story above the main floor of a building. The term was rarely used in the South.

1803 President Jefferson noted that "from the sum of 50,000 D. we shall take between 5, and 10,000 for covering the North wing of the Capitol and the President's house. The residue of 40 to 45,000 D. will be employed in building the South wing as far as it will go. I think it will raise the external walls to the uppermost window-sills, being those of the entresols." *The Correspondence and Miscellaneous Papers of Benjamin Henry Latrobe*, 1.

entry Access into a space through a gate or doorway; a vestibule, lobby, or entrance passage in a building or between buildings. Although commonly used in northern colonies to describe such a space, the term was less popular in settlements south of the Delaware River, where the term *passage* was predominant. See also **hall** (2), **passage** (1).

1657 A servant, "coming into the Entry" of a hall, "made a stopp." *Archives of Maryland*, 54.
1707 A glebe house was to be built with "two rooms and an entry below stairs." Christ Church Parish, Middlesex Co., Va., Vestry Book.
1712 The vestry hired a workman "to build A Passage or Entry from ye Vestry House Door to ye Church Door five foot wide." All Saints Parish, Calvert Co., Md., Vestry Book.
1748 A dwelling for sale in Charleston contained "a paved Entry 9 Feet wide." *South Carolina Gazette*.
1789 A plan for a dwelling in Charleston called for "two rooms in a floor and an entry leading to a stair case in or near the centre of the said house nine feet wide in the clear." Charleston Co., S.C., Deed Book R.
1812 Courthouse to be built in Murfreesborough, Tennessee, was to feature "an entry through the middle of the upper story, and partitions, so as to make two rooms on each side of the passage." *Nashville Whig*.

escutcheon (scutcheon) A protective metal plate surrounding the keyhole of a door.

1787 An estate inventory listed "12 Escutcheons" valued at "2/6." Norfolk Co., Va., Appraisements 1775–1800.

escutcheon
Prestwould, Mecklenburg County, Va.

espalier A framework or wall support system upon which ornamental and fruit trees were pruned and trained to protect plants from wind or weather. Avid gardeners hoped to taste the fruits of their labor much earlier than the fruit produced by trees which stood alone.

1804 "January. This month prune espalier trees." Gardiner and Hepburn, *The American Gardener*.

eustyle See **intercolumniation.**

exchange (change) An open space or building where merchants assemble for the transaction of business. Most gatherings involved the sale of bills of goods, securities, and bonds rather than actual merchandise. Above the open or arcaded space, one or two rooms were constructed for public meetings and entertainments.

> **1750** A woman was hired "twice every week to Sweep the Change." Wilmington, N.C., City Records.
>
> **1767** In Charleston an "exchange and custom-house [is to] be erected . . . extending on the Bay from north to south 92 feet, and from east to west 72, and to contain (besides several cellars to be lett) the collector's and naval offices, and a large room for the meeting of the inhabitants." *South Carolina Gazette.*
>
> **1804** In Savannah, "proposals will be received by the Building Committee on the Exchange for the finishing of the same." *Columbian Museum and Savannah Advertiser.*

extrados   The exterior curve or surface of an arch or vault. The term generally denotes the top of the arch voussoirs. See also **intrados.**

eye   See **hook and eye.**

fabric (fabrick)   A building or edifice, especially a church; the framing or construction of a building.

> **1673** A magistrate hired carpenters to erect "a fabrick or building an ordinary neere unto the Court house." Charles City Co., Va., Court Order Book 1672–1673.
>
> **1711** In New Castle, Delaware, "our Church is a stately Fabrick but still in distress by reason of the poverty of the people." SPG Letterbook A, SPGFP.
>
> **1737** Carpenters requested "to view the New Brick Church in Charles Town, and to Report . . . what repairs they judge necessary to be made, in any part of the said fabrick." St. Philip's Parish, Charleston, S.C., Vestry Book.

facade   The principal front or face of a building; more generally, any side of a building facing a street, garden, or public space. The term was seldom used during the colonial period and early national era.

face   *(n.)* The front of a building, or a finished or exposed surface of a member or object.   *(v.)* To apply a decorative molding or cover over a rough frame or unfinished surface, especially an architrave around apertures. See also **facing.**

> **1760** The vestry ordered that "the windows of said chapel to be sashed, faced, and glazed." Cunningham Chapel Parish, Clarke Co., Va., Vestry Book.
>
> **1799** Philadelphia carpenter John Langdon agreed to "make the window and Door frames, put them in, face the windows and Doors" for John Steele's house in Rowan County, North Carolina. Steele Collection, SHC.
>
> **1806** In William Nichols's restoration of St. Paul's Church in Edenton, North Carolina, "the front of the Galleries [is] to be framed in pannells with a moulding on the face." St. Paul's Parish, Edenton, N.C., Loose Vestry Papers.

facing   Decorative molding applied over framing members and other unfinished surfaces. Perhaps following Scottish usage, the term was frequently employed in the South to describe door, window, and fireplace architraves. See also **face** (*v.*).

> **1745** The "doors windows and seats" were to be finished "after the manner of the Upper Church & all proper facing and moulding." Truro Parish, Fairfax Co., Va., Vestry Book.
>
> **1758** Carpentry work on a building included "faising of 2 mantle trees." Chowan Co., N.C., Civil Actions, 1760, NCA&H.
>
> **1770** A bill was submitted for "making window sash & facing for the Store containing 12 lights . . . facing fire place & making wash & chair boards . . . making 3 plain doors & facing." Bedford Co., Va., Loose Court Papers.

factory   A building or group of buildings with machinery and other facilities for the manufacture of goods.

1805 In Fredericksburg, Virginia, "Davis & Southwick . . . have lately established a Cut Nail Manufactory . . . Blacksmith's work of any kind will be done at this Factory. . . . Also machines will be made to carry on the Cut-Nail business." *Virginia Herald*.

1808 Lexington, Kentucky, "abounds with factories. They manufacture here, annually, upwards of 200,000 yards of cotton bagging." *Charleston Courier*.

fall   See **fell.**

falling ax   See **ax.**

falling garden (falls, fall garden)   A formally landscaped area consisting of a series of terraced levels with sloping fronts and sides faced with turf. Each individual descent was known as a fall. Movement between levels was accomplished by means of grass ramps. Such gardens were sited on naturally sloping ground or on the bank of a river. Often when a dwelling house was newly built, the soil that came out of the excavated cellar and foundations were used to shape the terraced falls. See also **garden.**

1770 A visitor to Mount Clare, near Baltimore, "took a great deal of Pleasure in looking at . . . a very large Falling Garden. . . . You step out of the Door into the Bowlg Green from which the Garden Falls & when You stand on the Top of it there is such a Uniformity of Each side." *VMHB*, 45.

1783 At Westover in Charles City County, Virginia, there was "a view of a prettily falling grass plat . . . about 300 by 100 yards in extent an extensive prospect of James River and of all the Country and some Gentlemen's seats on the other side." Shippen, *Westover Described in 1783*.

1803 A house and grounds for sale in Stevensburg in Culpeper County, Virginia, contained "a handsome fall Garden." *Virginia Herald*.

falling wainscot   Partition wainscot that is hinged at its bottom or top rail, so that it can be lifted up or down to create a large space. Beginning in the third quarter of the 18th century, a number of Friends meetinghouses contained partition walls so constructed that divided the men's section from the women's. When services were held, the wainscotted partitions were folded up so that the meetinghouse was one open space. When segregated business meetings were held, the wainscotted partitions were closed, creating privacy for each of two groups. Although many of these wainscotted partitions operated like sash windows with pulleys and weights, a few were hinged and fastened to the ceiling when opened. Some courthouses also contained flexible partitions in jury room suites, which were thrown open for large meetings and public entertainments. Taverns and hotels likewise had these features for the same purpose. See also **wainscot.**

1793 "The partition to divide one of the end rooms on the upper story" of "Old East" at the University of North Carolina was "to be of falling wainscot." University Archives, UNC, Chapel Hill.

false (false + noun)   **1.** A subsidiary or supplementary element or member; something substituted for or serving in the place of the original or designated feature.

1724 A church was to be repaired with "false Rafters of Seven or Eight foot long" added to the roof. All Faith Parish, St. Mary's Co., Md., Vestry Book.

1790 On a Delaware farm was a "post and rail fence out of repair mostly supported by false posts pinned to the original posts, and the other original posts nearly rotten off." Sussex Co., Del., Orphans Court Valuations E.

1793 The town sergeant was ordered "to have a false partition made between the Cage, and the debtors Room." Norfolk, Va., Common Hall Order Book 1736–1798.

false plate
Granary, Marks Farm, Southampton
County, Va.

fanlight, fan sash
First Presbyterian Church, New Bern, N.C.

2. A nonfunctioning element added to match existing features for purposes of symmetry and balance. The most common features were false, blind, blank, or dummy doors, windows, chimneys, and chimney stacks. See also **blank window.**

> 1826 Revisions of specifications for the Goochland County, Virginia, courthouse noted that "the false chimnies were dispensed with." Cocke Papers, UVa.

false plate A board or scantling resting on top of the ends of joists or tie beams used to support common rafters. Developed in the Chesapeake region in the middle of the 17th century as a means of economizing the use of labor, the false plate allowed the roof framing system to be structurally independent of the wall frame. Characteristic of the upper South, colonial and early-19th century carpenters sometimes notched the false plate at a 45-degree angle over the joists, creating a tilted false plate. See also **raising plate.**

> 1673 A house was "to be jointed with false plate." Middlesex Co., Va., Court Records.
> 1688 A house for Captain William Whittington of Somerset County, Maryland, was to be "forty foot long over getted of each side one foot without the plates . . . rafters three & four inches thick in the flatt sides of them . . . Rafters eighteen foot & halfe Longe . . . plates forty foot long six & seven inches on the flatt sides . . . & the false plates for each side four & five inches on the flatt side." Touart, *Somerset.*
> 1771 A 40-foot Virginia tobacco house was to be built with "plates 12 inches squar, False plate 4 by 5 inches." Hubbard Papers, SHC.

fanlight, fan sash A semicircular window over a door. Such windows came into fashion in America in the late 18th and early 19th centuries. Although many fanlights were simple wood-frame sash, others displayed a virtuosity of ornamental design executed with thin metallic muntins. See also **D window, sidelight.**

> 1796 Architect Gabriel Manigualt of Charleston wanted "a Fanlight for a front door, made of the same materials as Mr. Macomb, Mr. Lynch, & a number of other handsome ones you have at New York, but of rather a plainer pattern than those I have mentioned." Manigault Papers, South Caroliniana Library.
> c. 1798 In John Dickinson's townhouse in Wilmington, Delaware, the entrance passage was "to be lighted by a door with a fan over it and by a small long window on each side." Dickinson Plantation Files, Delaware Bureau of Museums.
> 1817 A firm of painters in Alexandria, Virginia "engaged a first rate Plumber and Fan & side-light maker, either in lead or copper." *Alexandria Herald.*
> 1818 "Fan-Sash Making. METAL FAN-SASHES, of various descriptions, will be made by the subscriber at his shop. . . . The want of a Metal Fan-Sash Manufactory in Alexandria, has hitherto been severely felt by builders and others, who have been compelled to make use of wood, which is neither elegant nor durable." *Alexandria Gazette and Daily Advertiser.*

farmhouse A dwelling on a farm. The term was not very common until the early 19th century.

> 1773 South of "Acheepoo bridge" in South Carolina, a traveler "came sometimes to avenues leading from the high road terminated by farm houses at a quarter, half, and sometimes three quarters of a mile." Finlay, *Journal.*

farm quarter See **quarter** (3).

fascia (facia) A flat, horizontal, projecting band or division in an architrave that is broader than a fillet. In a more general sense, the vertical plane of any projecting band, belt, string course, or cornice member. See also **belting, fillet, platband.**

1811   Construction of a chimney piece included the "mantel, shelf, fascia & mould-ing." Riddell Accounts, Pleasants Papers, MHS.
1812   In the design of a college building in Pennsylvania, "I propose a stone or Marble fascia of 8 inches at every story." *The Correspondence and Miscellaneous Papers of Benjamin Henry Latrobe*, 3.

fashion   The make or form of an object. The customary mode of fabricating or shaping something; the particular pattern of an object. See also **fashionable, style, taste.**

1715   The brick of a church floor was "to be Laid Herring-Bone Fashion." St. Paul's Parish, Kent Co., Md., Vestry Book.
1725   Dwellings in Charleston were "glazed with Sash Window after the English Fashion." *South Carolina Historical Magazine*, 61.
1761   An addition to a church was to be "of the same weadth other demensions and fashion of the present building." Augusta Parish, Augusta Co., Va., Vestry Book.
1796   "The stile of houses of private Gentlemen" in Norfolk, Virginia, "is plain and decent, but of the fashion of 30 Years ago." *The Correspondence and Miscellaneous Papers of Benjamin Henry Latrobe*, 1.
1817   In ordering furniture from New York for Hayes, a plantation near Edenton, North Carolina, James C. Johnston advised a friend who was purchasing items for him that "it is unnecessary for me to say that I wish them of the plainest and neatest kind and not in the extreme of the fashion but what would suit a moderate liver in New York. A man by appearing very different from his neighbors is more apt to excite their ridicule and perhaps envy than their esteem & respect." Hayes Collection, SHC.

fashionable   In terms of architecture, something executed, finished, or conforming to the latest mode of fashion; stylish. Emerging in the early 18th century, this descriptive term was used in early America to distinguish the shape, proportion, and finish of certain architectural elements. Such elements conformed to standards of classical design as discussed and illustrated in English and European treatises and pattern books, and interpreted and promulgated by builders and craftsmen. Contemporaries generally recognized that fashionable forms were not part of the indigenous, commonplace manner of building, but part of a cosmopolitan design aesthetic. See also **genteel, neat, style, taste.**

1723   The cornice of a courthouse was described as "a fashionable over Jet." *Higher-Court Records of North Carolina*, 5.
1735   Specifications called for "fashionable stares to go into the court house chamber." Onslow Co., N.C., Court Minute Book, NCA&H.
1760   A church was to "be Compleatly Finished in the most Fashionable and Serviceable manner." Augusta Parish, Augusta Co., Va., Vestry Book.

featheredge (fether edge)   A sawn or riven plank, board, or shingle that has a thin edge on one side so that in section the piece is wedge shaped. Featheredged planks, boards, and shingles were applied to walls or roofs, so that the thick edge of one piece overlaps the thin or featheredge of one below it. The term appears in the late 17th century and goes out of usage in the first decades of the 19th century.

1698   The roof on a courthouse was "to be covered with featheredge poplar plank clear of sapp." Lancaster Co., Va., Court Order Book 1696–1702.
1730   A vestry house was to be constructed with a "Bastard frame weatherboarded with Clap boards roofed with Feather Edged Shingles." St. Luke's Parish, Queen Anne's Co., Md., Vestry Book.
1737   A North Carolina merchant recommended that "it is much better to Weatherboard with 3/4 boards and where ye Boards ly against ye Studs to dub it thin like ye feather edge so that between ye studs ye boards at ye upper edge remain 3/4 of

an inch when nail'd on which prevents them from splitting with ye heat of ye sun as ye feather edge, being generally thin generally does." Thomas Pollock Letterbook, NCA&H.

1818 The exterior of a courthouse was to be enclosed with "featheredge plank to be 9 inches wide of the usual thickness to raise 6 inches and nailed on with 20d nails." Northampton Co., N.C., Miscellaneous Court Records, NCA&H.

fell (fall)   To cut down a tree with an ax.

1658 "John Banister . . . shall fall, mall, and bring in place and readiness all such timber as shall be useful and necessary for the finishing and fitting of the two houses." Charles City County Court Order Book 1658–1661.

1686 In a letter to an English friend, a planter observed that "we have timber for nothing, but felling & getting in place, the frame of my house stood me in more money . . . than a frame of the same Dimensions would cost in London." *William Fitzhugh and His Chesapeake World.*

felling ax   See **ax.**

fence   A structural barrier of wood or iron used to define, separate, or enclose areas like fields, pastures, yards, and gardens. Among the earliest legislation in the southern colonies were directives for fencing in cultivated ground and other spaces requiring protection from animal and human intruders. Land was often characterized as "well fenced," "under a good fence," and "within fence." See also **ditch, pale, palisade, post and plank fence, post and rail fence, worm fence.**

1623 The Virginia General Assembly declared "that every freeman shall fence in a quarter of an acre of ground before Whitsuntide next to make a garden." Hening, *Statutes at Large*, 1.

1797 A plantation included an "outside fence and other Cross fences so as to lay the said plantation in four different fields or parts." Sussex Co., Del. Orphans Court Valuations F.

festoon
United States Bank (now City Hall),
Charleston, S.C., 1801

festoon   A decorative design consisting of a string of flowers, leaves, fruit, foliage, drapery, ribbons, and other ornaments suspended together in a curve or swag between two points. Occasionally, other elements were added to the design, such as skulls or bucrania, military arms, and cherubs. In the early architecture of the South, festoons were relatively unusual, appearing on some entablature friezes. They grew increasingly popular at the end of the 18th century, when they became a staple motif in the composition ornaments decorating chimney pieces. The pattern was also used on paperhangings. See also **encarpus.**

1763 The second stage of the steeple of St. Michael's in Charleston was described as having "Sashed windows and festoons alternately on each face, with pilasters and a cornice." Milligen Johnston, *A Short Description of the Province of South-Carolina.*

1797 Advertised for sale were "the much admired composition ornaments for chimneypieces" including "Rich flower festoons, Wheat, do. Neat small flower, do. Vine and ivey, do. Neat Husk, do." *Federal Gazette and Baltimore Advertiser.*

file   A metal bar with one or more of its surfaces covered with raised teeth or sharp edges, used for abrading or smoothing surfaces or sharpening the blades of various tools.

fill   1. To pack clay, brick, stone, or some other material between the wooden framing members of a wall to provide some insulation and structural rigidity. Brick or clay filled walls appeared in habitable

spaces as well as in some service buildings, such as kitchens. *Fill* rather than *nog* was the most common term for this method of insulation. See also **nogging.**

1681 The interior of a framed courthouse was "to be Lathed, filled, and white limed, or filled and sealed" only at the magistrates' end. Northumberland Co., Va., Court Order Book 1678–1698.

1702 "All the Particon Walls and Gable Ends above and below" in a courthouse were "to be well lathed and filled up with dirt and well plastered with well tempred Mortar and well mixed Lime and haire and white washed." Essex Co., Va., Will and Deed Book No. 10.

1727 A plantation owner sent to his overseer "10 M nails for lathing and filling in all my Quarters and pray let it be done out of hand that the quarters be made as warm for the people as we can." Robert Carter Papers, UVa.

1749 The Dashiell farm in Somerset County, Maryland, included a "fraimed Kitchen . . . wetherbarded with plank . . . the sides fild in with brick." Touart, *Somerset.*

1754 A seven by eight-foot slave cabin in Lancaster County, Virginia was to be built "and lathed and filled, so as to be thorough dry before cold weather." Joseph Ball Letterbook, LC.

1773 A theater was to be constructed with "a Brick Foundation at least ten feet in height above the surface of the ground and thereupon a wooden frame of good and Substantial materials [is] to be filled up with Bricks and also covered with brick on the outside." Charleston Co., S.C., Land Records Book 1779–1781.

2. To place clay or some other materials beneath groundsills to close gaps, or to raise the level of an earthen floor in a similar manner.

1759 Warehouses "want to be filled up under the sills with shells." Accomack Co., Va., Court Order Book 1753–1763.

1821 A poorhouse floor was "to be filled up twelve inches above the common level of the earth with dirt after being well rammed." King George Co., Va., Court Order Book 1817–1822.

fillet A narrow band or molding, often square in section. In general any rectangular molding that separates larger moldings, ornaments, or areas. The small bands separating the flutes of columns are also known as fillets. See also **fascia, list.**

fillister (philister) A rabbet or groove; a plane for cutting rabbets and grooves. For a more detailed description of the configuration and function of different types of planes, see **plane.**

finial An ornament that crowns the top of a canopy, pediment, newel, spire, or similar structures. See also **pyramid.**

fireback See **chimney back.**

fireplace (fier place) An open recess in a wall at the base of a chimney. It was only in the last two decades of the 17th century that the term came into use to define the opening of the chimney where the fire is made. Before that time the term *hearth* or simply *chimney* was used to describe this feature. *Hearth*, and occasionally *fire hearth*, appear through the first half of the 18th century as synonyms for *fireplace*. However, early in the century, *hearth* began to take on a more restricted meaning, signifying only the floor of the fireplace and the masonry that extended into the room beyond the chimney breasts. See also **chimney, hearth.**

> **1689** A brick courthouse was to have "in ye lower Roome two Chimneys or fier places att one End one below & another above ye Lower Room." Norfolk Co., Va., Deed Book 1686–1695.
>
> **1694** At one end of the statehouse in Annapolis, "a place of Judicature, in such forme as at the Stadt house now at St. Maryes is, at the other End a Chimney with a Fire place therein both belowe and above." *Archives of Maryland*, 38.
>
> **1707** A glebe dwelling was to be constructed with "double out side brick chimneys with fyer places above stairs at each end." Christ Church Parish, Middlesex Co., Va., Vestry Book.
>
> **1751** Plans were made for a minister's house with "a kitchen at one end 18 feet by 16 a stack of brick chimneys to contain three fire places and an oven." Christ Church Parish, Savannah, Ga., Church Records, GHS.
>
> **1758** A bricklayer was paid for "building one stack of chimneys with two angle fireplaces" and for "laying two hearths." Prince Edward Co., Va., Miscellaneous Court Papers.

fireproof Resistant to destruction by burning. Fires caused by lightning, arson, and inadvertent mishaps plagued a society wedded to wooden construction. Poor construction and maintenance caused sparks to ignite wooden chimneys and rain down on shingled roofs. Surprisingly, in an age when frame and log buildings dominated the southern landscape, actions to mitigate the causes of fire were slow to develop. City ordinances banning wooden chimneys were ignored for the most part, and no town had the equipment or organization to effectively combat a major conflagration. Even masonry buildings, as the burning of the government buildings in Williamsburg, New Bern, Raleigh, and Charleston so clearly demonstrated, were not exempt from the "fire fiend." Individuals occasionally took some precautions to combat fire by fireproofing the wooden portions of their buildings with framing timbers clear of resinous sapwood and by packing the spaces around joists and beneath floors with mortar, clay, sand, plaster, and other materials. In order to safeguard public records, states enacted laws in the late 18th and early 19th centuries requiring the construction of fireproof public records offices. In the 1790s, the state of Virginia required each county to have a fireproof clerk's office constructed with masonry floors, vaulted ceilings, tile or slate roofing material, and as little exposed woodwork as possible. Contemporary notions of fireproof construction are exemplified in Robert Mills's Fireproof Building, erected in Charleston in the mid-1820s.

> **1800** "PROPOSALS will be received at the office of Culpeper county . . . for erecting a CLERK'S OFFICE . . . of Stone . . . with one of the apartments arched with stone or brick, so as to be proof against fire." *The Virginia Herald*.

1812 Thomas Jefferson wrote about a type of fireproofing with which he was acquainted: "The first is by planking slips of lath in the inside of every joist at bottom, laying short planks closely on these and filling the interval between them and the floors with brick and mortar. This is usual to the northward under the name of counter sealing and is used in my own house, and has once saved my house by the floor resisting the taking fire from a coat of sawdust spaced over it and burning on it a whole night." Jefferson Papers, LC.

1822 A church office was to be built and "covered with Roman Cement, & the sides either with Roman Cement, or Rough Cast For the greater Security against Fire, the Roof to be covered with Plain Tile . . . the Window shutters to the No. & So. to be covered with Copper or Sheet Iron; & every other precaution taken which may be considered by Workmen as necessary to render the Building as completely Fire proof as possible." St. Michael's Church, Charleston, S.C., Vestry Book.

fireroom A room containing a fireplace.

1748 A workman was hired "to make a Door to shut in the Fire Room" of a courthouse. Accomack Co., Va., Court Order Book 1744–1753.

1764 A dwelling house for sale on the Patuxent River in Maryland was described as "consisting of one large wainscotted room 20 by 17, and two other small fire rooms; another Bed Room, and three closets; all below; Above, there is a handsome wainscotted Fire Room of the same size with the Hall below." *Maryland Gazette.*

firestone A heat resistant stone, often sandstone, used to line the inside of fireplaces and ovens.

1748 Rooms in a dwelling in Charleston contained "Marble Chimney Pieces, Hearths and Fire-stones." *South Carolina Gazette.*

fish pond In a pleasure ground near a dwelling, an artificial freshwater reservoir stocked with fish.

1733 The owner of a plantation at Goose Creek, South Carolina, boasted of having "a fish-pond well stored with pearch, roach, pike, eels, and cat-fish." *South Carolina Gazette.*

1743 At William Middleton's plantation near Charleston, there was "a large fish pond with a mount rising out of the middle—the top of which is level with the dwelling house and upon it is a roman temple. On each side of this are other large fish ponds properly disposed which form a fine prospect of water from the house." *Letterbook of Eliza Lucas Pinckney.*

1801 A garden in Wilmington, North Carolina, was "laid out in the English style— a Creek wound thro' the largest, upon its banks grew native shrubbery . . . a fish-pond, communicating with the Creek, both producing abundance of fish." *Autobiography and Diary of Mrs. Eliza Clitherall.*

fish pond
Charles Fraser, The Seat of Joseph Winthrop, Goose Creek, S.C.

flagstone (flagg) A flat piece of fissile stone used for paving. Sandstone and, occasionally, limestone flags were imported from England into the Chesapeake, coastal North Carolina, and the low country of South Carolina and Georgia, which lacked convenient sources of stone. Most of this material was used to pave the alleys of churches, parts of courtrooms, kitchens, entrance halls, and walks. See also **Bristol stone.**

1699 Specifications for "the Great Roomes" on the ground floor of the capitol in Williamsburg were to "be laid with fflagg stones." *Journals of the House of Burgesses,* 3.

1736 "All the floor back of ye Lawyers barr" in a courtroom was "to be laid with Flagg stone the other floors to be well laid with good inch and a half pine plank." Spotsylvania Co., Va., Will Book 1722–1749.

1737 Estimates made for repairing a church included "paving ye Steeple & West Porticoe with Flag Stones Laid in Mortar." St. Philip's Parish, Charleston, S.C., Vestry Book.

1760 "The Vestry . . . having measured the Area of the Church find the Contents to amount to 620 feet Square on which they agree to send to England for Flagg to lay the same." St. George's Parish, Harford Co., Md., Vestry Book.

flank window A sidelight. For a more detailed description, see **sidelight.**

> 1799 Architect Benjamin Henry Latrobe's design for a bank specified the use of marble for "the Impost mouldings of the Flank Windows." *The Correspondence and Miscellaneous Papers of Benjamin Henry Latrobe*, 1.

flat 1. The floor of a building.

> 1761 Noted in Virginia carpenter William Ellett's *Arithmetic Book:* "it is a Rule amongst workmen, that the Flat of any House, and half the Flat thereof, taken within the Walls is equal to the measure of the Roof of the same House; but this is when the Roof is true Pitch; for if the Roof be more flat or steep than the true Pitch, it will be more or less accordingly." William Ellett Arithmetic Book, Duke.

2. The level garden area on each terrace of a falling garden. See also **falling garden.**

flat arch A straight arch with a horizontal intrados. See also **jack arch, straight arch.**

flat point The broad, level, spoon-shaped end of the shaft of a wrought nail. Nails were fabricated with flat points to diminish the risk of splitting a wood surface when hammered and were favored by Chesapeake carpenters. See also **wrought nail.**

> 1741 In a disagreement over an invoice, a Williamsburg resident wrote to a merchant that "the nails are charged flat pointed but the greatest part are round pointed w[ch] takes a great deal of time to bore every board otherwise they will spit a driving and those few that are flat pointed the points are so thin and weak that they bend a driving so that they are of little use." John Custis Letterbook, LC.

flat roof A roof whose slope is very slight, being no more than a 20-degree angle; also a roof whose surface is horizontal. Following Italian treatises, English publications in the 17th and 18th centuries illustrated a number of flat roofs with slight slopes, which were supported in the center by short king posts and other struts. While fairly common in Boston and perhaps other parts of New England in the early 18th century, flat roofs were relatively rare in the South through the early 19th century. See also **square roof.**

> 1722 The public buildings in Williamsburg were covered with shingles "except the Debtors Prison which is flat roofed." Beverley, *The History and Present State of Virginia.*
> 1734 "Flat ROOF, . . is in the same Proportion as a Triangular Pediment. This is chiefly us'd in Italy and the hot Countries where little Snow falls." *Builder's Dictionary.*
> 1750 A glebe house was to be built "fifty foot long . . . thirty foot wide two story high the walls brick a flat roof without dormans." Christ Church Parish, Middlesex Co., Va., Vestry Book.

Flemish bond See **bond.**

flight An unbroken series of steps leading from one landing place to another. Stairs might ascend from one floor to another in a number of flights that are punctuated by one or more landings.

> 1746 Specifications called for "a flight of Stairs up into the garrets as in the plan" of Charles Pinckney's dwelling in Charleston. Huger Smith, *The Dwelling Houses of Charleston.*
> 1809 A two-story jail to be built in Greene County, Georgia, was to have "a flight of steps and landing place in the passage between" floors. *The Monitor.*

floating house A flat-bottomed boat with a roof fitted up as a floating dwelling or for some other function.

> **1773** Joseph Calvert asked the court "that he may have liberty for [his] floating house to remain at the side of the county wharf." Norfolk Co., Va., Court Order Book 1771–1773.
> **1813** A Charleston entrepreneur planed "to erect at the East Bay . . . a CIRCULAR FLOATING BATH HOUSE. . . . It will be 250 feet in circumference. . . . It will contain FORTY capacious private bathing rooms, lighted by VENETIAN windows: a large SWIMMING bath in the centre, of about 160 feet circumference: FORTY dressing CLOSETS attached to the swimming bath: two spacious SITTING rooms, one for the accommodation of LADIES, and the other for GENTLEMEN." *City Gazette and Daily Advertiser.*

floor, flooring (flore, flour, flower) The layer of boards, planks, framing, bricks, stone, clay, or other material that forms a walking surface in a building or structure. Many dwellings, outbuildings, and farm structures erected in the early South had no flooring system but used the natural surface of the earth. Earthfast structures erected by settlers in the Chesapeake in the 17th century and elsewhere at a later period frequently had no flooring system. Occasionally this was enhanced with rammed or crammed clay mixed with other materials to provide a hard, smooth surface. *Paved* masonry floors were used in many different situations, particularly for lining the surface of kitchens, dairies, cellars, stables, market houses, and parts of churches and courthouses. Framed floors were generally composed of a series of regularly spaced sleepers, joists, and girders tied into outer perimeter framing members. Across these horizontal members, floorboards were laid. Relatively unusual were *double floors* where large girders or *binding joists* carried small floor joists above and ceiling joists below, which were enclosed by lath and plaster or sheathing to form a ceiling. Wood flooring varied greatly in manner of finish and detailing. Most floorboards measured between an inch and an inch and a half in thickness, and between three and a dozen or more inches in width. Lengths varied significantly. In some situations, builders carefully lined up the end joints, staggered them, or hid them beneath partition walls. Although the surfaces of most floorboards were planed to some degree, their undersides were rarely planed. The underside of most common flooring in early buildings showed signs of *gauging* or roughly undercutting the area of the board that rests on the framing joists. The method of securing floorboards to the undercarriage also varied according to location and level of workmanship. In many subsidiary spaces such as lofts, lapped clapboards were sometimes used to provide a usable surface. Others had slabs or unjointed planks loosely laid across framing members. Jointed boards with squared sides could be *butted* against one another, *listed, lapped, doweled, splined,* or *tongue and grooved.* Depending on the quality of construction and location, boards were either face nailed or pegged so that the fasteners could be seen on top of the board. Other floors were *secret nailed,* leaving no visible evidence of nails. Pine and oak were among the most popular species of wood used by early builders in flooring. See also **binding joist, board, bridging joist, butt, dowel, earthen floor, gauge** (3), **joint, pave, secret nail, spline, tongue and groove.**

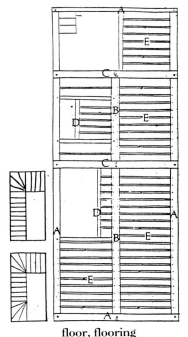

floor, flooring
Floor framing: (A) sill, (B) summer, (C) girder, (D) trimmer, (E) sleeper or joist

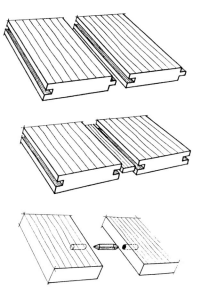

floor, flooring
Floorboard joint details:
tongue and groove (*above*),
spline (*center*),
dowel (*below*)

1656 An optimistic description of the Chesapeake colonies noted that the wooden dwellings were usually "daubed and white limed, glazed and flowered." Hammond, *Leah and Rachel.*

1666 A carpenter was to be hired "to laye a floore of plank" in a dwelling. Norfolk Co., Va., Will and Deed Book 1656–1666.

1713 Work on Bruton Parish Church included "the framing & raising the Floor at 10 sh pr Square." *Calendar of Virginia State Papers,* 1.

1723 The upper floor of a courthouse in Currituck County, North Carolina, was to be "plained Joynted and Close layed." *Higher-Court Records of North Carolina,* 5.

1755 Prices in London for "whole Deal boarded floors, shot clear of Sap . . . 25 s per Square.

Whole Deal boarded Floors, lifted and shot clear of Sap, 27s per Square.

Folding Joint-boarded Floors, plained, lifted, and shot clear of sap, at 30s pr Square.

Common streight-joint boarded Floors, clear of Sap, at 40s per Square.

Second-best boarded Floors, nailed, at 2l. 10s. per Square.

Second-best boarded Floors doweled, 3l. 5s. per Square.

Clean Deal boarded Floors dowled, at 5l. per Square.

Ditto, of long boards, 15 Feet long Boards, and upwards, at 6l. per Square.

Salmon, *Palladio Londinensis.*

1762 "It is agreed that Mr. John Tredway do lay the Stones for the Church floor." St. George's Parish, Harford Co., Md., Vestry Book.

1766 In Charleston, Henry Laurens wrote to a carpenter that "you have forgot that I told you I had no other flooring Boards than such as might be made serviceable for the additional buildings to Mepkin House where I should not much mind a Little piecing or patching. . . . the whole may be of the very best Yellow pine without blemishes or exceptions." *The Papers of Henry Laurens,* 5.

1774 Carpenter's work at William Corbit's house in Odessa, Delaware, listed "5 sqr 36 ft 6 ins Dowelled floor at 34/ sqr £15.19.2; 7 sqr 47 ft 2 ins floor boarding at 20/." Sweeney, *Grandeur on the Appoquinimink.*

1790 At Hampton near Baltimore, Charles Ridgely paid for "12 sqr 1 1/4 flooring blind naild at 45/ pr sqr £27.11.3." *MHM,* 33.

1793 "The floors in the sd. Ct. house to be Laid in the best manner Tounged and Grooved with well seasoned Pine plank one & a quarter inches thick and not to Exceed eight Inches wide." Henry Co., Va., Loose Court Papers.

flower garden Usually an enclosed piece of ground for the cultivation of flowers, sometimes mixed with practical or decorative herbs, fruits, or vegetables. See also **garden, knot** (2).

1709 "The Flower-Garden in Carolina is as yet arrived to a poor and jejune Perfection." Lawson, *A New Voyage to Carolina.*

1775 Charles Carroll of Annapolis advised a relative to "examine the Gardiner strictly as to . . . what Branch He had been Chiefly employed, ye Kitchen or Flower Garden." Charles Carroll Letterbook, MHS.

1796 "On one side of this lawn" at Mount Vernon "is a plain Kitchen garden, on the other a neat flower garden laid out in squares, and boxed with great precission." *The Virginia Journals of Benjamin Henry Latrobe,* 1.

1809 In the Moravian town of Salem, North Carolina, a traveler "visited a flower garden belonging to the female department. The flowers were very numerous, but none of them remarkable for their beauty or novelty." *The Journal of William D. Martin.*

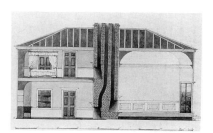

flue
John Izard Middleton, sectional drawing for a dwelling in S.C. showing the location of chimney flues, c. 1811.

flue (flew) A passage or duct to vent the smoke, gas, and heat created by a fire, especially the channel that runs from the throat of a chimney through the stack to the cap. See also **chimney, funnel.**

1756 A workman was hired "to build several flues at the several publick warehouses belonging to this county for burning tobacco." Richmond Co., Va., Court Order Book 1756–1762.

1772 "The fire places in the Hall and Dining Room" in a glebe house were "to be four feet wide and all the rest to be three feet with flews in the Funnell." St. Mark's Parish, Culpeper Co., Va., Vestry Book.

1784 In planning a greenhouse, George Washington inquired of another planter "whether the heat is conveyed by flues, and a grate, whether those flues run all around the House, the size of them without, and in the clear, Whether they join the wall, or are separate and distinct from it." Trostel, *Mount Clare.*

flush Two surfaces or objects that are contiguous, level, even, or forming the same plane. See also **cipher, lap.**

> 1740 Planters were given leave "to bild a gallery in the north wing of the church to reach from the north door till it comes flush with the main wall of the church." Christ Church Parish, Lancaster Co., Va., Vestry Book.
> 1742 A barn was to be "floared flush with plank full inch and half thick." Bristol Parish, Prince George Co., Va., Vestry Book.
> 1771 The corner posts of St. John's Church in Granville County, North Carolina, should "be got out fourteen Inches one way & twenty two Inches the other to be Rabited out so as to make flush walls with the other framing six inches." Francis Hawks Collection, Church Historical Society.

flute, fluting A groove or channel; usually a series of parallel upright channels in the shafts of classical columns and pilasters. Their number, profile, and stops varied according to the different orders and whether they were based on Greek or Roman precedent. The Tuscan column has no fluting. In the Doric order, there are twenty flutes separated by sharp arrises. In the Ionic, Corinthian, and Composite orders, there are twenty-four flutes separated by narrow fillets or lists. Fluting found on many Greek-inspired columns have elliptical channels, while those of Roman derivation are semicircular in profile. On columns and pilasters of the more ornate orders, the lower section of the fluted shafts are sometimes filled with a convex molding known as a *cable.* Although these rules were devised by architects and theorists in the Renaissance and promulgated in architectural publications imported into America, they were not always strictly followed in early southern buildings. Isolated examples aside, fluting, like many of the classical elements of architecture, began to appear in a significant degree in the second quarter of the 18th century. See also **arris, cable, order.**

> 1753 Church "galleries [are] to be supported with turned and fluted collums." Wicomico Parish, Northumberland Co., Va., Vestry Book.
> 1760 Specifications for a church included "five Pillars of Cypress on each side for the support of the Roof, the Columns to be 15 inches Diameter at the bottom of the Shaft, to be Fluted & the Capitols of the Dorick Order." Stratton Major Parish, King and Queen Co., Va., Vestry Book.
> 1777 At Bruton Parish Church in Williamsburg, "the Govrs. Pew is elegant, & elevated above the rest: a silk Curtain hangs on each Side & in Front of it from a Canopy supported by two fluted, gilt Pillars." *VMHB,* 62.

fly lattice, fly wire A thin wire mesh screen placed over windows to prevent insects from entering.

> 1770 The inventory of Governor Botetourt listed "100 feet fly Lattice" in the Governor's House in Williamsburg. *Inventories of Four Eighteenth-Century Houses in the Historic Area of Williamsburg.*
> 1771 A Williamsburg resident purchased from an English merchant "10 pieces of flywire 3 feet 1 inch square." *John Norton & Sons Merchants of London and Virginia.*
> 1772 A London merchant shipped "Iron wire for 14 Cellar Windows, 3 Feet 7 Inches wide, 2 Feet 4 Inches high" to a Virginia planter at Blandfield in Essex County, Virginia. Robert Beverley Letterbook, LC.

fodder house A shed or other loosely enclosed structure for the storage of coarse food, such as leaves and cornstalks for livestock.

> 1789 Outbuildings to be repaired at a glebe in Savannah included "a stable, corn house & fodder house." Christ Church Parish, Savannah, Ga., Records, GHS.
> 1821 On a farm in southern Delaware was an "old slab fodder House 12 by 13" feet. Sussex Co., Del., Orphans Court Valuations M.

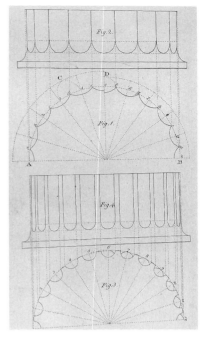

flute, fluting

folding door
Battersea, Petersburg, Va.

folding door (foulding door) A door consisting of two sections or leaves hung on opposite jambs, the edges of which meet when closed together. From the late 17th century onward, folding doors were used to accentuate primary entrances into public structures and grand houses as well as in utilitarian buildings such as barns, stables, stores, and warehouses that required wide openings. See also **double door** (1).

> 1680   The main entrance to a courthouse was to have "folding Wenscoatt dores." Talbot Co., Md., Court Judgments 1675–1682.
> 1698   There was to be "a pair of large folding dores att ye entrance into ye court house." Lancaster Co., Va., Court Order Book 1696–1702.
> 1711   A church was to have "two doors ones att the west end to be nine foot high and six foot wide folding doores, the Doore in the Chancell to be six foot four inches high and three foot wide." Christ Church Parish, Middlesex County, Va., Vestry Book.
> 1730   A barn was to be built with "one folding door and one single one opposite." Stratton Major Parish, King and Queen Co., Va., Vestry Book.
> 1757   It was ordered that a tobacco warehouse have "five folding doors in the front." Northumberland Co., Va., Court Order Book 1756–1758.

folding shutter   See **shutter**.

folly   An ill-considered and costly dwelling or other structure undertaken beyond the financial means of its builder to complete it. In many areas, particularly Maryland, the term *folly* was also given to a land patent or an estate, often for reasons of financial stress caused by the purchase or upkeep. The term does not appear in the colonial and early national period to have been used in the English sense, to describe an eyecatcher such as a temple or ruin built in a pleasure ground for some aesthetic reason.

> 1771   One of the most famous follies in colonial Maryland was the unfinished dwelling erected for Governor Bladen that was left exposed to the weather for many years. In a plea for money to repair St. Anne's Church in Annapolis, a poet observed that "With grief in yonder field, hard bye, A sister ruin I espy; Old Bladen's place, once so famed, And now too well 'the Folly' named, Her roof all tottering to decay, Her wall a-mouldering away." *Maryland Gazette.*

font
Christ Church, Lancaster County, Va.

font   A basin or receptacle made of stone, wood, or metal containing the water used in baptism. The body of the font was usually a large block of stone carved in the form of a baluster or column, with a hollowed-out bowl at the top. Many were covered with wooden canopies. In Anglican churches, the font was generally located at the back of the church near the west entrance.

> 1719   The churchwarden was requested to "make a New Font after the handsomest mannor he can; & put it up in the Church, the old one being Rotten." St. Anne's Parish, Anne Arundel Co., Md., Vestry Book.
> 1738   "Ordered that a Marble Font with Wooden Frame & Top with Pullys & Weights to Lift it off & on the Bason to be 18 Inches Deep & two feet Diameter be sent for the use of the Church in Annapolis." St. Anne's Parish, Anne Arundel Co., Md., Vestry Book.
> 1773   "William Copein [has] undertaken to make a stone Font for the Church according to a Draugh in the 150th plate in Langleys Designs being the upermost on the left hand for the price of six pounds." Truro Parish, Fairfax Co., Va., Vestry Book.

foot   The lowest part of an object; the end of a leg of a piece of furniture; the end of a rafter where it meets the plate or false plate.

> 1762   The wall of a church was to extend "twenty-two [feet] from the water table to the Foot of the Rafters." Frederick Parish, Frederick Co., Va., Vestry Book.

1763 The rafters of a church were to be "of old pine 14 by 8 inches at the foot and 8 inches square at the" top. "The ruff [is] to be framed after the New England manner." St. George's Parish, Accomack Co., Va., Vestry Book.

1767 Payment was made for "putting new feet to a bench." Cumberland Parish, Lunenburg Co., Va., Vestry Book.

footlace (foot less)   A rare term for a chamfered setoff or water table of a masonry building. See also **water table.**

1713 Brickwork at the parish church in Williamsburg consisted of "Rubbing & Cutting ye Foot lesses at one penny pr: foot." *Calendar of Virginia State Papers,* 1.

footpace   An intermediate landing at the end of a few steps; a raised area above floor level, such as a dais or the area around the altar in a church. The term had little currency in early America. However, the related term *halfpace* did appear in some instances to describe a stair landing. See **halfpace.**

1703   "Foot-pace, is a part of Stairs, whereon after four or six steps you arrive to a broad place, where you make two or three paces before you ascend another step; thereby to ease the legs in ascending the rest of the steps." Moxon, *Mechanick Exercises.*

foot
Prestwould, Mecklenburg County, Va.

footstone   An upright stone marking the lower end of a grave. See also **headstone.**

1825   "The Vestry resolved that head and foot stones & Wooden Monuments were as inconvenient as Tomb stones, and therefore extended the prohibition to them." St. Philip's Parish, Charleston, S.C., Vestry Book.

footway   A path set aside for foot passengers; a raised sidewalk, occasionally paved with tile, brick, or stone pavers in some of the larger cities in the late 18th and early 19th centuries. See also **sidewalk.**

1764   "The Commissioners, appointed to execute 'an Act for the keeping clean and in good repair the streets of Charles Town' GIVE NOTICE That they are ready to contract with any workmen, or others, for paving a regular foot-way (with good and well burnt brick, laid flat in mortar) on each side of the principal streets." *South Carolina Gazette.*

1786   In Blandford, a suburb of Petersburg, Virginia, "the Streets . . . are so very narrow they do not afford space sufficient for a foot way and gutter on each side, and Sufficient width for Carriages to Pass the middle." Petersburg, Va., City Council Minute Book 1784–1811.

1810   In Lexington, Kentucky, "the footways [are] neatly paved with brick, and the middle of the street with solid stone firmly bedded." *Virginia Argus.*

1820   At the White House in Washington, "the area north of the house has been graduated, and the carriage and foot-ways formed and gravelled." *Daily National Intelligencer.*

forge   **1.** A building in which cast iron is converted into wrought iron. Forges usually contained a finery mill for converting the cast iron into wrought iron and a chafery mill for shaping the wrought iron into usable bars known as *bar iron.* See also **cast iron, pig iron, wrought iron.**

1758   Property for sale near Baltimore contained "in the Forge . . . Three Fineries, and one Chafery, and a Stove for Bar-iron." *Maryland Gazette.*

1823   The Collin's property in Delaware contained "one Forge 32 by 35 Newly rebuilt." Sussex Co., Del., Orphans Court Valuations N.

2. A brick structure with a hearth in which a blacksmith heats iron to render it malleable.

form   A long backless seat. See also **bench.**

1654 "John Prosser of Wicocomocoe, Joyner, agrees to make for Thomas Brewer one table seaven foote long and one forme suddenly and two chaires and two joyned stooles." Northumberland Co., Va., Court Record Book 1652–1655.

1668 An agreement was made to construct "foure tables and foure joynt formes." Charles Co., Md., Court Proceedings 1668.

1702 Payment was made "to the joiner for windows, table, form and benches" for a church. St. Paul's Parish, Chowan Co., N.C., Vestry Book.

1705 A workman was hired to fabricate "two fourmes of Eight foot Long and two Benches to be sett up in the Jury Roome." Richmond Co., Va., Court Order Book 1704–1708.

fort A stronghold or fortified place, generally surrounded by a perimeter defense of walls, ditches, palisades, and earthworks. Forts varied in size, construction, and materials, ranging from the impressive stone walls of the Spanish Castillo San Marcos constructed in St. Augustine, Florida, in the late 17th century; palisaded enclosures of Indian villages near Roanoke Island, North Carolina; tabby-walled strongholds on the South Carolina and Georgia coasts; fortified domestic sites on the western frontier of the Shenandoah Valley; to the massive brick structures such as Fort Macon near Beaufort, North Carolina, erected early in the 19th century as part of a national coastal defense following the debacles of the War of 1812.

1607 At Jamestown, the first settlers constructed a "fort . . . which was triangle wise, having three Bulwarkes at every corner like a halfe Moone and foure or five pieces of Artillerie mounted in them." *VMHB*, 11.

1667 The General Assembly of Virginia passed "an act for fforts to bee built in each river. . . . commissioners . . . to advise and determine the most expeditious wayes and meanes to erect and finish the said fforts, taking care that in very ffort there be a court of guard and a convenient place to preserve the magazine; that each ffort be capable of eight greate guns at the least, the walls ten foote high towards the river or shipping tenn foot thick at least." Hening, *Statutes at Large*, 2.

1727 In the middle of New Castle, Delaware, "lies a spacious green in form of a square, in a corner whereof stood formerly a Fort." SPG Papers, Lambeth Palace Library.

1740 On the east bank of St. John's River in Florida, a Spanish general "gave orders for repairing this Fort raising parapets and Pallisading it all Round." Mereness, *Travels in the American Colonies*.

foundation The natural or prepared ground or base that supports a structure; also the lowest part of a building, usually masonry, resting below ground level; the groundwork.

1674 The statehouse at St. Mary's City was "to be built uppon a good secure and sound foundation of twenty eight inches thick from the bottom of the said foundation the water table which shall be three foote Cleere above the ground." *Archives of Maryland*, 2.

1698 Specifications noted that "ye wall of ye prison to be two brick thick ye foundation to be two foot and a halfe in the ground." Lancaster Co., Va., Court Order Book 1696–1702.

1753 "The foundation" of a church was "to be laid three feet under the surface of the earth and the foundation to be five feet thick and three feet and half from the surface of the earth to the water table." Wicomico Parish, Northumberland Co., Va., Vestry Book.

1810 The walls of the Bedford County, Tennessee, courthouse were "to be of brick and the foundation of stone, which foundation wall of stone shall be sunk two feet under ground and raised two feet above the ground." *The Democratic Clarion and Tennessee Gazette*.

foundation
Excavation of Corotoman, the home of Robert "King" Carter in Lancaster County, Va., revealed the foundation of the two-story brick dwelling erected in the mid-1720s.

foundry (foundery) An establishment in which iron is smelted and cast into molds. See also **ironwork** (1), **furnace.**

1776 "A Foundery" was to be erected "on the falls of the James River, for the purpose of casting cannon, etc. which will require a framed building 50′ square, and several other necessary houses." *Virginia Gazette.*

1777 "A little above Falmouth are Mr. Hunters Works. . . . He is now erecting a Mill for slitting & plating Iron, & is about building a Furnace for melting Iron Ore. At present he makes (from Pig Iron) Barr Iron, Anchors, all Kinds of common Black-smith's Work . . . & Nails." *VMHB*, 62.

fountain   In a garden or pleasure ground, a jet or stream of water made to rise or spout up artificially, including the structure built for such hydraulics. Fountains were rare features in early southern gardens.

fowl house   A henhouse or sheltered building for other domesticated birds such as ducks, turkeys, and guinea fowls. The term was used primarily in the southern low country, especially in South Carolina and Georgia. For a more detailed description, see **henhouse.**

1738   Among the outbuildings belonging to a house for sale in Charleston were "a Stable and a Fowl House with Gardens." *South Carolina Gazette.*

frame, framing (fraim)   *(n.)* The rough timber work of a building including walls, roof, and floors composed of posts, beams, braces, rafters, purlins, girders, sleepers, joists, studs, and plates, as well as individual structural parts of a building, such as door and window elements; the skeleton, carcass, or hull of a building; a building or structure assembled with rough timber work.   *(v.)* To fabricate and fit pieces of wood together with various joints in order to form a structure for enclosing or creating an opening. See also **doorframe, English frame, Virginia house, window frame.**

1643   It was agreed "to erect and build on some part of the 300 acres . . . one good and sufficient framed house." Surry Co., Va., Deed and Will Book 1652–1672.

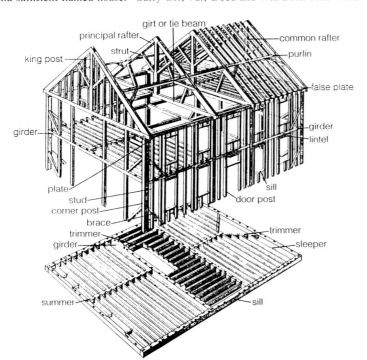

frame   Framing members of a typical late 18th- or early 19th-century, two-story dwelling

1659 "James Hall . . . sett up the fframe of howse twenty foot long, & fiveteene foot wide (all but the studds) at Hebdens Poynt." *Archives of Maryland*, 41.

1666 A carpenter was to be hired to make "two plaine frames for windows." Norfolk Co., Va., Will and Deed Book 1656–1666.

1676 Inventory of the estate of Francis Godfrey in Perquimans County, North Carolina, listed "1 framed house forty foot Long 20 foot wide; with a shade on the back side; and a porch on the front, being all sawed worke; and all Ready framed." Secretary of State Records, Wills and Inventories 1677–1701, NCA&H.

1731 Peter Porter produced his account for "getting the fraime of a house 20 feet by 16 & raising the Same & finding framing Timber £2.5.0." St. Anne's Parish, Anne Arundel Co., Md., Vestry Book.

1765 In Chowan County, North Carolina, William Luten charged client Joseph Sutton for "fraiming a house at 3/6 a square, 16 and 37 feet £2.17.0." William Luten Ledger Book, NCA&H.

1790 A carpenter's work on a house in Columbia County, Georgia, included "framing of rafters Sills & Joists £1.10.0." Thomas Carr Papers, UGa.

1797 In Charleston, "A PERSON Who is MASTER of the HOUSE CARPEN-

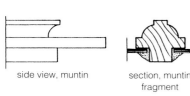

side view, muntin   section, muntin
fragment

frank
Muntin, Four Mile Tree, Surry County, Va.

frank   In the making of window sash and other joinery work, to cut a miter in two adjoining molded pieces only to the depth of their moldings. The rest of the two adjoining pieces are cut square to one another and secured by a tenon joint.

1807 Specifications for the New Orleans customs house called for the sashes "to be yellow pine 2 inch, Ovolo, franked and dowelled." *The Correspondence and Miscellaneous Papers of Benjamin Henry Latrobe*, 2.

1811 A building account for a dwelling house in Baltimore lists "72 Lights 8/4 Gothic Bar Sash 9 by 12 Single frank'd." Riddell Accounts, Pleasants Papers, MHS.

Franklin   1. An electrical conductor or lightning rod attached to roofs and chimneys to prevent lightning from striking the building by providing a direct path to the ground. Eponymously named for Benjamin Franklin, who pioneered experiments in electricity. See also **electrical conductor.**

1771 Plans were made "to erect a Franklin on the New Brick Prison." Norfolk Co., Va., Court Order Book 1771–1773.

1783 It was "ordered that the sheriff cause the conductor of the Franklin belonging to the Court House to be Repaired." Chowan Co., N.C., Court Minute Book 1780–1785.

1801 Listed in an estate inventory was a "Franklin or lightning rod..$2." Loudoun Co., Va., Will Book 1797–1802

2. An iron stove constructed in the form of a fireplace with an enclosed top, bottom, sides, and back, with a vent in the rear. The front had doors that could be opened to various positions to regulate the heat produced by the stove. Named after its inventor, Benjamin Franklin.

1791 For sale in a store in Alexandria: "Franklin Stoves." *Alexandria Gazette.*

1796 Merchant James Cavan "has on hand and for sale . . . a few very elegant Franklin stoves." *Alexandria Gazette.*

free of sap   See **clear of sap, sapped.**

freestone   Any fine-grained limestone or sandstone that can easily be sawn, cut, or shaped with a chisel in any direction without splitting.

1668 In England, "for paving with free-stone, as it is taken out of the Quarrie, the usual rate is 7d or 8d a foot square for Stone and Workmanship; but if the Stones be squared to a size, and ruled smooth, it is then dearer, as 12d or 14d a foot." Leybourn, *Platform Guide Mate for Purchasers, Builders, Measurers.*

1706 An undertaker agreed to build a courthouse for a specified price, "The flagg and free stone for pavement only excepted." Northumberland Co., Va., Court Order Book 1699–1713.

1769 The corners of a church along with "the Pedistals, and Doors with Pediment heads [are] to be of good white freestone." Truro Parish, Fairfax Co., Va., Vestry Book.

1802 The bill for stonecutters' work at John Tayloe's Washington residence included "Plain door soles & steps of Free Stone . . . marble Hearths squared & laid . . . Free Stone Jams and Mantle to D° . . . Run Free Stone to line Marble chimney Pieces." Tayloe Papers, VHS.

French window A type of casement window, in which the sash swings from the jamb of the opening, in the manner of a door.

1816 Discussing windows for a house in the District of Columbia, Benjamin Latrobe explained, "the French window opens as a door . . . which I have executed lately at Mr. Belthoovers, with excellent effect." *The Correspondence and Miscellaneous Papers of Benjamin Henry Latrobe*, 3.

fresco A wall or ceiling decoration or mural painted on wet plaster.

1744 In Annapolis, Samuel Rusbatch proposed "to carry on all the various branches of coach and herald painting, varnishing and guilding. . . . Also painting in fresco, cire-obscure, decorated ceilings for halls, vestibules, and saloons, either in festoons of fruits, flowers, figures, or trophies." *Maryland Gazette.*

1800 A design for a mausoleum for George Washington included a chamber decorated with panels "filled by representations, either in bas relief, or fresco painting, of the principal events of the life of Washington." *The Correspondence and Miscellaneous Papers of Benjamin Henry Latrobe*, 1.

fret An ornament consisting of a series of fillets or bands that are interconnected in a variety of rectangular patterns. See also **guilloche.**

1783 The frieze of a chimney piece in the council chamber of the Governor's House in New Bern "is a Siana fret laid in statuary" marble. Hawks Letter, Miranda Papers, Academia Nacional de la Historia, Caracas.

1790 Work at Hampton in Baltimore County, Maryland, included "2095 feet of outside moudilen and fret cornish quorter finished at 13d 1/2 pr . . . £117.16.10 1/2." *MHM*, 33.

fretwork An ornamental decoration in either openwork or relief consisting of a pattern of interlaced rectangular fillets, reglets, or bands.

1716 A sill was to be placed "under the frame of fret work at the North Door." St. Anne's Parish, Anne Arundel Co., Md., Vestry Book.

1783 In the drawing room of the Governor's House in New Bern, "the Base and Sur Base [were] inriched with fret work." Hawks Letter, Miranda Papers, Academia Nacional de la Historia, Caracas.

frieze (freeze) The middle section of a classical entablature between the architrave below and the cornice above, containing a long horizontal band that may vary in composition according to the different orders. A Doric entablature often consists of a series of regularly spaced triglyphs separated by metopes, which are sometimes decorated with carved ornament. A zoophorous frieze contains a band of carved or cast figures of men and animals. See also **entablature.**

1760 The canopy of the pulpit at St. Michael's Church in Charleston was carved with "a Swelling Freese [of] Cut Lawrel Leaves." Williams, *St. Michael's.*

1774 A craftsman fabricated "185 ft Archv Frieze & Cornice at 2/6 ft" for a dwelling in Odessa, Delaware. Sweeney, *Grandeur on the Appoquinimink.*

1783 In the council chamber of the Governor's House in New Bern, "the doors are flat Caps with contracted swelling Friezes." Hawks Letter, Miranda Papers, Academia Nacional de la Historia, Caracas.

French window
John Izard Middleton, design for a
dwelling with French windows,
South Carolina, c. 1811

fret

frieze
Doric frieze, Pavilion 1, University of Virginia. The principal elements of the frieze consist of an alternating series of triglyphs and metopes. The metope figure is based on a plate in Freart de Chambray's Parallele de l'Architecture.

frontispiece
John Wright Stanley House, New Bern, N.C.

1800 The composition ornament ordered for John Steele's dwelling in Rowan County, North Carolina, included "1 pair of Oak freezes & Large Wheat Sheaf Centre." John Steele Papers, SHC.

froe, frow A tool with a metal blade and a short wooden handle attached at right angles, used for splitting timber lengthwise into boards, shingles, palings, and other riven items. The tool was an integral part of clapboard carpentry, where it was used to rive four- and five-foot long clapboards. Along with the drawing knife, it was also the principal tool in shingle making. See also **rive.**

frontispiece The principal facade of a building, or more particularly, its decorative porch or doorway. In the 18th and early 19th centuries, the term was used generally to refer to a pedimented or ornamented doorway treated architecturally as a separate composition from the main facade. A few frontispieces fabricated in stone, such as the ones that frame the entrances to Westover in Charles City County, Virginia, were imported from England. Many wooden ones were inspired by designs published in English architectural books.

1718 In the review of the construction of a magazine on the statehouse grounds in Annapolis, it was discovered that "the Frontispiece is more then Concluded upon in the Agreement." *Archives of Maryland*, 33.
1749 A bricklayer was paid £3.10.0 for "A Frontispiece" at Marlborough, the home of lawyer John Mercer in Stafford County, Virginia. John Mercer Ledger G., Bucks Co., Pa., Historical Society.
1759 In Charleston John Landridge, "carpenter and joiner from London," advertised his skill in fabricating "neat chimney pieces and frontispieces." *South Carolina Gazette.*
1790 At Hampton in Baltimore County, Maryland, a craftsman constructed "one frontisepise fluted Pilasters . . . £10.0.0." *MHM* 33.
1792 Members of the North Carolina legislature sought to alter the plan of the statehouse in Raleigh by having "a brake in the center of the East and West front walls projecting two feet by twenty four feet in length, so as to have a Frontispiece East and West, something similar to the front of the public buildings in New Bern." Legislative Papers, NCA&H.

fronton A pediment surmounting the architrave or a door or window opening. The term is French and was rarely used in the South.

1747 A church was to have "a Fronton or Pediment over each Door Shingled." Albemarle Parish, Surry Co., Va., Vestry Book.

fulling mill A building where cloth was cleaned and thickened by beating with wooden mallets and washing in a variety of liquids.

1693 The Virginia General Assembly passed an "act for giveing encouragement to erect Fulling Mills." Hening, *Statutes at Large*, 3.
1748 "The Fulling-Mill on Curtis's Creek, five Miles distant from Patapsco Ferry, in Anne Arundel County," Maryland had been repaired and employed "a Man who is very well skill'd in Fulling, Dying, Shearing, and Pressing." *Maryland Gazette.*
1815 In Jefferson County, Kentucky, notice given of the erection of "a Fulling Mill on the south fork of Goose Creek, about 12 miles from Louisville. . . . The mill is so constructed as to be worked by horses when the water fails, and a house to dry in when the weather fails, so that no delay or disappointment need be feared. It is requested that all persons who may favor him with their custom, will mark their cloth with the first letters of their name, so as to prevent mistakes, and particular directions how to be dressed, and what purpose the cloth is for, so that the fuller may have it to suit any purpose. . . . Nimrod Dorsey." *Western Courier.*

funnel (funnil) **1.** A channel or passage for venting gases, heat, liquids; a chimney shaft. See also **chimney, flue.**

1733 "Agreed with Mr. Roger Mathews . . . to build a Brick Chimney . . . and to Carry ye Funnel a good heigth above the Roof." St. George's Parish, Harford Co., Md., Vestry Book .

1734 "FUNNELS of Chimneys. The Funnel is the Shaft, or smallest Part from the Waste, where 'tis gathered into its least Dimensions. Palladio directs, That the Funnels of Chimneys be carried through the Roof, three, four, or five Feet at the least, that they may carry the Smoke clear from the House into the Air." *Builder's Dictionary*.

1786 A city ordinance stipulated that "no person shall be permitted to keep a fire in a stove within this City . . . unless the hole in the Wall thro' which the funnell of the Stove passes, be lined with Sheets of Tin or iron sufficient to guard it against fire." Richmond, Va., Common Council Minute Book 1782–1793.

2. A soil pipe for a necessary house. See also **pissduit.**

1756 Jail to have "a funnel in each room to be made of good white oak plank for conveying filth." Northumberland Co., Va., Court Order Book 1753–1756.

1817 Needed "in the close room" of the jail, was a "new necessary lined with tin or lead & funnel." Elizabeth City Co., Va., Deed and Will Book 1809–1818.

furnace A structure or apparatus in which combustion takes place, transferring fuel into heat, used to smelt ores, produce steam, or warm buildings. At an ironwork, a furnace was a masonry structure with a chamber in which charcoal was burned for the purpose of smelting raw iron ore to produce pig iron. The term was often used to describe a *foundry*. See also **foundry, pig iron.**

1756 There was an order for "workmen to repair Roy's warehouse and build a furnace . . . repair Conway's Warehouse and build a furnace." Caroline Co., Va., Court Order Book 1755–1758.

1758 "To be sold . . . at ONION'S IRON-WORKS, on Gunpowder River, in Baltimore County . . . the said IRON-WORKS, in which are Furnace, forges. . . . In the Forge are Three Fineries, and one Chafery, and a Store for Bar-Iron. The Tide in the River Gunpowder makes to the Furnace Door." *Maryland Gazette*.

1771 In Williamsburg, Robert Carter wanted to purchase from the "Baltimore Furnace . . . the following Castings—2 large Chimney backs, for a Kitchen & Laundry, 6 small Chimney backs." Robert Carter Collection, MHS.

1803 In the Senate wing of the Capitol in Washington, "the erection of the furnaces intended to warm the room above, the clearing of the flues, and the building of one entire Stack could not be speedily accomplished." *The Correspondence and Miscellaneous Papers of Benjamin Henry Latrobe*, 1.

furring Strips of wood attached to a wall, ceiling, and other surfaces to support sheathing, plaster lath, weatherboards, and various finish materials. Furring provides a uniform and even surface on which to apply such material.

1802 A craftsman's bill to John Tayloe for work on the Octagon in Washington included "6288 [feet] Flooring Straight Joint, secret nail'd . . . 5988 [feet] Counter flooring . . . 6288 [feet] Joist 7 Ceilings; Furring & Dubbing." Tayloe Papers, VHS.

fust See **shaft** (1).

gable, gable end (gavel) The vertical triangular section of wall at the end of a pitched roof between the eaves and the ridge; a roof formed in the shape of an inverted V composed of rafter pairs of a single slope on each side. Treatment of gable ends varied. Some frame structures had one or both their gable ends constructed of brick. This was done in many instances to integrate the construction of a brick chimney. In a number of brick buildings, the area of the gable was sometimes framed rather than enclosed with brick to the apex of the roof. See also **Dutch roof, jerkin head roof.**

1674   At the statehouse in St. Mary's City, "the walls of the second story of the said house Porch and staire case to [be] nineteene inches thick upp to the wale plate and soe from the wale plate to the brest of the window of the Garrett att the Gable Ends and from the brest of the said windows upp to the point of Gable Ends fourteen Inches thick." *Archives of Maryland, 2.*

1706   A jail in Kent County, Delaware, was to have "the Gavell Ends . . . done with Penticos." Kent Co., Del., Court Records 1703–1718.

1753   The Stephens farm in Maryland had a "dwelling house 24 feet long and 20 feet wide 10 pitch with post in the ground one brick gable and chimney." Queen Anne's Co., Md., Deed Book D.

1791   The undertaker of the brickwork for a chapel "agreed to Run up the walls of the same for sixty four pounds, except the gable Ends above the Eve which are to be of brick for which he is to be Allowed one third more in proportion than for the lower work." Trinity Parish, Charles Co., Md., Vestry Book.

gadroon, gadrooning (godroon)   A convex molding consisting of a series of lobes or short reeds, often used as a decorative border. See also **reed.**

1768   Work at the Governor's House in Williamsburg included fabrication of "500 foot of Gooderoun Gilt moulding at 9 pr £18.15.0." Virginia Accounts, Botetourt (Badminton) Papers, Gloucestershire Record Office.

gallery (1)
Christ Church, Lancaster County, Va.

gallery (galery, gallary, gallory)   **1.** A platform, of greater length than width, projecting from the interior wall of a structure and usually containing additional seating in a church, courthouse, theater, or other public building. By the mid-18th century private galleries, built at their owners' expense, were often added to existing churches or included in original construction. See also **balcony, loft** (2), **hanging pew.**

1673   A building contract for a courthouse noted "a gallery to be made at the end of the house 5 foot wide and to have its length the whole breadth of the house." Westmoreland Co., Va., Deed and Patent Book 1665–1677.

1739   Parishioners petitioned "to build a Gallery at the West End of the said church for the reception and more easie accommodation of themselves and their families." Truro Parish, Fairfax Co., Va., Vestry Book.

1763   Design of an organ case depended upon the "dimensions of our Organ Loft or gallery." St. Michael's Parish, Charleston, S.C., Vestry Book.

1777   A carpenter was paid for "framing & flooring the Gallery with bench seats, breast work, dentil cornice and columns." Congregational Church, Charleston, S.C., Record Book.

2. A roofed but open-sided structure associated with various forms of outdoor entertainment. This meaning becomes evident in the early 19th century.

1801   In a Richmond public garden stood "an elegant Musical Gallery . . . calculated to contain an Organ of considerable magnitude." *Virginia Gazette & General Advertiser.*

1804   At a horse racing establishment in Powhatan County, Virginia, "in the field . . . a Gallery [is] erected on the highest part of the ground, eighty feet long, where the Racers may be seen on every part of the ground. In this Gallery, DINNER will be set." *Virginia Gazette & General Advertiser.*

galleting   Small pieces of brick, stone, or some other material inserted into mortar joints as a decorative device or to reduce the amount of mortar used.

galloping   Although the exact meaning of the term is not entirely clear, it probably referred to a framing member that rests on and rides over the top of another framing element, such as a bridging joist over a binding one or a common rafter carried on the back of a purlin. See also **bridging joist.**

> 1711   The joists of a courthouse were "to be all galloping joyce." Talbot Co., Md., Land Records Book No. 12.
> 1752   A market house roof in Annapolis was to have "Galloping Rafters." *Maryland Gazette.*
> 1790   Framing at Hampton in Baltimore, County, Maryland, included "6 sqr 88 feet of galoping joice fraiming." *MHM*, 33.

gallows   1. A wooden frame consisting of one, two, or three posts supporting cross beams on which condemned felons were hanged. In the late colonial period, the gallows in Williamsburg, Virginia, was triangular in form, patterned after the infamous one on Tyburn Hill in London. Most were of simple construction, consisting of two posts supporting a cross beam or even one post supporting an arm and brace. Until the second quarter of the 19th century, public hangings were popular affairs that provided titillation to the idle and a stern warning to the corruptible. Gallows generally stood beside a road on the outskirts of a village or town. See also **gibbet.**

> 1717   A carpenter was paid for "erecting a gallows." Middlesex Co., Va., Court Order Book 1710–1721.
> 1793   An order concerning "the place on which the gallows was to be built" was "rescinded, & that at the fork of the roads leading from Staunton to Miller's Iron works, . . . be considered as the place of execution of all condemned persons in the future." Augusta Co., Va., Court Order Book 1791–1793.
> 1796   In Richmond, "a negro, a notorious thief, was hanged. An exhibition of this kind is uncommon here. It of course attracted a great crowd of spectators . . . the criminal . . . walked from the [prison] to the Gallows, not only with composure but with cheerfulness, declaring his happiness in the prospect of death, and in the certainty of being soon with God." *The Virginia Journals of Benjamin Henry Latrobe*, 1.

2. Any type of wooden frame that consists of two posts crowned by a cross beam.

> 1731   A tobacco warehouse was to contain "four prizes with gallows and platforms." Northampton Co., Va., Court Order Book 1729–1732.

gambrel roof   A curbed gable roof divided into two sections of unequal slope. The term does not come into fashion in the South until after the first quarter of the 19th century. Before that time, contemporaries used the term *Dutch roof*. See also **Dutch roof.**

> 1765   "To be sold, a large building with two upright stories and a Gambrel Roof." *Massachusetts Gazette.*

gaol (goal)   A building for the confinement of prisoners awaiting trial or punishment. Also a place of detention for debtors awaiting better luck. The term was synonymous with the more common *prison* during the 17th and 18th centuries. In the late 18th century, the spelling of the term as *jail* came into currency. For a more detailed description, see **prison.**

garden   A piece of ground, often enclosed by a paled fence or wall, devoted to the cultivation of vegetables, herbs, flowers, fruits, shrubs, or grasses. The pleasure grounds surrounding a dwelling were also referred to as the garden in the 18th century. Most gardens in the colonial period were devoted to the purely practical production of food and medicines, while a few combined practical and pleasurable pur-

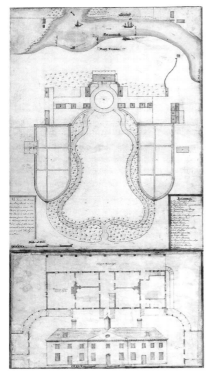

garden
Above: Charles Fraser, Wigton on St. James, Goose Creek, S.C.
Below: Plan of Mount Vernon, Fairfax County, Va., by Samuel Vaughan, 1787

suits. Private gardens often consisted of a piece of ground near a dwelling house appropriated for the cultivation of medicinal or food plants, fruits, and flowers. These were known as *kitchen gardens*. On wealthier estates, spaces devoted to flowers were called *flower gardens*, and those where fruit trees were grown were called *fruit gardens* or *orchards*. The plantings and functions of these garden types were often blended as well. The term *garden* also referred to ornamental planned spaces planted with grass, trees, and shrubs surrounding a dwelling. Although the term *formal garden* was seldom used in the 18th century, there were a number of gardens on larger estates and plantations whose plantings, walks, pools, fountains, statues, and other ornamental features followed a definite, recognizable plan, usually symmetrical with geometric forms. The placement of such pleasure gardens during this period depended upon the nearness of overland and waterborne transportation, the soil, the availability of fresh water, planting materials, and an impressive prospect. Because of their tranquil setting and the long distance to many churchyards, a number of southern gardens became family burial grounds. The term *public garden* began to appear in the late 18th century to describe a verdant landscape laid out in many southern towns where enterprising proprietors provided a variety of social entertainments. For a more detailed description of these public pleasure gardens, see **public garden.** For other types of gardens, see also **botanical garden, falling garden, flower garden, pleasure ground.**

1647 A tenant in York County, Virginia, agreed to "maintain the tobacco houses in repair, as well as the pales about the yard and gardens and other necessary fences." *W&MQ*, 1 ser., 5.

1686 Planter William Fitzhugh of Stafford County, Virginia, wrote about his orchard "of about 250 Aple trees most grafted, well fenced in with a Locust fence, which is as durable as most brick walls, a Garden, a hundred feet square, well pailed in, a Yeard wherein is most of the foresaid necessary houses, pallizado'd in with locust Punchens." *William Fitzhugh and His Chesapeake World.*

1701 A Middlesex County, Virginia, planter stipulated in his will that he "be buried in my own Garden, and Betwixt my first wife Frances and my last wife Margaret, and that, that place be either walled in with stone or brick twenty feet squear." Middlesex Co., Va., Will Book 1698–1713.

1717 John Custis of Williamsburg wrote to a London merchant that he had "lately got into the vein of gardening and have made a handsom garden to my house; and desire you will lay out 5£ for me in handsom striped hollys and yew trees." John Custis Letterbook, LC.

1739 "To be sold a Plantation . . . on Ashley River, within three Miles of Charlestown . . . the Gardens are extensive, pleasant and profitable, and abound with all sorts of Fruit trees, and resemble old England the most of any in the Province." *South Carolina Gazette.*

1754 It was "Ordered that there be a Gardain built on the Gleeb, where the Minister Orders itt, one Hundred feet square to be good saw'd pails of timber pine or poplar five feet high and pointed, the Railes of Good poplar saw'd to the usual size." Suffolk Parish, Nansemond Co., Va., Vestry Book.

1763 Merchant Henry Laurens of Charleston ordered from an English merchant "for my Garden about the Quantity of 15 or 20 Hogsheads of Gravel & small Stone Ballast." Later in the same year he thanked a member of the Moravian community of Bethabara, North Carolina, for sending him some "flower roots" but noted that "they were no novelty as we had such before in our Garden. . . . Mrs. Laurens is greatly disappointed, as she is not yet able . . . to get into our new House & become Mistress of that employment which she most delights in, the cultivating & ornamenting her Garden." *The Papers of Henry Laurens,* 4.

1804 Thomas Jefferson observed that "the kitchen garden is not the place for ornaments . . . bowers and treillages suit that better." *Thomas Jefferson, Landscape Architect.*

1806 An advertisement for a plantation for sale outside of Charleston boasted of "the handsomest Garden in the state, and laid out when belonging to the late Mr. Williamson, by English Gardeners. . . . and has since been much improved and additions made also by another English Gardener" containing "about 21 acres." *Charleston Courier*.

1806 An American gardening manual stated that "the kitchen garden is . . . ground allotted for the culture of all kinds of seculent herbs and roots for culinary purposes . . . generally placed detached entirely from the pleasure ground; also as much out of view of the front of the habitation as possible." M'Mahon, *The American Gardener's Calendar*.

garden house An ornamental structure in a garden or pleasure ground, often polygonal in form, dedicated to enjoyment of the surrounding landscape. Whether open or enclosed, these structures provided a setting for outdoor social activities. In some instances the term may have described a small building in which to store gardening implements. See also **summer house.**

1786 "I removed the garden houses which were in the middle of the front walls to the extreme points of them; which were done with more ease and less damage than I expected, considering the height one of them was to be raised from the ground." *The Diaries of George Washington*, 4.

1792 In Philadelphia, Thomas Jefferson complained to his landlord concerning work on a garden house completed in his absence: "I added that you need not do the inside finishing that is to say the plaistering of the garden house that i might arrange that to my own mind. . . . The object . . . was that I might have a place to retire & write in when I wished to be unseen & undisturbed even by my servants, & for this purpose it was to have a sky-light & no lateral windows. . . . When I returned from Virginia I found the garden house made with a window-door at each end; no sky-light, and a set of joists which were in the way. This rendered it absolutely useless for my purpose, & your work man having retained it long after as a shop, & left it without a floor, I have been able to make no other use of it than as a store room." Coolidge Collection, Massachusetts Historical Society.

1828 In Sussex County, Delaware, Orphans Court valuations for one property mention "a gardenhouse seven by seven feet in middling [repair]." Sussex Co., Del., Orphans Court Valuations O.

garner A building or enclosure for the storage of grain; a granary. See also **granary.**

1807 In a memorandum about storing grain, Thomas Jefferson directed that "the toll of the mill is to be put away in the two garners made, which are to have secure locks." *Thomas Jefferson's Garden Book*.

garret (garratt, garrett, garrit, garrot[t]) A room created partially or wholly from the space immediately beneath a roof. Unlike most lofts, garrets usually were finished, often heated, and designed for living or working. In the 17th century Chesapeake, the term appears to have been interchangeable with *loft*. See also **attic, loft.**

1674 A dwelling house in Charles County contained "a loft or Garrett . . . the said loft to be six foot high & sealed & lined with riven boards." *Archives of Maryland*, 60.

1748 A dwelling house for sale in Charleston contained "upper Lofts which may be converted into Garrets." *South Carolina Gazette*.

1786 A tavern in Richmond included "seven convenient lodging rooms in the garret, unconnected, two of which have fireplaces, and the whole apartments are so contrived to be independent of each other." *Virginia Gazette*.

gate **1.** A movable structure used like a door to control entrance and exit through an opening, but in a wall, fence, or similar free-standing barrier rather than a building. It is basically a rectangular frame of wood or iron, usually strengthened with a diagonal brace. Pales, bars, or boards may be added for additional security or ornament. Gates swing on hinges mounted along one vertical side and an adjacent post or jamb; they are used singly or in pairs.

1667   An act of the Virginia General Assembly required "that every person haveing a plantation shall, at the most plaine and convenient path that leades to his house, make a gate in his ffence for the convenience of passage of man and horse to his house about their occasions at the discretion of the owners." Hening, *Statutes at Large*, 2.

1743   The owner of a plantation in Lancaster County, Virginia, wrote "I would have a new Great Gate made out of the stuff that I have ready saw'd for that purpose; the Back & fore parts, that the bars are to be Mortois'd into to be of Locust; which must be faln [fallen] and ly to season a while, to keep it from splitting. And let it be Cross-brac'd, and pinn'd Cleaverly to keep it from swaging; and let their be a Good Latch & Catch put as Low as the old one, to keep it fast, that hogs may neither go in nor out: and give charge that it be always kept shut: and indeed it must be so hung as the old one was, and kept Greas'd, that it may shut itself." Joseph Ball Letterbook, LC.

1769   In Kent County, Maryland, a carpenter was "to make one good framed double gate each frame with good pine paling the said Gate to be hung to good locust posts with good iron hinges with an iron latch and ketch" for a churchyard. Chester Parish, Kent County, Md., Vestry Book.

1778   Magistrates in a Virginia county directed that someone be hired "to erect a Gate at each end of the Attornies Bar" in their courtroom. Northampton County, Va., Court Order Book 1777–1783.

2. An opening in an enclosing wall or fence, often treated as ornamental, defensive, or both and providing access to public, ceremonial, or other specialized spaces.

1806   In the District of Columbia, an Italian sculptor called Franzoni is "now engaged in a Free Eagle, also Colossal for the Gate of the Navy Yard." *The Correspondence and Miscellaneous Papers of Benjamin Henry Latrobe*, 2.

gauge (gage)   **1.** Any one of a number of tools with a calibrated arm used for measuring and marking lines.

2. To shape by rubbing or molding a brick into a consistent size and appearance. Gauged bricks were generally wedge-shaped in form and used to face the lintel of arched masonry openings. See also **brick, rubbed.**

1810   An account of work for the Riddell House in Baltimore listed "cutting & Setting 15 ft. Elliptical, rubbed, gauged arches." Riddell Accounts, Pleasants Papers, MHS.

1831   A brick courthouse was to have "all apertures nited and gaged arches on centers on the outside and ruff camber arches on the inside." Caswell Co., N.C., Court Minutes Book 1823–1831, NCA&H.

3. To cut or shape an object to bring it to a consistent or proper length, thickness, or measurement. The underside of floorboards were often undercut or gauged so that the upper side would form an even surface.

genteel   Fashionably refined, stylish, or graceful in shape or appearance. The term appeared in an architectural sense in the early 18th century, became common in the two decades before the American Revolution, and went out of use in the first quarter of the 19th century. It was used to connote a sense of appropriateness and polish in form and finish. See also **elegant, fashionable, neat, taste.**

1719   A churchyard was to have a brick wall "with a handsom Coopin Brick upon the Top and Genteely Rompt at each side of the Gates." St. Peter's Parish, New Kent Co., Va., Vestry Book.

gauge (2)
Blandfield, Essex County, Va.

1761 A church belfry was "to be compleated in a genteel and workman like manner." Elizabeth City Parish, Elizabeth City Co., Va., Vestry Book.

1777 Wanted in St. John's Parish, South Carolina, was "any Tradesman who is capable of executing a genteel Altar piece for this Church." *Gazette of the State of South Carolina.*

gibbet (jibbet) (*n.*) An upright post with arms on which the bodies of criminals were hung in irons or chains after execution. (*v.*) To hang or execute a convicted criminal on an upright post or gallows.

1707 A sheriff was paid for "his trouble in securing [two slaves] in prison & executing & gibbeting ye sd Negroes." Essex Co., Va., Court Order Book 1703–1708.

1713 An Indian slave convicted of stealing was ordered to "be hanged by the neck on a gibbet." Northumberland Co., Va., Court Order Book 1698–1713.

gild, gilding The application of gold leaf, gold flakes, or other material to produce a lustrous finish. Because of the expense of the material and the specialized skills required to properly apply gold leaf, gilding was rare in the early South. It was used to pick out various components of weather vanes, balls, finials, clock dials, and other exterior ironwork. In a few of the grander dwellings, some interior woodwork, especially capitals and architraves, received an application of gilding to highlight carved elements. Some churches, particularly Anglican ones, had various parts of the altar, pulpit, and other monuments gilded.

1727 The Anglican parish of St. James, Goose Creek, South Carolina, noted that the church was "decently beautified with paintings & guildings grave and commendable." SPG Letterbook A, SPGFP.

1752 A. Pooley advertised his services as "a Painter, either in the Limning way, History, Altar Pieces for Churches, Landskips, Views of their own Houses and Estates, Signs, or any other Way of Painting; and also Gilding." *Maryland Gazette.*

1753 The vestry ordered "that the Weathercock be repaired and gilded." St. Philip's Parish, Charleston, S.C., Vestry Book.

1770 Contained in the inventory of Lord Botetourt, governor of Virginia, was "a long Box of Gilt bordering intended for the supper Room." *Inventories of Four Eighteenth-Century Houses in the Historic Area of Williamsburg.*

1777 At Bruton Parish Church in Williamsburg, "the Govrs. Pew is elegant, & elevated above the rest: a silk Curtain hangs on each Side & Front of it from a Canopy supported by two fluted, gilt Pillars." Down the street at the capitol, the tympanum of the front pedimented portico formerly contained "the King's Arms (elegantly carved & gilt)." *VMHB,* 62.

1803 Estimates were made for "painting, Lettering and gilding Tables of commandments, Belief & Lord's Prayer, gilding the Sun, painting the Rays & Clouds in dome." St. Michael's Parish, Charleston, S.C., Vestry Book.

gimlet (gimblet) A tool with a screw point used for boring small holes. Gimlets were often used to create guide holes for nails and screws.

girder (girt) A large, horizontal, framing beam. From the 17th through the early 19th centuries, the name was applied to a variety of beams, often in a less than precise manner. Whatever the location, the chief purpose of these members was to provide additional rigidity to the frame. In floor framing, girders spanned the breadth of the interior space between the outer sills, breaking up the area into smaller units spanned by joists. For large floor spans, the framing was subdivided by even larger members known as summer beams, generally running from end sill to an interior girder, with a series of subsidiary girders tied into the summers at right angles. Sometimes, the terms *summer* and *girder* were used indiscriminately to refer to any large, internal flooring beam. This type of frame was occasionally called a girt floor. In two-story buildings, a girder was a beam in the outer or cross walls placed at the level of the upper floor, approximately halfway between the groundsill and upper wall plate at the eaves. At roof level, girders acted as tie beams spanning and binding the outer walls. See also **girt roof.**

1682 Specifications for a Quaker meeting house in Talbot County, Maryland, required a building "60 foote long 22 foote wide and to be Strong Substantiall Framed work with good white oak ground Sills and posts with girders and Summers and Small Joyst and ye upper Floors to be laid with plank." Third Haven Quaker Meeting, Minutes Book, 1.

1694 A church roof was to have "five Girders and five Principal Rafters." St. Paul's Parish, Kent Co., Md., Vestry Book.

1696 Payment was made for "covering the south side of the Courthouse and girding in the posts to the girders." Northumberland Co., Va., Court Order Book 1678–1698.

1747 A church was to have "a strong substantial Girt Floor." Albemarle Parish, Surry Co., Va., Vestry Book.

1752 Repair to a church included "a new Roof intire to the Church, which is eighty feet long, and forty feet wide, three Girders across the main Body." Christ Church Parish, Calvert Co., Md., Vestry Book.

1771 Specifications for St. John's Church in Granville County, North Carolina, called for the "Sills . . . to go the whole length of the Church to wit one on each side & one on each side of the Isle with such sufficient number of Girders or cross sills crossing the same as shall or is necessary in framing a House of these Dimentions so as to make it strong & substantial." Francis Hawks Papers, Church Historical Society.

1824 Plans for a courthouse specified that the "roof . . . be hipped & the joists . . . be 3 by 12 inches & framed into gearders & inter ties of a size suited to the proportion of the joists." Person Co., N.C., Miscellaneous Court Records, County Accounts, NCA&H.

girt roof A name occasionally applied to a principal rafter roof. Girders acted as tie beams, spanning the breadth of a building, and forming the lower chord of a principal rafter truss. The term had little currency outside 18th-century Virginia. See also **girder, principal rafter.**

1713 A glebe house was to have "a Good girt Roof." St. Peter's Parish, New Kent Co., Va., Vestry Book.

1745 A chapel was to be built with "a girt roof with principal rafters braced." Southam Parish, Cumberland Co., Va., Vestry Book.

glass A transparent material produced by mixing silica with other inorganic materials, such as soda and lime, known as flux. Once heated and in a molten state, glass was blown in two different manners. *Cylinder glass* or *sheet glass* was blown into a long cylinder, cut, and rolled into a flat sheet. *Crown glass* was made by blowing a large sheet into a round disc or table. Glass produced by this latter method was clearer and far more durable, and became the preferred glass of builders in the colonies and early republic. Although an early effort to manufacture glass in America occurred at Jamestown, glass production was later discouraged by English mercantile trade policies. Until the Revolution, all window glass was imported from Great Britain, chiefly from London and Bristol, the principal manufacturing centers. As an imported good, glass was a relatively expensive commodity, one that many Americans could not afford. As a result, the windows of many dwellings in the early South, particularly those in the backcountry settlements and those occupied by poorer tenants and slaves, were left unglazed. See also **crown glass, glazier, sheet glass.**

glaze (glase)   **1.** To furnish with glass; to install glass in windows. See also **glass, glazier.**

> **1656**   "Pleasant in their building," claimed a promotional tract that puffed the virtues of the Chesapeake colonies, "which although for the most part they are but one story besides the loft, and built of wood, yet contrived so delightfull, that your ordinary houses in England are not so handsome, for usually the rooms are large, daubed, and white limed, glazed and flowered, and if not glazed windows, shutters which are made very pritty and convenient." Hammond, *Leah and Rachel.*
> **1674**   The statehouse in St. Mary's City was to have "two iron Casements to every window in the said hous the frames and Casements to be . . . glased with good Cleer square glasse." *Archives of Maryland*, 2.
> **1772**   Payment was made "To William Smith for cuting & glazing 264 pains of glass." St. Helena's Parish, S.C., Vestry Book.

2. A transparent paint finish, composed of linseed oil tinted with transparent pigments.

> **1768**   "Colours which become transparent in oil, such as lake, Prussian blue, and brown pink, are frequently used without the admixture of white, or any other opake pigment; by which means, the tint of the ground on which they are laid retains in some degree its force; and the real colour, produced in the painting, is the combined effect of both. This is called GLAZING, and the pigments . . . are called glazing colours." Dossie, *The Handmaid to the Arts.*

glazier (glaser, glasier)   A workman who fits windows with glass. Professional glaziers plied their trade in the Chesapeake colonies by the middle of the 17th century. Until the 1730s and 1740s, when sash windows displaced leaded casements in all but the most humble and subsidiary structures, the work of a glazier consisted of cutting and arranging small glass panes or *quarrels* into leaded frames or *cames.* When sash windows came into fashion, the nature of the glazier's trade was transformed. Rather than working with lead and solder, the glazier cut larger panes of glass to fit into wooden frames and secured them against the back of the frame with small brads and putty. Glaziers had long combined their skills with those of other crafts, and by the late colonial period the trade was frequently combined with that of painters or joiners.

> **1657**   John Simpson of York County, Virginia, was identified in court records as a "glazier." Lancaster Co., Va., Court Record Book 1654–1666.
> **1688**   Payment was made "to Wm Harding Glazier for 2 days about Court house." Henrico Co., Va., Court Record Book 1688–1697.
> **1714**   "The Vestry hath agreed with William Mackey to make Moulds for the Glazier to put Stantions in the Windows Where it is Necessary." St. Paul's Parish, Kent Co., Md., Vestry Book.
> **1738**   A servant named John Minor, who ran away from his master in Gloucester County, Virginia, was described as "a plaisterer by trade, but can do Glaziers and Bricklayers work and has got a diamond, trowel, and other tools with him." *Virginia Gazette.*

glebe (gleeb, gleab, gleib)   A portion of cultivable land owned by an Anglican parish for the use of its minister. Glebes were established in Virginia from at least the middle of the 17th century and appeared in colonies in which the established church prospered. Although Anglican ministers often resided on their glebes, others were rented and the income applied to the maintenance of the living or the church fabric.

1635 "It is agreed by this vestry that a parsonage house should be built upon the gleeb land by Christyde next and that the said house shall be forty foot long and eyghteen foot wyde." *County Court Records of Accomack-Northampton, Virginia 1632–1640.*

1643 The Virginia General Assembly confirmed that "the east side of Nansimum River form the present gleab downewards to the mouth of the said River be a peculiar parish to which the gleab and parsonage house now is shall be appropriated and called the east parish." Hening, *Statutes at Large*, 1.

1661 "Bee it ordered that [for] the encouragement of ministers to come into the countrey and there better accomodation when [they] come there be glebes provided for every parrishe . . . with convenient houseing and stockes upon the same." Hening, *Statutes at Large*, 2.

1722 "The Church" at St. James, Goose Creek, South Carolina, "a beautiful Brick Edifice, was erected at ye Expense of ye parishioners, to which are annex'd 100 Acres of good glebe land." SPG Letterbook B, SPGFP.

1726 The vestry was to pay a planter "for the 200 acres of Land Where Mr. Francis Holland now Lives On purpose to make a Glebe of for the Use of the [parish of] St. Georges." St. George's Parish, Harford Co., Md., Vestry Book.

1756 The Reverend William Peasley wrote to his vestry that "I cannot . . . help thinking it a very great hardship that I am oblig'd to pay House-Rent, as you are not insensible that the Society [of the Propagation of the Gospel] sent me here on condition that a House would be provided for me, as the custom throughout this Province; and really the Society told me, before I left London, that there was a good Parsonage House on the Glebe, and on no other terms would I have come here. Besides Gentlemen, I believe the whole world will think it reasonable that the Inerest of the money given by the public for building a House on the Glebe, should be applied towards discharging the ministers House-Rent till the parsonage should be ready for his reception." St. Helena' Parish, S.C., Vestry Book.

1804 It was "resolved . . . that a sale be made of the Glebe Land Belonging to this parish . . . a tract of Land Adjoining the plantation of Capt. Thos. A. Reader, Containing by servey 241 1/2 Acres. Belonging to All Faith Parish." All Faiths Parish, St. Mary's Co., Md., Vestry Book.

glebe house   A dwelling provided by an Anglican parish for the incumbent of the living. The term was used primarily in Virginia from the late 17th through the early 19th centuries. In Anglican parishes in other colonies, *parsonage house* was the more common term. See also **parsonage house.**

1678 An agreement stated that "Mr. John Sheppard Minister should leave ye Glebe house in as good repair as when finished, its to be understood of ye 25 foot Dwelling, Closset & shed, and a Quarter repaired, the casualtys of violent gusts and Fire excepted. And for the other houses he builds at his own proper charge, he nor the next Incumbent shall be obliged to keep repaired." Christ Church Parish, Middlesex Co., Va., Vestry Book.

1702 Churchwardens were to "agree with some workmen for ye Building & ereckting a gleeb house upon ye gleeb plantation, six & thirty foot long & twenty foot wide with two outside chemneys two 8 foot square closetts plankt above & below, with two chambers above staires and ye staires to goe up in ye midst of ye house." Petsworth Parish, Gloucester Co., Va., Vestry Book.

1739 "The Revd. Mr. Patrick Henry . . . produc'd to the Vestry a plan of a Glebe House, proposed to be built by Mr. William Walker of Stafford County of the following Dimensions Viz., Thirty four feet Long, and Twenty Eight feet wide in the clear, to be of Brick." St. Paul's Parish, Hanover Co., Va., Vestry Book.

globe   A spherical ornament, fabricated out of solid wood or a metal shell, usually found on the tops of steeples and cupolas below the vane. Globes or balls were sometimes gilded.

1763 The spire of St. Michael's Church in Charleston was "terminated by a gilt Globe, from which rises a Vane, in the Form of a Dragon." Milligen Johnston, *A Short Description of the Province of South-Carolina.*

glue (glew)   A hard gelatin obtained from boiling animal hides, hoofs, and other scraps of material in water, which, after hardening, is then cooked with water in a double boiler to produce a strong adhesive. In an architectural context, joiners used hide glue in wainscotting to bond the edges of smaller pieces together in order to make broad panels.

> 1742   "Utensils us'd about a Pew in the Church" included pine plank, nails, holdfasts, and "Glew." St. Anne's Parish, Anne Arundel Co., Md., Vestry Book.
>
> 1793   At "Old East" at the University of North Carolina, "the outside doors and windows [are to be] put together with white lead the inside doors and framed partitions with glue." University Archives, UNC, Chapel Hill.

glyph   A decorative vertical groove or channel. See also **triglyph.**

gold leaf   See **leaf** (1).

Gothic (Gothick)   A style of architecture popular in Europe from the 12th to the 16th century, characterized by the use of the pointed arch, ribbed vaulting, and elaborate tracery, and moldings that owed little to classical architecture. A few elements of this style continued in England through the 17th century, particularly in rural church building and repairs. Early colonists in the Chesapeake found few opportunities to practice this style in the simple public buildings and domestic structures erected during the first century of settlement. The use of buttresses and molded mullions found on St. Luke's Church (1682), Isle of Wight County, Virginia, while not classical in form, were hardly Gothic in inspiration. It was not until the second half of the 18th century that Americans began to become cognizant of Gothic forms, largely through the publication of English architectural books. Unlike their counterparts on classical architecture, these books and essays were not based on a scholarly understanding of medieval building, but merely provided a catalog of forms thought to embody the spirit of the Gothic. For 18th-century Englishmen and Americans, the *Gothick,* symbolized by romantic ruins and irrationality, contrasted sharply with the Enlightenment ideas embodied in the harmonic proportions of classical architecture. Until the *Gothic Revival* took hold of the American imagination in the second quarter of the 19th century, there were few architectural references to the Gothic, it being little more than a minor fashion in the decorative arts. Here and there, cabinetmakers and joiners emulated the forms offered in English design books to produce furniture of a Gothic character. During this same period, a few observers of American architecture were inclined to describe a building as *Gothic* if it were old or had such superficial Gothic Revival features as pointed arch windows or spires.

Gothic
Library, Hayes,
Chowan County, N.C., c. 1817

> 1756   "GOTHICK—A wild and irregular manner of building, that took the place of the regular antique method at the time when architecture, with the other arts, declined. The Gothick is distinguished from the antique architecture by its ornaments being whimsical, and its profiles incorrect." Ware, *A Complete Body of Architecture.*
>
> 1767   A cabinetmaker in Williamsburg advertised that he was prepared to make "all sorts of Chinese and Gothick paling for gardens and summer houses." *Virginia Gazette.*
>
> 1774   A carpenter's account for work done at a dwelling in Odessa, Delaware included: "12 Lights Gothick sashes at 3/6 & Caseing windows..£2.10.6." Sweeney, *Grandeur on the Appoquinimink.*

1786 Estimates made for repairing the Congregational Church in Charleston included "building a Gothick pulpit." Congregational Church, Charleston, S.C., Church Records.

1803 A church near Annapolis that had been destroyed by fire "was the most gothic in the United States, and could vie with any church in the union in point of antiquity." *Charleston Courier.*

gouge A chisel having a partly cylindrical blade with the bevel on either the concave or convex side. Gouges were essential tools in carving and scribing. In an architectural setting, they were used for carving the ornaments of chimney pieces, friezes, and flutes. Repetitive gouged groves became especially popular as a decorative devise for chimney pieces in the early 19th century.

grain 1. The texture of a material such as wood or stone; the arrangement and size of their constituent parts. In wood, the grain consists of fibers growing in parallel, longitudinal veins or lines. Timber is far easier to cut or split along these grain lines than across them. Often sedimentary stones such as sandstone and limestone, which are composed of a series of layers, will readily split along a plane in which sediment was originally deposited. These layers may be extremely fine or very pronounced and will affect a stone's ability to be carved as well as its durability. The term was also used to refer to the texture of the stone.

1805 The ornaments of the Capitol in Washington were to be fabricated from "a yellowish Sand stone of fine grain, finer than the piperino or grey sandstone used in Rome. . . . This stone yields in any direction equally to the chissel, not being in the least laminated, nor hard enough to fly off before a sharp tool. It may therefore be cut with great precision." *The Correspondence and Miscellaneous Papers of Benjamin Henry Latrobe,* 2.

1812 The stone of the President's House in Washington "is like our Gloucestershire stone of a very good grain." Foster, *Jeffersonian America.*

2. *(v.)* To produce by painting an imitation of the natural grain of wood. The term did not come into general use until the antebellum period when there had been an upsurge in the imitation of wood graining for interior finishes. In the 18th century, the term *imitation* was used to describe this process of decoration. See **imitation.**

granary (granery, grainery) A building for the storage of threshed grain and occasionally other crops such as corn.

1624 An act passed in Virginia stated "that there shall be in every parish a publick garnary unto which there shall be contributed for every planter . . . at the crop after he hath been heere a year a bushell of corne." Hening, *Statutes at Large,* 1.

1715 Payment for "building a granary £8" was recorded in Anne Arundel County, Maryland. James Carroll Day Book, Georgetown Univ. Library.

1759 The vestry "ordered a Granary be Built . . . 30 foot long and 20 foot wide to be covered with cyprus shingles and weatherboarded with good fetheredge plank and floar'd." Suffolk Parish, Nansemond Co., Va., Vestry Book.

1808 On a plantation was "one framed planked granary twenty by thirteen." Sussex Co., Del., Orphans Court Valuations K.

granite A coarse-grained igneous rock composed chiefly of feldspar, quartz, and mica. The compact, crystalline character of granite makes it one of the most durable stones used in construction. However, in preindustrial America, it was one of the most difficult materials to shape. Granite appears in the South from the fall line to the eastern slope of the Appalachian Mountains. Quarries were opened in several areas of northern Maryland by the 1820s, after which time granite became a more common material in southern building. Unquarried granite was used much earlier in this region for foundations, chimneys, and rubble walling.

> **1800** In designing a pyramidal mausoleum for George Washington, architect Benjamin Henry Latrobe suggested that the material "be of Granite, which abounds in the Potomac." *The Correspondence and Miscellaneous Papers of Benjamin Henry Latrobe,* 1.
>
> **1802** Bids were accepted for supplying "the necessary quantities of Free stone of Granite, rough stone" for a jail in Washington, D.C. *Alexandria Advertiser and Commercial Intelligencer.*
>
> **1820** The architect in charge of work at the President's House in Washington reported the construction of the front gates and railing was nearing completion: "The pedestal work, which is of granite stone, has been completed, and the coping, circular, and straight, with piers to the carriage and foot-ways, and the iron railing, circular and straight have been prepared and put up." *Daily National Intelligencer.*

grate A frame consisting of a series of parallel metal bars, attached by cross bars at regular intervals and used for various purposes; a grille.

1. An iron frame of bars installed in prison windows, as well as the apertures of some stores and dwellings, to prevent entry or exit. Grates were also used to cover openings such as drains and chimney flues.

> **1698** A prison was to have "a window with iron grates." Lancaster Co., Va., Court Order Book 1696–1702.
>
> **1736** A prison "door [is] to be Grated with Iron th Squares not to exceed Six inches . . . and two Iron windows the Iron Grates of the Windows to be workt in the Brick." Middlesex Co., Va., Court Order Book 1732–1737.
>
> **1749** A prison was to have "a strong Door with sufficient Locks the door to be bound with Iron inside and outside and in form of grate work, an open grate in part of the Door for a window, another grate window on the opposite of the door for air." Westmoreland Co., Va., Court Order Book 1747–1750.
>
> **1768** Payment was made for "levelling the Yard" of the South Carolina statehouse, "sinking a Drain therefrom to the Common Sewer, laying a kerb, Grate &c." Journal of the Commons House of Assembly No. 37, SCA&H.

2. A frame of parallel metal bars used to hold fuel in a fireplace, furnace, or stove.

> **1747** A prison was to have "2 iron Grates 18 inches long and 12 inches wide each to be set on Brick Harths." Northumberland Co., Va., Court Record Book 1743–1749.
>
> **1748** Property for sale in Charleston contained "a large Kitchen grate, an oven and jack." *South Carolina Gazette.*
>
> **1768** Payment was made to "Laurens, Motte & Co. for a pair of stove grates for the Council Chamber" in the South Carolina Statehouse. South Carolina General Tax Receipts and Payments 1761–1769, SCA&H.
>
> **1802** Washington, D.C., artisan William Coltman charged John Tayloe for "the Brickwork at setting up Four Coal fire grates at 2 Doll.ʳ P. Grate...To Brick work at Setting up One Coal fire grate 2 [dollars]." Tayloe Papers, VHS.

gravel Small stones and pebbles, often mixed with other materials such as sand, clay, or loam. The most common use of gravel was for walks. However, in the 17th century it had limited use in roughcast and in later periods was sometimes inserted into mixtures of mortar.

> **1651** An indentured bricklayer from Barbados was hired by a Norfolk County, Virginia, planter in order "to ruffe cast" a dwelling in Kecoughtan "with lyme & gravell." Norfolk Co., Va., Will and Deed Book 1646–1651.
>
> **1767** Charlestonian Henry Laurens wrote to an English factor that if a ship "is coming this way in Ballast I beg the favour of him to remember 40 or 50 Ton of best Gravel for my Garden." *The Papers of Henry Laurens,* 5.
>
> **1806** The walls of a new brick meetinghouse in Fayette County, Kentucky, were "to be laid with fine gravel and lime, but a little clay may be added to lay the outside brick." *Kentucky Gazette and General Advertiser.*

grate (1)
Jail, Northampton County, Va.

grate (2)
Daniel Heyward House, Charleston, S.C.

gravestone A memorial stone placed over a grave. The term generally referred to any type of upright stone, but was also used to refer to all types of memorial stones including small flat ones and table tombs. Because of the paucity of natural stone in many areas of the coastal South, there were few specially carved memorial stones to mark the grave of an individual. By the second half of the 17th century, the wealthiest planters of the Chesapeake imported carved stones from English stonemasons, a practice that continued through the late 18th century. In South Carolina and other coastal settlements, a vigorous trade with New England gravestone carvers developed in the late colonial period. Stone carvers in Rhode Island supplied a number of slate figure stones for Charleston customers. From time to time, the city also had a few stone carvers who were capable of executing finely carved and lettered stones. See also **footstone, headstone, tombstone.**

1674 The will of Richard Cole specified that "my body be interred uppon Poynt pleasant uppon my plantation . . . in a neat Coffin of Black walnutt . . . a grave Stone of Black Marble be with all Convenient Speed sent for out of England with my Coate Arms . . . engraven in brasse & under it this Epitath: Here lies Dick Cole a grevious Sinner, That died a Little before dinner, Yet hopes in heaven to find a place, To Satiate his Soule with Grace." Westmoreland Co., Va., Deed and Patent Book 1665–1677.
1773 "JOHN BULL, Engraver of TOMB and GRAVE-STONES, From New Port, Rhode Island . . . carries on that business at his Shop on Champney's Wharf in Charles Town . . . where any Person may be Supplied with TOMB and GRAVE STONES, finished in the neatest manner . . . he has brought with him a few already cut, fit for engraving." *South Carolina Gazette and Country Journal.*

graveyard A place for the burial of the dead, often located on farms, in churchyards, or on public lots in cities and towns. Most graveyards were marked off by a fence or wall. As in other regions in early America, burial practices in the South varied over time and among different religious groups and social classes. The pattern of English burial in a parish churchyard scarcely survived the early years of settlement in the Chesapeake as the Anglican church struggled to become established. Parish boundaries often extended several hundred square miles and the location of churches did not become fixed in many regions until the late colonial period. Many families simply chose to bury their dead on a piece of land on their plantations. This practice continued for more than two centuries. In the second half of the 17th century and early 18th century, the English custom of burying important parishioners inside their respective churches enjoyed some popularity in established Anglican parishes in Virginia and elsewhere. At the same time, some parts of the churchyard were set aside as a graveyard. In a number of urban areas such as Charleston, this quickly led to overcrowding in small churchyards and regulations concerning the types and sizes of memorial stones and vaults were enacted. By the late 18th century and with increasing frequency in the early 19th century, most cities and large towns purchased land on their outskirts for public graveyards. See also **burial ground, cemetery.**

1679 A deed to several individuals "& the rest of the servts. of God frequently called Quakers," names "one house built by the sd people in the place called the Levy Neck Ould Fields near the Creek side . . . with ground sufficient for a Graveyard." Isle of Wight Co., Va., Will and Deed Book 1662–1715.
1768 On the Blakeford plantation on the Eastern Shore of Maryland was "one paled graveyard 20 feet square." Queen Anne's Co., Md., Deed Book H.

1800 In his will, builder John Ariss desired "to be buried, with permission of Mrs. Washington of Fairfield, in the graveyard at that place, and being a member of the Episcopal church, which I have ever considered as the best of Christian churches, I also request to be buried in a decent manner, according to the rites and ceremonies of that society." Berkeley Co., Va., Will Book 1796–1805.

great house The main or principal dwelling on a farm or plantation. The term did not necessarily imply that the dwelling was large or pretentious, but was only used to distinguish it from subsidiary build-ings. See also **manor house, mansion house.**

1730 On a glebe, the weatherboards of the "great house" were to be tarred. Stratton Major Parish, King and Queen Co., Va., Vestry Book.
1732 "To be sold, by Mr. John Moore all his Messuages and Tenements, situate on both sides of Mr. Trott's great House in Charlestown." *South Carolina Gazette.*
1760 At Mount Vernon, George Washington agreed with an undertaker "to build the two houses in the Front of my House . . . and running Walls for Pallisades to them from the Great house & from the Great House to the Wash House." *The Diaries of George Washington*, 1.
1763 Brickwork at Airwell in Middlesex County, Virginia, included "rubbing the bricks about the great house." Berkeley Papers, UVa.

great room The main or principal room in a building. This rela-tively uncommon term was not used to describe a room function but the relative size or position of a space.

1702 In assigning temporary spaces for various branches of the provincial govern-ment when it moved to its new capital in Williamsburg, it was agreed "that the building to the Westward next the College be appropriated to the use of the Genll Court and offices thereto belonging to wit: The great Roome below for the Genll Court to Sit . . . The great roome above stairs over the great Hall for the Council Chamber." *Journals of the House of Burgesses*, 3.
1751 In Charleston, "for the Benefit of Mr. Uhl at Mr. Gordon's Great Room in Broad Street . . . will be a Concert of Music." *South Carolina Gazette.*

gree, grece (gre) A flight of steps or staircase.

1689 A courthouse was to have a "hansum long gre." Norfolk Co., Va., Deed Book 1686–1695.

green Grassy, open space. The term usually referred to a private grassy area adjacent to a dwelling house in the 18th and early 19th centuries. Although more common in New England and the middle Atlantic colonies, it was occasionally used to describe an open area in the center of town or village used for public functions.

1727 "In the middle of the Town" of Newcastle, Delaware, "lies a spacious green in form of a square." Perry, *American Colonial Church*, 5.
1743 "A spacious bason in the midst of a large green presents itself as you enter the gate that leads to the house" of William Middleton outside of Charleston. *Letter-book of Eliza Lucas Pinckney.*

greenhouse A building, sometimes heated, with a large section of glazing in which delicate and tender plants and fruit trees were nur-tured and preserved during cold weather. See also **hothouse, oran-gery, stove house.**

1740 At Westover in Charles City County, Virginia, "Colonel Byrd . . . [had] a little green house with two or three orange trees." Bartram Papers, Historical Society of Pennsylvania.
1748 Property for sale in Charleston included "a large Garden, with two neat Green Houses for sheltering exotic Fruit-Trees, and Grape-Vines." *South Carolina Gazette.*
1770 At Mount Clare near Baltimore, a visitor took pleasure in viewing the "Green House with a good many Orange & Lemon Trees just ready to bear." *VMHB*, 45.

greenhouse
Wye, Talbot County, Md.

1784 In answer to some questions about the greenhouse at Mount Clare, Tench Tilghman "made a rough Plan of the Manner of conducting the Flues—Your Floor being 40 Feet long Mrs. Carroll recommends two Flues to run up the back Wall, because you may then increase the number of Flues which run under the Floor, and which she looks upon as essential—The trees are by that mean kept warm at the Roots . . . She recommends it to you to have the upper parts of your Window sashes to pull down, as well as the lower ones to rise—you then give Air to the Tops of your Trees—Your Ceiling she thinks ought to be Arched and at least 15 feet high . . . The Door of the House to be as large as you can conveniently make it— otherwise when the Trees come to any size, the limbs are broken and the Fruit torn off by moving in and out." Trostell, *Mount Clare.*

gristmill A mill for grinding grain. See also **mill.**

1683 Standing in St. Mary's County, Maryland, was "one Water Mill house with two Grist Mills." *Archives of Maryland,* 70.

1738 The will of John Thompson, a millwright of Craven County, North Carolina, left "all iron work and everything that belongs or connected with setting up a Grist Mill which iron work I brought into the said province" to his son. Secretary of State Records, Wills 1738–1752.

1792 Records describe "A Mill dam sett of Waste—Gates—An old Grist mill, 2 stories high, 20 feet square, and a shed adjoining 12 by 14 feet with 2 Water Wheels and 2 pair of Stones single-Geered, 2 boulting Chests with Cloths . . . all of which are in very bad Order and Repair. . . . Also one [corn] Kiln . . . 10 by 14 feet Built of Brick." Kent Co., Del., Orphans Court Valuations.

1801 It was declared that "one old Grist Mill 20 feet square must necessarily be rebuilt. . . . the [mill] house one and an half Stories high not to exceed the size of the present [mill] House, to be underpinned with Brick, and Cogg pitt to be done with brick, new throught and pier head, all the materials of the old Mill that will answer we recommend to be employed in the new Mill, the dam and flood gates also want some repairs." Kent Co., Del., Orphans Court Valuations.

groin The curved line formed by the intersection of two vaults.

1797 At the penitentiary in Richmond, architect Benjamin Henry Latrobe reported that "I pressed the necessity of beginning to make the Centers of the lower arches and the groins of the Cellar story." *The Correspondence and Miscellaneous Papers of Benjamin Henry Latrobe,* 1.

1820 In working on the Executive Offices in Washington, "the floors of the principal stories of the buildings, and which are supported by the groined arches of the basement, have been laid with stock brick." *Daily National Intelligencer.*

groove A rectangular channel cut in the edge of a plank or board to receive a projecting tongue of another piece or a spline. For a more detailed description, see **tongue and groove.** See also **spline.**

grotto An artificial subterraneous cavern in a garden, built for ornament, coolness, and bathing.

1752 "To Gentleman . . . as have a taste in pleasure . . . gardens . . . may depend on having them laid out, leveled, and drained in the most compleat manner, and politest taste, by the subscriber; who perfectly understands . . . erection of water works . . . fountains, cascades, grottos." *South Carolina Gazette.*

ground (*Usually pl.* grounds) Pieces of wood embedded in a wall that serve as plastering stops at the jamb of a doorway or the base of a partition. They also furnish a nailing surface for finish trim.

1774 A carpenter's account for work on the Corbit House in Odessa, Delaware, listed "2 Grounds undr Pilasters at 5/4." Sweeney, *Grandeur on the Appoquinimink.*

1802 The carpenter's bill for work on John Tayloe's elegant neoclassical house in Washington, D.C., included "Fram'd Circular grounds to Doors & Windows" for use in the circular rooms at the front of the house and "Dᵒ Straight" for the more conventional rectangular rooms elsewhere. Tayloe Papers, VHS.

1811 A Baltimore carpenter was paid for installing "fancy base, subase, and grounds." Riddell Accounts, Pleasants Papers, MHS.

ground floor   The floor in a building at or nearest ground level. By extension, the ground floor is also known as the *ground story* or, since the late 17th century, the *first story*. See also **story** (2).

> 1732   In a Charleston church, there were 47 pews built "on the Ground-Floor." Congregational Church, Charleston, S.C., Record Book.
>
> 1799   A design of a house "was made in consequence of a trifling Wager laid against me . . . that I could not design a house . . . which should have only 41 feet front; which should contain on the Ground floor, 3 Rooms, a principal Staircase, and back-stairs, and, which was the essential requisite, the front door of which should be in the Center." *The Correspondence and Miscellaneous Papers of Benjamin Henry Latrobe*, 1.

groundsill (groundsell, groundcell)   A horizontal beam at the bottom of a framed wall in which the lower ends of studs, posts, and braces are secured. An *interrupted sill* runs between the major wall posts and is lapped or tenoned into them. Groundsills sometimes sat on the ground or were raised off it on blocks or masonry foundations. The term was used primarily in the 17th century and had gradually disappeared from common usage in the South by the middle of the 18th century. The term *groundsill* may have been used by early builders rather than the shorter, synonymous *sill*, to distinguish it from other types employed in window and door construction. See also **interrupted sill, sill.**

> 1652   A builder was to "groundsell & brace" a dwelling "with 4 braces to the Groundsell." Surry Co., Va., Deed and Will Book 1652–1672.
>
> 1653   A tenant agreed to build on leased land "one good and sufficient framed house conteyning forty five foot in length and twenty foot in breadth with two chimneys and glass windows . . . and a cellar adjoining to it also of fifteen foot square the said house to be groundselled & underpinned with brick." Surry Co., Va., Deed and Will Book 1652–1672.
>
> 1681   "All the post" of a courthouse "and groundsells are to be of Locust, and the studs mortessed into the Groundsells." Northumberland Co., Va., Court Order Book 1678–1698.
>
> 1703   Payment was made for "removing an old Ground Sill" of a prison and "making a new one and studding underneath with locust studds." Essex Co., Va., Court Order Book 1703–1708.
>
> 1799   "The Ground Sills Guirders and Corner posts" of John Steele's dwelling in Rowan County, North Carolina, was "to be of good Sound post oak and all the other part of the frame to be made of Sound hewed and Sawed pine timber." John Steele Papers, SHC.

groundwork (ground frame)   The base on which a building is constructed; the lower part of a frame; a foundation. See also **foundation.**

> 1679   In an agreement to build a dwelling, "all the rest of the ground work [is] to be squared by" the carpenter. Henrico Co., Va., Deed and Will Book 1677–1692.
>
> 1711   Plans for a church required "the Ground Frame (vizt) the sills of the said Church the summers and Girders [to] be of the best White Oake to be quartered stuff and a foot square att least." Christ Church Parish, Middlesex Co., Va., Vestry Book.

grout   *(n.)* A thin, coarse, semiliquid mortar applied to masonry joints and other cavities as a sealant. *(v.)* To close a joint with such a substance. See also **mortar, putty.**

> 1763   Church walls were "to be well grouted every three courses." Wicomico Parish, Northumberland Co., Va., Vestry Book.
>
> 1765   "The bottom six courses" of a prison were "to be well grouted." Orange Co., Va., Miscellaneous Loose Papers.

1819 "The inner mortar" for the buildings at the University of Virginia were "to be one third lime and two thirds clean and gritty sand without any mixture of earth, the outer 1/2 lime and 1/2 such sand and the whole to be grouted with a mortar of the inner quality." *Lynchburg Press and Public Advertiser.*

grove A small woods or cluster of trees either occurring naturally and intentionally left in the landscape or purposely planted in the pleasure grounds around a dwelling. Often a grove consisted of large trees whose branches shaded the ground below. See also **clump.**

1742 "You may wonder how I could in this gay season think of planting a Cedar grove, which rather reflects an Autumnal gloom and solemnity than the freshness and gayty of spring. But so it is. . . . I intend then to connect in my grove the solemnity (not the solidity) of summer or autumn with the cheerfulness and pleasures of the spring, for it shall be filled with all kind of flowers, as well wild as Garden flowers, with seats of Camomoil and here and there a fruit tree—oranges, nectrons, Plumbs." *Letterbook of Eliza Lucas Pinckney.*

1776 George Washington wanted "to have groves of Trees at each end of the dwelling House . . . these Trees to be Planted without any order to regularity (but pretty thick, as they can at any time be thin'd) and to consist that at the North end, of locusts altogether, and that at the South, of all the clever kind of Trees (especially flowering ones) that can be got, such as Crab apple, Poplar, Dogwood, Sasafras, Laurel, Willow . . . to be interspersed here and there with ever greens such as Holly, Pine, and Cedar, also Ivy; to these may be added the Wild flowering Shrubs of the larger kind." *The Diaries of George Washington,* 2.

1807 At Monticello, Thomas Jefferson observed that "the canvas at large must be a Grove, of the largest trees, (poplar, oak, elm, maple, ash, hickory, chestnut, Linden, Weymouth pine, sycamore) trimmed very high, so as to give the appearance of open ground, yet not so far apart but that they may cover the ground with close shade." *Thomas Jefferson Landscape Architect.*

guardhouse A small building providing shelter for military or civilian sentinels. In Charleston, and perhaps other cities, a larger structure containing a lockup and various civic offices. The term was sometimes applied to small structures built near jails for officials to keep an eye on prisoners. See also **watch box.**

1733 In Savannah, Peter Gordon "mounted guard at eight o'clock at night, received orders from Mr. Oglethorp to fix two Centinells at the extream parts of the town who were to be relieved every two hours and then returning to guard house, which we had built of clapp boards upon the most convenient part of the Bluff, for commanding the river both wayes." *The Journal of Peter Gordon 1732–1735.*

1789 A court "ordered the sheriff [to] pay Venable and Venable £3.2.4 for building the Guard House." Prince Edward Co., Va., Court Order Book 1788–1791.

guesthouse A building for the reception and entertainment of travelers.

1620 Each of the four boroughs in the Virginia colony were required to "frame, build, and perfect, with all things thereto belonging, a common house, to bee called a Guest house, for the lodging and entertaining of fifty persons in each, upon their first arrivall. Of which houses, to be raised . . . shall be sixteene foot broad within, and nine score foot long, . . . And in each of them shall be set up all along on the one side, five and twenty Bedsteads of foure foot broad, sixe foot long, and two foot height from the ground . . . with partitions of Boords betweene them: And there shall be raised . . . five Chimnies. These houses we also require to be strongly built for continuance, with windowes well placed for wholesomenes of aire." *Records of the Virginia Company of London,* 3.

guildhall A place of assembly for a society of artisans, merchants, or citizens. When such a building was used for corporate purposes, the term was synonymous with the more common *town hall* or *market house.* For a more detailed description, see **town hall.**

1705 "An act for establishing ports & towns" allowed each Virginia town to "have a merchant guild and community with all customs and libertys belonging to a free burgh," with provision for a governing body of "eight of the principal inhabitants who shall be called benchers of the guild hall for the better rule and governance of the town." Hening, *Statutes at Large*, 3.

guilloche An ornamental pattern of interlacing curved bands. See also **fret**.

gula A cyma or ogee. For a more detailed description, see **cyma**.

gum A hardwood similar to yellow poplar, used primarily for framing members in building.

1771 The framing of a stable "below the plates [is] to be of good gum." Elizabeth City Parish, Elizabeth City Co., Va., Vestry Book.
1794 "The upper joists" of a barn in Delaware were "to be of the best gum 10 by 12." Dickinson Papers, Hall of Records.
1809 Part of a jail in Pasquotank County, North Carolina, was to be "lathed with gum laths 4 by 1 Inch." Pasquotank Co., N.C., County Accounts, NCA&H.

gunnery A place where arms are manufactured. See also **armory**.

1777 A visitor to Fredericksburg, Virginia, "went to see the Gunnery, as it is called. . . . About twenty Musquets, complete with Bayonets, are made here in a Week. About 60 persons are employed who have made all their own Tools, & do their Business with great Regularity & Expedition. They labor under some difficulty for want of proper Streams of Water, which increases manual Labor & makes the Manufactory more expensive." *VMHB*, 62.

gutta One of a series of small, cone-shaped projections located beneath the taenia of each triglyph and the underside of a mutule in a Doric entablature. See also **drop**.

gutter 1. A shallow channel or trough used to carry off rain water. Fabricated of wood, tile, or metal, roof gutters were used in several locations to convey water to a collection point at eaves level, where it ran off through a down spout or was funnelled to the ground or cistern by means of a pipe. Perhaps the most common roof gutters were located at the lower end of the roof, where they were either hung from the eaves or fastened to the ends of rafters. Less common but sometimes found on large, pretentious masonry buildings was a parapet gutter constructed along the lower edge of the roof but concealed from below by a parapet that carried up the side wall above the eaves. Double-pile houses, which were spanned by a set of parallel gable trusses known as an *M roof*, often had a gutter located at the junction of the two roofs. Altogether more unusual were sloping valley gutters, which were created at the angled intersection of two roofs. This intersection was sometimes known as a *gutter*, when the term was considered synonymous with *valley*, even if there were no channel for runoff. Ground gutters composed of brick or tile paving sometimes lined the perimeter of a building. Water flowing off the roof was channeled into this paving and conveyed away from the building or into an underground cistern. Beginning in the late 18th century, a few of the larger southern towns began to construct street gutters when roadways were graded and paved.

1703 An agreement was made "to make a new Gutter to ye Vestry house." All Saint's Parish, Calvert Co., Md., Vestry Book.

guilloche
54 Montague Street, Charleston, S.C.

1713   Payment was made to a workman for "makeing a gutter between the Court House and Jury House." Richmond Co., Va., Court Order Book 1711–1721.

1745   An estimate was made for "Sheet lead for 2 gutters one 23 feet long & one 20 Do @ £4.4.6 Sterl at 7lbs. for one." Huger Smith, *Dwelling Houses of Charleston.*

1756   A carpenter charged a client for making "a gutter with Spouts." Bertie Co., N.C., Court Actions, NCA&H.

1788   An agreement was made with a workman "to remove and take down the old Cornice" at St. Michael's Church in Charleston "and fix proper & sufficient Gutters or Aqueducts to convey the Water from the roof into four leaden pipes to be fixed at the four Corners." St. Michael's Parish, Charleston, S.C., Vestry Book.

1796   "The Street Commissioners" of Alexandria, Virginia, sought contractors to pave the streets of the city with stone of various sizes, "the largest in the centre, and the next in size to follow on each side, the smallest to be placed next to the gutters." *Columbia Mirror and Alexandria Gazette.*

1802   Stonecutters Shaw and Birth of Washington charged John Tayloe for "95 [feet] Spout and Gutter stones [at] 5/"; bricklayer Patrick Ferrell charged for "36 Run Gutter laid in mortar 1/6." Tayloe Papers, VHS.

1803   Leaking of the Capitol roof in Washington was caused in part "from the bad system of carrying off the Water. All the water is at present collected from every gutter and discharged into one deep cistern. After collecting in the gutters along the parapet, it is brought under the roof, in many gutters, into the internal Area of the roof, so that the chance of leakage is greatly multiplied." *The Correspondence and Miscellaneous Papers of Benjamin Henry Latrobe,* 1.

2. *(v.)* To cut a channel or corner off a framing member to prevent it from projecting into the room beyond the line of the plastering or sheathing. When the aesthetic preference for covering the frame with finished surfaces emerged in the 18th century, large corner posts and partition posts were often cut back to conceal them within the thickness of the wall. The term *guttering* appears to have been used in North Carolina and probably other regions as well to describe this practice.

1799   The corner posts of John Steele's house in Rowan County, North Carolina, were "to be hewed nine Inches Square guttored." John Steele Papers, SHC.

1818   The frame of a courthouse was to have corner posts "12 by 15 inches guthered." Northampton Co., N.C., Miscellaneous Court Records, NCA&H.

ha ha
18th-century ha ha rebuilt at Stratford, Westmoreland County, Va.

ha ha (ha haw)   A barrier between the pleasure grounds and the nearby pasture or wilderness to keep out large wildlife and livestock, and to extend the prospect into the adjacent countryside, so that the plantation appeared to be an unbroken continuation of the pleasure grounds. Three types of ha has were used in the 18th century. The wall and ditch variety was used if the land naturally fell away from the pleasure grounds, as when they bordered a meadow. The ditch ha ha relied upon the steepness of banks to keep out animals. The sunken fence ha ha was erected at the bottom of a ditch with the top of the fence kept below the upper ground level and out of view.

1783   The road to Westover on the James River in Virginia "is very spacious and very level bounded on either side by a handsome ditch & fence which divide the road from fine meadows whose extent is greater than the eye can reach." Shippen, *Westover Described in 1783.*

1785   George Washington noted in his diary that his workmen "began to wheel dirt into the Ha, Haws." Two years later he "brought the Ditchers to the home house . . . to compleat the sunk fence in the front of the lawn." *Diaries of George Washington,* 2, 3.

halfpace   A platform or landing between two flights of steps. See also **footpace, landing.**

1674   The statehouse at St. Mary's City was to have a "private doore to open into the garden of three foote wide and six foote high under the first halfe pace of the staires which staires shall be halfe pace of staires six inches and a halfe riseing & a foote in stepp for the first story . . . and a window uppon each halfe pace." *Archives of Maryland*, 2.

1726 "Square-flyers: These fly round the sides of a Square-Newel, either solid, or open, . . and at every corner of the Newel, there is a square Half-pace, that takes up 1/4 of a Circle, so they fly from one Half-pace to another." Neve, *City and Country Purchaser*.

1746 A two-story dwelling in Charleston was to have "one large Venitian window upon the half pace of the Stairs." Huger Smith, *The Dwelling Houses of Charleston*.

hall **1.** A large room or building used for the transaction of public business and the holding of courts of justice; also used for public assemblies, meetings, and entertainments. Occasionally, the body of a church was called the *hall* rather than the traditional English term *nave*.

1702 The provincial government appropriated the College of William and Mary building at the new capital of Williamsburg for temporary quarters, assigning "the great roome above stairs over the great Hall for the Council Chamber." *Journals of the House of Burgesses*, 3.

1712 An act passed by the South Carolina legislature called "for building a state-house" with "a handsome convenient room for the council, a large hall for the House of Commons, and closets for the papers belonging to the Council and House of Commons." *South Carolina Gazette*.

1753 A parish church was to be erected, "the Hall of the said church [to] be Thirty six feet in length by twenty feet in breadth." Antrim Parish, Halifax Co., Va., Vestry Book.

1773 In Charleston, "the Concert-house is a large inelegant building. . . . The Hall is preposterously and out of all proportion large, no orchestra for the performers, though a kind of loft for fiddlers at the Assembly. The performers were all at one end of the hall and the company in front and on each side." *Proceedings of the Massachusetts Historical Society*, 49.

1786 "Upon the third floor" of the market house in Richmond, there were "two rooms 14 feet by 10 feet, two rooms 14 feet by thirteen feet, three rooms 20 feet by 24 feet with necessary entries. These rooms are so constructed that they may occasionally be thrown into one large assembly hall 60 feet by 24 feet with a fireplace at each end." *Virginia Gazette*.

2. The principal, multipurpose room of a dwelling. Entrance into a dwelling opened directly into the hall or through a passage or lobby which led immediately into this large, ground-floor space. Because of its relationship to the door, the hall was sometimes referred to as the *outer room* or *outward room* in contrast to the more private *inner room* or *parlor*, which was the other principal ground-floor room. In the 17th century and throughout much of the 18th century, the hall served as the principal entertaining room, and also as a place to eat, cook, and sleep. The placement and function of the hall was slightly transformed in the second half of the 18th century with the introduction of double-pile plan houses that contained broad entrance spaces that were also called *halls*. In this capacity, the hall was no longer the primary entertaining space but served as a reception room in the center of the house, with the front entrance opening directly into it. Formal entertaining rooms and stairs and passages communicated with this space. In the grander houses, a saloon or large parlor was placed directly behind this central hall. Despite this association of *hall* with a circulation space, it was not until well after the first quarter of the 19th century that the term became synonymous with *passage* to define a *corridor*. See also **servants' hall.**

1643 An inventory of an estate listed goods "in the inward Roome within the Hall." *County Court Records of Accomack-Northampton, Virginia 1640–1645*.

hall (2)
B. H. Latrobe, William Pennock House,
Norfolk, Va., 1796

1657 A servant observed his "Maister comming forth of his owne chamber heareing some disturbance in the Hall finding John Salter with his wife in the Hall . . . [with] Salters breches downe in his hand & my Mrs. upon the bed with her coats up as high as her brest." *Archives of Maryland,* 54.

1721 "On Christmas Day, the Governor [Charles Eden] came into the outer room or hall and dined with the Company and that . . . in the evening he desired the Company to go into the parlour where . . . there was a large bowl of punch made." *Colonial Records of North Carolina,* 2.

1737 A dwelling to be built on a glebe was to have "four rooms on the ground or lower floor of the following dimensions viz: The Hall or entertaining room is to be fourteen foot wide, and sixteen foot long, with a room adjacent thereto, of fourteen foot in length, and eighte foot in breadth, and two other rooms of twelve foot long, and ten foot wide each." Truro Parish, Fairfax Co., Va., *Vestry Book.*

1767 "In the hall" of merchant David Galloway's dwelling in Northumberland County, Virginia, were "two looking glasses and one chimney glass; two arm'd and 17 plain mahogany chairs. 19 glazed pictures in black and guilded frames. Two large maps with rollers, one prospective glass. One set of fire tongs, shovel and poker. One chimney screen." Northumberland Co., Va., Court Record Book 1766–1770.

1783 "The principal floor" of the Governor's House in New Bern was "divided into seven rooms and two staircases. The Hall at entrance in the North front is 26 by 18 feet. The walls finished with stucco, pediments over the doors, niches in the walls, and a Modillion Cornice." Hawks Letter, Miranda Papers, Academia Nacional de la Historia, Caracas.

3. A house or building belonging to a guild, fraternal organization, or other social group.

1786 A building was erected in Charleston "called HARMONY HALL, for the Purpose of Music Meetings, Dancing and Theatrical Amusements. It is situated in a spacious Garden, in the suburbs of the City." *Maryland Journal and Baltimore Advertiser.*

1791 A lottery was allowed in Charlotte County, Virginia, to raise money "for erecting a Free Mason's Hall." Hening, *Statutes at Large,* 13.

4. The residence of a large planter or merchant.

1774 "Mr. [Robert] Carter has chosen for the place of his habitation a high spot of Ground in Westmoreland County [Virginia] at the Head of the Navigation of the River Nomini, where he has erected a large Elegant House, at a vast expence, which commonly goes by the name of *Nomini-Hall.*" *Journal and Letters of Philip Vickers Fithian.*

1799 "To be Sold" in Gloucester County, Virginia, was "the plantation named White Hall formerly belonging to Francis Willis decd." *Virginia Gazette.*

hall (4)
Archdale Hall, Dorchester County, S.C., first quarter 18th century. View of house following 1886 earthquake prior to demolition.

hall chamber   A room either directly above the hall on the upper floor or one opening off the hall on the ground floor. The hall chamber usually served as a sleeping room or storage space.

1667 An inventory of the estate of Mathew Huberd listed items "in the parlour . . . in the Hall . . . In the Parlour Chamber . . . [and] In the Hall Chamber: one featherbed, boulster, two down pillows Red Serrge Curtaines & Vallainces, one Red worsted Rugg, One blankett, bedsted & Cord & a buckerum Tester £12.00.00; featherbed, bolster, pillow, one blew yarne Rugg A trundle bedsted & Cord £4.00.00; one Featherbed bolster green yarne Rugg and blanketts £3.10.00." York Co., Va., Deed, Order, Will Book 1665–1672.

hammer   A tool consisting of a metal head connected to a short perpendicular handle, used for driving nails.

handrail   A wooden, stone, or iron rail supported by balusters, posts, brackets, and the like, erected on the sides of stairs or platforms to provide a rest for the hand and to prevent persons from falling or slipping. In terms of design, handrails of the colonial period often had molded sides and a curved upper section. In the very late 18th and first decades of the 19th centuries, neoclassical design aesthetics prompted a move toward thinner, rounded, or oval handrails supported by square or round balusters. See also **rail, railing.**

1746 Charles Pinckney's dwelling in Charleston was to have "one flight of stairs, under the great stairs with plain hand rail to go up to the first floar." Huger Smith, *Dwelling Houses of Charleston.*
1752 The "Communion Table Hand Rails and Ballasters" of a church were "to be all of Black Walnut." Trinity Parish, Charles Co., Md., Vestry Book.
1793 The stair in "Old East" at the University of North Carolina was "to be quite plain pine handrails & square bannisters." University Archives, UNC, Chapel Hill.
c. 1798 At John Dickinson's dwelling in Wilmington, Delaware, "the handrail of the principal staircase is to be one continued piece without any posts, so that the hand will not in the least be interrupted." Dickinson Plantation Research Files, Delaware Bureau of Museums.

hanging pew A small enclosed pew raised on posts and built by private subscription for the exclusive use of one or more families. Not part of a gallery but often built next to one, or standing alone along the wall of a church and reached by a private stairway, hanging pews came into fashion in many Anglican churches in Virginia in the 1730s and 1740s as a visible expression of the prestige of certain members of the local gentry. Conspicuous in location, yet not entirely visible from below and set apart from the seats of neighbors, hanging pews provided their occupants a means to separate themselves from their socials inferiors in a public setting.

1735 "On the motion of Col. Edward Moseley tis unanimously agreed and liberty given him to erect a hanging pewe on the north side of the new church at his own cost for himself his grandson Mr. Edward Hack Moseley, Capt. Anthony and Capt. Francis Moseley." Lynnhaven Parish, Princess Anne Co., Va., Vestry Book.

hanging post A post suspended from a roof truss or girder used to frame an element not supported from below, such as a gallery or hanging pew. The post in this case is acting in tension.

1758 It was "Ordered that Col. Henry Lee have Liberty to cut the hanging post in the gallary putting a pillar under the same gallary." Dettingen Parish, Prince William Co., Va., Vestry Book.

harbour See **arbor.**

hasp A metal fastener that fits over a staple and is secured by a padlock or pin. Most early hasps consisted of an iron bar attached at one end by a staple. The free-swinging end, shaped in the form of an eye, hooks over a second staple.

1640 A workman was paid for "lead soder and haspes." Maryland Patents Certificates & Warrants, MSA.
1788 Prison doors were "to be secured with hasps & padlocks two to each door." Prince William Co., Va., Deed Book 1787–1791.

hatch (hatchway)   **1.** A small gate; a half-door or wicket with an open space above; the lower section of a door that is divided into two sections. Although early southerners may have used this term to describe a variety of doors, the present connotation of a horizontal door to a scuttle or a trap door appears to be a 19th-century development. See also **scuttle.**

1702 In a courtroom, the raised magistrates' platform was "to be decently Railed and Banistered in with hatch wayes as by the platt." Essex Co., Va., Will and Deed Book No. 10.

hasp
Pruden cornhouse,
Isle of Wight County, Va.

1748 It was ordered that "A hatch be made to the poarch of the Lower Church." Stratton Major Parish, King and Queen County, Va., Vestry Book.

2. To draw a series of parallel lines in a sketch for purposes of rendering shadows or emphasizing wall thicknesses.

hatchet A cutting tool with a broad blade attached to a short handle, used by woodworkers to reduce the edges of boards and other material. Lathing hatchets had a poll on the back side of the blade and were used by plasterers for cutting lath to length and nailing them in place.

haymow A stack of hay; sometimes a place where hay is stored in a barn, such as a loft.

hayroom A place where hay for a stable is kept in bulk.

1743 The Crown Inn in Charleston contained "seven Rooms and a Shop, with a Kitchen, Store, Hay and Straw Rooms, 2 Chaise Rooms, Hay Loft, and a Stable that will contain 40 Horses." *South Carolina Gazette*.

1769 Among the outbuildings on a plantation in Prince George's County, Maryland, was "a Stable, built with Two Inch Plank let into the Posts, thirty-Six by Twelve Feet, with a large Hay-Room above." *Maryland Gazette*.

head In general, the top or upper section of an object or member, especially the upper part of a window aperture or the top of a nail.

1726 "Brads are a sort of Nails without Heads." Neve, *City and Country Purchaser*.

1751 "Instead of Square Arches to the windows they [are to] have compass heads." Upper Parish, Nansemond Co., Va., Vestry Book.

header **1.** In masonry bonding, a brick or rectangular stone laid so that its short end is exposed to the wall surface and its long end or stretcher extends back into the thickness of the wall. See also **bond.**

1711 "The front of the" courthouse was to be laid with "smooth bricks; with blue headers and stretchers to be rubbed from the sills of the windows upwards to the wallplate." Talbot Co., Md., Land Records Book No. 12, MSA.

2. A workman who attaches the head of nails to their shafts.

1809 At a nail manufactory in Petersburg, Virginia, "two good headers are wanted—to such, liberal wages and constant employment will be given." *The Republican*.

3. A trimmer. See **trimmer.**

headstone An upright stone placed at the head of a grave; a gravestone. See also **footstone, gravestone, tombstone.**

1773 "Whereas it has been found that the erection of head and feet stones and wooden monuments in the churchyard is attended with the same inconveniences as the erection of Tomb stones therein, Unanimously resolved that no person . . . be . . . allowed to reerect or repair the same in the said yard but that he or they may have liberty to place them even with the surface of the Earth or against the walls of the yard." St. Philip's Parish, Charleston, S.C., Vestry Book.

1817 A will requested that "a headstone be placed at his grave so that if any friends or relatives visit the city, they will know where his grave is located." Charleston Co., S.C., Will Book 1807–1818.

heart (hart) The hard, inner part of a tree. As a tree grows, the dead cells of the heartwood or *duramen* develop a tighter and more even grain which, along with the absence of sap, makes them more resistant to decay and insect damage than the outer sapwood. In many species such as pine and poplar, the heartwood is much darker than the sapwood. In the early South, specifications often called for heart-wood to be used for a structure's frame or covering, which would be exposed to the weather or wear most often. Perhaps the most common use of heart timber was for shingles and weatherboards.

1674 The roof of the Maryland statehouse in St. Mary's City was to have "laths for tile of heart of white Oke & one inch thick." *Archives of Maryland*, 2.

1763 It was "Ordered that the Rafters of the church already let out instead of oak the hart of old pine 14 by 8 inches at the foot." St. George's Parish, Accomack Co., Va., Vestry Book.

1808 The frame "and all other timbers exposed to the weather" on a courthouse in Columbia, Tennessee, were "to be of the heart of yellow poplar." *The Impartial Review and Cumberland Repository*.

hearth (harth, hearthstone, fire hearth) The place in a room or structure where a fire is made; the floor of the fireplace. From the 17th through the early 18th centuries, the term is nearly synonymous with *fireplace*, which only comes into use in the late 17th century. From the early 18th century onward, *hearth* became increasingly used in a narrower sense to mean the floor of the fireplace opening along with the paved area that projected beyond the chimney breasts. In some instances, the paved area in front of the firebox was known separately as the hearthstone. Metal hearths inserted into fireplaces were imported into the colonies from the second quarter of the 18th century onward. See also **chimney, fireplace.**

1688 A craftsman was sued for refusing to "lay a chimney hearth . . . as per agreement." Charles City Co., Va., Court Order Book 1687–1695.

1690 A bricklayer was hired to make "Bricks for backs of Chimneys fire Hearths and one Oven." Stafford Co., Va., Court Order Book 1689–1693.

1738 Imported from London into Charleston was "an Iron Hearth with Brass Facings." *South Carolina Gazette*.

1747 A prison was to have "iron Grates 18 inches long and 12 inches wide each to be set on Brick Harths." Northumberland Co., Va., Court Record Book 1743–1749.

1766 "The Harth" of a vestry house was "to be laid with Brick under the fire place & round the fire place to be laid with flag stone." St. George's Parish, Harford Co., Md., Vestry Book.

1770 "MARBLE SLABS fit for chimney hearths" were imported into Savannah. *Georgia Gazette*.

hedge Plantings of bushes or woody plants in a row, to act as defensive fences, decorative dividers, or windbreaks.

1705 "An act for prevention of trespasses by unruly horses, cattle, hogs, sheep, and goats" passed by the General Assembly of Virginia reckoned "an hedge two foot high, upon a ditch of three foot deep, and three foot broad" was "so close that none of the creatures aforesaid can creep through." Hening, *Statutes at Large*, 3.

1749 A garden in Charleston was "genteely laid out in walks and alleys, with . . . cassini and other hedges." *South Carolina Gazette*.

1805 "We are . . . going to surround" the orchard at Riversdale in Prince George County, Maryland, "with a hedge. It is incredible how they grow here—within seven years they are impenetrable." *Letters of Rosalie Stier Calvert*.

1812 Near Arlington in northern Virginia, "the fences were of hurdles to keep out pigs. The American thorn will not grow close enough and the cedar hedge though pretty is not strong enough for the purpose." Foster, *Jeffersonian America*.

helix See **caulicole.**

henhouse A structure providing a place for chickens and other fowl to roost and nest and a protective shelter from predators. Compared to *chicken house, fowl house,* and *poultry house, henhouse* was the most pervasive term for such buildings throughout most of the old South.

The term dominated in Virginia, almost to the exclusion of all others. In contrast, it rarely appeared in South Carolina, where *fowl house* and *poultry house* predominated.

> 1668 A craftsman in Charles County, Maryland, was paid for "Building a ten foot hen house." *Archives of Maryland*, 60.
> 1723 The Mason farm on the Eastern Shore of Maryland had "one old small ten foot raftered hen house much broke." Queen Anne's Co., Md., Deed Book IK.
> 1742 The vestry ordered the construction on a glebe of "a hen house 12 feet by 8 fraimed and inclosed with thick saped boards." Bristol Parish, Prince George Co., Va., Vestry Book.
> 1804 On a Delaware farm was a "loged Hen House Sixteen feet by fifteen in bad repair." Sussex Co., Del., Orphans Court Valuations Book IJ.

hermitage   A rustic hut or shady bower in a garden where an imaginary recluse could dwell.

herringbone   A diagonal pattern of arrangement in which adjoining vertical rows of rectangular elements are set at oblique angles to each other so as to create a *V*, inverted *V*, or chevron. Some wooden and many brick walks and floors were laid in a herringbone pattern in which the bricks or floorboards were set obliquely in alternating rows so as to form a zigzag pattern.

> 1715 In a church, the bricks in the aisles and altar area were "to be Laid Herring-Bone Fashion." St. Paul's Parish, Kent Co., Md., Vestry Book.
> 1788 For additional security, a door in a prison was "to be a good herringbone door lined." Prince William Co., Va., Deed Book 1787–1791.
> 1808 At Poplar Forest, Thomas Jefferson speculated that the floors "may be easier done in herring bone, as the hall floor at Monticello was." Coolidge Collection, Massachusetts Historical Society.

hew, hewed (hue)   *(v.)* To cut, shape, smooth, or roughly square timber or stone with blows of an ax, hammer, or chisel.   *(adj.)* Roughly squared materials such as stone, framing members, logs, or fence posts. See also **rive**.

> 1663 "Abraham Harman having occasion for such Tooles necessary for his employment demanded a Crosse cutt saw, a wrest to sett a saw with . . . narrow Axes & a broad Axe to hewe the Timber." *Archives of Maryland*, 49.
> 1668 "George Godfrey built for Daniel Johnson one Sixty foot Tobaccoe house & one ten foot Hen house & hewed timber for the frame of a forty foot hog house." *Archives of Maryland*, 60.
> 1697 "Severall peices of tymber now lyeing out in the woods adjacent to the Court House [are] ready squar'd and hew'd, also boards riven, etc. and other peices made ready for erecting and building a substantial prison." Westmoreland Co., Va., Court Order Book 1690–1698.
> 1748 A courthouse was "built with loggs hewed on both sides not laid close some of the cracks between the loggs quite open 4 or 5 inches." Augusta Co., Va., Court Order Book 1748–1751.
> 1767 Stonework of "the columns must be Round of the Plain Doric order and the Proportions Exact. . . . And those to which the Pilaster are to be Joined in one, and as I conceive Hewn out of the same Block or Blocks." Trostel, *Mount Clare*.

H hinge   A wrought-iron side hinge made with two parallel legs in the form of an H and joined in the center by a pivot. They were either surface mounted or mounted with one leg against the jamb behind the architrave. These hinges were among the most common ones used from the 17th through the second quarter of the 19th centuries. In the early colonial period, a number were made with foliated decorations at the top and bottom of each leg. See also **side hinge**.

H hinge
Christ Church, Lancaster County, Va.

1745 Church doors were "to be hung with H's." Fredericksville Parish, Louisa Co., Va., Vestry Book.
1745 A list of materials for a house to be built in Colleton Square for Charles Pinckney included "6 pr large 14 Inch H hinges with nails & screws." Huger Smith, *Dwelling Houses of Charleston.*
1789 A dwelling house was to be built with "the doors to be good batten rabbited and well nailed with good H Hinges." Northumberland Co., Va., Record Book 1787–1793.

high relief See **relief.**

hinge A jointed or flexible device on which a door, gate, or shutter pivots into an open or closed position. Made of wood, iron, brass, and other metals, hinges consisted of two plates or legs connected by a pin. See also **cross garnet hinge, dovetail hinge, H hinge, HL hinge, side hinge, strap hinge.**

hipped roof (hipt roof, hip roof) A roof type that has sloping rafters rising from two adjacent sides of a building. Hipped roofs appeared in the region in the late 17th century but only became common in the second quarter of the 18th century. Early references occasionally referred to them as an Italian roof, perhaps reflecting their appearance in classical design and influential architectural books, such as those by Serlio and Palladio. In contrast to hipped roofs, which had no gables, jerkin head roofs had their end rafter pairs hipped only above their collar beams.
1680 A courthouse was to be constructed with "an Italion or hip Roofe." Talbot Co., Md., Judgments 1675–1682.
1726 "A Hip Roof . . . hath neither Gable-heads, nor Shread-head, or Jirkin-head . . . For a Hip Roof hath Rafters as long and with the Angles at the Foot &c. at the ends of a Building, as it hath at the Sides, and the Feet of the Rafters on the Ends of such Buildings as have Hip-roofs, stand in the same Plain . . . and at the same Heighth from the Foundation with the Rafters on the Sides of the Roof. These Hip-roofs, some call Italian Roofs." Neve, *City and Country Purchaser.*
1765 The Willtown Presbyterian meetinghouse was to be built "forty feet square with hipt roof." *South Carolina Historical Magazine,* 62.

hip rafter A rafter at the junction of two planes of a hip roof. The upper side of the hip rafter is cut at two angles to respond to the slopes of the two intersecting roof planes.
1790 The carpenter's bill for work at Hampton in Baltimore County, Maryland, listed "23 sqr 25 feet of fraiming hip rafters @ 14s pr sqr." *MHM,* 33.
1819 Thomas Jefferson provided explicit specifications for framing his roof at Poplar Forest in Bedford County, Virginia, noting that "from each corner of the skylight to the corresponding corner of the wall, lay on a hip-ridge-rafter, and from these hips & the trimmers lay rafters towards East & West." Jefferson Papers, UVa.

H Lancaster hinge A variety of H hinges made in Lancaster, England, generally of a cheaper quality. See also **H hinge.**
1737 Imported into Charleston and to be sold by John Watsone were a "variety of iron ware, viz. hooks and hinges, H Lancaster hinges, ditto with rising joints." *South Carolina Gazette.*

HL hinge A variety of a wrought-iron *H* side hinge with a horizontal leg either at the top or bottom of the vertical leg that is attached to the door. Although these hinges could vary in size, they were especially popular for hanging large doors, since the horizontal leg provided extra strength not available with the H hinge. See also **H hinge.**

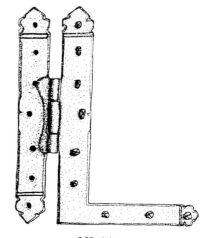

HL hinge

1731 Peter Porter was paid for putting up "1 pr of HL for the Out Door" of a building. St. Anne's Parish, Anne Arundel Co., Md., Vestry Book.

1771 At St. John's Church in Granville County, North Carolina, "in the West end shall be a Door nine feet High & four feet wide with good folding doors well lined a Hung with large HL Hinges." Francis Hawks Papers, Church Historical Society.

1788 A door in the "partition between the Gaolers Rooms to be a good 6 panel door with common HL or butt hinges." Prince William Co., Va., Deed Book 1787–1791.

hog court   An enclosed area where swine are kept; a piggery. See also **pen** (1), **sty.**

1640 Payment made a workman for "10 dayes work in railing in the hog court." Maryland Patents, Certificates, and Warrants 1637–1650, MSA.

hog house   A shelter for swine. In the mid- and late 17th century, a number of individuals in the Chesapeake and the Carolinas raised hogs for export to the Caribbean and other mainland colonies. In order to regulate the feeding and breeding of their herds and to protect them from predatory animals such as wolves, many colonists enclosed their animals in pens, a practice that diminished in the 18th century. At the center of these piggeries were long, open sheds or enclosed houses, which provided shelter. With the diminution in swine exports in the 18th century and the disappearance of predators, more and more animals were allowed to freely range in forests. With this change in practice, fewer hog houses were built throughout the southern colonies. However, such structures continued to be constructed on some plantations through the early 19th century.

1666 "Wee cleered fenced & planted what ground we could wee built a hogg howse of 80 foot Long & 20 broad with necessarie partitions on powells pointe" in the Albemarle Sound of North Carolina." Powell, *Ye Countie of Albemarle.*

1671 In Charles County, Maryland, "George Godfrey built for Daniel Johnson One Sixty foot Tobaccoe house & one ten foot Hen house & hewed timber for the frame of a forty foot hog house." *Archives of Maryland*, 60.

1682 "Hogs increase in Carolina abundantly, and in a manner without any charge or trouble to the Planter, only making them Sheds, wherein they may be protected from the Sun and Rain, and Morning and Evening to give them a little Indian Corn, or the pickings and parings of Potatoes, Turnips, or other Roots." Salley, *Narratives of Early Carolina.*

hoist   *(v.)* To raise or lift an object.   *(n.)* A beam with block and tackle for lifting goods, as sometimes employed above loading doors in the upper stories of stores and warehouses. A machine used on building sites for lifting heavy objects.

1740 Courthouse windows were "to [be] hoist[ed] with springs and pullys." Lancaster Co., Va., Court Order Book 1729–1743.

1804 Benjamin Latrobe wrote to John Letnall in Washington that "in the course of this week I shall send you, the hoisting machines of the Pennsylvania Bank" to be used on the Capitol. *The Correspondence and Miscellaneous Papers of Benjamin Henry Latrobe*, 1.

holdfast   **1.** An iron bar with a short arm that, when driven into a hole in a workbench, serves to secure an object such as a plank or board in a stationary position.

1703 "The Hold-fast, let pretty loose into round holes . . . in the Bench; Its Office is to keep the Work fast upon the Bench, whilst you either Saw, Tennant, Mortess, or sometimes Plain upon it." Moxon, *Mechanick Exercises.*

2. A device that holds, supports, clasps, or binds something.

1777   A house had "a stair-cloth with iron rods and holdfasts." *Maryland Journal and Baltimore Advertiser.*

1787   A workman attached "12 holdfasts [and] 2 electrical rods" to the chimneys of the South Carolina statehouse in Charleston. South Carolina Treasury Records Ledger, SCA&H.

1788   A church door was to be secured with "hold fasts and staples." Robert Carter Letterbook, MHS.

hollow and round planes   Matching pairs of molding planes with concave (hollow) and convex (round) blades. Often found in sets with graduated dimensions, hollows and rounds were used by joiners and cabinetmakers for all-purpose work, especially the fabrication of non-standard size moldings such as those employed in cornices. A cavetto and scotia are hollow moldings while a torus is a round one. See also **plane.**

home farm   A tract of cultivated land located adjacent to or including the environs of the landowner's dwelling. A term confined to Delaware; *home plantation* was more widely used. See also **dwelling plantation, home house, quarter** (3).

1813   Part of an estate was described as the "home farm where John Meridith lives." Sussex Co., Del., Orphans Court Valuations L.

home farm quarter   See **home farm.**

home house   That part of a farm or *plantation* incorporating the landowner's dwelling. The term was sometimes confined to the immediate environs of the owner's house, including domestic outbuildings like kitchens and smokehouses, as well as *quarters.*

1701   An inventory included items "at the home house." Middlesex Co., Va., Will Book 1698–1713.

1787   "Took a list to day of all my Negroes which are as follows at Mount Vernon and plantations around it . . . Muddy hole . . . Home House . . . River Plantation . . . Dogue Run Plantn . . . Ferry Plantation . . . Mill." *Diaries of Washington,* 4.

home house quarter   See **home house.**

home plantation   A farm or *quarter* containing the residence of the landowner, or adjacent to its environs. The term was used mainly in the upper South. See also **dwelling plantation, home farm, home house.**

1674   An inventory recorded "Serv.ts belonging to the home plantation," as well as "at the Dwelling house" and "at the English Quarter." Westmoreland Co., Va. Deeds, Patents, &c. 1665–1677.

1767   An orphans' account notes "the home plantation," in addition to two other quarters, and the main dwelling house. Queen Anne's Co., Md., Deed Book RT, No. H.

hook   A curved or angular piece of metal used for catching, holding, or suspending something. Hooks were used for a variety of purposes. Long curving hooks with tapering points were used by butchers to hang slabs of meat at market houses. In building, the most common hook consisted of a right-angled iron bar, the horizontal end of which was driven into a door or window frame, while the rounded vertical end served as a pivot for the eye of a strap hinge of a door, shutter, or gate. The modern term for this type of hook is *pintle,* but it does

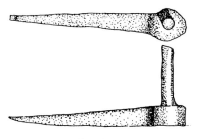

hook

not appear in earlier usage. A slightly different type of hook had a rectangular vertical end that acted as a support for a plank set across the inside of a doorway to prevent entry. A third hook commonly employed in early America was used to hold exterior shutters back against the wall. The vertical member of this type swivelled on a pin and eye, allowing the shutter to be pulled back against the wall and kept there when it resumed an upright position. Although the modern term *shutter dog* has been applied to this type of hook, it does not appear in the early records.

hook and eye hinge
Smokehouse, Cherry Walk,
Essex County, Va.

hook and eye hinge   A hook and hinge, known in modern terminology as a strap hinge. The hook is the pintle, the eye refers to the end of the strap that has been formed to fit over the pintle. See also **hook and hinge.**

> **1805**   The courthouse in Wilmington, North Carolina, was to receive "Strong substantial Venetian blinds, painted green, for each window, including raised joint or hook or eye hinges, hookes and staples for fastening them back, and bolts for shutting." *Wilmington Gazette.*
> **1806**   In Fayette County, Kentucky, a meetinghouse was to have "good folding batten window shutters, hung with hook and eyes, the doors hung with the same." *Kentucky Gazette and General Advertiser.*

hook and hinge   An elongated, forged hinge usually made into the form of a long narrow bar, tapering to a finial at one end and an eye at the other. The eye fits over a pintle, which in turn is driven into the jamb or gate post on which the hinged leaf will swing. Seventeenth- and early 18th-century hooks and hinges were often constructed so that the eye protruded on the rear of the hinge, causing the door or casement to which it was attached to abut its jamb. Common 18th-century hinges of this variety were made opposite, with the eye facing outward, and thus the leaf could sit flush with its jamb when closed. The modern term for a hook and hinge is *strap hinge.*

> **1737**   Imported into Charleston and sold by John Watsone were a "variety of iron ware, viz. hooks and hinges, H Lancaster hinges, ditto with rising joints, all sorts of nails, especially rose 5d, very proper for shingling." *South Carolina Gazette.*
> **1780**   Williamsburg blacksmith James Anderson made "3 pair hooks & hinges 40 lb. @ 1 /" for Samuel Beall. James Anderson Ledger Book 1778–1785, CWF.

hook and staple   An iron bar, bent at its end, used to fasten a gate, door, casement or shutter either in its open or closed position. The hook is secured when its crooked end is fitted into a staple that is driven into an adjoining leaf or jamb. Hooks are made of a square or flat bar, often twisted for decoration.

> **1745**   A vestry paid "Mr. Charles Pritchard for pailing in the spring and tarring the church and finding hooks and staples . . . 400 lbs. tob." Wicomico Parish, Northumberland Co., Va., Vestry Book.
> **1775**   "Hooks and staples for the courthouse windows" were provided at a cost of £.2.6. Cumberland Co., Va., Order Book 1774–1778.

horse block   A small step or platform of wood or stone set near the entrance to a building in order to facilitate mounting a horse. See also **upping block.**

> **1673**   A vestryman was to be paid "400 lb of Tobo for payling in the Church Yard and makeing the Horse Block." Christ Church Parish, Middlesex Co., Va., Vestry Book.

1731 "Richard Brookes hath agreed to Sett up three horse blocks at the Church with a Rail to Each of them for Eighty pounds of Tob'co." Saint Peter's Parish, New Kent Co., Va., Vestry Book.

hospital **1.** A building or group of buildings erected to house and maintain the poor, aged, or infirm of a city, county, or parish. The term in this sense is nearly synonymous with almshouse or poorhouse. See also **almshouse, poorhouse, workhouse** (1).

1735 The vestry of St. Philip's Church in Charleston noted that "whereas a number of Idle, Vagrant vitiously Inclined People . . . by Drinking and other sorts of Debauchery Speedily reducing themselves to Poverty and Diseases, have . . . become a great and dayly increasing Burthen on this Parish . . . ye Petitioners humbly conceiving that a Publick Workhouse & hospital under proper regulations will prove the most Effectual Remedies for these Evills." St. Philip's Parish, Charleston, S.C., Vestry Book.
1751 In Charleston, "the Workhouse or Hospital erected for the use of the poor of this parish is not at present properly applyed for the use intended." St. Philip's Parish, Charleston, S.C., Vestry Book.

2. A building for the care and maintenance of those declared insane. The first public institution for the care of the mentally ill was constructed in Williamsburg, Virginia, in 1773. Only those persons considered dangerously mad or curable were admitted to the hospital, where they were confined to small barred cells. This was a marked improvement and an architectural innovation in the care of the insane. Previously, people considered by the standards of the day to be mad were sequestered with felons and paupers in jails and poorhouses. At the public hospital in Williamsburg, inmates received medical attention from a doctor who tried to cure his patients through a variety of treatments, many of which involved bleeding or ducking.

1770 "A committee was formed for establishing an Hospital for the reception of Ideots, Lunatics, and persons of Insane Minds . . . It is to be a large commodious brick building, and to be erected in or near the city of Williamsburg." *Virginia Gazette.*
1772 A government official wrote to an English merchant asking him "to send over some Stone Steps for an Hospital the Country is building for the Reception of Lunaticks & other unhappy objects of insane Minds, which it is to be fear'd will Multiply too fast in this Country; we have been obliged to send four to the Hospital in Philadelphia for want of a proper place to accommodate them here." *John Norton & Sons Merchants of London and Virginia.*

3. A building used for the treatment of the sick, wounded, and those needing medical attention. Such structures required little in the way of specialized rooms or fittings. After battles, many buildings were appropriated for the treatment and recuperation of wounded soldiers. By the early 19th century, specialized structures were beginning to appear in a number of cities. See also **lazaretto, pesthouse.**

1805 In Charleston, "the Establishment of the MARINE HOSPITAL is now open, under the direction of the City Corporation, for receiving SEAMEN of all Nations. . . . The Captains are particularly requested to send their Clothes and Bedding, which will be returned when the Sailors are discharged from the Hospital. . . . Captains sending Sailors, are requested to do it as soon as taken sick, otherwise the good intention of the institution will be frustrated." *Charleston Courier.*

hot closet A small space adjoining an oven or fireplace, so as to capture their heat for drying various articles. See also **closet** (3).

1798 Benjamin Latrobe's plan for the remodelling of Green Spring in James City County, Virginia, included a "Dry^g or Hot Closet." Ludwell-Lee Papers, VHS.

hotel
Taylors Hotel, Winchester, Va.

hotel A building arranged for the lodging, feeding, and entertaining of travelers and other guests. The term came into fashion in southern cities in the last decade of the 18th century to distinguish the superior accommodations available at better taverns and inns. Far larger than earlier taverns, city hotels often stood two or more stories in height, had a number of private bed chambers, and large, public ground-floor dining and entertaining rooms.

> 1793 In Washington "the principal building of the Hotel" designed by James Hoban, "will have a front of 120 feet, and the largest room will be 40 by 60 feet: the stile of the whole will far exceed any building at present known in America." *Baltimore Daily Repository.*
> 1820 In Milledgeville, Georgia, "a brick edifice, to be 228 ft. long, and 3 stories high, is rearing on the spot. It is intended for a Hotel, and when completed will be inferior in size to few buildings of the kind in America." *Republican Star and General Advertiser.*

hothouse An artificially heated greenhouse for the cultivation of tender plants, often attached to a larger greenhouse. See also **pinery, stove house.**

> 1798 John Tayloe of Mount Airy in Richmond County, Virginia, constructed a "Green & Hot house" for £150; the smaller hothouses were attached to each side of the larger greenhouse. Tayloe Papers, VHS.
> 1801 In a garden in Wilmington, North Carolina, "were several Alcoves, Summer Houses, a hot-house." *Autobiography and Diary of Mrs. Eliza Clitherall.*

house (howse) A building for certain activities or, in general, any building. In modern usage, the term is synonymous with *dwelling*, a place of human habitation. However, from the time of settlement through the early 19th century, the term usually had a prefix to describe certain activities, occupants, or relationships associated with the building, such as *almshouse, back house, cowhouse, courthouse, meetinghouse, slave house, storehouse, smokehouse,* and *tobacco house.* Thus the term *dwelling house* was not redundant, as it would be today.

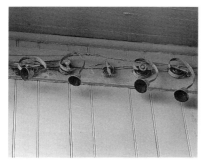

housebell
Nash House, Petersburg, Va.

house bell A spring-mounted bell used for calling servants. Connected by copper wires to activating devices or *pulls* throughout the house, one or more of these bells was often mounted on an outside wall facing the kitchen. In urban houses with attached kitchens, they were often mounted in the kitchen. First used in England during the 1740s, they appeared in the colonies about mid-century, but were not common until after the Revolution. Initially lines and pulleys were used to connect the bells to their pulls, but these quickly gave way to wire and *cranks*—metal pivots mounted wherever the wires changed direction. In the better installations, the wires were hidden within hollow wooden moldings or astragals and later in zinc *secret tubing.* For installations having more than one device, bells of varying size and tone were available to assist in distinguishing among calls from different parts of the house.

> 1749 In one of the earliest North American references to house bells, Stephen Callow advertised his services as an upholsterer, adding "N.B. He also hangs Bells in the best Manner." *The New-York Gazette, revived in the Weekly Post-Boy.*
> 1751 David and William Geddy of Williamsburg advertised an assortment of metal goods, including "House bells of all sizes." *Virginia Gazette.*
> 1756 In New York, John Elliot, "Lately come to this city from Philadelphia" announced his readiness to hang bells "in the neatest and most convenient manner, as done at London, with Cranks and Wires, which are not liable to be put out of order, as those done with pulleys." *The New-York Gazette or the Weekly Post-Boy.*

1772 Near Baltimore, Charles Carroll of Carrollton ordered "two bells with rings in different sounds with cranks for four rooms, also spare cranks and wires, some of the wire will be used on the outside of the house." Charles Carroll Letterbook, NYPL.
1795 For his new house in Mecklenburg County, Virginia, Sir Peyton Skipwith ordered a large assortment of bell hardware from a Birmingham firm, including "2 House Bells with Scrowl Springs . . . 3 doz Bell Cranks . . . 1 doz Bell slides" and "1 lb Iron Bell wire." Skipwith Papers, W&M.

houseboat A flat-bottomed boat with a roof fitted up as a floating dwelling. See also **floating house**.

1784 In Halifax County, Virginia, a workman was paid for "making one small House boat . . . £5." James Hunt Account Book, LC.

house carpenter The term was used occasionally to distinguish the house building trade from that of a ship's carpenter. See **carpenter**.

house joinery See **joiner**.

housekeeper's room, apartment A room or set of rooms in a large dwelling or public building reserved for the use and residence of a housekeeper, a person charged with running a household or the daily operations of a statehouse, hospital, prison or other public structure. In a domestic setting, household valuables such as table and bed linens and tablewares were sometimes locked in the housekeeper's room.

1758 Among the goods contained "in the House Keepers room" at Stratford in Westmoreland County, Virginia, was "a bed." Westmoreland County Record Book 1756–1767.
1763 The ground floor of the South Carolina statehouse in Charleston contained "Apartments for the House-keeper." Milligen Johnston, *A Short Description of the Province of South Carolina*.
1783 At the Governor's House in New Bern, "the Center room at the west end is about 16 by 12 feet, for the Housekeeper." Hawks Letter, Miranda Papers, Academia Nacional de la Historia, Caracas.
1803 Property for sale in Fredericksburg, Virginia, included a "kitchen 46 by 16, at one end a convenient room for an office, or a housekeeper, 3 lodging rooms for servants above and a dry cellar 16 feet square below." *Virginia Herald*.

house of correction A building or group of buildings erected to house vagrants and the poor of a corporation or parish. For a more detailed description, see **workhouse**.

1688 "The Court Caused to be entred that John Tutchbery is thought A fitt person to keep a house of Correct[ion]." *Records of the Courts of Sussex County Delaware 1677–1710*, 1.

1691 In Virginia, part of the money gained from the payment of certain fines was to be used for "erecting and supporting an house of correction." Hening, *Statutes at Large*, 3.

house of ease A necessary house; privy. For a more detailed description, see **necessary house**.

1774 In the paled garden of a Delaware farmstead was "a house of ease . . . about two feet square." Sussex Co., Del., Orphans Court Valuations A.

house of entertainment See **tavern**.

house of God, house of prayer A church or building where religious services were conducted.

1743 A minister noted that "there are other repairs made in our house of prayer, which deserve to be recorded as flowing from an Uncommon Instance of Piety." Fulham Papers 2, Lambeth Palace Library.

1763 A gift of velvet coverings meant that "the House of God not only Receives Considerable addition to its Present Decorations but also . . . adorn . . . the solemn Purposes they are appointed for." St. Michael's Parish, Charleston, S.C., Vestry Book.

house of industry A workhouse. For a more detailed description, see **workhouse** (1).

1818 A "HOUSE OF INDUSTRY established by the corporation, is now in operation . . . where donations from the benevolent will be thankfully received. . . . All persons wishing to have work done, either sewing, weaving, spinning, knitting &c. can have it done at a moderate price." *Alexandria Herald.*

house of mercy See **bettering house.**

house of office A necessary house; privy. For a more detailed description, see **necessary house.**

1677 Paid to "William Churchill for building a house of office for ye prison . . . [was] 525 pounds of tobacco." Middlesex Co., Va., Court Order Book 1673–1680.

1773 A craftsman received an order to build on a glebe a "house of office eight feet by six feet weatherboarded with pine plank and covered with cypress shingles, one Battand door with three lights of glass over it, proper seats put in, [and] the whole painted." Fairfax Parish, Fairfax Co., Va., Vestry Book.

house of rendezvous A tavern featuring bawdy entertainment.

1812 Near Colchester, Virginia, "in the middle of one of the woods we passed a wooden house which I was surprized to hear was a house of rendezvous, as it is called, where women receive the carters, riders, stage coachmen, etc., who pass by." Foster, *Jeffersonian America.*

housewright A carpenter. Although a common term in the North, few southern carpenters called themselves *housewrights.* See also **carpenter.**

1730 In a land transaction in Chowan County, North Carolina, James Potter was identified as a "housewright." Chowan Co., N.C., Deed Book C.

hovel A small, rude dwelling often open on one or more sides like a shed. See also **shed** (2).

1728 A family of settlers in the backwoods of North Carolina "liv'd rather in a Penn than a House. . . . The Hovel they lay in had no Roof to cover those wretches from the Injurys of the Weather. . . . The poor man had rais'd a kind of a House but for want of Nails it remain'd uncover'd." Byrd, *History of the Dividing Line.*

1786 A Charleston native found Washington, North Carolina, to be "great only in name, for it consists of only one miserable hovel, like the rest, in which we found two other gentlemen and their wives already lodged. We therefore pigged before the chimney all night on a bed spread on the floor." William Drayton, Journal of a Tour by Sea and Land from Charleston to New York, Charleston Museum.

1827 A geologist visiting western North Carolina complained that "the people lack industry. Some parts of the country . . . are as fine as the good parts of N. England & if the Inhabitants wd be industrious & cultivate them in a similar manner they might have painted frame houses instead of the present unsightly log hovels." Mitchell, *Diary of a Geological Tour.*

hull The body or frame of a building before it is enclosed with weatherboarding and roofing. See also **carcass.**

1729 "Philip Hamond . . . offers to Undertake the finishing the Hull of the house and . . . to have the same so Intirely Inclosed and Compleated as to free it from any Danger of Weather." St. Anne's Parish, Anne Arundel Co., Md., Vestry Book.

1757 Payment was made "to William Callaway for building the Hull of the Courthouse." Bedford Co., Va., Court Order Book 1757–1758.

1786 On a tenant farm in western Virginia was "one hull of a new log dwelling house, 2 story, 22 by 16 without a chimney." Jonathan Clark Notebook, Filson Club.

1791 An order read: "The hull of a framed House, which we order to have new doors and 2 new window Shutters and the Rest of the Windows closed up, the lower floor laid, and bourds laid on the Juice, the whole under pinned with brick and One Brick Chimney." Kent Co., Del., Orphans Court Valuations.

hurdle A movable rectangular barrier consisting of vertical sticks interwoven with strands of flexible twigs and branches known as wattles or withes. See also **wattle**.

1812 At Arlington in northern Virginia, "the fences were of hurdles to keep out pigs." Foster, *Jeffersonian America*.

hut (hutt) A building of impermanent or inferior construction intended for human occupation. A qualitative term applied by Europeans and Americans to temporary frontier shelters, the dwellings of the ethnically different, and, in general, structures housing the poor.

1674 Exploration of the Charleston region received assistance from "the Indians being diligent in making two barke-covered Hutts, to shelter us from the injury of the weather." Salley, *Narratives of Early Carolina*.

1773 "From hence [Portalago, South Carolina] we went on nine miles to a poor hut without windows called a Tavern." *Hugh Finlay Journal 1773–1774*.

1786 "Every little settlement [in eastern North Carolina] bore the appearance of poverty . . . their houses in general are log huts." William Drayton, Journal of a Tour by Sea and Land from Charleston to New York, Charleston Museum.

1816 An English army officer traveling in eastern North Carolina observed that "the houses are all built on scantling, and are worse than any thing in the form of dwellings, but the negro huts; for they are penetrable at every crevice; while, from the usual mildness of the weather, doors have become altogether released from the duty of being shut." Hall, *Travels in Canada and the United States*.

hydrant An apparatus consisting of an upright pipe with a spout or other outlet used for drawing water from a pipeline. Although far from common, a few southern towns had the rudiments of a public water system composed of underground pipelines by the early 19th century. Most supplied only a limited amount of the water used by town dwellers.

1808 Winchester, Virginia, had "an excellent supply of water conveyed through the streets in pipes, and rising as in Philadelphia, by means of hydrants." Caldwell, *A Tour Through Part of Virginia*.

icehouse 1. A subterranean or partly submerged structure, covered by a superstructure, used for the storage of ice collected from ponds, lakes, and streams during the winter. Square or conical pits, excavated to a depth of ten to twenty feet below the surface of the earth and from five to twenty feet across the bottom, were often lined with stone or brick for better insulation.

1795 A tavern for sale in Annapolis had "an ice-house built on the best construction, which will contain fifty large loads." *Alexandria Gazette*.

1809 In January 1803, Thomas Jefferson wrote that "if it is now as cold with you as it is here I am in hopes you will be able & ready to fill the icehouse. It would be a real calamity should we not have ice to do it, as it would require double the quantity of fresh meat in summer had we not ice to keep it." *Huntington Library Quarterly*.

1814 A proprietor of a resort at Shocco Springs in Warren County, North Carolina, advertised in June, 1814, that "additions and improvements have been made to his buildings, so as to render them more commodious and comfortable than heretofore. His Ice House is well stored with ice." *Raleigh Star*.

icehouse (1)
Rosewell, Gloucester County, Va.

2. A shop selling ice, ice cream, ice drinks, and other cold delights.

> 1820 In Raleigh, "DAVID SHAW has opened his Ice-House, and is prepared to furnish Ice-Cream, Punch or Lemonade, every day (the Sabbath excepted) from 10 in the morning til 10 at night. He will also sell Ice by the pound. . . . He still keeps on hand a full supply of Confectionary, Cordial, Lime-Juice, Candies, Spunge and Pound Cake, and nearly every article in the Confectionary line." *Raleigh Register.*

imitation   The representation of one material with another, generally the copying of the color and surface appearance of a superior material. The most common type of imitation was the marbling and graining of wood finishes in interior locations, such as chimney pieces, bases, wainscotting, and doors. Pine, for example, was occasionally painted to produce the color and grain pattern of more costly hardwoods such as mahogany and walnut. Another type of imitation consisted of using bevel-edged boards to replicate stone rustication. See also **scagliola, grain** (2).

> 1705 At the capitol in Williamsburg, "the wanscote and other Wooden Work on the first and Second floor in that part of the Building where the General Court is to be painted Like Marble and the wanscote and other wooden work on the two first flors in the other part of the Building shall be painted like Wanscote." *Journals of the House of Burgesses,* 4.
>
> 1736 An advertisement by a workman read: "House, Sign, and Ship-painting and Glazing Work done after the best manner, imitation of Marble, Walnut, Oak, Cedar, &c., at five Shillings a yard." *South Carolina Gazette.*
>
> 1747 "The outside" walls of the Anglican church in Savannah were "to be covered with a strong Cement, and neatly sett off in Imitation of Stone Work." *The Colonial Records of the State of Georgia,* 6.
>
> 1750 One room of a glebe house was "to be painted of a Lead Colour & the lower one of a Chocalate Colour. A plain Chimney piece in each room [is] to be Painted of a Marble Colour." Newport Parish, Isle of Wight Co., Va., Vestry Book.
>
> 1817 "The spaces between the columns" of the altarpiece in St. Paul's Episcopal Church in Baltimore "represents slabs of streaked marble, the whole resting on steps, apparently of clouded marble—the imitation uncommonly good." *American and Commercial Daily Advertiser.*

impost
Pavilion 7, University of Virginia

impost   The point where an arch springs. An impost block is a member that supports one side of an arch and is sometimes treated decoratively as a carved piece or as projecting stone or brickwork.

> 1774 Work on the Corbit house in Odessa, Delaware, included a "Frontispiece with Jaum caseing, impost, circular soffit &c. £18." Sweeney, *Grandeur on the Appoquinimink.*
>
> 1798 "The extra work" on the penitentiary in Richmond included "stone Pillars to support the Groins of 6 rooms, stone imposts to all the external Arches." *The Correspondence and Miscellaneous Papers of Benjamin Henry Latrobe,* 1.
>
> 1803 A church was designed by architect Robert Mills for an Episcopal congregation in South Carolina to have "two projecting Courses of Bricks at the feet of all the Arches to form Imposts." Johns Island Church Specifications, Charleston Library Society.

in antis   See **anta.**

infirmary   A room or apartment set aside in a hospital, prison, or workhouse for the care of the sick or injured.

> 1798 "Upon the second floor" of the west wing of the penitentiary in Richmond was "the infirmary for the Men." *The Correspondence and Miscellaneous Papers of Benjamin Henry Latrobe,* 1.

inn   A building for the accommodation of travelers and the entertainment of guests. Most inns had bedchambers, dining rooms, and other spaces for public entertainment and activities. The term was not as frequently employed as *ordinary* or *tavern*. See also **hotel, ordinary, tavern.**

> **1740** A house was for sale in Charleston "joining the Crown Inn." *South Carolina Gazette.*
>
> **1815** "Museum of Wax Figures" were on display "at Mr. Reardon's Inn, sign of the Spread Eagle, King Street" in Alexandria, Virginia. Alexandria Herald.

inside to inside The horizontal dimensions of a structure, excluding the width of the walls. See also **in the clear.**

> **1736** A bridge was to be "Ten feet wide from Inside to Inside of Each post." Spotsylvania Co., Va., Will Book 1722–1749.
>
> **1794** A clerk's office was to have "one room . . . twenty feet square from inside to inside and one room . . . with twenty by sixteen feet from inside to inside with a Partition wall between them of brick." Accomack Co., Va., Court Order Book 1793–1796.
>
> **1813** The tomb of an unhappy man was to be constructed of "brick and mortar six feet from inside to inside, and three and a half feet wide from inside to inside, and four feet from bottom to top" and covered with a stone engraved "I am gone where Woman cannot give pain." Princess Anne Co., Va., Will Book 1795–1871.

inspection house (inspecting house) A public warehouse used for the inspection of tobacco intended for export. In order to stop the flow of bad or trash tobacco from Virginia to England, the General Assembly passed a law in 1730 requiring that all exportable tobacco be shipped from specially designated locations. By the late 1730s, most counties had established at least two or three inspection houses along navigable rivers. Publicly appointed inspectors examined each hogshead to ensure the quality of the tobacco. A similar law was passed somewhat later in Maryland. Inspection houses varied in size but were generally clapboard-covered frame structures, with sheds attached to one or both sides. Tobacco was stored in the main section of the warehouse until shipment. A tobacco prize used for packing hogsheads was usually located in one of the shed rooms. See also **rolling house, transfer house, warehouse.**

> **1737** The county paid "Richard Tutt for building one inspecting house 40 by 20 feet." Spotsylvania Co., Va., Court Order Book 1730–1738.
>
> **1740** "On the motion of the inspectors at Bowlers, Joshua Fry and Philip Jones Gent. are appointed to agree with some person to build a warehouse at the said inspection forty foot long and twenty foot wide and sheded and to erect prizes at the said house, and to erect prizes at Piscataway Inspection." Essex Co., Va., Court Order Book 1738–1740.

insulated Detached, not connected or engaged with any other element, such as a free-standing column.

> **1796** At Mount Vernon, "there is a handsome statuary marble chimney piece in the dining room (of the taste of Sir Wm. Chambers), with insulated columns on each side." *The Virginia Journals of Benjamin Henry Latrobe,* 1.

intercolumniation (intercolumnation) The distance in the clear between two columns, usually measured at the lower part of their shafts in multiples of the diameter of the column. The Roman architect Vitruvius provided the terminology for the principal distances of intercolumniation, which, because of his status as an ancient codifier of the rules of classical architecture, was appropriated by Renaissance theorists and 18th-century English architectural publicists. In *pycnostyle*, the space is one and a half diameters distance; in *systyle*, the

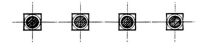

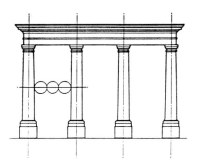

intercolumniation
Diastyle, 3 diameters width

columns stand two diameters apart; in *eustyle*, they are two and a quarter diameters apart; in *diastyle*, the distance is three diameters; and in *araeostyle*, the interval between columns is four or more diameters apart. In colonial America, few builders worried about the exact distancing of columns according to these classical rules until the introduction of English architectural books in the second half of the 18th century. Influenced by such books, a small number of individuals including Thomas Jefferson, sought to impose these rules upon their designs.

> **1756** "INTERCOLUMNIATION—A term used to express the spaces between columns, or the distances at which they are to be placed from one another. This is not arbitrary, but established rule. The intercolumniation is usually made smaller as the orders are more delicate, and larger as they are of the stronger kinds." Ware, *A Complete Body of Architecture.*
> **c. 1785** In devising the portico for the state capitol in Richmond, Thomas Jefferson noted that the proposed width "admits 6 columns & 5 intercolonnations . . . very nearly the Eustyle which is 2 1/4 diam." Jefferson Papers, Huntington Library.
> **1803** In supervising the construction of the Capitol in Washington, architect Benjamin Henry Latrobe insisted that "the Intercolumnations of the East and West fronts be equal." *The Correspondence and Miscellaneous Papers of Benjamin Henry Latrobe,* 1.

interrupted sill A horizontal beam at the bottom of a wall. Unlike a regular sill, which extends the length of the wall in one piece, an interrupted sill is composed of a series of smaller pieces that run between the main posts and are tenoned into them with the posts continuing vertically beyond the sill into the ground. The term is modern. See also **sill, Virginia house.**

> **1739** Tobacco warehouse to be built "forty foot long and twenty feet wide with a ten feet wide shed on each side thereof, the posts to be set in the ground and the sills tennented in the posts." Caroline Co., Va., Court Order Book 1732–1740.

interstices Spaces or intervals between things or parts, especially the gaps between building elements such as logs.

> **1785** "The poorest people build huts of logs, laid horizontally in pens, stopping the interstices with mud." Jefferson, *Notes on the State of Virginia.*
> **1811** In Halifax County, North Carolina, "the Negro huts are generally built of round pine or cypress logs, with dirt floors & dirt in the interstices between the logs." Thomas Henderson Letterbook, NCA&H.

intertie (interduces) A horizontal framing member used to bind upright posts together in walls and roof trusses, sometimes employed to bind multistory wall posts at intermediate levels.

> **1824** The roof a courthouse in Roxboro, North Carolina was "to be hipped . . . the Joists to be 3 by 12 Inches & framed into gearders & interties of a Size suited to the proportion of the Joists." Person Co., N.C., County Accounts, NCA&H.

in the clear The uninterrupted linear measurement of a space or interval, exclusive of the enclosing structural parts. See also **inside to inside.**

> **1674** Statehouse at St. Mary's City to have a "porch in front sixteene foote Long and twelve foote broad in the Clear on the Inside." *Archives of Maryland,* 2.
> **1680** A courthouse was "to be of three stories Pitch the first twelve foote in the cleere the second nine foote and the third eighte foote." Talbot Co., Md., Court Judgments 1675–1682.
> **1691** A brick church was "to be fourty five foot in length and twenty two foot in breadth Cleare within the walls." *VHM,* 3.
> **1802** A house in Washington, D.C., was described as being "22 feet by 29 feet in the Clear of the walls." INA Policy Record, CIGNA Archives.

in the extreme The overall dimensions of a structure, including the thickness of the wall. The meaning of the term is opposite of *in the clear*. See also **outside to outside.**

> **1788** The foundation of a jail was to "be thirty nine feet long & thirty three feet wide in the extreme." Prince William Co., Va., Deed Book 1787–1791.

intrados The inner curve or soffit of an arch or vault. See also **extrados.**

Ionic order (Ionick) One of the five orders of classical architecture, the details and proportions of which were codified by Renaissance writers in the 15th and 16th centuries. These scholars traced the origins of the order to the Ionian Greeks of Asia Minor. The most distinctive characteristic of the order is the capital, which is crowned by spiral scrolls or volutes. The frieze of the *Ionic* entablature is sometimes enriched with a continuous band of figures, swags, and other decorative ornaments. As with the other orders, the consciously correct use of the *Ionic order* with its system of proportions and details appears in the southern colonies in the second quarter of the 18th century, a period when several English architectural publications found their way into the hands of builders and clients in increasing numbers. See also **order.**

Ionic order

> **1756** "IONIC ORDER—One of the three original orders of the Greeks, of a middle nature between the Doric which was their plainest and the Corinthian which was their most ornamented. The base of the Ionic consists of a torus and two cavetto, with astragals between them. The shaft is . . . nine diameters, in height. The capital in the Ionic order consists of three parts, an abacus, a rind which is the hollow of the volute, and an ovolo under which is an astragal. The abacus supports the entablature, the rind produces the scrolls or volutes. . . . The Ionic entablature has its architrave divided into faces, its freeze is often made to swell, and the cornice has simple modillions." Ware, *A Complete Body of Architecture.*
> **1766** A church was to have "a handsom Altar piece of the Ionic Order." St. Andrew's Parish, St. Mary's City, Md., Vestry Book.
> **1769** "EZRA WAITE, Civil Architect, House-builder in general, and Carver, from London . . . calculated, adjusted, and draw'd at large for to work by, the Ionick entablature, and carved the same in the front and round the eaves, of MILES BREWTON, Esquire's House, on White-Point" in Charleston. *South Carolina Gazette and Country Journal.*
> **1771** "Whereas it appears that the dimentions of the alterpeace mentioned in the Articles with the undertaker for building the New Church are not according to the proportions of Architecture, the said undertaker is . . . to make the same according to the true proportions of the Ionic order notwithstanding." Truro Parish, Fairfax Co., Va., Vestry Book.

iron back See **chimney back.**

iron dog See **andiron.**

ironing room A space, often near a laundry or washroom, where clothes, table linen, and other items are pressed.

> **1799** A three-story dwelling for rent in Richmond contained "a brick kitchen with a cellar underneath, an ironing room on the second floor, sundry closets, and apartments for servants." *Virginia Gazette.*

ironwork 1. A building in which iron is smelted or heavy iron objects are fabricated.

> **1620** A contingent of workmen sent to Virginia; "the Comodities wch these people are dyrected principally to apply . . . are these ensuinge Iron for wch are sent 150

persons to sett upp three Iron worke proofe haveinge beene made of the extraordinary goodness of that Iron." *Virginia Company Records*, 1.

1681 Nicholas Spencer, president of the Virginia Council, noted that "the poverty of our Inhabitants, gives Checke to the Erecting of iron or pot Ash workes, both which wee have the natural means to produce great Quantities of." Colonial Office Papers, PRO.

1777 "A little above Falmouth are Mr. Hunter's Works which, with the Dwelling Houses for the Workmen, form a small Village. He is now erecting a Mill for slitting & plating Iron, & is about building a Furnace for melting Iron Ore. . . . He has a Grist Mill & Saw Mill, a Cooper's Shop, a Saddler's Shop, a Shoemaker's Shop, a Brass Founder's Shop, & Wheel-Wright's Shop." *VMHB*, 62.

2. The material fabricated of iron that is used in a building project. The term was used to describe all hardware, including locks, hinges, holdfasts, casements, hooks, staples, and straps. Sometimes nails were included under this general term.

1640 "Edward Lillie being at Mr. Hayes House the said Hayes asked him why he did not get forwarded the church work. The said Lillie answered that he could not go forward for want of nails and other iron work." Norfolk Co., Va., Court Minute Book of Lower Norfolk Court.

1661 "Jerrard Hawthorne [is] to build or make a paire of stockes and pillory and to fitt them with Iron worke." York Co., Va., Deed, Order, and Will Book 1657–1662.

Italian order See **Composite order.**

Italian roof See **hipped roof.**

ivory black A fine, soft, black paint pigment made by calcining ivory or bone.

1764 "JUST IMPORTED in the last Vessel from LONDON (via Philadelphia) and to be sold" in Annapolis, a list of paint pigments including "Ivory Black." *Maryland Gazette.*

1798 In Petersburg, Virginia, "COCKE & FIELD Have for sale . . . at their STORE on Bollingbrook street, . . PAINTS . . . Ivory Black." *Virginia Gazette and Petersburg Intelligencer.*

jack A machine consisting of gears and chains used in cooking for lifting and turning, especially spits.

1736 "Just imported" into Charleston "and to be sold by Peter Henry . . . kitchin jacks." *South Carolina Gazette.*

1748 The kitchen of a dwelling in Charleston contained "a large Kitchen grate, an Oven and a jack." *South Carolina Gazette.*

jack arch A straight or flat arch with a horizontal intrados. For a more detailed description, see **straight arch.**

1806 Plans for a market house in Charles Town, Virginia, included to have a "substantial jack arch over the front Door and also over the passage window opposite thereunto." Jefferson Co., Va., Deed Book 1806–1808.

jack plane See **plane.**

jack rafter A short rafter; one extending less than the full length of the roof slope, such as those that run from a plate to a hip rafter. See also **cripple.**

jack roof A short, single-sloped section of roof not extending to the ridge line but interrupted by an element such as a tower or chimney.

1753 "Wm Hall agreed . . . to do 85 sq ft of shingling . . . to the church at 50/ pr sqr & 16 sq ft of framing shingling . . . for the jack roof." St. Philip's Parish, Charleston, S.C., Vestry Book.

jail A building for the confinement of prisoners awaiting trial or for debtors. This spelling of the word *gaol* first appeared in the South by the 1750s, but was seldom used until the 1770s. By the early 19th century, *jail* had surpassed *gaol* as the common spelling and had overtaken *prison* as the general term for such a building. For a more detailed description, see **prison.**

> **1753** Justices reviewed the work "on the Prison" and were of the opinion that "the Posts tht Support the Porch should be framed and Underpind that the Ceiling of the under part of the Jail should be Plank'd." Spotsylvania Co., Va., Court Order Book 1749–1755.

jamb (jam, jamm, jambe, jaume) In general, one of the vertical sides of a doorway, window, or other wall opening. Specifically, the upright masonry sides of fireplaces or the pieces forming the side of a doorway or window.

> **1680** A courthouse was to have "two stacks of brick chimneys of fower harths of eight foote within the Gaumes." Talbot Co., Md., Judgements 1675–1682.
>
> **1746** The back parlor, study, and office of Charles Pinckney's dwelling was to have "a beed and facing to the window Jambs." Huger Smith, *Dwelling Houses of Charleston.*
>
> **1766** Specifications for a brick vestry house called for "the chimney to be four foot wide at the Back & to be properly flued & the Jam to be eighteen inches thick from the floor to the arch of the chimney four foot." St. George's Parish, Harford Co., Md., Vestry Book.
>
> **1802** A carpenter's accounts for construction of John Tayloe's Washington, D.C., residence included "Fram'd jaumb linings, moulded on pannels . . . D° D° plain . . . Back elbows & soffits . . . plain Jaumb linings to windows." The stonecutters' account included charges for "Free Stone Jams and Mantle to D°." Tayloe Papers, VHS.
>
> **1824** It was specified that "The jams of the 2 outer doors [are] to be panneled, the other two to be plane as also the window jams . . . the door jams & window jams to be painted white" in the brick courthouse at Roxboro, North Carolina. Person Co., N.C., Miscellaneous Court Records, NCA&H.

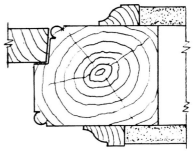

jamb
Door jamb formed by a stud

japan *(n.)* A hard varnish applied to metal and other materials to produce a black gloss. *(v.)* To varnish with a mixture of ingredients to create a high black gloss.

> **1739** An entry in the vestry records read: "The Aulter peace to be Neatly Painted: The Ground work of the Pannels to be Jappand; the Creed Lords Prayer & Ten Commandments to be Done in a Leagable hand In fair Gold Letters." Petsworth Parish, Gloucester Co., Va., Vestry Book.
>
> **1755** Work in a church included "1:8 Inch Japan'd Brass Knob'd Lock 0.14.0." Trinity Parish, Charles Co., Md., Vestry Book.
>
> **1773** In a glebe house "the room doors below [are] to have brass locks, and them above to have Jepaned locks with swirlls." Fairfax Parish, Fairfax Co., Va., Vestry Book.
>
> **1802** A notice read: "Richard Phillips, writer and ornamental gilder with burnished gold on glass. Names for Doors or Windows wrote in a superior style; chairs, &c. japaned and ornamented with gold equal to any imported." *Alexandria Advertiser and Commercial Intelligencer.*

jealous glass A type of slightly opaque glass cast with figures likes diamonds or lozenges, used to glaze windows lighting private spaces or to block views of service areas. Costly to manufacture, its use was confined to affluent households in Britain and was rarely used in early America. One known example of its use in Virginia was found in excavations at Rosewell in Gloucester County, Virginia, the large dwelling built by the Page family in the second quarter of the 18th century. The term was probably a corruption of *jalousie.*

1726   "Jealous glass—This is a sort of wrinkled Glass of such a Quality, that one cannot distinctly see what is done on the other side of it; but yet it admits the Light to pass thro' it. . . . is cast on a Mould, and is composed all over its Surface with a multitude of Oblong Circular Figures (which are concave,) somewhat resembling Weavers Shuttles; this is on one side of it, but the other consists of Figures a little Convex, and this last side is the side they cut it on. . . . This sort of Glass is commonly used, in and about London, to put into the lower Lights of Sash-windows, &c. where the Windows are low against the Street, to prevent People's seeing what is done in the Room as they pass by." Neve, *City and Country Purchaser.*

jerkin head roof (jirkin head)   A type of roof with the gable-end rafter pair sloped inward above the collar beam to form a hip. Although English writers used the term in the 18th century, colonists generally described the form more obliquely as being *hipped above the collars* or *windbeams*. See also **hipped roof.**

1711   A church was to "be hipp'd above ye wind beams." Christ Church Parish, Middlesex Co., Va., Vestry Records.

jet (jut, jetty, overjet, overset)   *(v.)* To cause to project or extend beyond a vertical plane.   *(n.)* A projection, often the eaves of a structure.

1674   "The Rafters [are] to Jett over a foot and a half on each side" of the statehouse. St. Mary's Co., Md., *Archives of Maryland,* 2.

1723   A courthouse in Currituck County, North Carolina, was to receive a "fashionable over jet." *Higher-Court Records of North Carolina,* 5.

1736   A market house was "Thirty foot long fifteen foot Wide, Six foot overset each Side the body of the House to be seven foot pitch (the overset the same) to have four good posts, each side to support the overset." Order Book of the Common Hall of Norfolk, Va. 1736–1798.

1796   Second floor joists of a jail were "to jet 10 inches over the Brick wall in order to receive the Box and Cornish." Stokes Co., N.C., Miscellaneous Court Records.

jib door
Hampton, Baltimore County, Md.

jib door (jibb, gib)   A door designed to blend into a wall, usually to provide service access with minimal visual impact. Typically, a jib door has no architrave and is hung on concealed hinges. The chair board and base are carried across the door with mitred seams to facilitate opening the door. The door is not paneled but finished with a smooth surface, sometimes of plaster. It is painted to blend with the surrounding wall and has a small and unobtrusive latch or doorknob. A jib door is the counterpart to a blind door, which is a false door designed to provide architectural balance. In modern usage, jib door has become interchangeable with *jib window*, referring to floor length windows that may also serve as doors, usually on the garden side of a house.

1802   A carpenter's accounts for the Tayloe house in Washington, D.C., include entries for "Circular fram'd grounds to Jib doors" and "To hanging 3 Jib Doors, 7/6 each." Tayloe Papers, VHS.

joggle   To fit or fasten two adjoining members with wooden pins or dowels. See also **dowel.**

1784   The walls of a log prison were "to be of hewed timber sixteen by sixteen inches, well Joggled together." Charlotte Co., Va., Court Order Book 1780–1784.

joiner (joyner, house joyner, shop joyner)   A carpenter specializing in the fitting together of paneling of other woodwork made of small pieces such as doors, windows, and mantels. At the time of American settlement, the woodworking trades in England were divided into the crafts of carpentry and joinery. Carpenters were responsible for framing a building and enclosing it, while joiners finished the interior work. Although powerful guilds in London and other English towns rigidly enforced this separation of the trades, the distinction was less precise in the countryside and villages. In the early South, joiners and carpenters shared most of these traditional responsibilities. In some documents an individual might be called a *joiner*, while in others he would be identified as a *carpenter*. Some members of the woodworking trades specialized in joinery work, which, by its nature, required them to possess a larger number of molding and carving tools such as planes and chisels that the average carpenter would not have carried in his tool chest. Until the last quarter of the 17th century, few buildings in the South required the full exercise of a joiner's skills. However, with the growing wealth of merchants and planters and the gradual improvement in housing conditions came the introduction of fashionable woodwork such as wainscotting, sash windows, paneled doors, staircases, and chimney pieces, all of which were fabricated by joiners in their shops and on building sites. See also **cabinetmaker, carpenter.**

1623 Among the immigrants to Virginia was "William Jones (about 17 aged) [from] London joyner." *VMHB*, 19.

1654 "John Prosser of Wicocomocoe, Joyner, agrees to make for Thomas Brewer one table seaven foote long and one forme . . . and two chaires and two joyned stooles." Northumberland Co., Va., Court Record Book 1652–1655.

1693 It was "Ordered that Jabell Alford be bound to Mrs. Susanna Hartley Widow untill he be one and twenty yeares of age and that the said Mrs. Hartley be bound and enter into bond to learne him the Trade of a Carpenter or Joyner within the same Time." *Higher-Court Records of North Carolina*, 2.

1702 Church accounts listed payment "to the joiner for windows, table, form and benches £6." St. Paul's Parish, Chowan Co., N.C., Vestry Book.

1726 "The Art of a Joiner" was "a Business requiring great Ingenuity, being the nicer and more delicate Part of wood-work; as Carpentry is the larger and rougher. . . . A good Joiner may more easily supply the Place of a Carpenter, than a Carpenter can do the fine Work of a Joiner." Neve, *City and Country Purchaser*.

1751 A newspaper item read: "Ran away from . . . the Naval Office in Charles County, Maryland . . . convict Servant . . . Jossath Rainherd, a cabinet-maker and joiner by trade. . . . He is a very smooth-tongued insinuating fellow, & an Englishman born." *Virginia Gazette*.

1769 "EZRA WAITE, Civil Architect, House-builder in general, and Carver, from London, HAS finished the architecture, conducted the execution thereof, viz. in the joiners way, all tabernacle frames . . . and carved all the said work in the four principal rooms; and also calculated, adjusted, and draw'd at large for to work by, the Ionick entablature, and carved the same in the front and round the eaves, of MILES BREWTON, Esquire's House" in Charleston. *South Carolina Gazette and Country Journal*.

joinery (joynery) The art and practice of framing and joining several small pieces of wood together to form decorative woodwork, such as panel doors, shutters, sash, wainscotting, staircases, and chimney pieces; the work performed by a joiner. See also **joiner.**

joint *(n.)* The place where two pieces or parts meet. *(v.)* To prepare boards, scantlings, or timbers for fitting together.
1. In masonry the space between two pieces may be treated in a variety of ways. When butted together without any mortar between them, they are said to be *dry* laid. Many masonry joints have putty or mortar laid between the two pieces. Bricklayers and stonemasons used a number of decorative treatments to finish exposed joints. This work

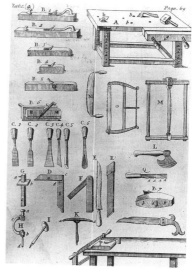

joiner

Joiner's tools. (A) Workbench: (a) hook, (c) mallet, (d) holdfast, (g) bench vise; (B1) foreplane, (B2) jointer, (B3) strike block plane, (B4) smoothing plane, (B5) rabbet plane, (B6) plow plane, (B7) underside of plane: (a) mouth, (b) sole; (C1) former, (C2) paring chisel, (C3) former, (C4) skew former, (C5) mortise chisel, (C6) gouge; (D) square; (E) compass saw; (F) bevel; (G) gage; (H) piercer; (I) gimlet; (K) auger; (L) hatchet; (M) pitsaw; (N) whipsaw; (O) tenon saw; (P) whetting block; (Q): handsaw; (R) mitre square

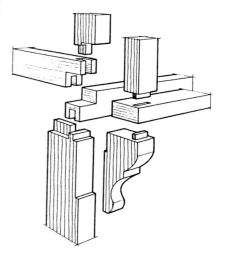

joint

The meeting of various framing elements sometimes required a complicated series of joints as illustrated in the second floor jetty of the Cupola House in Edenton, N.C., 1758.

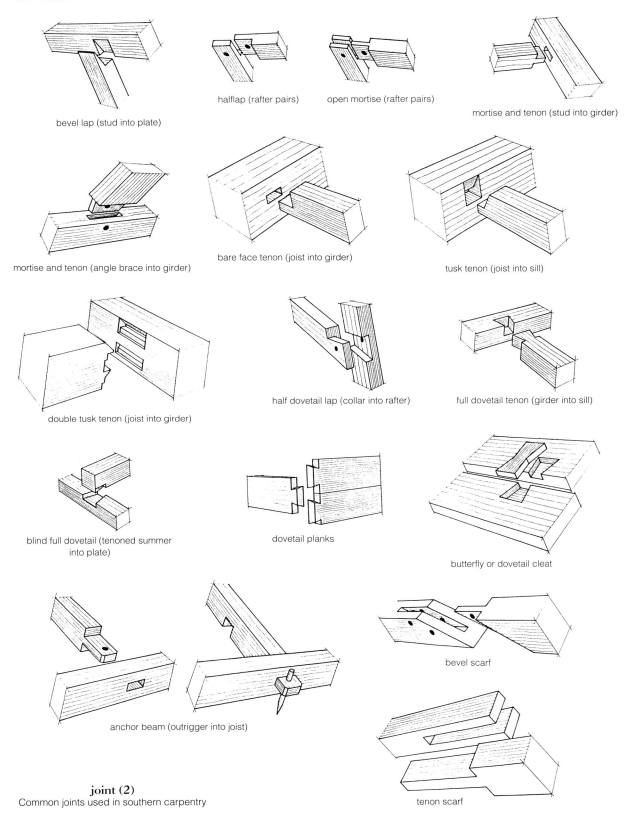

bevel lap (stud into plate)

halflap (rafter pairs)

open mortise (rafter pairs)

mortise and tenon (stud into girder)

mortise and tenon (angle brace into girder)

bare face tenon (joist into girder)

tusk tenon (joist into sill)

double tusk tenon (joist into girder)

half dovetail lap (collar into rafter)

full dovetail tenon (girder into sill)

blind full dovetail (tenoned summer into plate)

dovetail planks

butterfly or dovetail cleat

anchor beam (outrigger into joist)

bevel scarf

tenon scarf

joint (2)
Common joints used in southern carpentry

was known as *pointing*, the purpose of which was to protect the joint from the effects of weather and give the masonry surface a pleasing uniform finish. The simplest treatment was a flush joint, whereby the surplus mortar was scraped off with a trowel, leaving a smooth, even plane. Stonework often was finished with raised joints, whereby the mortar joint was higher than the corresponding walling material. The most common finish joint through the 18th century in the South was the tooled or scribed joint, which is commonly known today as a *grapevine joint*.

2. In carpentry and joinery, the connections made between two members or pieces were known as joints. These were secured by glue, nails, and pegs. The most common were the *lap, butt, mortise and tenon*, and *dovetail*. For a more detailed description of each type, see **butt** (2), **dovetail, lap, mortise and tenon.**

1673 A dwelling to be built was "to be jointed with false plate." Middlesex Co., Va., Court Order Book 1673–1680.

3. To plane smooth the edge of a board or shingle to fit snug against another piece.

1741 Thomas Williams contracted to "compleat the said house at his own expense & also saw & deliver so much inch plank from Pitt as will be sufficient to lay an upper floare of a house twelve by sixteen when the same is seasoned & joynted & will for consideration of two hundred pounds current money of Virginia to be paid." Bristol Parish, Prince George Co., Va., Vestry Book.

1772 A church was to be "covered with Chestnut or Yellow Poplar Jointed shingles." Shelburne Parish, Loudoun Co., Va., Vestry Book.

joist (joice, joyst, joyce, jist, gist) Horizontal framing members that support floorboards above and plaster laths and sheathing boards beneath. Joists span the major framing members and rest on masonry

joist

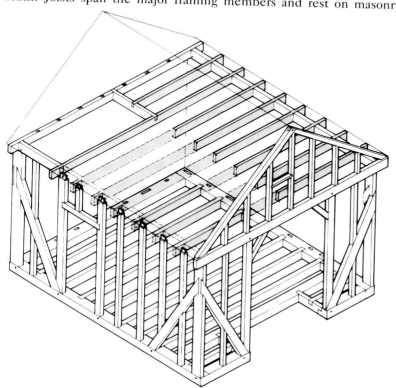

walls, plates, girders, summers, or sills. Those that support the ground floor of a structure were commonly known as *sleepers*. See also **sleeper**.

> 1661   A contract was made "to sufficiently floore with Boards and joysts" a building. *Archives of Maryland*, 41.
>
> 1680   Specifications for a prison called for the "joyce" to be spaced "not above six inches . . . and to be lofted with substantial rived boards." Lancaster Co., Va., Court Order Book 1680–1686.
>
> 1730   A carpenter was engaged to repair a parsonage house by putting up "Ceiling Joyce and ashlers for the plaistering above Stairs." Prince Frederick, Winyah Parish, S.C., Vestry Book.
>
> 1794   "The upper joists" of a barn in Delaware were "to be of the best gum 10 by 12—the sleepers or lower joists to be of white oak . . . 6 by 12—not more than two feet apart." Dickinson Papers, Del. Hall of Records.

journeyman   A craftsman who has finished his apprenticeship in a trade and qualified for wages, but does not work for himself. The journeyman is employed by others, usually at a daily rate. Also, a person employed by a master or building contractor for wages. See also **apprentice, master**.

> 1762   In Dumfries, Virginia, Mardun V. Eventon advertised for "TWO or Three Journeymen CABINETMAKERS who are versed in their Business, and can go on with any common Branch in the Cabinet way. . . . Such Journeymen as have a Mind to be employed by me, in the Business above-mentioned, may depend on agreeable Encouragement." *Maryland Gazette*.
>
> 1771   Samuel Spurr of Williamsburg "will give good wages, and accommodations, to two or three Journeymen Bricklayers, for the remaining part of the season, to work upon the Hospital building in this City. Plenty of Bricks and Lime is already, so there will be no Delay." *Virginia Gazette*.
>
> 1818   In Norfolk and Portsmouth, the master builders tried to establish a wage rate for those employed in the building trades. They noted that "Journeymen Carpenters' wages, at this place, are from $1.50 to $1.75 per day. . . . Journeymen Bricklayers' wages $2 to $2 1/2 per day." *American Beacon and Commercial Diary*.

juniper   A group of softwoods under the genus *Juniperus*. When used in the early South, the term referred to Eastern red cedar. See **cedar**.

> 1770   A church was "to be covered with Nineteen inch Juniper Shingles ends drawn and jointed." St. David's Parish, Craven Co., S.C., Vestry Book.
>
> 1800   "CASH will be given for twenty or thirty thousand of good well drawn Juniper Shingles, to be delivered in Wilmington," North Carolina. *Wilmington Gazette*.

jury house   A building constructed on the courthouse grounds for the deliberations of grand and petit juries. Jury houses contiguous to the courthouse or those which stood detached by several yards were particularly common in the northern neck counties of Virginia in the late 17th and first half of the 18th centuries.

> 1693   "Richard Haynie [is] to build a Jury House . . . twelve foot square, seaven foot pitche lofted and sealed with Clapboards, with a small table convenient benches." Northumberland Co., Va., Court Order Book 1678–1698.
>
> 1713   A workman was paid "for covering the Courthouse and Jury House" and "for making a gutter between the Courthouse and jury house." Richmond Co., Va., Court Order Book 1711–1716.

keeper   A device that secures the bar or bolt of a lock, thereby holding a door or other hinged element closed. See **catch** (1).

kerb   See **curb**.

kerf   An incision made in a piece of wood by cutting with a saw.

key 1. A metal instrument used to move the bolts of a lock forward or backward, so as to open or close it.

> 1670 A servant in Charles County, Maryland, was intrusted by his "master with the key of the Corne Loafte." *Archives of Maryland*, 60.
> 1723 An order was issued "that Locks be fixd upon the Assembly pew-doors for the Conveniency of Several house-keepers, and Free-holders . . . such house-keepers as shall pay to this Vestry half a Crown . . . shall have liberty to make use of the said pews, excepting in the time of Assembly. Order'd that the Church-Wardens provide Locks and Key for the said pews . . . and each Lock to have three keys." St. Anne's Parish, Anne Arundel Co., Md., Vestry Book.
> 1737 Notice: "Lost or Stolen out of the House in Church-street where Mrs. Pachelbel lives in, . . . a Key to the Parlour Door." *South Carolina Gazette.*

2. A wedge, bolt, or pin inserted into a hole or space to secure two pieces tightly together.

> 1809 Hinges in a prison were to be "revitted through the Door on a plate of Iron Extending across the Door the two middle hinges to . . . extend far enough to admit a mortice 2 1/2 inches by 3/4 inches beyond the edge of the door which mortice . . . to receive a bar of Iron 2 1/2 inches by 3/4 inches as a Key." Pasquotank Co., N.C., Miscellaneous Accounts, NCA&H.

keystone, key block A voussoir at the center of an arch, often decorated or embellished in some fashion. See also **arch** (2).

> 1674 "The porch" of the statehouse in St. Mary's City was "to have an arch in front six foote wide in the cleere and Eleven foote high to the Keystone of the Arch." *Archives of Maryland*, 2.
> 1820 Work at Bremo in Fluvanna County, Virginia, included arched windows with "key blocks." Cocke Papers, UVa.

keystone, keyblock
Nelson House, Yorktown, Va.

kiln (kill, keele) A furnace or oven for baking, drying, or burning a variety of materials. Three different kilns were used in building to fabricate or condition certain materials. A brick kiln or *clamp* consisted of green bricks stacked with spaces or flues running throughout the stack. Enclosed on the outside by a coat of mud, the stack was heated for several days by fires, allowing the green bricks to dry and then to vitrify. Although the system was inefficient by modern standards, with much wastage in underfired, salmon bricks and overfired, brittle clinkers, there was little improvement in this ancient process until the antebellum period. In some towns, permanent brick kilns were established, but most kilns were temporary structures erected on or near construction sites. Early planters in the Chesapeake and coastal settlements to the south found little natural limestone or chalk deposits that could be burned for lime. However, oyster shells provided a bountiful alternative. Lime kilns consisted of conical holes dug into the ground that were filled with shells and cord wood and covered over and left to burn for some time. Throughout the colonial period, planks and boards were seasoned in order to reduce the moisture content as the sap dried out. By the late 18th century, lumber was occasionally kiln-dried to speed this process by placing the material in a building where the air temperature could be raised through the use of stoves and fires. However, the process was never widespread and most timber, especially framing members, was used while still green. See also **season.**

> 1642 The court received the deposition of woman who, "being att her husband Brickhill shee did heare some body Cry Murder Murther." *County Court Records of Accomack-Northampton, Virginia 1640–1645.*

1668 "In every Clampe or Brick Keele . . . there are three degrees of Brick in goodness. . . . The first and best sort are those, which in burning, lie next the fire in the Keele, which if they have much Salt-peter in them, they will run, and be as it were glazed all over; and these for lasting, exceed all the rest in that Keele, although the Earth and making be the same. The second and most generall sort for building, are those which lie next in the Keele . . . The third and worst sort, are those that lie on the outside of the Keele, where the fire hath not so much power as it hath over those nearer." Leybourn, *Platform Guide Mate for Purchasers, Builders, Measurers.*

1735 A plantation for sale near Charleston contained "a Brick Lime Kiln." *South Carolina Gazette.*

1754 "Mr. Waite" the undertaker and "the vestry are of opinion that none of the bricks of the two first kilns are fit to be put into the Walls of the Glebe House but that what is done be pulled down & done with good bricks." Truro Parish, Fairfax Co., Va., Vestry Book.

1762 At Pope's Creek in northern Virginia, "the subscribers having erected a Lime Work, will supply any Person with a Quantity of Lime . . . those who choose to take it from the Kiln, may be supplied at 4d" per bushel. "Any Quantity of Shells will be delivered at any of the Places aforesaid." *Maryland Gazette.*

1789 "Mr. Henry Cooksey reported . . . that he had burnt a Kiln of Bricks containing Eighty Thousand Bricks, and the Vestry having viewed and Examined this said Kiln and conceiving it to be well burnt. . . . And Gerald Wood who was authorized to see the Lime that had been burnt by Mr. Cooksey measured and properly secured from the weather reported that he had seen the same done." Trinity Parish, Charles Co., Md., Vestry Book.

1799 Payment was made to a workman for "halling planks four days for 1st kiln. . . . To making the kiln, halling wood, attendance of Billy 15 days, making up the kiln that fell down, and all other work in drying the plank. . . . To two days and one Load halling the last kiln of plank. . . . To one day halling of all the plank from the kiln to the house." John Steele Papers, SHC.

1819 Available to builders at the University of Virginia were "lime kilns about 9 miles distant along the public road and the price of lime has been generally about 16 cents the bushel at the kilns." For carpenters who undertook work "unseasoned boards must be sufficiently kiln-dried." *Lynchburg Press and Public Advertiser.*

king post
King post roof frame

king post A vertical tension post in a roof truss connecting the tie beam with a pair of principal rafters at the ridge. The post flared near the bottom to provide shoulders into which were tenoned diagonally set struts connecting the post and the principal rafters. The diamond-shaped head at the top received the tenoned ends of the principal rafters. Occasionally, ridge boards or beams ran longitudinally from one king post head to another. Although king post roofs were in use in England in the 17th century, they did not appear in the colonial South until early in the next century, where they were used to cover the wide spans of public buildings and double-pile dwelling houses.

1760 In the construction of a 40-by-25-foot church, "the Roof to be Built with Principal and Purloins three main Girders and a King Post." Augusta Parish, Augusta Co., Va., Vestry Book.

1767 On viewing the roof construction of a church, the vestry determined "that in order to make the whole Frame Sufficient, the said Charles Tilden [undertaker] shall put or cause to be put King Posts . . . Seven Inches by Seven when squared with Sufficient Heads thereto, & to be straps with Clamps of Iron round the Coller Beams & up the said King Posts . . . with spur braces to the King Posts." Chester Parish, Kent Co., Md., Vestry Book.

1783 Carpenters advocated "securing the Roof" of a damaged church "by braces and King Posts, in such a manner, as not to need the use of Pillars, and at the same time to render the church, much more commodious." Congregational Church, Charleston, S.C., Record Book.

king's yellow One of a number of yellow paint pigments available in America in the 18th and early 19th centuries. The principal ingredient is arsenic trisulfide, a yellow crystalline substance.

1760 "JUST IMPORTED" into Maryland "from LONDON . . . SUNDRY Sorts of Paint and Colours, viz . . . King's, Prince's, and Naples Yellow." *Maryland Gazette.*

1798 For sale in a store in Petersburg, Virginia was a variety of paints including "King's Yellow, dry and in oil." *Virginia Gazette and Petersburg Intelligencer.*

kitchen (kitchin, kitching) A room or building in which food is prepared and cooked. At the time of southern settlement in the 17th century, English families cooked their meals in any one of a number of different spaces. In smaller houses, the hall served as the principal cooking chamber. Larger dwellings sometimes had rooms devoted entirely to cooking or separate buildings that served as kitchens. Excavations of early settlement sites in the Chesapeake reveal that few households had separate kitchens before the middle of the 17th century. In a few, such as the exceptional Bacon's Castle in Surry County, Virginia (1665), the kitchen was located in the cellar. Most people prepared, cooked, and ate their meals in the hall; if that space was devoted primarily to sleeping and entertaining, then cooking occurred in another, primary ground-floor room. However, by the second half of the 17th century, documentary and archaeological evidence suggests that a number of settlers were choosing to construct detached kitchens, a pattern that would predominate in the South through the Civil War. The decision to move the kitchen and other domestic functions out of the main house into a series of outbuildings stemmed from a complex blend of social, technological, and environmental factors. With the replacement of white indentured servants with black slaves, a separate building reinforced the spatial segregation of family and servants. The clapboard technology of the *Virginia house* favored the construction of a number of small, simply framed buildings over the fabrication of one large and intricately framed dwelling that housed all domestic functions. Finally, the heat generated by long periods of cooking could be confined to an outbuilding rather than permeating the entire house, a factor much appreciated in long, hot summers. With the increasing specialization of domestic functions in the 18th century, even modest households sought to remove cooking from its conspicuous place in the hall or main entertaining space. The most prominent feature of a detached kitchen was its chimney with its large cooking fireplace, which was sometimes accompanied by a bake oven. Many fireplaces contained trammel bars, long iron hooks for hanging pots. Other furniture found in these spaces included dressers, tables, and shelves that held the pots, pans, and cooking implements and provided work surfaces on which to prepare food. Many of the better kitchens had brick floors, plastered walls and ceilings, and a stair or ladder to garret rooms, which were used for storage or sleeping space for servants and slaves. See also **cookhouse.**

1635 A 40-by-18-foot parsonage house to be built on a glebe was to have "a chimney at each end . . . and upon each side of the chimneys a rome, the one for a study, the other for a buttery alsoe a pertition neer the midest of the house with an entry and two doures the one to goe into the kitchinge the other into the chamber." *County Court Records of Accomack-Northampton, Virginia 1632–1640.*

1642 The inventory of a millwright's estate listed goods in a hall and kitchen. "In the Kitchinge" were "one small brasse Kettle and three milk tubbs one pewter pott 3 brasse skillets 2 trayes and one sifting tray 3 sifters one frying pann 2 iron pestell one cowle and a tubb . . . 1 paire of pot racks two iron hooks." *County Court Records of Accomack-Northampton, Virginia 1640–1645.*

1666 An inventory of an estate listed "the little lodging roome . . . the great inward roome . . . the outward roome or kitchen." Norfolk Co., Va., Deed and Will Book 1666–1675.

1668 A carpenter was to be paid for "new Covering . . . [a] dwelling house of 40 foot long" and "for Building a Kitchen of 20 foot long and sixteen foot wide with a welsh chimney and a Lobs Corner 2 partitions and grouncell." Charles Co., Md., Court Proceedings, MSA.

1707 It was "Ordered that a kitchin be built up the said gleabe twenty four foot long & sixteen foot wide with a brick chimney and that ye same be lathed filled plastered and white washed with all necessary windows doors and partitions." Christ Church Parish, Middlesex Co., Va., Vestry Book.

1737 The vestry ordered to be built "a Kitching twenty foot long . . . sixteen foot wide, and eight foot pitch, with a good brick chimney, the upper floor to be laid with good inch pine plank . . . and the under floor with good brick or tyle, . . the inside of the said kitching to be lathed, filled in, and plaistered with shelves and water benches set up therein." Truro Parish, Fairfax Co., Va., Vestry Book.

1751 Money was subscribed to build a "Ministers House," which was to "26 feet by 18 two storys high to which a kitchen, at one end 18 feet by 16 a stack of brick chimneys to contain three fire places and an oven." Christ Church Parish, Ga., Vestry Records, GHS.

1766 "To be sold at Bath Town in North Carolina, A Good Dwelling-House, two stories high, with four rooms on a floor, and kitchen and cellars under the house." *Virginia Gazette.*

kitchen garden A fenced garden established primarily for growing vegetables, fruits, and herbs for domestic consumption. For a more detailed description, see **garden.**

knee A curved or bent member or element. The term was used specifically in the early South for two elements.

1. In roof framing, carpenters sometimes fabricated principal rafters from curved timbers. Their feet curved inward slightly just above the junction with the girder at the eaves. Workmen believed that such timbers would sit more firmly on the horizontal truss member if the joint was closer to a right angle. In modern terminology these curved rafters are known as *bent principals*, but during the colonial period they were called *knee rafters*. The garret walls or *knee walls* formed at this curved area are composed of short studs, which were known as *ashlers*.

2. Any molding that curves or flares at an angle, such as the end of an architrave where it meets a surbase, pedestal, or base.

1774 Carpenter's work done by Robert May for William Corbit's dwelling in Odessa, Delaware, included making "6 Knees to ye Ovolo," along with a chimney piece with "13 ft 8 ins Ovolo & 2 Knees." Sweeney, *Grandeur on the Appoquinimink.*

1783 The drawing room in the Governor's House in New Bern contained "kneed architraves to the windows." Hawks Letter, Miranda Papers, Academia Nacional de la Historia, Caracas.

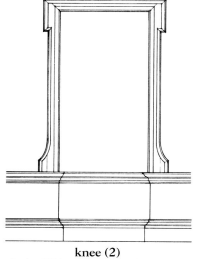

knee (2)
Parlor, Shirley, Charles City County, Va.

kneeling board A board raised slightly off the floor in front of a pew seat or altar rail, used for kneeling during worship service. Kneeling cushions were also in general use in a number of Episcopal churches by the late 18th century.

1745 Workmen were to add "ledges at the front of each Pew to lay books on, and kneeling boards to kneel on." St. Paul's Parish, Hanover Co., Va., Vestry Book.

knob An oval or round projection, especially a handle used to open locks, to pull open a drawer, or to slide a sash.

1737 "LATELY imported from London" and to be sold in Charleston were "Brass Knobs for Windows." Two years later, a new supply of "sash knobs" were available. *South Carolina Gazette.*

1760 A Savannah merchant wrote to his English supplier requesting "2 18 Inch spring Bolts with Brass knobs, 3 9 Inch Ditto." *Collections of the Georgia Historical Society*, 13

knocker A hinged knob, bar, or ring affixed to a door, used to announce the presence of a visitor.

1793 Stolen "from the stage doors" of a theater in Richmond was "a pair of brass knockers." *Virginia Gazette and General Advertiser.*

1802 Among a detailed list of "Iron mongery" in the carpenter's accounts for the Tayloe house in Washington, D.C., were "Mortise locks . . . 6 pr large hinges counter sunk . . . 6 latches . . . shutter locks . . . 20 rings . . . to shutters, 12 Draw'r handles 303 pair [shutter] hinges . . . 4 pʳ brass Dᵒ . . . 2 turnbuckles . . . 1 Knocker 2/6." Tayloe Papers, VHS.

knot **1.** A hard, cross-grained section in a piece of timber where a branch had formed in the trunk of a tree. Because knots sometimes shrank and popped out when dried and were difficult to work and plane, craftsmen carefully selected stuff that had as few knots as possible. In better quality buildings, clients often required exposed woodwork such as wainscotting and flooring to be free or clear of major knots.

1750 "The Floore" of a glebe house "to be laid with good quarter pine plank clear of knots." Newport Parish, Isle of Wight Co., Va., Vestry Book.

1792 In Washington "the Commissioners of the Federal Buildings" contracted for several thousand board feet of the "best yellow Pine Flooring Plank . . . to be free from sap and knots." *Virginia Gazette and Alexandria Advertiser.*

2. A flower bed laid out in an intricate design meant to please the eye especially when seen from a higher elevation such as a second-story window, mount, or belvedere. Designs were symmetrical and sometimes imitated the shapes and patterns of embroidery and cutwork of contemporary needleworkers. Beds separated by narrow paths were usually mirror images with patterns repeated at the ends and sides of quarters. See also **flower garden.**

1749 The residence of Alexander "Singing Sandy" Gordon in Charleston contained "a garden genteelly laid out in walks and alleys, with flower-knots, & laid round with bricks." *South Carolina Gazette.*

labyrinth A maze of walks bordered by high hedges, usually eight to twelve feet high, creating so intricate and difficult a path to the center that a person would lose himself in the walks. Such features were rare in Southern gardens.

1804 Thomas Jefferson suggested that "the best way of forming the thicket will be to plant it in labyrinth spirally, putting the tallest plants in the centre and lowering gradation to the external termination, a temple or seat may be in the center then leaving space enough to walk." Nichols, *Thomas Jefferson, Landscape Architect.*

lacquer (lacker) A protective, gold-colored coating of a resinous varnish, consisting primarily of shellac in alcohol. It is applied to wood and metal to produce a highly polished, lustrous, finish. See also **japan, varnish.**

1719 The vestry was to send to England for "flaggons washed over with Gold or Lacker." All Faiths Parish, St. Mary's County, Md., Vestry Book.

1803 The vestry voted to purchase in London "a double lackered Brass Chandelier with three Tier of Lights." St. Michael's Parish, Charleston, S.C., Vestry Book.

lacunar See **soffit.**

ladder A wooden structure consisting of two side pieces connected to each other at regular intervals by rungs used for climbing up or down. A stepladder is one that has steps rather than rungs. Both types were used in the process of construction. They were also commonplace features in dwellings that did not have permanent stairs to a cellar or loft. Ladders were occasionally fastened to the roof in an area near the chimney to provide easier access to it in case of fire.

1642 In the kitchen of a dwelling was a "ladder." *County Court Records of Accomack-Northampton, Virginia 1640–1645.*

1737 A workman was hired to construct "a door above [the] joyst" in the loft of a dwelling, "with a convenient ladder and neat rail to ascend up to the same." Truro Parish, Fairfax Co., Va., Vestry Book.

1742 Plans for a dwelling included a "covered way without into the seller with a broad step ladder and a private doar under the stares within, with doar ladder." Bristol Parish, Prince George Co., Va., Vestry Book.

1744 "The Fire-Masters" of Charleston required each household to have "one Bucket for each Fire Place, and a Ladder to reach the Eaves of the House." *South Carolina Gazette.*

1773 A dwelling was to have "the stairs . . . run up in the passage with handrail and banisters, and a door underneath to go down into the cellar with a broad step ladder." Fairfax Parish, Fairfax Co., Va., Vestry Book.

1788 On John Meriss's estate "a step ladder is wanting in stead of Stairs for Kitchen loaft." New Castle Co., Del., Orphans Court Valuations F.

lake A paint pigment of a reddish hue, obtained from mixing animal or vegetable coloring with a metallic oxide. A variety of lake pigments were available in early America, producing colors ranging from a dark crimson to a rose pink.

1734 "LAKE, especially the richest Sorts, is the best of all dark Reds, being a most pure crimson; 'tis a Colour that will grind very fine, and lies with a good Body; but there must be much Pains taken in grinding it; for if it be not well and thoroughly ground, its Colour will want much of its Glory; and besides this, 'twill work with some Difficulty; being apt to cling together like a Jelly, after 'tis laid on; just as warm Water does upon a greasy Trencher, when it is wash'd in it; to prevent which, it must be well ground, and tempered as thin, as it can well be work'd. There are several Sorts of *Lake* sold at the Colour Shops, very different, some being of a more dead and pale Colour." *Builder's Dictionary.*

1760 Imported from London and for sale in an Annapolis shop were "SUNDRY Sorts of Paints and Colours, viz . . . Lake." *Maryland Gazette.*

lampblack A fine, black paint pigment made from the carbon obtained from the soot of burning oil, pitch, and other fuels. Although imported from England, the pigment was also commonly produced in colonial America.

1727 There is an account for "lamp black" and "cash paid the painter for work done to the Church." St. Anne's Parish, Anne Arundel Co., Md., Vestry Book.

1761 Imported into Savannah from Bristol were "12 doz small barrels of Lampblack." *Collections of the Georgia Historical Society*, 13.

1812 In Orange County, Virginia, "Mr. Madison assured me that for several years an overseer on a neighbouring property had been in the habit of breaking off the branches and tops of his pine trees in order to make lampblack (the smoke of burnt pines collected on canvas being the process employed) which he sold at a considerable profit." Foster, *Jeffersonian America.*

Lancaster hinge See **H Lancaster hinge.**

landing 1. A place for the loading and unloading of goods and passengers. From the early 17th century onward, landings appeared at convenient locations along the numerous rivers and creeks that fed into the Chesapeake Bay and South Atlantic coast. Some were established by law as places for the inspection and export of tobacco, while others were developed by individuals to serve their plantations and commercial enterprises. Landings generally had a wharf of some type with storehouses, warehouses, mills, and other buildings crowding near the shoreline. See also **quay, wharf.**

>1692 An agreement was made to carry timber "to a convenient landing." Henrico Co., Va., Deed and Will Book 1677–1692.
>1694 An "English framed dwelling house with a . . . 15 foot Kitching about 200 yards from a good landing" was for sale. York Co., Va., Deed, Order, and Will Book 1694–1698.
>1787 At his plantation in Westmoreland County, Virginia, Robert Carter "finished the Wharff at the Landing." Robert Carter Day Books and Letterbooks, Duke.

2. A flat area or platform at the interval between two flights of steps or the area at the end of a stair flight. See also **halfpace.**

>1674 "The Roofe of the upper staire of the statehouse" at St. Mary's City was to be "of sufficient heighth that there may be Convenient landing & head way att the Topp of the staires." *Archives of Maryland*, 2.
>1809 The jail in Green County, Georgia, was to have "a flight of steps and landing place in the passage." *Monitor.*
>1811 There is an account for "Level Rail & Balusters on Landing" of a Baltimore dwelling. Riddell Accounts, Pleasants Papers, MHS.

landscape (landskip)   A pastoral painting mounted on canvas or paneling and generally placed above a chimney piece.

>1711 Specifications for a house in Charles County, Maryland, called for a "Chimney peace with very good Stone mouldings and a large Landscipp pannell." Rivoire, *Homeplaces.*
>1737 A new glebe house was to have "landskips over the chimneys." Truro Parish, Fairfax Co., Va., Vestry Book.
>1752 A painter advertised his services "in Limning way, History, Altar Pieces for Churches, Landskipps, Views of their own Houses and Estates, Signs, or any other Way of Painting." *Maryland Gazette.*
>1756 A Charleston merchant ordered from London "two handsome Landscapes of Kensington & Hyde Park which will just fill up two vacancys over the Chimney peices in the Hall and a large Parlour. . . . He would have handsome views of those two places with the adjacent Woods, Fields, & Buildings & some little addition of Herds, Huntsmen, &c., but not too expensive in the Painting. We cant form a Judgment of such peices." *The Papers of Henry Laurens*, 2.

landscape
Drawing of Principal Room, Bond Castle, Calvert County, Md.

lane   A narrow passage or road between fences, walls, and buildings. See also **alley** (2).

>1716 A description of a piece of property in York County, Virginia, noted that the boundary line ran "along Pegram's lane to Morris's Corn field." Jones Papers, LC.
>1739 It was "Ordered that Mr. Samuel Ball take possession of the Gleeb land and Houses and that he make a lane to the house." St. Mark's Parish, Culpeper Co., Va., Vestry Book.
>1800 In Baltimore, "a person, some nights ago, having been murdered in an house of ill-fame in Love-Lane, a large mob assembled on Wednesday noon, and tore it down, together with four adjoining houses of the same description." *The Telegraph and Daily Advertiser.*

lantern (lanthorn)   **1.** A small, open structure at the top of a roof or dome that provides light for the area below. See also **cupola, skylight.**

>1805 In the design of a dwelling, architect Benjamin Henry Latrobe noted that "the stairs will be lighted by a Lanthorn light in the roof. The difference between a Lanthorn light and a sky light is that, in the former the opening is surrounded by upright Sashes, in the latter it is covered by sloping Lights. The former always

keeps the house cool in Summer and never leaks, the latter heats it, and cannot easily be made watertight." *The Correspondence and Miscellaneous Papers of Benjamin Henry Latrobe*, 2.

1814 At the Governor's House in Raleigh, "you enter the anti-chamber; from this you pass into the rotunda in the centre of the building, which is lighted by a lantern window in the roof." *The Star.*

2. The room at the top of a lighthouse surrounding the light or beacon. See also **lighthouse.**

1795 "A complete and sufficient iron lantern in the octagonal form is to rest" on the masonry body of a lighthouse to be constructed at Cape Hatteras, North Carolina. *North Carolina Gazette.*

3. A transparent or translucent case enclosing a light to protect it from wind and rain, and to provide a housing from which to hang the light. In dwellings, lanterns often hung in entrance halls. In the late 18th and early 19th centuries, most of the major cities in America erected on major streets lampposts to support lights contained in lanterns.

1748 An estate for sale in Charleston contained "a paved Entry 9 Feet wide, a strait Arch for hanging a Lanthorn." *South Carolina Gazette.*

1794 A plasterer "is desirous of knowing whether you would like the passage ornamented, especially where the Lanthorn will hang." Izard Papers, LC.

1809 A Charleston visitor to Philadelphia marvelled at "the improved part of the City [wherein] most of the streets are wide; they are paved for carriages, & have side walks, very neat & commodious. They are illuminated every night, with a suitable number of lamps enclosed in Glass lanterns, fix'd on the top of high posts at the edge of the foot pavement." *Journal of William D. Martin.*

lap (lapt)   To set a timber, sheathing board, shingle, molding, or other building component partially or entirely over a lower layer or member. Early carpenters employed a variety of simple lap joints in the construction of buildings. One of the most common consisted of inserting one member into an open mortise cut into another member and securing the piece with either a peg or nail. Such lap joints were frequently employed in framing studs to wall plates; the head of the stud would be notched over or let into an open mortise in the lower side of the plate. Another common lap joint appeared at the apex of rafter pairs, where each rafter end was reduced in thickness by half, lapped together, and secured by a peg or nail. When carpenters employed these methods throughout a structure (eschewing more complicated and costly joints for reasons of economy), such buildings were referred to as lapped work. Bevel laps consisted of angling together the ends of two members in the same plane. Such laps appear in sheathing and moldings, where the intention was to maintain a continuous flush surface. Side lapped shingles provided a distinctive alternative to the more common methods of laying up a shingle roof. Rather than having their two sides butted together in the same plane, the shingles were laid with one of their long sides lapped over the adjoining shingle.

1725 The vestry house was to be covered "with good drawn Boards of red Oak, well lapp'd." St. George's Parish, Harford Co., Md., Vestry Book.

1747 An orphan's estate survey found "one 20 by 15 foot dwelling house lapt work . . . and one 30 by 20 foot tobacco ditto lapt work." Queen Anne's Co., Md., Deed Book C.

1767 Chapel "to be covered with lapped shingles." Frederick Parish, Frederick Co., Va., Vestry Book.

larder   A room or building in which food is stored; a pantry.

> 1781   Among the buildings destroyed or damaged on William Cary's property in Yorktown, Virginia, during the siege of the city were "a store house 24 by 16 feet . . . a smoakhouse, a dairy, a larder 8 feet square brick floor." York Co., Va., Claims for Losses.

latch   A devise for holding a door, gate, or shutter closed, consisting of a wooden or iron bar or bolt that slides or drops into a hole, groove, or catch. See also **bolt.**

> 1665   "He endeavoured to lift up the Latch & could not gett the Doore open." *Archives of Maryland,* 49.
> 1719   The vestry was to send to England for a "chest of window Glass Containing one hundred foot Square Iron Latches hasps and Doftaill hinges for Casements." All Faiths Parish, St. Mary's Co., Md., Vestry Book.
> 1737   Just imported from London into Charleston was a "variety of iron ware . . . several sorts of locks, thumb latches." *South Carolina Gazette.*
> 1745   An estimate made in building a large dwelling included "4 Dozen Iron latches & ketches for window shutters at 3 sh." Huger Smith, *Dwelling Houses of Charleston.*

lath (lathe)   Thin strips of sawn or riven wood used in roofing and walling. Roofing laths were placed at regularly spaced intervals across the backs of rafters, on top of which shingles and other roofing materials were nailed or occasionally pegged. In plastering, small lath, measuring no more than an inch or two in width and less than a half an inch in thickness, were nailed to exposed framing members with slight gaps between each stick so that the base coat of plaster would be keyed or secured into the interstices of this wooden formwork. The resulting material was known as lathing. Until the early 19th century, almost all plaster lath was riven rather than sawn. Occasionally lath were used as shims and nailers. See also **sheathing.**

> 1674   The Maryland statehouse was to have "the particions double Lathed and plaistered." *Archives of Maryland,* 2.
> 1683   Richard Harris of Somerset County, Maryland, was contracted to "hyre a thatcher and pay for Cutting of Sedge and nailes to naile the latthes upon the rafters." Touart, *Somerset.*
> 1704   The roof of a church was "to be lathed with Good oak lathes and Shingled with Good Siprus Shingles." Petsworth Parish, Gloucester Co., Va., Vestry Book.
> 1723   A workman was ordered to "Lath and plaster the walls of the house that he now lives in: and to seal it over head with laths and to plaster it with lime and heare thereon." Petsworth Parish, Gloucester Co., Va., Vestry Book.
> 1728   On the North Carolina-Virginia border "most of the Houses . . . are Log-houses, covered with Pine or Cypress Shingles . . . hung upon Laths with Peggs." Byrd, *History of the Dividing Line.*
> 1743   A church roof was to be recovered "with good new Cypress seasoned Shingles nailed upon good new Oak Laths of one inch thick and three inches broad." All Saints Parish, Calvert Co., Md., Vestry Book.
> 1782   A dwelling was "lathed inside but not plastered." Queen Anne's Co., Md., Guardian Bonds & Valuation Book SC.
> 1786   "Ch. Dickinson began to Rive laths & nail them on." Francis Taylor Diary, CWF.

lath
Mason House, Accomack County, Va.

lathe (turner's lathe, laythe)   A machine used for shaping objects of wood and metal. It operates by applying a variety of sharp-bladed instruments, such as a chisel, to a piece of material that is rapidly turned by means of a treadle connected to a reciprocating spring or a rotating wheel. Objects turned on a lathe for building primarily consisted of balusters, finials, and newels.

lathe   Parts of a pole lathe: (a) legs, (b) cheeks, (c) poppets, (d) screw, (e) rest, (f) handle, (g) tenons of poppets, (h) wedge, (i) treddle, (k) cross-treddle, (l) pole, (m) string

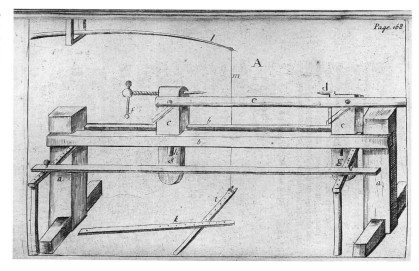

1679   In the estate of John Cumber were "2 heads for the head of a laythe." Henrico Co., Va., Court Records 1677–1692.

1773   An inventory of "the Estate of Mr. John Roberts supposed to be dead from his long absence beyond [the] Sea" listed "a Turners Laythe & Poppet Heads" valued at "£0.2.6." Princess Anne Co., Va., Deed Book 1772–1773.

lattice   A series of regularly spaced laths, bars, strips, or rods used as a screen to permit the flow of air through a structure. Dairies often had a lattice opening just below the wall plate to allow for the cooling circulation of air.

1730   Construction of a new dairy stipulated that it be "latticed as usual." Stratton Major Parish, King and Queen Co., Va., Vestry Book.

1775   "The Dairy shall be received" by a vestry "after a Lattice Window is made Opposite to the one already made." Bristol Parish, Prince George Co., Va., Vestry Book.

laundry   A room or building in which clothes are washed and cleaned. Often associated with kitchens, most laundries were located in outbuildings and contained a fireplace for heating water and large tubs for washing. They came into use by wealthier households in Virginia and neighboring colonies in the early 18th century. Farther south and in the northern Chesapeake the term *wash house* was used to connote a building housing this activity. See also **wash house.**

1735   A carpenter in Williamsburg charged a client for "2 1/2 Days Work Done About Door In ye Laundry £0.6.5." Jones Papers, LC.

1762   Outbuildings to be constructed on a glebe included a "kitchen and laundry 28 by 16 & 9 foot pitch." Cumberland Parish, Lunenburg Co., Va., Vestry Book.

1798   The owners of Ogle Hall in Annapolis constructed a "brick kitchen and laundry 16 by 32." U.S. Direct Tax, MSA.

lawn   An open area of cultivated grass or other ground cover in a pleasure ground adjacent to a dwelling, maintained for aesthetics and recreation.

1756   In Annapolis, the dwelling built for Governor Bladen stood "on an agreeable rising ground, in a beautiful Lawn, commanding the view of the Town." *Travels in the American Colonies.*

1794   At Belvedere in Baltimore, "the foreground possessed luxurious shrubberies and sloping lawns." Twining, *Travels in America 100 Years Ago.*

lattice
Kitchen, Hampton, Baltimore County, Md.

1799 In the of front of Mount Vernon, "the breadth of the whole building is a lawn with a gravel walk round it . . . The ground in the rear of the house is also laid out in a lawn." Weld, *Travels Through the States of North America.*

lazaretto A building to house those with contagious diseases. The term derived from the biblical Lazarus, a diseased beggar. See also **hospital (3), pesthouse.**

1767 Commissioners "for building a LAZARETTO upon the west end of Tybee Island," Georgia, advertised that the structure was to be 40-by-20-feet and constructed out of tabby. *Georgia Gazette.*

lead **1.** A heavy, malleable, bluish-white metal, frequently imported into the South in rolled sheets and used for flashing, gutters, window cames, and occasionally as a roofing material. See also **came, plumber.**

1684 In Charles City County, Virginia, William Byrd ordered from London "about 400 feet of glass of the large twelves, with drawn lead and soder proportionable." *Correspondence of Three William Byrds of Westover.*

1745 In estimating the cost of his dwelling in Colleton Square in Charleston, Charles Pinckney calculated that he needed sufficient "sheet lead for 2 gutters one 23 feet long & one 20 Do." Huger Smith, *Dwelling Houses of Charleston.*

1769 In Williamsburg, "at the LEAD MANUFACTORY, behind the church, may be had all sorts of sheet lead, pipes for conveying water from the tops of houses, cisterns, milkpans . . . and every other article in the plumbing business. . . . KIDD & KENDALL." *Virginia Gazette.*

2. Weights used to counterbalance window sashes made of cast lead. See also **cast iron, cord, pulley, weights.**

1745 An estimate of materials for Charles Pinckney's dwelling in Charleston listed "pigg lead to cast into window leads for 44 Sash Windows £5.11.6." Huger Smith, *Dwelling Houses of Charleston.*

1774 A carpenter's bill for work at William Corbit's house in Odessa, Delaware, recorded "lead for Window, Cord &c. £6.9.11 1/2." Sweeney, *Grandeur on the Appoquinimink.*

lead color A medium gray paint variously used as a primer, an interior color, and a finish for roofs. In most cases this color was composed of lampblack and white lead mixed in oil.

1726 Specifications for construction of a new courthouse called for an "arch over the court to be sealed with plank and that primed and painted of a led colour and alsoe the Banisters and barrs window fraimes staires and doors and door cases." Norfolk Co., Va., Order and Will Book 1723–1734.

1750 Concerning the exterior finishes of a new glebe house, the vestry of Newport Parish directed that "the Doors, Window Frames, and Cornish . . . be painted of a lead Colour." Newport Parish, Isle of Wight Co., Va., Vestry Book.

1762 The vestry directed that the steeple of a church be "painted white up to the roof, and the roof to be of a lead colour." Elizabeth City Parish, Elizabeth City Co., Va., Vestry Book.

1796 An invoice for paints ordered for the finishing of Peyton Skipwith's house at Prestwould included 2 kegs of "Lead Colour." Skipwith Papers, W&M.

leaf **1.** A thin sheet of metal, such as silver or gold, applied to various ornaments, including weather vanes, balls, sculptured figures, and capitals, to produce a glimmering surface.

1738 An agreement was reached with "Mr. Samuel Peacock that he . . . handsomly paint the aulter peace of popler spring church . . . and to find all the oyles & coulers except the leaf gould that is to be made use of for the carving work and other work that is to be done on the said aulter peace." Petsworth Parish, Gloucester Co., Va., Vestry Book.

1764 A Maryland merchant had for sale "Silver Leaf." *Maryland Gazette.*

1801 Alexandria painters MacLeod and Lumsdon submitted a bill for their work on the elegant Tayloe house "For finding paints, Oils, Gold leaf &ca with workmanship Painting &ca your drawing room in City Washington $180.00." Tayloe Papers, VHS.

2. One of two or more parts of a door, gate, or shutter turning upon a hinge. The term in this sense of a *fold* was uncommon in the early South. However, it was used in a similar sense to refer to a detachable or added part of a table, desk, or other piece of furniture. See also **double door (1), folding door.**

> 1699 A carpenter was paid for "making a table leaf." *Higher-Court Records of North Carolina*, 3.
>
> c. 1798 In designing his dwelling in Wilmington, Delaware, John Dickinson questioned whether "the front door fold or not? If it folds, should the leafs turn back upon the columns or intervals between the door and the small windows on each side, or should the doorway be so deep that the leafs may turn back flat against the sides of the doorway, or into recesses in it?" Dickinson Plantation Files, Delaware Bureau of Museums.

3. The part of a drawbridge that is hinged.

> 1809 "There are two draws" on the Potomac Bridge. "The construction of these draws, the manner in which they are hung, the machinery by which they are raised, are extremely ingenious, and combine strength with great facility and ease in raising. A boy of ten years old will be able to raise one leaf." *American and Commercial Daily Advertiser.*

lean-to (lean too)   A room or wing of a building enclosed beneath a single sloping roof, with the higher end abutting a wall or roof of a larger structure. In contrast to in New England, the term rarely occurs in the South. The preferred term for such a feature was *shed*. In dwellings, the space within lean-tos generally functioned as service rooms and bedchambers. See also **shed.**

> 1715 In Chowan County, North Carolina, a carpenter failed to build "one house of the dimention of twenty foot long & fifteen foote wide with a shade or lean too of eight foot wide." *Higher-Court Records of North Carolina*, 5.

leather   A tanned animal skin, used in building mainly as washers for hinges.

> 1747 "The munting sashes to be supported when up with Iron pins made fast to the frame with a Leather thong." Albemarle Parish, Surry Co., Va., Vestry Book.
>
> 1822 An estimate was made for "new leathering the Bellows of the organ." St. Michael's Parish, Charleston, S.C., Vestry Book.

ledge   **1.** A shelf, often supported by brackets, attached to the edge of a vertical member such as a panel.

> 1745 Harry Gaines was to build "ledges at the front of each Pew to lay books on." St. Paul's Parish, Hanover Co., Va., Vestry Book.
>
> 1752 A workman was hired "to fix a broader Ledge within the Barr for the Better Conveniency of the attorneys." Northumberland Co., Va., Court Order Book 1749–1753.

2. A transverse bar or strip of wood applied to a door, shutter, or gate; a batten. See also **batten.**

> 1746 In the cellar of his dwelling in Charleston, Charles Pinckney specified "2 four panel outside door—4 pair outside cellar window shutters panneld—All the rest of the Doors and window Shutters on this floar to be ledged." Huger Smith, *Dwelling Houses of Charleston.*

ledger   A horizontal pole used in scaffolding, lashed to the upright poles or standards and supporting one end of the putlogs. For a more detailed description, see **scaffold.**

length of board A 17th-century unit of measurement based on the length of a four- or five-foot clapboard used to define the dimensions of a structure. This board length regulated the spacing of the framing system. Thus two four-foot lengths of boards meant that the wall posts were spaced at eight-foot intervals.

> **1651** An "Agreement of John Dobbs to build a house of six lengths of boards with a Chimney" was recorded. Surry Co., Va., Deed and Will Book 1645–1672.
>
> **1657** To be built was "one small quartering house of twenty-five or thirty foot long and so much other out house as will make up the sum of ninety foot of housing. . . . Every length of boards so built allowing five foot to each length of boards." Surry Co., Va., Deed and Will Book 1645–1672.
>
> **1658** It was ordered that "One roome four lengths of boards [is] to be joyned to a house wch was then standing, and store of four lengths of boards at distance from the house, wch building was to be finished within one yeare." Charles City Co., Va., Court Order Book 1656–1658.
>
> **1675** A house was to be built "of five lengths of boards five & twenty feet longe and fifteen foote wide." Henrico Co., Va., Miscellaneous Court Records 1650–1717.

library A room or set of rooms in a dwelling house or public building or an entire building devoted to housing collections of books, manuscripts, etc., for reading and study. The term was relatively rare until the end of the 18th century. Most rooms in dwellings that served this function were generally called *studies*. See also **study.**

> **1710** At Westover, William Byrd noted that he had "put the pictures in the library," a separate outbuilding erected to house his books. Wright and Tinling, *Secret Diary of William Byrd.*
>
> **1724** An inventory of a gentleman's estate noted the presence of books "in the Library." Charleston Co., S.C., Will Book 1724–1725.
>
> **1802** John Tayloe was charged by a carpenter for "Ornamental Chimney pilasters to library" in the Virginia planter's Washington residence. Tayloe Papers, VHS.
>
> **1822** A church group was allowed to build two-story "library in the churchyard . . . of Brick, to be covered with Roman Cement." St. Michael's Parish, Charleston, S.C., Vestry Book.

light (lite) **1.** A window or aperture in a wall for the admission of light.

> **1668** A-ten-by-twenty-foot dwelling was to have "2 lights." Charles Co., Md., Court Proceedings 1668.
>
> **1691** An order was issued "to procure glass for the end light of the Court house." Westmoreland Co., Va., Court Order Book 1690–1698.
>
> **1711** A workman was paid for installing "2 small Lights at the Pulpit." Christ Church Parish, Charleston Co., S.C., Vestry Book.

2. A subdivision of a mullion or sash window. A transom window subdivided by two vertical mullions would be a three-light aperture. In the 18th and 19th centuries the term came to be used in a similar manner to describe the subdivisions of a sash window. Thus an eighteen-light window would be what is today called a nine-over-nine sash, that is, an opening with nine lights in the top sash and nine in the lower one. *Light* was used sometimes interchangeably with *pane* to refer to the glass in these subdivisions. See also **pane.**

> **1704** A courthouse was to have "one large sash window on each side of the house of three lights abrest to Reach from five foot high to ye wall plait and one window of two lights abrest against the Justices seat." Middlesex Co., Va., Court Order Book 1694–1705.
>
> **1710** The vestry gave permission to several of their parishioners "to cut a Window place in ye side of ye Church where their pew is, & to put in a transum two light window, according as of other windows in ye church are." All Saints Parish, Calvert Co., Md., Vestry Book.

1711 Courthouse windows were "to be well glazed with Led and Glass; Except the Lower Lights in the transume windows in front and End below the joyce which are to have shetters instead of glass." Talbot Co., Md., Land Records Book No 12.

1732 Carpenter James Wray of Williamsburg was paid for "mending a Light in an Iron Casement." Jones Papers, LC.

1745 In making an estimate of materials for his new house, Charles Pinckney noted "upon the Cellar floar 9 windows each sashd with 8 Pains of glass 11 by 9; Upon the first floar 16 windows with 18 Pains or lights in each." Huger Smith, *Dwelling Houses of Charleston.*

1791 It was "Ordered that the undertaker of the new jail do put an eight pane eight by ten light window in the front of the said jail." Prince Edward Co., Va., Court Order Book 1791–1793.

1806 Specifications called for a chapel in St. John's Parish, South Carolina, to have "eight windows . . . the size of the windows to be calculated for 18 light sashes, 10 by 12 inch glass." *City Gazette and Daily Advertiser.*

lighthouse   A tower with a beacon or light at the top to warn ships and other vessels of dangerous waters or to serve as guide into a channel or port. The treacherous Carolina coast made a necessity of such guides. See also **beacon house.**

1774 A notice stated that vessels were wanted to help transport "about 6,000 tons of stone from Mr. Brooke's quarry, on Rappahannock, and land the same on Cape Henry, for the lighthouse." *Virginia Gazette.*

1795 "A LIGHT HOUSE" was to be built "on the head land of Cape Hatteras on the coast of North-Carolina." The building was to be in the form of an octagon and stand more than 100 feet in height, topped by an iron lantern for the light. *North Carolina Gazette.*

lightning rod   An electrical conductor. For a more detailed description, see **electrical conductor, electrical rod.** See also **Franklin** (1).

1798 The vestry paid a workman for a "lightning rod and other work" about the church. St. Helena's Parish, S.C., Vestry Book.

1817 "Mr. [Lewis] Gibbes was appointed to purchase a lightning Rod, a Ball & a vane & to have the same put up" on the church. St. John's, Colleton Parish, S.C., Vestry Book.

lightwood   A hard, resinous wood created by girdling a pine. Because the sap is left in the tree when it is killed, the resulting lightwood is much more resistant to rot and termites. It was used in building for fence posts and foundation blocks. See also **block** (1).

1743 Plans called for a chapel "to be sett on good heart of Cypress Blocks the Sills to be of Good Lightwood Pine." Newport Parish, Isle of Wight Co., Va., Vestry Book.

1771 The posts in a glebe garden was "to be of Lightwood the Rails and Pales to be of Sawd Pine or Cypress." St. Stephen's Parish, Berkeley Co., S.C., Vestry Book.

lightwood
O'Quinn House, Moore County, N.C.

lime   A white, lumpy, water-soluble solid composed of calcium oxide; when combined with water or slaked to form calcium hydroxide, it is used as one of the chief ingredients in mortar, cement, stucco, whitewash, and plaster. In early America, lime was produced from two sources, limestone rocks and oyster shells. Because of the absence of the former in many southern coastal areas, the latter was the principal source of lime. Burned in a kiln, the *unslaked* or *quick lime* was placed in barrels and transported to building sites. In many areas, projects often came to a standstill as supplies of lime were exhausted.

1651 A bricklayer was hired to "plaister, White lyme & wash over the dyninge roome, yellowe roome & kitchinge, & chamber over the kitchinge" of a dwelling. Norfolk Co., Va., Will and Deed Book 1646–1651.

1666 The coast of South Carolina "abound[s] with Oyster bankes and such heapes of shells as which noe time cann consume . . . all rivers . . . are stored with this necessary material for lime for many ages, and lying soe conveniently that whatever neer River or Creeke you can thinke fitt to sett a house there you may place your lime kill alsoe and possibly in the banke, just by or very neere finde clay for your brick tile." Salley, *Narratives of Early Carolina.*

1734 "LIME, calcin'd Stone, Marble, Free-Stone, Chalk or other Matter, burnt in a large Fire in a Kiln or Furnace built for that Purpose; to be afterwards used in the Composition of Mortar for Building, the Fire taking away all its Humidity, and opening its Pores, so that it becomes easily reducible to Powder. . . . *Quick* LIME, or un-slak'd Lime, is that which is as it comes out of the Furnace. *Slak'd* LIME, is that wash'd or stepp'd in Water, and reserv'd for the making of Mortar." *Builder's Dictionary.*

1741 A church in Savannah was to be "lath'd and plaistered with oyster shells Lime [that] will last a great Number of Years." *Colonial Records of the State of Georgia*, 30.

1785 In Baltimore, the following notice appeared: "Wanted, a sober industrious Person, who understands turning the Arches of Lime-Kilns, and burning Lime. Also, two other Persons, who have been used to blowing and raising Lime-Stone." *The Maryland Journal, and the Baltimore Advertiser.*

limewash A coating consisting of lime and water used for whitening surfaces such as stucco and plaster. *Limewash* was mainly a British usage; the most common American term was *whitewash.* See also **whitewash.**

1681 A courtroom was "to be Lathed, filled, and white limed." Northumberland Co., Va., Order Book 1678–1698.

1702 An undertaker promised "to provide so much Lime as will wash the ceiling of the Chappel." St. Paul's Parish, Chowan Co., N.C., Vestry Book.

line, lining *(v.)* To apply a layer of material on the inner surface of something. To enclose the walls of a building with wood sheathing or some other material. *(n.)* Material that covers an interior surface, in contrast to casing, which encloses the exterior of a building. The term often appears in descriptions of or specifications for the framework of door and window jambs.

1678 A courthouse was "to be sealed and lined with . . . boards and the roome above . . . the porch chamber allsoe to be seiled and lined well with . . . boards." Charles Co., Md., Court and Land Records Book 1676–1678.

1747 In building an Anglican church in Savannah, the colonists were "directed . . . that the Inside Walls should be lined with Boards." *Colonial Records of the State of Georgia*, 6.

1774 A carpenter's account included "Lineing & hanging 2 Windows at 4/6" in a dwelling in Odessa, Delaware. Sweeney, *Grandeur on the Appoquinimink.*

lineal measure A one-dimensional measurement of a piece of material or workmanship. Generally used to calculate cornices, surbases, bases, and other moldings. The term *running measure* was also used. See **running measure, superficial measure.**

1820 An account of work done at Bremo in Fluvanna County, Virginia, included "Internal Cornice lineal 61.10 × 2.0 = 123.8 @2/6 = $58.52." Cocke Papers, UVa.

linseed oil A drying oil made by pressing flaxseed, used in paints and varnishes.

1674 "The frames and Casements" of the statehouse in St. Mary's City, Maryland, were "to be well laid in Lynseede Oyle according to art." *Archives of Maryland*, 2.

1704 Specifications called for the interior of a courthouse "roofe [to be] arched work and the ends and sides below it to be ceiled with half Inch plank and laid with Linseed Oyle and Colours, with weather boards to preserve the sills and face board down the gable ends." Middlesex Co., Va., Court Order Book 1694–1705.

1800   The vestry "Ordered that one Barrel of Linseed Oyl five Barrels Tar & 100 lb Red Ochre be purchased for Taring & painting the Roof of the Church at Chaptico." King and Queen Parish, St. Mary's Co., Md., Vestry Book.

lintel   A horizontal structural element of wood, stone, or iron spanning an opening. The lintel rests on the jambs of the opening, linking them together and supporting the weight of the wall above.

1786   An advertisement for goods imported to Charleston from Scotland noted "a quantity of free stone flags, lintels and jams." *Charleston Morning Post and Daily Advertiser.*

1811   Construction of a kitchen at Montpelier, Orange County, Virginia, included "4 lintels @ 9d." James Madison's Account with Dinsmore & Neilson 1810–12, Cocke Papers, UVa.

list, listel   *(n.)* A fillet.   *(v.)* To put a border or list to the edge of an object or piece.

1751   In Lancaster County, Virginia, several plantation buildings needed to "be well slabbed; and listed down every rafter with a Board of full breadth." Joseph Ball Letterbook, LC.

1823   "In the Corinthian capitels there is a want of the cavetto and listel of the astragal." Lambeth and Manning, *Thomas Jefferson as an Architect.*

little house   A necessary house; privy. For a more detailed description, see **necessary house.**

1725   A law passed regulating the construction of buildings on the low-water flats of Charleston noted the presence of "Cranes, Crane-Houses and Warehouses of ONE STORY, not exceeding TEN FEET in Height; and also, Little-Houses, commonly called Privies." *South Carolina and American General Gazette.*

1749   The court paid "James Rennolds for building a little house at the courthouse 500 pounds of tobacco." Caroline Co., Va., Court Order Book 1746–1754.

loam   A mixture of sand, clay, and other ingredients such as straw, which when moistened and combined with lime, was used as a mortar.

1752   The outside bricks of a church were "to be laid with good Mortar one third Lime and the other half Sand the Inside Bricks to be laid with Mortar one third Lime and two thirds Loam." Trinity Parish, Charles Co., Md., Vestry Book.

1809   The houses in the Moravian town of Salem, North Carolina, "are uncommonly well constructed—built chiefly of Brick, & a kind of yellow loam or mortar, to which is added great quantities of lime, which alters its nature & color, making it a brick yellow, & much harder than when in its natural state." *Journal of William D. Martin.*

lobby (loby)   A small entrance space, passage, or vestibule; an antechamber to a large public room. The term had limited currency in the South. See also **entry, hall** (2), **passage** (1).

1746   "The lobby and Star head" in Charles Pinckney's dwelling in Charleston was to be finished "with Surbase and skirting board round." Huger Smith, *Dwelling Houses of Charleston.*

1777   At the capitol in Williamsburg "you go into the Lobby of the House of Burgesses, & from thence into the Room where they sit." *VMHB,* 62.

1816   A courthouse in Jones County, Georgia, was to have "three doors in the lower story with circular tops and glazed, to wit one in the end wall entering the loby, and one in each side opening into the courtroom." *Georgia Journal.*

lock   A mechanism, usually operated with a key, intended to secure a door, drawer, or other barriers or containers in a shut position. The myth of an open, trusting society in the early South was belied by the extensive number of locks that were used to secure doors, furniture, pews, closets, boxes, chests, and gates from unwanted neighbors, strangers, servants, and family members. When not in use, public buildings such as churches and courthouses stood locked. Imported from England or fabricated locally, available locks ranged from padlocks, to stock and rim locks, to expensive brass locks. See also **padlock, rim lock, spring lock, stock lock.**

1665 "Raymond Staplefort att night caused a Boy his servant called Humphrey Jones to enter att a window, whereof Tow wooden Barrs had been broken eyther by himselfe or by the said Boy, where the said Boy having entered, opened the Doore, (which was fast shutt with a spring Lock) unto the said Staplefort." *Archives of Maryland,* 49.

1734 It was "Ordered that a lock be put on that Pew which is appropriated for Commanders of Vessells, and that Mr. Thomas Baker the Sexton do keep the key thereof, and suffer not to sit therein on Sundays but masters of Vessells, unless there be a vacancy after the first lessen is read." St. Philip's Parish, Charleston, S.C., Vestry Book.

1741 Imported into Charleston and sold by Robert Wilson were "banbury, plate and stock locks, stock and spring locks with knuts and screws, and fine locks for parlour and chamber doors." *South Carolina Gazette.*

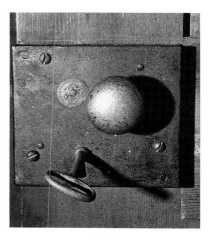

lock
Carpenter Patent Lock, early 19th century

locust Any of several trees of the genus *Robinia,* a member of the legume family. The black locust is one of the most durable hardwoods found in the Southeast. The heartwood is very resistent to decay and insect damage. Because of this durability, it became an important building timber, used for earthfast construction as well as fence posts.

1653 A fence was to be erected with "posts . . . of Locus or Chestnutt." Westmoreland Co., Va., Deed, Will, and Patent Book 1653–1657.

1681 "The posts . . . and groundsells" of a courthouse were "to be of Locust." Northumberland Co., Va., Court Order Book 1678–1698.

1686 A planter in Stafford County, Virginia, noted that "a Locust fence . . . is as durable as most brick walls." *William Fitzhugh and his Chesapeake World.*

1709 "The Locust, for its enduring the Weather, is chosen for all sorts of Works that are exposed thereto." Lawson, *A New Voyage to Carolina.*

1806 "The window frames at Poplar Forest may be of poplar dug out of the solid, with locust sills, tho' I do not know why the sides and top might not also be of locust dug out of the solid." Jefferson Papers, LC.

1806 The window and doorframes of a brick meetinghouse to be built in Fayette County, Kentucky, were "to be of good locust 5 by 7 inches, with a single architrave." *Kentucky Gazette and General Advertiser.*

lodging chamber, lodging room A room used for sleeping; a bedchamber. Through the early 19th century, the term *lodging room* was nearly synonymous with *bedchamber* or *bedroom.* In taverns and places of public accommodation, a lodging room was a chamber provided for overnight customers.

1655 In the Albemarle region of North Carolina, a carpenter constructed "a dwelling house of 20 foote square, wth a lodging chamber, and a Buttery, and a chimney." Norfolk Co., Va., Deed Book 1651–1656.

1666 Auditors of John Bateman's estate found "In Mrs. Batemans Lodging Chamber . . . one feather bed one boulster two pillowes one paire of sheetes one Match Coate a Counter Payne Curtayne Vallance and bedstead. . . . One Box of drawers one small Trunck for writings & one old Chest . . . one Couch and three Wooden Chaires . . . one small table and two Chaires . . . one paire of Andirons whereof one is broke a fire shovell a paire of tongs a paire of Bellowes and a tosting forke." *Archives of Maryland,* 57.

1729 A deposition given by Robert Pearce of Edenton, North Carolina, stated that he was "in his own lodging room in bed . . . did hear a noise in the next adjoining room . . . Mr. Richard Everard and Bremen went round to this Informants wooden window which was then closed shutt which they broke open." *Higher-Court Records of North Carolina,* 6.

1740 "WILLIAM CLEILAND in Charlestown give Notice, that he'll let the first story of his House, viz. a large Hall, Parlour, and Bed Chamber, a Kitchen distinct from his with a Lodging or a Store room above it." *South Carolina Gazette.*

1760 A notice read: "To be RENTED in Alexandria, THE GEORGE TAVERN which hath Three Fire-Places below Stairs, and a very good Bar: Six good Lodging Rooms above." *Maryland Gazette.*

1767 Edward Scott's dwelling in Chestertown, Maryland, contained "Eight genteel Rooms, Six of which are papered with most elegant Paper, Five of which are genteel Lodging-Rooms." *Maryland Gazette.*

1803 The property owned by Charles Yates in Fredericksburg, Virginia, had a "kitchen 46 by 16" with "3 lodging rooms for servants above." *Virginia Herald.*

lodging house   A building providing accommodation for a traveler or a temporary resident; a boarding house. See also **tavern.**

1777 In Charleston, "PAUL SNYDER, in Old Church Street, intends to leave off keeping a Lodging and Boarding House, on Account of the Dearness of Provisions, and returns his hearty Thanks to those Gentlemen who have favoured him with their Custom." *Gazette of the State of South Carolina.*

loft (loaft)   **1.** An upper floor, especially one immediately under or within the roof structure, given to the storage of crops, equipment, and other material, as well as to human occupation, particularly servants and slaves. Loft spaces often remain unfinished. A building containing such a space is often described as *lofted;* crops stored in such spaces are said to be *lofted* as well. See also **attic, garret.**

1640 A carpenter was paid for "5 daies work in laying the floore makeing doore and staires of the corn loft &c." Maryland Patents, Certificates and Warrants 1637–1650, MSA.

1665 A search for contested goods in a dwelling house resulted in their being found, "some in another Chest & some under his feather bed & some up in the Loft about the servants Beds." *Archives of Maryland,* 49.

1678 "The mens meeting . . . order[ed] yt the [Quaker] meeting house att Betties cove" in Talbot County, Maryland, "should be Lofted and p'titioned with falling Windows hung with hinges." Third Haven Quaker Meeting, Minutes, 1.

1727 Robert Carter wrote to one of his tenants in Lancaster County, Virginia: "I ordered your quarter and your overseers house to be lofted. It is very necessary not only for the warmth of the house but to lay the peoples corn up in." Carter Papers, UVa.

1784 A property included "One Saw'd log Kitchen the Other end of a dwelling House with an earthen floor and Brick Chimney the Loft Laid with Rough Pine Boards Cedar Roof in Tolerable Good Repair." Kent Co., Del., Orphans Court Valuations.

2. A raised space within a large room especially in public buildings. Many churches had lofts for organs. See also **gallery.**

1755 The vestry was to find someone "to build a Loft for an organ in the church in the city of Williamsburg and to set up the same." Bruton Parish, James City Co., Va., Record Book.

log construction (logg)   A method of building walls and chimneys by stacking round logs, hewn logs, sawn planks, or poles on top of one another so that they are notched or lapped over one another at the corners. Log construction was one of the most common building technologies employed by Southerners for all types of buildings from the late 17th through the middle of the 19th centuries. As in frame construction, the degree of workmanship and permanence in log building varied significantly, ranging from well-wrought plank dwellings to crudely fashioned cabins. Much effort has been made to discover the European precedents of this building technique. Since large forests with plentiful supplies of building timbers had long disappeared from the British landscape, immigrants from England and Scotland were unfamiliar with the form. Thus it has been presumed that the British settlers of the Chesapeake and Delaware Valley learned the technique from northern Europeans who came to the Delaware Valley colonies of New Sweden and, later, Pennsylvania. Sweden, Finland, Germany, and Switzerland had long traditions of building with logs. The Scandinavians of New Sweden, although small in number, certainly erected a number of log structures in the tiny colony by the time it was conquered by the Dutch. Besides the Scandinavian influence, another source of log building came from German-speaking settlers who immigrated to the Delaware Valley in the late 17th and early 18th centuries. Both groups used round, hewn, and plank log construction. Although the Germans certainly brought log building into the backcountry of Virginia and the Carolinas in the mid-18th century, settlers of British origin in the coastal regions of the Chesapeake had already adapted these foreign forms to their own needs. As early as the 1650s, Anglo-American settlers in Maryland, Virginia, and North Carolina constructed log dwellings, storehouses, prisons, smokehouses, and other structures. Many of these buildings were plank structures with finely sawn logs with tight joints, secured at the corners with dovetail joints. This method provided a measure of strength and security that a *Virginia house* could not provide and were thus used for prisons throughout the region in the late 17th and early 18th centuries. Even the simpler form of round log construction was evident in a number of areas. By the 1720s, it was the predominant form for dwellings on the Virginia-Carolina frontier. Crudely worked log buildings offered a relatively simple solution to the housing needs of many thousands of settlers. In more established areas of the Chesapeake and the Carolina lowcountry, cheap round log construction was used to house slaves and store agricultural produce. Between the laborious work of erecting a sawn plank building and a round log structure was a large middle ground of workmanship. The more permanent dwellings of small farmers in many regions were often fashioned out of logs that had been hewn on one or two sides with tight half-dovetail or V notches at the corners. Many had the log interstices chinked and daubed and covered over on the inside with plaster and enclosed on the exterior with weatherboards. Some of these dwellings were erected with solid masonry chimneys rather than with log hearths. Although the crude round log buildings fell into rapid disrepair and have all but disappeared from the modern southern landscape, the more durable log dwellings, built with considerable workmanship and pride, lasted well into the late 19th and early 20th centuries before they began to be considered inferior or outmoded forms of housing. See also **cabin, cabin roof, hew, plank house, round log, scalp, skinned.**

1663 In a domestic imbroglio in Charles County, Maryland, John Goold complained in court that John Lombroso "spoake to me in Giles Glovers loged hows and hee bid mee to speak to my wife that shee shoold give Consent to fulfill his lust." *Archives of Maryland*, 53.

1680 Following the disturbances of Culpeper's Rebellion in North Carolina, Thomas Miller was taken as a prisoner "to ye uppr end of Pasquotank River at one old Wm Jennings his house . . . and enclosed in a Logghouse about 10 or 11 foot square purposely built for him." *Colonial Records of North Carolina*, 1.

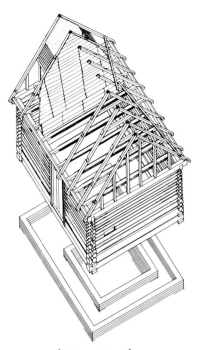

log construction
Council Kitchen, Southampton County, Va.

1683 On Governor Seth Sothel's plantation in the Albemarle region of North Carolina, Nicholas Gent charged for building a "Logg House" for a storehouse. *Higher-Court Records of North Carolina, 2.*

1690 A court was to build a prison "of the same dimensions as the logg'd prison by Accomack County Courthouse." Northampton Co., Va., Court Order Book 1689–1698.

1706 A prison was to be constructed whose "Walls [were] to be Oak Loggs Nine inches Thick the under loggs butt into the upper Swods ffashion." Kent Co., Del., Court Record Book 1703–1718.

1709 "A certain Indian . . . undermin'd a House made of Logs, (such as the Swedes in America very often make, and are very strong) which belonged to Seth Sothel Esq. Governor of North Carolina . . . this being the Indian Store-House, where Trading Goods were kept." Lawson, *New Voyage to Carolina.*

1728 On the Virginia-North Carolina border, "most of the Houses in this Part of the Country are Log-houses, covered with Pine or Cypress Shingles." Byrd, *History of the Dividing Line.*

1740 In Savannah, "they are underpinning the Court House (& Church) which being built of Loggs after the manner of our common built Houses, those Loggs beginning to decay, the whole begins to sink, as we find all other Houses so built to do sooner or later." Christ Church Parish, Savannah, Ga., Vestry Records.

1753 In Augusta County, Virginia, an agreement was made to build "two round Log Houses each twenty one feet Long and fifteen feet wide in the Clear to be eight Feet high under the joists which is to be square and three logs high above the joists beside the Wallplate. . . . the Houses and Chimnies to be Juncked and Daubed both outside and Inside, and Scutched or Squared both outside and inside of both Houses and the Gabel ends from the Logs to be Clapboard." Preston Papers, VHS.

1810 On the Milligan estate in Delaware was "a Granery of saw'd Logs . . . A Carriage House of Round Logs . . . two Stables of Logs . . . Two Corn Cribs, one of round and the other saw'd logs." New Castle Co., Del., Orphans Court Valuations I.

longhouse A modern term referring to buildings in which both principal domestic space and animal byre are housed, with shared entrance from outside. The remains of what may be early 17th-century longhouses have been found at Wolstenholme Towne and Jordan's Point on the lower James River in Virginia. The term was occasionally used during the colonial period to describe other buildings of impressive length, particularly the structures erected by Native Americans.

1674 Travelling in the backcountry of South Carolina, Henry Woodward came across an Indian settlement "which is built in a confused maner, consisting of many long houses whose sides and tops are both artifitially done with barke, uppon the tops of most whereof fastened to the ends of long poles hang the locks of haire of Indians that they have slaine." Salley, *Narratives of Early Carolina.*

long room A public entertaining room, sometimes attached to a tavern, designed for dancing, concerts, exhibitions, and social gatherings. See also **assembly room, ballroom.**

1753 In Charleston, there were "to be seen at Mr. Doughty's Long-Room . . . three most elaborate and curious Figures, German Wax Work . . . being an exact Representation of the present Queen of Hungary and Empress of Germany." *South Carolina Gazette.*

1790 A fifteen-year old contortionist was "to perform a variety of extraordinary FEATS of ACTIVITY . . . at McCrady's LONG ROOM, on the Bay" in Charleston. *The City Gazette or the Daily Advertiser.*

1818 In Augusta, Georgia "the second and last concert of Vocal and Instrumental Music will take place . . . at Mr. Bird's LONG-ROOM." *Augusta Herald.*

loom house A building or part of a building containing a loom for the weaving of yarn into cloth. See also **spinning house, weaving house.**

1775 On the Chance farm in southern Delaware stood "one Loom House." Sussex Co., Del., Orphans Court Valuations A.

1799 Appraisers of a plantation in Broad Creek Hundred in Sussex County, Delaware, noted a "loom house round oak logs 16 feet long by 16 feet wide with a shed to the end of it 8 feet wide shingle roof on each of them and brick chimneys in the loom house." Sussex Co., Del., Orphans Court Valuations G.

loophole   A small opening or narrow slit in a wall for admitting light and air and, in a military context, for firing weapons.

1737 The design of an Anglican church in Savannah called for "no windows from 10 feet high to the ground, but loop holes for muskets on occasion." *Journal of the Earl of Egmont.*

louver   A series of sloping, overlapping, horizontal slats set in a frame with an open space between each slat. Placed in an aperture, they provided ventilation and protection from direct light and view. Although the term was used in England at the time of American colonization, it rarely appeared in southern building documents. However, louvered windows were used where a measure of privacy or ventilation was desired, as in dairies and necessaries. Adjustable louvers appeared in the late 18th century and came into common use in the 19th century in window shutters. See also **slat, Venetian blind.**

louver
Dairy, Mattox Farm, Somerset County, Md.

lucarne (lutarne)   A dormer or garret window. See also **dormer window.**

1680 A courthouse was to have a hip roof "with Lutarnes hipt." Talbot Co., Md., Court Judgments Book 1675–1682.

lumber   Timber that is sawn or riven into planks, boards, and scantling.

1763 Charleston merchant Henry Laurens expected "a little Vessel from the West Indies & want the following Lumber to load her . . . 20 beams of 26 feet long 12 by 14, 40 M very best 2 In. plank, 2 M best Inch boards, Joist or Scantlin 3 × 4, 6 × 6, 6 × 7, 7 × 9, about 200 or 250 pieces I suppose will be sufficient and to be filled up with Shingles." *Papers of Henry Laurens,* 3.

1809 Materials needed for the construction of a Presbyterian church in Georgia included "the following descriptions of Lumber, viz. 2, 1 1/2, 1 1/4, and 1 inch boards, green and seasoned Scantling and hewed timber." *Augusta Chronicle.*

lumber house   A building in which a variety of articles, generally old and unused, were stored. Planks, boards, and scantling were sometimes kept in such structures as well. Lumber houses often served as general warehouses and utility buildings for commercial operations. See also **lumber room.**

1764 "At Pile's Warehouse in Charles County [stood] a Lumber House, at one End of which there is a Compting Room, and Bed Room." *Maryland Gazette.*

1796 Buildings on a plantation included "a framed Lumber House 8 feet Square in midling repair." Sussex Co., Del., Orphans Court Valuations F.

1801 Listed in an inventory was "a parcel of lumber in the lumber house @ $4 and 54 oak & pine stocks are valued @ $27." Spotsylvania Co., Va., Will Book F.

lumber room   An interior space devoted to the storage of miscellaneous, unused items. See also **lumber house.**

1761 In a dwelling house in Baltimore, "the apartments above are Three Rooms with Fire-Places, and other proper Rooms for Servants or Lumber." *Maryland Gazette.*

1773 On a glebe "a Dairy Sixteen by ten [is] to be built and one end to be fitted up Close for a Lumber Room." Bristol Parish, Prince George Co., Va., Vestry Book.

lumberyard, timberyard   A place where building materials are stored for sale. Most lumberyards were located in or near towns and usually had on hand prefabricated building frames and dimension lumber.

> 1736   In Charleston was "a Timber-Yard kept in Bedon-street by Henry Bedon, where any Person may be supplied with all sorts of Boards, Scantling, Laths, Cedar Posts for Gardens, and Frames for Houses." *South Carolina Gazette.*
>
> 1798   Thomas Preston of Alexandria had for sale "at his Lumber yard: A quantity of 1/2 inch, inch, and 2 inch Plank; Scantling of any dimensions, Walnut Plank and Scantling; 18 inches and 2 feet Shingles, Laths, Girders, Wall plates, Bond timber, and Sills of every dimensions, Cedar and Locust Posts, Scaffold and Ladder Poles." *Columbia Mirror and Alexandria Gazette.*

lunatic hospital   A benevolent institution providing shelter and support for those declared by a court by the standards of the day to be insane or dangerously mad. For a more detailed description, see **hospital (2)**.

> 1814   Visitors "went to the Lunatic hospital" in Williamsburg, "where there is between 20 and 30 poor unhappy Creatures Confined with madness." *W&MQ*, 2d ser., 3.

lunatic house   A dwelling built for the confinement of the insane. See also **hospital, lunatic hospital.**

> 1761   A court "ordered that Francis Heronimous build a house ten feet square to secure Paldos Heronimous a Lunitick Person until he recovers his reason that he be confined therein and that Thomas Owsley and William Owsley go there weekly and see that he is found with all Necessaries by the said Francis for his support." Loudoun Co., Va., Court Order Book 1757–1762.

lunette   A semicircular opening or surface. Lunette windows became fashionable in late 18th- and early 19th-century buildings, especially in gables and pediments, and over doorways. In Charleston and a few other cities, such windows also lit the upper story of stairwells. The term had limited use. See also **D window, fanlight.**

lyceum   A building where popular educational activities such as concerts, lectures, and exhibitions were held.

> 1800   On Sullivan's Island near Charleston, "a spacious, and well ventilated SALOON, is erected . . . in view of the beach and landing, to be distinguished as the SOUTH CAROLINA LYCEUM. Its object is the public accommodation, not merely as a THEATRE, but a HALL, to comprehend every purpose of meeting, for utility, amusement and instruction." *City Gazette and Daily Advertiser.*

M   The Roman numeral symbol for a thousand. Used in building as a shorthand symbol for the price of material per thousand, most commonly for bricks, nails, or, occasionally, lineal feet of boards.

> 1711   Materials needed to finish a church included "4 M Lath . . . £7, To 16 M Nails . . . £5, To 9 M Brick . . . £13.10.0, To 10 M Cypress Shingles . . . £12." Christ Church Parish, Charleston Co., S.C., Vestry Book.
>
> 1771   Bill for materials for the Chase House in Annapolis included: "346 M place bricks at 30/ per M at the Dock . . . £519." *MHM*, 33.

magazine
Williamsburg, Va., 1715

magazine   A building in which arms and other military supplies, especially gunpowder, are stored. Also the contents of a magazine. See also **armory, powder house.**

> 1667   An act was passed by the Virginia General Assembly for the construction of forts which were to have "a court of guard and convenient place to preserve the magazine." Hening, *Statutes at Large*, 2.
>
> 1714   "An act for erecting a magazine" in Williamsburg specified the construction of a "good substantial house of brick, which shall be called the magazine . . . In

which magazine, all the arms, gun-powder, and amunition, now in this colony belonging to the king . . . may be lodged and kept." Hening, *Statutes at Large*, 4.

1763 In South Carolina, Fort Prince George was rebuilt "with intire New Barracks & Store Houses, a New Stone Well, one New Stone Magazine." *The Papers of Henry Laurens*, 3.

mahogany (mahogony) A tropical American hardwood, reddish-brown in color. Mahogany was a costly wood imported into the South in the 18th and 19th centuries for the manufacture of furniture. In more important buildings it was used for doors, railings, mantelpieces, communion tables, and reredoses. Woodwork was sometimes painted a mahogany color in imitation of the costly wood.

1763 "Elfe & Hutchinson Cabinet makers, to make a Mahogany Communion Table." St. Michael's Parish, Charleston, S.C., Vestry Book.

1783 In the Governor's House in New Bern, "the hand rail, Baluster, and Carved Brackets to the best staircase are of mahoginy, the steps and risers of fine grain clear pine." Hawks Letter, Miranda Papers, Academia Nacional de la Historia, Caracas.

1804 Thomas Jefferson requested the fabrication of "a pair of folding doors, mahogany." Coolidge Collection, Massachusetts Historical Society.

mahogany color A paint treatment simulating the color of mahogany and sometimes its grained appearance as well. In the latter case, two prime coats of yellow were followed by a somewhat redder finishing coat. This final layer figured with *burnt umber* before it dried.

1752 Annapolis merchant Beale Bordley advertised an assortment of paint colors including "Spanish Brown, Stone Colour . . . Olive Colour and Mahogany Colour." *Maryland Gazette*.

1798 An agreement between Jeremiah Satterwhite and St. George Tucker stipulated that "The outer doors" of Tucker's house be painted a "dark mahogany colour." This was subsequently crossed out and changed to "Chocolate colour." Tucker Papers, W&M.

1812 New England house and ship-painter Hezekiah Reynolds offered the following instructions for producing a "Mahogany Color" scheme: "Prime with spruce yellow; when thoroughly dry, add to the yellow a small quantity of white Lead, say four ounces lead to one pound yellow, and lay the second coat. For the third coat take a sufficient quantity of Stone yellow pulverized; heat it on coals in iron; taking care to stir it constantly untill it changes to a red color; then let it cool; mix and grind it with clarified or boil'd oil; and it will be fit for use. Then for shading the work take umbre pulverized, and prepare it by heating as before untill it changes to a darker color; then mix and grind it in oil. When both are prepared lay a third coat; immediately shade it with the umbre, that the colors may more easily blend together. For shading use a graining or flat brush, and lay the paint in imitation of Mahogany wood, of which have a sample handsomely polished before you. When thoroughly dry, finish with a coat of Copal Varnish laid with a clean brush." Reynolds, *Directions for House and Ship Painting*.

mall A public open green space often used to connect one public area with another and used for recreation, usually promenading. The name derives from the fashionable late 17th- and 18th-century promenade in St. James Park, London.

mallet A hammer with a wooden head and handle used for driving wooden objects that would split or fracture if hit with a metal head.

manger (mainger) A trough or box for holding fodder for horses and cattle. Mangers usually are located in barns and stables, often in conjunction with racks.

1771 There were plans for a stable "to be built at the Glebe . . . 24 feet long and 16 feet wide. . . . to have stall, maingers and wrecks for four horses with a partition at one end 8 feet for a chair house." Elizabeth City Parish, Elizabeth City Co., Va., Vestry Book.

1792 "A Stall for two Cows 10 by 12" was to be built at Nomini Hall in Westmoreland County, Virginia, with "two maingers each to contain 3 Gallons." Robert Carter Papers, LC.

1802 The stable and coach house behind John Tayloe's Washington residence required carpentry charges for "45 [feet] 9 [inches] Run oak rabbetted manger Rail [at] 2/6 . . . 190 Superficial [feet] manger work [at] 8 [pence] . . . manger posts [at] 7/6." Tayloe also paid a blacksmith for "4 staples & 4 rings to a Manger 2/8." Tayloe Papers, VHS.

manor farm, manor plantation (maner)   The principal seat of a landholder, usually the location of the principal residence or *manor house*. In the old English feudal sense of a landed territorial estate farmed by tenants who owed a variety of obligations to a powerful individual, the *manor* as a legal and economic entity had a limited impact in the early South. Although there were many large landed estates in the southern colonies, few of these were more than large conglomerations of wilderness interspersed by a few cultivated acres and settlements of tenant farms. The term *manor* was often used to describe these large holdings. However, it was more commonly used to designate the primary plantation of an individual to distinguish it from other land holdings. On this home plantation was the *manor house*, a dwelling that may have been as humble as a cabin or as large as the best houses in the area. See also **home farm, mansion farm.**

1717 A man left to his wife his "manor plantation whereon my Son . . . now lives." Elizabeth City Co., Va., Deed and Will Book 1715–1721.

1734 "This is to give Notice to all Artificers . . . that the Manor commonly called, My Lady's Manor, but more properly, my Lord Baltimore's Gift, on the North Falls of Gun-Powder River, in Baltimore County, consisting of 10,000 Acres, will, the greatest Part of it, be divided into Lots or Farms, 50 or 100 Acres in each Lot or Farm, and will be let out either upon Lease, for Years, Lives, or otherwise, to such as are minded to settle there." *Maryland Gazette.*

1768 At Tadcaster on the Eastern Shore of Maryland "there is on the manor plantation a dwelling house 25 feet by 18 with a brick chimney." Queen Anne's Co., Md., Deed Book H.

1808 In southern Delaware the Gibbons estate contained "on the maner plantation . . . one ordinary Dwelling house thirty five feet by Sixteen . . . on the out plantation one Old Framed House Twenty feet by fifteen." Sussex Co., Del., Orphans Court Valuations K.

mansard roof   A roof with two inclined planes, or a curbed or gambrel roof, eponymously named for the 17th-century French architect Francois Mansart. The term had limited use in the early South, where the most common name for such a form was *Dutch roof.* By the mid-19th century, the term *mansard roof* had diverged slightly from its earlier British meaning and was used to describe a roof form having a double slope on all four sides. See also **Dutch roof.**

1796 The English emigrant architect Benjamin Henry Latrobe observed that "the inferior houses" of Norfolk "are chiefly framed and weatherboarded, and the sort of double roof, called by the french un Mansard (from the Architect who first employed them in France)—by the English Carpenters, a Curbroof, are very common." *The Virginia Journals of Benjamin Henry Latrobe,* 1.

mansion, mansion house (mantion)   A dwelling house; primary residence of a landowner; a glebe or parsonage house. The term was rarely used to distinguish a building of large size and good appearance. See also **glebe house, manor farm.**

1692 John Custis bequeathed to his grandson "the great Dutch presse and gilded looking glasse in the dineing roome of my mansion house Arlington." Northampton Co., Va., Court Order and Will Book 1689–1698.

1711 "James Moulder hath obtained a lycense to keep an ordinary att his Mansion house." Northumberland Co., Va., Court Record Book 1710–1713.

1722 "William West of Princess Anne County in Virginia devised to John Starke one mansion house, one kitchen, one garden, one orchard, thirty acres of arable plow land, 17 acres of meadow land, 70 acres of pasture, & 200 acres of woodland with appurtenances scituate lying and being on Perquimans River between Vosser's Creek and Sutton's Creek." *Higher-Court Records of North Carolina,* 5.

1740 A workman was hired "to build a mansion house upon the Gleeb . . . twenty four foot square." Truro Parish, Fairfax Co., Va., Vestry Book.

1775 On the Stephenson estate in southern Delaware "the Mention or dwelling house & log Citchin is in good Repair." Sussex Co., Del., Orphans Court Valuations A.

mansion farm, mansion plantation The primary farming lands and residence of an individual, including a dwelling and necessary out-buildings; the home farm. The term *mansion farm* was used quite commonly in southern Delaware in the late 18th and early 19th centuries to describe this landholding. See also **home farm, manor farm, out plantation.**

1782 "On the mansion place" at Lloyds Park on the eastern shore of Maryland was "one framed dwelling house with brick chimney 24 feet long and 18 feet wide." Queen Anne's Co., Md., Guardian Bonds and Valuations SC.

1810 The Burton estate in southern Delaware was divided into "mansion farm," "upper farm," and "Wolf Neck farm," each of which contained a dwelling house and outbuildings. Sussex Co., Del., Orphans Court Valuations K.

mantel (mantle) The decorative elements enframing the fireplace opening; a mantelpiece. In this sense, mantel appears to come into limited use in the late 18th century. Occasionally, the term may have been used to refer to the manteltree, or lintel, which supported the top of the fireplace opening. See also **mantelpiece, manteltree, chimney piece.**

1796 A Philadelphia supplier sent to Lewis Burwell in Richmond "Jambs & Mantles 21 feet @ 15/ per foot" and advised him to "be cautious in getting these chimney pieces set in with much care." Burwell Papers, UVa.

1814 At a Cecil County, Maryland, plantation, "a man came from Philadelphia to put our marble mantle in the dining room." *Diaries of Martha Ogle Forman.*

mantelpiece
54 Montague Street, Charleston, S.C.,
c. 1816

mantelpiece (mantlepiece) The decorative elements covering the jambs and manteltree of the fireplace opening, including the architrave, columns, pilasters, cornice, and shelf. The term was less common than the nearly synonymous *chimney piece.* See also **chimney piece.**

1713 Decorative woodwork in a glebe house included the "Mantle Pieces," to be painted Spanish brown. St. Peter's Parish, New Kent Co., Va., Vestry Book.

1751 In a brick dwelling in Queen Anne's County, Maryland, "the partitions and mantel pieces" were "wainscot." Queen Anne's Co., Md., Deed Book D.

1817 For sale in Baltimore were "an assortment of Elegant Marble Mantle PIECES with and without Columns." *American and Commercial Daily Advertiser.*

manteltree (mantletree) A beam spanning the opening of a fireplace that serves as a lintel to support the masonry or timber of the chimney above the opening. The term was sometimes used to refer to the decorative mantelpiece. See also **chimney piece, mantelpiece.**

1728 An estate inventory listed "china and other ornaments on the Mantle Tree in the Hall" of a dwelling house. Isle of Wight Co., Va., Inventory and Appraisement Book 1726–1734.

1755 A description read: "Chimney-Jaumbs, the sides of a Chimney, commonly coming out perpendicularly (tho' sometimes circularly) from the Back; on the Extremeties of which the Mantle-Tree resteth." Salmon, *Palladio Londinensis*.

1758 Carpentry work on a building included "faising of 2 mantle trees @ 5s pr." Chowan Co., N.C., Civil Actions, 1760, NCA&H.

marble (marvil) Metamorphosed limestone in a crystalline state. The attractiveness of this material is in its capacity to take a high polish. Although marble slabs for tombstones were imported into the colonies from the second half of the 17th century onward, it was not until the second quarter of the 18th century that a steady demand arose for marble chimney pieces and hearth slabs. The type and amount of marble imported into the colonies is difficult to judge, since most contemporaries failed to distinguish between polished limestone and true marble. Although the latter is absent in England, colonial Americans ordered *English marble* for tombstones, fonts, chimney pieces, and hearth paving. Much of this material was the dark gray *Purbeck marble* quarried in the south of England. The small amount of true marble that found its way to colonial America was first imported into Britain from Italy and other European countries. It was then worked by English stonemasons, who turned the material into highly valued architectural, sculptural, and sepulchral ornaments. Not until after the Revolution did Southerners begin to quarry native marble and limestone on a commercial scale. A number of quarries were opened but few proved enduring. Quarry operators found it difficult to compete with the well-established quarries and skilled carvers of England and Europe. As a result, foreign marble continued to dominate the growing southern market through the early 19th century. See also **imitation stone, statuary marble.**

1674 In his last will and testament, merchant Richard Cole instructed that he be buried on his plantation and "that a grave Stone of Black Marble be with all Convenient Speed sent for out of England with my Coate of Arms . . . and under it this Epitaph Here lies Dick Cole a grevious Sinner, That died a Little before Dinner, Yet hopes in heaven to find a place, To Satiate his Soule with Grace." Westmoreland Co., Va., Deed and Patent Book 1665–1677.

1747 Charleston merchant Henry Laurens wrote to his English factor in London that "I have sold all the Marble Slabbs you consign'd me. . . . One of the finest of them had been broken in England & Cemented together, & another had a piece broken off & Patched on again which people here discovered & dispis'd them so that it was not possible to obtain the same advantage for them as for other Goods besides their being an article of Luxury & not every Mans purchase." *The Papers of Henry Laurens*, 1.

1748 A dwelling for sale contained "four large convenient Rooms; with Marble Chimney Pieces, Hearths and Fire-stones, in one of the Rooms below and the dining Room above, . . . the Westernmost Room Chimney paved with black and white marble." *South Carolina Gazette.*

1767 Writing to his Bristol merchant for a supply of stone, Charles Carroll of Mount Clare in Baltimore County, Maryland, observed that "the Stone must come Cheaper from the Quarries near Bath than Else where as it is Easily Hewn and the water Carriage to Bristol Convenient and the Black and white Marble I suppose will be Equally Reasonable." Trostel, *Mount Clare.*

1769 Imported from England "For the Council Chamber in the Governor's House at Newbern in North Carolina [was] A large statuary Ionic chimney piece, the shafts of the columns sienna and the frett on the Frieze inlaid with the same. A Rich Vaze and Foliage on the Tablet; medals of the King & Queen on the Frieze over the Columns, the mouldings enriched, a large statuary marble slab and black marble covings. Mess[rs] DeVol & Grainger fecit." *Colonial Records of North Carolina*, 8.

1773 A Massachusetts visitor to Charleston's St. Philip's Church noted "that a much greater taste for marble monuments prevails here, than with us to the northward." *Proceedings of the Massachusetts Historical Society*, 49.

marble Chimney piece, Mount Vernon, Fairfax County, Va.

1802 John Tayloe paid stonecutters Shaw and Birth of Washington, D.C., for "marble Hearths squared & laid [at] 2/6 . . . Free Stone Jams and Mantle to D⁰ [at] 4/6 . . . Run Free Stone to line Marble Chimney Pieces [at] 4/6 . . . Marble Slab Border to Drawing Room [at] 15/." Tayloe Papers, VHS.
1806 "A large quarry of marble stone, of different colors, has lately been discovered on the plantation of Mr. John Henkel, near Harper's ferry [Virginia]. It is equal to the marble of Italy, or that of any other country." *The Journals of Benjamin Henry Latrobe*, 3.
1810 Payment was made to a Baltimore workman for installing "3 marble door sills . . . 11 marble window sills." Riddell Accounts, Pleasants Papers, MHS.

marbling, marbled See **imitation.**

market house (hall) A building or part of a building where goods and provisions are sold. Most towns of any size provided public land where vendors of goods could set up small stands and tables. At least once a week within this broad open market space, merchants and hucksters peddled goods ranging from basic necessities to exotic and expensive imports, while butchers and other traders set up stalls under the shade and protection of an arcaded or colonnaded space. The local market was not a free-wheeling, open-ended emporium of petty capitalists. It was, rather, a highly regulated system watched over by the clerk of the market and other corporate officials, who set the hours of market; determined the prices of meat, bread, and other commodities; and prosecuted those who would forestall or cheat their customers. The centerpiece of this corporate market was the market house, a one- or two-story, brick or wooden structure that provided permanent stalls and spaces for butchers and other vendors to display their wares. Following English precedent, most American market houses were rectangular structures that stood open on all or part of the ground floor. Arches or stout timber posts supported the second story or roof above as well as the large hooks and poles driven or embedded into their sides. These were used by butchers to hang sides of beef, game, and other items. Deep eaves often provided additional shade for the provisions on display. The most modest market houses were no more than large, open-sided sheds, while the more pretentious, such as the first one erected in Fredericksburg in the 1750s or 1760s, were arcaded brick structures that housed public entertaining rooms and courtrooms above the ground-floor market space. In some larger cities

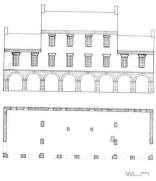

market house
Fredericksburg, Va., 1814.

such as Charleston, market activities were dispersed in different locations—a fish market was by the wharfs, and a beef and poultry market, farther inland. Because the market house often served as the venue for corporate and county courts, the term *courthouse* or *town hall* was sometimes applied to these structures. Occasionally, *market hall* was also used.

1730 An act of assembly authorized the town of Annapolis to acquire "part of the land laid out . . . for the Building A Custom House on, to & for the Building a Markett House." Anne Arundel Co., Md., Land Record Book 1729–1730.

1752 "The Corporation of the City of Annapolis . . . have determined to build a Market-House, 40 feet by 20, 10 feet pitch, underpinn'd with four courses of brick above the level of the ground with a brick floor below and a loft above; three doors on each side, and one at each end, each door to be eight feet high and six feet wide; the posts and rafters to be of yellow poplar, and the weather-boarding to be feather edged yellow poplar, a roof of Galloping Rafters, with small Turret for a Bell, in the middle of it, the roof and turret to be shingled with good cypress shingles; and the weather boarding to be painted red with oil colour; an entrance to be made to the loft, by a trap-door and ladder, and proper windows to be made above for the admission of the Air." *Maryland Gazette.*

1787 It was "Ordered, That the Commissioners formerly appointed to let out the Stalls in the Market House . . . make their report . . . [about] the Money received for the rent of the Stalls from the Butchers." Norfolk, Va., Order Book of the Common Hall 1736–1798.

marking iron (marking spike) A sharp-bladed instrument used to scribe and mark lines in woodwork.

marshalsea A prison for the confinement of felons and debtors so named for a jail in Southwark on the south side of the Thames in London. The term was rarely used in the colonial South. See also **prison.**

1701 "The prisoners now in the marshallcy or goale of this County as debters on their humble petition to this court [pray] that the rules to the said goale may be laid out in order to give them some release from close confinement." York Co., Va., Deed, Order, and Will Book 1698–1702.

mason A craftsman skilled in shaping and joining pieces of stone or brick together to form walls and other parts of buildings and structures. The terms *stonemason* and *stonecutter* were generally given to those who worked with stone and *brickmaker* or *bricklayer* used for those who made and laid bricks. The term *brickmason* was rarely used in the early South. See also **brickmaker, stonecutter, stonemason.**

1690 Robert Brent complained that he was bound to Robert Dunne "to doe so much worke of . . . a bricklayer or mason as should be really worth one Thousand pounds of Tobacco and . . . set to making of Bricks for raising him a Chimney." Stafford Co., Va., Court Order Book 1689–1693.

1734 "MASON is a Person employed under the Direction of an Architect, in the raising of a Stone Building. The chief Business of a Mason is to make the Mortar, raise the Walls from the Foundation to the Top, with the necessary Retreat and Perpendiculars to from the Vaults. . . . When the Stones are large, the Business of hewing or cutting them, belongs to the Stone-Cutters, though these are frequently confounded with Masons; the Ornaments of Sculpture, are perform'd by Carvers in Stone, or Sculptors. The Tools or Implements principally us'd by them, are, the Square, Level, Plumb Line, Revel, Compass, Hammer, Chissel, Mallet, Saw, Trowel, &c." *Builder's Dictionary.*

1773 Thomas Pritchett was apprenticed to William Wright, "Mason and Bricklayer" for a term of seven years "to learn the art of a mason." Richmond Co., Va., Court Deed Book 1768–1774.

masonry The art and practice of building with stone and brick. Work executed by a mason, especially stonework.

1744 In Savannah, "our Church Work [is] beginning to make some appearance above the ground in the Masonry, which is intended to be three foot above the Surface, and upon which the timber frame is to rest." *The Journal of William Stephens 1743–1745.*

1805 At the Capitol in Washington, "the North Wing . . . which is carried up, altho' the exterior is remarkably well finished as to its Masonry, is not a good building." *The Correspondence and Miscellaneous Papers of Benjamin Henry Latrobe,* 2.

mass house A name given by Protestants to Catholic places of worship.

1735 The Anglican minister in Cecil County, Maryland, noted that there was a "mass house" in his parish. Perry, *American Colonial Church,* 4.

master (master + bricklayer, builder, carpenter, joiner, mason, or workman) An individual of broad experience and training who is distinguished in the hierarchy of his craft from a journeyman or apprentice. Loosely, the term occasionally connoted an individual working for himself. In a legal sense, a master was bound to teach young apprentices the art and mystery of their craft as well as care for them and provide them with rudimentary education. The terms *master bricklayer, master carpenter, master joiner,* and *master mason* were not widely used in the South. When they were used, they implied a craftsman working in an entrepreneurial role, taking on large projects and supervising a diverse crew of journeymen, apprentices, and laborers. For a more detailed description of a master builder, see **builder** (2). See also **apprentice.**

1740 A building ordinance in Charleston regulated the wages of craftsmen: "for Carpenters and Joyners Master Workmen per day £2. For Negro Men Carpenters or Joyners per Day £1. For Apprentices (white or black) in the first year of their Time per day £0.7.6." *South Carolina Gazette.*

1748 "PATRICK MACLEIN MASTER-BRICKLAYER, just arrived from London, GIVES this public Notice, to all Gentlemen who are pleased to employ him, that he undertakes to finish any Kind of Building, or other Brick-Work." *South Carolina Gazette.*

1755 "Architect, a master-workman in a Building; and is he that supervises and gives the Draughts of Designs of a Fabrick . . . and also whose business it is to consider the manner and method of the Building." Salmon, *Palladio Londinensis.*

1767 Governor Tryon of North Carolina remarked that "the Pine (as Mr. [John] Hawks the Master Builder I took over with me from England, and who is a very able Worthy man) says is Vastly Superior to the . . . Norway Pine, for the Decking of Ships, as it is more Solid and filled with Turpentine which makes it very durable." *The Correspondence of William Tryon,* 1.

1768 "John Ariss Callis son of John Callis decd. late of the County of Westmoreland doth put himself apprentice to William Buckland Carpenter and Joiner of the County of Richmond to learn his art . . . after the manner of an apprentice to serve . . . four years . . . the said apprentice his master faithfully shall serve." Richmond Co., Va., Deed Book 1768–1774.

1818 "AT A MEETING Of the MASTER-BUILDERS of Norfolk and Portsmouth," a committee lamented the low wages paid in Hampton Roads compared with those found in "the Books of Prices of Master-Workmen in Washington and Baltimore." *American Beacon and Commercial Daily.*

maul (mawl) *(n.)* A round-headed wooden hammer or mallet used for driving the blade of a froe or a wedge. Many mauls were simply small logs measuring from 4 to 8 inches in diameter at the head with a tapered handle. They were used to rive rails, small framing members, lath, treenails, and shingles. *(v.)* To strike or split with a maul and wedge or froe. See also **froe, mallet.**

mausoleum   An elaborate tomb, often a burial place and commemorative monument to an important individual. The term was little used in the early South.

> 1800   Benjamin Henry Latrobe made designs for a "Mausoleum" proposed for George Washington. "The building is a Pyramid, upon a base of 13 steps, of 100 feet side and height. It contains one chamber, 30 feet square, in the Center of which is a plain Sarcophagus or tomb, and opposite the door a niche for the statue of the General. This chamber is lighted by 4 Windows, arched, one in each side. The pannels may be filled by representations, either in bas relief, or fresco painting, of the principal events of the life of Washington. The Platform encircles the upper part of the Pyramid." *The Correspondence and Miscellaneous Correspondence of Benjamin Henry Latrobe*, 1.

meal house, meal room   A building or room for the storage of ground cereal grain. See also **granary.**

> 1775   Repairs on a glebe noted that "the Meal Room is Plaistered." Bristol Parish, Prince George Co., Va., Vestry Book.
> 1793   Design of a market house in Richmond included a "meal house" measuring 12 by 18 feet with a door and window. Richmond, Va., Common Council Record Book 1793–1806.

mean relief   See **relief.**

measure   See **lineal measure, running measure, square** (1), **superficial measure.**

measurer   **1.** A public office held by a craftsman whose duty it was to see that materials sold at lumberyards were properly measured. Very few towns strictly regulated this activity.

> 1780   "William Munday is appointed Measurer of Scantling and Boards and was Accordingly sworn to Execute the said Office." Alexandria, Va., City Hustings Court Order Book 1780–1787.

2. In the English sense, a quantity surveyor; one who made estimates of timber and other materials necessary for a project or reviewed the work of a project in order to determine the value of the materials and workmanship.

> 1786   House builders in Annapolis advertised that they were willing "to design, estimate, measure and survey any building, and make out bills of scantling." *Maryland Gazette.*
> 1798   In calculating expenses, Benjamin Henry Latrobe stated that "all the English architects charge in 1795, five Guineas per day, and no surveyor or measurer less than one Guinea." *The Virginia Journals of Benjamin Henry Latrobe*, 2.

meat house (meet house)   A building in which meat or fish is cured by means of dense smoke. The distinction between *meat house* and *smokehouse* is not always clear. In most cases the terms appear to be synonymous, yet in a few instances meat house seems to refer to a building where the meat is stored rather than cured by smoke. For a more detailed description, see **smokehouse.**

> 1710   The inventory of the estate of "Mr. Samuell Wilsin" listed a "meat house." Princess Anne Co., Va., Deed Book 1708–1714.
> 1740   An orphan's estate contained "one old meat house 11 feet in length and 10 feet wide much out of repair." Queen Anne's Co., Md., Deed Book B.
> 1812   Outbuildings on a farm included "one meat house ten by ten in good repair one smoke House." Sussex Co., Del., Orphans Court Valuations L.

mechanic (mechanick) A workman or craftsman. *Mechanic,* like *workman,* was used in a general manner to refer to anyone working in the building trades. The association of the term with an individual skilled in the operation of machinery did not appear until after the early national period.

1763 Thomas Fields was bound to "John Coleman, mechanic" to learn the trade of "carpenter and house joyner." Fredericksville Parish, Louisa Co., Va., Indentures and Processioners Returns.

1767 In North Carolina, "Mechanicks for the building of houses and the making the implements of husbandry are in common with other colonies, tho' in a lesser degree of perfection: the materials for these purposes excepting timber lime and brick are imported from great Britain and the northern colonies." *Colonial Records of North Carolina,* 7.

1794 "To all the Architects and House Carpenters of the Eastern Shore of Maryland. By the request of a number of Fellow-Mechanicks, the Subscribers . . . give this public notice, that a meeting will be held . . . for the purpose of forming a society to adopt such rules and regulations as may be thought necessary for the better governing of that part of the Building Branch, and somewhat similar to those now existing in different parts of this Continent." *Maryland Herald and Eastern Shore Intelligencer.*

1828 In the North Carolina House of Commons, Charles Fisher asked his fellow delegates "what branch of mechanic have we in our country, in which we do not find negroes often distinguished for their skill and ingenuity? In every place we see them equalling the best white mechanics." *American Farmer,* 9.

meetinghouse A place of worship; a church. Also a place of public gathering. The term was used to refer to the structures erected by members of dissenting denominations and sects such as the Quakers, Congregationalists, Presbyterians, and Baptists. Many in these groups firmly believed that the term *church* should be applied to the members of a congregation and not to a place of worship, while others denied the sanctity associated by Anglicans and others to a church structure. They preferred the less emotive *meetinghouse* to describe the place where worshipers gathered. Among the first meetinghouses erected in the South were those built by Quakers in Maryland, Virginia, and North Carolina in the second half of the 17th century. The long, frame Third Haven Friends Meetinghouse in Talbot County, Maryland (1682–1684), is the earliest surviving meetinghouse in the South. As with most early meetinghouses, there are few if any embellishments to suggest the public nature of the structure. The building is domestic in scale and appearance, eschewing elements such as towers, crosses, compass-headed windows, and frontispieces associated with Anglican churches. Like Third Haven Meetinghouse, the interior of most latter dissenter meetinghouses were generally unadorned. Although some had enclosed pews, the vast majority of them contained rows of benches and forms arranged around a centrally placed pulpit. See also **church.**

1659 In Anne Arundel County, Maryland, "there was such . . . Land, reserved by the Inhabitants of this County, att their first coming . . . for their publik use . . . whereon att their common Charge they afterwards erected a meetinghowse." *Archives of Maryland,* 41.

1698 It was noted that the "Quakers have one new timber work meeting house built at West River; [and a] meeting house at Herring Creek" in Anne Arundel County, Maryland. Perry, *Colonial Church,* 4.

1726 In St. John's Parish, South Carolina, the Anglican minister wrote that "the Dissenters have built a meeting house on ye frontiers of our parish & do their upmost to gain Proselytes." SPG Letterbook B, SPGFP.

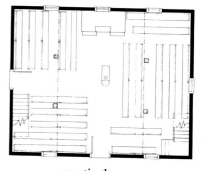

meetinghouse
Exterior and plan, Mauck's Meetinghouse,
Page County, Va., c. 1800

1769 "At a Meeting of the TRUSTEES for a PRESBYTERIAN MEETING-HOUSE to be built in Savannah, the following dimensions, &c. were approved of, viz. That it be 80 feet long by 47 feet wide in the clear, the walls to be 30 feet high from the foundation, with a handsome light steeple in proportion to the frame, a portico at one end of 50 by 10 feet, with galleries and pews." *Georgia Gazette.*

1816 In Columbia, South Carolina, "PROPOSALS WILL be received . . . for finishing the inside of the BAPTIST MEETING HOUSE—The walls to be plastered with lime mortar; overhead to be sealed with well seasoned boards, painted white; a decent plain pulpit, painted mahogany color; windows to be sashed and glazed with such other inside work as may be necessary for decency and comfort." *The Telescope.*

meeting rail   In a sliding sash window, the lower horizontal member or rail of the upper frame, or the upper rail of the lower frame, so called because of their adjoining position when the sash are closed.

1811 James Madison's account with the builders Dinsmore and Neilson at Montpelier in Orange County, Virginia, listed the construction of dozens of "meeting rails" and sash. Cocke Papers, UVa.

1820 John Neilson's work at Bremo in Fluvanna County, Virginia, included "2 pr meeting Rails 2/—6 each." Cocke Papers, UVa.

merchant mill   A large, commercial mill where grain is bought, ground, and resold.

1769 There was to be let at the Falls of the Potomac "a complete Stone Building, 151 Feet long, 36 wide, and 3 1/2 Stories high. In this Ediface are contained . . . a valuable Merchant Mill, with Two Pair of Stones, Bolting Mills. . . . Two large Granaries, 36 Feet by 30, on each Side the Mill. . . . I have . . . built a Grist Mill for Country Custom, and a Saw Mill." *Maryland Gazette.*

1774 In Westmoreland County, Virginia, "Mr. *Carter's* Merchant Mill begins to run to-day. She is calculated to manufacture 25.000 Bushels of Wheat a Year. . . . it is amazing to consider the work and Ingenuity—He told me his Bill for the materials and work was 1450£!" *Journal and Letters of Philip Vickers Fithian.*

1808 Thomas Jefferson "has a merchant mill, which he lets at a rate of 1200 dollars per annum, and a grist mill which he works himself." Caldwell, *A Tour Through Part of Virginia.*

messuage   A legal term used to describe a dwelling house, its outbuildings, curtilage, and the immediate lands associated with it. See **curtilage.**

1732 A notice stated: "To be sold, by Mr. John Moore all his Messuages and Tenements, situate on both sides of Mr. Trott's great House in Charlestown either together or in parts." *South Carolina Gazette.*

1753 There was "To be sold . . . that Corner Piece or Parcel of the Lot Numb. 73, with three Brick Messuages or Tenements thereon erected and built." *South Carolina Gazette.*

1761 A deed recorded the sale of "all that messuage or tenement situate, standing and being in the City of Williamsburgh. . . . adjoining the Lotts and Garden of Mr. John Coke and now in the possession of. . . . Thomas Cobbs together with the Lott or half acre of Land and all Houses, outhouses." York County, Va., Deed Book 1755–1763.

1804 "A Brick messuage and Kitchen, the messuage two Stories high, 37 feet in length, and 21 feet in breadth, a Celler underneath the whole, divided into 3 apartments in common Repair." Kent Co., Del., Orphans Court Valuations.

1825 An estate contained "A two storied brick Messuage of about 20 feet front by 33 feet deep." New Castle Co., Del., Orphans Court Valuations M.

metope   The area between the triglyphs in a Doric frieze, sometimes decorated with human and animal figures.

1822 Thomas Jefferson wrote to one of his workmen that "you are right in what you have thought and done as to the metopes of our Doric pavilion" at the University of Virginia. "Those of the baths of Diocletian are all human faces, and so are to be those of our Doric pavilion. But in my middle room at Poplar Forest I mean to mix the faces and ox-sculls, a fancy which I can indulge in my own case, altho in a public work I feel bound to follow authority strictly." Coolidge Collection, Massachusetts Historical Society.

mezzanine An intermediary floor level or story of low height between two other stories; usually constructed between the first and second floors of a building. The term was used infrequently in the early South. See **entresol.**

milk house (milke house) A room or building used for the storage of milk, butter, and cheese. For a more detailed description, see **dairy.**

1653 A room-by-room inventory of an estate listed items "in the milke house." Norfolk Co., Va., Deed and Will Book 1651–1656.

1664 A room-by-room inventory listed a "milke howse" and "milke house chamber." *Archives of Maryland,* 49.

1673 A carpenter was engaged to build "a ten foot [square] milk house." Middlesex Co., Va., Court Order Book 1673–1680.

1709 "A twelve feet square Milk house with plank shelves and plank doors" was to be built. St. Peter's Parish, New Kent Co., Va., Vestry Book.

1782 There is a notation of a "Small Milk House 4 by 3 feet." Kent Co., Del., Orphans Court Valuations.

mill (mill house) A building or part of a building equipped with machinery for grinding grain into flour or corn into meal. By extension, the term came to be used to refer to any establishment that used machinery to perform various operations, from the sawing of lumber or the production of cloth to the manufacture of tools. A *gristmill* contained millstones, gears, and other machinery connected to a source of power. From the 17th through the middle of the 19th centuries, that power was water or wind. Beginning in the early 19th century, steam machinery was used in some commercial mills in the South to grind grain and saw logs. See also **fulling mill, gristmill, merchant mill, sawmill, watermill, windmill.**

1609 "Mr. Trer acquainted the Court yt the 4 Dutch Carpenters [pro]cured by Mr. Deputye means for erecting of Sawinge Mills in Virginia are now com over for the service of the company and that in this next Ship are fitt to be shipped thither." *Virginia Company Records,* 1.

1641 It was "Agreed betweene Anthony Lynny Millwright . . . and Mr. Obedience Robins and Mr. John Wilkins . . . that the said Anthony Linny should build sett upp and finish a Wyndemill within the County of Accomack. . . . In consideration whereof the said Mr. Robins and Mr. Wilkins . . . to fynde all the Iron worke of belonging and apperteyneing unto the Finishing of the said Mill." *County Court Records of Accomack-Northampton, Virginia 1640–1645.*

1691 "Patrick Muckleroy . . . fitted a frame for a water mill and fitted himself with a pair of stones & other materials in order to the erecting a water mill thereon, prayed liberty to erect and build a mill on the . . . creek and to make and join his dam to the land opposite to his own land." Westmoreland Co., Va., Court Order Book 1690–1698.

1748 A plantation on Stono River in South Carolina contained "a pounding Mill for Rice, which beats out with two Horses four Barrels each Day." *South Carolina Gazette.*

1812 A property included "One frame Mill House 3 Stories high 40 by 36 feet in good repair except the lower floor which we allow to be made new, and there is within the said mill house, 3 run of Stones, 2 of which are Burrs, and the other Country Stones, the running Gears of which are in tolerable repair, 2 bolting Cloths and the running Gears belonging thereto in tolerable repair, and also the Machinary in tolerable repair.—2 water wheels pier head safe gates and floor gates in a decaying state and will want repair, the Sheathing on the end of the Mill house next the water wheels much be made new, the corner of the Mill house in a decaying State in consequence of the dash of the water and much be repaired, and we do allow the damn to be raised level with the Bridge." Kent Co., Del., Orphans Court Valuations.

1816 The city of Lynchburg, Virginia, contained "three Flour Manufacturing Mills . . . one Paper Mill." *Lynchburg Press.*

millwright A mechanic skilled in the construction and repair of mill machinery.

1642 "Anthony Lynny Millwright . . . [is to] build sett upp and finish a Wyndemill within the County of Accomack." *County Court Records of Accomack-Northampton, Virginia 1640–1645.*

1738 "Henry Chapman . . . [is] bound seven years to John Harford who is to teach him to read the bible distinctly to write a good Leadgable hand [and teach] the trade of a wind and water millwright." Princess Anne, Co., Va., Court Order Book 1737–1744.

1792 In Westmoreland County, Virginia, "Mr. Payne Millwright, is called here to repair the Cock-Pit Wheel of the Corn Mill and other Damage occasioned lately by George Moore for on Saturday last he moved the Beam which raises and lowers the uppermost Mill-Stone which occasioned a great crush breaking three Cogs of the Cockt-pit wheel." Robert Carter Papers, LC.

1805 In Charleston, "a Miller A YOUNG MAN, just arrived from Germany, and regularly bred to the Miller's and Millwright's business, wishes for employment in a Rice or Grist Mill." *City Gazette.*

mitre (miter) An oblique surface at the end of a piece of material, contrived so as to butt against an oblique surface of another piece joined to it. The line or plane of the joint between the two pieces makes an angle of 45 degrees, so that the adjacent sides of the two pieces meet at a right angle.

1747 A church was to have "each Door mitred at the Corners." Albemarle Parish, Surry Co., Va., Vestry Book.

1811 A carpenter's account was presented for "framed Door jambs fancy mitred moulding." Riddell Accounts, Pleasants Papers, MHS.

model (modell, modall) **1.** A building or part of a building that serves as a source of imitation; a standard or example for imitation or comparison.

1665 A church was to be built "according to ye Modall of ye Middle-plantacon Church in all respects." Christ Church Parish, Middlesex Co., Va., Vestry Book.

1743 When asked to devise a plan of a church for the town of Savannah, William Stephens, the leader of the colony, consulted with another settler and decided "that Covent Garden Church [in London] happening to be well known to both, I had recommended that to him as a Model in his Imagination to work by, as well for its being deemed a Curious piece of Inico Jones, as because the Work will come much Cheaper for being so very plain, wherefore I apprehend the less we vary from it the better." *The Journal of William Stephens 1743–1745.*

1746 "Marquis Calmes Gent. [was paid] for erecting a Ducking Stool according to the Moddal of that at Fredericksburgh £5.5.0." Frederick Co., Va., Court Order Book 1745–1748.

1792 A committee appointed "to let the building of a Courthouse for the use of this County to be of the same model of Franklin Courthouse except the justices seat." Henry Co., Va., Court Order Book 1792–1797.

2. A scheme or method for carrying out a building project; a set of designs for a building, including plans and written descriptions. See also **plan** (2).

1714 An undertaker was chosen to "Erect & Setup in New Brick Church in St. Paul's . . . Thirty four Pews, Pulpit & Reading Desk According to a Model by the sd Vestry drawn & agreed to by the said Vestry." St. Paul's Parish, Kent Co. Md., Vestry Book.

1727 It was decided that a chapel of ease was to be built and "that any workmen who have an inclination to Undertake the Same may repair to the Vestry at their next meeting where they may See the Model and be treated with in relation to the building thereof." St. Anne's Parish, Anne Arundel Co., Md., Vestry Book.

1748 "It is Agreed by Landon Carter Esq. . . . [to] Build an Addition to this Court house According to the Model Lodgd in the Clerks office." Richmond Co., Va., Court Order Book 1739–1752.

3. A three-dimensional representation or reproduction of a building or part of a building done at a small scale for purposes of study or to give an idea of the effect. Although not unknown in Great Britain in the 17th and 18th centuries, scale models of buildings made for the purpose of understanding what a structure would look like before it was constructed were extremely rare in the early South. Scaled representations in clay, wood, or some other materials were occasionally made of buildings after they had been erected. However, they served no purpose in the building process.

1793 "JERUSALEM. A MODEL of the Ancient and Magnificent CITY of JERUSALEM, as it stood when our SAVIOUR was upon earth, made agreeable to the description of Josephus, is now ready for exhibition, for the entertainment of the curious, it being famous in history for its superb and glorious temple, and other wonderful works all which are elegantly carved out in miniature . . . which is in a space of 16 feet by 9. . . . It may be seen at the Borough Tavern, at half a Dollar each, for grown persons, and half price for Children." *Virginia Chronicle and Norfolk and Portsmouth General Advertiser*.

modillion (modilion, mundillion, modalion)   A horizontal bracket or console placed in a series under the soffit of the cornice in the Composite, Corinthian, and less frequently, the Roman Ionic, orders.

1699 A "Courthouse [was] to have mondelion Eaves." Lancaster Co., Va., Court Order Book 1696–1702.

1707 Plans called for the roof of a courthouse "to be jetted nine inches on a side and cornish'd and mundillion'd round." Westmoreland Co., Va., Court Order Book 1705–1721.

1771 Carver paid "for 161 Modillions (to be finished by S. Chase). . .£20.2.6" at the Chase-Lloyd House in Annapolis, Maryland. *MHM*, 33.

1808 The courthouse in Columbia, Tennessee, was to have "a plain medillian cornice." *The Impartial Review and Cumberland Repository*.

modillion
Hook Store, Franklin County, Va., 1782

module   In classical architecture, a selected length, generally the diameter or semidiameter of the lower part of a column, from which the proportionate measurements of an order and the rest of the building are determined.

1734 "MODULE is a certain Measure or Bigness taken at Pleasure, for regulating the Proportions of Columns, and the Symmetry or Distribution of the whole Building. Architects generally chuse the Semi-Diameter of the Bottom for their *Module*, and this they subdivide into Parts or Minutes. . . . There are two Ways of determining the Measures or Proportions of Buildings. The *First* is, by fixt Standard Measure, which is usually the Diameter of the lower Part of the Column, call'd a *Module*, subdivided into 60 Parts, call'd Minutes. In the *Second*, there are no Minutes, nor any certain or stated Division of the *Module*; but it is divided occasionally into as many Parts as are judg'd necessary." *Builder's Dictionary*.

1804 In part of the design for the Capitol in Washington, the architect used the proportions in "Vignola's representation of the Doric of the Theatre of Marcellus" in Rome. "If the Columns be Eight Diameters high, the Diameter must be 3 f. 1 i. But they may be stretched so as to be only 3 feet in diameter. The module then will be 18 inches and the minutes 1 1/2 each." *The Correspondence and Miscellaneous Papers of Benjamin Henry Latrobe*, 1.

mold (mould)   A wooden or metal template used to form pliable materials such as clay, plaster, and composition into specifically shaped elements such as bricks, tiles, composition ornaments, and decorative plasterwork.

> 1701   "Thomas Jackson . . . agreed . . . to make one hundred thousand good and well burnt brick fit for building each and Every brick to be moulded in a shod mould 9 inches 3/4 in length and 4 3/4 in width and 4 inches 1/2 thick." St. Peter's Parish, New Kent Co., Va., Vestry Book.
>
> 1764   The vestry "did agree with Joseph Palmer for one hundred thousand good merchantable bricks . . . the said bricks to be made by the size of Mr. [Ville]pontoux's moulds." St. Stephen's Parish, Berkeley Co., S.C., Vestry Book.

molding (moulding)   A decoratively shaped piece of trim applied to or cut into the surface of a building element. Moldings embellish and emphasize structural members or shapes (e.g., planed edges of exposed framing and architraves carried around windows and doorways) or divert attention to purely decorative elements (e.g., overmantels and ceiling rosettes). Anglo-American moldings of the 17th and early 18th centuries are often free interpretations of ancient Roman moldings that had been revived during the Renaissance. The 18th century saw a growing academic correctness in both the composition of individual moldings and their assembly into architraves, cornices, and the like—in simple buildings as well as in costly edifices. Neoclassicism was first widely assimilated here in the form of moldings drawn from Greek rather than Roman sources. Whereas the Roman ovolo could be constructed with a single center point, the Greek ovolo was a compound curve requiring two center points to construct. In profile, Greek moldings had a more elliptical appearance. By the early 19th century, these new Greek moldings were often freely reworked in manners distinct from the classical language of composition. Well-constructed 18th- and early 19th-century buildings often incorporated a wide spectrum of moldings. Their relative richness reflected the intended social importance of the spaces where they were employed. See also **astragal, bolection, cavetto, cyma, flute, fillet, ogee, ovolo, quarter round, reed, scotia, torus.**

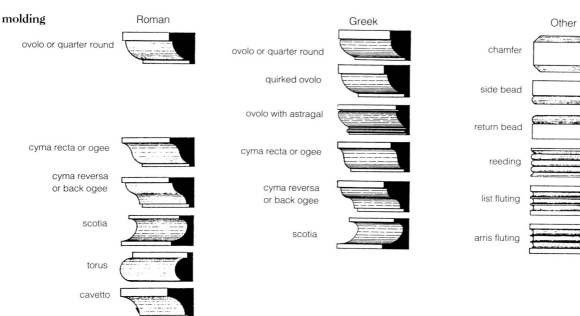

molding

Roman
- ovolo or quarter round
- cyma recta or ogee
- cyma reversa or back ogee
- scotia
- torus
- cavetto

Greek
- ovolo or quarter round
- quirked ovolo
- ovolo with astragal
- cyma recta or ogee
- cyma reversa or back ogee
- scotia

Other
- chamfer
- side bead
- return bead
- reeding
- list fluting
- arris fluting

1697 An order was issued "to Wainscot the Church round about Six foot high with a Good Moulding, or Balecion on Top." St. Paul's Parish, Kent Co., Md., Vestry Book.

1765 Joists in a glebe house were to have "well squared and plained, or moulding struck on each." Augusta Co., Va., Court Judgments.

1772 In a church, "the moldings on the top of the Pews [were] to be taken off and proper ones to be put in a workmanlike manner." Wicomico Parish, Northumberland Co., Va., Vestry Book.

1796 Gabriel Manigault of Charleston ordered from London composition ornament including "150 feet of ogee head moulding of one pattern 5/8th wide." Manigault Papers, South Caroliniana Library.

1811 At Montpelier in Orange County, Virginia, an account noted "50 feet rung of mouldings on windows & Doors @5/." Cocke Papers, UVa.

mopboard   A board placed around the floor at the base of a plastered, sheathed, or wainscotted wall. Although the term *mopboard* is synonymous with the more common *washboard*, its use was never widespread. See also **skirting board, washboard.**

1765 A workman was paid for constructing "mop and chear boards" in a Louisa County, Virginia, house. Garrett Minor Papers, CWF.

1826 Jury rooms in the Goochland County, Virginia, courthouse were to have "chair and mop boards." Cocke Papers, UVa.

mortar (morter)   A mixture of lime with sand and water, used as a bonding adhesive for masonry. Occasionally some other ingredient such as loam or cement was added into the mixture. On many projects, the proportions of the ingredients varied according to location. Mortar with a higher lime content was often used on the exterior face of the wall and one with more sand, on the interior. See also **cement, putty.**

1666 As part of a marriage contract, the husband was to see that "the Chimneys . . . be kept with Lime & Morter in good repair as they are now." Northampton Co., Va., Deed and Will Book 1655–1668.

1752 Specifications for a church stated that it was to have the "outside Bricks . . . laid with Mortar one third Lime and the other half Sand the Inside Bricks to be laid with Mortar one third Lime and two thirds Loam." Trinity Parish, Charles Co., Md., Vestry Book.

1766 The outside bricks of a church were "to be laid with mortar, two thirds lime and one third Sand, the inside Bricks to be laid with mortar half lime and half sand." Truro Parish, Fairfax Co., Va., Vestry Book.

1819 "The inner mortar" for the brickwork of the buildings at the University of Virginia at Charlottesville was "to be one third lime and two thirds clean and gritty sand without any mixture of earth, the outer 1/2 lime and 1/2 such sand and the whole to be grouted with a mortar of the inner quality." *Lynchburg Press and Public Advertiser.*

mortise (mortice, mortess)   A recess, notch, socket, or hole cut into a piece of timber or other material, so constructed to receive a tenon, the rectangular projection of another piece. The mortise and tenon joint was one of the most common carpentry joints found in early American building, employed in the joining of major framing members and the fabrication of window sash, doors, and wainscotting. In order to ensure solid construction in many key elements of a frame building, 17th-, 18th-, and early 19th-century clients often specified that mortise and tenon joints, which were stronger than simpler lapped joints, be used. To secure the joint from slipping, wooden pegs called *treenails* were often inserted into holes bored through the side of the mortise and tenon. See also **joint, treenail.**

1674 The principal rafters in the statehouse in St. Mary's City were "to be topped with mortice and Tennant and pinned att head & hipp." *Archives of Maryland,* 2.

1681 The frame of a courthouse was to have "the studs mortessed into the Groundsells." Northumberland Co., Va., Court Order Book 1678–1698.

1728 In northeastern North Carolina, fences were constructed "without any nails at all. . . . There are 3 rails mortised into the Posts." Byrd, *History of the Dividing Line.*

1735 In Anne Arundel County, Maryland, an agreement to build a dwelling specified that "the whole to be . . . Mortis & Tenant work." Waring Collection, MSA.

1766 In Annapolis, "the Roof of the great Building . . . which was intended for the Residence of the Governor, fell in, the Tenons being all rotten in the Mortises." *Maryland Gazette.*

mortise lock (mortice)   An iron lock intended to be let into the edge of a door and usually finished with brass escutcheons, cover plate, and handles or knobs. These relatively expensive locks came into fashion in the second half of the 18th century.

1762 Robert Carter ordered from London "Two mortice door Locks" for his dwelling in Williamsburg. Robert Carter Papers, LC.

1795 Gabriel Manigault of Charleston ordered from Bird, Savage, and Bird of London "18 best mortice Locks, one half right & 1 half left handed to cost about 10/ each." Manigault Papers, South Caroliniana Library.

1811 Installed in a dwelling in Baltimore were "10 Mortice Locks 100 ct each & 2 sunk bolts put on." Riddell Accounts, Pleasants Papers, MHS.

mount, mound   A pile of earth heaped up to be used as the base for a structure such as a summerhouse; or as an elevated site for surveying the surrounding landscape; or to cover a grave site; or to add variety to an otherwise flat ornamental landscape. Mounts were often formed from the digging of cellars and foundations. Walks leading up to their slope sometimes had their breadth contracted at the top to add to the illusion of greater length. Occasionally, as at Thomas Jefferson's Poplar Forest in Bedford County, Virginia, such mounts were planted with decorative trees and shrubs.

1743 William Middleton's pleasure grounds at Crow-Field outside of Charleston had "a large fish pond with a mount rising out of the middle—the top of which is level with the dwelling house and upon it is a roman temple." *Letterbook of Eliza Lucas Pinckney.*

1769 The garden at the Governor's House in Annapolis "is not extensive, but it is disposed to the utmost advantage; the center walk is terminated by a small green mount." Eddis, *Letters from America.*

1786 George Washington "set the people to raising and forming the mounds of Earth by the gate in order to plant Weeping willow thereon." *The Diaries of George Washington*, 2.

1801 In a garden in Wilmington, North Carolina, "A mound of considerable height was erected [with] a Brick room containing shelves and a large number of books— chairs and table and this wall call'd the family chapel." *Autobiography and Diary of Mrs. Eliza Clitherall.*

M roof   A roof formed by the junction of two parallel gable roofs with a valley between the back of the first and the front of the second roof. Such roofs were popular in the late 17th and early 18th centuries as a means of spanning deep buildings. Through the middle of the 18th century, many of the larger dwellings in Charleston had such roofs. Because of trouble with leaks at the junction of the two roofs, the form lost popularity in the late colonial period, supplanted by king post trusses and hip roofs.

mud house, wall (mudd)   A structure made of unbaked earth mixed with water and a binder, such as straw or twigs. Mud walls were constructed in a number of ways. Some consisted of individual pieces

M roof
Nelson House, Yorktown, Va.

packed in a mold and then stacked on top of one another. Others were made by pouring a mixture of materials into a wooden form, often with wooden vertical members such as puncheons acting as bonding agents. In England, and perhaps in the American South, a variation of this method involved the erection of a series of studs to which lathing was attached on both sides with mud rammed down the cavity. The outside surfaces of the wall were then parged or plastered. Because of the impermanent nature of such construction techniques, it is difficult to discover how pervasive such techniques were in the construction of dwellings, service buildings, and walls. See also **fill.**

1723 A deed recorded "a parcell of land in Norfolk Town . . . going out of Town, at the corner of Peter Cartwrights House formerly called the mudd house." Norfolk Co., Va., Deed and Will Book 1721–1725.

1748 In Virginia, "an act for the support of the Clergy" stipulated that the vestry of every parish were required to erect on the glebe "one convenient mansion house, kitchen, barn, stable, dairy, meat house, corn house, and garden well pailed, or inclosed with mudwalls." Hening, *Statutes at Large*, 6.

1770 In Richmond County, Virginia, "we have been putting in the sills under one side of the long tobacco house, commonly called the Mud house." *Diary of Landon Carter*, 1.

1818 "Laborers . . . are much wanted about Staunton, and indeed, in every part of Virginia west of the Blue Ridge. . . . Distillers, ditchers, builders of mud walls, mechanics of all sorts, particularly carpenters, are in great demand." *American Beacon and Norfolk and Portsmouth Daily Advertiser*.

mudsill A sill laid on or in the ground to provide support for the superstructure above. See also **bed sill, sill.**

1736 An agreement was made to build "a good and Substantial Bridge Ten feet wide from Inside to Inside of Each post which posts are to Extend Themselves from ye Mud Sils Three feet above ye sd Bridge." Spotsylvania Co., Va., Will Book 1722–1749.

1739 "Larkin Chew is to build one bridge across the River Po . . . the main posts of the bridge to extend from the Mud sills three foot above the said bridge." Spotsylvania Co., Va., Will Book 1722–1749.

mulberry A hardwood tree of the genus *Morus*. Because of the durability of some members of this family, mulberry was used occasionally in building for sills, window and doorframes, and other framing members. Its most common usage was for fence posts.

1714 A church was to have "ye window frames & Doore cases . . . made of Cedar Locust or Mulberry." Christ Church Parish, Middlesex Co., Va., Vestry Book.

1754 A dwelling on a plantation in Lancaster County, Virginia, was to have "sills of locust cedar or mulberry or other lasting wood laid part on the ground." Joseph Ball Letterbook, LC.

1770 Church "doors and windows [are] to be [built] with Compass Roofs, with good and Substantial well seasoned yellow poplar cases and frames with Mulberry Sills, well fixed in the Walls." St. John's Parish, Queen Anne's Co., Md., Vestry Book.

1803 In Talbot County, Maryland, an advertisement appeared for "LOCUST & MULBERRY POSTS, for sale and ready to be delivered as soon as the navigation will permit, a number of Locust and Mulberry posts, five feet long, designed for a Bank and Boarding Fence. The mulberry is of excellent quality." *Maryland Herald and Eastern Shore Intelligencer*.

mullion A fixed vertical bar separating a window that opens into two divisions. Casement windows of the 17th and early 18th centuries often had such divisions. The term should not be confused with *muntin*, which is a sash bar. See also **muntin, transom.**

mullion
Ware Church, Gloucester County, Va.

muntin
Slave quarter, Mulberry Plantation,
Berkeley County, S.C.

muntin A sash bar; small molded bars of wood for holding the edge of glass panes in a window sash.

> **1747** "The munting sashes [are] to be supported when up with Iron pins made fast to the frame with a Leather thong." Albemarle Parish, Surry Co., Va., *Vestry Book.*

museum A building or place where scientific specimens, works of art, and objects of curiosity and interest are kept and placed on display. The first collection of objects to be formally organized as a museum was that of the Charleston Library Society, which formed the Charleston Museum in 1773. After the Revolution, particularly in the first two decades of the 19th century, nearly every important town in the South had a small museum containing a diverse collection of art, natural history, and anthropological objects. Housed in dwellings, public buildings such as market houses or town halls, taverns, or in specially built rooms and structures, these museums served as cultural centers, the purpose of which was the intellectual and moral improvement of the general public. Run by individuals, societies, and even corporations, museums sought to edify the public through their collection of objects and books, and by sponsoring lectures and exhibitions.

> **1806** In Charleston, "the Proprietor of Paintings and Engravings, intending to establish a Museum, but not having been able to find in the city any apartment proper for such an establishment, has determined to have one built for that purpose, 30 by 30 feet, and 10 feet high. . . . The above room to have seven windows disposed on three sides with nine panes 11 by 8 to each, with a folding door in the middle 8 feet high and 5 feet wide; the ceiling and inside to be lined with boards on three sides; there must be a small door of communication on the unlined side which has no windows, and the floor of this room raised two feet above the surface of the ground." *City Gazette and Daily Advertiser.*
> **1808** A notice in the newspaper read as follows: "Baltimore Museum. The proprietor . . . finding it impossible to obtain a central situation, such as would suit with the plan he proposes, he has removed his extensive collection of CURIOSITIES To the Large Assembly Room, near Peter's Bridge, which from it airiness and coolness is admireably calculated, for a pleasant retreat in warm weather . . . where will be exhibited . . . more than 20 cases of BIRDS Which makes his present collection inferior to none in the U. States, (Mr. Peal's excepted) . . . a number of ANIMALS . . . SNAKES . . . Fifteen Wax Figures . . . Three Hundred Coins. . . . There are also Medallions of Washington, Bonaparte, Pain, Rochester, Priestly, Franklin, Newton, Broomfield, Ovid, Cato, Pythagoras, Aristides, Anacreon, Sappho, Cassandra, Homer, Plato, Seneca, A few Native and Foreign Fossils . . . add to this four different Views of the Battle of the Nile, Likenesses . . . of G. Washington, Alexander Hamilton, John Adams, Thomas Jefferson, Thomas M'Kean, C. C. Pinckney, Lord Nelson, Lord Dancan, Earl Howe and Charles James Fox. A large View of Richmond in England, six feet by four; a view of Boston, New York and the Falls of Niagara—Landscapes, &c. A very fine Organ of Astor's make is always ready to amuse the Visitors." *Baltimore Evening Post.*
> **1812** "Alexandria Museum. THE Members of Alexandria Washington Lodge, No. 22, have for some time had in contemplation the establishment of a Museum attached to their Lodge, to be composed of the works of nature and art. . . . They solicit the patronage of a generous public, their brethren in general, and particularly those whose occupations often call them to distant climes, where curiosities, both natural and artificial, are easy of attainment. . . . The subscribers therefore request that any article, suitable for such an institution, may be forwarded to them." *Alexandria Daily Gazette, Commercial and Political.*

mutule
Pavilion 4, University of Virginia

mutule A projecting flat block under the corona of a Doric cornice, corresponding to the modillions of other orders. The soffit of mutules were often decorated with a series of closely spaced circles. The latter consisted of hollow spaces cut into the mutule or slightly projecting applied pieces, known as *drops* or *guttae.*

1774 Carpentry work done for a house in Odessa, Delaware listed "78 ft 7 ins Cornice with mutules at 2/10 £11.8.2 1/2." Sweeney, *Grandeur on the Appoquinimink*.
1803 The entablature of an Episcopal church to be built "will also be of Brick with its mutules, except the four Corners which owing to the great projection of the Order will be necessary to have of Stone." Johns Island Church Specifications, Library Society of Charleston.

nail (naile, naille)   A fastening device intended to be driven by a hammer, used to join pieces of wood or other material together, or driven into a surface from which to hang various articles. Nails were usually made of iron or steel, but were occasionally fabricated from brass or other fine metals. Nails were made and sold by shape and size, the lengths being designated by *d* (pence). This nomenclature developed from the medieval English practice of describing the size of a nail according to its price per thousand. Common sizes in use in the early South included 2d, 3d, 4d, 5d, 6d, 8d, 10d, 12d, 20d, 30d, and 40d. Although nails were manufactured in blacksmith shops and naileries in the South, a sizable proportion of the nails used in building through the late 18th century were imported from England. Until the invention of the cut nail in the 1780s, all nails were manufactured by hand. See also **brad, cut nail, sprig, wrought nail.**

1645 Because of the scarcity of nails in the early Chesapeake, the Virginia General Assembly passed an act that tried to curb the practice of torching structures to obtain their nails: "it shall not be lawful for any person so deserting his plantation . . . to burne any necessary houseing that are scituated thereupon, but shall receive so many nailes as may be computed by 2 different men were expended about the building thereof for full satisfaction." Hening, *Statutes at Large*, 1.
1807 A notice read: "PRICES OF Nails, Brads & Sprigs, MANUFACTURED at the Penitentiary, and for sale by NICHOLAS HALLAM, agent for the Commonwealth, a few doors above the Swan Tavern, Richmond.

Wholesale	CUT NAILS	Retail
3d.	12 1/2 cents	13 1/2 cents
4d.	11 1/2	12 1/2
6d.	10 1/2	11 1/2
8d.	10	11
10d.	9 1/2	10 1/2
12d.	9 1/2	10 1/2
20d.	9 1/2	10 1/2."

Virginia Argus.

nailery   A building in which nails are made. See also **nail.**

1808 John Edwards Caldwell observed of Thomas Jefferson that "The only manufactories at present carried on by him, are at Bedford, of Smith's work, and at Monticello a nailery, the latter conducted by boys, but he is making arrangements for the manufacture of cotton and woolens, on his return to domestic life." Caldwell, *A Tour Through Part of Virginia*.

nail rod   A wrought iron strip or rod, square in section, from which nails are forged.

1784 An account of a large plantation in Westmoreland County, Virginia, listed "37 faggots Nail Rods in dwelling house cellar, weighing about 56 each—2072 pounds." Robert Carter Day Books and Letterbooks, Duke.
1807 A workman writing from Charlottesville to Thomas Jefferson noted that "We shall be wanting nail rod soon as it can't be got here." Jefferson Papers, UVa.

Naples yellow   One of a variety of imported yellow paint pigments sold in America by the middle of the 18th century.

1760 An advertisement appeared for "Just imported . . . from London . . . Sundry Sorts of Paint and Colours, viz . . . King's Prince's and Naples Yellow." *Maryland Gazette*.

neat Frequently joined with plain in 18th-century usage, this term connoted a substantial, workmanlike quality, a simple sufficiency, an absence of extraneous ornament. See also **plain.**

> **1674** Richard Cole desired to be buried "in a neat Coffin of Black walnutt if conveniently to be had." Westmoreland Co., Va., Deed and Patent Book 1665–1677.
>
> **1722** In St. Paul's Parish, South Carolina, "the church when finished as designed, which I believe may be in six months after ye Foundation is laid, will be a neat & regular building." SPG Letterbook B, SPGFP.
>
> **1735** By direction of local magistrates, the courthouse in Prince George's County, Maryland, was to be repaired and refitted, "the Seat of Justice to be Three Foot high all neat plain work." Prince George's Co., Md., Record Book 1734–1735.
>
> **1742** In Surry County, Virginia, the vestry of Albemarle Parish agreed with James Anderson for construction of a new church, "the two Doors in the South side to be made fast with Bars or Iron Hooks, that in the End with two Spring Bolts & a neat & strong lock . . . All the pews to be neatly cap'd plank seats on three sides . . . the Communion Table to be rais'd two steps above the floor of the Church and inclosed with Rails and neatly turn'd Ballasters . . . a Pulpit with a neat & suitable Canopy." Albemarle Parish, Surry Co., Va., Vestry Book.
>
> **1766** The justices of Amelia County, Virginia, directed that the new courthouse be built on the lands of Nathaniel Harrison, "the House to be finished of in a neat plain manner." Amelia Co., Va., Loose Court Papers.
>
> **1793** The provisions of the contract for construction of "Old East" at the University of North Carolina stated that it was "to be done & executed in a plain but neat substantial manner." University Archives, UNC, Chapel Hill.

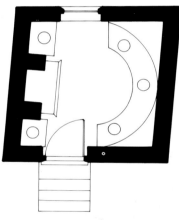

necessary house
Interior view and plan,
Westover, Charles City County, Va.

necessary house (necessary convenience, necessary office, necessary place) A small structure housing a latrine with an enclosed seat on a raised platform. Not all households possessed such conveniences. When they did appear in towns, necessaries were built at the back of the lot. In rural settings, they were often placed near gardens away from the dwelling. *Necessary house,* which is the most common term given to this building type, appears from the mid 17th century onward. *House of office,* and less frequently, *office house* and *house of ease* also appear in the records from the late 17th century but were less commonly used in many areas of the South. Except in South Carolina and, perhaps, Georgia, the term *privy* appears infrequently before the Revolution. Only in the mid 19th century does it begin to be used with any regularity across the region. See also **cloacina temple, little house, temple, water closet.**

> **1731** The court ordered the construction of a "necessary house." King George Co., Va., Court Order Book 1721–1734.
>
> **1738** It was "Ordered that a garden be built on the Glebe . . . and a necessary house eight by four feet." St. Paul's Parish, Hanover Co., Va., Vestry Book.
>
> **1783** A Savannah city ordinance required "all owners of lots . . . to sink every necessary house or privy at least five feet below the surface." *Gazette of the State of Georgia.*
>
> **1805** At a county courthouse, magistrates reported "that a brick necessary cannot well be dispurs'd with and imagine that one of the size of six feet by twelve with a division would be of convenience to the publick." Loudoun County, Va., Court Order Book 1805–1806.

neck, necking The space between the bottom of a capital and the top of a shaft in a column or pilaster; a group of moldings separating the shaft from the capital.

> **1798** In a critique of the dwelling built for Robert Morris in Philadelphia, architect Benjamin Henry Latrobe observed that "the pilasters are carried up . . . to their neckings and being diminished, they look horribly." *The Virginia Journals of Benjamin Henry Latrobe,* 2.

1811 A carpenter's work on a house in Baltimore included fabricating "8 Plain pilasters . . . 4 Imposts, Necks & Scallops." Riddell Accounts, Pleasants Papers, MHS.
1823 In reviewing the material sent to Charlottesville, Virginia, for the university building, Thomas Jefferson noted that "in the Corinthian capitels there is a want of the cavetto and listel of the astragal which intervenes between that and the necking of the shaft." Lambeth and Manning, *Thomas Jefferson as an Architect*.

Negro house   Term favored south of the Chesapeake, especially in South Carolina and Georgia, to identify a domestic structure occupied by African-American slaves. For a more detailed description, see **quarter** (1).

1735 An advertised plantation featured "new-boarded Negro-houses to hold 50 Negroes." *South Carolina Gazette*.
1789 Glebe buildings needing repair included "2 Negro houses 16 by 14." Christ Church Parish, Savannah, Ga., Records.

Negro hut   Especially in the lower South, a term for a dwelling house of African-American slaves. For a more detailed description, see **hut**.

1827 "At the Skirvey Plantation near Charleston, visitors proceeded to see the Negro huts about five hundred yards from the house. They are twenty-nine in number very neatly arranged. In each hut there are two apartments, one for sleeping in. Some of the huts had windows but very few, most of them having no light but what was admitted by the open door or an occasional separation between logs." Pope-Hennessy, *The Aristocratic Journey*.

Negro kitchen   A kind of *outbuilding* in which the functions of a *kitchen* and a *quarter* were combined. African-American slaves engaged in cooking and related domestic activities occupied a *loft* or upper story, a room adjacent to the kitchen proper, or the kitchen itself. See **quarter** (1).

1755 On a Colleton County, South Carolina, plantation "a negro kitchen" stood near a dwelling house. *South Carolina Gazette*.

Negro quarter   Variation of Chesapeake term for a dwelling built for African-American slaves or, less frequently, a group of such buildings or an agricultural division of a farm or *plantation*. For a more detailed description, see **quarter** (1), (2), (3).

1750 A decision was made "to build a Negro Quarter on the said Glebe 20 feet by 16, Brick Chimney & underpinned with Brick." St. Paul's Parish, Hanover Co., Va., Vestry Book.
1798 Outbuildings on a modest Baltimore County, Maryland plantation included a "round log negro quarter, 1 stry, 16 x 14." U.S. Direct Tax, MHS.

newel (newil)   A post that forms the support and axis of a winding stair. By extension, any post that supports the framing, handrails, and stringboards of a staircase at its beginning, turning points, and termination. Also, a short post placed at intervals in a balustrade to provide similar support.

1760 A carver was paid for "16 large newels for the staircase and tower" of a church. St. Michael's Parish, Charleston, S.C., Vestry Book.
1761 Churchwardens paid a workman for "turning 8 Newils for the alter front [and] 34 Bannisters for Do [and] 2 pannils for the alter dores." St. Michael's Parish, Charleston, S.C., Vestry Book.
1800 Carpenter John Langdon was hired to construct an "open newel stairs bracketed plain, the rails kneed and mitred in the posts" in John Steele's house in Rowan County, North Carolina. John Steele Papers, SHC.

newel
Prestwould, Mecklenberg County, Va.

niche
Mount Airy, Richmond County, Va.

newsroom   A public room in a coffeehouse, tavern, hotel, or other establishment where newspapers are kept on hand for the benefit of patrons.

> 1808   A visitor to Martinsburg, Virginia, noted that "the proximity to a much frequented sulpher spring . . . and the advantage of an excellent news-room, where the most respectable papers on the continent are taken, are additional inducements for strangers to frequent this place." Caldwell, *A Tour Through Parts of Virginia.*

niche   A recess or hollow place in a wall, generally intended to receive a statue, bust, or other ornament.

> 1783   The entrance hall in the Governor's House in New Bern was "finished with stucco, pediments over the doors, niches in the walls, and a Modillion Cornice." Hawks Letter, Miranda Papers, Academia Nacional de la Historia, Caracas.
> 1801   Washington plasterer William Foxton charged John Tayloe for "Nich at 3/6 & 2 nich heads . . . 3.8.6." Tayloe Papers, VHS.
> 1831   "Inside the Walls of the Court room [there] might be formed a few niches in which might be placed the Bust of some of Caswells most distinguished Jurists and statesmen . . . it may stimulate others to merit the same honor and distinction." Caswell Co., N.C., Miscellaneous Court Records, NCA&H.

nipper (knipper)   A tool for squeezing or compressing tightly an object, often used like pincers or pliers for gripping or pulling nails.

nogging   Brick, stone, or other material used to fill in the spaces between the wooden framing members of a wall. Nogging provided some insulation as well as structural rigidity. See also **fill.**

> 1808   A workman at Poplar Forest in Bedford County, Virginia, "has laid the flow in west rooms and is now studding the alcove, as soon as he is done with that I shall bricknog and plaster it." Coolidge Collection, Massachusetts Historical Society.

nosing (nose)   The projecting edge of a step, windowsill, porch, piazza, or some other raised platform that extends beyond the riser or upright surface below. The profile of the nosing is often shaped in the form of a torus or some segment of a curve.

> 1771   "The frames of the doors & Windows" of St. John's Church, Williamsboro, North Carolina "shall be worked out of the Sollid with good nose Sills." Francis Hawks Collection, Church Historical Society.
> 1802   A carpenter's accounts for the Tayloe house in Washington, D.C. included "Moulded nosing & riser." Tayloe Papers, VHS.
> 1806   "The floor of the Communion [area is] to be raised seven inches and fronted with a nosed step." St. Paul's Parish, Chowan Co., N.C., Loose Papers.

notch
Wilson Tobacco House,
Calvert County, Md.

notch   An angular cut or indentation at the edge of an object. In log construction, timbers were notched near their ends to prevent them from sliding out of vertical alignment. The most common log notching types were the *V* notch (where the top of the log was cut in an inverted V, and the log above it cut to fit over it) and the *half dovetail.* Perhaps just as pervasive was the simple *saddle* notch, in which the logs were left round and a curved cut made a few inches from the end of the log. Somewhat less common were the full dovetail and diamond notches. See also **dovetail, diamond.**

> 1775   "The new settlers are generally in such a hurry to get up their houses, that they pile up round trees one above another, notching them at the corners to hinder them from falling." M'Robert, *A Tour Through Parts of the North Provinces of America.*
> 1778   An owner of a lot at Berkeley Springs, Virginia, proposed to build a cabin "of Loggs or Poles . . . The Loggs to be . . . hewed on the outside after they are put up the Ends to be notched in Diamond way as is the method over the ridge." Yates Letterbook, UVa.

1789 At Coles Point in Westmoreland County, Virginia, a "Corn-house to be built of Logs to be notched at the Corners & pinned together." Robert Carter Papers, LC.

1793 In the Hampton Roads area of southeastern Virginia, "adjoining the house of the master was a hut for his blacks, formed of small pine trees laid one upon the other and fastened at the end with a notch; but they are not plaistered either on the inside or outside." Toulmin, *The Western Country.*

nursery   **1.** A room or apartment devoted to the care and training of infants and young children. Most references to nurseries are associated with large gentry houses, where they were generally located in wings, upper floors, or garrets.

1701   An inventory of Ralph Wormeley's dwelling house listed a "Nussery" and an "old Nussery."   Middlesex Co., Va., Court Records.

1767   Included in an inventory of an estate were "In the Nursarie. One featherbed and bedstead . . . three old chairs, one spinning wheel and one pine table." Northumberland Co., Va., Court Record Book 1766–1770.

1774   One of the wings at Mt. Airy in Richmond County, Virginia, was described as being used as "a nursery & Lodging Rooms." *Journal and Letters of Philip Vickers Fithian.*

1802   A brick dwelling for sale in Alexandria consisted "of 8 rooms, well finished, a full story and a half kitchen, nursery and lodging rooms above the same." *Alexandria Advertiser and Commercial Intelligencer.*

2. A plot or piece of ground where young plants such as trees and shrubs are grown before being transplanted.

1736   South Carolina planter Daniel Wesshuysen owned "a nursery of 5 or 600 mulberry trees about two years old, fit to plant out." *South Carolina Gazette.*

1749   A plantation on the Ashley River near Charleston included "a young nursery, with a great number of grafted pear and apple trees of the best sorts, with some thousands of orange trees, some of which are grown 8 feet since the last great frost." *South Carolina Gazette.*

1761   "I will endeavor to make amends and not only send the Seeds but plant a nursery here to be sent you in plants at 2 years old." *Letterbook of Eliza Lucas Pinckney.*

1801   "The garden and orchard" at Willow Brook in Baltimore "abounds with the greatest variety of the choicest fruit trees, shrubs, flowers . . . collected from the best nurseries in America and from Europe." *Federal Gazette and Baltimore Daily Advertiser.*

nut (nutt, knut)   A polygonal piece of wood or metal perforated in the center with a threaded hole, so arranged as to fit tightly around the shaft of a bolt or screw to hold together the objects through which the bolt or screw passes.

1741   Imported into Charleston were "stock and spring locks with knuts and screws." *South Carolina Gazette.*

1751   "There is to be an Iron handle and Brake to Each [city] well with upper and lower ropes well stapled and Iron bolts and Nuts for the Bolts to work on." Norfolk, Va., Common Hall Order Book 1736–1798.

oak   A highly decay-resistant hardwood of the genus **Quercus**; usually classified as red or white oak. Oaks are slow growing and long lived. There are more than three hundred species of oak. White oak, a select species, was often chosen for framing, because of its strength, and for cooperage. Because oak splits easily, the white oak was also used commonly for clapboards and shingles. White oak grows widely throughout the Southeast. It is generally harder and heavier than red oak. Red oak was favored for furniture and flooring because of its conspicuous rays or flecks.

1709 "Chesnut-Oak, is a very lofty Tree, clear of Boughs and Limbs, for fifty or 60 Foot. They bear sometimes four or five Foot through all clear Timber; and are the largest Oaks we have, yielding the fairest Plank. They grow chiefly in low Land, that is stiff and rich. I have seen of them so high, that a good Gun could not reach a Turkey, tho' loaded with Swan-Shot. They are call'd Chesnut, because of the Largeness and Sweetness of the Acorns. White, Scaly-bark Oak; This is used, as the former, in building Sloops and Ships. Tho' it bears a large Acorn, yet it never grows to the Bulk and Height of the Chesnut Oak. It is so call'd, because of a scaly, broken, white Bark, that covers this Tree, growing on dry Land. We have Red Oak, sometimes, in good Land, very large, and lofty. 'Tis a porous Wood, and used to rive into Rails for Fences. 'Tis not very durable; yet some use this, as well as the two former, for Pipe and Barrel-Staves. It makes good Clap boards. *Spanish* Oak is free to rive, bears a whitish, smooth Bark; and rives very well into Clap-boards. It is accounted durable, therefore some use to build Vessels with it for the Sea; it proving well and durable. . . . Bastard-*Spanish* is an Oak betwixt the *Spanish* and the Red Oak; the chief Use is for Fencing and Clap-boards. . . . The next is Black Oak, which is esteem'd a durable Wood, under Water; but sometimes it is used in House-work. . . . White Iron, or Ring-Oak, is so call'd, from the Durability and lasting Quality of this Wood. It chiefly grows on dry, lean Land. . . . This Wood is found to be very durable, and is esteem'd the best Oak for Ship-work that we have in *Carolina*; for tho' Live Oak be more lasting, yet it seldom allows Planks of any considerable Length. Live-Oak chiefly grows on dry, sandy Knolls. This is an Evergreen, and the most durable Oak all *America* affords. The Shortness of this Wood's Bowl, or Trunk, makes it unfit for Plank to build Ships withal. There are some few Trees, that would allow a Stock of twelve Foot, but the Firmness and great Weight thereof, frightens our Sawyers from the Fatigue that attends the cutting of this Timber. A Nail once driven therein, 'tis next to an Impossibility to draw it out." Lawson, *A New Voyage to Carolina.*

obelisk   A tall, slender shaft with sides tapering to a pyramidal head. In the southern landscape, a few were erected as commemorative monuments in public places, private grounds, and churchyards, or used as a decorative eyecatcher to terminate a vista in pleasure gardens. See also **pyramid.**

1756 "The general form of obelisks is to have eight or nine times their diameter at the bottom in height, and their thickness at top to be from half to three quarters what is at bottom." Ware, *A Complete Body of Architecture.*
1792 The French consul erected at Belmont, his home near Baltimore, "an obelisk to honour the memory of that immortal man—Christopher Columbus . . . in a grove in one of the gardens of the villa . . . on the 3rd of August, 1792, the anniversary of the sailing of Columbus from Spain." *Baltimore Evening Post and Daily Advertiser.*

obelisk
Charles Fraser, Monument to
Lt. Governor Bull, Charleston County, S.C.

ochre   A yellow, naturally occurring pigment, frequently used in house painting. Ochre varied widely in color and composition, as did the terminology associated with it. The pigment ($Fe_2O_2H_2O$) was a hydrated form of iron, of which the mineral goethite was the most common formulation. Used for interior and exterior work, it was sometimes referred to as yellow ochre or English ochre and was closely related to spruce yellow, a slightly darker compound. See also **red ochre.**

1761 "Yellow oaker" was among the pigments imported by the Charleston mercantile firm of Austin, Laurens and Appleby. *South Carolina Gazette.*
1764 In Annapolis, one shopkeeper advertised the sale of "Spruce Oaker," suggesting the equivalence of spruce yellow and yellow ochre. *Maryland Gazette.*
1766 In King William County, Virginia, was situated a dwelling house and numerous outbuildings, "all painted with ochre." *Virginia Gazette.*

office   1. A building, apartment, or room used for the transaction of public or private business, especially clerical work associated with business, government, law, printing, and other professions. Among the first offices to develop a special architectural character were those erected to house the papers of county courts. Although some of clerk's offices were constructed in courthouses, by the late 17th century, a large number, especially in Virginia, were built as separate structures. By the late 18th century, many were designed to be as fireproof as possible with masonry floors, tile or slate roofs, vaulted ceilings, iron-plated shutters, with as little exposed woodwork as possible on the inside. Distinct offices for commercial establishments may have developed in the South in the very late 18th century. By the first decades of the 19th century, many merchants, lawyers, and doctors moved out of their dwellings into specially built commercial structures or chose to erect small buildings on their house lots.

1678 The upper floor of a courthouse was "to be divided for an office for the Clerke." Westmoreland Co., Va., Court Order Book 1676–1689.

1709 At the capitol in Williamsburg, William Byrd "went to court and sat till noon when I went up to my office and did some business." *Secret Diary of William Byrd of Westover*.

1746 In Charles Pinckney's dwelling, "the back parlour, study and office [were to be finished] with only surbase & skirting boards round, & plain window seats." Huger Smith, *Dwelling Houses of Charleston*.

1749 Magistrates decided to "agree with some person to build an office sixteen feet by twelve with an outside chimney made of brick or stone with all other Conveniences for holding and preserving the Records and Papers belonging to this County." Cumberland Co., Va., Court Order Book 1749–1751.

1798 In Baltimore, an advertisement was published for an "Office of Intelligence. No. 179 Water Street. . . . the office will be open for the purpose of giving information, viz. Families may be supplied with servants, and servants with places. . . . Mechanics of all denominations who are out of employ, and master workmen who may want them, will find this office very accommodating for both parties. Also persons having house to sell or rent, lots to sell or lease, rooms to let." *The Telegraph and Daily Advertiser*.

2. The apartments below stairs and outbuildings arranged nearby in which household services were transacted. The term applied to such domestic service buildings as kitchens, pantries, dairies, wine cellars, laundries, and stables and was also used to refer to agricultural buildings in general.

1734 A dwelling for sale near Charleston contained "four rooms on a floor . . . very good underground Offices and Pump." *South Carolina Gazette*.

1759 A plantation for sale on Rock Creek in Frederick County, Maryland, had "a very good Dwelling-House on it, with Offices underneath, and convenient Out Houses." *Maryland Gazette*.

1782 For sale in "Scotchtown in Hanover County [are] 1000 acres, house 8 rooms with a large passage through it, the offices, of which there are all sorts, have been newly repaired." *Virginia Gazette*.

1783 Flanking the main block of the Governor's House in New Bern and connected by a colonnade were "the Kitchen and stable Offices . . . each 50 by 40 feet. . . . the one is a kitchen servants Hall cooks Larder Scullary [and] Brew house.. . . In the other Office are two la[rge] stables and a coach House and Bedrooms for the servants." Hawks Letter, Miranda Papers, Academia Nacional de la Historia, Caracas.

1798 In Annapolis, the Paca House was listed for purposes of taxes, along with the "kitchen and office 32 by 16 feet." U.S. Direct Tax, MSA.

3. A necessary house. See also **house of office, necessary house.**

1764 A plantation for sale on the Patuxent River in Maryland contained numerous outbuildings, including a "Garden and Office House, all newly paled in." *Maryland Gazette*.

ogee (O.G., oge, ogive) A molding consisting of a continuous double curve in the shape of an *S*. In academic language rarely employed in the South, English authors referred to the hollow and round ogee profile molding as a *cyma recta*. When the convex section of the molding was uppermost followed by the concave part, workmen called the molding a *back ogee* or, more formally, a *cyma reversa*. See also **cyma.**

> **1760** A bill for carving a pulpit listed "24 feet of Ogee Carved 5 leaved Grass in the Cornish . . . 22 feet Large Ogee full enriched." St. Michael's Parish, Charleston, S.C., Vestry Book.
>
> **1773** Door frames in a dwelling "to be cased with a large Oge and beed." Fairfax Parish, Fairfax Co., Va., Vestry Book.
>
> **1811** At Montpelier in Orange County, Virginia, a carpenter's bill listed "22 ft 8 Supal of framed door jambs 3/4 ogge & quarter round with astragals @ 4 . . . £2.5.4." Cocke Papers, UVa.

ogee roof A double-curved roof whose vertical profile is ogee shaped. Such roofs can be constructed like a bell roof with a convex lower section and a concave top, or the reverse, with a concave lower area and a convex upper section. Ogee roofs frequently crowned cupolas and could occasionally be found on small outbuildings.

oil In building this term generally referred to linseed oil, the preferred vehicle for housepaints. In preparation for mixing colors, raw linseed oil was boiled to improve its drying characteristics. In some instances dryers contained additives to improve the drying characteristics. For the same reason, raw linseed oil was always boiled before mixing. See also **linseed oil.**

> **1699** In Lancaster County, Virginia, an agreement for building a new courthouse stipulated that "ye dores windows and mondelions . . . be laid in oyle." Lancaster Co., Va., Court Order Book 1696–1702.
>
> **1729** In South Carolina, accounts for maintaining the buildings of St. Helena's Parish included charges for "12 lbs. of Paint" and "a Gallon of oyle." St. Helena's Parish, S.C., Vestry Book.
>
> **1798** A contract for painting St. George Tucker's house in Williamsburg noted that "St. George Tucker hath provided about 240 pounds of best white lead; half a hundred weight of Spanish brown,—and the like quantity of yellow Ochre, all ground in oil, and about sixteen gallons of boiled Linseed Oil; he is further to provide as much fish-oil as will be sufficient to paint the roofs, & sheds, as hereafter mentioned." Tucker Papers, W&M.
>
> **1800** In Gates County, North Carolina, exterior trim of the courthouse was to be painted white and "All other part of the house to be turpentine and oil mixed with red Oaker or spanish Brown mixed with Tar." Gates Co., N.C., County Accounts, NCA&H.
>
> **1812** "To prepare OILS for outside work" New England house and ship-painter Hezekiah Reynolds offered the following instructions: "Place red lead in the proportion of one pound to four galons of oil, at the bottom of the vessel—add the oil; then let them simmer or boil very gently over a slow fire, until clarified. When the red froth ceases to rise to the top, the oil is clarified and fit for use." Reynolds, *Directions for House and Ship Painting.*

olive color A green paint, generally used for interior work.

> **1739** William Beverley ordered "As much paint of a deep olive col^r ready ground with linseed oyl as wil paint 200 yds of wainscot." William Beverley Letterbook, 1737–1744, NYPL.
>
> **1748** The "Doors, Windows, & c." of Stratton Major church were to be "Painted with an olive color on the inside." Stratton Major Parish, King & Queen Co., Va., Vestry Book.

on center See **center to center.**

one-and-a-half story See **story and a half.**

one story See **story** (2).

orangery (orangerie) An enclosed building with glass panes where orange, lemon, lime and other fruit trees and tender plants are placed until warm weather; a greenhouse. The term was seldom used during the colonial period. Instead *greenhouse* was the most common term to describe such structures. See also **greenhouse.**

1790 A visitor to a Westmoreland County, Virginia, plantation noted the presence of "gardens, vineyards, orangeries and lawns which surround the house." Lockwood, *Gardens of Colony and State*, 1.

oratory A small chapel; a room for private devotions, especially one attached to a dwelling house.

1717 Anglican parishioners erected a "Chapel of Ease" ten miles from Newcastle, Delaware, "made of wood, in length 32 foot and breadth 22. . . . when thoroughly finished will make, we think as fair and compleat an oratory, as any not made of Brick within this Govt." Perry, *American Colonial Church*, 2.
1755 "Oratory . . . is a Closet or small Apartment near a Bed-chamber, furnished with a little Altar, or Image, for private Devotion (among the Romanists)." Salmon, *Palladio Londinensis*.

orchard An area for the cultivation of fruit trees, often enclosed by fencing.

1667 A planter in Somerset County, Maryland, stipulated in his will that his executors were "to make an orchard of 200 trees the one halfe winter fruite the other summer leaving sufficient fencing on it & aboute itt." *Archives of Maryland*, 44.
1686 William Fitzhugh of Stafford County, Virginia, described a Virginia orchard "of about 250 Aple trees most grafted, well fenced in with a Locust fence, which is as durable as most brick walls." *William Fitzhugh and His Chesapeake World*.
1736 On a plantation near Charleston was "an orchard well planted with peach, apple, cherry, fig, pomegranate and plumb trees." *South Carolina Gazette*.
1742 At Wappoo plantation near Charleston, "I have planted a large figg orchard with design to try and export them." *Letterbook of Eliza Lucas Pinckney*.
1784 An Englishman traveling through Virginia noted that the "plantations are generally from one to four or five miles distant from each other, having a dwelling house in the middle . . . at some little distance there are always large peach and apple orchards." *Gardens of Colony and State*, 2.

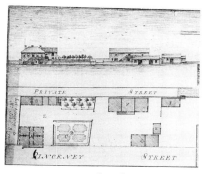

orchard
Small enclosed orchard on the lot and wharf belonging to Florian Mey on East Bay Street, Charleston, S.C., 1797

order The fundamental unit of design in classical architecture consisting of a column with base, shaft, capital, and entablature, detailed and proportioned according to one of five modes: Tuscan, Doric, Ionic, Corinthian, and Composite. The ancient Greeks developed the Doric, Ionic, and Corinthian orders and the Romans added the Tuscan and Composite. The codification of the rules of proportion and decoration was initiated by Italian theorists and architects such as Alberti, Serlio, Vignola, and Palladio in the 15th and 16th centuries. The precedents established during the Italian Renaissance affected 17th- and early 18th-century French and English writers and architects who did much to promulgate the codified laws of classical design through treatises and manuals that were imported into the American colonies in the 18th century. However, many elements of classical design appeared in southern architecture as early as the last decades of the 17th century, long before the torrent of publications which espoused and revealed the intricacies of its language were hawked by colonial booksellers. Much of this classicism probably arrived with skilled English builders, who had been trained in the new style of architecture in London and other metropolitan locations. Until the modern architec-

order

The Five Orders of ARCHITECTURE with their PEDESTALS.

tural profession evolved in the early 19th century around Benjamin Latrobe and his followers, few Americans grasped the nuances of proportioning and detailing inherent in this system. However, by the time of the Revolution, there were many clients and builders who lamented the propensity of builders to follow loosely the rules and insisted on their more correct application. Thomas Jefferson, for example, became a stickler for the correctness of detail based on his scholarly study of European treatises. Professional architects thought Jefferson a little too pedantic. Latrobe believed the president had "prejudices in favor of the architecture of the old french books, out of which he fishes everything." By the first decades of the 19th century, scholarship, carpenter's manuals, and the rise of an architectural profession inaugurated a long period when the adherence to the rules of the classical orders became commonplace in fashionable dwellings and public buildings, existing alongside a vast body of building that continued to exhibit looser interpretations of those rules. See also **Composite order, Corinthian order, Doric order, Ionic order, Tuscan order.**

1771 "Whereas it appears that the dimentions of the alterpeace mentioned in the Articles with the undertaker for building the New Church are not according to the proportions of Architecture, the said undertaker is . . . to make the same according to the true proportions of the Ionic order notwithstanding." Truro Parish, Fairfax Co., Va., Vestry Book.

1785 Thomas Jefferson dismissed the second capitol in Williamsburg as "a light and airy structure, with a portico in front of two orders, the lower of which, being Doric, is tolerably just in its proportions and ornaments, save only that the intercolumnations are too large. The upper Ionic is much too small for that on which it is mounted, its ornaments not proper to the order, nor proportioned within themselves. It is crowned with a pediment, which is too large for its span. Yet, on the whole, it is the most pleasing piece of architecture we have." *Notes on the State of Virginia.*

1804 "The rules that determine the proportions of what is called the orders, were, no doubt, arbitrary, among the ancients, as to all matters of detail. Palladio and his successors and contemporaries endeavor to establish fixed rules for the most minute parts of the orders. The Greeks knew no such rules, but having established general proportions and laws of form and arrangement, all matters of detail were left to the talent and taste of individual architects. This is amply proved in all their best buildings. Of this license in detail, I think it right to avail myself on all occasions." *The Correspondence and Miscellaneous Papers of Benjamin Henry Latrobe*, 1.

ordinary   A dwelling or purpose-built structure publicly licensed for the accommodation of travelers and the entertainment of guests. Prices for lodging, food, and alcoholic beverages were strictly regulated by the local courts. Ordinaries were frequently located in ports, ferry crossings, at crossroads, and on courthouse grounds, where they provided not only a place of accommodation but a venue for polite and raucous public entertainment such as assemblies, theatricals, lectures, dinners, gambling, drinking, and sporting activities. The term was by far the most common one to describe such places from the 17th to the middle of the 18th century in the Chesapeake. Gradually the terms *tavern* and, much later, *hotel* supplant it, so that it practically disappears from the records by the second quarter of the 19th century. **See** also **public house, tavern.**

> **1642**   A license was given to operate an "ordinary" for the "dyetting & accommodation of the commissioners" of the court. Norfolk Co., Va., Deed Book 1637–1646.
> **1679**   It was "Ordered by the Court that Mr. Thomas Hussy have a lycense for keepeing of an Ordinary at the house where hee now dwelleth (Viz) the Court house." Charles Co., Md., Land Record Book 1678–1680.
> **1684**   A petitioner was granted leave "to keep an ordinary att his Mansion house . . . [so long as he] doth constantly find and provide in his ordinary good wholesome & cleanly Lodging & dyett for Travellers and Stablage fodder & provender or pasturage & provender . . . and shall not suffer or permit any unlawfull gaming in his house nor on the Sabbath day suffer any person to Tipple or drink more than is necessary." Northumberland Co., Va., Court Order Book 1678–1698.
> **1751**   A minister admonished newspaper readers that "Ordinaries are now, in a great measure, perverted from their original Intention, and Proper Use; viz. the Reception, Accommodation, and Refreshment of the weary and benighted Traveller . . . and are become the common Receptacle, and Rendez-vous of the very Dreggs of the People . . . where not only Time and Money are, vainly and unprofitably squandered away, but . . . where prohibited and unlawful Games, Sports, and Pastimes are used, followed, and practiced." *Virginia Gazette.*
> **1774**   While in Annapolis, a recent British immigrant noted that he "Breakfasted at Rollins, a Public House, but in this Country called Ordinaries, and indeed they have not got their name for nothing, for they are ordinary enough." *Journal of Nicholas Cresswell.*

ornament   **1.** An accessory or addition used to adorn and embellish; the quality or circumstances of an object or building that confers beauty and enrichment. See also **composition ornament.**

> **1624**   In Virginia, "our Houses, for the most Part, are rather built for Use than Ornament; yet not a few for both, and fit to give Entertainment to men of good Quality." *Journals of the Houses of Burgesses*, 1.
> **1723**   The vestry believed that "building a pair of Stairs within the Body of the Church would not only be injurious to ye Propriety of some Pews therein, but likewise to ye Ornament and Beauty of ye Church." St. Anne's Parish, Anne Arundel Co., Md., Vestry Book.
> **1742**   At Bruton Parish Church in Williamsburg, "the brick ornaments of the Gavel ends [are] to be taken down, and finished with wood, answering the rest." *Records of Bruton Parish.*
> **1773**   At the College of William and Mary in Williamsburg, "the large garden before the College is of ornament and use." *Proceedings of the Massachusetts Historical Society*, 49.
> **1789**   Commissioners appointed to oversee the construction of a courthouse in Norfolk, "judging that a cupalo would be an ornamental addition thereto did contract with William Hobday to build the same." Norfolk Co., Va., Court Order Book 1788–1790.

2. The furnishings of a church, especially the accessories used to adorn the communion table, altarpiece, and pulpit of an Anglican church.

1694 Money was raised so that "there may be bought a Pulpett Cloath & Cushion for ye Chappell . . . and yt James Hill Churchwarden . . . send for ye sd ornament of a green colour." Kingston Parish, Gloucester Co., Va., Vestry Book.
1771 "£45 levied to purchase a compleat sett of crimson velvet ornaments for pulpit, communion and alter pieces on paste board. . . . Note the front of the pulpit cloth is to be mark'd Wicco comoco Parish 1771 in Gold Letters." Wicomico Parish, Northumberland Co., Va., Vestry Book.

orphans' house A building for the care and rearing of orphaned children. Establishments of this kind were rare in the southern colonies, where court-appointed guardians usually cared for such children and managed their inheritances, subject to the county court's supervision. In at least one case, an orphans' house was built by charitable donations solicited by the Anglican itinerant minister George Whitefield.

1764 "Governor James Wright carried me to visit the Orphan house, Bethesda on the bluf near the seashore which is large Substantial commodious Building, erected by Contributions collected from the charitable and benevolent, by the Rev'd. Mr. George Whitefield, and supported to this period in the same manner. Several Orphans have been reared and educated here, and put out to different Masters." *Travels in the American Colonies*.

outbuilding An independent structure devoted to some agricultural or domestic function. The term was seldom used. For a more complete description, see **outhouse.**

1767 After a parsonage house was constructed, a vestry was asked "to come to any determination about the Out Buildings" and they decided to "compleat them, as 'twas imposible the house coud be made use of else." St. Michael's Parish, Charleston, S.C., Vestry Book.

outchamber A term peculiar to Jefferson's writings, referring to the small building in which he lived while the main portion of Monticello was under construction. In 1771 he wrote to James Ogilvie, "I have here but one room, which, like the cobbler's, serves me for parlor for kitchen and hall. I may add, for bed chamber and study too. My friends sometimes take a temperate dinner with me and then retire to look for beds elsewhere. I have hopes however of getting more elbow room this summer." A second, matching structure was later built and both were connected to the main house by a terrace.

1775 In a memorandum about cutting stone for the house, Jefferson noted that 2 door sills would be needed "for Outchambers." Coolidge Collection, Massachusetts Historical Society.
1775 Another memorandum indicated designated 4 walnut sash were designated for the "N & S Outchamber." Coolidge Collection, Massachusetts Historical Society.

out farm A term used in Delaware to identify a tract of cultivated land not directly associated with the owner's place of residence. See also **out plantation, quarter** (3).

1827 Buildings at "one out farm" and "one other out farm" were noted and valued. Sussex Co., Del., Orphans Court Valuations O.

outhouse An independent, freestanding building generally associated with a dwelling house and designed for specific, subsidiary domestic and agricultural functions. Among the most common were *kitchens, smokehouses, cornhouses, barns, tobacco houses*, and *quarters*. The peculiarly southern practice of using multiple service buildings ap-

outhouse
Kitchen, office, and other outhouses, Tuckahoe, Goochland County, Va.

pears to be based partly in technological constraints of 17th-century construction, that is, the relative ease of building two small structures instead of one large one. An increasing preference for clearly expressed social distinctions also contributed to the physical separation of the residences and workplaces of indentured servants and slaves from the main dwelling. See also **outbuilding, quarters** (1).

> **1705** An act for constructing a house for the colonial governor in Williamsburg directed the overseer of building to "finish the aforesaid house and out houses." Hening, *Statutes at Large*, 3.
> **1753** A plantation near Charleston included "a commodious dwelling house . . . with other out-house, all new." *South Carolina Gazette*.
> **1810** In the town of Easton, Maryland, a lot with a dwelling house included "every convenient outhouse, including a good ice house." *Republican Star or Eastern Shore General Advertiser*.

out office An outhouse used for domestic or agricultural purposes. See **office** (2), **outbuilding.**

> **1796** For sale near New Bern was "a valuable plantation and tract of land containing about six hundred acres, with a commodious dwelling house and all necessary out offices on Trent Road—HEZEKIAH MERRET." *North Carolina Gazette*.
> **1805** Money was raised to publish a "Treatise on the mode of erecting Dwellings, Houses, Publick or private buildings, out-offices, or fencing walls." *Norfolk Gazette and Publick Ledger*.

out plantation A tract of land under cultivation, not including the environs of the landowner's dwelling house. A term confined to Delaware. See also **out farm, quarter** (3).

> **1790** Plantation buildings were identified and valued as the "home Place" and the "Out plantation." Sussex Co., Del., Orphans Court Valuations E.

outside to outside, out to out The overall dimensions of a structure from one extreme to the other, encompassing the thickness of the walls. In contrast, *in the clear* and *inside to inside* were terms used to define the internal dimensions of a space, room, or building. Describing buildings in terms of the outside dimensions seems to have been less common south of North Carolina.

> **1674** The statehouse at St. Mary's City was "to continue in length forty five foote from outside to outside." *Archives of Maryland*, 2.
> **1758** The length of the governor's house to be built at Tower Hill in Dobbs County, North Carolina was "to be Fifty Feet from Outside to Outside." *State Records of North Carolina*, 25.
> **1767** A lazaretto on Tybee Island, Georgia, was "to be 40 feet long, and 20 feet wide, from out to out." *Georgia Gazette*.
> **1806** In Fayette County, Kentucky, "Proposals will be received . . . for the building a Brick Meeting House, 40 by 50 feet, from out to out." *Kentucky Gazette and General Advertiser*.

oval window An elliptical or near circular window often found in gable ends, pediments, and above doors in public buildings. See also **bull's eye window, oxeye window.**

> **1704** At the capitol in Williamsburg, a proposal was made "to send for the Queens Armes in Glass for the Great window, the Armes of Virginia for One of the Ovall windowes and what other Ornament you may please for the other of the said Oval windows." *Journals of the House of Burgesses of Virginia*, 4.
> **1787** Alterations to a courthouse included "adding . . . an oval window over the door." Charlotte Co., Va., Court Order Book 1786–1789.

oven A chamber or device made of masonry or iron used for baking, cooking, heating, or drying. Generally circular with a domed cover-

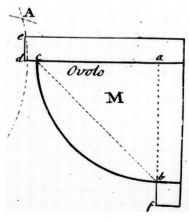

oven

Above: Seagle Farm, Lincoln County, N.C.

Below: Kitchen, Shirley, Charles City County, Va.

ing, ovens were located in conjunction with kitchen fireplaces or as free-standing structures sometimes protected by overhead coverings. See also **bakehouse.**

> 1688 A suit was brought against a workman for "refusing to make one brick oven." Charles City Co., Va., Court Order Book 1687–1695.
> 1742 A workman was hired to "buld to the Chichen a Chimny, and an Oven out of Doors." St. John's Parish, Colleton, S.C., Vestry Book.
> 1749 On the Dashiell farm on Maryland's Eastern Shore was "one brick oven and hous over it Covered with Clabbords." Touart, *Somerset.*
> 1759 A house in Alexandria, Virginia, for sale had "a Bake House 16 by 16, with a Shed 16 by 6, having a large Oven adjoining." *Maryland Gazette.*

overdoor A decorative element located above a door, such as a straight or pedimented entablature. See also **cap.**

> 1783 "Over the doors" in the council chamber in the Governor's House in New Bern "are flat Caps with contracted swelling Friezes." Hawks Letter, Miranda Papers, Academia Nacional de la Historia, Caracas.
> 1811 A craftsman fabricated "1 Pediment over door" at James Madison's house Montpelier in Orange County, Virginia. Cocke Papers, UVa.

overjet See **jet.**

overseer of building (overlooker) A person or committee charged with reviewing the progress of work on a building, especially a public structure. The term was sometimes used to refer to the builder or undertaker of the project.

> 1705 "The Committee Appointed to Inspect what Directions have been given about the Capitoll and Likewise to Consider what is further necessary to be Done to it Reported . . . that the Roof shall be painted white & the Cupolo to be painted in Such manner as Shall be Directed by the Overseer of the Building." *Journals of the House of Burgesses,* 4.
> 1714 Changes were made to a church "pursuant to the directions of ye overseers of ye worke." Christ Church Parish, Middlesex Co., Va., Vestry Book.
> 1717 It was "Ordered that the Gentlemen appointed by the Vestry overseers of the building of the said chappell acquaint the undertakers of the said building that they pursue the orders of the Vestry made relating to the pews in the said chappell." Christ Church Parish, Middlesex Co., Va., Vestry Book.

overseer's house A domestic structure provided for the manager of agricultural operations at a *quarter,* or an industrial establishment. Such buildings were often similar in quality, if not in form, to the houses of the slave labor force near which they were usually located. See **quarter** (3).

> 1727 In his instructions about a Lancaster County, Virginia, plantation, Robert Carter noted "I ordered your quarter and your overseers house to be lofted. It is very necessary, not only for the warmth of the house but to lay the peoples corn up in." Carter Papers, UVa.
> 1768 A tract of land in Hanover County, Virginia, contained "two tobacco house 29 by 16 one shedded 10 feet on the broadside, two quarters, a new corn house 16 by 12, an overseer's house . . . ground cleared for 4 or 5 hands." *Virginia Gazette.*
> 1789 Repairs on a glebe included a "fraim'd overseers house 25 by 16 feet." Christ Church, Savannah, Ga., Records, GHS.

overset See **jet.**

ovolo (ovelo, ovilloe) A convex molding whose profile is a quadrant of a circle or ellipse. In classical architecture, a Roman ovolo was a quarter of a circle, or quarter round, and sometimes called an *echinus;*

ovolo

while the Greek ovolo was flatter, more like a section of an egg. In the 18th century, classical-minded architects and authors in England preferred this term over the more common *quarter round* used by most workmen. *Ovolo* rarely appears in the American South before the middle of the 18th century, when it was employed most frequently by cabinetmakers. The Greek form of the ovolo gradually replaced the Roman ovolo in the early 19th century. See also **echinus, quarter round.**

> 1760   The carved work on the pulpit included "33 feet Ovelo for the Pannels." St. Michael's Parish, Charleston, S.C., Church Records.
> 1773   In the design of an unidentified building in Edenton, North Carolina, architect John Hawks specified that "the pillaster as in the plan is to project sufficiently from the Brickwork to receive at top (exclusive of the cap) the width of the ovolo and bead which is 3 1/2 inches." John Hawks Collection, SHC.
> 1793   Doors at "Old East" at the University of North Carolina were to have "pannels half an inch thick with an ovello on the framing." University Archives, UNC, Chapel Hill.
> 1819   "I should prefer however to have only the ovolo of the abacus carved, and it's cavetto plain, as may be seen in Scamozz[i]." Lambeth and Manning, *Thomas Jefferson as an Architect.*

oxeye window
Pompion Hill Chapel,
Berkeley County, S.C.

oxeye window   A round or oval window found often in gable ends, pediments, and above doors. See also **bull's eye, oval window.**

> 1753   A church was to be built with "three Ox eye windows one over each door." Wicomico Parish, Northumberland Co., Va., Vestry Book.
> 1786   Repairs to a church included "two ox eye sashes." Congregational Church, Charleston, S.C., Record Book.

padlock   A portable lock designed with a sliding and pivoted shackle that can be passed through a staple and then locked so as to engage a hasp. Padlocks were used primarily to secure prison doors, churchyard fence gates, and trunks.

> 1725   A blacksmith paid for "2 padlocks & keys & hasp & 2 staples" to secure the gates of a churchyard. St. Anne's Parish, Anne Arundel Co., Md., Vestry Book.
> 1788   Doors to a prison were "to be secured with hasps & pad locks two to each door." Prince William Co., Va., Court Order Book 1787–1791.

paint   A protective finish for architectural elements, most often composed of some coloring agent ground in linseed oil. Pigments could be purchased dry or already mixed in oil. White lead, whiting, lampblack, yellow ochre, red ochre, red lead, Spanish brown, verdigris and Prussian blue were among the most widely used of these agents, which were mixed in oil to produce a wide variety of colors. This mixing was a laborious process, accomplished using a muller on a marble slab or paint stone. For exterior painting, period specifications frequently called for two prime coats of paint, followed by a third, finish coat. References to painting are rare before 1700. They begin to appear in significant numbers only after 1720, when the notion of genteel finish began to manifest itself in buildings erected for the well-to-do. Before that time interiors were rarely painted, and exteriors were finished only with tar. By mid-century, interior trim, exterior siding and ornaments, and even roofs were routinely painted. See also **distemper, tar, whitewash.**

> 1701   For construction of a church in New Kent County, Virginia, the vestry of St. Peter's Parish directed Henry Wyatt to "send to England . . . for Ironwork, Glass for Sash Windows, and paint for the aforesaid Church." St. Peter's Parish, New Kent Co., Va., Vestry Book.

1711 In Talbot County, Maryland, justices directed that the "all windows front doore culloms pediments Dorments and Eaves of the said House and seat of Judicature to be well primed and painted." Talbot Co., Md., Land Records Book No. 12.

1738 John Carter wrote to his brother Charles that "If the Builder's Dictionary is at all to the purpose of your charge to the painter, it makes against you since in the cases supposed the oyl & colours are found by the workmen & how much soever you may Rely of the authority of this or the other author in my opinion Col Richd Randolph's rooms are as well painted as any I have seen at Mrs Pages & much better than some of them where the fingers stick to the paint which will perhaps never be dry and hard enough; and he once told me that 4d pr yard was more than any painter could deserve for plain work, & every Gentleman that has been in London and has made an inquiry about these matters must know that the best journeymen house painters may be hired for 2s 6 pr day." Carter-Plummer Letterbook, VHS.

1766 The vestry directed that the exterior woodwork of a church "be painted 3 times over with white lead." All Saints Parish, Calvert Co., Md., Vestry Book.

1771 For the new church of St. John's Parish, in Granville County, North Carolina, the vestry ordered that "every part of the [interior] work exposed to view shall be well painted of a Cream Collour. The out side of the Church except the roof shall be painted a Stone Collour & the roof shall be Painted with Spanish Brown." Francis Hawks Collection, Church Historical Society.

1812 New England house and ship-painter Hezekiah Reynolds offered the following advice for exterior painting: "New brushes may be used for priming, or the first coats; but for finishing, use only brushes about half worn. It is important that the hand of the painter, and the handle of the brush, be kept clean, and free from oil and paint; and that the brush be held while painting, firm by the handle—and that the building be prepared by filling the cracks and fractures with putty; and sweeping off the dust, spiderwebs, &c. In all cases, but especially in finishing; the paint should be laid strait and true, corresponding with the grain of the wood." Reynolds, *Directions for House and Ship Painting.*

painter A craftsman skilled in the preparation of pigments, the mixing of paint colors with linseed oil, and the application of paint, whitewash, tar, lacquers, and varnishes to wooden, plaster, masonry, and iron surfaces. Tools necessary for the trade included a stone slab for grinding colors and a variety of brushes, ranging from large round ones for field painting to thin, pencil-tipped ones for lettering and sash work. The first professional painters were working in the southern colonies by the beginning of the 18th century. By mid-century, a steady stream of professionally trained British immigrants, many of whom specialized in decorative painting of signs, heraldry, and coaches, supplemented the small number of locally trained painters. In the late colonial and early national periods, painters often combined their occupation with other trades such as plastering and glazing. See also **paint.**

1686 Anthony Dawson was responsible for "All Glaziers Work Carpenters Work Smiths Work and Painter Work" for the courthouse he was to undertake on the Eastern Shore of Maryland. Dorchester Co., Md., Land Record Book 1669–1683.

1705 "George Burton, Painter" witnessed the burning of the College of William and Mary in Williamsburg. *W&MQ*, 2nd ser., 8.

1739 "Agreed with Richard Cooke . . . that he Doe With all Convenient Speed provide Oyle & paint; to Do and proforme the work hear next mentioned that is to Say the Aulter peace to be Neatly painted: the Ground work of the Pannels to be Jappand; the Creed Lords Prayor & Ten Comandments to be Done in a Leagable hand In fair Gold letters and All Carving work to be Guilded And to paint all the Coving in the Angles whear it has been split or Defased And to handsomly paint Six Pues In the Church within and without of a Windscote Couler and to New Paint the Pulpit And Canopy And to new paint and Prime all the Doors of the Church window frames sashes Cornish Churchyard Gates And posts and to find and provide all the Oyle & Coullers Except the leaf Gould that is to be made use of for £20 when finished. . . . Scaffolding only excepted which the Gent. of the Vestory oblidge them selves to find." Petsworth Parish, Gloucester Co., Va., Vestry Book.

1744 "James Talbot was bound" an apprentice "to Daniel Badger, painter." St. Philip's Parish, Charleston, S.C., Vestry Book.

1744 "Samuel Rusbatch, late pupil to Robert Maberly, Esq. coach and herald painter; and varnisher to their majesties and the royal family; proposeth (under the direction of Joseph Horatio Anderson, architect in Annapolis) to carry on all the various branches of coach and herald painting, varnishing and guilding; as well plain as in the most decorated taste. Also painting in fresco, cire-obscure, decorated ceilings for halls, vestibules, and saloons, either in festoons or fruits, flowers, figures, or trophies. Carved ornaments in deception, guilding and burnishing in the neatest manner, as well house-painting, in distemper as dead whites, as in common colours, &c." *Maryland Gazette*.

1746 "ROBERT COCHRAN Painter and Colourist, hereby gives Notice, That he sells all Kinds of dry and mix'd Colurs, from one Pound to 100 Weight, and will supply Gentlemen in the Country with a Receipt how to use them, . . . and practices painting in the best Manner, and after the newest Fashions of Great Britain." *South Carolina Gazette*.

palace (pallace)   The official residence of an important dignitary. Specifically, the term was used in the colonial South to refer to a governor's residence. The governor's house completed by Governor Robert Dinwiddie in the 1710s in Williamsburg, Virginia, appears to have been the first such structure to be so called. Following this precedent, the building erected by Governor William Tryon as his residence and the meeting place of the provincial council in New Bern, North Carolina, was referred to as the *palace* after it was finished in 1770. See also **governor's house.**

1717   A resident of Williamsburg wrote to an acquaintance that "I assure you Sr it is so far from it (i.e. being a 'Court Favourite') that I have not bin wth: in the Governr: pallace doors nor exchanged one worth wth: the Governr: this nine months." John Custis Letterbook, LC.

1787   In New Bern, North Carolina, "the palace is a building erected by the province before the Revolution—It is a large and elegant brick Edifice two Stories high, with two Wings for the offices. . . . This House was formerly the residence of the Governors of this Country, as well as the place where the Legislature sat, to transact their business." Attmore, *Journal of a Tour to North Carolina*.

1816   Visitors to Raleigh wanted to be driven to the newly completed governor's residence. "The stage stopped at the post office. 'Here's a lady and gentleman wants to be drove to the Govern's—do you know whether they has moved into the Palace?'—'Palace!' repeated Sol[omo]n to me. 'Palace' said the gentleman to whom the driver spoke. 'I did not know what you meant, why don't you call it house, man, it's only a house, if you were in England now, palace might do.' The driver ventured to defend his anti-democratical expression only by saying, 'I heard most of the people call it palace, so I calls it so.' " Pattie Mordecai Papers, NCA&H.

pale (pail, paile, payle)   A split or sawn piece of wood vertically set in the ground or nailed to a horizontal rail supported by posts to form a fence. Pales were used where solid barriers were needed, especially for gardens and immediate environs of public buildings and dwelling houses. Pale tops were sometimes decoratively shaped; a simple, triangular point was most common in the southern colonies. In the later 18th and early 19th centuries, the term was confined increasingly to wide (averaging 2 to 6 inches), square-topped or pointed fence components, while the word *picket* was applied to thinner, more elaborately cut and less overtly functional varieties. From the mid-19th century to the present, *picket* has been used as a generic and somewhat imprecise term for all types of vertical fence elements. An entire fence containing pales was called a pale as well as a *paling* or *palisade*. *Pale* was also a name for an area so enclosed and was used in such phrases as *to pale in* a yard, garden, or other designated space.

pale
Paled lots, Savannah, Ga., 1734

1647 A rental agreement for a York County, Virginia, plantation required that the tenant "maintain the old dwelling house and quartering houses and Tobacco houses in repair, as well as the pales about the yard and gardens and other necessary fences." *W&MQ*, 1st. ser., 5.

1728 An agreement for enlarging a churchyard called for "500 foot of Pailing . . . the Posts thereof to be of Cedar or Locust to be of 7 foot Long & not less than 4 Inches Square and each post to stand not above 8 foot distance with 3 Rails between each post made in a triangular form of White Oak Mortiss'd & Tennanted the tennants let in to be tarr'd The Pails thereof to be of Yellow Poplar Saw'd five foot Long four Inches broad 3/4 Inches thick from the Saw, each Pail to Stand one Inch Differance and three Tenpenny Nails top each Pail." St. James Parish, Anne Arundel County, Md., Vestry Book.

1814 Robert Anderson wrote to Jane C. Charlton in Williamsburg: "In your next letter please inform me whether you prefer the lot to be enclosed with plank or pales . . . the last will be cheapest and such as I intend to put on the adjoining lot (Wright's) wch I bought a few days ago." Robert Anderson Account Books, VHS.

paled fence See **pale.**

paling See **pale.**

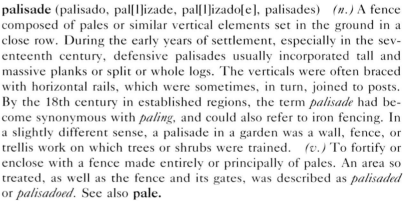

palisade
Palisaded garden, Virginia,
mid-18th century

palisade (palisado, pal[l]izade, pal[l]izado[e], palisades) *(n.)* A fence composed of pales or similar vertical elements set in the ground in a close row. During the early years of settlement, especially in the seventeenth century, defensive palisades usually incorporated tall and massive planks or split or whole logs. The verticals were often braced with horizontal rails, which were sometimes, in turn, joined to posts. By the 18th century in established regions, the term *palisade* had become synonymous with *paling*, and could also refer to iron fencing. In a slightly different sense, a palisade in a garden was a wall, fence, or trellis work on which trees or shrubs were trained. *(v.)* To fortify or enclose with a fence made entirely or principally of pales. An area so treated, as well as the fence and its gates, was described as *palisaded* or *palisadoed*. See also **pale.**

1610 Jamestown, Virginia, was enclosed "with a Pallizado of Planckes and strong Posts, foure foote deepe in the ground, of yong Oakes, Walnuts, &c." *Voyage to Virginia.*

1626 Indian attacks caused the Virginia government "to secure the forrest by running a pallizade from Marttin's hundred to kiskyack, which is not above six miles over . . . to secure the Necke." Letter to the Privy Council, *VMHB*, 2.

1686 A Westmoreland County, Virginia, property included "a Yeard wherein is most of the foresaid necessary houses, pallizado'd in with locust Punchens, which is as good as if it were walled in & more lasting than any of our bricks." William Fitzhugh Letters, VHS.

1783 The Governor's House in New Bern, North Carolina, contained "an Ionick portico Frontispiece to the North front and a range of Iron palisadoes from this to each Circular Colonade." Hawks Letter, Miranda Papers, Academia Nacional de la Historia, Caracas.

1801 In December 1801 and January 1802 John Tayloe took delivery of 42 pieces of "Paillisading" from foundry owner Henry Foxall to enclose the area ways surrounding his Washington residence. The bill referred to one piece as the "1st Cast" and based the price on the weight. The following month blacksmith James Worrell charged Tayloe for "Twenty four screw pins & nutts put in the pallisading 1.4.0." Tayloe Papers, VHS.

1824 Alexander Robison's town lot included "a Yard in front walled with stone and pallisade fence erected thereon." New Castle Co., Del., Orphans Court Valuations L.

Palladian window See **Venetian window.**

pane (pain)   One of the divisions of a window, consisting of a single sheet of glass held in place by a frame of lead or wood. Sash window panes were secured on the inside of the frame by putty and/or sprigs. Until the Revolution, window glass was imported into the colonies from Great Britain and was sold by merchants either in large *tables* or in smaller *panes*.   By the middle of the 18th century, windowpanes were frequently sold in standard sizes to fit sash light openings. The most common sizes were 8 by 10 inches, 10 by 12 inches, and 12 by 14 inches. The term was sometimes used interchangeably with *light* to refer to the subdivided openings of a sash window. See also **glass, light.**

1697   Glass ordered from England "for All faiths Church" included "3 Paines 2 feet one inch longe one foot and 1/2 broade . . . 3 paines more one foot and a 1/2 square . . . Six paines 3 foot 3 Inches long a foot and 1/2 wide." All Faiths Parish, St. Mary's Co., Md., Vestry Book.

1728   "Four duz: panes of London duble crond glass of about 11 & 12 size [are] to be sent for by the rev Emanuel Jones at the church." Petsworth Parish, Gloucester Co., Va., Vestry Book.

1745   Estimates made for glazing a house in Charleston were as follows: "Upon the Cellar floar 9 windows each sashd with 8 Pains of glass 11 × 9; Upon the first floar 16 windows with 18 Pains or lights in each; Upon the 2d Floar the same; Upon the Garret floar 8 windows with 8 lights in each." Huger Smith, *Dwelling Houses of Charleston.*

1755   A Charleston merchant wrote to a firm in Bristol, England, noting that "your Glass we have offer'd at prime cost in order to finish the Sale & none as yet will accept of it. . . . Shall push the Sale all that in our Power but the Box 9 × 7 we fear will never sell as we have no Windows that the pane is so small as that." *The Papers of Henry Laurens,* 1.

1762   A church to be built in Winchester, Virginia was to have "four windows on each side arched of forty pains of Glass each ten inches by twelve . . . two windows on each gable end upon the upper story arched of twenty eight paines of glass each ten inches by eight." Frederick Parish, Frederick Co., Va., Vestry Book.

panel (pannel, pannell)   1. Any surface enclosed by a border or frame or raised above or sunk beneath the plane of a wall, ceiling, or similar construction. In wainscoting, planed boards were set into rabbets in stiles and rails to form doors, shutters, wall sheathing, porch roofs, etc. Panels were often composed of a number of boards glued together. Raised panels were those with beveled edges tapering at the rabbets of the stiles, with a raised central section or field. Such raised fields commonly replaced flat panels by the early 18th century, and elaboration of the moldings between bevel and field came to represent the degree of expense and the relative social importance of the rooms in which they were used. A fashion for flat panels, which appeared at the time of the American Revolution, often led joiners to reverse the orientation, placing the raised face on the inferior space or elsewhere where it would not be seen. Such flat panels were sometimes enriched with fluting, reeding, incised frames, or decorative painting. Panel doors were generally a more expensive choice than doors consisting of battens nailed to sheathing. The two techniques were sometimes combined for security (sheathing secured to the rear of a panel door) or economy (stiles and rails nailed to the face of sheathing). Panel doors were often used in the best locations, with cheaper ones used in subsidiary spaces. The most common panel doors were six- and four-panel ones. The term *panel work* was sometimes

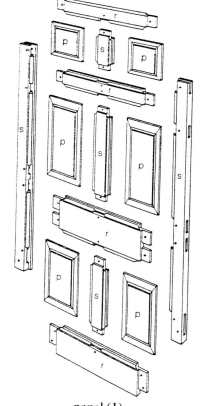

panel (1)
Constituent parts of a six panel door:
p = panel, r = rail, s = stile

used instead of *wainscotting* to describe this kind of woodwork. See also **wainscot**.

1688 A courthouse was to have a platform for the magistrates with a "panell overhead." Torrence, *Old Somerset*.

1726 In Caroline County, Virginia, a carpenter fabricated "2 six pannields door lin'd @ 12/." John Baylor Papers, UVa.

1733 In a church, "ye front of ye pews, pulpit, and desk [are] to be quarter round and raised panels." Blisland Parish, James City and New Kent Cos., Va., Vestry Book.

1739 The altarpiece of a church was to have the "Ground work of the Pannels . . . Jappand; the Creed Lords Prayor & Ten Comandments . . . Done in a Leagable hand." Petsworth Parish, Gloucester Co., Va., Vestry Book.

1773 In a glebe house, "all the doors on the lowere floor [are] to have six panels each, and frames to have double architrives, the doors on the upper floor to have four panels each, and the frames to be cased with a large Oge and beed, the room doors below to have brass locks, and them above to have Japaned locks with swirlls." Fairfax Parish, Fairfax Co., Va., Vestry Book.

1793 Specifications for "Old East" at the University of North Carolina stated that "the outer doors [are] to be folding doors three pannels in each square edge and flat pannel. . . . The pannels half an inch thick with an ovello on the framing. . . . The inner doors to be six pannel doors. . . . The pannels half an inch all square with an ovello on both sides." University Archives, UNC, Chapel Hill.

2. That part of a fence defined by two successive posts, or, in the case of a worm fence, the angles. Length and rail number as well as cost were often expressed in terms of panels. See also **post and rail fence, worm fence**.

1709 On the Walters estate on the Eastern Shore of Maryland were "419 pannels of old fencing, 121 pannels of new ditto." Queen Anne's Co., Md., Deed Book A.

1729 An advertisement for the sale of a Baltimore County, Maryland, plantation notes "1000 Pannels of worm Fence, 10 Logs high." *Maryland Gazette*.

1781 Damages claimed following the battle at Yorktown included "74 pannels of paling round the Stable Garden put up with Cedar posts sawed Oak pales & Rails, 3 Rails to a pannel . . . 57 pannels post and Rail round a Lot, six Rails to a pannel." York Co., Va., Claims for Losses.

pantile See **tile**.

pantry A room or building, generally near a kitchen or dining room, used for the storage of provisions as well as kitchen and dining implements.

1688 Among the rooms in William Stevens's dwelling in Somerset County, Maryland, was a dining room and nearby an "inward roome called the pantry." Maryland Prerogative Court Records, MSA.

1748 The outbuildings listed on a lot in Charleston included "a good pantry, poultry house, a large kitchen, wash house, and store rooms." *South Carolina Gazette*.

1766 Property for sale in Joppa, Maryland, contained "a Kitchen built of Brick, one Story high; on the lower Floor of which, are an inner and an out Kitchen; the inner Kitchen is joined to the Dwelling-House by a Passage, off which there is a large Pantry." *Maryland Gazette*.

1805 A large dwelling in Chestertown, Maryland, had "two kitchens, [and] a close and open pantry." *Republican Star or Eastern Shore General Advertiser*.

paperhanging
Prestwould, Mecklenburg County, Va.

paperhanging Interior wall covering consisting of strips of ornamental paper. Paperhanging came into general use in the southern colonies with the importation of English paper patterns in the middle of the 18th century. Although paper sizes varied, one of the most common consisted of individual sheets glued together and printed in strips 12 yards long and 21 inches wide. The term *wallpaper* gradually replaced *paperhanging* in the middle of the 19th century.

1749 For sale in Charleston were "Paper Hangings for Rooms." *South Carolina Gazette*.

1762 A Williamsburg resident wrote to his London merchant requesting "Paper to hang 3 Parlours." Robert Carter Letterbook, CWF.
1768 A house advertised for sale in Chestertown, Maryland, was "compleatly finished, with eight rooms, six of which are richly papered." *Maryland Gazette.*
1798 Samuel Irwin's Wilmington townhouse "in High Street . . . [is to] be papered the lower story." New Castle Co., Del., Orphans Court Valuations H.
1817 "Paper Hangings JUST received and for sale . . . a handsome assortment of Paper Hangings, among which are a few setts of Decorated Landscapes and Indian Scenery." *Alexandria Gazette and Daily Advertiser.*

papier mâché A substance composed of pulped paper and glue, molded wet and allowed to dry, producing light weight and inexpensive ornaments for ceilings, walls, and paper borders. The latter were often gilded.

1765 Charleston paper hanger John Blott advertised "Machee Ornaments for celings &c. to imitate Stoco work." *South Carolina Gazette.*
1765 In Fairfax County, Virginia, George William Fairfax ordered an extensive selection of paperhangings and accessories from Robert Stark of London. Among these were "paper mashé Ornaments for Ceiling agreeable to drawing for Room E . . . 46 yds Gadroon moulding in bur^d Gold . . . 72 yds White mashé border . . . mashé Ornaments for over Chimney." Fairfax Papers, VHS.

papier mâché
Miles Brewton House, Charleston, S.C.

parade **1.** A place where troops assemble for drills and ceremonial displays.

1754 On "His Majesty's Birthday . . . the Governour, attended by his Council and public officers, went down to Granville's Bastion and drank his Majesty's Health.. . . From there His Excellency went to the Parade and reviewed the Charles Town Regiment, who performed their Exercises, etc. to Admiration." *South Carolina Gazette.*

2. A public square or promenade.

1770 In Annapolis, money was appropriated by the Maryland General Assembly for building a statehouse and "for enlarging, repairing, and enclosing the Parade, not exceeding its present Length of 245 feet, and 160 in Breadth, designed to be enclosed with Stone or Brick Wall, and Iron Palisadoes . . . and to be laid with Flag, or other Stone or Gravel." *Maryland Gazette.*
1789 In Dover, Delaware, "four streets intersect each other at right angles, in the centre of town, whose incidencies form a spacious parade, on the east side of which is an elegant state-house of brick." Morse, *American Geography.*

parapet **1.** A low protective and sometimes decorative wall at the edge of a balcony, terrace, bridge, or above the cornice of a roof.

1737 Estimates were made for "making a Parapitt of Wood all along each front" of the roof of a church. St. Philip's Parish, Charleston, S.C., Vestry Book.
1783 At the Governor's House in New Bern, North Carolina, "a Block Cornice finishes [the front] pediment and Continues around the house with a parrapet wall and Ornament vause at each corner Brake." Hawks Letter, Miranda Papers, Academia Nacional de la Historia, Caracas.
1788 A workman was hired to "build a parapet Wall from the old foundations on the NORTH & SOUTH sides of the said CHURCH. . . . He shall also . . . remove and take down the old Cornice, & shall fix proper & sufficient Gutters or Aqueduct to convey the Water from the roof." St. Michael's Parish, Charleston, S.C., Vestry Book.
1805 "Mr. Lenthall has given me a regular account of the difficulties which have attended the ruinage of the roof of the President's house. I am almost in despair about parapet roofs in this climate." *The Correspondence and Miscellaneous Papers of Benjamin Henry Latrobe,* 2.

2. In military architecture, a defensive wall raised above the main wall or rampart.

1740 At a Spanish fort on the St. John's River in northern Florida, the "General gave orders for . . . raising Parapets and Pallisading it all Round." Mereness, *Travels in the American Colonies.*

parapet (1)
Bacon's Castle, Surry County, Va.

parastata(e) Free-standing pilasters, often supporting an arch and sometimes equated with antae. See also **pillar.**

pargeting Decorative or plain plastering of walls. This English term had little currency in the southern colonies and states.

> **c. 1609** At Jamestown, Virginia, dwellings "were at first, pargeted and plastered with bitumen or tough clay." *Voyage to Virginia.*

park A large, enclosed piece of ground associated with a substantial plantation comprised of woodland and pasture used for keeping deer, sheep, and cattle.

> **1727** A new governor of Virginia noted that his residence in Williamsburg contained "an handsome garden, an orchard full of fruit, and a very large Park." Gooch Transcripts, VSL.
> **1742** An estate map of Shirley in Charles City County, Virginia, located "the Orchards, Gardings, Park" near the James River. Carter Papers, UVa.

parlor (parlour, parler) A multipurpose entertaining and family sitting room located on the principal floor of most dwellings. Generally smaller and more private than the hall, the parlor was also used for sleeping and eating in many households through the early 19th century. By the end of the colonial period, many grander houses had a number of parlors, which were often well appointed with wallhangings, carpeting, and elegant chimney pieces and reserved for formal entertainment.

> **1653** An estate inventory listed a dwelling with a hall and "ould parlor." Norfolk Co., Va., Deed Book 1651–1656.
> **1674** Items found in John Lee's "parlowre Roome" included a "Spanish table 1 old turkey carpett, 3 cases of drawer" and "1 Spice box with drawers." Westmoreland Co., Va., Court Records.
> **1721** "On Christmas Day, the Governor [Charles Eden] came into the outer room or Hall and dined with the Company and . . . in the evening he desired the Company to go into the parlour where . . . there was a large bowl of punch made . . . and the Governor was very merry with the Company that night." *Colonial Records of North Carolina, 2.*
> **1793** In Chesterfield County, Virginia, a dwelling house was to be sold, with "six rooms on the lower floor . . . and a passage fourteen feet wide; This, with the dining room and parlor, is neatly wainscoted." *Virginia Gazette. And Richmond and Manchester Advertiser.*
> **1804** "In the front Parlor" of a house in Alexandria, Virginia, was "1 pair of Dining Tables old fashioned, 1 Scotch Carpet" and "In the back Parlour" was "1 side Cupboard, containing Sundry China Glass and Earthen ware, some Queens ware" and a "second side Cupboard." Alexandria, Va., Will Book 1804–1807.

parquet A floor composed of a series of short pieces of wood laid in various patterns, sometimes with inlays of other woods.

parsonage house A residence provided for a minister of a parish or congregation. The term was used in South Carolina and parts of North Carolina and Maryland to denote the dwelling specifically built to house the rector of an Anglican parish or other denominational minister. However, in Virginia, after the middle of the 17th century, the term *glebe house* was preferred by Anglicans to refer to such buildings. See also **glebe house.**

> **1635** The vestry agreed "that a parsonage house should be built upon the gleeb land . . . and that the said house shall be forty foot long and eyghteene foot wyde . . . and on each side of the chimneys a rome, the one for a study, the other for a buttery." *County Court Records of Accomack-Northampton, Virginia 1632–1640.*

1716 The minister of Christ Church Parish, South Carolina, complained that "neither the church and parsonage house [were] finished when I came into the parish [in] 1711." SPG Letterbook B, SPGFP.

1723 "The parsonage house" in St. John's Parish, South Carolina, "is of brick & in tollerable repair, but is five miles distant from the church." SPG Letterbook B, SPGFP.

1756 The Rev. William Peasley found it "a very great hardship that I am oblig'd to pay House-Rent, as you are not insensible that the Society sent me here on condition that a House would be provided for me, as is the custom throughout this Province; and really the Society told me, before I left London, that there was a good Parsonage House on the Glebe, and on no other terms would I have come here." St. Helena's Parish, S.C., Vestry Book.

1802 A payment was to be made to the builder of "the parsonage house so soon as the first box of tabbey is made." St. Helena's Parish, S.C., Vestry Book.

parterre A level or smooth area in a garden often occupied by an ornamental arrangement of flower, grass, or gravel beds of various shapes and sizes, edged with low growing shrubs and often somewhat raised for the better cultivation of plants. Also referred to as beds or squares, parterres were usually designed in geometric shapes and were separated by walks.

1796 When he visited Mount Vernon, the English-born architect Benjamin Henry Latrobe observed that "for the first time since I left Germany I saw here a parterre stripped and trimmed with infinite care into the form of a richly flourishing fleur-de-lis, the expiring groan, I hope, of our grandfathers' pedantry." *The Virginia Journals of Benjamin Henry Latrobe*, 1.

parting strip (parting bead, parting piece) A narrow strip of wood used to keep two pieces separate. Specifically, a thin piece of wood inserted into the side of a sash frame to separate the upper and lower sashes by creating two vertical channels.

1803 A church near Charleston was to have "Box'd Sash frames to all the lower Windows with beaded parting pieces." Johns Island Church Specifications, Library Society of Charleston.

1820 At Bremo in Fluvanna County, Virginia, John Neilson installed "pullies 6 @ 6 each, Hanging Treble Window 7/6....$1.75, Parting beads 3/....$.50." Cocke Papers, UVa.

partition (petition) A dividing wall within a building made of frame, brick, plank, or other materials.

1635 A parsonage house was to be "forty foot long and eyghteene foot wyde . . . a pertition neer the midest of the house." *County Court Records of Accomack-Northampton, Virginia 1632–1640.*

1645 A workman was hired "to weatherboard the partition" of a dwelling. *County Court Records of Accomack-Northampton, Virginia 1640–1645.*

1726 Repairs on a glebe included making "a partition in ye Tob'co house Eight foot." St. Peter's Parish, New Kent Co., Va., Vestry Book.

1736 A plantation house for sale near Charleston was "50 feet by 25 . . . divided into three rooms by brick partitions." *South Carolina Gazette.*

1768 On the Scrivener farm in Maryland was a "dwelling house 24 feet square with brick chimney plank floor above and below and a plank partition." Queen Anne's Co., Md., Deed Book H.

party wall A wall built on the line between two pieces of property. In row houses and other contiguous structures, party walls were built of sufficient thickness to serve as firebreaks.

1802 Each dwelling in a set of six row houses built in Washington, D.C. shared a "Party wall," which extended "1 foot above the Roof at Each End 9 Inches thick." INA Policy Records, CIGNA Archives.

party wall
Row of early 19th-century dwellings, Baltimore

1817 "AN ORDINANCE, to regulate party walls and partition fences" enacted in the city of Frederick, Maryland, specified that any person "who shall hereafter make use of . . . such party wall or partition fence, shall pay the original proprietor . . . one half part of the value of such party wall or partition fence." *Frederick-Town Herald*.

passage (passageway) 1. A long, narrow space providing access to various rooms, apartments, or parts of a building; a corridor. Though references to passages in dwellings occur as early as the 1680s, they did not appear in any significant numbers until about 1720. This new space, which generally ran through the center of the building from the front to the rear door, transformed the circulation plan of southern domestic architecture and greatly enhanced the privacy of the house. Before the advent of the passage, communication in the house was through one room into another. The passage provided independent access to all the principal ground-floor rooms and to the upstairs as well. It also functioned as a waiting room for servants and visitors whose social credentials did not warrant an invitation to join the planter or merchant and his family in the main rooms. Soon the advantages of this space as a refuge from summer heat became evident. By the middle of the 18th century, wealthier families spent an increasing portion of their time there. In response, the passage and the stair to the upper floor tended to grow in size and became more elaborate during this period. The term continued in use well into the 19th century and was only displaced by the term *hall* at a very late period.

passage (1)
Westover, Charles City County, Va.

1677 In laying out church fittings, the vestry ordered that there be "6 foot allowed for ye reading desks & passage into ye pulpitt." Petsworth Parish, Gloucester Co., Va., Vestry Book.
1696 In laying out the statehouse in Annapolis, it was ordered "that there be two or three Jury Rooms made and a Passage through the midst of the House so that on one side the said Rooms may lye & On the other side the Offices and at the end of the Passage will be the Entrance into the Porch Chamber by which means all the Rooms will be Private." *Archives of Maryland*, 19.
1715 An estate inventory in Prince George's County, Maryland, listed items "in the Hall passage." Maryland Prerogative Court Inventories and Accounts 1716–1717.
1717 "I desire you will lay out 40 Sh 50 Str in good Comicall diverting prints to hang in the passage of my house." John Custis Letterbook, LC.
1724 An English writer remarked that some Williamsburg dwellings contained "A passage generally through the middle of the house for an air-draft in summer." Jones, *Present State of Virginia*.
1746 A glebe house was to have "a passage through the house eight feet wide and the staircase run up in it with banisters." Wicomico Parish, Northumberland Co., Va., Vestry Book.
1767 The furnishings "in the passage" of a merchant's house in the northern neck of Virginia included "one large leather couch, three walnut chairs, one small damask carpet, one pair back gammon tables . . . one water jug and one wooden can, two glazed picktures and one map, one leather trunk and one glass lamp." Northumberland Co., Va., Court Record Book 1766–1770.

2. A long and relatively narrow walk or space between two buildings or between a freestanding wall and a structure. Also, a sheltered walk connecting two parts of a building or two separate structures. See also **covered way**.

1766 For sale in Baltimore, "a large convenient Dwelling-House, Passage and Kitchen." *Maryland Gazette*.
1794 A property included "a Log dwelling house with two Rooms below two Rooms above stairs and a log Kitchen with a passage between the House and Kitchen which passage must be weather boarded with rough boards." New Castle Co., Del., Orphans Court Valuations H.

1797 A house for rent in Alexandria, Virginia, contained "a covered passage leading to a convenient kitchen in the yard below." *Columbia Mirror and Alexandria Gazette.*

1816 "The passage" in a tavern in Person County, North Carolina, "is 10 feet wide and 30 feet long, and is between two separate frame buildings." *Raleigh Register.*

passway A narrow passage between buildings; an alley. See also **alley** (2).

1825 The city council "Ordered that the sergeant take down the steps leading in the courthouse yard and erect a passway similar to that at the clerks office." Fredericksburg, Va., City Council Minute Book 1801–1829.

patera (patra, petra) A circular ornament resembling a shallow disk or other flat medallion worked in bas relief and used as an ornament in friezes and fasciae, often accompanied with festoons of flowers and other decorative elements.

1811 Payment was made to a carpenter for "20 circular patras's @ .50 . . . $10.00." Riddell Accounts, Pleasants Papers, MHS.

pave, pavement *(v.)* To cover or lay a surface with masonry such as brick, tile, and stone so as to create a smooth, level surface. *(n.)* A covering of stone, brick, or tile laid over the surface of a hearth, floor, yard, footway, or street. Brick, tile, and stone pavers were used in work areas of heavy traffic, such as entrances, kitchens, and yards, and in subterranean spaces such as cellars and dairies, where dampness militated against the use of wood flooring. Paving was also an important part of public architecture, used in the public areas of courtrooms and in alleys of churches. In the late colonial and early national period, a sign of urbanity in towns and city was paved streets and walks. Although most southern towns suffered in comparison to Philadelphia and New York, some did have pavings of cobblestones, freestone, and brick tiles in important thoroughfares. See **pavior.**

1674 The ground floor of the statehouse in St. Mary's City was to "be paved with flatt paveing Stone or Brick." *Archives of Maryland, 2.*

1695 The chancel of a church was "to be pav'd with Tile, and a Six foot Ile the length of the Church to be pav'd with Tile." St. Paul's Parish, Kent Co., Md., Vestry Book.

1705 In Williamsburg, it was ordered "that Twelve hundred ffoot of fflage Stone to pave the walks that leads to the Capitol be Sent for to England." *Journals of the House of Burgesses, 4.*

1753 A plantation for sale in Prince William Parish, South Carolina, contained "a good dwelling house with a piazza . . . a garden in the south front, and yard lately paved in." *South Carolina Gazette.*

1756 Henry Laurens of Charleston wrote to a Philadelphia merchant requesting shipment of "two hundred flat Tyles for paving Chimney Hearths, one half red & one half of the blueish colour. We are told these Tyle are made in Pensilvania & are as cheap there as any where else . . . and we are inform'd you have a kind of Stone in your Colony much us'd for pavements before Streets, Doors, Jamms of Windows &c." *Papers of Henry Laurens, 2.*

1802 A Washington bricklayer charged John Tayloe for "256 Yards Herring Bone pavement flat [at] 2/6 . . . D° Plain 1/10 . . . 249 1/2 D° Herring Bone D° Edge [at] 3/9." Tayloe Papers, VHS.

1811 In Alexandria, Virginia, an announcement read: "Notice to Pavers . . . proposals will be received for regulating and paving Commerce-street in a substantial manner, from the end of the present pavement to the east side of West-street, in length about 530 feet, and in width 32, the side stones to be of falls stone, not less than 15 inches deep and well jointed. . . . the largest paving stones to be placed in the gutter and sides thereof towards the centre of the street." *Alexandria Daily Gazette, Commercial and Political.*

pavilion   An ephemeral or ornamental building standing in a garden or pleasure grounds, used for entertainment or shelter like a summerhouse; a projecting subdivision of a larger building, often forming a terminating wing and distinguished by variation in height and roof form.

> 1777   Commenting on his garden structures, Charles Carroll of Carrollton wrote that "I like my pavilions: they are rather small." Charles Carroll Letterbooks, MHS.
> 1807   Thomas Jefferson wrote to one of his brickmakers telling him that "as soon as the spring will possibly permit, we must have the bricks moulded and burnt, and the south pavilion [of Monticello] done before you go to Bedford." Coolidge Collection, Massachusetts Historical Society.
> 1822   Thomas Jefferson wrote to a workman about construction work at the University of Virginia noting that "my frieze is 5 I wide, very nearly, I believe, of the breadth of those of the Ionics you have to do for some of the rooms of the Pavilions." Coolidge Collection, Massachusetts Historical Society.

paving tile   See **tile.**

pavior (paviour)   Material used in paving. See **pave.**

> 1720   "Instead of 1,000 foot of board paviour which I wrote to you for before, I now desire you to send me in two thousand foot." *Letters of Robert Carter 1720–1727.*

pearl color   A greenish white paint, composed of white lead, Prussian blue, and spruce yellow. It was used primarily for interior work.

> 1727   At the Governor's House in Williamsburg, "the great Dining room and Parlor thereto adjoining [are] new painted, the one of pearl colour the other of cream colour." *Executive Journals of the Council of Virginia,* 4.
> 1812   "Pearl Colour" was compounded as follows: "To one pint of white Lead add one teaspoonfull of Prussian blue; and one teaspoonfull of Spruce Yellow, or in that proportion." Reynolds, *Directions for House and Ship Painting.*

pebbledash   Small stones applied to a fresh coat of plaster on an exterior wall to create a textured surface. In contrast to *roughcast,* which is composed of a variety of crushed aggregates mixed with sand and lime and applied with a trowel, pebbledash consists of pebbles that are thrown against the base coat. This form of exterior rendering probably appeared in the South in the early 19th century but never gained widespread popularity. See also **roughcast.**

> 1822   The owner of a house in Prince George's County, Maryland, wrote to architect James Hoban noting that he was "about to plaister & pebble dash my House." Private Papers, Compton Bassett.

pedestal (pedistal)   A support for a column, pilaster, statue, urn, window architrave, or similar structure. Typical of many classical design features, the pedestal is subdivided into three parts: the lowest section known as a base or plinth; a large, flat middle section called a dado or die; and a crowning molded part known as a cornice or cap.

> 1726   A carpenter requested payment for "putting the pedistall and weather cock up repairing the Shingling of the Church." St. Anne's Parish, Anne Arundel Co., Md., Vestry Book.
> 1783   In the library of the Governor's House in New Bern, North Carolina, there were "pedestals on the dado to receive the Window architraves." Hawks Letter, Miranda Papers, Academia Nacional de la Historia, Caracas.
> 1790   A carpenter's work at Hampton in Baltimore County, Maryland, included "making 5 pedistils for orns to stand on a 30 pr £7.10.0." *MHM,* 33.
> 1798   "The pedestals on the South front" of the theater in Alexandria "are designed for the Statue of Shakespeare, with the Tragic and Comic Muse at the West and East corners." *The Times and Alexandria Advertiser.*

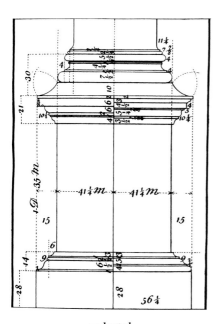

pedestal

pediment (pedement)   A low, triangular gable with a horizontal cornice and raking cornices surmounting a portico, colonnade, wall, or aperture. The raking cornices may be straight, scrolled in the form of an ogee, or part of a curved segment. Pediments whose raking cornices stop or return before they reach the apex were known as *open* or *broken*. Pediments first appear in the Chesapeake in the mid-seventeenth century. They were representative of the artisan mannerist style found in brick buildings such as Bacon's Castle (1665) and Newport Parish Church (1682), where they accentuate the entrance openings. Pedimented porches and overdoors soon followed at the end of the century and the beginning of the next. See also **fronton**.

pediment
John Wright Stanley House,
New Bern, N.C.

1711   A courthouse was to have "a hemsome Peddiment over the front doore supported with well turned Collums and bases of Cedar and Locust." Talbot Co., Md., Land Records Book No. 12.

1746   The design of Charles Pinckney's dwelling in Charleston had "a proper Pediment in the front of the roof over the Balcony." Huger Smith, *Dwelling Houses of Charleston.*

1767   "The Pediments to the doors" in a church were to be "Rubed work in the Tuscan Order." Fairfax Parish, Fairfax Co., Va., Vestry Book.

1771   "Over the Door of" St. John's Church in Granville County, North Carolina, there was to "be a Circular Pediment or shell." Francis Hawks Collection, Church Historical Society, Austin.

1783   A description of the Governor's House in New Bern by its architect John Hawks noted that there were "pediments over the doors" in the hall; the tabernacle frame in the council chamber contained "the proper Entablature fully inric[hed] and an open pediment;" and "in the center of the North front" of the building, "a pediment spans 32 feet, in the Tympan of which is the Kings Arms in alto relievo." Hawks Letter, Miranda Papers, Academia Nacional de la Historia, Caracas.

1785   A courthouse was to have "a Seat for the Judge a pediment over the Seat." Rockbridge Co., Va., Will Book No. 1.

peg (pegg)   A wooden pin of a cylindrical or tapered shape driven through a hole in order to hold two or more parts of a structure together. Carpenters commonly used pegs or, as they were more frequently called, *treenails,* to secure mortise and tenon joints of major framing members. In roofing, pegs were used occasionally to hold shingles and slates to sheathing or laths. See also **treenail**.

1728   On the North Carolina-Virginia border, "most of the Houses in this Part of the Country are Log-houses, covered with Pine or Cypress Shingles, 3 feet long, and one broad. They are hung upon Laths with Peggs." Byrd, *History of the Dividing Line.*

1808   Repairs to an orphanage house roof required "All the slate and boards to be taken off, the slate to be hung on laths with cedar pegs." *Charleston Courier.*

pen (penn)   **1.** A small enclosure for domestic animals such as cows, sheep, swine, and fowl. See also **coop, sty**.

1658   On the Williams plantation in St. Mary's County, Maryland, was a "Cow pen." *Archives of Maryland,* 41.

1670   Several servants "did goe to the hogg penn and killed a barrow." *Archives of Maryland,* 60.

1784   A note read: "Counted the Sheep carefully & their were 32 head including the sick one in the Cow house & the two in the fattening Sheep pen." Richard Henry Lee Memorandum Book, Huntington Library.

2. An enclosure for the confinement or safekeeping of goods or for dwelling. In this sense, *pen* often meant a roughly fabricated log structure. The term came into currency in the late colonial period.

1771   Planter Landon Carter of Richmond County, Virginia, noted that "I find there is no making my carpenters understand me. I only ordered those two roofs of the

penciling
University of Virginia

Riverside cornfield to be put on pens made of logs to lap in across one another; And they have got plates, posts, and sills as if for a new tobacco house." *Diary of Landon Carter.*

1786 A tenant farm in western Virginia contained a "round log cabbin 26 by 20 with inside cat and clay chimney; two round log pens 16 foot each with 14 foot floor between them, the rafters raised but no cover." Jonathan Clark Notebook, Filson Club.

penciling The practice of ruling mortar joints with a narrow white line to enhance the appearance of brick masonry. Penciling was applied after the entire wall had received a coat of red paint nearly matching the color of the brick. The term derives from the small brush used in this sort of work, referred to as a *pencil*. The technique saw widespread use by the early 19th century, when the practice of painting masonry surfaces became common.

1808 The outer walls of a new building for the Bank of Kentucky were to be "faced with stock brick, neatly penciled." *The Reporter.*

1810 In Baltimore, James Mosher's account with Judith Riddell included a charge for "rubbing down, oiling and penciling the front" of her house. Riddell Accounts, Pleasants Papers, MHS.

1831 Brick walls of the new courthouse were to be "laid in Flemish bond and penciled down." Caswell Co., N.C., Court Minutes, 1823–1831.

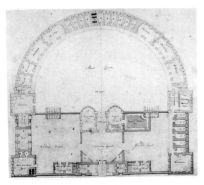

penitentiary
B. H. Latrobe, drawings of the Penitentiary House, Richmond, 1797.
Above: View in perspective of the gate
Below: Ground plan

penitentiary A place of imprisonment and reformation of inmates through discipline, work, and reflection. The prison reform movement in England and America in the late 18th century slowly transformed the way in which society treated its miscreants. In the colonial period, those convicted of a felonious crime were subjected to corporal and shaming public punishments. Under the watchful and reveling gaze of a court day crowd, felons were whipped, branded, pilloried, and hanged on courthouse grounds. Correction of antisocial behavior was swift and humiliating. Advocates of penal reform believed that such cruel punishment failed to curb crime and wasted human potential. They argued that those who broke the law should be given a chance to redeem themselves and reform their behavior through confinement and work in a prison designed to promote reflection and regeneration. Prison discipline included enforced silence, manual labor, and chapel services. By the last decade of the 18th century, Southerners began to accept the need for penal reform. The Virginia legislature revised the state's penal code in 1796 and called for the construction of a large, centralized prison or *penitentiary house.* The next year, architect Benjamin Henry Latrobe won the competition for the design of the building. Penitentiary design made a strong break from prison architecture of the colonial period. Rather than being thrown together in a common dungeon or crowded jail, prisoners in a penitentiary were given private cells so that they would not be corrupted by their fellow inmates. These cells were arranged around long corridors that extended out from a main block or formed a curved segment around a central administrative core. Workshops and exercise yards were interspersed around this central observation post, which provided a post from which to monitor and regulate activities. See also **prison.**

1797 Benjamin Henry Latrobe wrote to the governor of Virginia "to offer my services in the design of the Penitentiary houses voted by the last Legislative Assembly." *The Correspondence and Miscellaneous Papers of Benjamin Henry Latrobe,* 1.

1815 "The improvement of Milldedgeville . . . is a source of gratification. . . . Among several new houses recently erected, is the Penitentiary or State-Prison. This stupendous building adds greatly to the appearance of the town." *Georgia Journal.*

pent (appentice, pent-house) A lean-to or shed attached to a structure, with a single sloped roof and either open or enclosed on the sides.

1683 Repairs to a church required "that ye earth be firmly ram'd under the sells, and a convenient pent house made to keepe the raine off them." Christ Church Parish, Middlesex Co., Va., Vestry Book.

1704 A courthouse was to have "a handsome pent-house over the interior dore." Middlesex Co., Va., Court Order Book 1694–1705.

1725 A carpenter was ordered "to take off the Roof of the pent house Round the Church . . . and to raise the Roof higher and put on new Rafters and Cover it with good Boards." All Saints Parish, Calvert Co., Md., Vestry Book.

perch (pearch) A solid measure used for stonework, generally considered to be sixteen and a half feet long, one and a half feet thick, and one foot high. However, measurements varied widely in different localities.

1772 An account for building a dwelling in Odessa, Delaware listed "laying 109 Perch of Stone [in] Seller at 3/9 per perch £20.8.9." Sweeney, *Grandeur on the Appoquinimink.*

1792 A payment was made "to Brewer Reeves for 7 2/3 pearch's of Mason work at 6/ pr pearch in raising the court house more than was in the agreement or contract of letting, It appearing to the court that the same was necessary to allow room for the cornish above the windows." Rockingham Co., Va., Court Order Book 1791–1794.

1794 "PROPOSALS will be received . . . for Building a stone chapel in" Hagerstown, Maryland, "for the use of the Roman Catholic congregation." The undertaker "must mention what he will do it for by the perch of the wall—that is sixteen feet and one half a foot in length and one foot in height of the whole thickness . . . 20 inches thick." *Washington Spy.*

1814 Thomas Jefferson wrote to a stonemason that "I have about 80 or 100 perch of stone work to be laid at Poplar Forest in Bedford, 10 miles from Lynchburg: and also from one to two hundred perch to lay at this place; in all of which I should be willing to employ you. The work in Bedford might be done by the perch; but for that here I would rather pay you a reasonable monthly hire, because difficulties and delays in hauling materials sometimes unavoidably occur, which I would rather should be at my own loss, than to have complaints." Coolidge Collection, Massachusetts Historical Society.

peripteral In classical architecture, a building, especially a temple, surrounded by a single row of columns. See also **peristyle.**

c. 1786 In Thomas Jefferson's notes for the design of the Virginia state capitol, he referred to "The example of the Peripter, temple Vitruv. pa. 67." Jefferson Papers, Huntington Library.

peristyle In classical architecture, a building surrounded by a colonnade or a courtyard or room wholly or partially ringed by a series of freestanding columns. See also **astylar, prostyle.**

1821 In architect William Nichols's remodeling of the statehouse in Raleigh, "the Commons Hall is of a semi-elliptical form to contain four rows of desks and chairs arranged as in the Senate with a gallery and vaulted ceiling supported by a peristyle of columns of the same order." *Raleigh Register, and North Carolina Gazette.*

pesthouse A building to quarantine those with contagious diseases. Pesthouses were often built in or near port cities to confine sailors and slaves infected with such diseases. See also **hospital (3), lazaretto.**

1747 It was ordered that the "Church wardens pay Mr. Motte his expenses of twenty shillings for sending down a Negroe Wench who has the Leprosye to the Pest House & also pay the charges of keeping her there which is 15/ pr week & provide a gown for her." St. Philip's Parish, Charleston, S.C., Vestry Book.

1756 A Charleston merchant wrote to a business associate in Barbados that "our Pest House where the slaves are to be placed during their Quarantine is in good order." *The Papers of Henry Laurens, 2.*

1787 The sheriff was ordered to repair "the Pest House so as to be commodious for persons infected with the small Pox or any other contagious disorder to resort to." Norfolk Co., Va., Court Order Book 1786–1787.

1793 "Whereas it is reported . . . that a negro in the service of Mr. John Moody hath lately broken out with the Small Pox, to the great alarm of many of the inhabitants of the City," a committee was formed "to procure a pest-house, and have the said negro removed thereto." Richmond, Va., Common Council Records, 1793–1806.

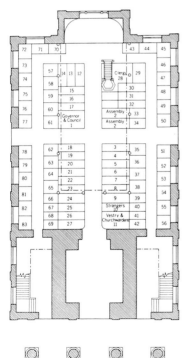

pew
Above: St. James Santee, Charleston County, S.C.
Below: 1760 pew plan, St. Michael's Church, Charleston, S.C.

pew (pugh) One of a number of fixed benches enclosed by paneled partitions and doors used to seat some or all members of a congregation in a church or meetinghouse. These fixtures came into common use in Anglican churches in Virginia in the last quarter of the 17th century and continued to be used throughout the South in many churches and meetinghouses until they went out of fashion in the second quarter of the 19th century. Members of the congregation generally sat in pews assigned or purchased by them. Except for some dissenting congregations such as the Baptists and Friends, seats in many churches were assigned to individuals according to social status, sex, and age. Some had specially designated pews for local magistrates, vestrymen, and occasionally for strangers. With the addition of cushions, curtains, shelves, and warming devices, pews provided a greater sense of privacy, warmth, and comfort during the long hours spent in communal worship. They were generally arranged in squares or rectangles interspersed by aisles or alleys. Supported by brackets, benches within a pew often lined three or four sides, with the result that many worshipers sat with their backs away from the pulpit or communion table. By the beginning of the second quarter of the 19th century, this pattern of seating began to give way to ones where all members of the congregation faced forward toward the pulpit and communion table in seats known as *slip pews.* Not all churches or meetinghouses were pewed. Many only had benches or forms for their members. Others had only part of the building pewed, with areas away from the pulpit and communion table having only benches. While some galleries had pews, many contained only benches. Among some dissenting groups such as the Friends, such comfortable and costly seating arrangements were an anathema to their notions of worship.

1677 Directives for building a church specify "2 wainscoate double pews one of each side of ye Chancell, Joyning to ye Scrime with ballisters suitable to ye pulpitt & deske Joyninge to ye Scrime, all ye rest of ye pews of both sides of ye said church to be double, and all to be done wth wainscoate Backs." Petsworth Parish, Gloucester Co., Va., Vestry Book.

1711 An Anglican church was to have "five high framed Pewes, three of the south side and two of the north side, the Rest of the Church to be Divided into pewes five foot wide to be seated round." Christ Church Parish, Middlesex Co., Va., Vestry Book.

1726 It was "Ordered that Certificates be made ready to give each person a title to the Pew they have purchased." St. Helena's Parish, S.C., Vestry Book.

1741 "Mr. Simon Duffe agrees with the Vestry to Build & finish a Pew fronting Mr. Dulanys also a Pew next Adjoyning in the new addition for the use of the

Honble Speaker of the Lower House of Assembly of four feet wide." St. Anne's Parish, Anne Arundel Co., Md., Vestry Book.
1789 It was "Order'd that John Callinder be employ'd to paint on the Door of the Pew opposite the Pulpitt in Black or White Letters the Word Strangers." St. George's Parish, Spotsylvania Co., Va., Vestry Book.

piazza (piaza, piazer, peazer, peazor, peeaza)   **1.** In Italy, the piazza was an open public square or space surrounded by buildings. In 17th-century England, by misapplication the term referred to the covered walk or gallery surrounding an open square, as at Covent Garden or the Royal Exchange. In the colonial South, this meaning of the term appears in Virginia by the end of the 17th century to indicate an arcaded space found in public buildings such as the College of William and Mary, the first capitol, and county courthouses. See also **arcade.**

> **1699** The cross wing of the Williamsburg capitol was to be "raised upon piazza, and built as high as the other parts of the building." Jefferson Papers, LC.
> **1732** In Yorktown, Virginia, "they are just finishing a Court house or Town hall of Brick with a Piazza before it [which is] very handsom and Convenient." *VMHB*, 22.
> **1736** A new courthouse was "to have Eight Arches or Piazas in the outside wall frunting ye Courte." Spotsylvania Co., Va., Will Book 1722–1749.

piazza (1)
Courthouse, Hanover County, Va.

2. A covered open porch or veranda supported by columns or pillars and attached to the outside of a building. The use of the term in this sense appears in South Carolina by the second quarter of the 18th century and slowly moves up the seaboard. By the end of the century, this meaning of the term becomes the most common and appears throughout the South. In domestic architecture, piazzas were used as reception areas for visitors and provided a relatively cool and shady place to sit or entertain. See also **balcony, porch.**

> **1738** A minister was "requested to confer with a workman about Building a piazza on the back side" of the parsonage house. St. John's Parish, Berkeley Co., S.C., Vestry Book.
> **1739** "A shade or PA*" was to be added "on the front of the Parsonage House." Prince Frederick, Winyah Parish, S.C., Vestry Book.
> **1748** For sale in Charleston was a dwelling house with "a piazza 12 feet wide and 48 long paved with good square stone." *South Carolina Gazette.*
> **1773** In Edenton, North Carolina, James Iredell "Spoke to Mr. Jones in his Piazza, walked with him in his Garden, but was not asked in to his house." *The Papers of James Iredell,* 1.
> **1773** An orphan's estate was described as having "a framed dwelling house 56 feet long and 32 feet wide with an 8 feet piazza on one side." Queen Anne's Co., Md., Deed Book K.
> **1787** In New Bern, "there are to many of the houses Balconies or Piazzas in front and sometimes back of the house, this Method of Building is found convenient on account of the great Summer Heats here." Attmore, *Journal of a Tour to North Carolina.*
> **1795** A dwelling was described as having "a porch or a piazza on the easternmost side of the house about 21 feet long by 7 feet wide plank floor with seats." Worcester County, Md., Orphans Court Proceedings 1792–1797.
> **1809** At an ordinary in Halifax County, Virginia, "it was now morning, & many of the young people . . . were seated or walking for their amuzement in the cool shade of a long piazza, enjoying the morning breezes." *Journal of William D. Martin.*

piazza (2)
Above: Charles Fraser, Brabrant, French Quarter Creek, S.C., 1800.
Below: B. H. Latrobe, Mount Vernon, Fairfax County, Va.

3. An enclosed passageway or room between two buildings, generally the main structure and an ancillary space such as a kitchen or workroom. It contained the principal stair. Although this meaning of the term can be found in the South, its use in this sense was not as common as it was further north in Philadelphia and the Delaware Valley.

1799 For sale in Richmond was a three-story house. "Adjoining this building is a kitchen, laundry, office, coach house . . . lodging rooms for domestics. This building is connected to the house by a double piazza." *Virginia Gazette.*

1800 Ground floor rooms of a large house sold by auction in Baltimore had "an entry, parlor, dining and housekeeper's room which by a piazza and pantry communicate with a spacious brick kitchen." *The Times and District of Columbia Daily Advertiser.*

picked in In painting, this term referred to the use of a contrasting color to highlight carved or raised ornament.

1805 At the Bank of Pennsylvania, Benjamin Latrobe recommended the following color scheme for one of the ceilings: "The ridges of the ceiling pale blue, moulding white, the rose white, picked in with blue." *The Correspondence and Miscellaneous Papers of Benjamin Henry Latrobe, 2.*

picture slip A horizontal wooden strip from which to hang pictures, generally found in the best or most important room of a house.

1798 An agreement between Jeremiah Satterwhite and St. George Tucker stipulated colors for the "picture slips, windows, & other parts of the front & back passage." Tucker Papers, W&M.

picket (picquet) A narrow wooden stake pointed at one end to facilitate driving into the ground. Pickets were used collectively to construct fences, much like *palisades*. Rails and other bracing elements were sometimes incorporated. The term made only rare documentary appearances until about the middle of the nineteenth century, by which time it had also acquired another meaning. During the early 1800s, relatively thin, decorative fence pales came to be specified as *pickets*. By 1900 the term denoted all pales, regardless of size, finish, or even material, a meaning that persists today. See also **pale.**

1811 The garden at Poplar Forest in Bedford County, Virginia, was "to be inclosed with a picquet fence, 7. feet high, & so close that a hare cannot get into it. it is 80. yards square, & will take, I suppose about 2400. rails 8 f. long, besides the running rails & stakes. the sheep to be folded in it every night." *Thomas Jefferson's Garden Book.*

pier
Slave quarter, Upper Brandon,
Prince George County, Va.

pier (peer) **1.** A short piece of masonry, square or rectangular in section, used to support the frame of a building; also a masonry or wood piling support for a bridge.

1712 It was "Ordered that Mr. Alexander Graves build Jetts & Peers of brick for ye Sleepers to be laid on." Christ Church Parish, Middlesex Co., Va., Vestry Book.

1806 A chapel was to be built "near Black-Oak in St. John's Parish [South Carolina], 25 feet square, on brick piers three feet high." *City Gazette and Daily Advertiser.*

1809 The Potomac Bridge in Washington "is supported by 201 piers, 25 feet opening. Each pier is composed of 5 piles on the flats, 6 in the channel, and 7 at the draw." *American and Commercial Daily Advertiser.*

2. A mass of masonry in a wall between apertures; the mass of masonry between arches in an arcade.

1734 A church was to have a "galery at the west end as long as the peer will admitt." Bristol Parish, Prince George Co., Va., Vestry Book.

1804 An architect charged with finishing the Capitol in Washington noted the shortcomings of earlier designs saying that "the arrangement of Columns either of 32 or 24 in number, has no possible reference to the piers and windows." *The Correspondence and Miscellaneous Papers of Benjamin Henry Latrobe, 1.*

3. A pillar or post on which a gate or door is hung.

1719 A wall was to be built around a churchyard with "Two Wide Handsom Gates made after the form of Iron Gates with Handsom Square Peares (or Posts) for the

Gates, with a hollow Spire at Top." St. Peter's Parish, New Kent Co., Va., Vestry Book.
1774 A churchyard wall was "to have three pier gates." Truro Parish, Fairfax Co., Va., Vestry Book.

pigeonhole One of a series of recessed compartments or boxes in a cabinet, desk, or bookpress, used for sorting and storing papers, letters, and documents. Named for their similarity to nesting roosts in pigeon houses, pigeonholes in domestic and public furniture came into fashion in the early 18th century. In order to keep track of the voluminous paperwork of court cases, county clerks began to install numerous bookpresses subdivided by pigeonholes in their offices by the second quarter of the 18th century.
1731 Payment was made to a carpenter for building "a Case of pigeon holes." Jones Papers, LC.
1802 "To be erected in the record room" of a county clerk's office were "shelves pigeon holes and sliding doors." Culpeper Co., Va., Court Order Book 1802–1803.

pigeon house A structure housing doves or pigeons, with multiple entrances and internal niches or boxes for roosting and nesting. Some pigeon houses are freestanding buildings, often round in plan or raised above ground level on posts. Some are essentially enclosed rows of boxes affixed to walls of dwelling houses or outbuildings. Regardless of size and configuration, pigeon houses are designed to ensure a ready supply of pigeons and facilitate the retrieving of eggs and birds. See also **dovecote.**
1724 Standing on a plantation in Kent County, Maryland, was a "pigeon house ten foot square." Kent Co., Md., Court Records.
1751 A plantation had a "pigeon house 8 feet square." Queen Anne's Co., Md., Deed Book D.
1764 In Richmond County, Virginia, "Colo. Tayloe's Ralph [was] sent back here to cut my dishing capstones for my Pigeonhouse posts to keep down the rats." *Diary of Landon Carter*, 1.

pigeon roof A tall pyramidal roof of four equally sloped sides, so named after the type often constructed on pigeon houses. See also **hipped roof.**
1735 It was "Ordered that there be built for the Reverend Mr. John Becket on the Gleeb land a meat house ten foot square eight foot pitch pigeon roof." St. Mark's Parish, Culpeper Co., Va., Vestry Book.
1773 A twelve-foot square dairy was "to have a pidgion roof . . . covered with the best juniper cypress shingles." Fairfax Parish, Fairfax Co., Va., Vestry Book.

pig iron Smelted ore that is cast into ingots or pigs. Pig iron was used to produce wrought iron or steel.
1767 Charles Carroll of Mount Clare near Baltimore wrote to merchants in Bristol that "I shall Ship you in the first of your Ships that arrive here Bar and Pig Iron that will Amount in Value to about one hundred and thirty Pounds Sterling." Trostel, *Mount Clare.*
1777 At the ironwork of Mr. Hunter of Falmouth, Virginia, workmen made "(from Pig Iron) Bar Iron, Anchors, all Kinds of Blacksmith's Work, Small Arms, Pistols, Swords, Files, Fuller's Shears, & Nails." *VMHB*, 62.

pigment A pulverized substance made of organic or inorganic matter that when combined with a liquid vehicle such as linseed oil, becomes a paint. Throughout the colonial and early national periods, most paint pigments were imported from England. See also **paint.**

pigeon house
Bowman's Folly, Accomack County, Va.

pilaster
United States Bank (now City Hall),
Charleston, S.C., 1801

pilaster (pillaster) An engaged pier or square column projecting slightly from a wall and furnished with a base, capital, and entablature. Pilasters were frequently used in frontispieces, chimney pieces, and altarpieces, and also served to mark the ends of balustrades, colonnades, galleries, piazzas (2), porticos, and other columnar spaces. See also **column, pier, pillar.**

1767 The owner of Mount Clare in Baltimore County, Maryland, planned to construct a portico in front of his house with imported English stone consisting of "Round Columns . . . and Pilasters." Trostel, *Mount Clare.*
1774 A carpenter fabricated "49 ft 10 ins fluted Pilasters . . . 6 ft 6 ins Caps to Pilasters . . . 1 Pediment" in a house in Odessa, Delaware. Sweeney, *Grandeur on the Appoquinimink.*
1783 In the council room in the Governor's House in New Bern, "the Ornaments over the marble Chimney Commonly called Tabernacle Frame consists of Corinthian Columns and pillasters fluited with the proper Entablature fully inric[hed] and an open pediment." Hawks Letter, Miranda Papers, Academia Nacional de la Historia, Caracas.
1802 Carpentry charges for construction of the Tayloe house in Washington, D.C., included "open pilaster run 1/6 . . . Ornamental Chimney pilasters to library 3/ . . . ornamental Pilaster, Base & Cap 3/6." Tayloe Papers, VHS.

pile 1. One of a series of large timbers driven into marshy or soft ground to form a solid foundation for the superstructure of a building or structures such as wharves and bridges.

1736 "Resolv'd forthwith to rebuild the Battery before Johnson's Fort, for which there will be wanted a large quantity of Bricks, Lime, Piles, Mud, Earth, and Ballast Stone." *South Carolina Gazette.*
1768 A notice read: "Wanted by the COMMISSIONERS of FORTICATIONS, three thousand Pine-PILES, from four to five inches diameter, and from eight to ten feet long, with a thickness sufficient to square six inches." *South Carolina and American General Gazette.*
1773 In the design of a prison for Edenton, North Carolina, architect John Hawks noted that "it may be a necessary precaution to drive piles close to the Walls on the inside and three or four feet below the Foundation to prevent undermining in case the floor is broke up or any person on the outside should attempt giving assistance, the tops of these piles after drove should be level with the underside of the oak joist that receive the floor." Hawks Papers, SHC.
1785 A wharf builder "professes . . . the capacity of building a complete pile-driver . . . and recommends the driving of large piles on the outside walls of every wharf, which is the custom in Baltimore." *Virginia Journal and Alexandria Advertiser.*
1809 "Each pier" of the bridge spanning the Potomac River in Washington "is composed of 5 piles on the flats, 6 in the channel, and 7 at the draw. These piles are driven from 20 to 30 feet into the mud, and strongly braced and bolted." *American and Commercial Daily Advertiser.*

2. A large or imposing building.

1741 The College of William and Mary in Williamsburg was described as "a lofty pile advanced with a Cupola." Oldmixon, *The British Empire in America.*
1775 The outside of the statehouse in Annapolis "is compleated & is a noble, spacious pile of building & I think in a very good Taste." *Dr. Robert Honyman's Journal.*
1796 The Capitol in Williamsburg "is a heavy brick pile with a two story-portico towards the street." *The Virginia Journals of Benjamin Henry Latrobe,* 1.

3. The depth of a building measured by the number of rooms. A double-pile dwelling is two rooms deep, arranged from front to rear. *Pile* in this sense was not used in the early South.

pillar (piller, pillow) In the broadest sense, any vertical support made of wood, masonry, metal, or other material, used to sustain the weight of a superstructure. Pillars were either round, square, or rectangular in plan and varied from plain to elaborate in ornamentation and finish.

The term was used loosely and interchangeably in the colonial and early national periods to refer to a *column, pier, pilaster,* or *post.* See also **underpin.**

> 1727 The Anglican church built at St. James, Goose Creek, South Carolina, was adorned with "two rows of round timber pillers, painted marble." SPG Letterbook A, SPGFP.
>
> 1742 Plans for a barn required that it be "under pined with good brick pillers laid in good mortar." Bristol Parish, Prince George Co., Va., Vestry Book.
>
> 1755 A "poarch [is to] be built to the Glebe House nine feet square, sett on brick pillows." Stratton Major Parish, King and Queen Co., Va., Vestry Book.
>
> 1760 A church was to have "five Pillars of Cypress on each side for the support of the Roof, the Columns to be 15 inches Diameter at the bottom of the Shaft, to be Fluted & the Capitols of the Dorick Order." Stratton Major Parish, King and Queen Co., Va., Vestry Book.
>
> 1766 The exterior walls of a church were "to have four Columns or Pillars in each carried up in the Bricks half a brick thick from the outside." Chester Parish, Kent Co., Md. Vestry Book.
>
> 1767 "The lower Floor [is] to be a girt Frame with a Pillar of Brick under each girder." Amelia Co., Va., Loose Court Papers.
>
> 1770 "There shall be proper Joints and Buttresses made to support a Gallery in the West end of the Church with neat turned posts or pillars erected for the same purpose." St. John's Parish, Queen Anne's Co., Md., Vestry Book.
>
> 1788 A market house to be built in Charleston was "to be on brick pillars arched." *City Gazette or the Daily Advertiser.*
>
> 1821 Joseph Freeman of Gates County, North Carolina paid Jethrow Harrell ten dollars "for Building one Chimney an underpillering of his house." Joseph Freeman Papers, Private Papers.

pillar
Mount Airy, Richmond County, Va.

pillory An instrument of punishment composed of a post with boards with holes to secure the head and hands, used to subject felonious offenders to public ridicule. Far more brutal than the stocks, the pillory was reserved for those who committed serious offenses such as rape, perjury, forgery, counterfeiting, and hog stealing. Those who were placed in the pillory had one or both ears nailed against the headboard. When the offender was removed from the pillory after an hour or a day, part of the ear was cut off, marking the guilty as a person of *evil fame.* Required by law in Virginia and other colonies, pillories and other public instruments of punishment stood in a prominent position on the courthouse grounds. With changing sensibilities and notions of punishment, pillories gradually disappeared from public places in the second quarter of the 19th century. See also **stocks.**

> 1619 A servant convicted of false accusations against his master was sentenced to "stand fowere dayes with his eares nayled to the Pillory." *Records of the Virginia Company,* 3.
>
> 1648 Convicted of perjury by the Kent County, Maryland, court, John Goneere was "to be nailed by both ears to the Pillory with 3 nails in each ear and the Nailes to be slitt out, & afterwards to be whipped with 20 good lashes. And this to be executed immediately before any other business of Court be proceeded upon." Maryland Patents, Certificates, and Warrants 1637–1650, MSA.
>
> 1688 "Whereas Mary the wife of John Cole hath in a most notorious & insolent manner in contempt of his Majesties Lawes & Authority . . . losed & pulled out a naile fastened to the ear of Micha Wardell in the Pillory for a fact by him committed the Court think fitt as a just reward for her said offence and to warn others from the Same that She Stand two howers tyed fast to the Pillory with her back thereto & her face to the Court house with a Paper fastened to her breast written in Capital Letters viz. for her contempt of authority." Accomack Co., Va., Will and Order Book 1682–1697.

pin (pinn) A small, cylindrical piece of wood or metal used to fasten or support. The terms *pin, peg, dowel,* and *treenail* were all used to describe the wooden piece used to secure two members together. Pins were used to keep the lower sash of a window open by inserting them into holes drilled into the lining of the window frame.

> **1717** It was ordered that the churchyard fence "rails . . . be well Tenoned into the posts with Shoulders and the upper most Rail . . . be pinned into the post." All Saints Parish, Calvert Co., Md., Vestry Book.
>
> **1747** In a church, "the munting sashes [are] to be supported when up with Iron pins made fast to the frame with a Leather thong." Albemarle Parish, Surry Co., Va., Vestry Book.
>
> **1813** The under floor of a jail in Reynoldsburg, Tennessee, was "to be laid first with hewed logs, 12 inches thick well pined." *The Clarion and Tennessee Gazette.*

pincer (pincher, pinser) A metal tool similar in shape to a pair of pliers, used mainly for pulling nails. See also **nipper.**

> **1667** Inventory of the goods of a Somerset County, Maryland, household listed "a paire of pinsers." Maryland Testamentary Proceedings 1666–1668, MSA.
>
> **1783** Tools owned by a Fairfax County, Virginia, man included "1 pair of pinchers & nippers." Fairfax Co., Va., Will Book 1776–1782.

pine (pyne) One of the most common softwoods used in building, pine consists of a number of species of reddish yellow wood. Southern yellow pine, which includes the *loblolly, shortleaf, slash,* and *longleaf* varieties, flourishes throughout the South and became the principal building material in the colonial and early national periods. Pine, the most versatile of woods, was used in framing, flooring, weatherboards, shingles, wainscotting, and other interior woodwork. Northern white pine was imported into the South in a limited supply, especially in the late 18th and early 19th centuries.

> **1674** The floors of the statehouse in St. Mary's City were "to be laid with quartered planck inch & quarter thick after plained either good white Oke or Pine of this Countrey sawen while the Turpentine is in them." *Archives of Maryland,* 2.
>
> **1709** "Of Pines, there are, in *Carolina,* at least, four sorts. The Pitch-Pine, growing to a great Bigness, most commonly has but a short Leaf. Its Wood (being replete with abundance of *Bitumen*) is so durable, that it seems to suffer no Decay, tho' exposed to all Weathers, for many Ages; and is used in several Domestick and Plantation Uses. This Tree affords the four great Necessaries, Pitch, Tar, Rozin, and Turpentine; which two last are extracted by tapping, and the Heat of the Sun, the other two by the Heat of the Fire. The white and yellow Pines are saw'd into Planks for several Uses. They make Masts, Yards, and a great many other Necessaries therewith, the Pine being the most useful Tree in the Woods." Lawson, *A New Voyage to Carolina.*
>
> **1734** "To be sold by John Lining" in Charleston, "a Pine Frame of a Dutch roof'd House . . . ready to raise." *South Carolina Gazette.*
>
> **1763** It was "Ordered that the Rafters of the church already let out instead of oak the hart of old pine 14 by 8 inches at the foot and 8 inches square at the Corner and that the coller Beams be the same wood 12 deep by 8 inches." St. George's Parish, Accomack Co., Va., Vestry Book.
>
> **1792** "THE Commissioners of the Federal Buildings" in Washington "will contract for the following quantity of best yellow Pine Flooring-Plank . . . 10,000 feet, 32 feet in length, 5 inches wide, and 1 1/2 do thick—20,000 feet, 30 feet in length, 5 inches wide, and 1 1/2 thick . . . to be free of sap and knots—the logs to be quartered, and the hearts taken out. They will also contract for 150,000 feet of Northern, clear, white Pine Plank—one half of inch thick." *Virginia Gazette and Alexandria Advertiser.*
>
> **1797** "I was not very well informed respecting the difference of Virginian and Northern pine. . . . I have [now] particularly examined the two sorts, and seen them worked upon, and find that they differ exactly as yellow and white deal do in Europe. The former is more durable, resists the effects of Wet, and retains a better color than the latter. It is fuller of turpentine. On this account it is more usefull for all external works, for floors, and for every thing that is not to be painted. The clean

and best sort works well under the plan, and for general uses it is as good as the best plank in the World. But it has qualities which peculiarly and wholly unfit it for the purpose of centers. It cannot be nailed without boring, and when nailed it holds the nail so fast and splits so easily that the nail, or plank, or both, is lost, in taking the Center asunder." *The Correspondence and Miscellaneous Papers of Benjamin Henry Latrobe*, 1.

pineapple   In early usage, the seed cone of a pine tree. An ancient symbol of fertility, this natural form came to be frequently used as a terminal element in 18th-century design. It appeared as the finial for a hipped roof, the crowning feature of a pulpit, and the central element of an ogee pediment.

1760   In Charleston, Henry Burnett's bill for carving the pulpit at St. Michael's Church included a charge of £12 for "1 Pine Apple of the top of the Pulpit." Williams, *St. Michael's*.

pinery   A heated stove house used for growing pineapples. See also **stove house.**

1770   A visitor to Mount Clare near Baltimore noted that its owner, Charles Carroll, "is now building a Pinery where the Gardr expects to raise about an 100 Pine Apples a Year. He expect to Ripen some next Sumer." *VMHB*, 45.

pinnacle   A small ornamental turret, generally terminating in a pyramid or ball, which rises above the roof of a building. See also **finial, pyramid.**

pintle   See **hook.**

pissduit   A channel or drain to carry off urine and waste from a necessary house.

1696   In Annapolis, a proposal was made "to Contrive a Pissduit and House of Office some where near the State House." *Archives of Maryland*, 19.

pit (pitt)   **1.** The lowered space at the front of a theater abutting the stage, containing the cheapest seats in the house. See also **box, theater.**

1796   In Petersburg, a lot was "to be purchased or Leased for a Fram'd Theatre of the following dimentions—Eighty five feet—in length—Forty five feet wide and thirty five in hight. The foundation to be built with Brick or Stone Seven feet high—The Building to Consist of a Stage upper and under Boxes, a Pitt, & proper Offices, together with two Dressing rooms under the Stage." Petersburg, Va., Hustings Court, Deed Book 2.

1797   In the newly opened Petersburg theater, an evening's performance included "A New Comedy, called The Rage; or A Picture of present Manners. . . . The Comic Song of 'The Learned Pig,' by Mr. Turnbull. To which will be added the Comic Opera of Peeping Tom of Coventry. Tickets to be had at Mr. Armistead's Tavern at the Printing Office, and at the Office of the Theatre! Boxes 6s Pitt 4s 6d." *Virginia Gazette & Petersburg Intelligencer*.

2. A hole excavated underneath scaffolding on which logs are placed to be sawn into boards. Two sawyers—one on top of the log and one in the pit—use a whip or pit saw to cut the log into separate pieces, stopping short of the log's end. After all cuts are made the remaining, uncut ends of the boards are split loose. Marks left on boards that have been pit sawn are characterized by groupings of relatively vertical and straight striations, with the marks occasionally changing their angle relative to the board's edge as the angle of the saw is altered to accommodate the sawyers stepping in the direction of the cut.

pineapple
Gunston Hall, Fairfax County, Va.

1760 "Mike and Tom began sawing in the Pit some considerable time after Sun rise and Cut 122 feet of Scantling." *Diaries of George Washington*, 1.

3. The heartwood of a tree. In many wood species the heartwood was valued for its durability and resistance to rot.

1741 Thomas Williams contracted to "compleat the said house at his own expense & also saw & deliver so much inch plank from Pitt as will be sufficient to lay an upper floare of a house twelve by sixteen when the same is seasoned & joynted & will for consideration of two hundred pounds current money of Virginia to be paid." Bristol Parish, Prince George Co., Va., Vestry Book.

pitch 1. The height of a wall measured between the sill and the plate. Nearly all 17th- and 18th-century references to pitch imply wall height rather than roof angle. By the middle of the 19th century the use of the term with this meaning had all but disappeared.

1641 A Norfolk County, Virginia, "store [is] to be built 60 feet long and 20 wide, 8 feet pitch." VMHB, 41.

1646 "It is inacted, that there be two houses built . . . of forty foot long apeece with good and substantial timber, the houses to be twenty foot broad apeece, eight foot high in the pitche and a stack of brick chimneys standing in the midst of each house." Hening, *Statutes at Large*, 1.

1736 It was ordered that a prison be constructed with the "pitch or Distance between the Floore and floore withinside to be not less than seven Foot." Carteret Co., N.C., Court of Pleas and Quarter Sessions.

1744 A house was to be built with a "ten foot pitch between the upper part of the Syll & lower side of the Plate." Truro Parish, Fairfax Co., Va., Vestry Book.

1824 "The pitch of the [court] house [is] to be 14 feet from floor to ceiling." Person Co., N.C., Miscellaneous Court Records, NCA&H.

2. The angle of a roof, or the proportion between the height and the span of the roof. The meaning of the term in this context rarely appeared before the late 18th century but became standard usage by the mid-19th century. See also **square roof.**

1726 "Pitch. The angle of a Gable End and consequently the whole Roof of a Building. If the Length of each Rafter be 3/4 of the breadth of the building, then the Roof is said to be True Pitch. If the Rafters are longer, tis said to be a high or sharp pitch'd Roof; if shorter, which seldom happens, is said to be a low or flat pitch'd Roof." Neve, *City and County Purchaser*.

1761 A Virginia carpenter noted that "it is a Rule amongst workmen, that the Flat of any House, and half the Flat thereof, taken within the Walls is equal to the mesure of the Roof of the same House; but this is when the Roof is true Pitch; for if the Roof be more flat or steep than the true Pitch, it will be more or less accordingly." William Ellett Arithmetic Book, Duke.

1799 Specifications for a North Carolina house modeled after stylish Philadelphia examples noted that the "pitch of the roof to be rather flatter than the common run of the Buildings in or near Salisbury." John Steele Papers, SHC.

3. A gable roof. This meaning of the term seems confined to South Carolina through the late 18th century.

1755 A house to "be erected on part of the public ground near the work-house . . . with a pitch roof." *South Carolina Gazette*.

1815 A wooden church was "to be hip at one end & pitch at the other." St. John's, Colleton, S.C., Vestry Book.

4. A tarry, resinous substance obtained from pine trees and used for coating wood surfaces for protection, or used as a binding agent.

1759 A rafter in a church was to be repaired with a splice after "having filled the inside with good pitch, so as to stop all the Crevices." St. George's Parish, Harford Co., Md., Vestry Book.

place brick See **brick.**

plain Unadorned, without patterning or elaboration. Because the term was used so widely, its meaning was never precise. It was used to provide a general guideline for the level of elaboration or detailed ornamentation desired for a building or part of a building. When used for specific details, it signified little or no embellishments. In working out the meaning of this term on the building site, this generally implied unbeaded edges, no moldings on a jamb, no carved enrichments on a molding, and a cornice without modillions. See also **enrich, fashionable, neat.**

1666 A dwelling was to have "two plaine frames for windows." Norfolk Co., Va., Will and Deed Book 1656–1666.

1698 In Somerset County, Maryland, the "Dissenters hath a house at Snow Hill, Quakers one at the Road going up along the Seaside, & one at Nearoakin about 30 feet long, plain country buildings, all of them." Perry, *American Colonial Church,* 4.

1721 The interior of a chapel was "to be common plain work." Bristol Parish, Prince George Co., Va., Vestry Book.

1793 "Old East," the first building on the campus at the University of North Carolina was to be "executed in a plain but neat substantial & workmanlike manner." University Archives, UNC, Chapel Hill.

1800 In making an estimate of the costs of finish carpentry for John Steele's house in Rowan County, North Carolina, the Philadelphia carpenter John Langdon noted that "Surbase plain pr foot 7 cts, If frett or fluted add pr foot 6 cts." John Steele Papers, SHC.

1806 An Episcopal chapel to be built in St. John's Parish, South Carolina, was to have "a plain cornice under the eves." *City Gazette and Daily Advertiser.*

plan 1. A drawing or diagram depicting a horizontal layout of a building, part of a building, or a building and its surroundings. The use of the term *plan* to connote a graphic representation does not come into general use until the second quarter of the 18th century. Before this time, *plat* or *draft* had greater currency. Most plans of buildings were created as design sketches rather than as working drawings used by craftsmen on the site. While many plans were drawn to scale and included the location of openings, partitions, and fittings, others were simply crude sketches and provided only general spatial relations rather than specific and detailed information.

1736 It was noted that "To Edward Voss for two plans of the Brick Church to be paid French Strother . . . £5." St. Mark's Parish, Culpeper Co., Va., Vestry Book.

1740 A church agreed to construct a steeple and vestry room "according to a Plan Delivered into the Vestry drawn by" William Walker, the builder. St. Peter's Parish, New Kent Co., Va., Vestry Book.

1743 In preparing to build a church in Savannah, the president of the colony noted that "knowing my own Incapacity in Architecture, dared not Venture without proper help to form a plan, and Assign the just Dimensions &c. The first thing I thought necessary was to employ a person capable of laying down such a Draught as should be approved of, for building the same." *The Journal of William Stephens 1743–1745.*

1784 Charleston builders were invited to view "the Ground-Plan and Elevation" of an assembly room before submitting bids on its construction. *The South Carolina Gazette, and Public Advertiser.*

2. *(n.)* A scheme, procedure, or method for carrying out a design, program, or action. *(v.)* To develop a proposal for a design. The wording of many colonial contracts and specifications makes it difficult to distinguish whether the term is used in its first meaning, that is, a drawing, or in its second sense, as a program of action.

1773 The congregation agreed "that the great width of the proposed plan [of the new meetinghouse] renders it almost impossible to proceed with" and that it should instead be constructed "upon a plan of sixty six feet by fifty in the clear." Charleston, S.C., Congregational Church Record Book.

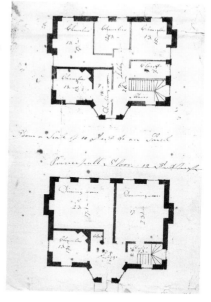

plan (1)
Dwelling, Virginia, late 18th or
early 19th century

1815 A new courthouse was to be built "upon the following plan, the [building] to be sufficiently large to have two Jury Rooms upon the lower floor." Essex Co., Va., Court Order Book 1812–1815.

planceer, plancier (plancher)   The underside of a corona; generally, any soffit of a cornice.

1820 An account of the work on the exterior entablature at Bremo in Fluvanna County, Virginia, included "planceers of all the Portico 219 feet 10 inches @ 1/6." Cocke Papers, UVa.

plane (plain)   One of a large number of woodworking tools used for shaping rough pieces of wood, fitting them with slots, grooves, rabbets, fillets, and finishing them with smooth surfaces and molded edges. Perhaps the most important tool in the chest of woodworking implements, the plane consists of an adjustable metal blade known as an iron housed in a wooden body or stock, often made of beech, and a wedge to secure the iron in a fixed position. Among the most common planes found in the early South for rough dimensioning were long jack planes, which had convex irons that were used for removing waste wood with thick shavings. For more refined smoothing, the try plane or fore plane, with a slightly curved iron, was used. To ensure that planks and boards butted together with a very fine joint, a jointer was used to shape their sides. Finally, smaller finishing planes were used to smooth surfaces to a clean and even finish. Their stocks were often coffin-shaped. This general group of planes were often called bench planes. For specialized shaping, the most common planes were a set of hollows and rounds, fillister, ogee, ovolo, panel raising, plough, bead, sash, cornice, and rabbet planes. Each performed a specific task and often came in various sizes.

plank   A long, flat piece of wood measuring at least two inches in thickness and more than eight inches in width used primarily for sheathing, flooring, and log wall construction. The term was loosely applied in the early South: many buildings were weatherboarded with planks measuring less than two inches in thickness.

plank house
Evans Smokehouse,
Perquimans County, N.C.

plank house   A type of log construction consisting of sawn planks or logs laid horizontally and notched at the corners. This method differed from other types of log construction in the amount of labor exerted in sawing logs into two to six inch-wide, close-fitting, planks. Also known as *sawed log* houses, this construction method first appeared in the South in the late 17th century and was used for a variety of purposes. Because of the solidity and regularity achieved by this labor-intensive method of construction, buildings that required a measure of security, such as storehouses, smokehouses, and prisons, were built in this manner. As field evidence indicates, log plank construction was not limited to these functions. It was common throughout the South in the 18th and early 19th centuries, even in older settled areas such as the Chesapeake and the coastal plain of the Carolinas and Georgia, where numerous plank dwellings, stables, and kitchens survive. See also **log construction.**

1762 For sale at a watermill was "a good Plank Granary and Mill house in one, two Story, and . . . a small Plank Dwelling-house." *Maryland Gazette.*

1773 To be built on a glebe was "one stable 24 feet by 16 feet, the body to be sawed logs four inches thick, to be dowld and dovetailed." Fairfax Parish, Fairfax Co., Va., Vestry Book.

plantation   1. During the earliest years of settlement, any region inhabited by colonists, a place in which they had planted a residential community.

> **1624** Virginia legislation directed "that there shall be in every plantation, where the people use to meete for the worship of god, a house or roome sequestred for that purpose." Hening, *Statutes at Large*, 1.

2. A tract of cultivated land owned or rented by an individual. Throughout the colonial era and, at least in the upper South, into the 19th century, the term remained synonymous with farm. It was also used to designate the component *quarters* of larger holdings. Agricultural development of the land, not necessarily sustained with the labor of slaves, was the principal characteristic of the plantation. See also **quarters** (3).

> **1626** The "said Arbitrators shall view the works & houses w'ch have been built & done . . . upon ye plantation of Martin Brandon" in Prince George County, Virginia. *VMHB*, 26.
>
> **1751** A "Plantation [is] to be sold by the name of Lilleput within two miles of Brunswick [North Carolina], 1280 acres fronting river with very good rice land and very good Brick Dwelling House." *North Carolina Gazette.*
>
> **1769** An announcement read: "To be sold in Augusta [Georgia] . . . as compleat and well-found a Farm or Plantation as any in this province." *South Carolina and American General Gazette.*
>
> **1812** In Richmond County, Virginia, there was "one cart from each plantation with mule wagon hauling stone, timber &c. to the C House." Tayloe Papers, VHS.

plaster (plaister)   A composition of lime, sand, and water, occasionally mixed with hair, applied as a paste in several coats to interior walls and ceilings. The term was sometimes used to refer to *roughcast*, which contained an aggregate such as gravel and was used on the exterior of buildings. Interior plaster was generally applied directly to brick walls and was applied over lath on frame ones. After an initial scratch coat, a plastered surface received one or two more coats, the last usually a thin white coat of a high lime content. Decorative plaster work, also known as *stucco*, was relatively rare in the early colonial period. In the late 17th century, walls, overmantels, and ceilings of a very few houses were sometimes decorated with plaster flowers, garlands, and animals, which were fabricated on the site by a skilled plasterer or stuccoist. The Governor's House in Jamestown and the Mount, the home of John Taliaferro in Caroline County, Virginia, had decorative plaster work on their chimney pieces or ceilings that probably dated from the last quarter of the 17th century. In the late colonial and early national period, neoclassical design motifs fashioned in stucco appeared in a number of dwellings, including Kenmore in Fredericksburg, Virginia. See also **composition ornament, papermâché, stucco** (2).

plaster
Above: Fragment from late 17th-century building, Jamestown, Va.
Below: Plaster chimney piece, Archdale Hall, Dorchester County, S.C., first quarter 18th century.

> **1651** Bricklayer William Eale agreed to "substantially plaister, White lyme & wash over the dyninge roome, the yellowe roome & kitchinge, & chamber over the kitchinge" of Francis Yeardley's dwelling. Norfolk Co., Va., Will and Deed Book 1646–1651.
>
> **1734** It was "Agreed with Mr. Peter Secare to Plaster the Church at 2/6 pr yd to supply him with Lime & hair and Boards for Scaffolding and Laborers to attend. . . . Agreed with Mr. Jno. Lane for two Negroes to attend the Plasterers at 6/10 1/

2 per day for each Slave." Prince Frederick, Winyah Parish, S.C., Vestry Book.

1747 Workmen consulted by colonists intending to build the first Anglican church in Savannah computed "the different Expences betwixt Plaistering and Boarding, We found the latter would exceed the former at least one third: These Things being duly considered induc'd Us to send for the Workmen, when we contracted to finish the walls in the manner following viz: To be watled betwixt the Studs with white Oak Watling, and filled up on each Side with a strong Plaister . . . the Inside when finished to be a clean plaistered White Wall." *Colonial Records of the State of Georgia,* 6.

1758 The church paid a builder "William Waite for a plaister cornice." Dettingen Parish, Prince William Co., Va., Vestry Book.

1758 "Any Person willing to undertake to rough cast the Outside and plaister the Inside of St. Michael's Church in Charles-Town with or without furnishing materials, are desired to give in their proposals." *South Carolina Gazette.*

1779 A visitor to Virginia noted that "the houses are most of them built of wood, the roof being covered with shingles, and not always lathed and plastered within, only those of the better sort that are finished in that manner, and painted on the outside." Anburey, *Travels Through the Interior of America.*

1786 In an Orange County, Virginia, dwelling, "Dickinson laid on the first coat of Plaister on the two least rooms above & about the other two." Francis Taylor Diary, CWF.

1801 John Tayloe's accounts for the construction of the Octagon in Washington included a bill for "Stucco and Plasters Work done by M^r [William] Foxton." Among dozens of entries were "354 yds 2 Coats Plastering [at] 11d . . . 2711 yds 3 $^{Do\ Do}$ [at] 1/2." Tayloe Papers, VHS.

plastered chimney A rarely used term for a wooden chimney. For a more detailed description, see **chimney**.

> **1754** A framed glebe house incorporated "at each end a Dirt or Plaistered chimney." Antrim Parish, Halifax Co., Va., Vestry Book.

plasterer (plaisterer) A craftsman responsible for applying plaster to walls and ceilings; a stuccoist. In the division of labor on a building site, a plasterer nailed laths to stud walls, mixed the ingredients to make plaster, and applied the various coats. As a distinct trade, plasterers appeared in the South by the late 17th century. However, many combined their skills with that of bricklayer or painter, especially in rural areas where craftsmen were often versatile and the separation of crafts was often blurred.

> **1698** The vestry agreed with "Gideon Gamble of Cecil County Plaisterer . . . to plaister the Church . . . on the Inside where Plaistering is Necessary . . . and to find Lime sufficient for the Same and other Necessary stuff." St. Paul's Parish, Kent Co., Md., Vestry Book.
>
> **1703** "James Knott, plaisterer . . . agreed . . . to drive and naile on the lathes and doe all the lathing, plaistering and painting work that is to be done in, on or about a Brick Church now built in this parish." St. Peter's Parish, New Kent Co., Va., Vestry Book.
>
> **1768** The churchwardens were to "bind William Fentress as an apprentice to George Shores until he attains the age of 21, to learn the Trade of a Brick-layer and Plaisterer." Princess Anne Co., Va., Court Minute Book 1762–1769.
>
> **1789** Joseph Kennedy, "Stucco-workman, Plasterer, and Plain Painter, from Dublin, Has settled in Baltimore. . . . He will undertake to perform the several Branches of his Profession, in the most approved and latest Fashions—Having been regularly bred under as good Workmen as any in Ireland, he flatters himself, that he shall be able to satisfy those who may employ him. A specimen of his Work may be seen at Mount-Clare, near Town." *Maryland Journal and the Baltimore Advertiser.*

plaster of paris A calcined gypsum plaster pulverized to a fine white powder, used as an additive for regular plaster or for making ornamental casts. Because of its capacity to set rapidly after mixing with

PLATE **281**

water, plaster of paris could be formed into precisely molded forms. See also **composition ornament.**

> 1765 Carver Nicholas Bernard of Charleston advertised for sale "a variety of neat figures and busts in plaister of Paris, with brackets for ditto." *South Carolina Gazette.*
>
> 1784 "Just imported, and landed at Dumfries and Alexandria, from New York, ABOUT Forty Tons of PLASTER-OF-PARIS. As few persons in this State are acquainted with its qualities, it may be necessary to inform such, that nothing is equal to it for plastering or covering houses, as also for stucco work, but of late more particularly valuable for manure, two bushels being found sufficient for an acre of land." *Alexandria Gazette.*
>
> 1794 Ralph Izard wrote to John Kean of Philadelphia that "Mr. Owen has employed a Man to plaster my new House in Charleston who has informed him that Stucco may be procured in Philadelphia for 4 1/2 dollars pr Ton. . . . I suppose he must mean Plaster of Paris, if so, he must be mistaken about the price. . . . If it is sent in the Stone, I do not think there are machines there to pulverize it, & if it is pulverized in Philadelphia, it must be packed in Caskes. He wishes to have three Tons, which I must think much more than will be necessary." Izard Papers, LC.

plat (platt) **1.** A sketch of a building especially the ground plan. In the 17th century the term is nearly synonymous with *draft* to connote the graphic design of a building. This meaning of plat is occasionally used after the mid-18th century but is superseded by its second meaning.

> 1680 Specifications for a courthouse referred to the "Ruff Plott heere annexed." Talbot Co., Md., Court Judgment Book 1675–1682.
>
> 1702 The design of a courthouse was "sett downe and portra'ed in a certaine Mapp Platt or draught." Essex Co., Va., Will and Deed Book No. 10.
>
> 1804 Architect Robert Mills submitted "Drawings consist[ing] of a View of the Church with the proposed Elongation, Drafts of [the] Altar Pulpit and Reading Desk, accompanied with a Ground Platt." St. Michael's Parish, Charleston, S.C., Vestry Book.

2. A survey plan or map of a piece of land or property with natural and man-made features delineated.

> 1748 A surveyor was requested to "return a Platt and Survey" of the prison and courthouse bounds. Brunswick Co., Va., Court Order Book 1745–1749.
>
> 1796 Commissioners "returned a platt and survey" of the market house lot. Fredericksburg, Va., City Council Minute Book 1782–1801.

3. A small area or bed of ground usually planted in grass on the pleasure grounds adjacent to a dwelling. See also **plot.**

> 1743 "From the back door" of William Middleton's plantation house near Charleston "is a spacious walk a thousand foot long; each side of which nearest the house is a grass plat ennamiled in a Serpentine manner with flowers." *Letterbook of Eliza Lucas Pinckney.*
>
> 1783 Westover in Charles City County, Virginia, stood on the banks of the James River, "commanding a view of a prettily falling grass plat." Shippen, *Westover Described in 1783.*

plate (plait) A horizontal framing timber laid upon the tops of walls to receive other timbers. Generally, the term referred to a *wall plate* that rested upon a masonry or timber frame wall on which joists or trusses rested. A secondary plate, which sat on top of the joists and supported the rafters, was known as a *false plate* or, in some cases, a *raising plate.* See also **false plate, raising plate, wall plate.**

> 1697 "Robert Norris doth oblige hemself to Arch the Church . . . fit for Plaistering . . . from the plate to the Wind beam, being about Seven foot Perpendicular." St. Paul's Parish, Kent Co., Md., Vestry Book.
>
> 1741 A chapel was to be built "eleven foot in pitch between sill and plate." St. Paul's Parish, Chowan Co., N.C., Vestry Book.

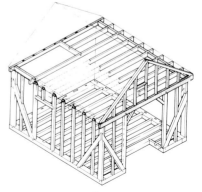

plate

1792 There was recorded a "Bill of scantling for the House 18 feet by 22 feet, 2 stories high . . . 2 End plates 18 ft 8 in by 13 in . . . 2 Middle plates 22 ft 11 in by 13 in." Hubard Papers, SHC.

playhouse A building in which entertainments, such as plays and musical performances, are given; a theater. For a more detailed description, see **theater.**

1745 "The Play-House in Williamsburg, being by order of the Common Hall of the said City, [is] to be fitted up for a Court-House, with all the necessary Alterations and Repairs." *Virginia Gazette.*

1772 In Norfolk, minister Joseph Pilmore "preached in the Play-house at seven. . . . Afterwards I was much edified by Mr. Davis's sermon in the Church, and at six o'clock went to the Play-house; but it would not contain one half of the people so I stood in the open air." *The Journal of Joseph Pilmore Methodist Itinerant.*

1801 In Charleston, "a Correspondent who witnessed the alarm and confusion created by the rabble in the gallary of the theatre . . . suggests . . . shutting up that part of the house altogether. . . . The noise proceeding from the gallery, frequently destroys all the effect of a good play; and renders the attendance of a band of music of no consequence. Few ladies retire from the play-house without a severe headache." *The Times.*

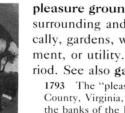

pleasure ground
Francis Guy, Pleasure ground at Bolton, near Baltimore

pleasure ground The gardens, lawn, and planted area immediately surrounding and belonging to a dwelling or other buildings. Specifically, gardens, whether public or private, intended for beauty, amusement, or utility. The term was seldom used during the colonial period. See also **garden.**

1793 The "pleasure grounds of David Meade, Esq., of Maycox" in Prince George, County, Virginia, noted that "these grounds contain about twelve acres, laid out on the banks of the James river in a most beautiful and enchanting manner. Forest and fruit trees are here arranged as if nature and art had conspired together to strike the eye most agreeably. Beautiful vistas, which open as many pleasing view of the river." *Collections of the Massachusetts Historical Society,* 3.

1799 "One hundred acres of ground, toward the river are left adjoining to the" White House in Washington "for pleasure grounds." Weld, *Travels Through the States of North America.*

1803 At "that elegant and highly improved Villa called the Hermitage" near Wilmington, North Carolina, "the Gardens and Pleasure Grounds of about two acres, are disposed with much taste and in point of beauty and improvement equal to any in the United States." *Wilmington Gazette.*

1806 "The district commonly called the . . . Pleasure Ground, may be said to comprehend all ornamental compartments, or divisions of ground, surrounding the mansion; consisting of lawns, plantations of trees and shrubs, flower compartments, walks, pieces of water &c. whether situated wholly within the space generally considered as the Pleasure-garden, or extended to the adjacent fields, parks, or other out grounds." M'Mahon, *The American Gardener's Calendar.*

plinth **1.** The plain square member under the base moldings of a column, pilaster, or pedestal; a socle. Also a low, continuous base beneath a building in the form of a low, flat projection. See also **socle.**

1811 For a pair of interior columns in a dwelling in Baltimore, a workman fabricated "2 pair of mahogany sunk plinths & Caps." Riddell Accounts, Pleasants Papers, MHS.

1812 The portico at Montpelier in Orange County, Virginia, had four columns with "bases as well as plinths." Foster, *Jeffersonian America.*

1821 A workman made "8 Plinths for Ionic Columns in the Commons Hall" of the statehouse in Raleigh. Treasurers and Comptrollers Papers, Statehouse, NCA&H.

2. The base of an exterior brick or stone wall up to the offset or water table, where it diminishes in thickness. In 18th-century England, and perhaps rarely in America, the term was also used to refer to a projecting belt course between floors of building. See also **belt course, water table.**

> 1734 "Plinth of a Wall is a Term us'd by Bricklayers for two or three Rows of Bricks, which advance out from the Wall, or it is us'd in General for every flat, high Moulding, serving in a Front Wall to mark the Floors." *Builder's Dictionary*.

3. In interior woodwork, the flat, plain member at the bottom of a wall, architrave, or dado. Specifically, the plinth is the broad, flat part of a base, mopboard, or skirting board. A plinth block terminates a door or window architrave before it reaches the floor and serves as a stop for a plinth or base.

> 1811 Carpentry work at Montpelier in Orange County, Virginia, included "29 ft 6 rung of Base & Plinth in passage." Cocke Papers, UVa.

plot In gardening, a plat or piece of ground of small or moderate size designated for a specific purpose, usually the growing of grass. See also **plat.**

> 1775 In selecting a gardener, one gardening advocate advised that he should inquire as to "whether he is an expert at levelling, making grass plots & Bowling Greens, Slopes, & turfing them well." Charles Carroll Letterbook, MHS.

plug A small piece of wood embedded in the face of masonry walls to serve as a nailing block to attach interior and exterior trim, including architraves, mantels, and paneling.

> 1802 A carpenter's account for John Tayloe's house in Washington, D.C., included "Torus skirting, plugg'd to walls." Tayloe Papers, VHS.

plumber (plumer) Traditionally, a craftsman skilled in the working of lead by fitting and soldering of pipes, flashing, cisterns, and roofs. The term gradually came to be used to describe artisans working with other metals such as copper, zinc, and tin.

> 1712 In building a church, John Hipkins undertook the "carpenters plumers and glasiers work." Christ Church Parish, Middlesex Co., Va., Vestry Book.
>
> 1769 Working in Williamsburg was "a person from England, well acquainted with the useful branches of PLUMBING, GLAZING, and PAINTING." *Virginia Gazette*.
>
> 1796 In Alexandria, "JOHN EMERY Plumber and Shot Manufacturer . . . rented a shop at the head of Fairfax Street; where he intends to carry on the above business in all its various branches-such as sheet lead, either cast or milled, from four pounds the square foot to fourteen; Wall Pipes, for conveying water from the roof of the house, with ornamented heads, which come cheap and are durable; water pipes of any bore for conveying of water to any distance; lead pumps put down to any depth, which will come cheaper than wood, considering its durability, and is sweeter and colder. . . . Likewise sash leads for windows." *Columbia Mirror and Alexandria Gazette*.

plumb rule An instrument for determining whether a post, wall, or other element is vertically aligned. It consists of a pointed weight known as a *plumb bob* tied to a line that is connected at the top through a hole with a *plumb board*. The plumb board is a narrow piece of wood with two long, parallel straight edges. The plumb line swings freely, denoting a piece of work as even if the line matches the kerf mark on the board.

> 1767 In a review of work on a Presbyterian meetinghouse, it was observed that "the whole of the Pews are not put up by Line or Plum." Records of Willtown Presbyterian Church, *South Carolina Historical Magazine*, 62.

podium A long, continuous pedestal. See also **pedestal.**

plinth (1)
Pavilion 2, University of Virginia

plinth (2)
Hungar's Glebe House,
Northampton County, Va.

plinth (3)
Ridout House, Annapolis, Md.

point, pointing *(v.)* To fill the exposed joints of a piece of masonry with mortar or putty in order to preserve it from the effects of weather. *(n.)* The mortar or putty finish of a masonry joint often done in a decorative fashion. The simplest form was known as *flat* pointing, where the mortar was scraped flush with the face of the brick. One of the most common finishes used from the 17th through the early 19th centuries was tooled smooth and then scribed or ruled in the center of the joint to create an even line. The modern term *grapevine* has been applied to this type of pointing. In the early 19th century, *V* pointing became fashionable. The mason formed this by striking the upper and lower edges to create a projecting ridge in the center of the joint. Finally, one of the most expensive forms of pointing was *tuck* work, which consisted of creating a *grapevine* joint and filling in the scribed line with a hard lime mortar or putty. Occasionally, the rest of the joint was painted the color of the masonry, so that a thin white line of the tuck point stood in sharp contrast. See also **joint, pencil.**

> **1674** At St. Mary's City, the statehouse walls were to be "well pointed without with good lime." *Archives of Maryland, 2.*
> **1760** "The foundation" of a church was "to be underpinned with stone and pointed with lime." Frederick Parish, Frederick Co., Va., Vestry Book.
> **1769** The vestry reached an agreement with a workman to "point the gable ends" of St. Stephen's Church "with mortar." St. Stephen's Parish, Berkeley Co., S.C., Vestry Book.
> **1786** A tenant farm in western Virginia contained an "indifferent stone spring house not pointed," while a neighbor had a dwelling house "with a stone chimney not pointed." Jonathan Clark Notebook, Filson Club.
> **1796** Stone walls of a jail were "to be Laid in lime morter and neatly pointed with lime." Stokes Co., N.C., Miscellaneous Court Records, NCA&H.
> **1811** In Charleston, an account listed "the following measurement of workmanship to be correct Done for Isaac Ball, Esq. by Robert Roulain. 3,623 feet whole Tuck pointing at 5 pr. foot 75.9.7; 5,504 Ditto half Tuck ditto at 3 pr ditto 68.11.9; 168 Ditto Flat Pointing at 2 pr ditto 1.8.0." Ball Family Papers, SCHS.

pole (pol, poole)   **1.** A unit of linear measurement equal to the length of a surveyor's pole or *rod*—about sixteen feet. Multiplied by itself, the pole became a unit for measuring area, a square pole or rod being about 16 by 16 feet, or about 256 square feet.

> **1668** An English author suggested that "a Bricklayer with a diligent labourer . . . may lay 1000 Bricks and upwards in a day; and 4500 Bricks will make one Rod of Wall or of the side of a Building, at one Brick and half thick, the Rod, Pole, or Perch, containing 16 foot and a half of superficial measure." Leybourn, *Platform Guide Mate for Purchasers, Builders and Measurers.*

2. A slender log or shaft of wood used as a structural member, with or without the bark removed.

> **1706** The floor of a prison in Kent County, Delaware, was "to be laid on Pooles Eighteen inches deep & twelve inches thick of White Oak to be let into the Ground so that the Lower floor may rest on the surface of the earth." Kent Co., Del., Court Record Book 1703–1718.
> **1778** A new house in Berkeley Springs, Virginia, was to be of "Loggs or Poles." Yates Letterbook, UVa.
> **1786** In preparation for building a chimney in Orange County, Virginia, workmen brought "Bricks, earth for mortar and poles for Chimney Scaffold." Francis Taylor Diary.
> **1807** In Nelson, County, Virginia, an account for framing William Massie's barn included a charge for "weight poles & eve bareers." Massie Papers, Duke.

poorhouse A building or group of buildings erected by a parish or corporation for the charitable reception of the poor. The term was synonymous with the less frequently used *almshouse*. Poorhouses erected by rural parishes were generally small, cheaply constructed houses or groups of houses surrounded by garden plots and service buildings. By the late 18th and early 19th centuries, poorhouses in some urban areas were being converted into workhouses, where the poor were expected to labor at various jobs. Occasionally, walls were erected around these city poorhouses, giving the institution a less benevolent appearance. See also **almshouse, workhouse.**

> 1751 Money was levied by the parish "for maintaining the poor house." Elizabeth River Parish, Norfolk Co., Va., Vestry Book.
> 1762 Agreement for "the Building of a Poor House in the Town of Winchester for the use of the Poor" specified a log building 36 by 16 feet. Frederick Parish, Frederick Co., Va., Vestry Book.
> 1821 The county court ordered "the building of five cabins for the accomodation of the poor . . . 14 feet Square, in the clear, the floors to be filled up twelve inches above the common level of the earth with dirt after being well rammed, the pitch of the cabins above the floor to be seven feet." King George Co., Va., Court Order Book 1817–1822.

poplar When used in the early South, the term typically referred to yellow poplar because true poplars, which are in the willow family, genus *Populus*, were not used in building. See also **yellow poplar.**

> 1729 A glebe house was "wetherboarded with feather edged quarter . . . poplar nine inches broad & one inch thick." Stratton Major Parish, King & Queen Co., Va., Vestry Book.
> 1737 Two tobacco houses and two dwelling houses "are to be with frames of good white oak or poplar timber." Elizabeth City Co., Va., Deeds, Wills, Bonds, Etc.

porch (poarch, portch) An exterior structure forming a covered shelter at the entrance to a building. From the time of settlement through the second quarter of the 18th century, the principal entrance of many public buildings and dwellings had small porches, squarish in plan, which were enclosed in varying degrees by walls or balustrades. In domestic architecture, the upper part of these entrance towers often contained porch chambers connected to the second floor, which functioned as service or sleeping rooms. As early as the 1690s, a few buildings had completely open porches whose roofs were supported by columns or posts. However, it was not until the middle of the 18th century that this form became relatively common in the South. A few porches were treated as open sitting rooms with cornices, plastered ceilings, sheathing, surbases, washboards, and built-in benches on the wall next to the entrance. The term virtually disappears in the lower South in the 1730s and 1740s as long *piazzas*, stretching the full length of the facade, became the most common form of entrance shelter. Gradually, the piazza form and term moved northward into coastal North Carolina and Virginia, and appeared in Maryland and Delaware by the time of the Revolution. From the middle of the 18th century through the antebellum period, contemporaries began to refer increasingly to an open, pedimented entry porch by its classical name, *portico*. As a result, the term *porch* was slowly eclipsed, until it was revived in the late 19th century to indiscriminately describe most varieties of sheltered entrance structures. See also **piazza** (2), **portico.**

porch
Above: Enclosed porch, Bacon's Castle, Surry County, Va. The original door has been blocked.

Below: Open pedimented porch, Shirley, Charles City County, Va.

1653 A contract was made to build a dwelling 50 by 20 feet with "a porch six foot wide, and tenn foot longe." Surry Co., Va., Deed and Will Book 1652–1672.

1674 A dwelling house in Charles County, Maryland, was "twenty & five foot in Length & twenty & two foot in breadth, with a porch tenne foot long & eight food wide thereunto Adjoyneing with a room over the first roome & another over the said porch." *Archives of Maryland*, 60.

1676 In Perquimans County, North Carolina, a carpenter had constructed a "framed house forty foot Long 20 foot wide, with a shade on the back side, and a porch on the front." Secretary of State Records, Wills and Inventories 1677–1701, NCA&H.

1686 A courthouse was to have "a large Porch att the end of the house with rails and Banisters about it." Dorchester Co., Md., Land Record Book 1669–1683.

1701 It was ordered that "the porches of the said Capitoll [in Williamsburg] be built circular fifteen foot in breadth from outside to outside, and that they stand upon cedar columns." *Journals of the House of Burgesses*, 3.

1742 "Two poarches" were to be added "to the dwelling house six feet square closed on each side." Bristol Parish, Prince George Co., Va., Vestry Book.

1745 "Mr. Lyell is to build two porches at the two doors of the Glebe house one at the front 8 foot square with back boards and benches . . . one other at the Back Door 6 foot square to be built and finished in a like manner." Christ Church Parish, Middlesex Co., Va., Vestry Book.

1773 A glebe house was to have "Two Portches Ten, by Seven feet out, Weatherboarded hand rail high, with Good featheredge Plank and Good flours, Neatly finished with out side cornice's, and Sealed in side, with Good wide benches &c." Bristol Parish, Prince George Co., Va., Vestry Book.

1795 An orphan's estate contained a "framed dwelling house hip roof'd about 17 1/2 feet by 40 . . . [with] a porch or piazza on the easternmost side of the house about 21 feet long by 7 feet wide plank floor with seats." Worcester Co., Md., Orphans Court Proceedings 1792–1797.

1803 A minister wanted to "let My House, in Fredericksburg" containing a "commodious close porch in front, and an open portico in the rear." *Virginia Herald*.

1808 A two-story brick courthouse in Columbia, Tennessee, was "to have a porch and portico on each side 12 by 20 feet . . . of open work, supported by brick columns." *The Impartial Review and Cumberland Repository*.

porch chamber **1.** A second- or third-floor room located directly above the entrance porch. These small, unheated rooms functioned as service and sleeping chambers in 17th- and 18th-century dwellings. Porch chambers gradually went out of fashion with the displacement of enclosed porch towers by open porches in the middle of the 18th century.

1668 "In the porch Chamber" of Major John Croshaw's house were "three Feather beds, three bolsters, one Rugg, one bedstead, one old Trunke, 1 Chest, a piece of a Deske." York Co., Va., Deed, Order, and Will Book 1665–1672.

2. A small, usually unheated room enclosed at one or both ends of an open porch or piazza. It was often entered only from the porch and was not accessible from the rest of the house. By the 19th century it was traditionally called the *preacher room*.

1709 A Quaker in Perquimans County, North Carolina, willed his wife three "feather beds to be kept in the porch chamber for Gods Messengers and Ministers to Lodge." Secretary of State Records, Wills 1712–1722, NCA&H.

portal A large gate, door, or entrance, especially one of imposing appearance.

portico A covered entrance or porch with a roof supported by a regular series of columns. The term was particularly used to distinguish a pedimented projection characteristic of a classical Greek or Roman temple front. Contemporaries sometimes referred to a long porch or piazza as a *portico*. Following the English practice of the 18th century, the term was occasionally employed to characterize covered spaces supported by an arcade. See also **piazza, porch.**

> **1737** Workmen at St. Philip's Church in Charleston recommended the construction of "a large Cornish under ye eves & round ye Porticoes." St. Philip's Parish, Charleston, S.C., Vestry Book.
> **1769** A Presbyterian meetinghouse to be built in Savannah, Georgia, was to be "80 feet long by 47 feet wide . . . with a handsome light steeple in proportion to the frame, a portico at one end of 50 by 10 feet." *Georgia Gazette.*
> **1786** On a farm in the Shenandoah Valley of Virginia, there was a "framed dwelling house 26 by 20 . . . and a portico the length of the house five feet wide." Jonathan Clark Notebook, Filson Club.
> **1807** A 30-by-20-foot dwelling was for sale near Wilmington, North Carolina, "with two piazzas to the east and south, and a portico to the west." *The Wilmington Gazette.*
> **1838** The two-story courthouse in Spotsylvania County, Virginia, was to have a "portico in front 12 feet wide with a pedimented roof. . . . Four columns to the portico, each about 23 inches at the base, and running up to the cornice." *Political Arena.*

portico
St. Philip's Church, Charleston, S.C.

Portland stone A fine, white, durable Jurassic limestone quarried from the Isle of Portland off the south coast of England in Dorsetshire. A creamy white color when quarried, Portland stone had the tendency to turn whiter with age. Because of its color, durability, and ability to be quarried in large blocks, it became one of the most popular limestones in England in the late 17th and 18th centuries. Wren faced the facade of St. Paul's Cathedral with it, and used it as a decorative trim to contrast the brick walls of Hampton Court and in many of his churches in the city. In Dublin it was used in many of the public buildings erected in the 18th century. In the 1750s, Portland stone was used for the decorative dressings of Trinity College. As with most imported English stone, the material had limited use in America, employed occasionally as a facing material but more widely for paving in important dwellings and public buildings. See also **Bristol stone.**

> **1734** A church was to have a center "Isle Eight foot wide Laid with portland stone or Bristol marble." Bristol Parish, Prince George Co., Va., Vestry Book.
> **1747** A survey of materials at the unfinished Governor's House in Annapolis found "that there is Round the outside of the said House a Quantity of Portland Stone, Bremen Stone, several Casks of Stucco, and some wrought Country Stone." *McDowell Hall at St. John's College.*

post A substantial vertical timber, used in various places to support horizontal framing members and roof trusses. Posts also provided a point for lateral attachments for doors, gates, and fences. For a description of specific types of posts and their uses, see **bollard, corner post, doorpost, hanging post, king post, post and rail fence, post in the ground, prick post, prize post, sure post.**

> **1659** A workman was employed to "putt upp the Posts of the Welch Chimney." Proceedings of the Provincial Court of Maryland 1658–1662, MSA.
> **1692** A courthouse was to be built with "foure girders groundsills and outside posts." Richmond Co., Va., Court Order Book 1692–1694.
> **1755** It was "Ordered, That the Bell be hung in the Church Yard, and Secure as may be, between two Posts." St. Anne's Parish, Anne Arundel Co., Md., Vestry Book.

post and rail fence A type of fence composed of regularly spaced, groundset posts linked with horizontal rails to create a contiguous, ladderlike barrier. Rails were usually mortised into, but sometimes nailed onto, the posts. Typical examples contained three to five rails and averaged five feet in height. Durable woods like locust, cedar, and chestnut were favored for posts, while strong, resilient species like oak, poplar, and heart pine constituted the best choices for rails. Posts and rails were either hewn or sawn. Sawn boards sometimes replaced rails, producing a variation called a *post and plank fence;* this arrangement was more prevalent in the 19th century than earlier. The *post and rail fence* was rarely painted; it was more often tarred for protection from the elements. Post and plank fencing was usually painted. *Post and rail fencing* enclosed many different kinds of areas, from urban lots and yards of public and private buildings in both town and countryside, to pastures, orchards, and cultivated fields.

> **1653** Francis Sherwood agreed to build 150 "pannell of post and railes five railes to the pannell sufficiently performed by the sd Sherwood to keepe out hoggs and Cattle." Westmoreland County, Va., Deed, Will, and Patent Book 1653–1657.
>
> **1719** A vestry hired a carpenter to "Rail in the Church yard 100 foot Square, with Seven Rails in a pannel; five foot high each pannell, to be Eight foot in Length & well Tarr'd." St. Paul's Parish, Hanover County, Va., Vestry Book.
>
> **1764** A Maryland vestry decided "to Post & Raile in the Church Yard according to the following Dimension Viz. The Post to be of Good sound Locust Six & Half feet in Length & Six inches deep & four inches Broad & Plac'd Eight feet Distance. The Plank of Good Sound White Oak. Six inches Broad & Two inches Thick. The first Plank five inches from the Ground. Between the first and second the same distance between the second and third eight inches distance the fourth plank to range with the Top of the Post. Each Plank to be let in the Post two Inches & Spik'd on With four Inch Spikes." St. George's Parish, Harford Co., Md., Vestry Book.
>
> **1794** It was ordered "to post and rail the garden." Kent Co., Del., Orphans Court Valuations.

post in the ground An earthfast framing system wherein the principal vertical members are embedded several feet in the ground and bound together at the eaves by wall plates. Known to Chesapeake colonists as a *Virginia house,* this framing technique was comparatively cheap but impermanent, since it eliminated much of the complicated joinery of a carefully constructed box or *English frame* and made masonry foundations unnecessary. However, *post in the ground* construction required numerous repairs if a building's usefulness were to be prolonged for more than one or two decades. Southern builders constructed *post in the ground* structures as dwellings, churches, outbuildings, and commercial structures for more than two centuries. By the early 19th century, this construction method was relegated primarily to subsidiary outbuildings and poorer farm dwellings. For a more detailed description, see **Virginia house.**

> **1623** In Virginia "the platacons are far asunder & their houses stande scattered one from another, and are onlie made of wood, few or none of them being framed houses but punches sett into the Ground and Covered with Boarde." *Records of the Virginia Company,* 4.
>
> **1680** It was stipulated that a prison have "the maine posts . . . three foote and a halfe in the ground." Lancaster Co., Va., Court Order Book 1680–1686.
>
> **1701** Churchwardens were "to agree with a workman for building a Church 25 feet long posts in the ground and held to the Collar beams." St. Paul's Parish, Chowan Co., N.C., Vestry Book.
>
> **1704** A survey of a county jail revealed that "several posts [are] wanting and most of them [that] are standing to be rotten off by the ground so that . . . there must be a new set of posts all round." Middlesex Co., Va., Court Order Book 1694–1705.
>
> **1735** A plantation near Charleston contained "two new Barns . . . one 35 by 80

post in the ground
Above: Wilson Tobacco House,
Calvert County, Md.
Below: Post mold of a hole-set post,
Gray Farm Barn, Suffolk, Va.

Posts in the Ground, the other well fram'd and finished of good yellow Pine 30 Feet by 40." *South Carolina Gazette.*

1750 In western Virginia, a planter "has built two tobo Houses and Tarred posts in ye ground." *Diary of Robert Rose.*

potato house, potato hole   A building or part of a building, often semisubterranean, used for the storage of potatoes during the winter; a subterranean storage cellar for root crops.

1766 A workman was paid for "building a potato house 10/, filling up the walls 20/ . . . £1.10.0." Francis Jerdone Account Book, W&M.

1791 In Florida, the naturalist William Bartram visited "the town of Cuscowilla, which is the capital of the Alachua tribe," which contained a large building, part of which was "closed on all sides by notched logs; the lowest part is a potatoe house, and the upper story over it a granary for corn and other provisions." *Travels of William Bartram.*

1803 Work on the Spencer estate in southern Delaware included "potato hole walling fire sill & harth." Sussex Co., Del., Orphans Court Guardian Accounts IJ.

pot house   A building where pottery and other ceramics are made.

1749 Buildings for sale on a lot in Philadelphia included "a good pot-house, a kiln and kiln-house, a good mill, with yard room, and all utensils fitting and necessary for the business of a potter." *Pennsylvania Gazette.*

1797 A carpenter was paid for "casing pot house doors." Stokes Co., N.C., Miscellaneous Court Papers, NCA&H.

poultry house   A henhouse. The term appeared throughout the lower South and in Maryland in the 18th and early 19th centuries but was rarely used in Virginia. For a more detailed description, see **henhouse.**

1733 A plantation near Goose Creek, South Carolina, contained a "poultry house." *South Carolina Gazette.*

1744 For sale on St. Johns Island near Charleston was a plantation with "a poultry house, 30 Feet by 15." *South Carolina Gazette.*

1770 On the Blake farm in Queen Anne's County, Maryland, was a "poultry house 16 feet square covered and weather boarded with clapboards." Queen Anne's Co., Md., Deed Book I.

poultry yard   See **yard** (3).

powder house, powder magazine   A building in which gunpowder and other explosives were stored. The more common terms used in the region for such a structure were *magazine* and *armory*. See also **armory, magazine.**

1791 The "contract for a powder house [is] to be let; brick building 16 feet wide and 30 feet long; 10 feet high in the clear and 18 inch wall." *Virginia Gazette and Alexandria Advertizer.*

pozzolana   A siliceous material named for the fine volcanic rock from Mount Vesuvius that was used by the ancient Romans as an additive to make a very hard cement. With the growth in the early 19th century of engineering projects that required a more durable form of hydraulic cement, builders experimented with new materials and new combinations of old materials. A few sought to replicate the successful recipe used by the Romans. For a more detailed discussion of various types of cement, see **cement.**

1818 "NEW CEMENT. David Meade Randolph . . . of Virginia, announced that he has discovered a cement that answers to the character of the puzzolona, and becomes hard after a short time in water. This is a valuable discovery if the inventor has confidence in its principles. The Roman cement which has become so hardened with time as to become durable as stone, has long been lost. . . . This cement is invaluable in all species of stone work and masonry, in bridges, in puddling canals, in tanks or cisterns, and we trust that the experiments will continue to be made." *American Beacon and Norfolk and Portsmouth Advertiser.*

prick post   A secondary post in a frame located between the major corner posts. While the term appears in New England during the colonial period, it was rarely used in the South.

principal joist   A girder; a large internal floor beam.

> 1798   Proposals were made for "planing and fixing the principal joists of the Galleries" in a penitentiary "in Locust." *The Correspondence and Miscellaneous Papers of Benjamin Henry Latrobe*, 1.

principal rafter, roof
Principal rafter roof with kneed principals, Bruton Parish Church, Williamsburg, Va.

principal rafter, principal roof   One of a pair of large diagonal framing members forming a roof truss. The foot of a principal rafter is framed into a tie beam. Principal rafters support purlins, which in turn support the weight of the smaller common rafters. Principals were often shaped with a diminished size above the purlin toward the apex of the roof. Some had kneed feet where the lower part of the rafter curved downward and tenoned into the tie beam at a more obtuse angle. In a *king post* roof, the head of the principals are tenoned into the head of the king posts. Principal rafter roofs, often called *principal roofs*, were used for deep spans in churches, courthouses, and other sizeable structures as well as on a number of buildings that supported a heavy covering such as slate or tile. See also **common rafter, king post, purlin.**

> 1674   The roof of the statehouse at St. Mary's City was to have "Rafters Eighteene foot & halfe long standing twelve inches a sunder with six paire of principalls and double purloines framed in even with the rafters & to be morticed in & every paire of Principalls to be braced in . . . every paire of Principalls to be tenn & Eight inches square." *Archives of Maryland*, 2.
> 1682   The Third Haven Quaker Meeting House constructed in Talbot County, Maryland, in 1682–1684 survives to the present. The 1682 specifications offered an uncommon usage of principal rafter in describing the closely spaced, heavy common rafter pairs that were employed. "Ye Roofe to be Double Raftered and good principle Rafters every t[w]o foote and to be Double Studded below, and to be well Braced." Third Haven Quaker Meeting, Minutes, 1.
> 1694   A 52-by-26-foot church was to have "five Girders and five Principal Rafters, and other Timber proportionable to Such a Building." St. Paul's Parish, Kent Co., Md., Vestry Book.
> 1711   "The principall Rafters of the sd Church [are to] be Sawed of good white Oake to be six and nine inches Square att the foot and six and four inches att the Top. . . . the small Rafters be of three and four inches Square." Christ Church Parish, Middlesex Co., Va., Vestry Book.
> 1767   "The Roof [is] to have three pair of Princeapal Rafters or as the Workmen Call it a princeapal Roof." Fairfax Parish, Fairfax Co., Va., Vestry Book.
> 1771   St. John's Church in Granville County, North Carolina, was to have "substantial pair of Principal Rafters at every six feet with large Coller Beams King Post & Purlings from one Principal Rafter to the other well Braced." Francis Hawks Collection, Church Historical Society, Austin.
> 1806   The roof of a brick meeting house in Fayette County, Kentucky, was to have "king post 10 by 12, principal rafters 8 by 9, tapered from the purlins to the top by 5 by 5; purlins 8 by 8, braces 5 by 7, small rafters 3 by 5, two feet from centre to centre, the principal rafters 10 feet apart." *Kentucky Gazette and General Advertiser.*

prison   A place for the incarceration of those awaiting trial or those convicted of a crime awaiting sentencing or execution. Prisons were also used for the confinement of debtors. Until the early 19th century, prisons were not used to keep individuals locked up as part of their punishment. As a result, most structures erected in the early South were relatively small brick, frame, or stone structures built on the courthouse grounds. The early prisons erected in the Chesapeake colonies were no more than *Virginia houses* of simple earthfast construction, with little attention paid to security in construction. By the beginning of the 18th century, this attitude had been transformed, perhaps because so many desperate prisoners easily made their escape from these frame buildings. In the late colonial period, greater attention was paid in making prisons as strong as possible. Many were lined with two or three layers of sheathing of stout planks, logs, and stone and brick walls. Doors and windows were lined or barred. These tiny rooms, measuring no more than 16 by 16 feet at best, may have had a place for the prisoners to ease themselves. Straw, blankets, and a few other provisions were the most a prisoner might expect during his confinement. As a result, the interiors of these structures were dark and, no doubt, very unhealthy places. Debtors who unfortunately were forced to reside in such dark holes were given the liberty to walk about the prison bounds on a regular basis. While most prisons contained only one or two rooms at most, there was an effort made in the second half of the 18th century to divide the incarcerated according to their status, sex, and race. The most elaborate structures contained rooms for black and white criminals, debtors, and, occasionally, women. The terms *prison* and *gaol* were synonymous during the colonial period. By the beginning of the 19th century, *jail* came to be used more frequently to describe these structures, although *prison* continued in common usage well into the 19th century. See also **bridewell, gaol, jail, marshalsea, penitentiary.**

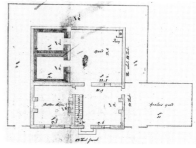

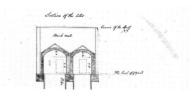

prison
John Hawks, elevation, plan, and section for a prison, Edenton, N.C.

1662   An act was passed "for prevention of escapes for prisoners . . . that sufficient prisons should be built in each county, and that a house built after the form of a Virginia house (our ability not extending to build stronger) should be accompted a sufficient prison, and that any person being a prisoner for debt or crime, and breaking one of those prisons, should be proceeded against as a fellon." Hening, *Statutes at Large, 2.*

1692   "Thos. Chamberlayne . . . committed to ye County Gaol . . . did . . . violently break off several boards from ye sd prison and come out at ye sd breach (ye subsheriff . . . said that he was in sight and forbad it) & that being again apprehended & ye sd breach made up he did again by some means gett out & make his escape home." Henrico Co., Va., Court Order Book 1678–1693.

1747   A "prison [is] to be 20 feet long and 12 foot wide in the clear, to be framed work & planked with Plank 4 inches thick of white oak plank Set up End Mortised & Tenanted into the sill and plate the house is to be Seven foot pitch in the clear . . . & two Petitions. . . . the Joists is to be Sett as Near one another as they Can and flore to be laid on them of Inch Plank the lower floor is to be laid of white oak plank two inches thick with Half Crown Nails and the Sleepers as Close to one another as they can be sett. . . . to be three Duble doors with Good Sufficient Locks there is to be 3 Iron Plates the whole Bigness of the Doors well nailed on and one window on the front side in the Debter Room one foot Square to be well done with iron bars and 2 iron Grates." Northumberland Co., Va., Court Order Book 1743–1749.

1765   The court ordered "the building of a new Prison . . . to be 24 Feet long & 16 feet wide, with a Brick Chimney & two fire places in it near the middle and a Brick partition . . . with a small window about 6 Inches square. . . . The walls to be 3 Bricks thick to the Surface of the Earth & 2 afterwards . . . the Sleeprs in the Ground & 7 feet from the Top of the Sleepers to the Joists, the Sleeprs to be 10 inches deep and laid close. . . . On the inside to have Wall of Saw'd logs of sound

Oak 6 Inches thick and dovetail'd at the corners & windows and Tenoned into large posts at the doors. . . . ceiled with Oak plank 1 1/2 inches thick & railed perpendicular & across the Logs. . . The roof to be laid with good bricks on a bed of mortar on the joists & Brick Walls, to be 6 course thick at the ends & sides then rise to the middle the height of 3 feet & a half at least in form of a hip'd roof . . . & covered with a strong Clap board roof & that Tarr'd." Orange Co., Va., Loose Court Papers.

privy A structure or room housing a latrine with a bench with holes. This term was little used in many areas of the South until the late 18th century. It appears to have enjoyed some currency before that time in South Carolina and, perhaps, Georgia. For a more detailed description, see **necessary house.**

> 1737 On a glebe, "a privy house of five foot square and six foot pitch with a door thereto" was to be built. Fairfax Parish, Fairfax Co., Va., Vestry Book.

prize house (priz, prise, press) A building that housed a *prize*, the term commonly applied to a variety of mechanical devices used to compact cured tobacco into large wooden barrels known as hogsheads, prior to shipment. In the colonial period tobacco was inspected at designated stations along the tidal estuaries, often requiring that hogsheads be opened and then repacked. Thus tobacco prizes might be found on individual plantations and at the inspection warehouses. By the early nineteenth century, the inspection warehouses had largely disappeared, and tobacco houses often included a *prize shed* on one side. See also **inspection house, rolling house.**

> 1718 On a plantation in Richmond County, Virginia, was "a good large Tobacco house called ye press house." Richmond Co., Va., Miscellaneous Record Book.
> 1744 At Morattico in Lancaster County, Virginia, "the roof of the Prise house, and the shades must be pulled off; and it must be new posted." Joseph Ball Letterbook, LC.
> 1776 At Sabine Hall in Richmond County, Virginia, a wind "broke to Pieces my Prize house full of tobacco stemmed for Prizing quite down." *Diary of Landon Carter*, 2.

prize post The principal member of the tobacco prize or press. Set vertically in the ground, it was the fulcrum on which the horizontal *tongue* pivoted to press tobacco into a hogshead below. In its broadest sense, the term could also refer to the entire prizing mechanism. See also **prize house.**

> 1759 Repairs made to the Pocomoke warehouses included "new tongues in the prize posts and a bolt through the top as they are all Split at the top." Accomack Co., Va., Order Book 1753–1763.

profile An outline of an object, especially a molding revealed by a transverse section.

promenade A place for strolling for pleasure and sociability. Walks were laid out in private and public pleasure grounds and along river banks, public squares, and other open areas for such amusement.

> 1786 "Along the river" in Savannah "there is a sand bank called the Bluff that remains partly dry in the winter and serves as a public promenade." Castiglioni, *Travels in the United States of North America.*
> 1815 Improvements to the state capital in Milledgeville included "the enclosure of the State-House square and avenues of trees planted in it, which in a few years will form an agreeable and beautiful prominade." *Georgia Journal.*

proportion   The comparative relationship between various elements or parts in terms of magnitude, quantity, and size. From the Renaissance through the 19th century, architectural theorists believed that the purpose of proportion was to establish a demonstrable harmony of parts in a building. The application of this principle to building occurred on two planes—in the overall conception of a building and at the level of individual components of a building. Some architects sought to establish precise rules of proportion based on the ratios they observed in the classical orders of architecture. British architectural books that set out the proportioning of individual elements such as doors, windows, and cornices came into use in the American colonies by the middle of the 18th century. The more comprehensive system of a singular modular proportion for all elements in a building rarely appeared in American design until the late 18th and early 19th centuries when architects and scholars such as Thomas Jefferson carefully absorbed the tenets espoused in European and British treatises on classical architecture. Before that time and long afterward, most builders thought of proportion in terms of traditional dimensioning modules. Taking the standard sizes of individual elements such as openings, framing members, and wall thicknesses, they would scale or *proportion* them to meet the aesthetic or structural requirements of the building under consideration. See also **symmetry.**

1679   Major framing members of a church were to be "of a substantial substance as the proportion of the sd church in reason doth require." Accomack Co., Va., Deeds, Wills, and Order Book 1678–1682.

1704   A dwelling was to be built "forty foot in length, with breadth proportionable." Wicomico Parish, Northumberland Co., Va., Vestry Book.

1733   A church was to have "six windows in ye body of the church and two in ye east end in proportion to the pitch of the walls." Blisland Parish, James City and New Kent Cos., Va., Vestry Book.

1756   "PROPORTION—The relationship which the several members of a column, or other part of a building, have to the whole of that column, or part; and which that column, or part, has to the ediface." Ware, *A Complete Body of Architecture*.

1771   "Whereas it appears that the dimentions of the alterpeace mentioned in the Articles with the undertaker for building the New Church are not according to the proportions of Architecture, the said undertaker is authorized and desired to make the same according to the true proportions of the Ionic order notwithstanding." Truro Parish, Fairfax Co., Va., Vestry Book.

1804   Benjamin Henry Latrobe explained to Thomas Jefferson why he had to make changes to the design of the Capitol in Washington: "It is necessary that the Columns of the Rotunda should be three feet longer than the Pilasters, in order to get rid of the blocks (Des) on which the Pilasters are raised. This contrivance which throws the Columns out of all proportion to the Entablature, is one of the innumerable bad consequences of a design radically defective in the harmony of its exterior decoration, with its internal distribution." *The Correspondence and Miscellaneous Papers of Benjamin Henry Latrobe*, 1.

1812   At Montpelier in Orange County, Virginia, the home of James Madison had "a massive portico to it of the plainest and most massive order of architecture, but which Palladio gives a specimen of the Tuscan. Mr. Madison himself superintended the building which he had executed by the hands of common workmen to whom he prescribed the proportions to be observed at the suggestion of Thomas Jefferson." Foster, *Jeffersonian America*.

1825   In the design of St. Matthew's Church in Hillsborough, North Carolina, architect William Nichols "has made a farther alteration in the plan . . . making it 35 by 45, saying that a less width would not be proportionate to the length." Cameron Family Papers, SHC.

1828   A builder submitted "estimates of the Cost of your Court House," including "A Tuscan Cornice with full entabliture, Drawn in Proportion to its Hight." Malcolm Crawford Papers, VSL.

prospect 1. An extensive or commanding sight or view, an important element in choosing a site for a dwelling or garden in the 18th century.

> 1733 "There is scarce a shrub in view to intercept your prospect, but grass as high as a man on horseback. Towards the woods there is a gentle ascent, till your sight is intercepted by an eminence, that overlooks the whole landscape." Byrd, *A Journey to the Land of Eden.*
>
> 1734 A notice read: "To be Let or SOLD an Island . . . which commands an entire prospect of the Harbour" of Charleston. *South Carolina Gazette.*
>
> 1777 "Col. Grayson has lately purchased a Hill at the Back of Dumfries, [Virginia,] on which he intends to build, it commands a fine Prospect of the Town, Quantico & its Shores, Part of Patowmack, adjacent Fields, Woods, etc." *VMHB,* 62.
>
> 1783 Architect John Hawks of New Bern sent a foreign visitor "an original sketch of the situation of the House and Gardens for the residence of the Governor . . . of North Carolina. It was agreed for the advantage of a prospect down the river, that the South front should be thrown more to the Eastward which leaves the Gardens not quite so regular as appears in the sketch." Hawks Letter, Miranda Papers, Academia Nacional de la Historia, Caracas.
>
> 1788 Belvedere, the home of Governor John Howard, was "situated upon the verge of the descent upon which Baltimore stands, its grounds formed a beautiful slant toward the Chesapeak. . . . The spot, thus indebted to nature and judiciously embellished, was as enchanting with in its own proper limits as in the fine view which extended far beyond them. . . . Both the perfections of the landscape, its near and distant scenery, were united in the view from the bow-window of the noble room in which breakfast was prepared, with the desire, I believe, of gratifying me with this exquisite prospect." Twining, *Travels in America 100 Years Ago.*

2. A pictorial representation of a scene or a building.

> 1737 It was announced that there was "JUST PUBLISHED . . . the West Prospect of ST. PHILLIPS CHURCH in CHARLES-TOWN." *South Carolina Gazette.*
>
> 1740 "All persons who had subscribed to Mr. Bishop Roberts (late of Charlestown deceased) for the Prospect and Plan of the said Town, are desired to send for them to Mary Roberts . . . at her House in Tradd Street, where they are ready to be delivered." *South Carolina Gazette.*

prostyle In classical architecture, a building that has freestanding columns in front. See also **astylar, peristyle.**

Prussian blue A bright blue pigment extensively used for interior painting. Patented in 1704, the color was made by heating scrap iron and organic materials (horn, hoof parings, hair, and scraps of hide) together with potash, saltpeter, and sand. The resulting blue substance was then ground to produce the pigment.

> 1756 Charleston merchant Samuel Carne listed "Prussian blue" among the pigments he offered for sale. *Maryland Gazette.*
>
> 1768 Before coming to Virginia, Governor Botetourt purchased "50lb of the Best Verditer" and "24lb of prussian blew" with which to color new paperhangings in the ballroom of the Governor's House in Williamsburg. Beaufort Papers, Gloucester Records Office, England.
>
> 1773 In Virginia, Captain John Billups paid William Houghson "12/ and sixpence for painting the Hall in Prussian Blue." Billups Papers, W&M.

public garden (pleasure garden) An urban pleasure ground laid out with walks, plantings, and buildings, which offered a variety of entertainments, recreations, and diversions to a paying public. Although many early public gardens were no more than taverns with gardens attached, where customers could participate in leisurely pursuits such as lawn bowling or fishing, by the late 18th and early 19th centuries a number of enterprising individuals laid out more ambitious schemes in most of the larger southern towns. Some were organized on a grand

prostyle

scale in imitation of English pleasure gardens and were named after such famous London ones as Vauxhall and Ranelagh. The proprietors of these public gardens tried to attract various classes of urban society not only with a pleasing surrounding but also with a number of well staged events such as concerts, sporting events, and firework displays. Many public gardens came to life at night under the illumination of lanterns and served as a stage for merriment and assignations.

> **1784** A public pleasure garden in Baltimore boasted "convenient Summer-Houses . . . now ready for the Reception of Ladies and Gentlemen." The proprietor offered a variety of beverages as well as "cold Collations" to his visitors. *Baltimore Daily Repository*.
> **1801** "The arrangements" of Chatsworth Gardens in Baltimore "are said to be extremely neat, such as forming pleasant summer houses, serpentine walks, shady groves, and every other rural appearance, which may give a pleasing relaxation to the leisure hours of the industrious citizen. A band of music generally attend in the summer months, three times a week. Accommodations and refreshments are likewise provided." Warner and Hanna, *Baltimore City Directory, 1801*.
> **1804** In Richmond was "Hay Market Garden. Now in a high state of accommodation for ENTERTAINMENTS, being provided with excellent Musicians and a Fire Worker of great celebrity, will be prepared to amuse visitors during the races, with CONCERTS, BALLS, FIRE-WORKS, & ILLUMINATIONS, in the most splendid style." *Virginia Argus*.

public hospital See **hospital** (2).

public house (publick house) A house or building licensed by local officials for public entertainment through the sale of wine, ale, brandy, and other spirits and the boarding and accommodation of travelers. The term was less commonly used than *ordinary* and *tavern*. See also **ordinary, tavern.**

> **1669** Harsh words were spoken at a Charles County, Maryland, dwelling house "being a house of publick resort & entertainment." Archives of Maryland, 60.
> **1715** Leave was given to erect "a publick house of entertainment with the bounds of the courthouse land." Northumberland Co., Va., Court Order Book 1713–1719.
> **1783** An ordinance was passed "that any master or keeper of any public house, or tavern in Charleston, who shall permit it or suffer any tragedy, comedy, farce, interlude, or other theatrical entertainment to be acted, performed, or exhibited therein, without permission first . . . shall forfeit his license." *Ordinances of the City Council of Charleston*.
> **1826** A boastful hostler claimed "that I keep as good a Publick House as any in the State of Virginia; my Stables are as good and as well provided as any gentleman's stable—my Bed Rooms are good and clean enough for the President of the U.S. to sleep in." *The Intelligencer, and Petersburg Commercial Advertiser*.

pug To pack or fill the space under a floor with mortar, clay, sawdust, or other material for the purposes of fireproofing or soundproofing a room or space.

> **1801** Washington artisan William Foxton's bill for "Stuco & Plasters Work done . . . for John Tayloe Esq" included "666-2/3 [yds] Pugging between Joists [at] 1/8 28.10.10." Tayloe Papers, VHS.
> **1820** At the White House in Washington, "the garret and second story floors have been laid of best 5/4 heart pine, and the whole of these stories counter-floored and pugged, to guard against fire." *Daily National Intelligencer*.

pulley (pully) A small moveable wheel with a grooved rim for carrying a rope, that turns in a frame or block and serves to change the direction of a weight. In a single sliding sash window, a pulley was often set near the top of the window casing, with a rope connected to the lower sash at one end and counterbalanced by a lead or iron weight at the other. Most 18th-century pulleys consisted of a wood case with an iron or brass pin on which a wood wheel rotated. In the early 19th century, iron and brass were substituted for the wood portion of the pulley. See also **cord, sash, weight.**

> 1733 Church windows were "to be hung with leads and pulleys." Blisland Parish, James City and New Kent Cos., Va., Vestry Book.
>
> 1738 It was "ordered that Marble Font with Wooden Frame & Top with Pullys & Weights to Lift it off & on the Bason . . . be sent for the use of the Church in Annapolis." St. Anne's Parish, Anne Arundel Co., Md., Vestry Book.
>
> 1745 Charles Pinckney of Charleston calculated the cost of "Pigg lead to cast into window leads for 44 Sash windows £5.11.6; Lines for Pullies for Do." Included in these calculations were "14 sash window frames, for glass 11 × 9—18 pains in each window, to run with double pullies." Huger Smith, *Dwelling Houses of Charleston.*
>
> 1808 One of Thomas Jefferson's workmen wrote that "we also want two doz. brass pulleys to finish hanging the sashes." Coolidge Collection, Massachusetts Historical Society.

pulpit
Christ Church, Lancaster County, Va.

pulpit (pulpet)   An elevated structure consisting of an enclosed platform with a desk and seat, used in churches and meetinghouses by the minister to deliver the sermon and conduct other parts of the service. For most Protestant denominations, the pulpit served as the central organizing force that governed the layout of churches. Because of the importance of the sermon and reading the Bible, the ideal plan was one that was a square or squarish rectangle with the pulpit located at the center of one of the longer walls so that all worshipers could hear the minister. In many Anglican churches as well as some dissenting meetinghouses, the pulpit was elaborately embellished with fine carvings, molded paneling, an elaborately shaped base, and crowned overhead by a sounding board or type. With the introduction of English architectural books into the American colonies in the second quarter of the 18th century, many pulpits erected in the South, especially those constructed in urban Anglican churches, followed metropolitan design precedents. See also **church, meetinghouse.**

> 1677 Specifications for a church called for the "pulpit to be of wainscoate 4 foot diameter, & made with 7 sides, 6 foot allowed for ye reading desks and passage into ye pulpitt: ye ministers pew to be under ye pulpitt, & raised 18 Inches and ye readers deske under it." Petsworth Parish, Gloucester Co., Va., Vestry Book.
>
> 1760 At St. Michael's Church in Charleston, carver Henry Burnett's account listed "a Swelling Freese Cut Lawrel Leaves; 24 feet of Ogee Carved 5 Leaved Grass in the Cornish; 22 feet Ovelo for the pulpit; 22 feet Large Ogee fully Enriched; 22 feet 3/4 Ogee Carved 5 Leaved Grass; 33 feet Ovelo for the Pannels; 16 Bracketts for the Stairs of the pulpit; Carving a Swelling Torus cut with Foliage Flowers & cut through & Relieved on the Backside; 40 feet of Ogee on ye Architraves; 1 Pine apple on the top of the pulpit; 6 Bracketts or Supports under the pulpit; 2 Corinthian Capitals for the Columns that Support the Type of the pulpit." Williams, *St. Michael's.*
>
> 1762 It was ordered that "a Pulpit [be] Fixed at a proper Height from the floor and of a Sufficient size wainscotted with a Door hung upon Proper Hinges to it and a pair of Stairs to lead up to it a cushion board to it and a seat in it and a well worked canopy fixed over it." Frederick Parish, Frederick Co., Va., Vestry Book.

pulvinate   A convex profile, cushion-shaped. The frieze in some Ionic orders has a pulvinated configuration. The term was not common in the South. See also **swelling.**

pump   A device placed over a well for raising water. Most pumps consisted of a tube in which suction is created by means of a plunger or piston activated by a handle, forcing water upward to a spout.

1736 A house to be let in Charleston contained "a convenient Kitchin, yard, garden, brick-well and pump." *South Carolina Gazette.*

1751 It was "Resolved, that the serjant put up the four wells, that are to be made in this Borough. . . . There is to be one Pump in each Well made of old Pine with Spout and Caps to Each Well. There is to be an Iron handle and Brake to Each well with upper and lower ropes well stapled and Iron bolts and Nuts for the Bolts to work on. . . . the Pumps and Covers to be Tarred." Norfolk, Va., Common Hall Minute Book 1736–1798.

punch   **1.** A short metal rod tapered at one end used for piercing or driving. Carpenters used nail punches to drive the head of a nail below the surface of the wood.

2. To pierce or cut an object so as to make a hole through it.

1784 A blacksmith charged a client for "punching 3 holes in hinges." James Anderson Account Book, CWF.

1796 A jail was to have vertical, 1 3/4-inch iron bars across the windows with "Cross Bars 3/4 inch square 5 Inches apart checked & punched throu the 1 3/4 Inch bars." Stokes Co., N.C., Miscellaneous Court Records, NCA&H.

3. A short, upright framing member; a stud. *Punch* in this sense is an abbreviation of *puncheon.* For a more detailed description, see **puncheon.**

1623 "Few or none" of the dwellings in Virginia were "framed house but punches sett into the Ground and Covered with Boarde." *Records of the Virginia Company,* 4.

1765 A log glebe house was to have "a partition across the house of punch and pennel work." Augusta Co., Va., Court Judgments.

puncheon (punch, punchen, punchin)   A short, thick, split or hewn piece of timber, sometimes roughly finished on one or more surfaces. In the southern colonies, puncheons often appeared as sturdy, upright elements or *pales* in fences and *palisades.* Puncheons also were used for roofing and, from the late 18th century, for flooring, especially in log structures. Quicker and easier to produce than sawn or even carefully riven boards, puncheons were much employed in frontier situations or wherever economy and speed in construction were desired.

1686 A domestic yard in Stafford County, Virginia, was described by its owner as "pallizado'd in with locust Punchens, which is as good as if it were walled in & more lasting than any of our bricks." *William Fitzhugh and His Chesapeake World.*

1725 Old Estotoe, a Cherokee village in Oconee County, South Carolina, was "a large Town and very well fortifyed all round with Punchins and also ditched on the Outside of the sd Punchins." Mereness, *Travels in the American Colonies.*

1791 In Kentucky, "puncheon floors are all right as long as it is cold enough to let them be covered with furs." Jillson, *Tales of the Dark and Bloody Ground.*

1804 In Maryland, "houses or cabins . . . are generally made of heavy timber logs covered with split timbers called 'puncheons' which they pin to the rafters with wooden pins." *MHM,* 4.

punk   Partially decayed or rotten wood.

1736 A builder promised to fill or "stop the punk holes in the wall." Lynnhaven Parish, Princess Anne Co., Va., Vestry Book.

1819 The windows at Poplar Forest in Bedford County, Virginia, were "exposed to danger . . . The water can't be fenced off better. The woodwork all around the sash was as dry as punk." Coolidge Collection, Massachusetts Historical Society.

Purbeck stone   A grayish, shelly limestone quarried from the Isle of Purbeck in Dorset in the south of England. Although not a true marble, the stone could take a high degree of polish, which turned it a dark gray, as is evident in the colonnettes in Salisbury and York cathedrals. Exported through London and Bristol, the material was used in the colonies primarily as a paving stone, often in contrasting patterns with white limestones. As a paving stone, Purbeck was less polished and thus lighter gray in color.

1740 The vestry charged "£84 payable to Capt Hooper for freight on a parcel of Purbeck Stones Capt Jolleif sent to pave the Church being four pounds 10/ sterling pr bill lading." St. Philip's Parish, Charleston, S.C., Vestry Book.

1756 A notice read: "Wanted about 280 feet of purbeck and 80 feet of balne shrosberry stone for completing the piazzas of the capitol in Williamsburg. . . . The size of the stone that will best answer is 18 inch square." *Virginia Gazette.*

purlin (purline, purloin) A longitudinal roof timber carried by principal rafters or gable-end walls and, in turn, providing support for common rafters or vertically applied sheathing boards. Some purlins sat on the back of the principal rafters in shallow trenches; others were morticed into the sides of the rafters; a few were clasped or supported in the angle between the collar and the principal; and yet others stood on short posts and had the edge of the principal rest against them.

1674 The roof of the statehouse in St. Mary's City was to have "six paire of principalls and double purloines framed in even with the Rafters & to be morticed in." *Archives of Maryland, 2.*

1760 A church roof was "to be built with Principals and Purloins three main Girders and a King Post on each." Augusta Parish, Augusta Co., Va., Vestry Book.

putlock, putlog A horizontal scaffolding member placed perpendicularly into a wall, on which are laid planks to create a work platform. Putlock holes are the spaces in masonry buildings that are occupied by one end of the scaffold poles or putlocks during construction. These were sometimes left open after completion of construction.

1755 "Putlogs, [are] pieces of Timbers, or short Poles, (about seven Feet long) used by Masons and Bricklayers in building Scaffolds to work on. The Putlogs, are those pieces which lie horizontal to the Building, one end resting upon the Ledgers; which are those pieces that lie parallel to the side of the Building." Salmon, *Palladio Londinensis.*

1769 The vestry hired a workman to "Stop the Putlock holes" of their new brick church. St. Stephen's Parish, S.C., Vestry Book.

1772 The vestry ordered that "the putlock or Scaffold holes to be stop'd." Wicomico Parish, Va., Vestry Book.

putty (puttey) A compound of whiting and linseed oil with a pasty consistency, used to secure windowpanes in sash and as a bond for brickwork where tight, clean joints were required. Beginning in the early 18th century, brick frontispieces and arches that were not bonded with a fine lime mortar were often laid with putty. Like lead, glass, paint, and some hardware, putty was frequently imported from Great Britain. See also **glaze, mortar.**

1746 Work at a glebe house in Fluvanna County, Virginia, included "glass and putty" for the windows. Cabell Papers, W&M.

1766 "The Arches and Pediment heads of the Doors & Windows" of a church were "to be of bricks rubbed, gauged and set in putty." Truro Parish, Fairfax Co., Va., Vestry Book.

1766 Church windows were "to be glazed with Crown Glass & to be put in with such Putty as will be proof against Wind & water." All Faiths Parish, St. Mary's Co., Md., Vestry Book.

1767 In ordering columns from an English merchant, a Maryland lawyer specified that they were to "be Composed of Different Blocks or Pieces of Stone to be Placed upon the other Putty or Cement for Joining must be sent in with them or Instructions How to make it." Trostel, *Mount Clare.*

1798 For sale in a store in Petersburg, Virginia, was "Putty in bladders." *Virginia Gazette and Petersburg Intelligencer.*

pycnostyle   See **intercolumniation.**

pyramid   Any element shaped with sloping sides that taper to a point, such as a spire, finial, or obelisk. Because of symbolic associations with Egyptian funerary practices, pyramidal monuments were occasionally imported into the South and erected in churchyards. These were mainly of tall, slender proportions rather than the squat form now associated with the term. See also **obelisk.**

> 1674   The roof of the statehouse in St. Mary's City was to have "Bargeboards att the Gable Ends & Piramedes." *Archives of Maryland,* 2.
> 1699   St. Anne's Church in Annapolis was to have "Pyramedes at the four Corners of the Topp and the like att the Porch and Room Opposite." *Archives of Maryland,* 22.
> 1766   A church was to have a front "Portico with two Pyramids" crowning the flanking towers. St. Andrew's Parish, St. Mary's Co., Md., Vestry Book.
> 1771   "If it is proposed to have" a monument to Lord Botetourt "in the Form of a Pyramid, it can be placed conveniently in no part, except at the Bottom of the Isle fronting the Pulpit" in the chapel at the College of William and Mary. *Tyler's Quarterly Historical Magazine,* 3.

quadra   See **socle.**

quarrel (quarry)   A square or lozenged-shaped piece of glass set diagonally in a window frame. Through the first half of the 18th century, many casement and transom windows consisted of several such small-sized quarrels secured in place by slender lead pieces known as *cames.* See also **diamond** (1).

> 1698   Shipped to a planter in Virginia was "a box of glass in quarries with lead answerable in Diamond Cut containing about 80 or 100 feet." *William Fitzhugh and His Chesapeake World.*
> 1731   In the Anglican church in Annapolis, part of the glazing work consisted of "180 new Qua put in at 2d . . . £2.10.0." St. Anne's Parish, Anne Arundel Co., Md., Vestry Book.
> 1734   "QUARRELS of Glass—a Pane or Piece of Glass cut in a Diamond Form. They are two Kinds, *viz.* Square and Long, each of which is of different Sizes, express'd by the Number of them which makes a Foot, *viz.* 8ths, 10ths, 12ths, 15ths, 18ths and 20ths; but all the Sizes are cut to the same Angles, the Acute Angle being 77 Degrees 19 Min. in the Square Quarrels, and 67 Degrees 21 Minutes in the Long ones." *Builder's Dictionary.*

quarry   An open-air excavation from which building stone is obtained by cutting with picks, wedges, and drills. Except for parts of northern Maryland, much of the southern seaboard lacked quarriable stone for building. One of the earliest commercial operations in the South was located at Aquia Creek in Stafford County, Virginia, where buff-colored sandstone was quarried by the 1750s. Builders used the stone from this quarry for decorative trim on neighboring churches and dwellings as well as for a number of public buildings in Washington, D.C., including the Capitol and White House. From the 1780s through the 1820s, several quarries opened for business near Baltimore and in western Virginia, offering customers a growing supply of native sandstone, limestone, granite, marble, and slate. The important slate quarries in Buckingham County, Virginia, provided an alternative roofing material that appealed to many public building commissioners. Despite these efforts, many coastal towns continued to import stone from England, Italy, and northern states. Not until the advent of canals and railroads, which made shipment of material from

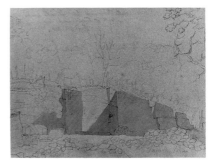

quarry
B. H. Latrobe, Mr. Robertson's Quarry, Aquia, Va., 1806

remote locations economically feasible, did southern quarries have a major impact on local building.

> **1734** "A Plantation call'd Epsom Wells, situated in St. John's Parish . . . affords good Stone for building, a Quarry being now open'd." *South Carolina Gazette.*
>
> **1794** The stone for a Catholic chapel to be built in Hagerstown, Maryland, "can be had on the lot where the house is to be built, and the quarry is already opened, which will save a great deal of expence in hauling." *Washington Spy.*
>
> **1796** An announcement appeared as follows: "FREESTONE, Warranted equal if not superior in quality and colour to any on the continent. WE have commenced the Stone-cutting business at JOHN DUNBAR'S Quarry on Aquia Run, Stafford County, Virginia, which we mean to carry on in its various branches. . . . Those gentlemen engaged in building at any seaport in the United States may be supplied (with at least) the ornamental parts of their houses at moderate expence, as by preparing the stone at the quarry, there will be a great saving in waste and carriage." *Alexandria Gazette.*
>
> **1817** In Buckingham County, Virginia, "THE Subscribers are now engaged in working a SLATE QUARRY . . . and have now on hand ready for delivery about 200 square of excellent SLATE, which will be delivered to any purchaser either in Richmond, or any other place on James River." *Richmond Commercial Compiler.*

quarry-faced Ashlar masonry whose visible side is roughly dressed with a hammer.

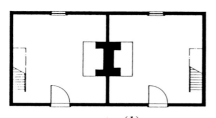

quarter (1)
Plan of double quarter, Tuckahoe, Goochland County, Va.

quarter **1.** A domestic structure devoted to the accommodation of slaves. Like the *quartering house*, it was a type of *outbuilding* that provided both functional and social separation between servants and those they served. The *quartering house* sheltered any combination of indentured Europeans, African-Americans both free and enslaved, and Native American Indians of varying status. The quarter reflected the increasing acceptance and codification of slavery that began in the mid-17th century and thus existed to house one particular group of people. Quarters, like *quartering houses*, were often architecturally indistinguishable from the dwelling houses of the free population. The slaveholder's resources, both economic and humane, and the degree to which he chose to expend them, dictated the form and quality of quarter structures. Typical examples were single story, one- or two-room buildings with gable end chimneys, earthen floors, unglazed, shuttered windows, and unfinished interiors. This use of the term, and its variant *Negro quarter*, were confined mostly to the Chesapeake region and environs, though the building type appeared throughout the South. See also **Negro house, Negro hut, quarter house.**

> **1754** Directions were given "for building a quarter on the Glebe Sixteen feet square and an outside Chimney." Southam Parish, Cumberland Co., Va., Vestry Book.
>
> **1770** Appraisal of a plantation noted "one negro quarter 20 by 16 brick gable end and chimney weather boarded with clapboards and covered with feather edge shingles together with a shed on one side." Queen Anne's Co., Md. Deed Book RT, No. 1.

2. A group or cluster of houses occupied by slaves. By extension, this use of the term indicated a distinct residential or community area of relative autonomy, somewhat removed from the immediate vicinity of the slaveholder's dwelling or located at an associated farm or *plantation*. It is this meaning of *quarter* that enjoyed the longest currency, persisting well into the 19th century throughout the South. See **quarter** (3).

> **1733** Developing a Virginia plantation involved a search for "a place to fix yr Quarter . . . ye woods are so very thick now yt we cou'd not see about us, but the best place yt [we] cou'd find free from dispute was ye old feild next ye branch towards the Range." Latane Papers, UVa.

quarter (2) Early 19th-century quarter at Lavington, Colleton County, S.C.

1746 As observed in the Chesapeake, "a Negro Quarter is a Number or Huts of Hovels, built at some Distance from the Mansion-House; where the Negroes reside with their Wives and Families, and cultivate, at vacant Times, the little Spots allow'd them." Kimber, "Observations in Several Voyages and Travels in America," *London Magazine*.
1792 In Orange County, Virginia, "I walked to the Quarter, Moses about framing a house there." Francis Taylor Diary, CWF.
1820s A former slave recalled that at a Union County, South Carolina, plantation, "the quarter had nine houses." Yetman, *Life under the 'Peculiar Institution.'*

3. Part of a larger holding of land devoted to agricultural production. These component farms or *plantations* were worked by slaves, generally supervised by overseers or foremen, both black and white. A quarter was provided with some combination of appropriate domestic and agricultural structures, often limited to quarters, an *overseer's house*, a *tobacco house* or other crop-related buildings, and a *corncrib* for food supplies. Quarters could be part of, adjacent to, or quite separate and distinct from the tract on which the landowner lived. The term and its infrequent variant *Negro quarter* largely belong to the upper South, although the division of land into agricultural production units occurred throughout the region. See also **dwelling plantation, home farm, home plantation, out farm, out plantation.**

> **1678** A deed described the parcel sold as "a ridge of land known as Francks Quarter on Coulchester Creek." Norfolk Co., Va., Deed Book 1675–1687.
> **1688** Observations on establishing a plantation in Virginia noted the possibility of "a Quarter to settle hands upon, for the larger support of the Riverside plantation." *William Fitzhugh and his Chesapeake World.*
> **1771** An advertisement of a thousand-acre tract in south-central Virginia claimed "amongst many things that may be justly said in Favour of the Land, it is well situated for a Negro Quarter, being convenient to Mills, and remote from Courthouses and Very public Roads." *Virginia Gazette.*
> **1807** In Virginia, "when the estate, however, is so large as to be divided into several farms, then separate quarters are attached to the house of the overseer on each farm." Weld, *Travels Through the States of North America*, 1.

4. Another name, chiefly British, for *stud*. For a more detailed description, see **stud.**

5. A British term for *shed*. For a more detailed description, see **shed.**

quartered Lumber that is sawn from the log at a perpendicular angle to the growth rings. In contrast to flat sawing where all the boards or planks are sawn from a log in one direction producing lumber with a tangential or flat-grained face, quarter sawing divides a log into four wedge-shaped sections or quarters. Each quarter section is then sawn perpendicular to the growth rings, producing a tighter radial face. Such radially sawn lumber was easier to dry without warping and shrinking and thus much in demand for flooring and weatherboarding.

> 1674 Stairs at the statehouse in St. Mary's City were "to be made of good white Oke quartered Planck." *Archives of Maryland,* 2.
> 1711 The sills of a church "which were ordered to be of quartered stuff being too difficult to be gott, Itt is now ordered that the said peices be of ye best ring oake squared with ye saw of the same dimensions." Christ Church Parish, Middlesex Co., Va., Vestry Book.
> 1760 "The flooring of the Pews &c. [are] to be laid with well season'd quarter'd Pine Plank clear of Sap." Stratton Major Parish, King and Queen Co., Va., Vestry Book.

quartering house   A domestic *outbuilding* devoted to the accommodation of servants. Located apart from the dwelling of those served, the quartering house represented the increasing functional and social separation evident in English building practice beginning in the late medieval period. The term is confined in use to the 17th century and geographically to the Chesapeake region. See also **quarter** (1).

> 1647 A York County, Virginia, agreement stipulated that a tenant "maintayne the dwelling house, Quartering house & Tobacco house standing uppon the premises." York Co., Va., Deeds, Orders, Wills 2.
> 1657 A carpenter agreed to build "one small quartering house of twenty-five or thirty foot long and so much other out house as will make up the sum of ninety foot of housing." Surry Co., Va., Orders, Deeds, Wills 1645–1672.
> 1661 Proceedings of the provincial court noted that one "Judith Loue was present at Mr. Gerrards Quartering howse at Mattapenny when Captaine Hinfield brought thither certain Iresh Servants to sell unto Mr. Gerrard." *Archives of Maryland,* 41.

quarter round (1/4 round)   A convex molding, the profile of which forms a quadrant of a circle; sometimes referred to as an *ovolo* by 18th-century architects, writers, and some classically minded craftsmen. For a more detailed description, see **ovolo.**

> 1733 The moldings in "ye pews, pulpit, and desk [are] to be quarter round with raised panels." Blisland Parish, James City and New Kent Cos., Va., Vestry Book.
> 1745 In a church "ye side of the pews [are] to be square panneld work 4 feet high, rais'd three inches the doors and faceing to be 1/4 round pannel'd work." Fredericksville Parish, Louisa Co., Va., Vestry Book.
> 1806 A chapel in St. John's Parish, South Carolina, was to be built with "weatherboards on the outside plained and beaded, or struck with a quarter round." *City Gazette and Daily Advertiser.*

quay (key)   A landing place for the loading and unloading of ships along the edge of a body of water, especially one with a battered wall of masonry or logs; a dock. See also **landing, wharf.**

> 1741 "There are several fair Streets" in Charleston "and some very handsom Buildings; as Mr. Landgrave Smith's House on the Key, with a Draw-Bridge and Wharf before it; Col. Rhett's on the Key." Oldmixon, *The British Empire in America.*
> 1816 Lumber for sale in Baltimore "at the head of Hughes' Quay." *Federal Republican and Baltimore Telegraph.*

quick lime   See **lime.**

quincunx   In the design of a formal garden, trees or shrubs planted in squares of five with one at each corner and one in the middle.

quirk   In moldings, a quirk is a sharp return from the extreme projection separating the one part from the other. It has a sharply angled channel which separates the convex part of a molding from the fillet. The channel of a quirked bead terminates at an angle, rather than

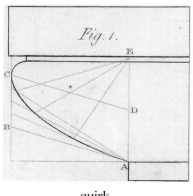

quirk

perpendicular to the bottom. Quirked Greek and Gothic moldings appeared in the South at the beginning of the 19th century.

> 1801 William Foxton's bill for "Stuco & Plasters Work done . . . for John Tayloe Esq" included an array of elaborate decorative work for Tayloe's Washington residence, including "206 [feet] 10 [inches] Bead [at] 0/3 . . . 324 [feet] 6 [inches] Quirk Dᵒ/ 0/1." Tayloe Papers, VHS.
>
> 1811 The interior trim of a dwelling house was to have "Splayed Elbows [with] quirk ovolo" moldings. Riddell Accounts, Pleasants Papers, MHS.

quoin (coin) The external angle of a wall, especially the stones or bricks that form the corner of the wall. Decorative quoining was occasionally used to accentuate the termination of a wall plane in the 18th and early 19th centuries. This was done either through the use of contrasting materials such as stone in a brick wall, or through the use of painted or rubbed brickwork. Another method consisted of raised or rusticated quoins, whereby bricks or stones projected beyond the surface of the wall and generally had bevelled edges. Occasionally imitation quoins were executed in wood on frame houses. See also **rusticated.**

quoin
Bevel-edged quoins, Mount Airy, Richmond County, Va., c. 1758

> 1749 A bricklayer was paid for constructing "900 coins and returns" at Marlborough in Stafford County, Virginia. John Mercer Ledger, Bucks Co., Pa., Historical Society.
>
> 1766 "The outside Quoins" of a church in southern Maryland were "to be Built with Stock Bricks, as also all the outside Walls." St. Andrew's Parish, St. Mary's City, Md., Vestry Book.
>
> 1767 "The Quoins and arches" of a church in northern Virginia "to be of Rub'd Brick." Fairfax Parish, Fairfax Co., Va., Vestry Book.
>
> 1771 A committee reviewing the work done on a church observed "that the Stone coins are coarse grained and rather too soft, they desire the same may be painted with white lead and oyle, which they think will make them sufficient." Truro Parish, Fairfax Co., Va., Vestry Book.

rabbet (rabit, rebate) A long channel, groove, or recess on or near the edge of a surface, cut at right angles to receive another member or element such as the frame of a door or window. See also **tongue and groove.**

rabbet
B. H. Latrobe, Detail of a rabbet at meeting of the leaves of a folding door, Decatur House, Washington, D.C., 1818

> 1704 At the justices' end of a courtroom, "the floor [is] to be groved or Rabbitted." Middlesex Co., Va., Court Order Book 1694–1705.
>
> 1742 A kitchen "door [is to be] made to fall in a Rabit." Bristol Parish, Prince George Co., Va., Vestry Book.
>
> 1771 The corner posts of St. John's Church in Granville County, North Carolina, were to "be got fourteen Inches one way & twenty two Inches the other to be Rabited out so as to make flush walls with the other framing." Francis Hawks Collection, Church Historical Society.
>
> 1796 The door frame of a jail was "to be made of White oak timber 4 Inches thick & 21 Inches wide" and installed in the jamb "so as to leave a Rabit on the Inside for the Shetter to fall in." Stokes Co., N.C., Miscellaneous Court Records, NCA&H.

rack An open frame of wood or metal for holding fodder, usually hay and straw, for animals. A rack is often fixed to a wall above a manger in a stable or barn but may also be freestanding and placed in fields and yards when required.

> 1742 "The present Kitching" to be "set upon sells and moved & fitted up for a stable with Rack and manger." Bristol Parish, Prince George Co., Va., Vestry Book.
>
> 1792 "A Stall for two Cows 10 by 12 in the clear" was to be built with "two racks, rounds of which to stand upright and not Angularly as is customary." Robert Carter Papers, LC.
>
> 1802 Carpenter's charges to John Tayloe for work on the stable behind his Washington residence included "Rack Staves 1/ 156 holes 6ᵈ." Tayloe Papers, VHS.

rafter Any one of a series of paired scantling or poles, set at an angle, used to support the covering of a roof. For a description of various types of rafters, see **common rafter, hip rafter, jack rafter, principal rafter.**

> 1674 The roof of the statehouse in St. Mary's City was to have "rafters Eighteene foot & halfe long standing twelve inches a sunder with six paire of principalls and double purloines framed in even with the Rafters & to be morticed in & every paire of Principalls to be braced in & every paire of Rafters to have two buttoned braced to the Collor beame every paire of principalls to be tenn & Eight inches square . . . the small Rafters four and three Inches square to be topped with mortice and Tennant and pinned att head & hipp tennanted at the foote." *Archives of Maryland*, 2.
> 1759 A courthouse roof was to have "rafters 4 inches by 3 inches." Johnston Co., N.C., Court Minute Book 1759–1766.

raftered house An impermanent building type constructed without side walls so that its rafters sit directly in the ground. Such buildings appeared in the Chesapeake in the 17th century and were often used as tobacco houses and storage buildings.

> 1658 "I owe Mr. Bushrode for the tobaccoe house Three score foot with Rafters upon the ground." York Co., Va., Deed, Order, and Will Book 1657–1662.
> 1670 A plantation in Surry County, Virginia, contained "3 sixty foot walplate tobacco house [and] one 50 foote raftered house." Surry Co., Va., Deed and Will Book 1652–1672.

rail In general, a horizontal member framed between two uprights to form a piece of wainscot, fence panel, or barrier or support such as a handrail or bar. In joinery, a flat horizontal member framed by mortise and tenon joints into vertical stiles. Also, the horizontal members of a sash frame. See also **bar** (4), **fence, meeting rail, handrail, stile, wainscot.**

railing An open-framed barrier of various types consisting of a horizontal rail supported by a series of uprights such as balusters or posts. A balustrade or fence; the horizontal members of a balustrade, fence, staircase, or bar. See also **baluster, bar** (4), **fence.**

> 1640 A workman's account listed "10 dayes work in railing in the hog court." Maryland Patents, Certificates, and Warrants 1637–1650, MSA.
> 1711 Churchwardens listed in their accounts "railing in the Communion Table." Christ Church Parish, Charleston, Co., S.C., Vestry Book.
> 1723 "To Mr. James Glenn for railing the Fork Church yard, in part of payment 2500 lbs. tob." St. Paul's Parish, Hanover Co., Va., Vestry Book.
> 1777 The statute of Governor Botetourt in the capitol in Williamsburg was "surrounded with a neat Iron Railing." *VMHB*, 62.

raising hinge
Prestwould, Mecklenburg County, Va.

raising hinge A hinge with a spiral thread on one part of its pivot or a beveled barrel at its pin that forces the door or shutter to lift up as it is opened to clear an obstacle, such as a carpet. See also **skew hinge.**

> 1795 Gabriel Manigault of Charleston ordered from Bird, Savage, and Bird of London "24 best 4 Inch butt hinges half left & half right handed, & 6 of them raising hinges." Manigault Papers, South Caroliniana Library.

raising piece, raising plate Chiefly English, a wall plate. The term also may have been used to describe what was then a new feature in architecture, a second plate that sat on top of ceiling joists and carried the feet of the rafters. This secondary plate was also known as a *false plate*. See **false plate, wall plate.**

1703 "The four Corner Posts called the Principal Posts . . . should be each of one piece, so long as to reach up to the Beam of the Roof, or Raising-plate. . . . Its lower end is to be Tenannted, and let into a Mortess made near the corner of the Ground-plate Frame; and its upper end hath also a Tennant on it to fit into a Mortess made in the Beam of the Roof, or Raising-piece." Moxon, *Mechanick Exercises*.
1755 "BEAM-FILLING is Bricklayers work, tis only filling up the vacant spaces betwixt the Raising-Plate and the Joists." Salmon, *Palladio Londinensis*.
1774 Carpenter's work on the Corbit House in Odessa, Delaware, listed "3 sqr 29 ft Raising pieces & Wall plates at 10/." Sweeney, *Grandeur on the Appoquinimink*.

rake, raking A term applied to any member or element inclined or sloped from the horizontal.

1797 A carpenter's work at a parsonage house included "34 feet Raking Modillion cornice to the pediment." St. Michael's Parish, Charleston, S.C., Vestry Book.
1811 A stairway was installed with "raking Skirting." Riddell Accounts, Pleasants Papers, MHS.

ram To pack or compress materials such as soil to form a hard, dense surface. In a building context, earthen floors of clay, lime, straw, and other materials were often combined and rammed to produce a durable surface. Fence posts and building posts were often rammed after they had been inserted into their hole in order mitigate subsidence and lateral movement. See also **cram, earthen floor.**

1730 Payment was made to a workman for "digging of post holes and Raming." St. Anne's Parish, Anne Arundel Co., Md., Vestry Book.
1806 The foundation of a market house was to be filled "with earth well rammed inside, and outside, ready to be received a good pavement of hard brick, which shall be laid throughout the same next year, upon a good bed of sand." Jefferson Co., Va., Deed Book 1806–1808.
1821 Cabins built for the poor in King George County, Virginia, were to have "floors . . . filled up twelve inches above the common level of the earth with dirt after being well rammed." King George Co., Va., Court Order Book 1817–1822.

ramp An inclined plane; specifically, a pronounced, concave, sloping curve of a handrail, wainscot, or coping as it rises from an incline to a higher horizontal level. Many of the most elaborate stairs in the 18th and early 19th centuries contained ramped and twisted balustrades with curved handrails that turned with the direction of the stair and were ramped at the landings. See also **twist.**

1719 A brick wall around a churchyard was to be finished "with a handsom Coopin Brick upon the Top and Genteely Rompt at each side of the Gates." St. Peter's Parish, New Kent Co., Va., Vestry Book.
1746 In the design of his Charleston house, Charles Pinckney specified that there were to be "one pair of great stairs up the 2nd floar with ramp Twist & Brackets." Huger Smith, *Dwelling Houses of Charleston*.
1800 In the "open newel stairs" of John Steele's house in Rowan County, North Carolina, carpenter John Langdon was to construct "Ramps in the hand rail." John Steele Papers, SHC.

ramp
Stair, Carter's Grove,
James City County, Va.

rampart A broad, elevated, earthen wall raised as a defensive fortification around a site.

1716 Jamestown "is built on an island, it was fortified with a small rampart with embrasures, but no all is gone to ruin." Fontaine, *Memoirs of a Huguenot Family*.

range 1. (*v.*) To set in a straight, even, or level fashion. (*n.*) Any element that runs in a straight manner. In masonry, a row or course of stonework, or a wall laid up in courses. Range work may vary from the regularity of ashlar to random range work, with rectangular stones of different heights and widths laid in irregular but discernible courses.

1762 The walls of a church were "to be Built entirely of ranged stone . . . with Two folding wainscot doors . . . the upper parts of them to range with the Tops of the windows." Frederick Parish, Frederick Co., Va., Vestry Book.

1764 The last plank in a post and rail fence was "to range with the Top of ye Post." St. George's Parish, Harford Co., Md., Vestry Book.

1808 A courthouse in Columbia, Tennessee, was to be built "set on underpinning of stone ranged work." *The Impartial Review and Cumberland Repository.*

2. A cooking apparatus in a kitchen fireplace.

rasp A kind of coarse *file*, its cutting surface formed by raised points rather than incised, straight grooves. Rasps were used for rough, preliminary shaping of surfaces.

rebate A rabbet. For a more detailed description, see **rabbet.**

recess A receding part or space, such as a cavity in a wall for a door, bed, sideboard, or piece of furniture; an alcove or niche.

recess
McIlwaine House, Petersburg, Va.

> **c. 1798** In designing his front door, John Dickinson wondered if it should "be so deep that the leafs may turn back flat against the sides of the doorway, or into recesses in it?" Dickinson Plantation Research Files, Delaware Bureau of Museums.
> **1803** In part of the design for the Capitol in Washington, "the return angle must necessarily be a hollow vile corner, as that of the recess on the East front . . . alias, a pissing corner." *The Correspondence and Miscellaneous Papers of Benjamin Henry Latrobe,* 1.
> **1815** A woman was shocked at the "vitiated style of dress" of female guests at a local wedding in Raleigh. "Oh, surely, the ladies have forgotten that even dress was necessary, or at least that they have anything to conceal. Their backs and bosoms were all uncovered. My heart was indignant at the sight, and as I saw these shameless women surrounded by the beaux, I shrank yet farther into the recess, and turning abruptly away hid my face with a handkerchief." Susan Davis (Nye) Hutchinson Diary, SHC.

red lead A bright orange pigment frequently used in housepainting, either by itself for coloring, as a drier, or as an inexpensive extender for more costly red paints. It was a monoxide of lead (PbO) formed by heating melted lead in a furnace until it calcined into a powder.

> **1764** An Annapolis merchant advertised an assortment of colors including "White and red Lead." *Maryland Gazette.*

red ochre An iron oxide pigment occasionally used in housepainting. Natural deposits of this material were mined near Shotover, Oxfordshire, but the pigment was also manufactured by heating and calcining yellow ochre. The quality and color of the synthetic product varied with the time of calcination. The artificial pigment was relatively inexpensive and much used in distemper painting. The terms *ruddle* and *red chalk* were sometimes mentioned in reference to the natural product; however, this usage was rare in America. See also **ochre.**

> **1764** In Annapolis, one shopkeeper distinguished between "Red and yellow Oker" in his advertisement for the sale of various paints. *Maryland Gazette.*
> **1800** A courthouse in Gates County, North Carolina, was to be painted with "turpentine and oil mixed with red Oaker or Spanish Brown mixed with Tar." Gates Co., N.C., County Accounts, NCA&H.

reed, reeding A small convex molding, usually one of a series of parallel, half-round moldings. It is the convex equivalent of *fluting. Reeding* became a fashionable decorative motif from the late 18th through the middle of the 19th centuries and was often used to enrich columns, pilasters, chimney pieces, and door and window architraves.

> **1812** A carpenter's account of work done in Charleston listed "one Sette of Astragal one sette of Reeded Jambs with Blocks, Hearth and fixings. $80." Ball Family Papers, SCHS.

reglet A fillet, especially a narrow, flat molding used in a fret molding. See also **fillet, fret**.

relief A decorative feature that is raised or embossed above a uniform surface. A bold or deep embossing was known as *high relief* or *alto rilievo*; a moderately raised surface, as *middle relief* or *mezzo rilievo*; and a low or *bas relief*, as *basso rilievo*. See also **emboss**.

> **1783** The chimney piece in the council chamber in the Governor's House in New Bern "is of statuary marble fully inriched and supported by two Ionick Columns of Siana marble, on the Tablet in the Center is an Urn in Bas relieve with foliages, to the Frieze is a Siana fret laid in statuary and a Bust of the King over one Column, and Queen over the other in mozzo relievo at each end of the Frieze. . . . In the center of the North front [of the palace] a pediment spans 32 feet, in the Tympan of which is the Kings Arms in alto relievo." Hawks Letter, Miranda Papers, Academia Nacional de la Historia, Caracas.
>
> **1800** In a design for a mausoleum for General Washington, architect Benjamin Henry Latrobe proposed a pyramid with an arched chamber "the panels" of which "may be filled by representations, either in bas relief, or fresco paintings, of the principal events in the life of Washington." *The Correspondence and Miscellaneous Papers of Benjamin Henry Latrobe*, 1.

render To cover with plaster.

> **1680** A workman was "to Calk render wash and stopp the whole building." Talbot Co., Md., Judgments 1675–1682, MSA.
>
> **1737** In London, the trustees of the colony of Georgia designed a church for Savannah and called for the "walls to be 3 feet thick, 10 feet high, and 2 brick & half upwards, all to be render'd and white wash'd on the Inside." *Journal of the Earl of Egmont.*
>
> **1808** An orphans' house in Charleston was "to be rendered inside." *Charleston Courier.*

rent (wrent) A split, tear, check, or plane of cleavage.

> **1766** A merchant ordered several thousand feet of "well seasoned 2 Inch Pine plank, good lengths & free from Sap & wrents." *The Papers of Henry Laurens*, 5.

return The continuation of a building part, especially a decorative element such as a molding, in a different direction. The change or bend from the original line is usually a right angle. The continuation is sometimes brief, a mere turn of the corner.

> **1740** An order was issued for a brick courthouse with window and door "jams and returnes to be rubbed brick." Lancaster County, Va., Court Order Book 1729–1743.
>
> **1769** "The Returns and Arches of the Windows" in a church were "to be of rubbed Brick." Truro Parish, Fairfax Co., Va., Vestry Book.

reveal The side of an opening in a wall between the framework for a door or window and the face of the wall. When the reveal is cut diagonally, it is called a *splay*. See also **splay**.

> **1811** Carpentry work in a dwelling included fabricating "reveal boards." Riddell Accounts, Pleasants Papers, MHS.

rib (ribb) An arch supporting a vault or dome.

> **1802** Washington carpenter Andrew McDonald charged John Tayloe for "Circular ribbs to arches . . . 1.18.6." Tayloe Papers, VHS.

reed, reeding
LeMoine House, Petersburg, Va.

1804 Thomas Jefferson observed that although "I have spoken of a Spheriodical roof" for the chamber of the House or Representatives in the Capitol in Washington, "that will not be correctly the figure. Every rib will be a portion of a circle of which the radius will be determined by the span and rise of each rib." *The Correspondence and Miscellaneous Papers of Benjamin Henry Latrobe*, 1.

rider   See **worm fence.**

ridge   The horizontal line at the meeting point of the upper edge of two sloping surfaces of a roof; the apex of the roof.

1689 Anticipating the construction of his house, William Byrd I of Westover ordered a quantity of "flat tile . . . with ridging tile proportionable." *Correspondence of Three William Byrds of Westover.*
1773 The chimneys of a glebe house were "to be seven feet above the ridge." Fairfax Parish, Fairfax Co., Va., Vestry Book.

ridge board, ridgepole   A horizontal timber or member at the top of the roof, to which the upper ends of rafters are fastened. Although rarely used for common rafter roofs until the late 19th century, such pieces were standard features on most *cabin roofs* and were occasionally used in *principal rafter* roofs. See also **ridge.**

1745 "The Gable ends of the Glebe House [are] to be Brickt up . . . to the ridge pole." Christ Church Parish, Lancaster Co., Va., Vestry Book.
1818 The roof of a courthouse was "to be a square roof with a ridge pole and two supporters, the joists to be braced in order to support them." Northampton Co., N.C., Miscellaneous Court Records, NCA&H.

rim lock (rimb)   An iron lock with an iron case. See also **stock lock.**

1749 Merchant Francis Jerdone of Yorktown sold to Abraham Archer "1 8 inch Rimb lock 0.7.6, 1 stock lock 0.2.6." *Journal of Francis Jerdone*, VSL.
1785 Material for sale in Alexandria included "iron-rimed and wood stock locks." *Virginia Journal and Alexandria Advertiser.*

rim lock
Brass rim lock, Ridout House,
Annapolis, Md.

riser   The upright face of a step, or the vertical piece connecting two treads. This distance between each tread was the rise.

1764 The steps in a kitchen step ladder, "to be eased at the bottom and risers of 7 inches." Cumberland Parish, Lunenburg Co., Va., Vestry Book.
c. 1798 In Wilmington, Delaware, John Dickinson wanted "a sufficient elevation . . . for the platform of the principal stairs . . . without requiring more than 6 inches rise to each step." Dickinson Plantation File, Delaware Bureau of Museums.
1802 Among the charges to John Tayloe for carpentry on his house in Washington, D.C., was an entry for "Moulded nosing and riser." Tayloe Papers, VHS.

rising joint   An H or HL hinge whose pin is offset to give additional clearance.

1737 Imported into Charleston and to be sold by John Watsone was a "variety of iron ware, viz. hooks and hinges, H Lancaster hinges, ditto with rising joints." *South Carolina Gazette.*
1738 A church to be built was to have doors "Hung with rising Joints as also the pew Doors." Bristol Parish, Prince George Co., Va., Vestry Book.

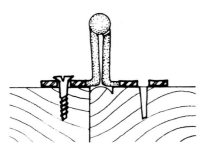

rising joint
Section of a pew hinge,
Prince George,
Winyah, Georgetown, S.C.

rive   To split a log longitudinally with a bladed tool such as froe, hatchet, or ax; to cleave. The labor-saving cheapness of splitting wood with the grain, compared to the lengthy operation involved in sawing framing members and cladding materials, made *riving* the preferred method of fabrication of early 17th-century settlers of the Chesapeake. Practically all elements of an impermanent *Virginia house* could be riven rather than sawn. Riven work continued to play an important role in southern carpentry through the early 19th century. Clapboards, laths, rails, and shingles were almost always riven. Other building elements, such as balusters and studs, were partially riven, sometimes before they were finished with planes, chisels, and other tools. See also **cleave, split, Virginia house.**

> **1651** In an agreement "to build a house of six lengths of boards," carpenter John Dobbs promised "to rive all the boards." Surry Co., Va., Deed and Will Book 1652–1672.
>
> **1680** A prison was "to be lofted with substantial rived boards." Lancaster Co., Va., Court Order Book 1680–1686.
>
> **1727** "I have already ordered very good cabbins made for my people . . . if this is not yet done pray let it be done out of hand there is such a large timber there that the carpenters may very well by riving thick boards & hewing them make them answer the place of plank." Carter Papers, UVa.
>
> **1772** Carpenter William Luten of Chowan County, North Carolina, charged his client for "riving and draying 1500 shingles at 10d....£0.12.6." William Luten Account Book, NCA&H.
>
> **1786** In Orange County, Virginia, "Ch. Dickinson began to Rive laths & nail them on." Francis Taylor Diary, CWF.
>
> **1821** It was ordered that the roofs of county poorhouses "be covered with rived slabs and nailed on." King George Co., Va., Court Order Book 1817–1822.

rivet (rivit) An iron pin forged with a head on one end, and used to secure two or more members together. The end of the pin was cold-hammered to form a second head, locking the pieces together. Rivets were often used to securely fasten hinges and grated windows together. See also **bolt.**

> **1742** "Patrick Creagh produc'd the following Acct viz. . . . To 10 pa Hinges & Rivets for the Pews 3.10.0." St. Anne's Parish, Anne Arundel Co., Md., Vestry Book.
>
> **1773** At the prison in Edenton, North Carolina, "the Locks . . . should be fixed in the Doors and a strong Iron plate over the lock on the inside the door riveted on." Hawks Papers, SHC.
>
> **1809** In Greensborough, Georgia, the jails windows were "to be secured by iron bars on each side the wall rivetted together through the wall." *Monitor.*

rod 1. A measure of length equal to sixteen and a half feet. Brickwork was sometimes measured by the square rod. Strips of wood known as *rods,* with incremental measurements marked on them and measuring either sixteen and a half feet or ten feet, were used by craftsmen to lay out and measure work. See also **superficial measure.**

> **1668** "4500 Bricks will make one rod of Wall, or the side of a Building, at one Brick and half thick, the Rod, Pole, or Perch, containing 16 foot and a half of superficial measure." Leybourn, *Platform Guide Mate for Purchasers, Builders, Measurers.*

2. A thin metal or wooden strip used as a stiffener or fastener.

> **1730** "John Key [was paid] for Rods & Staples for eastern shore [chapel] window shutters." Lynnhaven Parish, Princess Anne Co., Va., Vestry Book.
>
> **1763** There is an account for "mending the Curtain rods which are now fixed up in the Organ Gallery." St. Michael's Parish, Charleston, S.C., Vestry Book.
>
> **1777** A dwelling for sale in Baltimore contained "a stair-cloth with iron rods and holdfasts." *Maryland Journal and Baltimore Advertiser.*

3. See also **electrical conductor, nail rod.**

rolling house A tobacco warehouse, so named because it was a place of storage for large hogsheads of prized tobacco, which were rolled along paths to river landings. See also **inspection house, transfer house, warehouse.**

roof
Common roof forms used in the early South

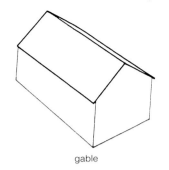

gable

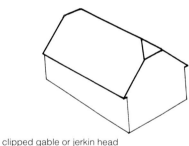

Dutch or gambrel

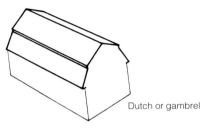

clipped gable or jerkin head

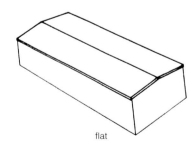

flat

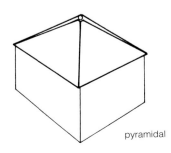

pyramidal

1705 The Virginia General Assembly passed an act "that all such landing places, as have store-houses, commonly called rolling-houses, built at or near them, or have heretofore been commonly used for bringing tobacco unto, and to which there are plain roads already made, shall be held and accounted public landings." Hening, *Statutes at Large*, 3.

1748 Property to be let at Elk Ridge included "a Store House, with all Conveniencies, ready fitted for keeping a Store, situate near the said Landing, at the Head of Patapsco River; where is a Dwelling House, a Large Rolling House with weights and scales." *Maryland Gazette.*

rolling mill A machine for rolling metal—such as iron, copper, and lead—into sheets. To roll iron, it first must be softened by heat, and then fed through the mill.

1782 An advertisement stated: "To be sold, at Stevenson's Refinery, (for ready MONEY only) A LARGE Quantity of PLATES of fine COPPER, fit for stills and other Uses, warranted to roll; and proper allowance will be made for carrying to the rolling-mills. . . . The first rain that comes to enable the rolling-mill to work, a quantity of sheet-copper will be set to Baltimore." *Maryland Journal & Baltimore Advertiser.*

Roman cement See **cement, pozzolana.**

Roman order See **Tuscan order.**

roof The covering of a building, including the framing or other structural elements, as well as the sheathing or roofing material. For more detailed descriptions, see **cover** and the various roof types: **cabin, curb, dome, Dutch, flat, gable, gambrel, girt, hipped, jack, jerkin head, M, mansard, ogee, pigeon, principal rafter, square.**

room A space within a building separated by walls or partitions. A specific regional use of the term appeared in the tobacco-growing colonies in the colonial period, where the interior of tobacco houses were subdivided every four or five feet by a series of horizontal tier poles. Sticks holding leaves of tobacco were hung over these tier poles. The space between each set of tier poles was known as a *room.*

1757 On his plantation in Richmond County, Virginia, Landon Carter "ordered the overseer to take some sticks in the 3 tier above the ground tier, vizt that above the joice and that below it the 2nd room from the gable end." *Diary of Landon Carter,* 1.

rope walk A long, narrow yard or structure where rope is made.

1756 James Reid of Charleston advertised the sale of "his house and land contiguous to his rope-walk." *South Carolina Gazette.*

1810 In Lexington, Kentucky, "there are now at work 9 rope walks." *Virginia Argus.*

rostrum A platform or elevated area used for addressing an audience.

1787 In Charleston, a theater was to be converted into an assembly room "for the purpose of reading Lectures, Poems, Odes, and Orations . . . also for concerts. . . . the stage . . . formed into an Orchestre, for the Music, and a Rostrum for the Lectures." *Columbian Herald.*

rotunda A large circular hall or room, especially one surmounted by a dome such as in the main building at the University of Virginia and the central space of the Capitol in Washington, D.C.

1804 In a change in the design of the Capitol in Washington, Benjamin Henry Latrobe noted that "the Columns of the Rotunda should be three feet longer than the Pilasters, in order to get rid of the Blocks on which the Pilasters are raised." *The Correspondence and Miscellaneous Papers of Benjamin Henry Latrobe*, 1.

1814 At the Governor's House in Raleigh, "you enter the anti-chamber; from this you pass into the rotunda in the centre of the building, which is lighted by a lantern window in the roof. In this is a circular staircase." *The Star*.

1823 In a letter to Thomas Appleton in Livorno, Italy, Thomas Jefferson wrote that "I am now authorized to apply to you for the capitels of the columns of our Rotunda, agreeable to the following specifications. Ten Corinthian capitels of marble . . . two Corinthian semi-capitels for Pilasters." Lambeth and Manning, *Thomas Jefferson as an Architect*.

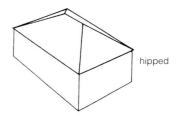

hipped

roughcast An exterior wall covering composed of a crushed aggregate of gravel and sand mixed with a lime mortar or, in the late 18th and early 19th centuries, a cement mortar. The mixture was applied by a trowel over a wet mortared undercoat. Following English practice, Chesapeake builders in the early and mid-17th century occasionally roughcast frame and masonry structures, but the practice eventually fell into disuse. Roughcasting reappeared in the low country of the lower South in the second quarter of the 18th century, where it flourished for more than a century. In the early 19th century, following a national fashion for mortared plaster facades, roughcasting spread throughout the South. By the middle of the century, the term was eclipsed by *stucco*. See also **stucco** (1).

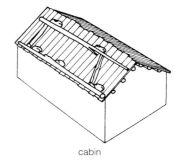

cabin

1651 A bricklayer agreed to "ruffe cast" the exterior brickwork of a dwelling house "with lyme & gravell." Norfolk Co., Va., Deed and Will Book 1646–1651.

1727 The vestry instructed a workman to "plaister & rough cast all the outside of the Church." Christ Church Parish, Charleston Co., S.C., Vestry Book.

1768 Bricklayers were paid for "Rough Casting the State House" in Charleston. Journal of the Commons House of Assembly, No. 37, SCA&H.

1793 A building committee examining a prison found "it to be compleated according to contract except as to the rough cast which they have Judged best not to be put on til May next . . . because the cement is judged not to be properly hardened for receiving the rough cast." Charlotte Co., Va., Court Order Book 1792–1794.

1806 "The Orphan House Church" in Charleston "has been lately roughcast, and it will give you pleasure to hear that it has been well done, and looks remarkably handsome, particularly the front of the building." Manigault Papers, South Caroliniana Library.

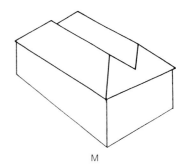

M

rough laid Rudely finished, unplaned lumber installed as flooring.

1770 A carpenter was paid for "3 Sq & 50 feet flooring rough laid without Plaining being the store loft." Bedford Co., Va., Loose Court Papers.

round A convex molding plane. For a more detailed description, see **hollow and round planes.**

octagon

round log A felled tree cut to certain lengths and laid horizontally to form a wall. A log left in the round, unhewn. The term was used to distinguish a type of construction whereby unhewn logs were piled on top of one another and crudely notched at the corners. In terms of economy and skill, it was the least expensive and simplest form of log building, often used for domestic and agricultural structures as well as for dwellings. Round log construction was pervasive throughout most of the South from the early 18th century through the 19th century. A form familiar to all ethnic groups in the South, it could be found on the western frontier as well as the settled regions of the

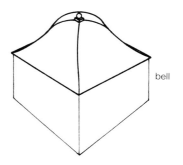

bell

rubbed
Frontispiece, Christ Church,
Lancaster County, Va., c. 1732

Chesapeake. The term *round* was occasionally used to distinguish individual logs in a wall. See also **log construction.**

> 1744 On a plantation on the Eastern Shore of Maryland stood "one old post in the ground boarded tobacco house about 30 feet in length and an old 20 feet round rough logged tobacco house." Queen Anne's Co., Md., Deed Book C.
>
> 1768 There was "to be Sold . . . in Frederick County, Maryland . . . a round Log Dwelling House and Kitchen. . . . There is also on the above land . . . a Square Log Dwelling-House, Two Stories high." *Maryland Gazette.*
>
> 1769 A chapel of ease was to be built "24 feet by 20 round loggs for the body a clapboard roof." Camden Parish, Pittsylvania Co., Va., Vestry Book.
>
> 1778 A farmstead contained "an old log barn and stable, wanting three rounds of logs." New Castle Co., Del., Orphans Court Valuations.
>
> 1786 On the Vance farm in western Virginia stood a "1 1/2 story log dwelling house, logs scalp'd, the inside, outside round . . . one round log barn 54 by 20 cover'd with straw which is rotten . . . round log shop 20 by 16 . . . round log stable 18 by 14 covered with straw; one scalp'd log stillhouse 20 by 20." Jonathan Clark Notebook, Filson Club.
>
> 1811 In Halifax County, North Carolina, "the Negro huts are generally built of round pine or cypress logs, with dirt floors & dirt in the interstices between the logs. They are small, crowed, & smoky, & as might be expected very filthy." Thomas Henderson Letterbook, NCA&H.

rowlock A brick laid on its narrow side so that one of the ends is exposed. Rowlock courses were used on occasion at the bottom of foundation walls, as a make-up course to bring adjacent masonry course into level alignment, or as the simplest form of decoration across a rectangular fireplace, window, or door opening. In the latter case, a flat piece of iron or other structural material was required since a rowlock course lacked the inherent strength of an arch.

rubbed A decorative finish obtained by rubbing a brick with a stone, brush, abrasive tool, or another brick so as to produce a smooth surface of consistent color. The practice appeared in colonial architecture by the first quarter of the 18th century. It was used to highlight door, window, and arcade openings, arches, bands, water tables, medallions, cartouches, frontispieces, and the corners of facades. In contrast to the variegated brickwork of a wall, the uniformity of the red hues of rubbed bricks accentuated these special features. Rubbed bricks the width of a stretcher or more often ran down the side length of a window opening, while the arched lintel above was decorated with gauged bricks with thin mortar joints set with lime putty. See also **brick, gauge** (2).

> 1711 The bricks of a courthouse were "to be rubbed from the sills of the windows upwards to the wallplate." Talbot Co., Md., Land Records No. 12, MSA.
>
> 1736 Specifications for a courthouse called for the "corners of ye building round the Doors and Windows to be made of good Rubbed Brick." Spotsylvania Co., Va., Will Book 1722–1749.
>
> 1767 In a new church, "the Quoins and arches [are] to be of Rub'd Brick the Pediments to the doors Rub'd work in the Tuscan Order." Fairfax Parish, Fairfax Co., Va., Vestry Book.
>
> 1771 "The Vestry are . . . of Opinion that the rub'd bricks at the returns of all the windows ought to be painted so near as possible the same colour with the Arches." Truro Parish, Fairfax Co., Va., Vestry Book.
>
> 1810 A Baltimore bricklayer's account included "cutting, & Setting 15 ft. Elliptical, rubbed, gauged arches @ 150 cts. pr ft $22.50." Riddell Accounts, Pleasants Papers, MHS.

rule A straight-edged strip of wood or metal calibrated with lines to aid in the measuring of distances and marking of straight lines. Early woodworkers often worked with one- and two-foot rules. Jointed folding rules made of boxwood came into common use in the early part of the 19th century.

rule joint   A joint between two hinged pieces, consisting of a quarter round and a fillet fitted against a cove and fillet.

rules   See **bounds.**

Rumford fireplace   1. A specially configured fireplace invented by the American-born Benjamin Thompson, Count Rumford (1753–1814), for improved heating efficiency. Rumford's design involved lowering the fireplace opening, splaying its sides, constricting the throat, and bringing the back of the fireplace forward to create a smoke shelf. These changes were calculated to maximize reflected heat and better control the flow of smoke. Rumford popularized this invention through publication of his *Essay IV: Of Chimney Fire-places, with proposals, to save fuel; to render Dwelling-houses more Comfortable and Salubrious, and effectually prevent Chimnies from Smoking* (1796). Rumford also invented a cooking stove and a roaster which he also promoted successfully. See also **Rumford roaster, Rumford stove.**

> **1804**   To Benjamin Latrobe, Thomas Jefferson wrote: "I should ask the favor of you to select for me in Philadelphia 3. of the handsomest stoves, of the kind called Open stoves, or Rittenhouse stoves, which are in fact nothing more than the Franklin stove, leaving out the double back and flues formed in that for supplying warm air. The Rittenhouse stove is commonly used in Philadelphia, and was the model & origin of the Rumford fireplace, which is a Rittenhouse stove in brick instead of iron." Jefferson Papers, LC.
>
> **1810**   In Baltimore, James Mosher's bill to Judith Riddell included a charge for "rumfordising 4 fire places." Riddell Accounts, Pleasants Papers, MHS.

Rumford roaster   A cylindrical metal oven for roasting meat, invented by Benjamin Thompson, Count Rumford (1753–1814). Rumford's roaster included a drip pan to catch juices and prevent their burning and affecting the taste of the meat. A system of blowpipes and dampers allowed for better control of temperature and moisture in the roasting process. Rumford promoted his invention through various publications.

> **1810**   In Baltimore, Judith Riddell paid James Mosher for "casing kitchen fireplace for Rumfords Roasters &c." Riddell Accounts, Pleasants Papers, MHS.

Rumford stove   1. A cooking range invented by Benjamin Thompson, Count Rumford (1753–1814). Developed from a prototype designed for Baron von Lerchenfeld in Munich, Germany, Rumford's range was a flat-topped, brick structure, equipped with a series of cooking vessels set snugly into the range top to improve cooking efficiency. Each vessel had its own fireplace and damper for controlling the heat under each vessel. Southern records contain few if any references to such stoves. See also **stove.**

2. A cast-iron stove made on the pattern of Count Rumford's fireplace. See **Rumford fireplace.**

> **1805**   In reply to Thomas Jefferson's request for three iron stoves, Benjamin Latrobe asked "whether You could not make a less size, constructed on Rumfords plan . . . answer your purpose." *Papers of Benjamin Henry Latrobe, 2.*

running measure   A one-dimensional measurement of a piece of material or workmanship. Used to calculate moldings, bases, surbases, and cornices. It was also referred to by workmen as *lineal measure*. See also **lineal measure, superficial measure.**

> 1741   An agreement was made with Simon Duffe "for the Seats and Brackets in the pews three pence per foot running measure." St. Anne's Parish, Anne Arundel Co., Md., Vestry Book.
> 1811   Work at Montpelier in Orange County, Virginia, included "12 feet rung of skirting" to a kitchen staircase, "50 feet rung of mouldings on window & Door." Cocke Papers, UVa.

rusticate, rustication
William Gibbes House, Charleston, S.C.

rusticated, rustication (rustick)   Stonework that had deep sunk joints between blocks so as to create a bold, striking visual effect. The joints were sometimes channeled or beveled to separate the individual stones. The surface of the stones were sometimes either smoothly finished, roughly hammered to produce an uneven surface, or cut with a series of sinuous, wormlike channels known as *vermiculation.* Rustication was most often employed on the basement or lower floor of a building to suggest strength and solidity. Keystones, voussoirs, quoins, and banded architraves were rusticated. In the 18th century, a fashion appeared in the stone-poor regions of the South that imitated rustication in wood, where thick planks were beveled at regular intervals to simulate rusticated ashlar stonework. At Mount Vernon in Fairfax County, Virginia, George Washington had the exterior walls treated in this manner, with sand included in the paint as well to imitate the texture of stone. More unusual are the rusticated drum of the cupola at the Cupola House, built in Edenton, North Carolina, in 1758, and the rusticated tower at the base of the steeple that rises out of the pedimented portico of St. Michael's Church in Charleston, South Carolina (completed 1761).

> 1777   At Dumfries, Virginia, "the Court House is small, but a neat tasty Brick Building, rusticated with Stone." *VMHB,* 62.
> 1778   Robert Carter of Nomini Hall in Westmoreland County, Virginia, wanted to have "a wall 22 feet . . . raised all around my dwelling House Rustic of Plank." Robert Carter Day Books and Letterbooks, Duke.
> 1790   A carpenter charged for "5 yds 5 feet of Rustick in gevil ends of portico" at Hampton in Baltimore County, Maryland. *MHM,* 33.
> 1796   Mount Vernon "is a wooden building, painted to represent champhered rustic and sanded." *The Virginia Journals of Benjamin Henry Latrobe,* 1.

Rustic order   1. As the simplest of all the classical orders, another name for the Tuscan order. For a more detailed description, see **Tuscan order.**

2. Simply finished with rough work, sometimes in the sense of *rustication.* The meaning of the term derives from its association with rural simplicity.

> 1736   Charles Pinckney offered a plantation for sale near Charleston on which was "a tollerable Dwelling-house, (built indeed after the Rustic Order)." *South Carolina Gazette.*

sacristy   A space or room within a church where sacred vessels and vestments are stored. Such rooms were rare in colonial churches, only appearing with increasing frequency in the early 19th century, especially in Episcopal churches.

> 1817   In St. Paul's Church in Baltimore "on the north side of the Chancel, and communicating with it, is the Sacristy." *American and Commercial Daily Advertiser.*

saddle (sadle)   A raised wooden sill fastened to the floor at the threshold of a doorway to hide a floor joint.

> 1811   At Montpelier in Orange County, Virginia, a carpenter was paid for "2 sadles under doors @ 6/." Cocke Papers, UVa.

saloon, salon   A large, spacious room on the principal floor of a building used for the formal reception and entertainment of guests; an elegant room often located in the center of a dwelling; a drawing room. The term appears in the colonies from the middle of the 18th century through the early 19th century.

> 1769   An English visitor observed that the house and grounds of the Governor's House in Annapolis "commands an extensive view of the bay and the adjacent country. The same objects appear to equal advantage from the saloon and many apartments in the house." Eddis, *Letters from America*.
> 1779   "These saloons" at Tuckahoe in Goochland County, Virginia, "answer the two purposes of a cool retreat from the scorching and sultry heat of the climate, and of an occasional ball-room." Anburey, *Travels Through the Interior Parts of America*, 2.
> c. 1790   "An apartment like this, extending from front to back, is very common in a Virginia House; it is called the saloon, and during summer is the one generally preferred by the family, on account of its being more airy and spacious than any other." Weld, *Travels Through the States of North America*, 1.
> 1800   For sale in Baltimore was a residence that contained "on the second floor of the house . . . a saloon with two fire places, occupying the whole front of the house (34 feet in clear)." *The Times and District of Columbia Daily Advertiser*.
> 1814   In the front of the Governor's House in Raleigh "is a portico by which you enter the anti-chamber; from this you pass into the rotunda in the centre of the building. . . . In this is a circular staircase. Beyond this is the saloon, and on one hand the drawing, and the on the other the dining room." *The Star*.

sanctuary   That part of the church around the altar; a chancel. The term was rarely used in the early South, *chancel* being the more common name applied to the area where the communion table and altar-piece were located.

> 1807   In his design for the Roman Catholic Cathedral in Baltimore, Benjamin Henry Latrobe advised against making "the sanctuary or chancel . . . a receptacle for the dead." *The Correspondence and Miscellaneous Papers of Benjamin Henry Latrobe*, 2.

sanding   A paint treatment in which sand was thrown against a wet finish coat until the entire surface was covered with aggregate. The resulting finish was intended to simulate the appearance of stone and was believed to offer superior protection as well.

> 1793   From Philadelphia George Washington sent instructions to Anthony Whiting on the painting of his house: "the Mansion house must be examined and repaired . . . after which I will have both sides of it and the ends painted and sanded." *The Writings of George Washington*, 32.
> 1799   "Sanding is designed to answer two purposes, durability, and presentation of Stone; for the latter purpose, and in my opinion a desirable one; it is the last operation, by dashing, as long as any will stick, the Sand upon a coat of thick paint. This is the mode I pursued with the painting at this place, and wish to have pursued at my houses in the City. To this, I must add, that as it is rare to meet with Sand perfectly sifted; the fine dust must be separated from the Sand by a gentle breeze, and the sifter must be of the finess the sand is required and . . . It must be dashed hard on, and as long as any place appears bare." *The Writings of George Washington*, 37.

sapped (sap'd)   Specifications often called for the use of durable heart timber that was *sapped* or free of the softer sapwood. See also **clear of sap.**

> 1742   A henhouse was to be "inclosed with thick saped boards." Bristol Parish, Prince George Co., Va., Vestry Book.

1756 "A new 30 foot tobacco house [was] covered and weather boarded with sapt clapboards." Queen Anne's Co., Md., Deed Book E.
1760 "The plank that is to be used" on a courthouse roof was "to be of pine and shingles of chestnut sapped." Fauquier Co., Va., Court Order Book 1759–1762.

sash (shash) A wooden or metal frame for holding windowpanes, which slides vertically or horizontally within a window frame. Sash windows differed from casement windows in that they slide open within the same plane, whereas casements pivot open. Although sash windows appear as early as the mid-1690s at the College of William and Mary and with increasing frequency in the first quarter of the 18th century, they did not generally replace casements in the Southern colonies until the 1730s and 1740s. Through the colonial period, most sash were single hung, that is, only the lower sash were movable, the upper fixed. The well-hung 18th-century sash had lead (later iron) counterweights, but most colonials satisfied themselves propping up sash with pins or sticks. See also **casement, cord, double hung, single hung, pulley, weight.**

1699 At the capitol in Williamsburg, "the Windows to each Story of the s^d Building shall be Sash Windows and y^t the Roofe shall be a Hip Roof with Dormand Windows." Jefferson Papers, LC.
1701 Henry Wyatt agreed "to send for England this present shipping for Ironwork, Glass for Sash windows and paint for the . . . Church." St. Peter's Parish, New Kent Co., Va., Vestry Book.
1725 In a letter from Mrs. Margaret Kennett to her mother living in England in the village of Wye in Kent, she noted that "the Buildings in Charles Town . . . are of Brick Lime and Hair, and Some very fine Timber Houses and are generally glazed with Sash Windows after the English Fashion." *South Carolina Historical Magazine*, 61.
1738 A church was to have "Shash windows proportion'd to the Building Glaz'd with diamonds Glass." Bristol Parish, Prince George Co., Va., Vestry Book.
1740 Plans for a courthouse included "four sash windows in the body, two at the ends of the house. . . . The windows to hoist with springs and pullys and to be glazed with Crown Glass." Lancaster Co., Va., Court Order Book 1729–1743.

saw A hand tool made of an iron or steel blade with sharp teeth and a wood handle, intended to cut a piece of wood, metal, or stone in two. Saws were available in different designs, depending on their intended use. *Frame saws*, and their smaller counterparts known as *bow saws*, had a long, thin blade (known as a web) stretched between two points of attachment within a wood and metal frame. A *handsaw* had a wide blade, often with a taper, and a wooden handle. Depending on how the teeth are sharpened, this tool was used either for ripping boards or as a cross-cut saw. A whip saw likely refers to a *pit saw*. Pit saws were used to convert logs into boards. Pit saws came in two general varieties. A framed pit saw was an elongated version of a frame saw. With the improvements in steel production in the second half of the 18th century, open pit saws without a supporting frame became popular. A *tenon* (or tenant) saw was used for cutting tenons. It was a small handsaw with a metal capping on the blade to keep it from flexing. A *panel saw* was a small handsaw used for cross-cutting when a clean finish was required. See also **pit, saw box.**

saw box The wooden, removable handle on a pit saw of the variety without a frame. These handles were removable for convenience when traveling, and when the saw needed to be taken out of the kerf.

sawmill An establishment for the sawing of timber into planks, boards, and scantling; the machinery used to cut timber consisting of a carriage with a long blade attached to a frame that moves in a reciprocating motion when turned by gears attached to a waterwheel. Beginning in the second quarter of the 18th century and continuing through the 19th century, sawmills on the lower Cape Fear River of North Carolina manufactured hundreds of thousands of board feet of lumber each year, most of which was exported to the Caribbean and northern ports. Despite the presence of these mills, very little framing timber in many areas of the South was sawn by a water mill until the early 19th century. Most framing, scantling, boards, and planks were either pit sawn, hewed, or riven.

sawmill
Mill sawn roof sheathing,
54 Montague Street, Charleston, S.C.

> **1620** The Virginia Company procured "Dutch Carpenters from Hamborough, men skillfull for the erectings of Sawinge Mills who were shortlie to come for England and to goe for Virginia for the use and benefitt of the Company to sett up Sawinge Mills there." *Virginia Company Records*, 1.
>
> **1710** "I rose at 3 o'clock and ate milk about 4 and then we went over the river and were a—horseback by 5 and so rode to Falling Creek, where we got about 7, and we found Mr. G-r-l getting ready the mill for a wager and a little after 8 o'clock the mill began to saw and sawed 2,000 feet in five hours and finished the rest in four hours more by which we won a wager of £40 of John Woodson, who laid that the mill could not saw 3,000 feet of planks in ten hours. There was abundance of company there, the best of which I treated with wine." *The Secret Diary of William Byrd of Westover 1709–1712*.
>
> **1766** In a letter to the English Board of Trade, Governor William Tryon of North Carolina noted that "lumber a considerable staple in this port, exported to the West Indies is returned in sugar, rum, & molases. . . . Of lumber exported, plank and scantling are sawed in the mills. There are but few of these in the province, but what are on the creeks on the northeast and northwest branches of the Cape Fear River. Of these creeks, there are fifty saw mills now in repair & more building, each with two saws. These mills wil saw upon a medium two hundred thousand feet apiece per annum. I sent some pine plank that was sawed by hand (being too great a length for the carriage of the mills, the carriages not exceeding thirty feet) to Mr. Hughes Commissioner of the dock yard at Portsmouth." *Colonial Records of North Carolina*, 7.

sawpit A long, narrow excavated area in the ground over which timbers are placed on a framework to be cut into planks, boards, and scantling by a long-bladed pit saw. One man stood in the pit and another on top as they moved the saw in a reciprocating motion. Pit sawing was perhaps the most common form of sawing in the early South. An alternative to excavating a sawpit was building two large tressels. This method was inherently less stable than a sawpit and was more laborious since large timbers needed to be lifted on top of the tressels. See also **pit** (2), **saw**.

> **1738** A church was to be "weather Boarded with feather edge Plank with a Bead Rough from the pitt." Bristol Parish, Prince George, Co., Va., Vestry Book.
>
> **1768** Henry Laurens of Charleston wrote that William Bruce "has a mind to settle some Saw pits in Copartnership with me at Turtle River but desires first to be satisfied about the goodness of the Pine. . . . He has been told that the Pines there are very ordinary & very low." *Papers of Henry Laurens*, 5.

saw set A tool used to bend saw teeth alternatively to the left and right, causing the groove that is cut in a board to be slightly wider than the blade, thereby reducing friction while sawing.

sawyer See **pit** (2).

scaffold, scaffolding

scaffold, scaffolding (scafeld)   A temporary platform erected on a building site to provide access to areas above the ground and support for workers and materials during construction and repairs. Most scaffolding consisted of a series of poles connected at various levels by a series of horizontal ledgers. Perpendicular to the ledgers were putlocks or putlogs that were attached at one end to the outer scaffold poles and nailed to framing or inserted into holes of the brickwork at the other. Boards or planks laid across the putlocks provided a working surface for builders. See also **putlock.**

> **1713**   An estimate of materials for constructing a new church in Williamsburg listed "the whole scaffolding stuff, chords & plank at 3 Pounds." *Calendar of Virginia State Papers,* 1.
> **1734**   It was "Agreed with Mr. Peter Secare to Plaster the Church at 2/6 pr yd to supply him with Lime & hair and Boards for Scaffolding." Prince Frederick, Winyah Parish, S.C., Vestry Book.
> **1786**   At a building site in Orange County, Virginia, "Peter with Cart & oxen brought Bricks, earth for mortar and poles for Chimney Scaffold." Francis Taylor Diary, CWF.

scagliola   A highly polished, variegated plasterwork made to imitate marble or some other stone, and used as an interior decoration for columns and walls. See also **imitation.**

> **1817**   "The nave" of St. Paul's Episcopal Church in Baltimore "is bounded on the sides by four ranges of lofty columns, twenty-four in number . . . these columns are finished in scagliola in imitation of yellow clouded marble." *American and Commercial Daily Advertiser.*

scale   In architectural delineation, the proportion that a drawing of a structure bears to the actual object. Such drawings are laid out by the use of a *scale,* an instrument with a series of graduated lines representing proportionate sizes, such as one quarter of an inch to the foot. Although many surviving design drawings from the 18th and early 19th centuries were not done to any scale, a few were done in a carefully delineated fashion. With the emergence of professional builders and architects in the late 18th century, more and more plans, elevations, and sections were done in scaled representation.

> **1773**   Among the items owned by builder William Rigby Naylor, the designer of the Exchange in Charleston, were "drawing Instruments and Scales." *South Carolina Gazette and Country Journal.*
> **1818**   Commissioners appointed to decide upon a plan for a new courthouse reported that "the plan furnished by Ethelwald Sandford seems . . . the most elegable and also the cheapest. The demensions of the building may be seen by reference to an accurate draft and scale thereof furnished by the said Sandford." Westmoreland County Deed and Will Book 1814–1819.

scale house   A building or part of a building in which weights, measures, and scales are housed. Because scales were used to measure produce and merchandise, buildings housing these instruments were erected at market houses, tobacco warehouses, and wharves.

> **1754**   "Proprietors of Nomini Warehouses do . . . build a scale house 12 foot by 16 near the warehouse on the lower side." Westmoreland Co., Va., Court Order Book 1752–1755.
> **1790**   There was to be built at the tobacco warehouses in Dumfries, Virginia, "a compting house, scale house, funnell, and wharf." *Virginia Herald and Fredericksburg Advertiser.*
> **1826**   A committee was appointed "to contract for the erection of a public scale house and the purchase of a suitable pair of scales." Lynchburg, Va., Proceedings of the Common Council 1826–1828.

scallop   A decorative motif consisting of a series of segmental curves, often employed to finish the outer edge of an element.

> 1774   A carpenter installed "3 Scallopt Shelves" in William Corbit's house in Odessa, Delaware. Sweeney, *Grandeur on the Appoquinimink.*

scalp (skelp)   To remove the bark and sometimes partially square a log by hewing; to remove part of the edge of a log, producing a flat surface on one or more sides.

> 1761   Appraisers of an orphan's estate on the Eastern Shore of Maryland listed "one lapt log house 20 feet by 16 wants covering one side . . . one round log stable 16 by 8 want no repair . . . one scalpt log house 16 by 20 wants no repair." Queen Anne's Co., Md., Deed Book F.
> 1786   On the western frontier of Virginia, William Vance lived in a "1 1/2 story log dwelling house, logs scalp'd the inside, the outside round & one end cas'd with plank," while nearby John Feller dwelt in a "scalped rough logg'd house almost new 40 by 18." Jonathan Clark Notebook, Filson Club.
> 1803   Benjamin Blackston's guardian was ordered "to build a smoke house of hewed or Scalped Logs 12 feet square and 10 feet Story." Kent Co., Del., Orphans Court Valuations F.

scantling (scantlin, skantlin)   The dimensions of a piece of timber in breadth and thickness. In the broader sense, the term refers to any dimensioned structural framing member. Beginning in the early 18th century, *bills of scantling*, also called *bills of lumber*, were produced by carpenters and millwrights. These listed the size, length, and number of framing members necessary for the construction of a building.

> 1692   A prison to be erected was patterned after "the same forme work and scantlings" of the previous building. Richmond Co., Va., Court Order Book 1692–1694.
> 1737   Carpenters produced "a Bill of Scantlings for repairing the roof of St. Philip's Church which is as follows Vizt.: 8 plates 6 by 8 [inches], 30 foot long; 200 rafters 3 by 5 [inches] 20 foot long." St. Philip's Parish, Charleston, S.C., Vestry Book.
> 1769   In framing a house, specifications called for "the Scantling to be of a Size and proper Proportion to the Building." Truro Parish, Fairfax Co., Va., Vestry Book.
> 1786   House builders in Annapolis advertised that they were willing "to design, estimate, measure and survey any building, and make out bills of scantling." *Maryland Gazette.*
> 1797   A sawmill advertised as for sale "a large quantity of SCANTLING, of the following sizes. 3 by 3, 3 by 4, 3 by 5, 3 by 6, 3 by 9, 3 by 10, 3 by 11, 3 by 12, 4 by 4, 4 by 5, 4 by 6, 4 by 8, 4 by 10, and 6 by 6; from 20 to 30 feet in length, all cut of Edisto pine, and on application bills of Scantling will be cut at the shortest notice." *South Carolina State Gazette and Timothy & Mason's Daily Advertiser.*

scapple (scabble)   Generally, to reduce the face of stone or timber without working it entirely smooth. Specifically, to roughly dress a stone surface with a chisel or pick, producing a coarse, textured finish. See also **scalp.**

> 1812   In designing a monument to the victims of a theater fire in Richmond, architect Benjamin Henry Latrobe proposed that "the whole of the exterior I would build of . . . common granite . . . the outside walls scappelled, or hammered." *Correspondence and Miscellaneous Papers of Benjamin Henry Latrobe*, 3.

scarf   A joint in which two members are joined together in the same plane by means of lapping their ends over one another in a variety of ways and securing them with pegs, straps, or bolts. Scarf joints were commonly used to form long horizontal framing members such as sills, plates, and purlins.

> 1803   Plans for an Episcopal church near Charleston required the builder to "lay Wall plates all around the building properly scarf'd and lapp'd for the footing of Rafters, and floor joists." Johns Island Church Specifications, Library Society of Charleston.

scheme A method, plan, or procedure for carrying out a design or program of building. The term could imply a drawing. See also **plan** (2).

> 1707 "A Scheme of the said church being this day laid before the vestry and the said vestry after mature deliberation are of opinion & accordingly order that ye church be fifty six foot long." Christ Church Parish, Middlesex Co., Va., Vestry Book.
>
> 1754 Court to "agree with Persons to undertake to build a wooden Prison . . . according to a scheem lodged with the Clerk where the same may be seen by any person who is willing to undertake the same." Accomack Co., Va., Court Order Book 1753–1763.
>
> 1808 "The Church [is] to be built at or near the foundation of the old Church and of such dimensions and materials as a majority of the Vestry and Churchwardens shall hereafter determine on. . . . We the subscribers agreeing on the above scheme for building an Episcopal Church." St. Paul's, Stono Parish, S.C., Vestry Book.

schoolhouse A structure built or appropriated for the use of a school. Although some buildings were erected near churches and meetinghouses, in towns and cities, or on the grounds of large plantations, most Southerners received little or no formal education throughout the colonial and early national period. Itinerant teachers and ministers reached some of the young, but few had the benefit of a specialized structure catering to their educational needs. In some Friends meetinghouses, an upper room was used as a formal schoolroom. Occasionally, vestry rooms, town hall chambers, or rooms in dwellings served as classrooms. Only when academies were built in the late colonial period did schoolhouses take on a distinctive architectural character. See **academy**.

> 1692 Carpenter Michael Webb agreed to build for William Bennett "a twenty foot school house." Westmoreland Co., Va., Court Order Book 1690–1698.
>
> 1760 A Chowan County, North Carolina, carpenter's account listed "7 squar of Sealing joists to the school hous @ 9s pr 3.3.0; to 3 Squar of Smith work @ 9s pr 1.7.0; . . . to faising of 2 mantle trees @ 5s pr 0.10.; to making 1 Scuttle Door & faising 0.6.0; to puting Scurting board round the School house 0.7.0." Chowan Co., N.C., Civil Actions, NCA&H.
>
> 1766 An Anglican minister in New Bern noted that "the schoolhouse is at length inclosed & that it is a large & decent Edifice for such a young country, forty five feet in Length, & Thirty in Breadth; & has already cost upwards of 300£. . . . The floors are not laid, nor the chimnies built. . . . Twould give me great satisfaction to see a little flourishing Academy in this place. I have this affair much at heart & the difficulties I have met with have given me much Uneasiness." SPG Letterbook B, SPGFP.
>
> 1774 At Nomini Hall, the home of Robert Carter in Westmoreland County, Virginia, the Princeton-educated tutor wrote that "at the North East corner" of the dwelling "& 100 yards Distance stands the School House. . . . the School House is forty five feet long . . . & twenty-seven from North to South; It has five well-finished, convenient Rooms, three below stairs, & two above; It is built with Brick a Story & a half high with Dormant Window; In each Room is a fire; In the large Room below stairs we keep our School. . . . The Room above the School-Room Ben [Carter] and I live in." *Journal and Letters of Philip Vickers Fithian.*
>
> 1779 "Upon the Representation of the Inhabitants of Leesburg for leave to build a School house on the courthouse lott ordered that forty square feet of land on the southwest corner of the said lott be appropriated for that purpose." Loudoun Co., Va., Court Order Book 1776–1783.
>
> 1804 Records describe "A frame School House in Duck Creek cross Roads 30 by 15 feet weatherboarded with pine, 5 windows with Sash and 60 panes of Glass therein with window Shutters—one Story high covered with a cedar Roof." Kent Co., Del., Orphans Court Valuations.

scotia (scocia) A deep hollow molding generally employed at the base of a column. The profile of a scotia is more than a quadrant of a circle or ellipse, which distinguishes it from a cavetto.

> 1811 A workman was paid for making "16 Steps of Stairs with Scocias." Riddell Accounts, Pleasants Papers, MHS.

scraper 1. A metal blade held in the bare hand or mounted in a wooden stock, used for the final smoothing of wooden surfaces.

2. An apparatus consisting of a horizontal metal blade fixed to steps or near a door, used to wipe dirt and mud from boots and shoes before entering a building.

> 1810 Ironwork for the Riddell dwelling in Baltimore included "3 foot Scrapers." Riddell Accounts, Pleasants Papers, MHS.

screen (scrime) Any moveable or fixed device of various materials that serves as a barrier, filter, or partition in order to separate, seclude, or protect an area. In Anglican churches, balustraded screens were sometimes erected to separate the chancel from the body of the church, a practice that gradually disappeared in the early 18th century. See also **fly lattice.**

> 1677 "The Chancell [is] to be 15 foote and a Scrime to be runn a Crosse ye Church wth ballisters." Petsworth Parish, Gloucester Co., Va., Vestry Book.
> 1711 A church was to have "A Commendable Screene to Divide the Church from the Chancell." Christ Church Parish, Middlesex Co., Va., Vestry Book.
> 1765 "In the dining room" of an attorney in Charleston was a "Six leaved Screen India Figures on Gilt Leather." Charleston Co., S.C., Will Book 1763–1767.
> 1767 Property "in the hall" of a dwelling mortgaged by a merchant in the northern neck of Virginia included "one set of fire tongs, shovel and poker. One chimney screen." Northumberland Co., Va., Court Record Book 1766–1770.

screw (scrue) A slotted iron pin with a spiral groove cut along its length to facilitate its movement when driven either into a piece of wood or into another piece of metal. Most screws during the period had a slotted head. Although wood screws in the 17th century often were pointed on the end opposite their head, they became blunt pointed in the 18th century. Not until machine-made screws became widely available during the second quarter of the 19th century did the point reemerge on the screw. Before machined screws were invented they were manufactured in one of three ways. They could either be hand filed to shape, turned on a lath, or the grooves could be cut by a screw plate. Screws are most often used as a method to attach hardware. See also **screw driver, screw plate.**

> 1745 To build a house for Charles Pinckney in Colleton Square "6 pr large 14 Inch H hinges with nails & screws" and "6 Dozen strong 1/2 inch wood screws" were needed. Huger Smith, *Dwelling Houses of Charleston.*

screw bolt A threaded rod, usually with a square head; a bolt.

screwdriver A tool used to drive a screw. A screwdriver usually consists of a flat iron bar with a slightly tapered end made to fit the slot in the head of a screw.

scribe *(v.)* To fit the edge of one surface to another uneven or irregular one, such as cutting and planing the edge of a washboard to meet the floorboards. Such a method is also known as coping. *(n.)*

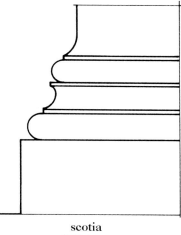

scotia
Ionic base

screen
Laird-Dunlop House, Washington, D.C.

A sharp-bladed instrument used to mark timbers when laying out a frame. Certain types of gouges are used to make a cut in a straight line for scribing a molding. See also **coping.**

> 1726 "Scribe, A Term us'd by Joyners, when they are to fit one side of a piece of Stuff against the side of some other piece of Stuff and the side of the Piece they are to fit it to is not regular." Neve, *City and Country Purchaser.*

scroll
Fullerton House, 15 Legare Street, Charleston, S.C.

scroll (scrowl, scrole) A wave or spiral ornament, used singularly to terminate an element such as a modillion, bracket, broken pediment, or stair rail, or used in a repeating manner as in a frieze. Scrollwork was an important decorative motif in ironwork. Also, another name for the *volute* of a capital.

> 1753 "JAMES LINGARD, Smith and Farrier, makes all kinds of scroll work for grates and stair cases." *South Carolina Gazette.*
> 1772 A glebe house was to have "a genteel pair of stairs with scrolls brackets." St. Mark's Parish, Culpeper Co., Va., Vestry Book.
> 1783 "Each window Architrave" in the council room of the Governor's House in New Bern "forms a scrole at Bottom and is supported by a pedistal." Hawks Letter, Academia Nacional de la Historia, Caracas.
> 1790 At Hampton in Baltimore County, Maryland, carpenter Jehu Howell charged for "16 scrowls on dormont windows at 15s pr £12.0.0." *MHM*, 33.
> 1811 The termination of the stair in the Riddell House in Baltimore consisted of a "mahogany Scroll & curtail Step." Riddell Accounts, Pleasants Papers, MHS.

scutch To dress, smooth, or square the surface of stone, brick, or timber by a variety of means including cutting, hammering, rubbing, and adzing. See also **scalp.**

> 1753 A log house in Augusta County, Virginia, was "to be Scutched or Squared both outside and inside." Preston Papers, VHS.

scuttle A small framed opening in a ceiling or roof. See also **bulkhead (1), trap door.**

> 1760 A carpenter charged a client for "making 1 Scuttle Door & faising £0.6.0." Chowan Co., N.C., Civil Actions, NCA&H.
> 1778 A request was made "that Proper Workmen be Employed to repair the leaks in the Stepple & Roof of the Church and that the Scuttle be Stopt up." St. Michael's Parish, Charleston, S.C., Vestry Book.

sea green A yellow-green paint color composed of white, verdigris, and spruce yellow.

> 1799 An invoice for paints ordered for the finishing of Peyton Skipwith's house at Prestwould in Mecklenburg, County, Virginia, included "Fine Sea Green, 2 kegs." Skipwith Papers, W&M.
> 1812 New England house and ship-painter Hezekiah Reynolds wrote that sea green is made in the following manner: "To one pint of white Lead, add one table spoonful of Verdigris; one do. of Spruce Yellow. Mix and grind them well together; and if upon experiment it should be too light, add of the coloring ingredients at discretion." Reynolds, *Directions for House and Ship Painting.*

seal (seale, seil, ceil, ciel) To provide an internal surface of a room or other enclosed space with a solid cover or sheathing of boards, planks, or lath and plaster. By the 1720s, the meaning of *seal* had narrowed to indicate the application of only wooden materials to an inner wall or ceiling. Sealing a room made it somewhat more impervious to the elements as well as more finished in appearance. It was a technique of greater economy and simplicity than plastering and occurred in all kinds of domestic, agricultural, and public buildings.

1674 Directives for building a dwelling house near Port Tobacco, Maryland, called for "all the roomes to be well plankt on the floores, the lower roome to be well wainscoted, the upper roome well daubed & sealed with morter white limed & sized, & the shead sealed & lined with riven boards." *Archives of Maryland*, 60.

1676 "It was thus concluded . . . that the [Quaker] meeting-house att Betty's cove" in Talbot County, Maryland, "Should be finished as followeth: viz. to Seale the Gable End and the Loft with Clapboard and Make a partition betwixt the new Roome and the old three foot high Seiled and with windowes to Lift up and Down and to be hung with hinges." Third Haven Quaker Meeting, Minutes 1.

1735 A county court wished its new "court house to be ceiled with plank where the justices sitt." Onslow County, N.C., Court Minutes.

1740 An addition to a glebe house was "to be celed with plank as the other part of the house or lathed and plastered and well white washed." St. Mark's Parish, Culpeper Co., Va., Vestry Book.

1767 A building contract on the lower eastern shore of Maryland called for "the whole Chapel to be Sealed over Head with plank Three Quarters of an Inch thick" and "the Insides of the Wall to be Well Plastered and White Washed up to the Sealing." Touart, *Somerset*.

1802 "A new frame Barn 24 feet in length and 20 feet in breadth [is to] be built & roofed & weather boarded with oak Clapboards and ceiled inside to a sufficient height to hold wheat or other grain." Kent Co., Del., Orphans Court Valuations F.

1816 Specifications for a Baptist meetinghouse in Columbia, South Carolina, called for "the walls to be plastered with lime mortar; overhead to be sealed with well seasoned boards, painted white." *The Telescope*.

season To dry wood by lowering its moisture content through exposure to the air or the heat of a kiln. Depending on the climate, the species of wood, and the process, seasoning lasted anywhere from a few weeks or months to a year. Although many framing members were used when they were still green with a high moisture content, southern clients and builders were often concerned that floorboards and other interior woodwork be sufficiently seasoned so as not to warp or shrink after installation.

1726 Carpenters "generally rough plane their boards for Flooring, before they begin any thing else about the Building, that they may set them by to season; which they do thus. They lean them one by one on End a-slant, with the Edge of the Board against a Balk . . . somewhat above the Heights of half the length of the Boards, and set another Board in the same Posture on the other side of the Balk, so that above the Balk they cross one another; then on the first side they set another Board in that Posture, and on the second side another, and so alternately till the whole Number of Boards are set on end: Being set in this Posture, there is left the Thickness of a Board between every board, all the length, but just where they cross one another, for the Air to pass through to dry and shrink them." Neve, *City and Country Purchaser*.

1730 Offered for sale in Maryland was "a well-seasoned sawn frame, for a very commodious small house, with two rooms on a floor; well-seasoned inch pine plank, half inch pine plank, oak, gum, and poplar inch plank, featheredge poplar plank." *Maryland Gazette*.

1760 In a church, "the flooring of the Pews &c. [are] to be laid with well season'd quarter'd Pine Plank clear of Sap . . . the Wainscot for pews to be of well season'd Pine or Cypress Plank." Stratton Major Parish, King and Queen Co., Va., Vestry Book.

1763 "If tis in your power to send me about Three thousand feet of Inch, Inch & quarter, & Inch & half Cypress, that is well season'd, I shall be very thankfull to you but it should be quite dry being for my own use at Ansonborough." *Papers of Henry Laurens*, 3.

seat **1.** A place to sit; something built to support individuals while sitting down, such as a stool, chair, cricket, form, or bench. See also **window seat**.

1678 A courtroom was to have "a table and seat round the end of the house for the judge with a chaire and a desk before it." Westmoreland Co., Va., Court Order Book 1676–1689.

1763 At a Presbyterian meetinghouse in Lancaster County, Virginia, James Gordon "agreed with Mr. Atkins to have more double seats & less single ones. I understand people are displeased with the single seats, which we thought would be more convenient for the People, as they faced the minister. But as it seems disagreeable to some . . . as it is cheaper to have them double, thought it proper to order more made. But I have great reason to fear that there is much more pride than piety among us." *W&MQ*, 1st ser., 12.

2. The site or location of a residence, especially one in the country.

1711 In South Carolina, Anglican minister Francis Le Jau mentioned that Colonel Broughton, the builder of Mulberry Plantation, had departed three months earlier to "live upon his fine seat fourteen miles off." *The Carolina Chronicle of Dr. Francis Le Jau.*

1777 Mardun Evington advertised his skills as a "master workman in the various branches of architecture, either in publick and private buildings, from the most elegant and superb, down to the gentleman's plain country seat." *Virginia Gazette.*

1791 Upon his arrival in South Carolina, George Washington noted, "Breakfasted at the Country seat of Governor Pinckney about 18 miles from out lodging place." *Diaries of George Washington*, 6.

secret nail In flooring, sheathing, wainscotting, and other woodwork, to secure planks and boards to joists, beams, and other supports by driving nails diagonally into their edges, so that the heads of the nails are concealed by the adjoining plank or board. The blind nailing of floors was often reserved for the most important spaces in a wellbuilt dwelling house or public building. See also **blind nail.**

1771 "The Isle & the floor where the Communion Table stands [is] to be Secret nailed . . . with good Brads." Granville Parish, Granville Co., N.C., Francis Hawks Collection, Church Historical Society.

1792 In the statehouse in Raleigh, "the floors shall be laid of 1 1/2 inch pine plank, 6 inches wide tongued & groved & secretly nailed." Cameron Papers, SHC.

1793 The floors of "Old East" at the University of North Carolina were "to be nailed with flooring brads through the boards not secret nailed." University Archives, UNC, Chapel Hill.

1811 A dwelling was to have "5/4 Secret nailed flooring" and "1 Secret nailed & hung 6/4 Cellar Door." Riddell Accounts, Pleasants Papers, MHS.

section An architectural drawing depicting the internal elevation of a structure or part of a structure cut through at an imaginary plane. Such a rendering provided builders and clients with a better understanding of the relationship of room heights and decoration, stair configurations, and roof construction. However, such drawings were not common in the colonial or early national eras. Master builders and professional architects were among the first to use sections to explain their designs to clients. See also **elevation, plan** (1).

1765 "ROBERT KIRKWOOD, Carpenter, Carries on his business at his house in Tradd Street . . . and is ready to undertake building and finishing of houses and other buildings. . . . He likewise draws plans, elevations and sections of buildings." *South Carolina Gazette.*

1769 "EZRA WAITE, Civil Architect, House-builder in general, and Carver, from London . . . flatters himself to give satisfaction to any gentleman, either by plans, sections, elevations, or executions, at his house in King-street." *South Carolina Gazette and Country Journal.*

1803 In his plans for an Episcopal church near Charleston, architect Robert Mills called for the "Foundation Walls [to be] Eighteen Inches above the ground level proportion'd in thickness to what is shown in Sections." Johns Island Church Specifications, Library Society of Charleston.

sentinel box (sentinel house)   A small structure providing shelter for watchmen or sentinels involved in various civic and military duties. See also **watch box.**

> 1664   At St. Helena's on the southern coast of South Carolina, English travelers came across the ruins of a French settlement that included a "house like a Sentinel-house, floored ten foot high with planks, fastened with Spikes and Nayls, standing upon substantial Posts." Salley, *Narratives of Early Carolina.*
>
> 1789   A workman was paid for "building a centinell box" on the courthouse grounds. Prince Edward Co., Va., Court Order Book 1788–1791.

Serliana   See **Venetian window.**

servants' hall   A common room in the cellar of a large dwelling or a subsidiary outbuilding such as a kitchen where servants gathered and dined. Beginning in the late 18th century, a number of such halls were equipped with bell systems, which could summon servants to the primary domestic spaces.

> 1777   The inventory of the estate of Sir John Colleton of Charleston listed a "Servants Hall" and a "Closet in Servants Hall." Charleston Co., S.C., Will Book 1776–1778.
>
> 1782   The estate Scotch Town in Hanover County, Virginia, contained a framed dwelling with "eight rooms upon one floor, with most delightful cellars under them, together with a dairy and servants hall with fire-places." *Virginia Gazette, or the American Advertiser.*

servants' house   A dwelling for slaves or indentured servants, especially one near an urban residence or the main house of a plantation. See also **negro house, quarter.**

> 1760   A plantation for sale at the head of the Severn River in Maryland contained "a very good Dwelling-House of Brick and Stone . . . a good Stone Kitchen joining the House; Two Houses for Servants and Negroes." *Maryland Gazette.*
>
> 1820   A tavern at Culpeper Courthouse, Virginia, had "a new house 16 feet square for the reception of servants." *Virginia Herald.*

settlement (settling)   A gradual sinking of a building or structure due to structural failure caused by rot, poor construction, removal of bearing members, or the subsidence of the soil below.

1823   "With regard to the Fissures in the old wall at the north west corner of the church, which have been discovered . . . the Vestry have been assured by three respectable workmen . . . that no injury can arise therefrom; for these cracks having occurred by the settling of the wall at an early period of the building of the Church, will not become worse and they can be stopped with good gravel mortar." St. Philip's Parish, Charleston, S.C., *Vestry Book.*

sewer   A conduit or drain for carrying off wastewater and refuse from a dwelling or city street. Few houses or cities were equipped for the efficacious removal of sewage, a problem that exacerbated the spread of contagious diseases well into the 19th century.

1768   In work on the statehouse in Charleston, bricklayers Peter and John Horlbeck were paid for building "a well in the Yard, Carting earth to and levelling the Yard, sinking a Drain therefrom to the Common Sewer, laying a kerb, Grate &c." *Journal of the Commons House of Assembly, No. 37,* SCA&H.

1798   A report on the work at the penitentiary in Richmond noted that "the Sewers are dug out." *The Correspondence and Miscellaneous Papers of Benjamin Henry Latrobe,* 1.

shade   A protective screen or cover to shield an area from light, heat, or water. In the sense that it is a protective covering above a door or window, the meaning of the term is synonymous with *shed* or *pent.* See also **blind.**

1744   A prize house was to have "Door posts stroungly Mortoised into the Cill; and a shade made over the door, in the manner there is before the Henhouse Door; It must be two lengths of boards long." *Joseph Ball Letterbook,* LC.

1768   An order was given "to make shades over the church windows." Christ Church Parish, Lancaster Co., Va., *Vestry Book.*

shade (variant spelling for shed)   See **shed.**

shaft   **1.** The body of a column or pilaster between the capital and the base. See also **column.**

1760   A church was to have "five Pillars of Cypress on each side for the support of the Roof, the Columns to be 15 inches Diameter at the bottom of the Shaft, to be Fluted & the Capitols of the Dorick Order." Stratton Major Parish, King and Queen Co., Va., *Vestry Book.*

2. The narrowest portion of a chimney located above the throat, which contains the funnels and rises to a cap above the roof. See also **chimney, stack.**

1788   "A fireplace of 1 1/2 feet in the clear in each of the gaolers rooms [is] to run up in one shaft intirely in the insides of the main wall with a grating of sufficient iron barrs where it goes through the ceiling of the Debtors Rooms to go into the sd shaft." Prince William Co., Va., *Deed Book 1787–1791.*

1797   Lightning struck the chimney of a dwelling in Richmond; "A small part of the Shaft which remained above the ridge was most singularly shattered, the bricks being taken out in holes, and those which remained, standing in the most whimsical and critical positions." *The Virginia Journals of Benjamin Henry Latrobe,* 1.

shake   **1.** A fissure or cleft in a piece of timber caused by rapid loss of moisture in drying, wind stress, felling, or natural formation. See also **rent.**

1759   An inspection of the timber used in a church noted "that the said Rafters are sufficient, but . . . there is a wind Shake therein." St. George's Parish, Harford Co., Md., *Vestry Book.*

1811   Timber for a project "must be of heart yellow pine, clear of shakes, rents and knots." *Norfolk Gazette and Publick Ledger.*

2. A modern term for shingle. It was not used in the early South.

shank **1.** The straight part of a nail between the head and the tapered point. Also the blank part of a screw between the head and the thread. See also **nail, screw.**

2. The plain area between the triangular channels of a triglyph in a Doric frieze. See also **Doric order, triglyph.**

shave (round shave, spokeshave) A woodworking tool consisting of a molded metal blade set in a block with a handle on each side, used for planing curved work such as handrails and wainscot.

sheathing (sheeting) A covering or lining fastened to the framing members of a structure over which sometimes another finish layer is placed. Specifically, unjointed or ciphered boards fixed to the top of rafters, on top of which are nailed shingles or other roofing materials such as slate or tin.

> **1793** The shingles for the roof of "Old East" at the University of North Carolina were to be "made of heart pine eighteen inches long gage not rounded but laid square & nailed to sheeting of oak plank with six penny nails." University Archives, UNC, Chapel Hill.
> **1799** Estimate of materials for John Steele's dwelling in Rowan County, North Carolina, listed two thousand feet of boards "for sheathing roof" and "10,000 joint shingles." John Steele Papers, SHC.

shed (shade, shead, shedd) **1.** A room or wing of a building enclosed beneath a single sloping roof with the higher end abutting a wall or roof of a larger structure. Shed extensions appeared in domestic and agricultural buildings from the early 17th century onward and functioned as service rooms, bedchambers, and workspaces. In this sense, the shed is closely related to the *outshot* in England and *lean-to* in New England. By extension, a shed roof had a single slope.

> **1653** A dwelling was to be built "fiftye foote long, twentye foote wide with a shedd all along the side, and a shedd at one end." Surry Co., Va., Deeds and Wills Book 1652–1672.
> **1657** A servant "toke my Mrs. & carried her into the shed chamber & theare she remained that night." *Archives of Maryland*, 54.
> **1715** A carpenter in Chowan County failed to build "one house of the dimention of twenty foot long & fifteen foote wide with a shade or lean too of eight foot wide." *Higher-Court Records of North Carolina*, 5.
> **1752** "Workmen [were hired] to make bricks at the Glebe sufficient to build a Chimney . . . to the back shed of Glebe House for the Ministers study." St. James, Northam Parish, Goochland Co., Va., Vestry Book.
> **1797** A farm had a "carriage house 16 feet by 11 feet with a shed 8 feet wide and the length of said carriage house." Queen Anne's Co., Md., Guardian Bonds and Valuations SC.

2. A freestanding structure built for storage or used as a covered workspace or shelter for animals or goods. Such buildings were often completely open on one or more sides.

> **1682** "Hogs increase in [South] Carolina abundantly, and in a manner without any charge or trouble to the Planter, only to make them Sheds, wherein they may be protected from the Sun and Rain." Salley, *Narratives of Early Carolina*.
> **1709** A workman was engaged "to make a Curb and Windless for the well, and a Shed over the Well." St. Peter's Parish, New Kent Co., Va., Vestry Book.
> **1766** A farm in Frederick County, Maryland, had "a shed for Horses in the Summer 41 Feet by 12, with a Conveniency for keeping Oats, Saddles, &c." *Maryland Gazette*.
> **1800** In Yamacraw, Georgia, a brickyard had "a shed 100 feet long, 38 feet wide, to contain [bricks] when dried." *Columbian Museum and Savannah Advertiser*.

shed (1)
Burrage's End, Tobacco House,
Anne Arundel County, Md.

sheet glass (common glass, cylinder glass) An inferior type of window glass produced in England and the early American republic. It was manufactured by blowing a cylinder several feet long and about one foot in diameter. After cracking off the blowpipe, the cylinder was slit open and the glass rolled to produce a flat sheet. This method produced glass that was brittle and apt to have more streaks and waves than *crown glass*. See also **crown glass, glass.**

> 1753 In Charleston, "GEORGE SMITH, hath just imported in the Live-Oak, from Bristol . . . sheet glass in cases." *South Carolina Gazette.*
> 1770 Payment for glazing a church included a number of boxes of "Sheet Glass." St. John's, Colleton Parish, S.C., Vestry Book.

sheeting See **sheathing.**

sheet iron Wrought iron either forged or rolled into sheets for a variety of uses, such as lock cases, roof coverings, and lining of shutters and doors.

> 1803 At the Capitol in Washington, Benjamin Latrobe noted that it was "my full intention to take off the whole roof of the North wing, and put on one the Presidents zigzag roofs of sheet iron." *The Correspondence and Miscellaneous Papers of Benjamin Henry Latrobe*, 1.
> 1805 In a kitchen, "the stove room floor should have sheet Iron placed on it in such manner as to prevent fire." Loudoun Co., Va., Court Order Book 1805–1806.
> 1809 Clerk's office "doors and window frames and shutters to be lined with sheet iron." Richmond, Va., Hustings Court Order Book No. 8.
> 1811 Montpelier, James Madison's home in Orange County, Virginia, workmen installed "17 ft 6 rung of sheet Iron gutters @ 6/." Cocke Papers, UVa.
> 1813 The double walls of a prison were to be "lined between with Sheet Iron." Wayne Co., N.C., Miscellaneous Court Records, NCA&H.

sheet lead Lead milled into sheets and used for flashing, lining gutters, and covering roofs. See also **lead.**

> 1745 Materials needed for Charles Pinckney's house in Charleston included "sheet lead for 2 gutters one 23 feet long & one 20 D°." Huger Smith, *Dwelling Houses of Charleston.*
> 1807 At Monticello, Thomas Jefferson wrote to the firm of Jones and Howell: "Be pleased to send me the quantity of sheet lead below stated, to be rolled, and of the thickness suitable for covering houses." Coolidge Collection, Massachusetts Historical Society.

shelf **1.** Boards on which to store or display objects in settings ranging from closets and milk houses to shops and parlors. Generally supported by sawn brackets, ledgers, or slots in wooden stanchions. Shelves employed for display in entertaining rooms were occasionally sawn in a curvilinear plan, creating decoration at the cost of storage space.

> 1691 In a courthouse, "the little closett [is to] be fitted up with a bench or table to write upon with some shelves to lay bookes and papers on." Westmoreland Co., Va., Court Order Book 1690–1698.
> 1709 Richard Littlepage agreed to build "a twelve feet square Milk house with plank shelves." St. Peter's Parish, New Kent Co., Va., Vestry Book.
> 1742 A kitchen was to be built "with the dressers and necessary shelves." Bristol Parish, Prince George Co., Va., Vestry Book.
> 1770 There is an account of a workman installing "Shealves Counter & other Conveniencys in the Store." Bedford Co., Va., Determined Cases 1770.

2. The cornice or cap of a mantelpiece or fireplace surround.

> 1783 In the council chamber of the Governor's House in New Bern, "the Chimney Cap or shelf is of statuary marble fully inriched and supported by two Ionick Columns of Siana marble." Hawks Letter, Miranda Papers, Academia Nacional de la Historia, Caracas.

shell lime Lime made from oyster shells. For a more detailed description, see **lime**.

shingle One of a series of thin, narrow pieces of wood laid side by side and lapped over one or two lower courses to protect roofs, and occasionally walls, from the weather. Shingles came into common use in the Chesapeake by the middle of the 17th century and became the most common roofing material in the early South. The most typical woods used in the fabrication of shingles were pine, cypress, cedar, oak, poplar, and chestnut. Workmen rived or sawed shingles from small sections of logs into long, thin pieces with wedge-shaped profiles. Most were from one-half to a full inch in thickness at the end to be exposed, and tapered to a thin wedge at the other end. In an effort to prevent warping, the edges of exposed ends were occasionally rounded off or scalloped. As with tiles and slates, shingles were nailed or pegged to laths or sheathing. In many parts of the South, some shingles were applied over a clapboard covering. Shingles were laid from the eaves upwards to the apex of the roof, with workmen installing a starter course at the eaves level, over which the first course of exposed shingles were attached. Measuring on average between one foot and two feet in length, only the lower five to seven inches were exposed to the weather, the rest providing an undercovering for upper courses. Besides having each course lapped over the lower one, some shingles were also partly laid over adjoining ones in the same course in a pattern that is now referred to as *side lapped*.

shingle
Prestwould, Mecklenburg County, Va.

1649 In Virginia, "they have . . . Houses and Chimneys built of Brick, and some of Wood high and fair, covered with . . . Shingell for Tyle." *A Perfect Description of Virginia*.

1711 Specifications called for a church to have "shingles . . . of the Heart of Cypress three quarters of an inch att least att the Thickest end to be sixteene inches long and to shew when laid five inches out." Christ Church Parish, Middlesex Co., Va., Vestry Book.

1728 On the Virginia-North Carolina border, "most of the Houses . . . are Loghouses, covered with Pine or Cypress Shingles, 3 feet long, and one broad. They are hung upon Laths with Peggs." Byrd, *History of the Dividing Line*.

1744 In Savannah, members of the Anglican congregation had "prepared a Sufficient quantity of Shingles for the purpose" of finishing the church. The shingles had been "drawn out of Cypress, about 20 Inches long, and Inch thick at the lowest end, and taper'd upwards to the Thickness of a Knife Blade." *The Journal of William Stephens 1743–1745*.

1752 The Virginia General Assembly specified that "all shingles" for export "shall be eighteen inches and a half long, five inches broad, and five-eighths of an inch thick." Hening, *Statutes at Large*, 6.

1760 A log dwelling was "to be covered with lap Shingles." Augusta Parish, Augusta Co., Va., Vestry Book.

1764 At Reviving Spring plantation in Maryland, "there is one framed dwelling house . . . covered with round shingles six inch show on one side, and the other side feather edge shingles." Queen Anne's Co., Md., Deed Book G.

1786 A survey of Epraim Leith's tract on the western frontier of Virginia listed an "old log dwelling house . . . covered with round shingles and a very old round log kitchen . . . covered one side with long shingles, the other side with slabs." Jonathan Clark Notebook, Filson Club.

shod Edged or lined with metal.

1701 "Every brick [is] to be moulded in a shod mould of 9 inches 3/4 in length and 4 3/4 in width and 4 inches 1/2 thick in the cleer." St. Peter's Parish, New Kent Co., Va., Vestry Book.

shop joiner See **joiner.**

shore A timber, sometimes set at an oblique angle to a wall or roof, that acts as a brace to provide support while the structure is under construction or repair.

> 1798 "The South front" of a dwelling in Philadelphia "is not yet raised from the ground in the Center part, but part of each side is quite finished. The roof in the mean time is carried by shores." *The Virginia Journals of Benjamin Henry Latrobe, 2.*

shoulder 1. The sharp break in the thickness of the butt end of a framing timber where a tenon projects. The shoulders of joists, rafters, and other members are fashioned in a variety of ways to better secure and strengthen the joint. See also **tusk.**

> 1681 Rafters were "to be so dubd that they may have a square shoulder to come upon the plate." Northumberland Co., Va., Court Order Book 1678–1698.
> 1717 Fence "rails [should] be well Tenoned into the posts with Shoulders." All Saints Parish, Calvert Co., Md., Vestry Book.

2. Any projection or element with a sharp change in width or thickness or direction that resembles a human shoulder. See also **crossette.**

shrubbery Shrubs in general or a grouped planting of shrubs in a pleasure ground.

> 1785 George Washington recorded that he "removed from the Woods and the old fields, several young Trees of Sassafras, Dogwood, and Red bud, to the Shrubbery at the No. side of the grass plat." *Diaries of George Washington, 2.*
> 1794 At Belvedere in Baltimore, "the foreground possessed luxuriant shrubberies and sloping lawns." Twining, *Travels in America 100 Years Ago.*

shutter
Exterior shutter, Lipsett's Store,
Eastville, Va.

shutter (shetter) A paneled or battened wood leaf hinged to a window frame used for security and to regulate light. Louvered shutters or *Venetian blinds* with movable slats offered a specialized solution that became increasingly common in the early 19th century. A folding shutter was an interior shutter with a secondary leaf (shutter flap), usually a plain board hinged to the principal leaf. When open, folding shutters block the full width of the sash; when closed, the flap folds behind the principal leaf in a pocket of the window reveal. See also **Venetian blind** (2).

> 1656 The rooms in dwellings in the Chesapeake "are large, daubed and white limed, glazed and flowered, and if not glazed windows, shutters which are made very pritty and convenient." Hammond, *Leah and Rachel.*
> 1692 A workman was "to make two window shutters for the two windows below and to make a fram'd shutter for the sd windows." Charles Co., Md., Court and Land Record Book 1690–1692.
> 1711 The courthouse windows were "to be well glazed with Led and Glass; Except the Lower Lights in the transume windows in front and End below the joyce which are to have shetters instead of glass." Talbot Co., Md., Land Records Book No 12.
> 1746 For his new dwelling in Charleston, Charles Pinckney specified that there be "4 pair outside cellar window shutters panneld, All the rest of the Doors and window Shutters on this floar to be ledged." Huger Smith, *Dwelling Houses of Charleston.*
> 1769 The sheriff was ordered to appoint someone "to see that the Doors & window shutters of the courthouse be constantly shut after the using of the court and that at all times the court is not setting that the windows, tables, benches etc. so may be preserved & kept clean & that he provide Iron bolts for the window shutters." Amelia Co., Va., Court Order Book 1766–1769.
> c. 1798 The front windows in John Dickinson's house in Wilmington, Delaware, were to have "inside shutters only, and scarcely to show any frame—The 8 windows

on Market Street to have very strong thick shutters of the common kind—the nine windows to the south and west to have for shutters the best contrived Venetian blinds, for excluding the rays of the sun." Dickinson Plantation Research Files, Delaware Bureau of Museums.

1805 "The shutters" of a church to be built near the Santee Canal in South Carolina were "to be plain batten with substantial hooks, hinges, &c." *City Gazette and Daily Advertiser.*

shutter dog   See **hook.**

sideboard   A closet for the storage of tablewares—often with some sort of sliding door or shutter. The term goes out of use in this sense by the middle of the 18th century. See also **buffet, closet.**

1720 An estimate for the cost of finishing the Governor's House called for "4 yards of [paint] on the Side board Shutter." *Journals of the House of Burgesses of Virginia,* 5.

1728 Following the death of Nathaniel Harrison, appraisers found an extensive collection of china, glass, and silver, which they listed in their "Inv'y Side Boards in the Hall." Surry Co., Va., Deed and Will Book 1715–1730.

side hinge   A wrought-iron hinge forged in the shape of an H; an H hinge. A side hinge with a leg is an *HL hinge.* See also **H hinge, HL hinge.**

sidelight   One of a series of window lights flanking a door or other opening. Sidelights came into fashion along with fanlights in the late 18th and early 19th centuries as a means of providing light in newly prevalent entrance passages. See also **fanlight, flank window.**

1802 A carpenter in Washington, D.C., charged John Tayloe for "Side lights 2/ and 6 Sq^{rs} sash to D^o 1/6" for the garden entrance to his elegant town house on 18th Street and New York Avenue. Tayloe Papers, VHS.

1811 At Montpelier in Orange County, Virginia, workmen constructed "2 Venetian doors with side lights." Cocke Papers, UVa.

1817 A firm of painters and glaziers "engaged a first rate Plumber and Fan & sidelight maker, either in lead or copper." *Alexandria Herald.*

sidelight
Bragg House, Petersburg, Va.

sidewalk   A raised footpath on the side of a street; a paved footway. The term does not come into general use until the early 19th century with improvements in public amenities in a number of American cities and towns. See also **footway.**

1809 A South Carolina visitor to Philadelphia noted that "in the improved part of the City most of the streets are wide; they are paved for carriages, & have side walks, very neat & commodious. They are illuminated every night, with a suitable number of lamps enclosed in Glass lanterns, fix'd on the top of high posts at the edge of the foot pavement, which adds very much to the splendor, brilliancy & convenience of the city." *Journal of William D. Martin.*

sill (sell, cell, cill)   A horizontal timber that is the lowest part of a frame, used to support or connect vertical members of a superstructure. The term is used to define two specific elements: the bottom, exterior members of a house frame; and the lower part of a door or window frame. The roughly squared house frame sills, also known as *groundsills* in the early South, stood on masonry foundations or on wooden blocks or rested on or in the ground. At the corners, end sills and long wall sills were generally lapped over one another or joined by a mortise and tenon joint. Corner posts, intermediate posts, and smaller members such as studs and braces were either lapped, butted, or mortised into them at regularly spaced intervals.   Occasionally, the

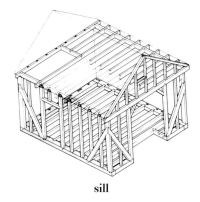

sill

term *sill* was indiscriminately used to refer to any large ground frame member. Windowsills varied in materials, construction, and style. Made of brick, stone, or wood, they often projected beyond the face of the wall and were decoratively treated with moldings or tooling, or left plain. Some were built as integral parts of the frame, while others were installed as separate elements. Doorsills could be just as varied in construction and materials. See also **groundsill, interrupted sill.**

> **1683** Repairs to a church included "ye earth be firmly ram'd under the sells, and a convenient pent house made to keepe the raine off them." Christ Church Parish, Middlesex Co., Va., Vestry Book.
> **1711** It was required that "The sills of the . . . Church the summers and Girders be of the best White Oake . . . be of quartered stuff and a foot square att least." Christ Church Parish, Middlesex Co., Va., Vestry Book.
> **1742** "The Sill of the [church] Door [is] to be of Stone." St. Anne's Parish, Anne Arundel Co., Md., Vestry Book.
> **1744** In the repair of a prize house, there should be "Good stout End cills of white oak or Chestnut, laid upon the Ground, or not let above an inch or two into it." Joseph Ball Letterbook, LC.
> **1760** At Smith's Neglect on the Eastern Shore of Maryland, there was "an old dwelling house full framed . . . and the sills very rotten so that many of the posts stands in the ground." Queen Anne's Co., Md., Deed Book F.
> **1792** "Large Log dwelling House with a Cellar under part thereof the west end of the house required to have new under Logs or Sills." New Castle Co., Del., Orphans Court Valuations G.
> **1806** Repairs to St. Paul's Church in Edenton, North Carolina, included "eight pairs new sashes with circular heads, double hung, in boxed frames with Oak Sills." St. Paul's Parish, Chowan Co., N.C., Loose Papers.

single house A term used in Charleston to describe a dwelling with a center stair passage flanked on either side by a single depth of rooms. The dwelling's shorter end was turned toward the street and usually had a piazza stretching across the long entrance facade. The form of the single house probably appeared in Charleston in the late colonial period as a response to developmental pressures as well as social and climatic circumstances.

> **1789** Contract made in Charleston to build "a compleat well-finished dwelling house commonly called a single house, three stories high . . . twenty-two feet wide or thereabouts and forty-six feet long or thereabouts, with two rooms on a floor and an entry leading to a stair case in or near the centre of the said house nine foot wide in the clear . . . with two stacks of chimneys so as to allow one fire Place in each room." Charleston Co., S.C., Land Records Book R.

single hung A term applied to any window having one movable, counterweighted sash. This was always the lower sash, the upper being fixed in place. Judging from surviving evidence, sash lines were made of cotton cord, the sash weights of iron or, more commonly, of lead. See also **double hung, sash.**

> **1811** A bill for work on James Madison's house at Montpelier included charges for "7 windo Single Hung @ 2/6." Cocke Papers, UVa.

single work See **work.**

sink 1. A drain or sewer, often of brick.

> **1772** A vestry was to "lett the digging and planking a Sink to the cellar at the Glebe." St. Andrew's Parish, Brunswick Co., Va. Vestry Book.
> **1803** In a report on construction of the Capitol in Washington, Benjamin Latrobe mentioned "a small court which becomes necessary for light as well as domestic use, for it must contain a pump or cistern, and a sink to take off water." *The Correspondence and Miscellaneous Papers of Benjamin Henry Latrobe,* 1.

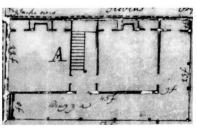

single house
Above: 123 Tradd Street, Charleston, S.C.
Below: Plan of a house, 240 Meeting Street, Charleston, S.C., 1789

2. A built-in basin to hold water for washing.

> 1748 A house to be sold in Charleston included a well-equipped kitchen, "compleatly fitted with Stoves and a Sink for washing Dishes." *South Carolina Gazette.*

sitting room A small, informal parlor. The term comes into fashion in the South in the late colonial period to describe a room in a dwelling where members of a family would gather. Compared to a more formal entertaining space such as a *saloon* or *drawing room*, the *sitting room* was used for minor domestic tasks, reading, and conversation. See also **parlor.**

> 1774 A wine merchant lived in a two-story dwelling house in Charleston, which consisted of "of a very large and airy dining Room, and sitting Room on the first Story." *South Carolina Gazette and Country Journal.*
>
> 1787 Near Tarboro, North Carolina, a visitor lodged at "Mrs. Cobbs' house [which] consisted of two Apartments, one was the sitting Room, the floor was of Clay or dirt, and there was one Bed in the Room. The other Apartment was floored with Boards and contained four good Beds." Attmore, *Journal of a Tour to North Carolina.*
>
> 1813 In Washington, "the President's house is a perfect palace. . . . On the side opposite to the entrance are doors opening to four rooms. The corner is the dining room and is very spacious. . . . This room opens by a single door into Mrs. Madison's sitting room which is half as large. This is furnished equally well, and has more elegant and delicate furniture. . . . This room in the same way, enters into the drawing-room, which is an immense and magnificent room, in an oval form. . . . Next to the drawing room is the President's sitting-room which has no communication with the form and opens to the hall. This corresponds to Mrs. Madison's parlour, and is handsomely furnished." *Diary of Elbridge Gerry, Jr.*

size, sizing A glutinous substance applied to plaster and occasionally wood, used for filling the pores of the surface so as to provide a better surface for painting, whitewashing, or an adhesive ground for gold leaf.

> 1674 The upper room of the Charles County, Maryland, courthouse was "to be well daubed & sealed with morter white limed & sized." *Archives of Maryland,* 60.

skew To set off in an oblique manner; having an oblique direction, shape, or form, or cut at an oblique angle. Used collocatively to describe a tool in which the blade is set at an angle to the cutting surface.

> 1774 An account of carpenter's work at William Corbit's house in Odessa, Delaware mentioned "17 ft 8 ins skew Wainsct at 14d £1.17.11." Sweeney, *Grandeur on the Appoquinimink.*

skew hinge A hinge that lifts a door over an obstacle such as a carpet. See also **raising hinge.**

> 1795 An invoice for hardware ordered from Birmingham, England, included "12 prs 7 ins Skew H hinges." Skipwith Papers, W&M.

skim A thin, lime-white layer of plaster. The skim coat is the last coat of plaster applied to a surface. The term may date only from the first half of the 19th century.

skinned Logs that have had their bark removed. See also **scalp.**

> 1821 "The logs [from] which the houses" for the poor "shall be built are to be skinned pine." King George Co., Va., Court Order Book 1817–1822.

skirting board A narrow board placed around the floor at the base of a plastered or wainscotted wall. *Washboard* was the more common name given to this protective border. See also **base** (3), **mopboard, washboard.**

> 1750 A house was "to be carried up with skirting & Chair boards in both Rooms." Newport Parish, Isle of Wight Co., Va., Vestry Book.
> 1771 One of the balls fired in a tavern duel became "lodged in the Skirting Board" of the parlor. *South Carolina Gazette.*

sky blue A light blue paint, probably composed of Prussian blue and white lead or whiting.

> 1772 In Cumberland County, Virginia, the vestry of St. Mark's Parish ordered the "inside work" of the new Glebe House was "to be painted sky blue." St. Mark's Parish, Cumberland Co., Va., Vestry Book.
> 1809 For a new clerk's office, a Henry County, Virginia, justice ordered that "all the wood part of the inside . . . to be painted of a sky blue." Henry Co., Va., Order Book 1808–1811.

skylight A sloping, glazed opening in the roof, used for lighting an area such as a stair or room below. See also **cupola, lantern** (1).

> 1783 At the Governor's House in New Bern, the main staircase was lit "by a sky light 9 feet Diameter of an octagon plan or domical section. . . . The Back staircase which is likewise in the Center of the House receives its light from a hiped skylight." Hawks Letter, Miranda Papers, Academia Nacional de la Historia, Caracas.
> 1806 The architect of the Capitol in Washington, Benjamin Henry Latrobe, wrote to President Jefferson that "in a correspondence on the subject of *ribbed Skylights* . . . I declared freely my opinion of them. It was: that however beautiful their effect in the Hall au bled at Paris, they ought not be used in the Hall of Rep. principally on acct. of probable leakage." *The Correspondence and Miscellaneous Papers of Benjamin Henry Latrobe*, 2.
> 1818 "We are building a new courthouse in Fincastle and the planning and direction devolve on me. It is to have a skylight and your to let me know whether glass suitable for that purpose can be got in Richmond. I understand that there is a glass factory." Breckenridge Papers, VHS.

slab 1. A plank sawn or riven from the outside edge of a log; any roughly worked plank with uneven edges. Slabs were used primarily as a roof covering, siding, and flooring.

> 1751 "You must cover the dwelling house as soon as you can and the other houses for the present must be well slabbed; and listed down every rafter with a Board of full Breadth." Joseph Ball Letterbook, LC.
> 1786 James Leith's farm on the western frontier of Virginia contained an "old log dwelling house, 18 by 16, covered with round shingles, and a very old round log kitchen, prop'd, covered one side with long shingles, the other side with slabs." Jonathan Clark Notebook, Filson Club.
> 1794 In Orange County, Virginia, a "cart went to Herndons Mill & brought a load of Slabs for Cornhouse floor." Francis Taylor Diary, CWF.
> 1821 Roofs of the cabins for the poor in King George County, Virginia, "to be covered with rived slabs nailed on and not to leak." King George Co., Va., Court Order Book 1817–1822.

2. Any thick piece of stone, used for paving, hearths, tombs, and other purposes.

> 1762 Robert Carter of Williamsburg ordered from England "three marvell hearth Slabs." Robert Carter Letterbook, CWF.
> 1774 "TO BE SOLD . . . A quantity of Slabbs, proper for tileing a kitchen floor or yard." *Virginia Gazette, or Norfolk Intelligencer.*
> 1814 At the Wickham House in Richmond, "the floors of the porticos are square slabs of Marble of different colours." Calvin Jones Papers, SHC.
> 1825 A committee looked into the merits of "prohibiting the laying of Slabs & building of Monuments, in the church yard." St. Philip's Parish, Charleston, S.C., Vestry Book.

slake See **lime.**

slat A thin, narrow strip of wood, often one of a series used within a framework to regulate the passage of light and air into an aperture. They were used in Venetian blinds and often appeared in louver windows in dairies and necessaries.

1805 Benjamin Henry Latrobe wrote to Thomas Jefferson about problems he was encountering in controlling the light entering the legislative rooms in the Capitol in Washington. He suggested the use of Venetian blinds in which "the Slats of the blind, which are hung on pivots in the frame . . . [with] a rod to which the upper edges of the Slats are attached by staples." *The Correspondence and Miscellaneous Papers of Benjamin Henry Latrobe*, 2.

1810 On a Delaware farm were "two small corn Cribs walls with pine poles and pine Slats." Sussex Co., Del., Orphans Court Valuations K.

1811 Thomas Jefferson wrote to James Oldham, that "Judge Cabell having consulted me as to some things to be done to his house, I advised him to apply to you to make some Venetian blinds with moveable slats. The kind I had in view may be seen in a house Dr. Currie inhabited in Richmond about a dozen years ago." Coolidge Collection, Massachusetts Historical Society.

slate A fine-grained, brittle metamorphic rock formed from clay or shale. The material splits readily along the parallel planes of its natural cleavage lines. Split into thin pieces, it was used in early America chiefly as a roof covering and occasionally as paving. In the 17th and early 18th centuries, what little slate was used in the South was imported from Britain, chiefly from Wales, the west country of Devon and Cornwall, and the northwest Lake District. By the middle of the 18th century, Charleston imported large amounts of slate to roof public buildings and domestic structures. As settlement moved westward into the Piedmont, a number of slate beds were discovered, which, by the end of the century, were actively quarried. Perhaps the most important early-19th-century quarry was located in Buckingham County, Virginia. As a nonflammable material, slate along with tile received a boost during this period in the rush to construct fireproof public buildings such as clerks' offices. Despite its durability and the presence of regional quarries, slate never replaced wood shingles as the principal roofing material in the early South. The difficulty of transporting it over long distances kept the cost of the material beyond the means of most individuals.

1705 The Governor's House in Williamsburg is to have "a covering of stone slate." Hening, *Statutes at Large*, 3.

1752 In Charleston, "just imported by Othniel Beale and Comp. a quantity of best grey stone (or slate) for covering houses." *South Carolina Gazette*.

1755 Winchester, Virginia, was "a town built of limestone and covered with slate with which the hills abound. The inhabitants are a spurious race of mortals known by the appellation of Scotch-Irish." *W&MQ*, 1st ser., 10.

1765 "ANY Cumberland SLATER, or other PERSON, that can undertake to cover a House with Slate, may hear of a JOBB on applying to the Printing-Office" in Annapolis. *Maryland Gazette*.

1784 Payment was made to "Roger and Peter Smith for 43 Tons Slate purchased of them for the State House" in Charleston. South Carolina Treasury, Journal 1783–1791, SCA&H.

1797 "Valuable Slate Land, &c. to be LEASED OR SOLD; LYING in the county of Buckingham, about sixty miles above Richmond, in Virginia;—from which one of the warehouses in Manchester is covered, and the Capitol in Richmond now covering; where the quality of the slate may be seen and judged by those who wish to possess themselves of so valuable a property. With respect to the quantity, it seems inexhaustible. It is easily raised, and lies in large bodies immediately on the river bank, from whence it may be transported to any of the large towns in America where it will be most wanted, without any of the inconveniences or deductions of land carriage. . . . From the small experiments already made, even with raw hands taken from among the common labourers of the field, at a time, too, when the comparative value of that kind of covering with others of a less safe and durable nature was little known in this part of America . . . the profits have been found to be considerable." *Virginia Gazette and General Advertiser.*

1800 "Slate Work. THE subscriber proposes roofing houses with SLATE in the best maner, and on moderate terms, as he has a large supply of the first quality. Application to be made at Joseph Townsend's, Baltimore, or the subscriber, living in Frederick County. JOHN ROBERTS." *Federal Gazette and Baltimore Daily Advertiser.*

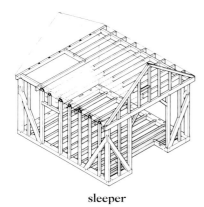

sleeper

slaughterhouse A building where animals are butchered for meat; an abattoir.

1793 A gallows was to be erected "within 30 feet of the road leading from Staunton to Peter Haner's, opposite to the slaughter house." Augusta Co., Va., Court Order Book 1791–1793.

1798 Behind a dwelling in Bloomsbury Square in Annapolis was a "frame slaughter house 16 by 10 feet." U.S. Direct Tax, MSA.

slave house See **Negro House, quarter.**

sleeper A horizontal framing member laid on the ground or set just above it to support the lower floor of a building or the superstructure of a bridge. By the late 17th century, the term almost invariably referred to ground-floor joists rather than a larger timber that supported those joists. See also **joist.**

1680 A bridge was to be built with "good hewd timber clear of any Sapp to be layd cross . . . sound & strong sleepers, well supported in the middle." Isle of Wight Co., Va., Wills, Deeds, etc. 1662–1715.

1750 "The Sleepers of the lower floor [of a house] to be of good White Oak Sawed, 8 by 5 inches. The joists [of the second floor] to be of Timber Pine, sawed 8 by 4 inches." Newport Parish, Isle of Wight Co., Va., Vestry Book.

1754 A house in Augusta County, Virginia, was to have "Sleepers Squared with a Beam of a foot square under the middle of the sd Sleepers also to put in Joysts of eight Inches by five square with a Large Beam under the middle of them." Preston Papers, VHS.

1788 Specifications called for "The sleepers in the Criminals Rooms [of a prison] to be 12 by 4 inches & laid 6 inches apart & the joists on the second floor as well as those above to be 19 by 4 inches all laid 6 inches apart." Prince William Co., Va., Deed Book 1787–1791.

sliding door
William Mason Smith House,
Charleston, S.C.

sliding door A door, or more generally, a pair of doors hung from rollers seated in tracks that move sideways across an opening. When opened, it retracts into a pocket or cavity in the wall. Sliding doors first appeared in the South at the beginning of the 19th century but only became a standard feature in most double parlor dwellings in the 1830s and 1840s, where they separated the two principal entertaining spaces. See also **folding door.**

1802 The "first story" of a row house in Washington, D.C., had "two fire Places wood Petiton with Sliding doors 6 feet wide 8 feet high." INA Insurance Policy, CIGNA Archives.

1802 Building commissioners were to "cause to be erected in the record room" of a clerk's office "the shelves pigeon holes and sliding doors in that part of the house as they may think most advantageous." Culpeper Co., Va., Court Order Book 1802–1803.

slip **1.** Any added member such as a stud, rafter, joist, or lath that is used to enclose, cover, or frame the space of an area. Specifically, a sill that just fits between the space of a window opening and does not extend into the walls of the jamb.

1738 Repairs to be made to tobacco inspection house included "making sills and slipp studds between every post." Spotsylvania Co., Va., Court Order Book 1730–1738.

2. A sliding movement, to move in a sliding fashion up and down or back and forth.

1769 "Ordered that a glass window (with four lights eight by ten inches) be made to the closet in the mansion house at the Glebe and that the same be so contrived as to slip up and down." Cumberland Parish, Lunenburg Co., Va., Vestry Book.

slope In a falling garden, the inclined piece of ground between a horizontal terrace; a fall. For a more detailed description, see **falling garden.**

1773 At Nomini Hall in Westmoreland County, Virginia, "is a curious Terrace covered finely with Green turf & about five foot high with a slope of eight feet, which appears exceedingly well to persons coming to the front of the house. . . . This Terrace is produced along the Front of the House, and ends by the Kitchen, but before the Front-Doors is a broad flight of steps of the same Height & slope of the Terrace." *Journal and Letters of Philip Vickers Fithian.*
1785 An entry reads: "Planted . . . Brown Berries in the west square in the Second plat . . . next the Fall or slope." *Diaries of George Washington, 2.*

sluice An artificial channel for conducting water.

1773 After heavy rains, a traveler in North Carolina found it "no small risk of being drown'd in passing the rivers in flats (a kind of boat very ill calculated for passing the rivers in their present state, for they run like mill sluices)." Finlay, *Journal.*
1817 Work on a plantation in Maryland involved laying "a sluice in the grave yard marsh." *Diaries of Martha Ogle Forman.*

smith's shop (blacksmith's shop) A building containing one or more forges in which blacksmiths work iron bars into a variety of items for building and other purposes. See also **forge.**

1733 On a plantation near Goose Creek, South Carolina, was "a House built for a Smith's Shop." *South Carolina Gazette.*
1751 For sale in Fairfax County, Virginia, was "a Smith's Shop, eighteen feet square with a brick chimney in the middle. Also a likely Negro Fellow, that hath been near three years at the Blacksmith's Trade." *Maryland Gazette.*
1769 The "smith's shop" in operation at the Falls of the Potomac contained "Two fires." *Maryland Gazette.*

smokehouse (smoak house) A building in which meat, especially pork and fish, are cured by concentrated exposure to enveloping smoke. Generally ranging in size from 8 to 14 feet square, frame smokehouses were usually double studded or built of tightly dovetailed planks to support the weight of the hanging meats. Smoke came from an open fire in the center of the floor. The smokehouse as a distinctive building type first appears in the early 18th century and soon became one of the most common types of domestic outbuildings in the South. See also **meat house.**

1716 A craftsman rented a plantation in York County, Virginia, which included a "smoak house." Jones Papers, LC.
1732 There was to be built on a glebe "a Smoak house eight foot square planked Dore." Newport Parish, Isle of Wight Co., Va., Vestry Book.
1751 The vestry hired a "Workman to build a smoke house on the Glebe well framed ten feet squar underpining with brick the sides to be cyphered with inch plank and covered with boards or planks and well shingled." Elizabeth City Parish, Elizabeth City Co., Va., Vestry Book.
1795 "His smokery for bacon, hams, etc. is a room about twelve feet square, built of dry wood a fireplace in the middle, the roof conical, with nails in the rafters to hang meat intended to be smoked. In this case a fire is made on the floor in the

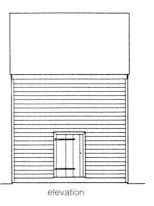

elevation

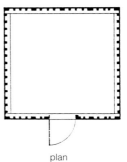

plan

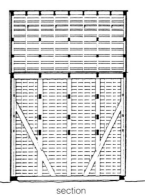

section

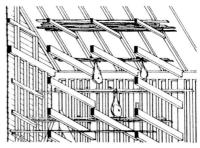

sectional perspective

smokehouse
Bacon's Castle, Surry County, Va.

middle of the building in the morning, which is not necessary to renew during the day. This is done for four or five days successively. The vent for the smoke is through the crevices of the boards. The meat is never taken out 'till it is used." Cooper, *Some Information Respecting America.*

snake fence A type of fence composed of stacked, split rails describing in plan a series of interlocking angles. The term gained currency in the 19th century. For a more complete description, see **worm fence.**

soapstone A soft, smooth, greasy stone composed of talc, used for hearths, floors, and ornaments.

> 1802 Charges for interior decorative stonework at John Tayloe's Washington residence included "Soap Stone to Chimneys . . . 62.12.6 . . . Marble Hearths squared & laid . . . 8.0.0 . . . Free Stone Jams and Mantle to D° . . . 18.0.0." Tayloe Papers, VHS.
> 1811 At the Riddell dwelling in Baltimore, payment was made to a workman for "fixing Chimney peice, & Cutting & fixing Soap Stone to Ditto." Riddell Accounts, Pleasants Papers, MHS.
> 1826 Bids were to be taken for "laying a floor in the Clerks office of this County with soapstone, the same to be less than three inches thick, to be dressed smooth and square." Henry Co., Va., Court Minute Book 1820–1827.

socle (zocle, zoccolo) A flat, plain block or unmolded support beneath the base of a pedestal, column, or building; a plinth. See also **plinth** (1).

> 1816 In designing the Washington Monument in Baltimore, architect Robert Mills noted in his diary "made drawing of Zocle of W. Monument." Pocket Memorandum Book, LC.
> 1817 A "zoccolo marbled and cushioned" supported the columns of a church chancel in Baltimore. *American and Commercial Daily Advertiser.*
> 1819 A pavilion at the University of Virginia campus was to have "a zocle of 12 I. under the whole colonnade to raise it's floor above the ground." Lambeth and Manning, *Thomas Jefferson as an Architect.*

soffit (soffet) The underside of any component of a building. Specifically, a ceiling; the lower side of a vault or arch; the under surface of the corona of a cornice.

> 1773 In the design of an unidentified building in Edenton, North Carolina, architect John Hawks noted that "the Soffite or underside of the arch from Pillaster to column of a single row, should be the exact width of the column at the top which is 10 inches." John Hawks Collection, SHC.
> 1790 Work on the pediment at Hampton in Baltimore County, Maryland, included fabricating "8 pannels in soffett." *MHM,* 33.
> 1811 At Montpelier in Orange County, Virginia, carpenters made "57 ft run of framed window jambs & soffits." Cocke Papers, UVa.
> 1820 A bill of work at Bremo in Fluvanna County, Virginia, specified woodwork for windows with "Circular Arch . . . [and] Circular Soffits." Cocke Papers, UVa.

solder (sodder, sawder) *(n.)* An alloy of varying composition used to join pipes, gutters, window cames, and other surfaces together. *(v.)* To bond a joint together with a metallic alloy.

> 1640 Materials used in repairing a house included "lead soder and haspes." Maryland Patents Certificates and Warrants, 1637–1650.
> 1704 The vestry was to order from England "glass, lead sodder and casements for the chappell." St. Peter's Parish, New Kent Co., Va., Vestry Book.
> 1726 "Solder, or Sodder—There are several kinds . . . Solder for Lead, which is made of Lead and half as much Block-tin. This is for Plumbers use; for Glaziers use it may be somewhat finer." Neve, *City and Country Purchaser.*
> 1738 "Richard Lovel [was paid] for saudering the Organ pips." Petsworth Parish, Gloucester Co., Va., Vestry Book.

soffit
Pavilion 10, University of Virginia

solid To work an element such as a window frame or sill out of a single piece of wood, rather than framing it together with several different pieces.

> **1771** In St. John's Church, Williamsboro, North Carolina, "the frames of the doors & Windows shall be worked out of the Sollid with good nose Sills & to show as if Architrave." Francis Hawks Collection, Church Historical Society.
>
> **1773** In a prison for Edenton, North Carolina, architect John Hawks specified that the "Gutter [be] wrought out of the solid to convey the water thro' the wall to the outside of the prison." John Hawks Papers, SHC.
>
> **1795** The window frames of a courthouse in Woodstock, Virginia, were "to be made of good white oak worked out of the solid with a place for fixing weights to hoiste the sash." Shenandoah Co., Va., Court Order Book 1795–1798.

sounding board **1.** A wooden canopy placed above a pulpit. Sounding boards were symbolic of the honor attached to the minister's office and the word of God preached from the pulpit. The board also reflected the sound of the minister's voice out into the church. By the 18th century, the most elaborate sounding boards constructed in churches and meetinghouses were polygonally shaped with an ogee roof terminated by finials. The flat soffit was often decorated with an inlaid sun pattern. In the colonial period, Virginians eschewed this term in favor of *type*. See also **canopy, pulpit, type.**

> **1711** A South Carolina Anglican vestry observed that their unfinished church still lacked a "Desk, Pulpit & Sounding board." Christ Church Parish, Charleston Co., S.C., Vestry Book.
>
> **1770** Construction of a new church called for "the Pulpit and Sounding Board of polished black walnut To be built together with the Clerks Desk stair case and Bannister After the model of George Town Pulpit as near as possible." St. David's Parish, Craven Co., S.C., Vestry Book.

2. Short boards set transversely between floor joists that support plaster or coarse mortar used to muffle sound.

> **1727** Church repairs called for "more sounding Bords" to be installed. St. Helena's Parish, S.C., Vestry Book.

spa A resort associated with a mineral spring and frequented at certain times of the year by the well-to-do. Here they gathered to bathe in the springs or drink its waters—or simply to enjoy the company of others. These resorts replicated, in a modest way, the pattern set by such watering places as Bath and Tunbridge Wells in England. Spas were the principal object of many who traveled for pleasure in the late 18th century, and by the 1820s they provided diversion for a growing middle class. It was this later period that saw intensive development of the springs.

> **1808** At Sweet Springs in Monroe County, Virginia, one traveler described a nearby resort: "About one mile from these springs is another spa;—a considerable sum of money has been expended in building houses and accommodations for company, but it is now totally deserted, and I am told that the present possessor is involved in a chancery suit respecting the premises." Caldwell, *A Tour through a Part of Virginia.*

spandrel (spandril) The triangular area between the extrados of two arches, extending from the spring line to a horizontal tangent line at the crown of the arches.

> **1798** Extra work on the penitentiary in Richmond consisted "of Stone Pillars to support the Groins of 6 rooms, stone imposts to all the external Arches, stone Corbels in the Spandrils of the Arches, and Keystones to the large Groins." *The Correspondence and Miscellaneous Papers of Benjamin Henry Latrobe*, 1.

Spanish brown   A highly variable, naturally occurring pigment, reddish brown in color, extensively used in the 18th century as a primer, and as an inexpensive finish color.

> 1723   "Spanish Brown . . . dark, dull red, of a Horseflesh Colour, 'tis an Earth, it being dug out of the ground, but there is some of it of a very good Colour and 'tis of great use among Painters, being generally used as the first or priming Colour, that they lay upon any kind of work, being cheap and plentiful." Smith, *The Art of Painting in Oyl.*
>
> 1734   Window frames of a church were to be "twice primed first with Spanish brown then with white lead." Blisland Parish, James City and New Kent Cos., Va., Vestry Book.
>
> 1771   The vestry of St. John's Church, Granville County, North Carolina, directed that the new building be painted "a Stone Collour & the Roof to be painted with Spanish Brown." Francis Lister Hawks Collection, Church Historical Society.
>
> 1800   A courthouse was to be painted with "turpentine and oil mixed with red Oaker or spanish Brown mixed with Tar." Gates Co., N.C., County Accounts, NCA&H.

Spanish whiting   A white paint pigment and filler made from chalk. See also **whiting.**

> 1764   Imported in Annapolis was "Spanish whiting." *Maryland Gazette.*
>
> 1798   "COCKE & FIELD Have for sale . . . at their STORE" in Petersburg "Spanish Whiting." *Virginia Gazette and Petersburg Advertiser.*

specification (Usually *pl.* specifications)   A written description of the particular materials, dimensions, construction methods, payment, and quality of workmanship of a projected work to be followed by a builder. Although such documents had long been part of the British building tradition inherited by the 17th-century settlers of the Chesapeake and Carolinas, the earliest surviving descriptions of building projects provided little more than the bare outlines of the work, generally listing the size of the structure, the types of materials to be used, and the obligations of client and undertaker in terms of supplying labor and materials. Much was left unsaid because the work usually progressed under the watchful eye of the client who resolved many building details with his craftsman on the construction site. The brevity of contractual agreements also stems from the fact that most clients wanted structures which conformed to the traditional way of building. Thus there was little need to spell out the commonplace. Both parties knew what they meant for a building to be *good, sufficient,* and *workmanlike.* For much of the colonial period, building projects were modest in scope, and the choice of detailed finish work was limited by custom and craftsmanship. If the client was more ambitious and looked to a form or manner of building that was outside the regional vernacular, more of these details would be written into a contract, citing, for example, a specific way of fashioning a type of wainscotting, or noting the type of cornice detailing found in a neighbor's dwelling. Even so, to modern eyes, most specifications of the colonial period provide only the barest glimpse of the building process. The term *specifications* did not come into use until the very end of the 18th century, not surprisingly at a time when professional builders and architects were making an effort to distinguish their role in the building process from that of common carpenters and workmen. Before that time, these written descriptions were sometimes called *articles of agreement* or simply *plans.* With the advent of professional architects, a growing range of specialty materials and construction techniques, the emergence of specialized building types, and the growing wealth and ambition of the new nation, specifications became more detailed than their colonial predecessors. The generalities of design ideals of that earlier period had given way to self-conscious specifics of detail, spelling out a web of obligations, novel techniques, and a variety of new materials in a manner that profoundly influenced the shape of architecture in the early 19th century. See also **plan** (2).

> **1806** The English-born architect William Nichols devised a plan for the repair of St. Paul's Church in Edenton, North Carolina, and set down the "specification of the Carpenter's and Joiner's work to be done." St. Paul's Parish, Chowan Co., N.C., Loose Papers.
> **1824** A document was titled "Specifications for the building the Court House in Roxborough, N.C. to be built after the following manner, to wit." Person Co., N.C., Miscellaneous Court Records, NCA&H.
> **1826** "On the 17th day of January 1826 Dabney Cosby and Valentine Parrish entered into an Agreement with the Commissioners appointed by the County Court of Goochland, to build a Courthouse for the said County according to the foregoing specifications." Cocke Papers, UVa.

spike A large nail with either a round or square head, used to join large framing members and fasten thick planks. See also **wrought nail.**

> **1739** A prison was to be repaired "by laying down a new floor a cross the upper floor with two inch plank to be layed down with spike nails." Spotsylvania Co., Va., Court Order Book 1738–1749.
> **1764** In specifications for a post and rail fence around a churchyard, "each Plank [is] to be let in the Post two inches & Spik'd on with four Inch Spikes." St. George's Parish, Harford Co., Md., Vestry Book.
> **1813** The wall of a jail was "to be sealed with 2 inch plank all of which is to be nailed with 30d or spikes to be set at the distance of 4 inches from each other." Wayne Co., N.C., Miscellaneous Court Records, NCA&H.

spindle A short, turned piece of woodwork.

> **1716** "Paid Mr. Bladen for takeing down and mending the Spindle of ye Golden Ball" on the Anglican church in Annapolis. St. Anne's Parish, Anne Arundel Co., Md., Vestry Book.

spinning house A building in which to carry on the manufacture of thread and related tasks, generally associated with the larger rural estates. In some cases, spinning was relegated to a spinning chamber or spinning room in the planter's house. Spinning houses were sometimes furnished with bedding and with ironing equipment as well as one or more spinning wheels, a grouping that suggests servants' living space as much as work. Because spinning was regarded as a woman's task, the spinning house or room may have acquired a female association. Whether whites worked among the slaves here remains unclear. Spinning houses were rare before 1730. In subsequent decades the natural increase of the slave population provided surplus labor for such activities and well-to-do planters began to invest in spinning and weaving equipment as a profitable outlet for this labor. See **loom house, weaving house.**

> **1732** In Lancaster County, Virginia, Robert Carter's spinning house and the "Spinning House Chambers" above were furnished with several beds, flat irons, a pair of tailor's shears, a mortar and pestle, and 3 physic sieves, but no spinning equipment. Carter Papers, UVa.

1768 Appraisers listed a bed, an "old spinning wheal," several flat irons, a table, 2 chairs and a bag of feathers "In the spining house" at Traverse Tarpley's plantation in Richmond County, Virginia. Richmond Co., Va., Will Book 1767–1787.

1781 Rawleigh Downman's house had a "Spinning Chamber" with a bed, "1 Flax Wheel and rule . . . 1 Cotton do. & 2 Chairs . . . 1 Clothes Basket." Lancaster Co., Va., Will and Deed Book 1770–1783.

spire   In general, a conical, sharp-pointed termination to an object. Specifically, a pointed, polygonal, pyramidal roof forming the upper stage of a steeple or tower. See also **steeple**.

1717 Churchyard gate posts were to have "Spires on the Top." All Saints Parish, Calvert Co., Md., Vestry Book.

1719 A churchyard was to have "two Wide Handsome Gates made after the form of Iron Gates with Handsom Square Peares (or Posts) for the Gates, with a hollow Spire." St. Peter's Parish, New Kent Co., Va., Vestry Book.

1761 An Anglican church to be built in Winchester, Virginia, was to have "a Steeple with a Spire 56 Feet high from the Surface of the Earth." *Maryland Gazette*.

1791 "A CONTRACT For building the Steeple to the Presbyterian Church in Alexandria" noted that "the brick and stone work are to be 95 feet high from the foundation, on which will be erected a spire of wood, of 65 feet high." *Alexandria Gazette*.

splay   Any sloped surface or oblique angle that creates a larger opening on one side than on the other. Splayed jambs are often found at windows, doorways, and niches.

1811 Windows in a house had "Splayed Elbows [with] fancy mitered mouldings." Riddell Accounts, Pleasants Papers, MHS.

splice   To join two pieces of timber together in a continuous plane through the use of a lap or scarf joint.

1779 Recommendation "to splice the sill under the back part of the house as far as is judged necessary." New Castle Co., Del., Orphans Court Valuations F.

spline   A long, narrow strip of wood inserted into the grooves of the edges of two adjoining boards; a loose tongue. See also **tongue and groove**.

split   To divide a material such as wood along the grain by cutting it with an ax, froe, or some other bladed instrument. Split timber was far more economical to produce than sawn stuff and was the predominant method of fabricating many building materials such as shingles and laths. Although the term is nearly synonymous with *rive*, for the most part, contemporaries used *split* to refer to the cutting of larger pieces such as rails and framing timbers rather than smaller elements such as laths and clapboards. See also **cleave, rive**.

1733 The first settlers of Savannah were "sett about sawing and splitting boards eight feet long in order to build clapp board houses." *The Journal of Peter Gordon 1732–1735*.

1737 A plantation to be sold near Charleston was "well fenc'd in with split Rails." *South Carolina Gazette*.

1756 On the Wells farm on the Eastern Shore of Maryland was "one house with hewed logs 20 by 16 covered with smooth boards in indifferent repair, one smiths shop with split logs 16 feet square covered with smooth boards in good repair, one log stable with split logs 16 by 12 covered with smooth boards in indifferent repair one ditto with round logs 12 feet square." Queen Anne's Co., Md., Deed Book E.

1773 A building account for William Corbit's dwelling in Odessa, Delaware, listed "Laths Splitting &c £6.10.0." Sweeney, *Grandeur on the Appoquinimink*.

1816 On a tract of land in Angola Neck in southern Delaware was a "rail or split log corn crib." Sussex Co., Del., Orphans Court Valuations L.

splitwood   Material that has been prepared by riving it out of round log segments such as shingles or clapboards.

> 1729   "The wall part" of a church in West Chester, New York, "is likewise cover'd with Laths & upon which them are nail'd as on the Roof splittwood which they call shingles." SPG Letterbook B, SPGFP.

sprig   A small, wedge-shaped, headless nail used primarily in sash glazing; also a small, square-bodied brad. See also **brad**.

> 1720   The vestry of a church purchased from a London merchant "Sprigs for Cazments." All Faiths Parish, St. Mary's Co., Md., Vestry Book.
> 1741   "Just imported . . . from London . . . glaziers and sash sprigs." *South Carolina Gazette*.
> 1789   "The machine for making nails and sprigs, constructed by Mr. Fulsom . . . now of Harrisburg, in Pennsylvania, effects all its operations from rolled strips of iron, without any further use of fire." *Maryland Gazette or Baltimore Advertiser*.
> 1797   Along with composition ornaments for sale, a Baltimore merchant noted that "small neat sprigs may also be had for putting on the above." *Federal Gazette and Baltimore Advertiser*.

spring   **1.** A flat, iron bar, bent in tension and used to put pressure on another member. A spring can either be a single leaf or a double leaf in the shape of a V, referred to as a "double spring." Springs are used in stock and rim locks to enable the bolt to be activated, and are used in spring bolts to keep the bolts from slipping out of the locked position when mounted vertically.

> 1726   Payment made "for a large Springbolt & Staples" and "for one large double Spring box Lock." St. Anne's Parish, Anne Arundel County, Md., Vestry Book.

2. The point where an arch or vault begins to curve.

> 1831   The outside doors of a courthouse were "to have double eliptical arches sprung over them." Caswell Co., N.C., Court Minute Book 1823–1831.

3. The setting of board sheathing together with bevel joints to produce a flush face.

> 1745   The vestry agreed with carpenter Thomas Byrn "to weather board the Church round with inch pine plank Sprung and plaind." All Saints Parish, Calvert Co., Md., Vestry Book.
> 1794   The carpenter's report for work done on George Washington's threshing barn at Dogue Run in Fairfax County, Virginia, included charges for "Jointing & springing & puting up the weather boarding Round the Outside of the treading house." Manuscript Collection, Papers of George Washington, LC.

spring bolt   A bolt with a sliding bar that is held in position by means of a leaf spring. See also **bolt** (1).

> 1745   Josiah Smith supplied the Norfolk courthouse "two spring bolts 1/6." Norfolk Co., Va., Miscellaneous Court Records 1652–1748.
> 1766   The vestry house was to have "good sufficient window shutters with spring bolts to the Same." St. George's Parish, Harford Co., Md., Vestry Book.

springhouse   A structure erected over a natural spring or a watercourse to preserve it from impurities and to serve as a larder and cool place for keeping milk and cheese. Springhouses often had troughs and shelves for these functions.

> 1762   A farm for sale near Annapolis contained "a Dwelling-House and Barn, Spring-House, and a very convenient Still House." *Maryland Gazette*.
> 1786   A settlement on the western frontier of Virginia contained a "spring house with cellar, logg'd 18 by 15, 10 years built." Jonathan Clark Notebook, Filson Club.
> 1798   "Major Moore's Joe came here to underpin floor of spring house, but the water at the bottom would not admit of working on it, drained off part." Francis Taylor Diary, CWF.

spring lock An iron lock, originally made with an open face, but later enclosed within an iron case. The bolt on a spring lock is activated by a handle that is pushed horizontally against the tension of an internal spring. Spring locks can only be operated from one side of the door.

> 1665 "Raymond Staplefort att night caused a Boy his servant called Humphrey Jones to enter att a window, whereof Two wooden Barrs had beene broken eyther by himselfe or by the said Boy, where the said Boy having entered, opened the Doore, (which was fast shutt with a spring Lock) unto the said Staplefort." *Archives of Maryland*, 49.
>
> 1748 Specifications for a dwelling house included "one good spring lock for the front door iron rim's eight inches the other seven doors to have locks five inches." Southam Parish, Cumberland Co., Va., Vestry Book.
>
> 1772 A glebe house included "brass spring locks to each of the inside doors . . . one of the passage doors to have a strong spring lock the others to be fixed with Staple hook and barr." St. Mark's Parish, Culpeper Co., Va., Vestry Book.

square 1. A superficial or two-dimensional measurement of an area. Carpenters calculated their framing, flooring, and roofing work by the *square*, a measurement of 100 *superficial* or *square* feet. See also **superficial measure.**

> 1668 "Carpenters do commonly work by the square of 10 foot, in erecting their Carcas, that is the framing and setting up with their Partitions, Floors, Rafters, and such like." Leybourn, *Platform Guide Mate for Purchasers, Builders, and Measurers.*
>
> 1713 At Bruton Parish Church in Williamsburg, carpenter Lewis Deloney's account listed "16 Square flooring done at the Church @ 3/6." Further accounts listed "framing, raising and covering the Roof at 18 sh 6d pr Square, the framing & raising the Floor at 10 sh pr Square." Jones Family Papers, LC; *Calendar of Virginia State Papers*, 1.
>
> 1726 "Floor boards are commonly measur'd by the Square (of 100 superficial Feet) by multiplying the Length of the Room in Feet, by the Breadth in Feet, and the Product is the Content in Feet; then measure the Chimney-ways, and Well-holes for Stairs by themselves, and deduct their Content in feet from the whole Content in Feet." Neve, *The City and Country Purchaser.*
>
> 1790 In Columbia County, Georgia, a carpenter's account for building a dwelling listed "laying the Lower floor—tongue & grovd four Squares & half @ 8/ pr square £1.16.0. . . . To Seiling three squares & half @ 12/6 pr Square £2.3.9." Thomas Carr Accounts, UGa.

2. A level or smooth piece of planted ground in a garden or pleasure ground usually slightly raised for the better cultivation of plants. Squares were often referred to as *beds* and occasionally as *parterres*. In the 18th century, squares were usually geometric forms, more often than not in the shape of a rectangle, and separated from one another by walks. On occasion, a sunken piece of ornamental grassy ground such as a bowling green was also called a *square*.

> 1784 In Williamsburg, a gardener "sowed Pease in the Square next Chimney . . . Glory of England, sowed same Day in Square next Street." Joseph Prentis Garden Book, UVa.
>
> 1792 In Annapolis, William Faris "planted the Walnut Tree Square full of plants and the Square in the lot." William Faris Diary, MHS.

3. The arrangement of dwellings and streets around a central open area. Also the intersection of two or more streets. Following English fashion of constructing squares in cities such as Bath and London, a few speculators in southern towns laid out suburban squares. Few of these squares had the architectural uniformity characteristic of many English ones, but were rather developed in a piecemeal fashion.

> 1764 The sale of a dwelling in Portsmouth listed its location "in Cavendish Square." Norfolk Co., Va., Deed Book 1764–1765.
>
> 1774 In Charleston, there was "to be LET . . . A BRICK TENEMENT in Colleton Square, on a Corner Lot." *South Carolina Gazette and Country Journal.*

4. One of a number of different instruments for laying out carpentry and joinery work as well as for drafting. Most squares consisted of a long blade with either another blade at right angles or an adjustable second blade used for measuring and laying out angles. A *carpenter's square* consisted of two arms attached at right angles to one another and was used to set out roofing, staircases, and other framing elements. The *mitre square* was used for laying out angles and the *try square* used for laying out right angles. The *T square* was used by draftsmen to mark horizontal lines on paper or serve as a perpendicular support for angled squares.

square head An aperture or a covering for one that has a straight rather than arched or compass head.

> **1815** Church to have "ten Window frames & three door frames with circular heads with pannel doors & pannel shutters of Square heads." St. John's, Parish, Colleton Co., S.C., Vestry Book.

square roof A roof whose angle is 45 degrees, also known as true pitch. See also **pitch** (2).

> **1755** Specifications for a 30-by-20-foot tobacco warehouse called for a "square roof." Perquimans Co., N.C., Court Minute Book 1755–1761.
> **1794** A clerk's office was "to be arched with brick and a square roof of wood upon the top of the whole, meaning the Rafters to be at right angles to one another." Accomack Co., Va., Court Order Book 1793–1796.
> **1810** An overseer at the Goose Pond in Hanover County, Virginia, wrote to the owner that "thare are not aney timbers gotten for the portico not knowing the sise & plan of it—I am still at a loss about what form you intend it to be bult. . . . I wish Mr. Rootes would say what cise it is to be & wheather a Sqeuar rugh simeler to a dorment . . . & wheather the portico is to be in the center of the house." Williams Berkeley Papers, Duke.

stable A building used to house horses. Planters and merchants wealthy enough to own a carriage often would build a structure to store both the vehicle and board their horses. These structures were typically laid out with a room for carriages at its center, stalls for the horses in flanking spaces, a small harness room for the storage of tack, and a loft for the storage of hay. See also **carriage house, chaise house, coach house.**

> **1674** Payments were made for "clapboards to build a stable & smoak house." Norfolk Co., Va., Wills and Deeds 1666–1675.
> **1751** On a glebe was "a Log Stable Sixteen feet Square and Seven feet pitch one Folding Door at the End, with Racks, Mangers and Stalls for four Horses." Wicomico Parish, Northumberland Co., Va., Vestry Book.
> **1758** Specifications noted "a stable of Brick, of the same Dimensions as the Kitchen [24' x 44'], Part whereof for a Coach Room, and the rest fitted in the Inside with Stalls and proper Conveniences." *State Records of North Carolina,* 25.
> **1823** The vestry decided to build a new two-story "carriage house and stable" with "two good rooms for servants" on the second floor. St. Philip's Parish, Charleston, S.C., Vestry Book.

stack The mass of a chimney or group of chimneys and funnels extending from the base to the cap of the shaft. Modern usage has often narrowed the meaning of the term to refer only to the shaft, the narrowest portion of the chimney mass, which contains the funnel and rises above the roof. See also **chimney, shaft** (2).

> **1680** A courthouse was to be built "with two stacks of brick chimneys of fower harths of eight foote within the Gaumes." Talbot Co., Md., Judgement Book 1675–1682.

stack
Holloway House, Port Royal,
Caroline County, Va.

1729 On a farm in Baltimore County, Maryland, was "a Kitchen 30 feet long and 15 wide, with a stack of Chimneys in the middle." *Maryland Gazette.*

1750 A dwelling house was to have "a stack of chimneys in the middle that shall make four fire places in viz.: two in the fore rooms and two in the shade." Elizabeth River Parish, Norfolk Co., Va., Vestry Book.

1751 A "Ministers House" in Savannah was to be "26 feet by 18 two storys high to which a kitchen, at one end 18 feet by 16 a stack of brick chimneys to contain three fire places and an oven." Christ Church Parish, Ga., Church Records, GHS.

1799 Plans for John Steele's dwelling in Rowan County, North Carolina, called for "the frame of the walls to be five Inches thick and the Stack of Chimneys to run up in the Center of the partition that Divides the two parlours." John Steele Papers, SHC.

stair (usually *pl.* stairs; stares)   A series of steps leading from one level to another. Stairs are formed by a carriage containing horizontal *treads* and vertical *risers.* The outer edge of a stair is known as a *string.* If the edges of the treads and risers are exposed, it is an *open stringer,* and if they are covered by a *stringboard,* it is a *closed stringer.* A *flight* of stairs is an unbroken series of steps leading from one landing to the next. Stairs are described by their construction and geometrical shape. Many early stairs in the colonial South made a quarter turn around a central *newel* post in one corner of a room, often enclosed with partition framing. Such stairs were sometimes known as *winding stairs* because at or near the lower end of the flight, a number of treads were wedge shaped, with their narrow edges terminating in the newel. *Dog-leg stairs* consisted of two flights of stairs parallel to one another, broken in the middle by a landing. *Open well stairs* have an opening or *well* between the outer strings of each flight and landing. The fashion for geometrical stairs appeared in the South in the late colonial period and continued through the antebellum period. Pulpit stairs were among the first curving or *twisted* stairs to appear in the South. The pattern books of William Pain and others introduced grand *circular* and *elliptical stairs,* which became showpieces of the joiner's trade in the dwellings of a number of merchants and planters. These geometrical stairs were lighter in detail than the straight-legged stairs of their Georgian predecessors, often sweeping up in a curvilinear or elliptical space in a dwelling.

1640 An account of work performed for a planter included "5 daies work in laying the floore makeing doore and staires of the corn loft." Maryland Patents, Certificates and Warrants 1637–1650, MSA.

1740 The raised magistrates' platform in a courthouse was to have "a paire of Stairs to go into it handsomely made and neatly railed." Lancaster Co., Va., Court Order Book 1729–1743.

1778 Carpenter William Luten of Chowan County, North Carolina, charged a client for "framing, weatherboarding, shingling, and making 2 doors and running up the stairs." William Luten Ledger Book, NCA&H.

1826 St. Philip's Church in Charleston contained "spiral Stairs leading to the Steeple." St. Philip's Parish, Charleston, S.C., Vestry Book.

staircase (staire case)   A flight of stairs including its framework, balusters, handrail, and other decorative details. The term was often interchangeable with *stairs.* In the 17th century and throughout the 18th century in most dwellings, staircases were small with a number of winding stairs turning around a central newel, often enclosed in a narrow opening in one corner of the room or next to a chimney. With the emergence of the center passage in domestic architecture in the early 18th century, the staircase became an element of considerable elaboration. In the best merchant and gentry dwellings, carved brackets, turned balusters, ramped and twisted handrails, and wainscotting executed in costly woods made the staircase a symbol of status. This rich elaboration decreased after the Revolution, replaced by simplified, attenuated elements such as unmolded handrails and square balusters, characteristic of neoclassical design aesthetics. With this transformation in the late 18th and early 19th centuries, spiral and elliptical staircases displayed the virtuosity of the joiner. See also **stair.**

staircase
Shirley, Charles City County, Va.

> **1673** Specifications called for "a staire case to goe up into the Chamber over the court house." Westmoreland Co., Va., Deed and Patent Book 1665–1677.
> **1680** A courthouse was to have "a fayre open well stare Casse up into the Roofe." Talbot Co., Md., Judgements 1675–1682.
> **1746** Plans for a dwelling included "a passage through the house eight feet wide and the staircase run up in it with banisters." Wicomico Parish, Northumberland Co., Va., Vestry Book.
> **1764** Henry Laurens of Charleston advised a Liverpool merchant that "mohogany is the thing by all means for your Stair case. (I believe you would agree in opinion with me if you saw mine.) The expence is very little more than of Cedar in the first Cost & in time it becomes abundantly cheaper, as it is firm, durable, & gains beauty whether you will or not with age." *Papers of Henry Laurens*, 4.
> **1783** In the Governor's House in New Bern, "the hand rail, Baluster and Carved Brackets to the best staircase are of best are of mahoginy, the steps and risers of fine grain clear pine, the light is conveyed to this staircase by a sky light 9 feet Diameter." Hawks Letter, Miranda Papers, Academia Nacional de la Historia, Caracas.
> **1803** An Episcopal church near Charleston was to have "a common winding staircase upon a circular base, 1 1/2 inch oak steps, 1 1/4 inch risers, with a center Newel." Johns Island Church Specifications, Library Society of Charleston.

stairway A synonymous term for *stair* that came into use in the late 18th or early 19th century.

> **1806** Regarding work under way at his estate in Bedford County, Virginia, Thomas Jefferson wrote that "The porticos & stairways will require some more digging." Coolidge Collection, Massachusetts Historical Society.
> **1824** In Charleston the vestry of St. Philip's parish approved a charge "for rough casting stairway wall of steeple and other repairs." St. Philip's Parish, Charleston, S.C., Vestry Book.

stake and rider fence See **worm fence.**

stall **1.** An enclosure in a stable, shed, or cowhouse for the accommodation of an animal, often equipped with a manger and rack. See also **manger, rack.**

> **1732** Thomas Sherman was employed to build "a stable for the horses at this courthouse of the Dimension of 36 foot long and suitable width for stalls on each side." Westmoreland Co., Va., Court Order Book 1731–1739.
> **1766** A "stable [is to] be built for the Gleeb of sawed loggs of 20 foot by 16 with a shed of 8 foot the length of the stable . . . to have eight stalls with a passage between." Cumberland Parish, Lunenburg Co., Va., Vestry Book.
> **1792** At Nomini Hall in Westmoreland County, Virginia, "a Stall for two Cows 10 by 12 in the clear [is] to be built, near the Necessary House." Robert Carter Papers, LC.

2. A booth or stand in which merchandise or food is displayed for sale. Most corporations fitted out their market houses with stalls where butchers, farmers, and other merchants could sell their produce and wares. While most stalls were rented on a yearly basis, a few were set aside free of charge for farmers and others from the surrounding countryside. See also **market house.**

1740 An act was passed prohibiting encroachment upon the public right-of-ways in front of buildings in Charleston, "saving only that it shall be lawful for the Inhabitants to suffer their Stall Boards (when their Shop Windows are set open) to turn over and extend Eleven inches, and no more, from the foundation of their Houses into the Streets, for the better Conveniency of their Shop Windows." *South Carolina Gazette.*

1782 In Fredericksburg, "Country people who come to this market suffer many inconveniences for want of stalls. . . . ordered that two stalls be immediately erected in the market . . . for their convenience, and that the proprietors of private stalls in the market shall pay the clerk the sum 7 1/2 d for each stall." Fredericksburg, Va., City Council Minute Book 1782–1801.

1817 "The market house [is to] be laid out into five Butcher Stalls." Portsmouth, Va., Town Minute Book 1796–1821.

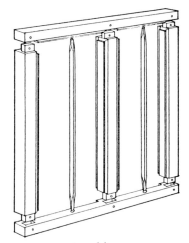

stanchion
Casement window frame with stanchions, Holly Hill, Anne Arundel County, Md.

stanchion (stantion)   An upright prop, such as an iron bar support, of a casement window.

1714 The vestry hired a workman "to put Stantions in the Windows." St. Paul's Parish, Kent Co., Md., Vestry Book.

1795 A lighthouse on the North Carolina coast was to be crowned by an "iron lantern in the octagonal form. . . . The eight corner pieces of stanchions of which, are to be built in the wall to the depth of ten feet. These stanchions to be nearly three inches square in the lower ten feet, and 3 1/2 inches by 2 1/2 inches above." *North Carolina Gazette.*

stand   1. A raised platform of wood for a minister or orator. See **rostrum.**

1833 At a Methodist camp meeting, near St. Michael's, Maryland, Frederick Douglass noted that "The ground was happily chosen; seats were arranged; a stand erected." Douglass, *My Bondage and My Freedom.*

2. A plot of land; a plantation.

1796 Near Williamsburg, "Judge Tyler termed his estate on York river, an excellent stand for good living without thinking of anything further." *Virginia Journals of Benjamin Henry Latrobe,* 1.

3. A site or building for a business.

1787 "A bargain will be given in that excellent stand now occupied by Mr. Mark Pringle." *Maryland Journal, and the Baltimore Advertiser.*

1788 One subscriber offered for sale a property suited "to those who would wish for the best Stand for a Dry or Wet Store." *Maryland Journal, and the Baltimore Advertiser.*

standard   An upright timber; a vertical framing member.

1788 Jail walls were to be built with "six inches square oak standards or studs at six inches asunder." Prince William Co., Va., Deed Book 1787–1791.

1817 A workman was engaged to construct "a strong post between each standard of the sheds" of a market house. Portsmouth, Va., Town Minute Book 1796–1821.

staple   A piece of wrought iron forged into the shape of a *U* and driven into wood, often used to receive either a hook, hasp, bolt, or the bolt of a lock. See also **hasp, hook and staple.**

1712 In York County, Virginia, "Mr. Thomas Nelson Junr. is paid by county levy 65 lbs. tobacco for a large lock and staple for the prison door." York Co., Va., Deeds, Orders, and Wills Book 1711–1714.

1725 "For Smiths work done for the church by Order" Thomas Jobson was paid £0.6.0 "for a large bolt 2 foot long & 3 staples." St. Anne's Parish, Anne Arundel County, Md., Vestry Book.

1739 Payment was made to John Holybush for "2 locks 30/ 2 bolts 12/6 2 staples & hasp." Christ Church Parish, Charleston Co., S.C., Vestry Book.

statehouse   A building where members of the provincial and later state legislatures and courts met for deliberation. The accommodations provided by each colony for their provincial assemblies varied significantly with the nature and structure of authority and power within each province. Where assemblies were weak and the authority of the executive branch strong, many public functions were housed in makeshift quarters. Some were accommodated in the governor's house, which served as a public meeting space as well a as private residence. For example, the Governor's House erected in New Bern by William Tryon in the late 1760s housed the provincial council in a grand chamber, while the lower body of the General Assembly usually met elsewhere. Many statehouses also housed the provincial courts, the public records, and occasionally the colony's stock of gunpowder. Most buildings by the late colonial period contained one or two large rooms on the ground floor for the courts and assemblies, connected by a large lobby and stairhall. On the second floor were additional meeting spaces as well as offices of various officials. As a recognizable form, the statehouse was slow in developing. Through the first half of the 17th century, the governments of Virginia and Maryland sat in a variety of buildings, including taverns. Tired of the dishonor of having "all our laws being made and our judgments given in alehouses," the General Assembly of Virginia in 1663 sought to build or rent accommodations that provided the necessary status and respect they believed the body deserved. This search for the appropriate form of public building was evident at Jamestown, where the Governor's House was fitted with decorative plasterwork that included some symbols of the province. The first important statehouse erected in the South that was a self-conscious assertion of provincial authority was the two-story brick structure erected at St. Mary's City, Maryland in 1674. This structure served the provincial courts as well as the legislature for nearly twenty years before the capital was moved to Annapolis. Although constructed of brick in a region where most structures were of wood, the St. Mary's City statehouse had few exterior features that set it apart as a public structure. The first interjection of English public building forms such as cupolas, compass-headed window, arcades, vanes, and dials appeared in Williamsburg at the beginning of the 18th century with the building of the first capitol. In the late colonial period, South Carolina and Maryland constructed large brick structures that further defined the form of the provincial statehouse. Built in the 1750s, the South Carolina statehouse was a nine-bay, two-story stuccoed structure with a central pedimented projection, making it one of the most important colonial interpretations of English Palladianism. The statehouse in Annapolis had a large dome that became a critical iconographic image of the type, made all the more emphatic with construction of a domed capitol in Washington.

> **1674** An act was passed "for the building of a state house and Prison att St. Maries." *Archives of Maryland*, 2.
>
> **1774** At the northwest corner of Broad and Meeting Streets in Charleston was "the State House where the members of the assembly meet to transact all the business of the province and the judges sit to hear and try causes, etc. It is a large handsome substantial building and looks well." *South Carolina Historical Magazine*, 9.

stately Dignified, elegant. The term was rarely used to describe buildings.

> **1708** "The Church" in Newcastle, Delaware, "is a fair and stately Building and one of the largest in this government." SPG Papers, Lambeth Palace Library.

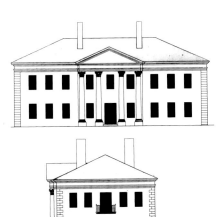

statehouse
Restored south and east elevations,
South Carolina Statehouse,
Charleston, S.C. 1753

1772   In approaching a plantation near Goose Creek, South Carolina, there was "a very long avenue of wood and a part of it stately Live oaks." *South Carolina Historical and Genealogical Magazine*, 36.

statuary marble   White Italian marble imported into the South in the form of chimney pieces and statues.

1783   In the drawing room of the Governor's House in New Bern, "the Chimney [is] of plain statuary marble with a frame for a picture or landscape over it." Hawks Letter, Miranda Papers, Academia Nacional de la Historia, Caracas.

1796   At Mount Vernon, "there is a hansome statuary marble chimney piece in the dining room (of the taste of Sir Wm. Chambers), with insulated columns on each side. This is the only piece of expensive decoration I have seen about the house." *The Virginia Journals of Benjamin Henry Latrobe*, 1.

1817   The baptismal font of St. Paul's Episcopal Church in Baltimore "is of statuary marble, resting on a sub-plinth of dark marble." *American and Commercial Daily Advertiser.*

statue
Canova's statue of George Washington in the statehouse in Raleigh, N.C.

statue   A representation of a figure, animal, deity, eminent person, or other image, either sculpted from stone or cast in lead, bronze, or other metals. The most important public statues in the colonial south were that of Governor Botetourt, which was originally erected in the capitol in Williamsburg, Virginia and that of William Pitt, which stood upon a pedestal at the intersection of Broad and Meeting Streets in Charleston, South Carolina. Commissioned by the provincial legislatures in each colony as tokens of respect and admiration, both pedestrian statues were sculpted by English artists in the early 1770s. Patriotism and a desire for a national cultural identity stimulated the commissioning of statues in the early republic, especially in the wave of nationalist fervor after the War of 1812. The seated figure of George Washington in Roman garb, commissioned by the state of North Carolina from Italian sculptor Antonio Canova at Thomas Jefferson's suggestion, was regarded by many as the finest piece of sculpture in the South. Installed in the North Carolina statehouse, it perished in 1831 when the building burned. If public statuary was sparse in early America, statues appeared in a number of gardens throughout the South, where they often were placed at the termination of walks or at the meeting of axes. Most of these were of allegorical figures or deities, or were copies of classical statuary.

1773   "There is a large colossal statue of Mr. Pitt in Charlestown much praised by many. The drapery was exquisitely well done: but to me, the attitude, air and expression of the piece was bad." *Proceedings of the Massachusetts Historical Society*, 49.

1774   At Mount Airy in Richmond County, Virginia, was "a large well formed, beautiful Garden, as fine in every Respect as any I have seen in Virginia. In it stand four large beautiful Marble Statues." *Journal and Letters of Philip Vickers Fithian.*

1777   At the capitol in Williamsburg "is an elegant white marble pedestrian Statue of Lord Botetourt in his Robes, made by Richard Hayward, London, 1773 . . . the workmanship of the Statue is exquisitely fine. The whole is placed upon a Free-Stone Foundation, & surrounded with a neat Iron Railing." *VMHB*, 62.

1800   "A very striking proof of the folly of expecting that any statue will be always respected exists in Williamsburg, where Lord Botetourts statue which had remained untouched during the whole war, was mutilated, and decapitated by the young collegians, in the first frenzy of French revolutionary maxiums, because it was the statue of a Lord. The statue now graces Mrs. Hunt's Garden in a very mutilated state." *The Correspondence and Miscellaneous Papers of Benjamin Henry Latrobe*, 1.

1805   At the botanical garden in Charleston, "some evil minded person, taking advantage of the Gardener's absence, knocked at the Gate, and on being admitted . . . went directly to the Statue of Mercury, which was standing in the middle of the Garden, and threw it down, by which means it is entirely destroyed." *Charleston Courier.*

1819 In North Carolina, a letter from architect William Nichols to "the committee appointed to confer with the superintendent of public buildings as to the disposal of the Statue of Washington" by Antonio Canova, described the possible locations for the sculpture: "Had it been equestrian a space in centre of the west front [of the statehouse] would have been suitable, or had it been pedestrian, then a kind of Monopteros Temple or Canopy supported by twelve collumns and open all round might have been a sufficient appendage and protection. But from its being formed in a sitting posture an enclosed building either circular or parallelogram with a dome & portico would be proper." Treasurer's and Comptroller's Papers, NCA&H.

stay Any piece that acts as a stiffener, strut, or brace for another member.

1801 At the Octagon in Washington, a blacksmith charged his client for "two grates and stays for the nursery" and "two stays to the frontispiece of a Door." Tayloe, Papers, VHS.
1811 A house in Baltimore was constructed with "joists framed in Smaller Girders Cambered & Double Stayed." Riddell Accounts, Pleasants Papers, MHS.

steel A manufactured alloy of iron containing small amounts of carbon, which produces a hard malleable metal. It was distinguished from the more brittle cast iron by its elasticity and lower carbon content. Steel was used in building mainly as blades for cutting tools such as saws. See also **iron.**

1777 At Falmouth, Virginia, "Mr. Hunter has erected Works for making Steel (this Business he is just beginning upon)." *VMHB*, 62.

steeple A tall, ornamental structure attached to a church, meeting-house, or other public building, generally consisting of a tower, surmounted by a series of diminishing stages, often ornamented with arches, pilasters, and moldings, crowned by a pointed polygonal spire. One of the upper stages of the steeple often contained bells. Steeples became popular in England following the Great Fire of London in 1666 when a number of parish churches were rebuilt according to the designs of Christopher Wren. Wren's steeples set the standard of architectural treatment of this nontraditional church appendage throughout England and her American colonies. A series of publications, including James Gibbs's *Book of Architecture* (1728), provided colonial builders with patterns for church steeples that were adapted and used with increasing frequency in the late colonial period. The steeple at St. Michael's Church in Charleston owes much of it design vocabulary to English sources. At the end of the 18th and beginning of the 19th centuries, many denominations chose to ornament their churches and meetinghouses with steeples, often competing with one another within towns to construct the tallest or most elaborate structures. The term was often used in the early South to refer to any appendage of this kind, whether a tower, spire, or combination of the two. See also **belfry, spire, turret.**

1685 The vestry debated the cost of construction of "a steeple and a ring of bells" for the church at Middle plantation in Virginia. *Records of Bruton Parish.*
1737 Churchwardens were to "agree with a carpenter to repair the steeple & get the Bell hung." St. Helena's Parish, S.C., Vestry Book.
1740 The vestry reached an agreement with "Mr. William Walker of the Parish of St. Paul, in the County of Stafford, builder, to Erect & Build a Steeple & Vestry Room according to a Plan . . . drawn by the said Walker for the consideration of one hundred and thirty pounds." St. Peter's Parish, New Kent Co., Va., Vestry Book.
1755 In a petition for more money, the builders of St. Michael's Church wrote to

steeple
Steeple designs for
St. Martin-in-the-Fields, London

the General Assembly that the church was "of such Dimensions as would the better accommodate a growing Town, & with such decent Ornaments of Architecture as are suitable to the Public Use of divine worship for which it is intended. That the Steeple is carried up on a Massy Foundation to such an Height, as besides being an Ornament to Charlestown the Metropolis of this Province, it is of extraordinary Use to the Navigation on our Coast. It is so high as to be discerned at Sea before the Land is seen, & so properly situated as to be a plain leading mark for the Bar of this Harbour, and therefore effectually answers the Purpose and Intention of building a beacon." Williams, *St. Michael's*.

1755 In Annapolis, "a Petition [is to] be drawn and presented to the General Assembly, to have their Assistance in Building a Steple or Belfry, wherein to hang the new Parish Bell." St. Anne's Parish, Anne Arundel Co., Md., Vestry Book.

1795 The design for a stone courthouse in Woodstock, Virginia, included "a steeple . . . on the house, and . . . the petition walls, which are to be made of brick and be made strong as to bear the said steeple." Shenandoah Co., Va., Court Order Book 1795–1798.

steeple house A name used by Quakers to refer to a church, so called in part because of the belief that a church consisted of persons gathered together for worship and was not the building itself.

1702 The Quaker "George Fox, in some of his Printed Pamphlets, makes a great outcry and noise against the Steeple Houses in England, as he calls them, for having Crosses on the Tops of them, and that it is Popery; what can the Quakers say to this? Are their Bretheren of Rhod-Island guilty of Popery, for having the Cross on the top of their Meeting-House." Keith, *A Journal of Travels from New-Hampshire to Caratuck*.

stepladder See **ladder.**

stereobate In classical architecture, a solid mass of masonry serving as the base of a temple. See also **stylobate.**

stick and clay chimney A rare term for a variety of wooden chimney. See also **chimney.**

1786 On a Frederick County, Virginia, plantation was a "low log dwelling house 22 by 16, half stone chimney, the other part sticks and clay, floor of slabs." Jonathan Clark Notebook, Filson Club.

stile **1.** In joinery, a vertical member framing a panel; the outer, upright member of a sash frame or gate. See also **rail.**

1737 Repairs at a church included "60 Rails, Stiles & Parts." St. Philip's Parish, Charleston, S.C., Vestry Book.

1803 Doors in an Episcopal church were to have "rais'd pannels one side, flat the other, Stiles struck with quarter Round." Johns Island Church Specifications, Library Society of Charleston.

1819 A workman at Poplar Forest in Bedford County, Virginia, wrote to Thomas Jefferson that "I have pine enough for stiles and rails of 6 windows. I have got them all ready to put together that is the mortising and tenionton." Coolidge Collection, Massachusetts Historical Society.

2. A series of steps, especially ones that ascend and descend over a fence or wall.

1707 A workman was engaged "to make a gate & a Stile" for the fence enclosing a churchyard. All Faiths Parish, St. Mary's Co., Md., Vestry Book.

1797 A young woman in King and Queen County, Virginia, "walk'd to the stile after sunset to meet with the girls from Riccohoc carri'd them a watermellon and some fine Peaches, we stood there talking till it was dark, then part'd." *Early American Literature Newsletter*, 2.

still house A building in which distillation is carried on; a distillery consisting of a vessel in which liquid is heated and vaporized and a cooling apparatus or coil for condensing the vapor. See also **brandy house.**

> **1718** A carpenter's work on a plantation included "a good Still house and another good small house by it." Richmond Co., Va., Miscellaneous Record Book.
> **1745** Listed in an estate of a Charleston man were "coppers and Utensils for a Still House." *South Carolina Gazette.*
> **1785** Property for sale in Loudoun County, Virginia, included "a large still-house, well finished, built but two years, with two stills, one 110, the other 60 gallons." *Virginia Journal and Alexandria Advertiser.*

stock (stocke) 1. The wooden part of a tool that holds the blade, such as the body of a plane.

2. Another name for a brace. See **brace** (2).

stock brick See **brick.**

stock lock Any kind of wrought-iron lock encased in a wooden box and mounted on a door, pew, gate, etc.; often used in utilitarian locations. The wooden lock cases were often made from riven oak. See also **Banbury lock, rim lock.**

> **1640** A carpenter installed "4 stock locks" in a dwelling. Maryland Patents, Certificates, and Warrants 1637–1650, MSA.
> **1688** Stephen Crump paid for "a Stock lock and key for the lower Church." St. Peter's Parish, New Kent Co., Va., Vestry Book.
> **1745** A list of materials for Charles Pinckney's dwelling included "9 7 inch Iron plate Chamber locks with brass furniture, 6 wood stock locks 10 inch." Huger Smith, *Dwelling Houses of Charleston.*
> **1749** A Yorktown merchant sold to Abraham Archer "1 8 inch Rimb lock at 0.7.6 and 1 stock lock at 0.2.6." Journal of Francis Jerdone, VSL.

stocks A instrument of punishment consisting of a framework with two hinged boards with circular cutouts for securing ankles, used to expose a petty offender to public ridicule. Most were built on courthouse grounds, along with a pillory and whipping post, symbols of judicial authority and the chief forms of punishment used in the colonial South. Those who had the temerity to disrupt a courtroom session with drunken or calumnious outbursts often found themselves uncomfortably seated in the stocks for an hour or two, where they were subjected to the jeering of a boisterous and sometimes hostile crowd. As a means of chastisement, stocks survived in many areas of the South until the second quarter of the 19th century, when changing sensibilities about the nature of punishment rendered them outmoded. See also **pillory.**

> **1635** Henry Charleton said that if he had met William Cotton "without the Church yeard he would have kickt him over the Pallyzadoes calling him . . . a black cotted raskoll." The court ordered Charleton to "build a pare of Stocks and gett in them three severall sabouth days in the tyme of Dyvine servis and their aske Mr. Cotton forgiveness." *Court Records of Accomack-Northampton, Virginia 1632–1640.*
> **1671** A court ruled "that noe person presume to smoake tobacco, or to be covered in ye Face of this Court; upon ye penaltie of lying in the stocks one houre." Lancaster Co., Va., Court Order Book 1666–1680.
> **1706** "Whereas Arthur fframe came into court drunk behaved himself irreverently in disturbing ye court setting the court therefore order the sheriff to put ye sd Arthur fframe into ye stocks wch was by the sheriff accordingly done sum time after ye sd Arthur fframe petitioned this court in an humble manner acknowledging his offence prayed to be released ye court out of their Clemency ordered ye Sheriff to release him." Accomack Co., Va., Court Order Book 1703–1709.
> **1808** "Ordered that Joseph Snodgrass be put in the stocks for one hour for contempt by fighting." Giles Co., Va., Court Order Book 1806–1809.

stone color A light gray, almost white, paint color, useful in interior work for setting off colored wall treatments. The color was composed primarily of white lead mixed in oil with small amounts of Prussian blue, spruce yellow, and umber. The color was used in exterior as well as interior applications.

> **1771** In Granville County, North Carolina, the yard of St. John's Church was to be enclosed with a post-and-rail fence having "three Pallisadoed Gates painted a Stone Colour with Locks." Likewise, the "out side of the Church except the Roof" was to be painted "a Stone Collour." Francis Lister Hawks Collection, Church Historical Society.
> **1794** With regard to his houses in Alexandria, George Washington instructed his overseer that "Thomas Davis must paint the outside of both houses there; the lower part of a stone color, and the roofs red." *Writings of Washington*, 33.
> **1798** In Williamsburg, an agreement between Jeremiah Satterwhite and St. George Tucker stipulated that "The platform for the Steps . . . is also to be painted of a light stone Colour." Tucker Papers, W&M.
> **1812** New England house and ship-painter Hezekiah Reynolds wrote that "Light Stone Color" be made in the following manner: "To one pint of white Lead, add two teaspoonfuls of Prussian blue; four do. of Spruce Yellow; one do. of Umbre." Reynolds, *Directions for House and Ship Painting*.

stonecutter A craftsman engaged in the fabrication of dressed stonework for buildings, chimney pieces, ornaments, and gravestones. See also **stonemason.**

> **1767** Charles Carroll of Mount Clare wrote to an English merchant about purchasing stone for a new addition to his dwelling in Baltimore County, Maryland: "I need not I hope Desire the Greatest Exactness in the Stone Cutter and Person of whom you Git the stone and marble as they must be sensible that the Least Deviation, Mistake, or variance from the Plan Can not be Remedied here and must Render the whole that will be sent useless to me." Trostel, *Mount Clare*.
> **1786** George Allen acquainted "the Citizens of South-Carolina, that he carries on the MARBLE and STONE-CUTTING BUSINESS in its various branches, at Providence, in Rhode Island, where may be had Side Boards, Chimney Pieces and Hearths of white or variegated light or dark blue and white Marble; Hearth Stones of fine Slatestone . . . also Gravestones, Tombstones, and other Monuments, done in Slate or Marble, with Coats of Arms, Crests, or any other carvings, done in the most elegant manner, and a very reasonable rate. . . . Samples of the different kinds of Stone may be seen by calling at the Printing Office in Elliott-street." *Charleston Morning Post and Daily Advertiser*.
> **1798** At the President's House in Washington, "the stone cutters are now employed at the balustrade which finishes the stone work of the building." *Observatory*.
> **1804** Church accounts listed payment to "Walker & Evans Stone Cutters for Ornamental Stone Work for three Pillars 28D Each $84." St. Michael's Parish, Charleston, S.C., Vestry Book.

stonemason An artisan skilled in the hewing, dressing, and laying of stone for building and other purposes. Masons often did much of the carving work associated with *stonecutters*. See also **mason, perch, stonecutter.**

> **1763** The Churchwardens were to bind out James McCoy, age 6, to William Fielder "who is to learn him the trade of a stone mason." Loudoun Co., Va., Court Order Book 1762–1765.
> **1792** In Orange County, Virginia, Francis Taylor "went with uncle Taylor to Capt. Burnley Two Scotch Stonemasons are raising him a Chimney." Francis Taylor Diary, CWF.
> **1819** At the University of Virginia, "STONE MASONS are to say for how much they will lay the stone and find the mortar and grout of the composition . . . leaving the gauging and harding for a particular arrangement. The quantity of this work to be done is about 300 perch." *Lynchburg Press and Public Advertiser*.

stoop A small, raised, open platform at the entrance to a house containing seats or benches. Originally a Dutch term, it rarely appeared south of northern Maryland and Delaware, where contact with Dutch-speaking settlers was more common.

> 1754 A dwelling had "a stoop at the south door of the said house six feet long and five feet wide and seats to the same." Queen Anne's Co., Md., Deed Book D.

stop 1. The molding on the inside face of a door or window frame used as a surface against which a door, shutter, or sash closes. Stops could be integral or applied to the frames.

> 1725 A carpenter's work at a church included "making new stops at the back door and vestry door." St. Anne's Parish, Anne Arundel Co., Md., Vestry Book.
> 1787 "All the sashes requisite for the . . . house with beads and stops." Charleston Co., S.C., Land Records Book 1787–1788.

2. A chamfer that curves back to an arris, usually occurring near the intersection of two members or pieces, such as where the joist meets a wall plate. See also **chamfer.**

store A building in which merchandise is sold. Also a room or building where goods are kept. By the middle of the 18th century, many stores contained a salesroom with fenestration limited to the front wall to accommodate shelving on the other walls. By the late 18th century, fashionable stores often had bow windows which not only brought more light into the salesroom but provided a means of attractively displaying wares. A counter formed a barrier between the customer and the goods. A *counting room* for handling accounts adjoined the salesroom and often was visually connected by a glazed door. Storage rooms could be located on the same floor, in the cellar, or in the attic when constructed as a one-story building. Usually an apartment was provided in the upper story for the shopkeeper. In more elaborate urban stores built in the 1790s and later, the upper floors of stores were rented out as apartments. See also **storeroom** (2).

storehouse A building used for the storage or sale of goods or supplies. The term was used to describe a place for the storage of domestic, agricultural, and commercial items.

> 1609 The settlers of Virginia were to have "in every plantacon . . . a Comon Graunge and Storehowse of Corne." *Virginia Company Records*, 3.
> 1709 "A certain Indian . . . undermin'd a House made of Logs, (such as the Swedes in America very often make, and are very strong) which belonged to Seth Southwell Esq, Governor of North Carolina . . . this being the Indian Store-House, where Trading Goods were kept." Lawson, *A New Voyage to Carolina*.
> 1752 Property advertised for sale in Fairfax County, Virginia, contained "a Store House 24 Feet Square, in which is a Counting Room 12 Feet by 18, with a Division in the back Part 24 Feet by 8, Brick Chimneys to the Whole, and Weatherboarded with Plank." *Maryland Gazette*.

storeroom 1. A room set aside for the storage of goods or supplies, especially those of a household. See also **lumber room.**

> 1732 Dwelling on Church Street in Charleston consisted of "9 rooms, 8 of which have fire places in them, There is likewise a Kitchen, store room and other conveniences backward." *South Carolina Gazette*.
> 1773 François Villepontoux agreed "to Build a Store room and Milk House under one Roof 12 feet by 25 feet." St. Stephen's Parish, Berkeley Co., S.C., Vestry Book.

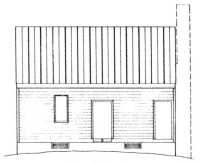

southeast elevation

section, north wall

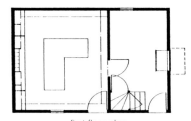

first-floor plan

store
White Store, Isle of Wight County, Va.

storehouse
Charles Fraser, A Bason and Storehouse belonging to the Santee Canal, S.C., 1803

2. A store; a place where merchandise is sold. See also **store.**

> 1764   A two-story merchant's dwelling for sale in Baltimore County, Maryland, contained "a good Cellar the whole Width of the House, a Parlour, large Store Room and Warehouse on the first Floor; Two Lodging Rooms and a large Warehouse on the second Floor." *Maryland Gazette.*
>
> 1803   An advertisement read: "To Merchants! I will RENT for one year, or during my Life, A House and Lot in the town of Stevensburg. There is a Store Room in the house well fitted for the reception of Goods, a Compting Room adjoining the store, a large dining room and chamber, with two fireplaces below stairs, four lodging rooms." *Virginia Herald.*

story (storey)   **1.** The height of a wall measured from the sill to the plate. The use of the term in this sense seems to be limited to the low country of North Carolina, South Carolina, Georgia, and, perhaps, surrounding regions. See also **pitch** (1).

> 1767   A lazaretto was to be built in Georgia with the wall 12 feet "in height from the foundation, and 9 feet story." *Georgia Gazette.*
>
> 1790   The vestry sought "some Person to undertake to Saw and Build a House on the Glebe thirty feet long, and eighteen feet wide with Piazza nine feet wide, the Story is to be twelve feet with a Pitch Roof." St. Stephen's Parish, Berkeley Co., S.C., Vestry Book.
>
> 1797   In Charleston, a proposal was made to build "FIVE substantial ENGINE HOUSES; of the following Dimensions; 15 feet deep, 10 feet wide, and 8 feet story, from the floor to the plate." *City Gazette and Daily Advertiser.*

2. A horizontal subdivision of a building, with a room or set of rooms situated above another. In this sense, the term is nearly synonymous with *floor*. In enumerating the number of stories in a building, colonial Americans in the South departed from English standards relatively early. Thus each story was equated with each floor so that the ground floor was the first story and the second floor was the second story. In contrast, by English reckoning, the term *first floor* applied to the second story above the ground floor. See also **story and a half.**

> 1674   The statehouse in St. Mary's City was to have "halfe pace stairs six inches and a halfe riseing & foote in stepp for the first story, and six inches riseing and foote in stepp for the second story." *Archives of Maryland, 2.*
>
> 1768   "To be Sold" in Frederick, Maryland, was "a very good Three Story House 45 by 20 Feet; the First or Ground Story is of Brick and stone, and in it is an excellent Kitchen and dry Cellar; the Second has Two very good Rooms, with Fire Places, a Ten Feet Passage and Stair-Case leading to the Third Story, on which is Three very genteel Rooms." *Maryland Gazette.*
>
> 1807   In Columbia County, Georgia, "will Be Let . . . The building of a good Brick Court-house of the following size, Viz. fifty feet long & thirty feet wide, two story high . . . the first story to be eleven feet pitch, and the second nine." *Augusta Chronicle.*

story and a half (one and a half story)   A building whose front and back walls rise a short distance above the height of the ceiling joists of the ground floor but do not extend far enough to be considered a full second story. In frame buildings, the corner posts continue a few feet past the plate that supports the joists for the second floor. The plates are mortised into the side of the posts. Occasionally, small windows lit these short front and back walls on this half story. Buildings whose garret space was lit by dormer windows and whose rafters rested on plates on or near the level of the ceiling joists of the story below were not considered to be a story and a half in height but only one story. A story and a half building provided more usable and habitable space above than a one-story structure.

1757 In Annapolis, a piece of property for sale contained a house "60 feet by 21, one End of which, 20 Feet long, is built with Brick and Stone, a Story and 1/2 high, in which is Two Fire-Places below, and one above." *Maryland Gazette.*

1796 "For Sale" in Alexandria "at Harper's Wharf . . . HOUSE FRAMES of the following dimensions, 24 by 18 feet square, two stories—14 by 18 do—14 by 18 single story—12 by 16 story and a half." *Columbia Mirror and Alexandria Gazette.*

1800 On Beacon Island in the Pamlico Sound of North Carolina, "a dwelling house" was to be erected "38 feet long by 26 feet deep, three rooms and a passage on the lower floor . . . the pitch below to be 8 1/2 feet, the posts to run above the Joists 2 1/2 feet so as to form a half-story. Two other Houses each 26 feet by 12 same length of posts. Barracks 60 feet long by 16 feet, the length of the posts same with foregoing: as all the buildings are intended to be a story and half high." *Newbern Gazette.*

stove **1.** A raised masonry structure for cooking, having one or more holes on the top surface and vaults below with iron gates on which to burn charcoal. Iron grates or trivets on the top of each hole supported pots and pans. Stoves were often built under a window or near a chimney for better ventilation. Besides the convenience of a raised cooking surface, these structures offered greater heat control in the cooking of delicate sauces and "made dishes" (fricassees, ragouts, etc.). To obtain the slow, continuous heat needed for simmering gravies and sauces or preserving fruits in sugar syrup, period "receipts" frequently called for a "chafing dish of coals," or stove, to be employed. Stoves of this kind were popular in France during the 17th and 18th centuries, where they were referred to as *potagers.* The growing acceptance of French cuisine in Britain and America led to the widespread adoption of these stoves and associated techniques of cookery among the well-to-do. See also **Rumford stove.**

stove (1)
Kitchen, Hampton, Baltimore County, Md.

1731 A stove was defined as "a Sort of Furnace, where they dress Pottages, and where they prepare Ragoes. It is made of Brick-Work, furnish'd with Chaffing-Dishes above, and an Ash-Pan underneath." *Builder's Dictionary.*

1748 Property for sale in Charleston had "a Kitchen, compleated fitted with Stoves and a Sink for washing Dishes, a large Kitchen grate, an Oven and a jack." *South Carolina Gazette.*

1759 British cook William Verral described stoves as "little round machines of iron fix'd in brickwork about three feet from the ground." *A Complete System of Cookery.*

1770 Harriott Pinckney Horry of Charleston directed that "Beef Collops" be placed into a "Stew Pan when the butter is hot and set them on the stove over a slow fire till they are warm enough." *A Colonial Plantation Cookbook: Receipt Book of Harriott Pinckney Horry.*

1775 The estate inventory of South Carolina Governor Lord William Campbell listed "8 Fixed Stoves" in the kitchen of his Charleston house. Public Record Office, London.

1809 From Henry Foxall, Thomas Jefferson ordered stove parts for Monticello like those he had seen at the President's house in Washington. These included "Some irons of casting for the stoves or stew-holes in the kitchen in which the box part and the grills or bars were all solid together and that you make them of three sizes. I must ask the favor of you to make 8. for me, to wit 2. of largest size & 3. of the middle & 3. of the smallest size. . . . I must pray you act without delay . . . as they are indispensable in a kitchen." Foxall replied: "I observe the information you have received respecting our Method of Making Stew holes is not agreeable to our practice, we cast the cheeks, and grates sepperate and not sold together, the reason is that one set of cheeks will last as long as many sets of grates. I have sent you a double set of grates two to each Stew hole, believing it might be difficult for you to obtain the others when the first set of grates might become useless." *Thomas Jefferson's Farm Book.*

1824 In the making of preserves, Mary Randolph of Virginia explained, "When a chafing-dish cannot be procured, the best substitute is a brick stove with a grating to burn charcoal." *The Virginia Housewife.*

stove (2)
Mauck Meetinghouse, Page County, Va.,
dated 1799

2. A metal heating apparatus installed inside fireplace openings to radiate heat from a coal or wood fire. Most contained a raised grate fully or partially enclosed on the sides, back, and top. Stoves were sometimes installed in tobacco warehouses to preserve the crop from excessive dampness. Large, freestanding stoves were sometimes installed in a few dwellings and public buildings, such as the ballroom of the Governor's House in Williamsburg. Stoves of all varieties appeared with greater frequency in the second half of the 18th century but did not become standard features in most dwellings until late in the next century. See also **Bath stove, Franklin** (2).

> 1755   A dwelling for sale in Baltimore contained "4 fireplaces and room for 4 stoves." *Maryland Gazette.*
> 1756   A "workman [was to be employed] to build a stove at Laytons warehouse according to the act of assembly." Essex Co., Va., Court Order Book 1754–1757.
> 1768   Payment was made "to Laurens, Motte & Co. for a pair of stove grates for the Council Chamber for the courtroom" in the statehouse in Charleston. South Carolina General Tax Receipts and Payments 1761–1769, SCA&H.
> 1798   "Sixty dollars [is] allotted for the purpose of purchasing and erecting a stove in the courthouse . . . it to be fixed up . . . for the use of the good folk of this county." Goochland Co., Va., Court Order Book 1797–1799.

stove house   A structure with a heating system for growing plants year round indoors; a hothouse. See also **greenhouse, hothouse, pinery.**

> 1799   A nurseryman offered for sale "to Botanists, Gardeners and Florists, and to all other gentlemen, curious in ornamental, rare exotic or foreign plants, flowers, cultivated in the green, hot-house, or stove house." *Federal Gazette and Baltimore Advertiser.*

stove room   A space heated by a stove, generally found in areas of German settlement in the backcountry of Maryland, Virginia, and the Carolinas. Many German settlers in the South installed ceramic stoves in their dwellings to heat various rooms. By the end of the 18th century, such stoves, along with improved cast iron ones, appeared more frequently in households and public buildings throughout the South.

> 1766   For sale in western Maryland was a "Frame Dwelling-House 24 Feet by 20, with a Stone Chimney, and a Stove Room, and a Stove in it." *Maryland Gazette.*
> 1805   At the county jail, "it would be necessary that the stove room floor should have sheet Iron placed on it in such manner as to prevent fire." Loudoun Co., Va., Court Order Book 1805–1806.

straight arch   A flat arch with a horizontal intrados. In brick construction, finely crafted straight arches had specially molded, and sometimes rubbed, brick voussoirs that tapered from a thicker extrados to the thinner intrados. A thin putty joint between voussoirs accentuated the decorative effect of the arch and provided greater structural stability.   See also **arch, flat arch, jack arch.**

> 1711   The front of a courthouse was to be laid with "smooth bricks; with blue headers and stretchers to be rubbed from the sills of the windows upwards to the wallplate with streight arches over the windows." Talbot Co., Md., Land Records Book No. 12.

straight joint   A line created by the meeting of two or more separate elements or pieces, often extending over several rows or courses. Straight joints often occurred when a particular area was added to, reworked, filled in, or patched. A straight joint floor is one in which the joints between the sides of the boards or planks continue in a straight line from one end to the other. See also **break**.

> 1797   In Lexington, Kentucky, carpenters undertook "broken joint flooring" at $3.50 per square and "Straight dº per dº'" at $3.00. *Kentucky Gazette*.
>
> 1806   Architect Benjamin Latrobe estimated the cost of "One square of floor and joists, joist 3 x 12, best heart pine straight joint askew nailed floor, lathed and two coat plaistering in the Cellar to preserve the timber and Church from damp, 8 joists in each square." *The Correspondence and Miscellaneous Papers of Benjamin Henry Latrobe*, 2.

strap   **1.** A bar of iron bent to fit around large framing members to hold them securely together. The strap is usually held in place by a bolt, but sometimes wrought and cut nails are used. See also **bolt**.

> 1767   To settle a dispute between the vestry of Chester Parish, Maryland, and the builder, Charles Tilden, it was determined that "the said Charles Tilden shall put or cause to be put King Posts Seven Inches by seven when squared with Sufficient Heads thereto & to be strap's with Clamps of Iron round the Collar Beams & up the said King Posts." Chester Parish, Kent Co., Md., Vestry Book.
>
> 1814   After an inspection of the steeple at Saint Michael's Church in Charleston, for damage caused by winds, John M. Schnierle informed the vestry that "All the Work [is] in the Steeple Roof, inside where the large Iron Straps & Some Wooden braces are to be fixed." St. Michael's Parish, Charleston, S.C., Vestry Book.

2. A bar of iron used to secure a pair of window shutters closed, and mounted to the face of the jamb. Often the strap pivots on an iron pin and for exterior shutters, was secured on its opposite end by driving a second pin through a hole in the bar and jamb, and wedging it from the interior. For interior shutters, the bar was dropped into an iron bolt. See also **bolt**.

> 1809   The clerk's office at Henry County, Virginia, was to include "strong window shutters to each window, with iron straps and bolts across the same." Henry Co., Va., Order Book 1808–1811.

straw color   A pale yellow paint composed of a mixture of white lead and a small quantity of spruce yellow mixed in oil. This color was similar to *light stone color*. See **stone color**.

> 1798   An agreement between Jeremiah Satterwhite and St. George Tucker stipulated that woodwork in the front and back passages was to be painted "a pale Stone Color or straw Colour." Tucker Papers, W&M.
>
> 1805   Benjamin Latrobe wrote to Samuel Fox that "The walls of the Great room will in my opinion have a good effect if painted of a pale, but warm Oker, or straw color." *The Correspondence and Miscellaneous Papers of Benjamin Henry Latrobe*, 2.
>
> 1812   New England house and ship-painter Hezekiah Reynolds wrote that straw color be made in the following manner: "Lay on the first two coats white; or slightly tinged with yellow; and for the last coat; to every ten ponds of white lead, add one pond of Spruce Yellow, or English Ochre well ground and mixed." Reynolds, *Directions for House and Ship Painting*.

stretcher   A brick laid with its long side parallel to the face of a wall. See also **bond, header** (1).

> 1711   The front of a courthouse was to be laid with "blue headers and stretchers." Talbot Co., Md., Land Record Book No. 12, MSA.
>
> 1803   Architect Robert Mills specified that the bricks used in an Episcopal church were to be "well burnt laid in flemish bond, no two Courses to be stretchers." Johns Island Church Specifications, Library Society of Charleston.

striga   See **flute, fluting**.

string (stringer)   The sloping support members that form the carriage for the treads and risers of a stair. See **stair**.

strut
Bruton Parish Church, Williamsburg, Va.

stucco (1)
Orphan's Chapel, Charleston, S.C.

stucco (2)
Kenmore, Fredericksburg, Va.

stringboard A board or facing of thin pieces covering the ends of the steps in a staircase. The stringboard served as a decorative element, applied over the structural string of the stair carcass.

> 1790 A carpenter's work at Hampton in Baltimore County, Maryland, included "1 flite of stringboard stairs." *MHM*, 33.
> 1793 At "Old East" at the University of North Carolina, the "stair [is] to be quite plain . . . the lower side of the stairs to be lined with 3/4 boards from one string board to the other." University Archives, UNC, Chapel Hill.
> 1797 The parsonage house contained a stair with "mahogany bannisters . . . string board, half hand rail dado, & Moulding Skirting." St. Michael's Parish, Charleston, S.C., Vestry Book.

stringcourse See **belt course.**

struck A decorative cut made in a piece or member; generally a molding that is cut rather than applied.

> 1735 A dwelling in Maryland was to be weatherboarded "wth Plank ye frunt plaind & Struck . . . wth a Bead." Waring Collection, MSA.
> 1748 An order stated that floor "Joists [are] to be Plained & a bead struck on Each Edge." Augusta Parish, Augusta Co., Va., Court Judgements.
> 1771 Specifications called for a church "to be covered with featheredged plank well lapt plained & struck with 1/4 Round & Nailed on with 20d nails." Granville Parish, Granville Co., North Carolina, Francis Hawks Collection, Church Historical Society.

strut A brace in a roof truss acting in compression. Struts were often placed at an angle, the lower part resting on a tie beam, collar beam, or shoulder of a king post and the upper end supporting a principal rafter. See also **brace.**

> 1771 "Each Principal Rafter with the Collar Beams Struts King Posts & Braces" of a church in Granville County, North Carolina, was "to be Seven Inches by Twelve." Francis Hawks Collection, Church Historical Society.

stucco (stuco, stoco) **1.** A granular, calcareous cement used to protect exterior walls or imitate decorative stonework. See also **roughcast.**

> 1764 The Stafford County, Virginia, jail was to be "well covered with stucco, to keep out the weather." *Virginia Gazette.*
> 1807 A recipe in a Richmond newspaper "for a composition in imitation of Portland Stone" noted that it could be "used for water proof stuccoing." *The Enquirer.*
> 1810 Estimates made for repairing St. Michael's Church in Charleston listed the costs for "Rough Casting, Slating . . . Stucco Work & Plaistering." St. Michael's Parish, Charleston Co., S.C., Vestry Book.
> 1811 Architect Benjamin Henry Latrobe wrote to a client that "without the aid of a man who has practice in covering houses wi[th] stucco or roughcast, or other external coat, I advise you not to meddle with it." *The Correspondence and Miscellaneous Papers of Benjamin Henry Latrobe*, 3.

2. A very fine plasterwork composed of pulverized limestone, used on the inside of buildings for ornamental details such as cornices and dadoes. See also **composition ornament.**

> 1734 "STUC (in Masonry) is a Composition of Lime and Dust of white Marble pounded together and sifted; of which Figures and other Ornaments in Sculpture are made." *Builder's Dictionary.*
> 1775 In Williamsburg, "JAMES WILSON Carver, from LONDON" advertised that he "MAKES all Kinds of Ornaments in stuco, human Figures and Flowers, &c. Stuco Cornishes in Plaster." *Virginia Gazette.*
> 1783 The walls of the hall at the entrance to the Governor's House in New Bern were "finished with stucco." Hawks Letter, Miranda Papers, Academia Nacional de la Historia, Caracas.
> 1804 Specifications for the new exchange in Savannah called for "the walls and ceiling to be plaistered and a large stoco cornice in the front room." *Columbian Museum and Savannah Advertiser.*

stud (studd) One of a series of slender vertical timbers interspersed between larger structural posts, used in framing walls and partitions. In dwellings and smaller outbuildings, most riven or sawn studs generally measured 2 to 3 inches in width and 3 1/2 to 5 inches deep. They were either butted and nailed, lapped and nailed, or mortise and tenoned into major framing members such as sills, plates, braces, and rafters. They provided a nailing surface for exterior and interior sheathing and laths. Smokehouses, prisons, tobacco houses, and other structures that required additional structural support or security were sometimes *double studded*, which meant that the size of the studs were increased proportionally or the studs were more closely spaced. Studs forming the short walls in garrets were known as *ashlers*. See also **ashler.**

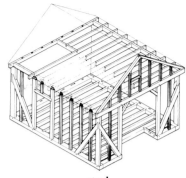

stud

> **1668** A craftsman demanded payment for "adding to the Dwelling house 10 foot long and twentie foot wide double raftered Studded, and groundceld and making an incide Chimney 400 lbs of tobaccoe." Charles Co., Md., Court Proceedings 1668.
> **1678** It was "ordered that the shedd belonging to the Courthouse have two studds put betweene each studd that now is standing." Lancaster Co., Court Order Book 1666–1680.
> **1726** A "Workman [is] to Erect and build a New Prison which is to be . . . Double Studded with good oak Studds." Princess Anne Co., Va., Court Minute Book 1717–1728.
> **1759** A courthouse was to be built with the "posts 8 inches by 4 inches, studs 4 inches by 3 inches." Johnston Co, N.C., Court Minute Book 1759–1766.
> **1781** In Yorktown, Virginia, there was a "smoke house 12 feet square double studded." York Co., Va., Claims for Losses.

study A room in a dwelling house or other building devoted to reading, writing, and the storage of books and papers. In many Anglican parishes, the study was a common feature in the ground floor of a parsonage house. The term was gradually eclipsed by *library* in the late 18th and early 19th centuries but did not entirely disappear from usage in the South to define a room for contemplative exercise. See also **library.**

> **1635** On the Eastern Shore of Virginia, a parsonage house was to be built with "a chimney at each end of the house, and upon each side of the chimneys a rome, the one for a study, the other for a buttery." *County Court Records of Accomack-Northampton, Virginia 1632–1640.*
> **1719** Found at the house of Orlando Jones in Williamsburg, was "In his Study: his Library & a parcell of Old Books." York Co., Va., Court Order and Will Book 1716–1720.
> **1740** It was ordered that "a convenient additional building of twelve feet for a study be made to the gleeb house." St. Mark's Parish, Culpeper Co., Va., Vestry Book.
> **1808** "Mr. Jefferson . . . is engaged in his study, either in drawing, writing or reading." Caldwell, *A Tour Through Part of Virginia.*

stuff Materials used for building. Wood that is to be used by carpenters and joiners is referred to generically as *stuff*.

> **1698** A plasterer of a church was "to find Lime sufficient for the Same and other Necessary Stuff as Need shall require." St. Paul's Parish, Kent Co., Md., Vestry Book.
> **1705** Carpenters were asked to report "what stuff will be necessary" for the repair of a church in James City County, Virginia. *Records of Bruton Parish.*
> **1754** Vestrymen were to "purchase Timber & stuff to build a Kitchen on the Glebe Land." St. Helena's Parish, S.C., Vestry Book.

sty An enclosed area where swine are kept. See also **pen** (2).

> **1640** Payment was made for "50 dayes work in building hog sties which were left imperfect." Maryland Patents, Certificates, and Warrants 1637–1650, MSA.

style (stile)   A distinctive or characteristic mode or form of construction or execution of an object, structure, or landscape; especially the manner in which a garden, building, or parts of a building are shaped, distinguished by the arrangement, form, and particular characteristics of their structure and ornamentation. The mode of building of an individual, country, or period. The term came into use in the late 18th century as a synonym for *taste*. See also **fashion, taste.**

> 1769   "The Buildings in Annapolis were formerly of small dimensions and of inelegant construction; but there are now several modern edifices which make a good appearance. There are few habitations without gardens, some of which are planted in a decent style and are well stocked." Eddis, *Letters from America.*
> 1796   "The stile of the houses of private Gentlemen" in Norfolk "is plain and decent, but of the fashion of 30 Years ago. They are kept very clean and independent of papering, which is not universal, fitted up much in the English style." *The Correspondence and Miscellaneous Papers of Benjamin Henry Latrobe,* 1.
> 1799   "AMERICAN MANUFACTURED Composition Ornaments" were for sale in Baltimore. "The designs are all in the newest style, chiefly cut on brass." *Federal Gazette and Baltimore Daily Advertiser.*
> 1805   "I submit to you two designs" for the Roman Catholic Cathedral in Baltimore, "the one in the Gothic, the other in the Roman style." *The Correspondence and Miscellaneous Papers of Benjamin Henry Latrobe,* 2.
> 1805   A house in Chestertown, Maryland, was "finished according to the most approved style in modern architecture." *Republican Star or Eastern Shore General Advertiser.*

stylobate   In classical architecture, the uppermost step or platform forming the stereobate on which columns stand. See also **stereobate.**

subfloor   A rough floor beneath a finished surface; a counterfloor. Subfloors were relatively rare in the early South, as they were used only in extraordinary circumstances such as for security in the construction of prisons or the fire or soundproofing of a structure. See also **counterfloor.**

subplinth   A secondary plinth placed beneath the principal plinth. For a more detailed description, see **plinth.**

> 1804   "In fixing the Subplinth or Base block on which the Colonnade is to stand, its width must be sufficient to receive the bases and plinths of the Columns." *The Correspondence and Miscellaneous Papers of Benjamin Henry Latrobe,* 1.
> 1811   An account for carpenter's work for a house in Baltimore listed "51 [feet] 9 [inches] base subplinth & grounds." Riddell Accounts, Pleasants Papers, MHS.

suburb   A populated area lying outside the corporate limits of a city or town. Most of the larger cities in the early South, and even smaller ones such as Williamsburg, had suburban developments created by large property owners who subdivided their land, laid it out into lots and streets, and sold individual lots to interested buyers.

> 1741   The Quaker meetinghouse in Charleston was located "in the Suburbs, . . . property so call'd on the other Side of the Draw-bridge, in the Half Moon, toward Ashley River." Oldmixon, *The British Empire in America,* 1.
> 1789   Savannah "is regularly built in the form of a parallelogram, and including its suburbs, contains 227 dwelling houses." Morse, *American Geography.*
> 1809   A visitor to Richmond believed himself "fortunate enough to enter its suburbs at that part, from which its appearance is most advantageous. Emerging from a thick wood, . . . this noble city was in full view. How happy the transition!" *Journal of William D. Martin.*

summer (summertree)   A large bearing beam running the length or breadth of a building that provides support for the floor. Summer beams are supported by either ground sills or girders and have the ends of common joists set into them at regularly spaced intervals. In the colonial Chesapeake, craftsmen employed summer beams along with girders and other large framing members in the construction of solidly framed dwellings or structures that required relatively broad spans, such as churches and courthouses. Often times, this type of construction was known as an *English frame* to distinguish it from the much more pervasive and simpler framing referred to as the *Virginia house* which developed in the 17th century.

> **1674** The second story of the statehouse at St. Mary's City was "to be Nine foote in the Cleere from the upper side of the [floor]board to the lower side of the summer." *Archives of Maryland, 2.*
>
> **1707** A brick courthouse was to have "a good substantial English frame with summers girders and half joists." Westmoreland Co., Va., Court Order Book 1705–1721.
>
> **1760** "The main Body" of a church was "to be well fram'd with Poplar or Cypress Timbers, the Girders to be 12 Inches Square the Summers 12 Inches Square, the Jists to be 12 by 3." Stratton Major Parish, King and Queen County, Va., Vestry Book.
>
> **1806** Specifications for a brick meetinghouse to be built in Fayette County, Kentucky, included "a summer in the lower floor 14 by 16 and split in the middle." *Kentucky Gazette and General Advertiser.*

summerhouse A building in a private or public pleasure garden designed to provide a cool, shady place in the heat of summer. These structures varied in architectural elaboration from rustic, open sheds to formally treated, classical designs and were often placed at the termination of a view in a pleasure ground.

> **1703** The estate inventory of a merchant in St. Mary's County, Maryland, listed a "Summer house." Maryland Prerogative Court, Inventories and Accounts, MSA.
>
> **1705** At Westover in Charles City County, Virginia, "Colonel Byrd, in his Garden, which is the finest in that Country, has a Summer-House set round with the Indian Honey-Suckle." Beverley, *The History and Present State of Virginia.*
>
> **1740** A tenement for sale in Charleston contained "a handsome garden with a summerhouse at the end thereof." *South Carolina Gazette.*
>
> **1777** A survey of the possessions of John Randolph of Tazewell Hall in Williamsburg listed "five green Windsor Chairs, one green Settee belonging to the Summer House." Randolph Papers, UVa.
>
> **1801** The public pleasure grounds known as "Chatsworth's Gardens . . . about half a mile from" Baltimore were arranged "to be extremely neat, such as forming pleasant summer houses, serpentine walks, shady groves, and every other rural appearance, which may give a pleasing relaxation to the leisure hours of the industrious citizen." Warner and Hanna, *Directory.*

sun blind See **blind.**

superficial measure (supal) A two-dimensional measurement of an area, specifically the length times the width of a piece of material or workmanship. Carpenters often calculated their framing and roofing work by the *square*, a measurement of 100 *superficial* feet. Glazing, painting, paving, wainscotting, and plastering were all measured in superficial lengths of feet or yards. See also **square** (1).

> **1726** "Wainscot is generally measur'd by the Yard square, i.e. nine Superficial Feet.. . . when Joyners would take the Dimensions of a Room they have Wainscoted; they take a Line on the top of the corner of the Room, and as they carry it down to the bottom, they press it (with their Fingers) into all the Mouldings; this they account the breadth and (they measure) the Circumference of the Room from the length. . . . The Dimensions being this taken in the Feet, they multiply the length by the breadth, and the Product is the Content in Feet; which being divided by 9, the Quotient is the Content in Yards." Neve, *City and Country Purchaser.*

1772 "To be LET to the lowest Bidder . . . in Loudoun County, in the Parish of Cameron, THE building a Brick Church, 53 by 42 Feet in the Clear, 28 Feet high, or not to exceed 2226 Feet superficial Measure, with a Gallery." *Maryland Gazette*.

1774 An account read: "Paid George Smith Jr. for the timber, scantling &c. for the roof of this church delivered at Thrice, vizt. 22,560 feet superficial measure of timber and scantling 35/ . . . £394.16.0." Congregational Church, Charleston, S.C., Record Book.

superstructure That part of a building erected above its foundation or basement.

1744 In Savannah, "the Stone Work of the Church being now near carried to its Height intended, the Carpenters stood next ready with their Frame Work for the Superstructure." *The Journal of Williams Stephens 1743–1745*.

1806 "I herewith transmit to the Committee of the Catholic Congregation at Baltimore for your use, the plan of the foundation story of the Cathedral with the necessary Sections. On studying this plan you will easily understand it. The red parts of the plan represent the foundation, over which is shaded in Indian ink the plan of the body of the Church, by which means, the manner in which the superstructure is supported becomes evident at one view." *The Correspondence and Miscellaneous Papers of Benjamin Henry Latrobe, 2*.

surbase (sirbase, subase, sub-base) The molding separating the lower panelling of a wainscotted room or defining the top of a dado or plinth. See also **chair board**.

1746 Charles Pinckney's dwelling in Charleston contained "the best parlour . . . with double cornice round, surbase, window seats . . . the back parlour, study and office with only surbase & skirting boards round, & plain window seats . . . the entry with Surbase and Skirting board round . . . the stairs to be wainscotted hand rail high." Huger Smith, *Dwelling Houses of Charleston*.

1773 A glebe house was "to have wash & chair boards & Sir base." Bristol Parish, Prince George Co., Va., Vestry Book.

1783 In the drawing room of the Governor's House in New Bern, "the Base and Sur Base [were] inriched with fret work." Hawks Letter, Miranda Papers, Academia Nacional de la Historia, Caracas.

1793 Specifications for dormitory rooms called for "the chair board [to be] three inches broad with surbase." University Archives, UNC, Chapel Hill.

1797 Composition ornaments for sale included "Base and Surbase mouldings." *Federal Gazette & Baltimore Advertiser*.

sure post A vertical timber placed beneath a sill, girder, or beam to provide support or additional reinforcement.

1757 Payment made for "3 Sure posts put to a Tobo House" in Orange County, Virginia. James Madison Account Book, Shane Collection, Presbyterian Historical Society.

1772 Repairs on a glebe included "setting up three sure posts to support the lower floor of the dwelling house." St. Andrew's Parish, Brunswick Co., Va., Vestry Book.

sweating room A space where persons are sweated as part of a curative treatment, especially at thermal springs that became popular spas in the late 18th and early 19th centuries. See also **spa**.

1808 "The Hot Springs are in Bath county. . . . Here are three baths, one of vital heat, or 96 degrees . . . one of 104, and it is said the hottest is 112. . . . The patient on coming out of the two latter, is wrapped in blankets, and lies stewing in the swetting room adjoining the bath, until the perspiration has freely spent itself from every pore of the body." Caldwell, *A Tour Through Part of Virginia*.

sweep **1.** An instrument used for drawing water from a well, consisting of a long, flexible pole connected to an upright post that acts as a lever to raise and lower a bucket.

1755 A workman was paid "for setting up a sweep and finding two buckets for the well at St. Pauls Church." Albemarle Parish, Sussex Co., Va., Vestry Book.

sweep (1)
Lavington, Colleton County, S.C.

2. (sweeper) A person who cleans chimney flues.

1756 "Sweep, Sweep, Sweep, Peter Wilson in Annapolis, [has] with great application, and Industry, acquired the curious art of cleaning or sweeping chimnies in the neatest manner." *Maryland Gazette.*

1756 "Solomon (not improperly sirnamed Gundy) Chimney-Sweeper in Annapolis, Having acquired the ART in his Youth, with painful study and application, and not just taken up as a certain person has done, hereby gives notice, that he can sweep chimneys as well as, if not better than, Peter Wilson, and that he can climb up Chimneys, without either ladder or rope, of any height, and not do as he is inform'd a certain Person sometimes does, that is come down them, as indeed any Body might do if they were but to go up a ladder and fling themselves in at top; but he goes up and comes down, and makes clean work, with care and expedition . . . for six pence a Funnel." *Maryland Gazette.*

1772 In Charleston, "SEVERAL CHIMNIES having taken FIRE since the late cool Weather set in, the FIRE-MASTERS are sorry there should be so much Reason to censure the Inhabitants of this Town, for their shameful Inattention. . . . it is expected, and will be insisted on, that all thos Chimnies, the Vents of which are so narrow as not to admit a Sweeper, shall be pulled down and properly rebuilt." *South Carolina and American General Gazette.*

swelling An element or part of an element that is wider in the center than at the ends, presenting a convex profile. The term was applied in two specific ways in early architectural language.

1. In order to overcome an optical illusion of concavity, some columns were given wider girths in their lower portions with a slight tapering at the top. This is also known as *entasis*.

2. An ogee-shaped profile with a boldly projecting, convex lower section and a concave upper one; also a simple convex profile. See also **pulvinate.**

1760 Carving work on the pulpit in St. Michael's Church in Charleston included "a swelling Freese Cut Lawrel Leaves . . . a Swelling Torus cut with Foliage Flowers." Williams, *St. Michael's.*

1783 The council room in the Governor's House in New Bern contained overdoors with "flat Caps with contracted swelling Friezes." Hawks Letter, Miranda Papers, Academia Nacional de la Historia, Caracas.

symmetry The mutual relationship in size, form, and arrangement of parts of an object; a balance and harmony of constituent elements with each other and as a whole. The term was used in the 18th and early 19th centuries in the same manner as *proportion*, to describe the comparative relationship of various parts in terms of magnitude, position, and quantity. The variety of meanings implicit in the term in the early period has narrowed in modern usage to refer to what Isaac Ware called *respective symmetry* and is known today as bilateral symmetry with mirror image elements on either side of an imaginary vertical center line. See also **proportion.**

1804 The roof of the north wing of the Capitol in Washington was "to be thoroughly repaired. Is it necessary to aim at something like a symmetry with the roof of the South wing? Or is that practicable at all?" *The Correspondence and Miscellaneous Papers of Benjamin Henry Latrobe*, 1.

1817 In St. Paul's Episcopal Church in Baltimore, "the aisles of all the galleries are on a level, so that the wainscot of the back pews are on a level, and these, and the dado of the aisle, present a uniform and unbroken line, by which both convenience and symmetry are preserved." *American and Commercial Daily Advertiser.*

synagogue A building or place of meeting for Jewish worship and religious instruction.

swelling (1)
Colonnade, East Lawn,
University of Virginia

swelling (2)
Overdoor, Shirley, Charles City County, Va.

1789 In a survey of the new American nation, a gazetteer noted that Charleston had "two Jewish synagogues, one for the Portuguese, the other for the German Jews." Further south, Savannah also had a "Synagogue." Morse, *American Geography*.

systyle See **intercolumniation.**

tabby
Fort Dorchester, Dorchester County, S.C.

tabby (tabbey, taby, tappy) A building material used primarily in coastal Georgia and South Carolina consisting of sand, lime, oyster shells, and water. The mixture was poured into plank formwork and allowed to settle and harden for a number of days. Tabby was used to construct a variety of buildings, from forts and churches to dwellings and outbuildings, from the late 17th century to the middle of the 19th century.

1746 A description of Frederica noted that there were "many good Houses, some of Brick, some of Tappy (which is a Cement of Lime and Oyster Shells)." *London Magazine*, 16.

1759 In Charleston, "proof of the Goodness of our fortifications has more than once been made, and TABBY-WORK is fully proved to be the best." *South Carolina Gazette*.

1770 Specifications "for building of a CHAPEL OF EASE, on Eidsto-Island; the Walls [are] to be of Tabby Work." *South Carolina Gazette and Country Journal*.

1800 The vestry "prepared to build the tabby wall round the church yard." St. Helena's Parish, S.C., Vestry Book.

tabernacle **1.** A house of worship, especially one for a large congregation and often applied to those of nonconformist denominations and sects. The term is sometimes applied to temporary places of worship.

2. A receptacle for the sacraments placed over the altar; also a decorative niche in a church, often housing a statue and surmounted by a canopy.

1805 In developing the plans for a Catholic Cathedral in Baltimore, architect Benjamin Henry Latrobe observed that "if the width of the Altar be less than 6 feet, the Tabernacle, and the Lights will not have sufficient room in width." *The Correspondence and Miscellaneous Papers of Benjamin Henry Latrobe*, 2.

tabernacle frame An ornamental frame generally consisting of a pediment, entablature, and pilasters or columns erected around a niche or window, over a doorway, or above the shelf of a chimney piece. See also **frontispiece.**

1769 "EZRA WAITE, Civil Architect, House-builder in general, and Carver, from London, HAS finished the architecture, conducted the execution thereof, viz. in the joiners way, all tabernacle frames, (but that in the dining-room excepted) and carved all the said work in the four principal rooms" of the Miles Brewton House in Charleston. *South Carolina Gazette and Country Journal*.

1777 A "Master Workman in the various Branches of the Cabinet business" advertised the fabrication of "plain Tabernacle chimney pieces." *Virginia Gazette*.

1783 In the council chamber of the Governor's House in New Bern, "the Ornaments over the marble Chimney Commonly called Tabernacle Frame consists of Corinthian Columns and pillasters fluited with the proper Entablature fully inric[hed] and an open pediment." Hawks Letter, Miranda Papers, Academia Nacional de la Historia, Caracas.

tablet A flat slab, panel, or surface, especially one bearing an inscription, image, or carving.

1797 Composition ornaments offered for sale included "Landscape tablets, with rich flower festoons, Vase tablets, with wheat festoons." *Federal Gazette and Baltimore Daily Advertiser*.

1800 John Steele "bot of Lane Chapman & Wellford" for his Rowan County, North Carolina, dwelling "1 Women figure Tablet & fruit Canopy Centre." John Steele Papers, SHC.

1815 Because of the growing shortage of space, "it was resolved that should application be made for leave to erect a Monument in the Churchyard, the Vestry shall only allow a tablet against the wall, or a headstone not exceeding 4 1/2 feet in length." St. Philip's Parish, Charleston, S.C., Vestry Book.

taenia The fillet that separates the architrave from the frieze in the Doric entablature. See also **Doric, fillet.**

talon See **ogee.**

tan house, tanyard A building and its associated workspaces where hides were converted into leather. Hides were dressed or curried by soaking, scraping, beating, and coloring. A tannery contained vats filled with lime, bark, urine, and other ingredients where hides were soaked before they were finished in a tan house. Because of the noxious odors produced in the process, many municipalities tried to keep tanyards on the outskirts, away from the built-up area of a town. See also **bark house.**

1662 In an effort to encourage home manufactures, the Virginia General Assembly passed an act stipulating that "there be erected in each county at the charge of the county one or more tanhouses, and they provide tanners, curryers, and shoemakers, to tanne, curry and make the hides of the country into leather and shoes." Hening, *Statutes at Large*, 2.

1733 "To be Sold or Let, A Dwelling-House, Tan-House, and Tan-Yard, in the Town of New-Castle. . . . Also near Four Hundred Hides, with several Dozens Skins, the major Part now a tanning." *Pennsylvania Gazette.*

1753 In operation near Charleston was a "tan yard, at Ashley Ferry, consisting of two lots of ground, with a dwelling house and tan house thereon, about 30 tan vats, four lime pits, handlers, &c." On hand were "about 40 cords of new bark." *South Carolina Gazette.*

1757 "TO BE SOLD, A CONVENIENT TANYARD, lying in Annapolis, adjoining to a good Landing, with all the Appurtenances, thereunto belonging: In which are 14 Vats, 2 Lurches, 5 Handles, 4 Limes . . . and 2 large Water-Ponds." The "Lime-House and Bark-House" were "covered with Shingles." *Maryland Gazette.*

1782 On the Bishop property in Queen Anne's County, Maryland, was "one small tanhouse, yard and vats." Queen Anne's Co., Md., Guardian Bonds and Valuations SC.

1810 Standing in Delaware was "A Tanyard . . . a Curriers Shop adjoining the Brick dwelling together with the Cellar under the Brick dwelling.-back of said Houses is a Mill house 42 by 28 feet wants repairing, a Bark house 45 by 28 feet, with a Shed 18 feet wide in tolerable repair, a Beam house wants repairing, 48 laying vats— 3 lime vats, 4 bate vats, 2 pool vats." Kent Co., Del., Orphans Court Valuations.

tar A viscous, generally dark-colored liquid obtained by distilling resinous wood or coal. Pine tar was used extensively in the South as a protective and preservative coating for shingle and board roofing, weather- and clapboarding, groundset posts, and other exterior wooden and some metal elements. Tar and its by-product, pitch, were valued particularly as naval stores and emerged in the 17th century as important export commodities.

1717 Instructions were given by a vestry "to tar the shingles & featheredge boards of the church." Christ Church Parish, Charleston, S.C., Record Book.

1791 A courthouse "roof [is] to be painted with Spanish Brown & Tar." Amelia Co., Va., Deed Book 1789–1791.

1803 Gutters at the Capitol in Washington "though of lead . . . are coated with tar and sand so as to prevent the possibility of seeing where they are faulty." *The Papers of Benjamin Henry Latrobe*, 1.

tassel **1.** A decorative ornament consisting of bunched threads or cords that hang from a knob and are found most often as an element in fabric designs.

> **1768** The pulpit of a Anglican church in Maryland was to be decorated with "the best Green Velvet . . . with Gold fringe & tassels . . . and a Green Velvet Cushion . . . with a Gold Tassel at Each End." Chester Parish, Kent Co., Md., Vestry Book.

2. (torsel) A short piece of wood inserted at or near the edge of a masonry opening, on which the ends of a larger timber such as a lintel or manteltree rest.

> **1703** "When you lay any Timber on Brickwork, as Torsels for Mantle-Trees to lye on, or Lintols over Windows, or Templets under Girders, or any other Timbers, lay them in Loam, which is a great preserver of Timber." Moxon, *Mechanick Exercises*.
> **1746** A client specified that the "brick layers to be bonded throughout for cutting lintells, Tossells." Huger Smith, *Dwelling Houses of Charleston*.

taste **1.** The mode of design associated with an individual, country, or period; the manner of expressing the formal qualities of an object. In this sense, the term came into use in the early 18th century to refer to what is now loosely known as *style*, that is, a set of visual characteristics and conventions that distinguishes a particular form. See also **fashionable, genteel, style.**

> **1744** In Annapolis, "Samuel Rusbatch . . . proposeth . . . to carry on all the various branches of coach and herald painting, varnishing and guilding; as well plain as in the most decorated taste." *Maryland Gazette*.
> **1751** Undertaker John Ariss had nearly completed a number of buildings "after the Modern Taste" in Westmoreland County, Virginia. *Maryland Gazette*.
> **1756** A house for sale in Charleston was "made after the Chinese taste." *South Carolina Gazette*.
> **1773** A New England visitor to Williamsburg observed that "there is but two private buildings of note, the Governor's and the Atty. General's. The first is not remarkable: the other is in the Chinese taste, and is the handsomest of the two." *Proceedings of the Massachusetts Historical Society*, 49.
> **1774** In Williamsburg, "GEORGE HAMILTON, CARVER and GILDER, just from Britain . . . intends carrying on this Business, viz. Looking-Glass Frames in Burnish or Oil Gilding Girandoles, Ornaments and Decorations for Gentlemens Houses, Chimney Pieces, Door and Window Cornices, Mouldings and Enrichments, Hall and Staircase Lanthorns, Picture Frames black and gilded, Ladies Toilet and Dressing Glasses; all the above after the new Palmyrian Taste." *Virginia Gazette*.
> **1774** A stucco worker in Charleston advertised "plaistering and Carving in Stucco in all its Branches, either in the Modern or Gothic Taste." *South Carolina and American General Gazette*.
> **1796** At Mount Vernon, "there is a handsome statuary marble chimney piece in the dining room (of the taste of Sir Wm. Chambers), with insulated columns on each side." *The Virginia Journals of Benjamin Henry Latrobe*, 1.

2. An aesthetic discernment; a sense of what is appropriate, harmonious, and excellent.

> **1763** "That Lady has a wonderful inclination & some taste for Gardening." *The Papers of Henry Laurens*, 4.
> **1777** "In the midst of this Desolation" on Jamestown Island in Virginia "appears a large Brick House (delightfully situated, with large Rooms, well-papered, lofty Ceiling, Marble Hearths & other Indications of Elegance & Taste)." *VMHB*, 62.
> **1809** "The face of the country, & its appendages, from Richmond to Fredericksburg, must delight the traveller of every description. It is almost a continued plane: on every side lies extensive farms, neatly planed, & highly cultivated: on most of these, emerging behind clusters of trees, selected for their beauty, usefulness & novelty: planted by the hand of taste & reared by the attention of honest & industrious farmers, are seen, neat, comfortable, & not unfrequently handsome buildings." *Journal of William D. Martin*.

tavern A dwelling or purpose-built structure for the accommodation of travelers and the entertainment of guests. Prices for lodging, food, drinks, and stableage were strictly regulated by the local courts. Besides a haunt for those in search of alcoholic refreshment, taverns became the venue for a number of public and private entertainments including assemblies, balls, concerts, business meetings, dinners, and sporting activities and amusements such as gambling, billiards, cockfights, and horse races. By the middle of the 18th century many taverns had specialized rooms and fixtures such as well-appointed assembly and long rooms, dining rooms, and bars. The term appeared infrequently until the mid-18th century. Before that time *ordinary* was the most commonly used term to describe these structures in the Chesapeake and other parts of the South. See also **hotel, inn, ordinary.**

> **1747** In Charleston, there was "to be lett . . . or sold . . . the house and lot at Ponpon Bridge, where Mr. Samuel Davidson lately kept tavern; the house contains eleven rooms with sash'd windows and a very convenient bar; is very suitable for a store or tavern." *South Carolina Gazette.*
>
> **1760** A notice read: "To be rented, In Alexandria—The George Tavern. There are three fire places below stairs, a very good bar, and six rooms above, a dining room, 24 feet by 18, a room of the same dimensions above it, in which is a very good London Billiard table." *Maryland Gazette.*
>
> **1772** "To be sold" in Halifax, North Carolina, were "two lots . . . adjoining the Courthouse and Jail, well suited for Tavern keeping. There is one House forty four Feet long and twenty feet wide, with three large Lodging Rooms up stairs, and four Closets to the House, ten feet wide, with a large Bar Room at one End, and a Cellar underneath; also a Dwelling house adjoining, thirty two Feet long and sixteen Feet wide, with three Rooms below and two above, and a Piazza on the front side . . . also a Billiard House twenty eight feet long and eighteen feet wide, with two good lodging Rooms above, and a good Billiard Table; likewise a Kitchen sixteen feet square, and a good smokehouse, stable, horse lots &c., a large garden in good order, wherein are many fruits and herbs, all well paled in." *Virginia Gazette.*
>
> **1788** A celebration of George Washington's birthday in Richmond was capped by "an elegant ball . . . provided at the Union Tavern, where a most brilliant company of Ladies and Gentlemen assembled, which gave lustre to the joyous festival." *The Virginia Independent Chronicle.*

temper To mix, moisten, and knead clay or lime to bring it to the proper consistency and desirable state for making bricks, mortar, or plaster.

> **1712** A church was to be "built with brick well tempered & well burnt." Christ Church Parish, Middlesex Co., Va., Vestry Book.
>
> **1797** "It is intended to burn some thousand better and cleaner moulded bricks, for this purpose, in the second kiln. . . . I have small hopes of their proving very good. The earth has never been well tempered and is not the best sort. The Brick maker is not much in fault." *The Correspondence and Miscellaneous Papers of Benjamin Henry Latrobe,* 1.
>
> **1821** The wooden chimneys of the cabins to be built for the poor were required "not to smoke, with backs to be well made and sufficiently large to guard against fire, of good and well tempered mortar." King George Co., Va., Court Order Book 1817–1822.

template (templet, timplett) A pattern or mold made of wood or metal, used as a guide for shaping of a molding, cutting the miter on sash bars, and other repetitive tasks.

> **1810** "John Hemings is just entering on a job of sash doors for the house at Poplar Forest, and tells me he cannot proceed without his sash planes and the templet belonging to them." Coolidge Collection, Massachusetts Historical Society.

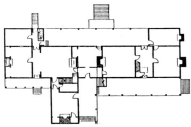

tavern
Exterior and plan,
Hanover Courthouse Tavern,
Hanover County, Va.

temple
Montpelier, Orange County, Va.

temple   In the classical world of Greece and Rome, a building dedicated to the honor or worship of a deity or deities. In early America, the term occasionally appeared as a rhetorical device to refer to a place of worship such as a church, meetinghouse, or synagogue. With the spread of classical education in the South in the 18th century, the term took on more of an architectural meaning to describe a porticoed building or one that was inspired by the buildings of antiquity. The association of classical meanings with modern garden designs in 18th-century England and continental Europe led to the construction of classically inspired summerhouses and other buildings at strategic focal points in many gardens. Often called *temples* because of their architectural references to classical structures, these buildings were used for many pleasurable recreations. The term also became a euphemism for a *necessary house.*

> **1734**   The churchwardens of St. Thomas Parish in North Carolina wrote to London noting that "we are now build at our own proper Costs a small Church . . . but, we fear, that our abilities will be far short of compleating & adorning the same as becomes a temple of God." Fulham Papers, Lambeth Palace, Library.
> **1743**   In the pleasure ground of William Middleton's plantation near Charleston, there was "a large fish pond with a mount rising out of the middle—the top of which is level with the dwelling house and upon it is a roman temple." *Letterbook of Eliza Lucas Pinckney.*
> **1791**   The prison bounds for Petersburg, Virginia, encompassed Robert Armistead's "temple" at the back of his lot. Petersburg, Va., Deed Book No. 2.
> **1804**   At Monticello, Thomas Jefferson planned a "Tuscan temple . . . at the Point. . . . The kitchen garden is not the place for ornaments of this kind. Bowers and treillages suit that better, & these temples will be better disposed in the pleasure grounds." *Thomas Jefferson Landscape Architect.*
> **1808**   "Our old ice-house near the house" at Riversdale in Prince George's County, Maryland, "was not good, because it leaked. We have built a new one in the wood beyond the stables. It is covered with straw and surrounded with great fine trees and looks like a little hut. A little farther on, a negro cabin gives the same effect and another we intend to build supported by columns will look like a temple." *Letters of Rosalie Stier Calvert.*
> **1822**   Thomas Jefferson intended "to ornament the frieze" in one of the rooms in his house at Poplar Forest in Bedford County, Virginia, after "the Ionic of the temple of Fortuna virilis." Coolidge Collection, Massachusetts Historical Society.

tenant house   A dwelling occupied or rented by someone other than the owner of the property. See also **tenement**.

> **1816**   On an 170-acre tract of land was "a one story house frame tenant house in good repair." Sussex Co., Del., Orphans Court Valuations L.

tenement   Land or any real property that is owned by one person and occupied or rented by another. Throughout the early national period, the term had not yet taken on the pejorative meaning it acquired later in the 19th century to apply to rented housing and rooms of a substandard quality. See also **tenant house**.

> **1740**   In Charleston, there were "to be let, Two convenient Tenements . . . with a good Kitchen, washhouse, storehouse and a handsome garden with a summerhouse at the end thereof." *South Carolina Gazette.*
> **1745**   A survey of a property noted "there is likewise a small tenement on the same tract of land where there is a 20 foot dwelling house 16 feet wide." Queen Anne's Co., Md., Deed Book C.
> **1750**   A deed was for land in the city of Norfolk "on Cambridge Lane fronting 23 feet 4 inches with tenement in occupation of Mary McNeil . . . and adjoining tenements." Norfolk Co., Va., Deed Book No. 1746–1750.
> **1768**   Devised in a will was a "middle brick tenement in Dock Street [and] also my lower brick tenement now occupied by Doctor Eustace" in Wilmington, North Carolina. Secretary of State Records, Wills, NCA&H.

tenement
Blake Tenements, Charleston, S.C.

tenon (tennant) A rectangular projection at the end of a piece of timber or other material formed to fit into a mortise or hole of the same dimensions in another member. The mortise and tenon joint is secured from slipping by inserting a wooden pin or treenail into a hole bored through the sides of the mortise and tenon. One of the most common of all woodworking joints, it was used by craftsmen to fasten major framing members, window sash, doors, and wainscotting. To ensure a strong frame, clients often specified that a structure was to be *mortise and tenon work* to distinguish the framing from the more common and less strong lap joints frequently employed by southern builders. See also **cock** (1), **lap, mortise, tusk.**

> 1674   Rafters of a statehouse were "to be topped with mortice and Tennant and pinned att head & hipp tenanted att the foote." *Archives of Maryland*, 2.
> 1717   A churchyard fence was to have "the rails . . . well Tenoned into the posts with Shoulders." All Saints Parish, Calvert Co., Md., Vestry Book.
> 1739   Specifications for a tobacco warehouse stated that the "posts [are] to be set in the ground and the sills tennented in the posts." Caroline Co., Va., Court Order Book 1732–1740.
> 1811   "On the Western side of the Balcony, one of the lower rails is a little decayed as also the tenents of the Bannisters." St. Michael's Parish, Charleston, S.C., Vestry Book.

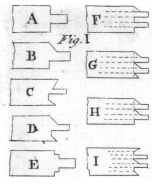

tenon

tenon to tenon (tenant to tenant) The height of a wall from sill to plate. The term was relatively uncommon. See also **pitch** (1).

> 1708   An agreement was reached to build "a church of forty foot long and twenty-four wide fourteen feet from the tenant to tenant for hight." St. Paul's Parish, Chowan Co., N.C., Vestry Book.

terrace 1. A raised platform or flat roof of a building used as a walkway or place to sit.

> 1774   Construction of the William Corbet House in Odessa, Delaware, included the fabrication of "3 sqr 24 ft 5 ins boarding on ye Terrass at 25/ . . . 2 sqr Frameing undr Ditto at 9/ . . . [and] 69 ft 8 ins Chineas Lattis at 3/6." Sweeney, *Grandeur on the Appoquinimink.*
> 1816   An advertisement for zinc as a roofing material noted that it "can be made use of in cases where lead, tin or copper are employed; such as covering terraces." *Federal Gazette and Baltimore Daily Advertiser.*

2. A raised, embanked walk in a garden with a level top and sloping sides. Flat grassy or planted garden areas often appeared as part of a series of terraced falls with sloping fronts and sides faced with turf, usually on the garden facade of a house sited on a naturally sloping ground or on the bank of a river. Movement between levels or terraces was accomplished by means of grass ramps. Each individual descent was referred to as a *fall*. See also **falling garden.**

> 1773   At Nomini Hall in Westmoreland County, Virginia, there "is a curious Terrace covered finely with Green turf & about five foot high with a slope of eight feet, which appears exceedingly well to persons coming to the front of the house . . . This Terrace is produced along the Front of the House, and ends by the Kitchen, but before the Front-Doors is a broad flight of steps of the same Height & slope of the Terrace." *Journal & Letters of Philip Vickers Fithian.*
> 1806   A gardening book noted that "regular terraces either on natural eminences or forced ground were often introduced . . . for the sake of prospect . . . being ranged single, others double, treble, or several, one above another, on the side of some considerable rising ground in theatrical arrangement." M'Mahon, *The American Gardener's Calendar.*

thatch A roof covering of straw, reeds, or similar material, usually arranged in bundles and attached to laths in consecutive overlapping rows like shingles. By the 18th century, thatch was confined largely to agricultural outbuildings, especially tobacco houses and barns.

> **1763** At a plantation landing in Craven County, South Carolina, stood "a thatch'd House too near to our Rice Store which endangers it greatly in case of fire." *Papers of Henry Laurens*, 3.
>
> **1771** In Richmond County, Virginia, "the Carpenters [are] thatching the new raised Old tobacco house near Riverside. I made them reap and thrash out the wheat to get the straw and to thatch on each side regularly . . . then Mangorike tobacco house shed to new sill and to thatch, for covering rots and slabbing will not do." *The Diary of Landon Carter*, 2.
>
> **1775** Michael Dushane's estate included "one log thatched stable." New Castle Co., Del., Orphans Court Valuations E.
>
> **1786** A "one half worn round log barn 44 by 22, thach'd with straw which is pretty rotten" was recorded in Frederick County, Virginia. Jonathan Clark Notebook, Filson Club.

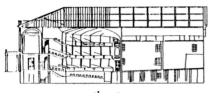

theater
Charles Busby, Section through
Bollingbrook Theater, Petersburg, Va.,
1816

theater (theatre) A building in which entertainments, such as plays and musical performances, are given. Buildings such as warehouses and barns were often fitted for use as a theater; the only essential requirements were a stage and a place for an audience to sit or stand. After the Revolution, substantial theaters were constructed in American towns of a refined nature that included more specialized stages, better seating for the audience, and various rooms to be used by the cast. Such theaters might have bench seating in the *pit* for those of modest means and *box* seats in a series of balconies for the more well-to-do. The *stage* is raised and might contain a *fly* for controlling the *sets*. *Dressing rooms* are provided at times for the convenience of the cast. See also **box** (5), **pit** (1), **playhouse**.

> **1759** Rev. Andrew Burnaby noted in his diary while travelling in southern Maryland: "I here met with a strolling company of players, under the direction of one Douglas. I went to see a theatre, which was a neat, convenient tobacco house, well fitted for that purpose." Burnaby, *Travels Through the Settlements in North America*.
>
> **1770** An advertisement for the sale of a lot in Fredericksburg, Virginia, included "a large building erected for a Blomary, with three lots of ground, there might easily be converted into a glass house, which is much wanted in this colony. . . . The above building would make a good theatre, which might be beneficial to the town in general, and country adjacent, if proper persons, and of a good demeanor, were to perform." *Virginia Gazette*.
>
> **1796** A proposal was made in Petersburg for "a piece of ground to be purchased or Leased for a Fram'd Theatre of the following dimentions-Eighty five feet-in length-Forty five feet wide and thirty five in hight. The foundation to be built Brick or Stone Seven feet high-The Building to Consist of a Stage upper and under Boxes, a Pitt, & proper Offices, together with two Dressing rooms under the stage." Petersburg, Va., Deed Book 2.

thicket A dense growth of bushes, shrubs, or small trees. In the design of pleasure grounds, an intentionally planted or natural collection of woods and undergrowth left to add variety to the view and to attract songbirds.

> **1743** "On the right hand" in William Middleton's plantation near Charleston "is what immediately struck my rural taste, a thicket of young tall live oaks where a variety of Airy Chorristers pour forth their melody." *Letterbook of Eliza Lucas Pinckney*.
>
> **1784** "The best way of forming a thicket will be to plant it in labyrinth spirally, putting the tallest plants in the centre and lowering gradation to the external termination." *Thomas Jefferson Landscape Architect*.

T hinge A cross garnet hinge. For a more detailed description, see **cross garnet**.

threshing floor (thrashing floor)   A plank floor in a barn, often laid in the center section of a multiple bay building, used to separate grain or seeds from the chaff by beating with a flail. See also **barn, winnowing house.**

> **1666**   As part of a marriage contract, Alexander Fleminge promised to "new Cover the Barne with Clapboard & the Loft & threshing flore with plank." Northampton Co., Va., Deed and Will Book 1655–1668.
> **1748**   A 40-by-20-foot barn was to be built with "a threshing floor of two inch plank fourteen feet by twenty." Augusta Parish, Augusta Co., Va., Vestry Book.
> **1750**   It was "Ordered that Coll Samll Buckner have for laying a Thrashing Floor in a Tobacco house at the Glebe 20 feet by 12 . . . 420 lbs. tobo." Petsworth Parish, Gloucester Co., Va., Vestry Book.

throat   The narrow opening in a chimney just above the fireplace and below the flue, occasionally closed by a damper to regulate the draft.

thumb latch   A wrought or cast iron handle and fastener for a door. Thumb latches consists of a U-shaped grasp for opening the door. A thumb press passes through the door and is activated on the side with the handle. The thumb press is used to lift the locking bar out of its keeper.

tie beam   The principal transverse framing member connecting the front and rear wall plates. Primarily part of the roof structure, the tie beam served as the lowest member of a truss in which the feet of the principal rafters are framed, restraining them from an outward thrust against the wall. In a king-post truss, the lower end of the king post acted as a tension member, tenoned and often strapped with iron bars to the tie beam to prevent the tie from sagging. The term *tie beam* only came into use in the early 19th century. Before that time the terms *beam, cross beam,* or *girder* were used to describe this member. See also **intertie.**

> **1824**   A courthouse roof was "to be hipped . . . the joists to be 3 by 12 inches & framed into gearders & inter ties of a size suited to the proportion of the joists." Person Co., N.C., Miscellaneous Court Records, NCA&H.
> **1830**   "The tenon, connecting the king post with the tie beam, is not required to be more than two inches long." Benjamin, *The Architect, or Practical House Carpenter.*

tier   One of a series of rows arranged one above the other. The term was especially applied to the vertical divisions of a tobacco house on which sticks of drying tobacco leaves were placed. See **tobacco house.**

> **1746**   An absentee owner ordered the construction of "a Thirty foot double tir'd Tobacco-house shade on one side" on his Lancaster County, Virginia, plantation. Joseph Ball Letterbook, LC.
> **1757**   An entry read: "Ordered the overseer to take some sticks in the 3 tier above the ground tier, viz that above the joice and that below it the 2nd room from the gable end." *Diary of Landon Carter,* 1.
> **1795**   "On top of the Pyramid" of a lighthouse to be built at Shell Castle in the Pamlico Sound of North Carolina, there was "to be a strong framed tier of joists." *North Carolina Gazette.*

tile (tyle)   A small, thin slab or plate of fired clay, variously shaped according to its application. Used in quantity primarily for covering roofs, especially as a means of fireproofing, and for paving floors. Tiles, often decoratively finished, were also applied to vertical surfaces. Three

types of tiles were particularly favored in the southern colonies. *Paving tiles* were usually square and flat, most often red, blue, or black in color, and used as a flooring largely for kitchens, dairies, church aisles, and hearths. *Dutch tiles* were also square and flat, though generally smaller than paving tiles. They were made of a whitish clay, glazed, and often decorated with figures or other designs, usually in a blue color. Dutch tiles were most commonly applied to the jambs of fireplace openings, hence the synonym *chimney tile*, which came into use in urban areas around the mid-18th century. *Pantiles* were rectangular, sometimes glazed, and transversely curved into an S-profile. They provided a more watertight covering than plain, uncurved tiles. The term sometimes appeared as a generic name for roofing tile.

> **1741** An agreement was made with a workman "to lay the Alloys [aisles] in the New Church [wi]th Good Smooth well burnt tiles instead of plank." Christ Church Parish, Lancaster Co., Va., Vestry Book.
>
> **1750** In a glebe house "the Hearths [are] to be laid with Tile 9 inches square." Newport Parish, Isle of Wight Co., Va., Vestry Book.
>
> **1751** Imported from England to Annapolis "painted Dutch tiles for chimney pieces." *Maryland Gazette.*
>
> **1771** An advertisement appeared for "PAN TILES (either of the crooked or flat Sort) for covering of Houses" imported from England to Charleston. *South Carolina Gazette.*

tin A sheet of hammered or rolled iron that has been dipped into molten tin for a protective coating. By the middle of the 19th century, tin was a popular choice as a roof covering because it provided a cheap, durable alternative to wood shingles.

tippling house (tipling house) A building where spirituous beverages were sold. The term occasionally appears in the 17th and 18th centuries. The more common names for such places were *ordinaries* and *taverns*. See also **ordinary, tavern.**

> **1668** An act was passed by the Virginia legislature "for suppressing and restraint of the exorbitant number of ordinaries and tipling houses." Hening, *Statutes at Large,* 2.
>
> **1783** The keeper of the prison in Richmond complained that because "the present Prison being surrounded by tippling houses, liquor is conveyed to them by the guards, by disorderly people plying round the Pickets." *Calendar of Virginia State Papers,* 3.

tobacco house A building used to store and cure tobacco. As developed in the second quarter of the 17th century in the Chesapeake, such buildings were divided by a series of tier poles into four- or five-foot spaces known as *rooms*. Tier poles extended from a few feet above ground to the rafters. Tobacco leaves were strung around four- or five-foot long sticks and then hung on the tier poles in each room to dry. In order to expedite the curing or drying process, most tobacco houses had two or three large doors that allowed the free flow of air throughout the building.

> **1627** A servant pulled off three boards from the side of one of his master's "tobacco houses and stole as much tobacco as himselfe could carry away under his arme." James City Co., Va., Minutes of the General Court, *VMHB,* 28.
>
> **c. 1680** A Virginia tobacco house "is usually built of clapboard about 20 or 25 foot wide; at every 5 foot their goes a range or rail quite cross the house, the Joists are ranges themselves, & there are usually three tire above, and one below. These are to bear up the sticks on which the Tobacco is hung like shingles on a lath." Banister, *The Natural History.*

tile
Above: Branford-Horry House, Charleston, S.C.
Center: Slave quarter, Boone Hall, Charleston County, S.C.
Below: Pompion Hill Chapel, Berkeley County, S.C.

1757 There was a contract to build a "Tobo. House 40 by 20 [feet] Double tier'd, end cills fram'd and 6 Doors" for £5 in Orange County, Virginia. James Madison Account Book. Shane Collection, Presbyterian Historical Society.

1777 "Houses for curing Tobacco in (called here Tobacco Houses) . . . are generally large & consist of only the outside Shell; in Appearance they resemble our [New England] Barns." Anne Arundel Co., Maryland. *MHM*, 46.

tombstone A horizontal memorial stone covering a grave. The term may have been used loosely to apply to any type of gravestone, including an upright stone, headstone, or footstone. See also **gravestone**.

1736 In Charleston, "any Person that wants Letters to be cut in Tomb stones . . . may have the same done by David Murry . . . in Elliot's Street." *South Carolina Gazette*.

1748 In his will, Benjamin Berryman stipulated that he was to be buried "in the ground next my dear wife Sarah Berryman and my dutiful daughter Hannah in a Decent manner but no Funeral Sermon and within twelve months to have a handsom Brick Voaught and a tomb stone to Cover the head of the Voaught with the time of My Daughter and my wife and my death and our ages Cut on the stone." Fairfax Co., Va., Will Book 1742–1752.

1795 In his will, Alexander Campbell hoped "that no tombstone will be raised over me; because it will merely hinder something from growing on the Spot; and as Lands now sell, it is pity to lose so much of the Earths surface which maybe used for the sustenance of the living. If all men had Tombstones erected over their graves the earth would in a few Centuries be one entire pavement." Richmond, Va., Hustings Deed Book 1792–1799.

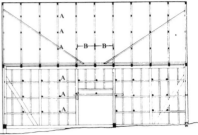

tobacco house
Above: Ballard Farm,
Somerset County, Md.
Below: Section through a tobacco house.
A = tier pole, B = room

tondino See **astragal**.

tongue and groove An edge joint of two planks or boards consisting of a continuous raised fillet or *tongue* on one edge that fits into a corresponding rectangular channel or *groove* cut into the edge of the other member. The most common use of this joint was for flooring and sheathing. See also **spline**.

1746 The plan for a dwelling in Charleston called for "the floar to be well laid & grovd or tongued." Huger Smith, *Dwelling Houses of Charleston*.

1787 One floor of a house was to be "groved and tongued plained on the top," while the other was to be "rough and square joint." Charleston Co., S.C., Land Book 1787–1788.

1793 "The lower floor" of "Old East" at the University of North Carolina was "to be laid with square edged boards. The second floor to be tongued & grooved the boards not to exceed seven inches in width." University Archives, UNC, Chapel Hill.

1805 A dwelling with a store on the ground floor in Wilmington, North Carolina, was to be constructed with "the first or lower floor . . . well planed and Jointed, and the floors of the second and third stories . . . planed, jointed and groved and tongued." McKoy, *Early Wilmington*.

tombstone
Governor Nott tomb, Bruton Parish
Churchyard, Williamsburg, Va.

topiary The shaping of trees and shrubs by clipping and training. In the designs of formal gardens around dwellings and public buildings, especially during the first half of the 18th century, the clipping of yew or other hedging into realistic and fanciful shapes—columns, balls, or obelisks—enjoyed some popularity in the South. The term *topiary* was seldom used. Instead, contemporaries referred to *clipped* or *cut* trees and shrubs.

1777 "At this Front of the College" of William and Mary in Williamsburg "is a large Court Yard, ornamented with Walks, Trees cut into different Forms, & Grass." *VMHB*, 62.

torsel See **tassel** (2).

topiary
College of William and Mary,
Williamsburg, Va., c. 1737

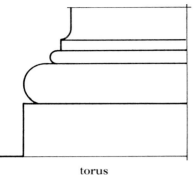

torus
Tuscan base

tower
St. Peter's Church, New Kent County, Va.,
tower added 1740

torus A large, projecting, convex molding generally forming the lowest section of the base of a column just above the plinth.

> **1734** "TORUS is a thick, round Moulding, us'd in the Bases of Columns: It is the bigness that distinguishes the Torus from the Astragal." *Builder's Dictionary.*
> **1760** The pulpit was carved with "a Swelling Torus cut with Foliage Flowers." St. Michael's Parish, Charleston, S.C., Vestry Book.
> **1803** A church was to have "Torus moulding capping to all the Pews." Johns Island Church Specifications, Library Society of Charleston.
> **1811** A carpenter's account for interior woodwork in a dwelling in Baltimore included a "Torus Base & Subase." Riddell Accounts, Pleasants Papers, MHS.

tower A building or part of a building characterized by its tallness in comparison to its lateral dimensions. The term was generally used to describe defensive structures associated with forts, or the lower stage of a steeple. See also **steeple.**

> **1737** Trustees of the colony of Georgia discussed "the building a church in Georgia of brick, the same to be 80 feet long, & 40 feet broad in the clear, with a Square tower 40 feet high, and 20 feet square from out to out." *Journal of the Earl Egmont.*
> **1799** In Orange County, Virginia, "I walked to C. Taylors, The Workmen raised the tower part of the frame of his house." Francis Taylor Diary, CWF.
> **1816** The vestry of St. Michael's Church in Charleston solicited help from the city government to help pay for repairs to the steeple. They noted that "experience renders it unnecessary to dwell upon the advantages derived from its use, as a Land Mark, Watch Tower, And from whence our most effectual alarm is Sounded." St. Michael's Parish, Charleston, S.C., Vestry Book.

town hall (town house) A public building housing the offices and meeting spaces of a civic corporation. Town halls were often built to contain other civic facilities such as a market, lockup, and courtroom. Many were also used for assemblies, museums, lectures, concerts, and similar public entertainments. It never developed into a distinctive building type. In fact, the most common terms used for buildings that served in this capacity were *market house* or *courthouse.* Some incorporated cities, including Williamsburg and Norfolk, never had a purpose-built town hall during the colonial period. With the widespread incorporation of municipalities at the end of the Revolution, construction of town halls was spurred but not all cities had such facilities. Like English prototypes, the few early town halls built in the South often combined an arcaded ground floor given over to market activities with one or two floors above divided into rooms for meetings of members of the common hall or city council. See also **market house.**

> **1682** Charleston "is regularly laid out into large and capacious Streets. . . . They have reserved convenient places for Building of a Church, Town-House and other Publick Structures." Salley, *Narratives of Early Carolina.*
> **1732** At Yorktown, "they are just finishing a Court house or Town hall of Brick with a Piazza before it (which is) very handsom and Convenient." *VMHB,* 22.
> **1782** About forty planters, merchants, and people living in the vicinity of Fredericksburg, "having a due sense of the great utility afforded the Country in general as well as the inhabitants of the town of Fredericksburg by the commodious situation of the Town House in the said town, which rendered accommodation, not only to the polite, and numerous assemblies, by which youth were greatly benefitted, but also to all sorts of ancient and modern societies of Fellowship, and viewing with regret the ruinous situation which is brought by the depredations of War, Do oblige ourselves to pay on demand the sums affixed to our names towards the repairs of that useful building." Fredericksburg, Va., City Council Minute Book 1782–1801.
> **1784** It was ordered that "a Town Hall of forty feet long and thirty two feet wide be built on the Public Land . . . and Resolved, That as Taxes are High the Com-

missioners shall only agree for the Outside work, Windows, doors, laying of the floors, and a Staircase, to be finished" at a later date. Norfolk, Va., Common Hall Order Book 1736–1798.

1824 A reception was held for "General Lafayette at the town hall." Fredericksburg, Va., City Council Minute Book 1801–1829.

trabeated   Constructed with a beam or lintel.

trabeation   An entablature. See **entablature**.

trammel   1. An instrument for describing large ellipses.

2. A moving iron instrument consisting of rings or links bearing crooks or hooks suspended from a transverse bar in a chimney on which pots are hung.

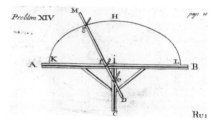

trammel (1)

transept   The transverse part of a cruciform church crossing the main east-west axis at right angles; one of the arms projecting from the central crossing of a church. The term was little used in the early South. Although there were a number of early cruciform church plans, the arms were almost always referred to as *wings*. In Christian architecture of the medieval period, the transepts were often used as chapels, a practice that probably continued in the cruciform church constructed by the Catholics in St. Mary's City, Maryland, in the 1660s. The Reformation in England changed the use and configuration of church interiors. Rather than subdividing the space into a number of discrete areas, the auditory church plan emphasized the centrality of the pulpit. Nearly all the early churches of the southern colonies followed the pattern of centrally planned structures. Some Anglican churches, like the Bruton Parish Church in Williamsburg, Virginia (1715), were built with a cruciform plan. Others, like as St. Andrew's Parish Church on the Ashley River near Charleston, had wings added to an early rectangular structure to create a cruciform plan (1723). In these and other buildings, the short arms acted as wings to house additional parishioners whose pews and benches were oriented toward the pulpit near the center of the crossing. The term *transept* came back into use in the South in the early 19th century, especially at the advent of the Ecclesiology movement in the Episcopal church. See also **chapel, church, meetinghouse, wing**.

1805 Benjamin Henry Latrobe advised members of the building committee of the Baltimore Catholic Cathedral that "a Cathedral of the Latin Church, has a prescribed form, from which that propriety, which ought to be uniform in practice, to produce the respect which is always given to consistency, does not permit the Architect to deviate. This form is that of a cross, the *style* of which is longer than the head, or either of the arms. The head of the cross is also *necessarily* the Choir, the Arms, the *Transepts*, and the Style the Nave of the *Church*. This form and this disposition govern imperiously the *Minimum* of the size of the Cathedral." *The Correspondence and Miscellaneous Papers of Benjamin Henry Latrobe*, 2.

transfer house   A public warehouse used for the storage of tobacco. Planters exchanged their loose, unpacked tobacco for transfer bills of credit. See also **rolling house, warehouse**.

1779 A workman was engaged to "to repair the Transfer Warehouse at the Upper Warehouse on Totuskey." Richmond Co., Va., Court Order Book 1776–1784.

1784 "The Charge for Erecting two new Warehouse four new prizes and repairing two other warehouse and the Transfer house for the reception of Tobo. at Fredg. warehouse amounts to £377.4.9." Spotsylvania Co., Va., Court Order Book 1782–1786.

transom
St. Andrew's Church,
Charleston County, S.C.

transom (transum)   A fixed horizontal bar separating an aperture into two separate divisions. In the traditional English sense, a transom bar divided a mullion window into at least two lights in height. In early America, many casement windows lighting churches, important rooms in dwellings, and other large spaces were so divided by transoms. By the time of the American Revolution, the term's meaning had changed slightly and was used primarily to describe the bar that separated a light or row of lights from a door below. Such an arrangement was sometimes known as a *transom door* or, somewhat confusingly, a *transom window*. Finally, the row of lights itself became known in the 19th century as a transom. See also **fanlight.**

1674   "The windows of the Hall" in the statehouse in St. Mary's City "shall be Eight in number with double lights divided with a transome att two thirds of the hight of the said windows." *Archives of Maryland*, 2.

1710   A parishioner was given leave "to cut a Window place in ye side of ye Church where their pew is, & to put in a transum two light window, according as of other windows in ye church are." All Saints Parish, Calvert Co., Md., Vestry Book.

1711   The front of a courthouse was to have "lights over the Door worked with Archytrive Transome windows all the other windows to be plain transome windows except the Dormers which are to be without transome." Talbot Co., Md., Land Records Book No. 12, MSA.

1785   A carpenter's estate contained "2 Transum door Frames" in his workshop. Fairfax Co., Va., Will Book 1783–1791.

1802   A dwelling in Washington, D.C., had a "front Door folding 4 feet wide with a Circular Transom Sash." INA Fire Insurance Policy, CIGNA Archives.

1811   A carpenter constructed "4 Transom Door frames" in a Baltimore dwelling. Riddell Accounts, Pleasants Papers, MHS.

transverse   Lying in a cross direction; a cross section.

1755   "Transverse, A term in Joinery, signifying to plain a Board, (or the like) across the Grain." Salmon, *Palladio Londinensis.*

trap door   An access door to an opening in a horizontal or nearly horizontal surface, such as in a floor or roof. See also **bulkhead (1), scuttle.**

1752   "An entrance [is] to be made to the loft" of the market house in Annapolis "by a trap-door and ladder." *Maryland Gazette.*

1802   A row house in Washington, D.C., had "a shingle roof [and] a Trap door at the Chimneys." INA Fire Insurance Policy, CIGNA Archives.

1827   A two-story brick house needed "a new trap Door on the Ruff." New Castle Co., Del., Orphans Court Valuations M.

tread   The horizontal part of a stairstep on which the foot rests. See also **riser.**

1805   In his design of the Roman Catholic Cathedral in Baltimore, architect Benjamin Henry Latrobe noted that "the platform round the Altar must be aleast 2 feet in width to permit the Officiating priest to stand and turn round upon it; and if there be seven steps, i.e., six treads to the platform, of only 8 inches in width . . . the whole of the 18 feet is taken up." *The Correspondence and Miscellaneous Papers of Benjamin Henry Latrobe,* 2.

treble sash   A large window divided into three sash frames. As the neoclassical fashion for elongated proportions emerged in the South in the late 18th and early 19th centuries, treble sash were often used in principal apertures. With their sills standing at floor level, many such windows faced onto balconies where the lower two sash could be raised to allow access outside.

1796 In his design for the "pavilion between Hall and Entry" at Monticello, Thomas Jefferson planned to install "Treble windows." Coolidge Collection, Massachusetts Historical Society.

1811 At Montpelier, James Madison's home in Orange County, Virginia, carpenters constructed "90 ft 2 rung. treble sash frames @ 1/8." Cocke Papers, UVa.

treenail (trenail, trunnel) A wooden pin or peg used to help secure framing members together at their joints. The term was used to refer to dowels that anchored floorboards to sleepers or plank sheathing to wall framing. See also **dowel, peg.**

1672 A laborer "mauled logges stakes and trunnels." Accomack Co., Va., Court Order and Will Book 1671–1673.

1717 Bridge specifications called for posts to "be traneld with good inch and a quarter trunnels square pieces" into the sleepers. Northampton Co., Va., Court Order Book 1716–1718.

1773 Barn to be "floor'd with Inch and a half plank trunneled Down and Proper Sleepers." Bristol Parish, Prince George Co., Va., Vestry Book.

trellis (treillage) A framework for the support of vines in a garden.

1804 "The kitchen garden is not the place for ornaments . . . bowers and trellages suit that better." *Thomas Jefferson Landscape Architect.*

triglyph In a Doric frieze, a raised, decorative, rectangular block consisting of two chamfered channels or grooves in the center known as *glyphs* and two chamfered edges or half glyphs. The spaces between triglyphs are known as *metopes*. See also **Doric, metope.**

1802 In Washington, a carpenter charged John Tayloe for "Ornamental Chimney pilasters to library . . . D° Frieze and Triglyph." Tayloe Papers, VHS.

1804 In planning a design for the Capitol in Washington, architect Benjamin Henry Latrobe stipulated that "if the Columns be Eight Diameters high, the Diameter must be 3 f. 3 i. But they may be stretched so as to be only 3 feet in diameter. The module then will be 18 inches . . . The Entablature is always 2 Diameters or 4 Modules . . . The Frieze 1 1/2—2, . . . Width of the Triglyph 1 Mod." *The Correspondence and Miscellaneous Papers of Benjamin Henry Latrobe*, 1.

trim The visible, finished woodwork of a building such as the cornice, base, architrave, wainscot, etc. The term was seldom used in the early South.

1807 At Poplar Forest, John Hemmings reported to Thomas Jefferson "that the flat roof over the hall Lakes [leaks] very bad. The lake is in the center and comes out right at the face of the trimm." Coolidge Collection, Massachusetts Historical Society.

trimmer A short beam that frames a stair or hearth opening, usually referred to as a *header* in modern usage. Trimmers were used to carry the ends of joists, which could not extend across the area of the opening.

1726 "Trimmers . . . are those pieces of Timber fram'd at right Angles to the Joysts, against the Ways for Chimneys, and Well-holes for Stairs." Neve, *The City and Country Purchaser.*

1774 A carpenter's account for work done at the Corbit House in Odessa, Delaware, listed "17 sqr 95 ft 5 ins Joices at 7/ sqr 137 ft 4 ins large Trimr, Girds, &c. at 5d ft." Sweeny, *Grandeur on the Appoquinimink.*

1790 A carpenter in Columbia County, Georgia, installed "two trimers @ the fireplaces." Carr Accounts, UGa.

1819 Thomas Jefferson ordered the fabrication of a skylight at Poplar Forest in Bedford County, Virginia, with "2 cross trimmers [tenoned] into . . . girders." Jefferson Papers, UVa.

triglyph
Pavilion 1, University of Virginia

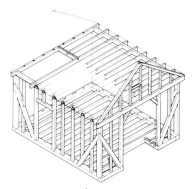

trimmer

trochilus   A scotia. See **scotia.**

trough   A long, narrow channel used to hold water or food for animals. Also a boxlike conduit used for channeling fluids or dry materials from one point to another.

> 1697   In repairs of a mill in North Carolina, carpenters charged for "hanging the Grindstone and trough." *Higher-Court Records of North Carolina,* 3.
> 1759   A prison required "a Trough and passage to carry the excrements of Prisoners." Loudoun Co., Va., Court Order Book 1757–1762.
> 1795   In Amherst County, Virginia, a carpenter was paid for "building a Stable at the Court house 23 by 28 feet, with Stalls, racks, and trough." Cabell Papers, W&M.
> 1804   Construction problems at the President's House in Washington included "leakiness of the roof. . . . This important defect arose from two principal causes: the very injudicious manner in which the gutters, and the troughs conveying the water to the Cistern were constructed, and the badness of the Slating." *The Correspondence and Miscellaneous Papers of Benjamin Henry Latrobe,* 1.

trowel   A flat, lozenge-shaped tool with a handle, used for spreading and shaping mortar and plaster.

true   Accurately or exactly shaped, well fitted, or conforming to a pattern; straight, level.

> 1800   A tile manufactory in Charleston claimed that their "tiles are manufactured with greatest care. They are all of a true line, calculated to lie close into each other, and they do not require to be pointed on their outside." *Times.*

true pitch   See **pitch** (2).

truss   **1.** A rigid triangular framework consisting of chords, struts, and other supporting members. In roof framing, a pair of common rafters tied together by a collar beam or a pair of principal rafters anchored by tie and collar beams.

> 1790   Carpenter's work at Hampton in Baltimore County, Maryland, included "2 sqr 16 feet of Trus fraiming . . . of boath porticoe." *MHM,* 33.

2. A bracket or modillion projecting from the face of a wall that serves as a support for a cornice.

> 1798   The theater in Alexandria, Virginia, was praised for its "external appearance. . . . It is a lofty edifice decorated with handsome pediments and deep cornices, the window-frames, trusses, and rustic work are of stone." *The Times and Alexandria Advertiser.*
> 1799   Composition ornaments for sale included "capitals, pilasters, keystones, shutters, trusses." *Federal Gazette and Baltimore Daily Advertiser.*

tunck (yunk)   An Anglicized borrowing of the German word for whitewash or limewash. It derived from *tünchen* and was used by some English-speaking settlers in the western parts of Virginia, where the

truss
King post truss: (1) tie beam, (2) king post, (3) strut, (4) principal rafter

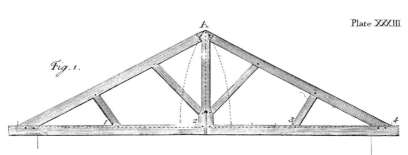

Plate XXXIII

influence of German-speaking immigrants was strong. See also **white-wash.**

> 1747   A clerk was requested to draw up "the charges the Co. has been at for yunkling and dawbing the Co. Ho." Augusta Co., Va., Court Order Book 1745–1747.
> 1753   In Augusta County, Virginia, Benjamin Harris agreed to build for James Patton "two round Log Houses" with log chimneys and central "shade" connecting the two sections. "The Houses and Chimnies is to be Tuncked and Daubed both outside and Inside and Scutched Square both outside and inside." Preston Papers, VHS.

tun timber   A unit of measure for selling timber. A solid measure containing 40 feet of round timber or 50 feet of hewed timber was called a tun or load. This amount of timber was said to contain a tun weight, which was calculated to be 2000 pounds.

> 1767   In North Carolina, sawmills operated on the "Cape Fear, & on its branches and creeks there are fifty erected and more constructing; chiefly with two saws. Upon a medium each mill is supposed to saw annually one hundred and fifty thousand feet of Board and Scantling. Ton timber is hewed or squared where the timber is fallen, what is not consumed of these articles in the province is exported to the West Indies. These mills are constructed to saw plank of 25 to 30 feet in length." *Colonial Records of North Carolina,* 7.

turkey coop   See **coop.**

turkey house   A covered enclosure for turkeys. For a more detailed description of domesticated bird shelters, see **henhouse.**

turkey paint   A bright red paint composed of sulphonated castor oil.

> 1770   "The doors & door Cases, Windows & Window Frames & Shutters" of a church were "to be well primed with Spanish Brown or well ground Turkey paint." St. John's Parish, Queen Anne's Co., Md., Vestry Book.
> 1772   "Barge boards and corner boards" of a glebe house were "to be painted white the rest of the outside roof and all to be painted with turkey paint or Spanish Brown." St. Mark's Parish, Culpeper Co., Va., Vestry Book.

turner   A craftsman who fashions or shapes objects on a lathe. The principal objects turned on a lathe for building were balusters, newels, finials, and columns. As in all the woodworking trades of the early South, some turners had enough work to specialize in their crafts, while most practiced a versatile trade of furniture making, carving, and joinery. See also **cabinetmaker, joiner, lathe.**

> 1619   Among the craftsmen that were needed in Virginia were "turners." *Virginia Company Records,* 1.
> 1708   Edward Holmes was bound to Tully Smith "to Learn . . . the trade of a turner & Joiner." Princess Anne Co., Va., Court Order Book 1691–1709.
> 1760   The cabinetmaking firm of Elfe and Hutchinson of Charleston were paid for "Turning 50 Seader Banisters for the Pulpit Staircase" in St. Michael's Church. Williams, *St. Michael's.*
> 1777   Maurice Evington of Henrico County, Virginia, offered for sale "a complete Set of House Carpenters and Joiners Tools, also 12 books of Architecture, a Set of Carving Tools, a Set of Turners Tools, and the Bench with 2 Screw and Points." *Virginia Gazette.*

turnkey   An arrangement with a builder to undertake the construction of a building from foundation to finish. On completion, the keys are turned over by the builder to the client, signifying the formal acceptance of the building according to the terms of the contract.

> 1702   "The Chappel being viewed by all the Vestry here present are satisfied therewith and to receive the house and keys from Mr. John Porter." St. Paul's Parish, Chowan Co., N.C., Vestry Book.

1762 "Charles Smith hath undertaken the Building of a Church in the Town of Winchester for the sum of Five Hundred and ninety-nine pounds . . . and finish off the whole in a workmanlike manner and turn the keys & deliver them to the churchwardens . . . on or before the fourth day of February 1764." Frederick Parish, Frederick Co., Va., Vestry Book.

1767 "The Consequences of this meeting" of the vestry "was to receive of Messrs. Miller & Fullerton the Keys of the Parsonage House &c. as information had of them that the same was Compleated in a Workmanlike Manner accordg to agreement." St. Michael's Parish, Charleston, S.C., Vestry Book.

turnpike A barrier or gate across a road or bridge, used to stop traffic in order that tolls may be levied. In the late 18th and early 19th centuries, turnpike roads were built across parts of the South and tolls were paid at turnpikes.

1748 Magistrates of the Hanover County, Virginia, court were to "receive Subscriptions . . . to apply the same towards building a bridge over Pamunkey River, from Newcastle to the Land of Edmund Littlepage, in King-William County, and to design, direct and agree with Workmen for building the same, and for the Support and Maintenance thereof; That the said Justices . . . to set up and erect Gates and Turnpikes on or across the said Bridge, through which no Person should be permitted to pass, without paying a Toll or Duty." *Journals of the House of Burgesses*, 7.

1809 A bridge across the Potomac designed by Robert Mills improved transportation between Washington and Alexandria. Until that time, "the largest mail route passes over a ferry, frequently difficult, and sometimes impossible to cross, is twelve miles from the Capitol to Alexandria, and is a circuitous, hilly, and a miry road. On an average, it takes three, and when the roads are bad, four hours to travel it." With the bridge, "the distance from the Capitol to Alexandria is less than six miles; is straight, level, and beautifully turnpiked by the Alexandrians, and can be travelled with ease in fifty minutes." *American and Commercial Daily Advertiser.*

turnstile (turn style) A gateway composed of four radiating arms at right angles to each other which revolve horizontally around a central post, used to regulate passage.

1823 It was "Resolved that the market house committee enquire into the cost of . . . fixing turn styles between the pillars" of the arcaded market house. Fredericksburg, Va., City Council Minute Book 1801–1829.

turpentine An oleoresin derived from viscous substances extracted from coniferous trees, especially pines. Turpentine was sometimes used as a thinner in grinding paint pigments. It was also used to flatten or dull the gloss of a paint.

1674 Floors of the statehouse in St. Mary's City were "to be laid with quartered planck inch & quarter thick . . . either good white Oke or Pine of this Countrey sawen while the Turpentine is in them." *Archives of Maryland*, 2.

1774 It was "ordered that the Roof of the upper Church and Vestry House be painted and the posts and rails fence round the Yard thereof be well painted with turpentine and red Paint." Truro Parish, Fairfax Co., Va., Vestry Book.

1797 Compared to southern yellow pine, white pine imported from the North was "more durable, resists the effects of Wet, and retains a better color. . . . It is fuller of turpentine. On this account it is more usefull for all external works, for flooring, and for every thing that is not to be painted." *The Correspondence and Miscellaneous Papers of Benjamin Henry Latrobe*, 1.

1800 The roof and walls of the courthouse in Gates County, North Carolina, were to be covered with "turpentine and oil mixed with red Oaker or spanish Brown mixed with Tar." Gates Co., N.C., Accounts, NCA&H.

1808 In New Bern, James McKinlay recommended painting the outside of a brick dwelling "in the following manner Viz. 50 lbs of red lead mixed with 30 lbs of Venetian red. . . . if the Venetian Red cannot be procured Spanish Brown will do but will not make quite so good a colour. Add to this 2 lb of Rosin & Mix with Oil till it is of a proper thickness to paint with, add to this . . . spirits of Turpentine and lay it on the wall with a paint Brush so as to cover the whole face of the Wall Joints & all." Ernest Haywood Papers, SHC.

turret A small tower or superstructure projecting from the peak of a roof. In the early South, turrets appeared on some churches to carry a bell. See also **belfry, cupola.**

> 1699 St. Anne's Church in Annapolis was to have "a Strong Cubalo or Turrett to hang a Large Bell in." *Archives of Maryland,* 2.
> 1752 The roof of the market house in Annapolis was to have a "small Turret for a Bell, in the middle of it, the roof and turret to be shingled with good cypress shingles." *Maryland Gazette.*
> 1796 "The miserable four legged turret" of the Episcopal Church in Norfolk was "tumbling down." *The Correspondence and Miscellaneous Papers of Benjamin Henry Latrobe,* 1.

Tuscan order The plainest of the five classical orders of architecture. The form developed in ancient Italy and was recognized as a distinctive type by Renaissance theorists in the 16th century. Since it had few distinctive ornaments and required little carving, the Tuscan order became very popular in late colonial America. During the early years of the 19th century, the form was extensively used in public buildings such as courthouses as a relatively inexpensive symbol of the links between ancient traditions of Roman law and democracy and their modern embodiments. See also **order.**

> 1756 "TUSCAN . . . is of Roman origins, and much resembles the original *Doric* of the Greeks. The *Tuscan* is the plainest, strongest, and most massy. The base of the *Tuscan* column consists only of a single torus, resting upon a plinth, and crowned with a cincture; the shaft has six diameters in height, and its diminution is a fourth or a fifth part, for in these things architects vary. The capital is very plain; it consists of an abacus, a quarter-round, astragal, and fillet; under the neck there is another astragal and fillet, but these belong to the shaft of the column. The entablature is plain and large, it consists of an architrave of one face, a plain freeze, and a cornice with a few plain mouldings." Ware, *A Complete Body of Architecture.*
> 1767 "The Pediments to the doors" of a church were to be "Rubed work in the Tuscan Order." Fairfax Parish, Fairfax Co., Va., Vestry Book.
> 1811 Workmen installed at Montpelier in Orange County, Virginia, "2 Tuscan pilasters with proper Caps & Bases." Cocke Papers, UVa.
> 1826 A courtroom was to have a "gallery . . . supported by 2 columns of wood of Tuscan order, supporting a tuscan entableture." Cocke Papers, UVa.

Tuscan order

tusk A bevelled shoulder on a tenon made to give it added strength. Tusk tenons are often found on the ends of floor joists mortised into girders.

twist A feature with a curve or turn, specifically a curved stair railing that makes a radial turn with the change in direction of a staircase. See also **ramp.**

> 1746 In the design of his Charleston house, Charles Pinckney specified that there was to be "one pair of great stairs up the 2nd floor with ramp Twist & Brackets." Huger Smith, *Dwelling Houses of Charleston.*
> 1777 A workman advertised his ability to fabricate "Ramp and twist Pedestals; geometrical, circular, plain and common Stair Cases." *Virginia Gazette.*
> 1797 An account of work in a parsonage house listed "1 Story Stairs with Circular cornices rampt & twist Mahogany, hand rail turned Mahogany Bannisters." St. Michael's Parish, Charleston, S.C., Vestry Book.

tympanum (tympan) The recessed triangular space between the horizontal and raking cornices of a pediment. Also, the area enclosed within an arch between the intrados and lintel of the aperture below.

> 1783 "In the center of the North front" of the Governor's House in New Bern, "a pediment spans 32 feet, in the Tympan of which is the Kings Arms in alto relievo, and attributes painted." Hawks Letter, Miranda Papers, Academia Nacional de la Historia, Caracas.

twist
Pompion Hill Chapel,
Berkeley County, S.C.

tympanum
Aquia Church, Stafford County, Va., 1757

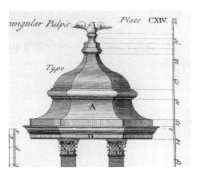

type

1803 An Episcopal church designed by Robert Mills included "Tympanum of Pediment" to be carried "to the underside of Rafters." Johns Island Church Specifications, Library Society of Charleston.

type   A wooden canopy over a pulpit. This term was used primarily, though not exclusively, in Virginia in the 18th century. In the 19th century it was replaced by *sounding board.* See **canopy, sounding board.**

1734 An Anglican church was to have "a decent pulpet & Type." Bristol Parish, Prince George Co., Va., Vestry Book.
1760 A carver was paid for "2 Corinthian Capitals for the Columns that Support the Type of the pulpit." St. Michael's Parish, Charleston, S.C., Vestry Book.

umber   A brown, siliceous earth consisting of hydrated iron oxide with some amounts of manganese oxide, used as a brown paint pigment. When it is calcined, it turns a reddish brown and is known as *burnt umber.*

1797 Among the pigments offered for sale by a Petersburg merchant was "umber." *Virginia Gazette and Petersburg Intelligencer.*

umbrella   A cloth sun screen. See also **shade.**

1752 A committee was appointed to hire someone "to make proper Umbrillo's for such of the Court House windows as they think require them." Spotsylvania Co., Va., Court Order Book 1749–1755.

under floor   The lower floor of a building, in contrast to the upper one at the second-story level. The term was not used during this period to connote a subfloor.

1766 "The under floor" of a vestry house was "to be of good Quartered pine plank an inch & half thick." St. George's Parish, Harford Co., Md., Vestry Book.
1808 "The floor at Poplar Forest" in Bedford County, Virginia, "being intended for an under floor must be laid with oak. Poplar would not hold the nails, and pine is too distant & dear. . . . Good nailing will secure it against warping." Coolidge Collection, Massachusetts Historical Society.
1810 In a two-story courthouse in Shelbyville, Tennessee, "the under floor [is] to be laid with brick edge up. . . . The second floor . . . to be laid with quarter plank 1 1/2 inches thick tongued and grooved, all of yellow poplar." *The Democratic Clarion and Tennessee Gazette.*

under frame   The lower part of a frame; the sills, sleepers, girders, and summers of a building. See also **groundwork.**

1772 In a church to be built, "the under frame [is] to be all of White Oak." Shelburne Parish, Loudoun Co., Va., Vestry Book.

underpin, underpinning   *(v.)* To support or prop up a building from below by laying a solid foundation, piers, or blocks; to form a base on which to build a superstructure. To replace or strengthen the foundation or system of support in a structure. *(n.)* A system of supports beneath a wall; the materials or system of support used beneath the sills of a building or structure.

1643 A dwelling was "to be groundselled & underpinned with brick." Surry Co., Va., Deed and Will Book 1652–1672.
1680 A discussion is recorded about building a "twenty foot Square house English frame under pinned with brick." *Journals of the House of Burgesses, 2.*
1736 The "Body of the [market] House [is to be] underpinned with Brick three Brick high from the Surface of the Earth." Norfolk, Va., Common Hall Order Book 1736–1798.

1740 In Savannah, "they are underpinning the Court House (& Church) which being built of Loggs after the manner of our common built Houses, those Loggs beginning to decay, the whole begins to sink, as we find all other Houses so built to do sooner or later." Christ Church Parish, Savannah, Ga., Church Records, GHS. 1786 In Orange County, Virginia, "C. Dickinson began to underpin Kitchen with stone having first levelled the house." Francis Taylor Diary, CWF.

under sash (lower sash) The lower, movable frame of a two-part sash window. The upper sash projected in front of the *under sash* as viewed from the outside and, for the most part, stood fixed in the window frame. In single-hung sash, it was the lower one that was made to open by being connected to a cord that ran through a pulley and was counterbalanced by lead weights. See also **double hung, sash.**

1793 At "Old East" at the University of North Carolina, "the under sash [is] to be hung." University Archives, UNC, Chapel Hill.

undertaker 1. A person who is engaged to build a structure; one who undertakes to carry out a project. The undertaker of a building was not necessarily a craftsman or professional builder, but anyone who entered into an agreement to see that a building was completed. By the middle of the 18th century, some craftsmen were occasionally called *undertakers*, referring to their status as building *contractors*. The term was common in the upper South, but less so in Georgia and the Carolina lowcountry until the very late 18th century. See also **builder, contractor.**

1665 It was resolved that "the Mother Church be forthwith built by the Undertakers Capt. Cuth: Potter and Mr. John Appleton." Christ Church Parish, Middlesex Co., Va., Vestry Book. 1698 A courthouse was to be built with "the railes and banisters and seats to be left to ye directions of ye undertakers. . . . Mr. Robert Carter doe undertake and agree with ye Court for ye building of ye aforesaid work according to demencons for five and fourty thousand pounds of tobacco." Lancaster Co., Va., Court Order Book 1696–1702. 1740 Articles of agreement were made with "William Walker undertaker and Arthiteck of the County of Stafford for building certain bridges over the creeks called Rappahannock and Totusky." Richmond Co., Va., Court Order Book 1739–1746. 1767 The churchwardens were "to Sett up Advertisements for Any Person that will undertake to build the pews in All faiths Church to Meet the Vestry. . . . Ordered that the Undertaker of the Pews for the Chaple Doe Raise them Six Inches Above the Floor." All Faiths Parish, St. Mary's Co., Md., Vestry Book. 1771 "Whereas it appears that the dimentions of the alterpeace mentioned in the Articles with the undertaker for building the New Church are not according to the proportions of Architecture, the said undertaker is authorized and desired to make the same according to the true proportions of the Ionic order notwithstanding." Truro Parish, Fairfax Co., Va., Vestry Book. 1819 "Ethelwald Sandford the undertaker of the courthouse" was to be paid "the sum of $2000 that being his second payment agreeable to contract." Westmoreland Co., Va., Court Order Book 1819–1823.

2. A person who makes funeral arrangements. Although this sense of the term was known in 18th-century England, it was rarely used in the American South until the very late 18th and early 19th centuries. Most of such undertakers had professional training in the woodworking trades, sometimes specializing in the fabrication of coffins and coffin furniture.

1795 Alexandria upholsterer and cabinetmaker John Hubball announced "that he has commenced the UNDERTAKING of FUNERALS . . . N.B. Bells hang'd and venetion blinds made in the neatest manner." *Columbia Mirror and Alexandria Gazette.*

1806 "THE novelty of an UNDERTAKER'S Business, in Charleston, having excited much enquiry by some as to what is meant by the term *Undertaker*, and by others . . . how far extends the supplies of one—In order, therefore, to explain both, and to the public generally, the following plan is submitted, viz. To any written or personal application, He will instantly attend at the house of the deceased, and arrange with a friend of the family, every thing necessary for the funeral. Every article of mourning, such as Scarfs, Hoods, Hats, and Bands &c., &c. that may be ordered, will be sent to the house of the deceased, at an early hour, all ready made up. A coffin, substantially and neatly made, of any description, will be furnished, and sent in proper time. Dress furnished, of all sizes, ready made, or made to order. . . . To a family labouring under every affliction of grief for the loss of one of its members, it must be evident an establishment of this kind is desirable; it not only prevents the feelings of the surviving relatives from being harassed by the unavoidable hurry and confusion in providing for a funeral. . . . every delicacy observed that the solemn occasion of a Funeral requires by the UNDERTAKER. . . . N.B. The bill for any funeral expences will be presented a few days after interment when it will be expected to be punctually paid." *City Gazette and Daily Advertiser.*

upbrace   See **brace** (1).

upping block   A step or platform used to help mount a horse. For a more detailed description, see **horse block.**

> **1730**   A carpenter was engaged "to make one Uping Block fram'd at the West Gate of the Church yard." All Saints Parish, Calvert Co., Md., Vestry Book.

urella   See **caulicole.**

urn   A large decorative vase with straight sides terminating in a broad mouth, often mounted on a pedestal in gardens, on balustrades, and on acroteria on roofs. Urns in bas-relief appear in the tympanum of broken pediments. See also **vase.**

> **1783**   In the center chimney piece in the council chamber in the Governor's House in New Bern was "an Urn in Bas relieve with foliages." Hawks Letter, Miranda Papers, Academia Nacional de la Historia, Caracas.
> **1790**   Work at Hampton in Baltimore County, Maryland, included "making 5 pedistils for orns to stand on." *MHM*, 33.

valley
Cupola House, Edenton, N.C.

valley   The internal meeting of two inclined planes of a roof. The opposite is a *hip*, where there are two projecting, outward intersections. The rafter that forms this junction was known as a *valley rafter*. The board placed on the valley in order to affix a lead gutter was called a *valley board*. A *swept valley* was one where the juncture was shingled over in a curving or swept series of shingles rather than provided with a gutter.

> **1776**   A workman was hired "to reshingle the valleys of the roof if necessary." Blisland Parish, James City and New Kent Cos., Va., Vestry Book.
> **1798**   If the roof of the penitentiary in Richmond "be covered with Slate, the Hips of the Hip-roof must be leaded, and also the Vallies." *The Correspondence and Miscellaneous Papers of Benjamin Henry Latrobe*, 1.
> **1811**   An account for building the Riddell dwelling in Baltimore listed "55 [feet] 4 [inches] Valey & Reveal Boards . . . gutter on Roof." Riddell Accounts, Pleasants Papers, MHS.

vane   A metal banner that turns around a pivoted point, moving with the prevailing wind, to indicate the direction of the wind. Vanes were also used to regulate the flow of air in and out of a chimney. They were placed atop steeples, cupolas, and towers of important structures. The banners often had carved tails and were sometimes gilded.

Many had elaborate decorative scrollwork attached to the rod above and below the banner as well as letters marking the cardinal points. See also **weathercock.**

> 1718 Payment was made to a craftsman "for makeing & Setting the Vane of said Belfry," St. Anne's Parish, Anne Arundel Co., Md., *Vestry Book.*
>
> 1795 A lighthouse to be built in the Pamlico Sound of North Carolina was to be capped by a lantern, "over which is to be a copper funnel; through which the smoke may pass into a large copper ventilator in the form of a man's head . . . this head to be turned by a large vane, so that the hole for venting the smoke may be always to leeward." *North Carolina Gazette.*
>
> 1817 A vestryman "was appointed to purchase a lightning Rod, a Ball & vane & to have the Same put up" on a church. St. John's Parish, Colleton Co., S.C., *Vestry Book.*

vane
Courthouse, Williamsburg, Va., c. 1771

varge board See **bargeboard.**

varnish A hard, glossy, transparent coating consisting of a variety of resins such as copal, lac, gum, gamboge, and mastic mixed in a solvent such as linseed oil or turpentine, used to protect wood and metal surfaces against the debilitating effects of moisture, air, and light.

> 1772 John Alwood agreed with the vestry of St. Michael's Church in Charleston "to Varnish all the Fronts of the Galleries, the Pillars & Capitals, the Pulpit &c. & to be done three times over in the Best Manner." Afterward, the vestry was "not altogether approving of the Varnishing the Gallery Pulpit &c. and agreed to give Mr. Alwood Thirty Pounds for the addition of Painting the whole a Mahogany colour." St. Michael's Parish, Charleston, S.C., *Vestry Book.*
>
> 1772 "HIGH VARNISHING fit for Altars in Churches, Coaches, Chariots, Chaises, Cornishes in houses, and all other Things, if Painted in Oil-Colours, done at the cheapest Rate: It is greatly superior to the high Varnish of London and Parish, which Varnishes crack by a violent Heat of the Sun, but this resists the greatest Heat for a great Length of Time without Cracking. Enquire of Mr. Christian Smith in King-street" in Charleston. *South Carolina and American General Gazette.*
>
> 1817 Advertisement for "House & Sign Painting, gilding, Glazing and Varnishing" in Alexandria, Virginia. Members of the firm noted that they kept on hand the "best Copal Varnish and a few other articles in their line." *Alexandria Herald.*

vase A decorative vessel, usually higher than it is wide, used to contain various things such as flowers. In an architectural setting, vases and urns were used as ornaments, often set upon pedestals, balustrades, and on acroteria on roofs. See also **urn.**

> 1783 The roof of the Governor's House in New Bern had "a parapet wall and Ornament vause at each corner Brake and center of the pediment." Hawks Letter, Miranda Papers, Academia Nacional de la Historia, Caracas.
>
> 1798 In Charleston, "MARBLE [was] received on Consignment from Amsterdam, and for sale . . . A FEW ELEGANT Marble Chimney Pieces, Various Colors, with Ornaments and Figures. Do. SLABS, VASES AND FIGURES, in Groupes." *City Gazette and Daily Advertiser.*

vault 1. An arched roof over a space. Generally, an underground chamber in a cellar, used for storage. During the 18th century, some contemporaries referred to such spaces as *arched* rather than *vaulted.* See also **arch.**

> 1705 The Governor's House in Williamsburg was to be built "with convenient cellars underneath, and one vault." Hening, *Statutes at Large,* 3.
>
> 1755 "TO BE LETT . . . the house and stores (with a good vault underneath) in Broad-street." *South Carolina Gazette.*
>
> 1795 For sale: "That beautiful seat, Society Hill . . . in King George County . . . with four rooms and a passage on each floor and a cellar under the whole house, with a well finished vault for liquors." *The Columbia Mirror and Alexandria Gazette.*

2. A burial chamber either within a church or in a churchyard.

> **1718** The vestry in Annapolis granted the widow of a governor "liberty to make a vault not exceeding ten foot square." St. Anne's Parish, Anne Arundel Co., Md., Vestry Book.
>
> **1748** A will required the executors "to have my Body put in the ground next my dear wife . . . and within twelve months to have a hansom Brick Voaught and a tomb stone to Cover the head of the Voaught . . . And then to have our bodies with Slip Coffins to be put in the Voaught." Fairfax Co., Va., Will Book 1742–1752.
>
> **1801** "Mr. Wagner, a Member of this Church applied for Permission to build a VAULT under the South Pavement." St. Michael's Parish, Charleston, S.C., Vestry Book.
>
> **1825** "The practice of appropriating certain portions of the Church yard as Family burial grounds, by means of Vaults and palings, seems to be of very ancient date & probably was almost with the use of the church." St. Philip's Parish, Charleston, S.C., Vestry Book.

3. A fireproof room or compartment used for the storage of valuables.

> **1800** In fleeing a fire in Savannah, bank employees "were obliged to leave in the vault . . . the gold, the silver, and all their books." *Raleigh Register.*

vendue house, vendue office   A building or room where public sales and auctions occurred. See also **exchange.**

> **1767** "When the new Exchange" in Charleston "shall be opened, the old one or vendue house is to be levelled." *South Carolina Gazette.*
>
> **1784** The Hustings court in Petersburg, Virginia, was authorized "to licence a vendue office or offices in some convenient publick place . . . and to appoint a vendue master." Petersburg, Va., City Council Minute Book 1784–1811.

veneer (vaneer)   A thin layer of wood of a superior quality applied over another, more common type.

> **1734** "VENEERING, VANEERING is a Sort of Marquetry, or inlaid Work, whereby several thin Slices, or Leaves of fine Woods of different Kinds, are applied and fastened on a Ground of some common Wood. There are two kinds of inlaying; the one which is the more ordinary, goes no farther than the making Compartments of different Woods; the other requires a great deal more Art, and represents Flowers, Birds, and the like. The first kind is what we properly call Veneering, the latter is . . . Marquetry." *Builder's Dictionary.*

Venetian blind   A louvered wooden screen that regulates the amount of light and air that passes through an opening. The term begins to appear in this region in the third quarter of the 18th century and was used concurrently through the early 19th century to define two distinct types of screens. See also **blind.**

1. A flexible hanging screen fixed to the inside of a window jamb, composed of a series of movable wooden slats held together by strips of webbing and controlled by cords. By pulling the cords, they can be raised or lowered to adjustable levels and the slats can be turned at various angles to allow the passage of air and light.

> **1770** A Williamsburg carpenter advertised that he made "the best & newest invented Venetian sun blinds for windows, that move to any position so as to give different lights, they screen from the scorching rays of the sun, draw up as a curtain, prevent being overlooked, give a cool refreshing air in hot weather, & are the greatest preservatives of furniture of any thing of the kind ever invented." *Virginia Gazette.*
>
> **1787** Writing from Philadelphia to a correspondent at Mt. Vernon, George Washington noted "I may get a Venetion blind, such as draws up and closes, and expands made here, that others may be made by it, at home." *The Writings of George Washington,* 29.

2. A fixed louvered shutter with adjustable wooden slats. Through the

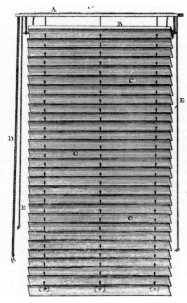

Venetian blind (1)

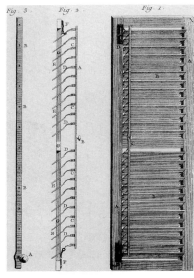

Venetian blind (2)

Venetian blind
French examples of both types
of Venetian blinds

second quarter of the 19th century, this second meaning of the term seems to have been the more predominant one. See also **shutter.**

> **1805** Repairs to a courthouse in Wilmington, North Carolina, called for "Strong substantial Venetian blinds, painted green, for each window, including raised joint or hook or eye hinges, hooks and staples for fastening them back, and bolts for shutting" them. *Wilmington Gazette.*
>
> **1816** The academy building in Sparta, Georgia, was to have "Venecian shutters." *The News.*
>
> **1820** A Culpeper, Virginia, tavern for sale was "painted white with green Venetian blinds." *Virginia Herald.*
>
> **1820** In Raleigh, "the white frame houses, with their neat Venetian blinds, which the heat renders almost indispensable to the smallest house, give the town a clear and interesting appearance." Hodgson, *Remarks During a Journey Through North America.*
>
> **1826** Courthouse specifications included "Venetian blinds to all windows with hooks to fasten them back when open and bolts to fasten them in the inside when shut," to be painted "green 3 coats." Goochland Co., Va., Cocke Papers, UVa.

Venetian door   A three-part doorway with an arched central section flanked by narrow, flat-topped windows. The central opening generally has a glazed arch over the door with the shorter window sections partly or entirely lit by sidelights. Such doorways gained popularity throughout the South in the late 18th and early 19th centuries. Occasionally the fanlight extended over the sidelights.

> **1811** Work at Montpelier in Orange County, Virginia, included the construction of "2 Venetian Doors with side lights @ £45." Cocke Papers, UVa.
>
> **1823** A tenement entrance in Charleston was to be improved "by a Venetian Door in front of the present one, so as to allow the old work to remain, highly objectionable in its present State, as affording a hiding place & shelter for children & loungers." St. Michael's Parish, Charleston, S.C., Vestry Book.

Venetian red   A red pigment made from iron oxide. Imported into America from the mid-18th century onward, it produced a dark shade of orangish red.

> **1760** An advertisement read: "JUST IMPORTED . . . from London" into Annapolis, "SUNDRY Sorts of Paints and Colours . . . fine Venetian Red." *Maryland Gazette.*
>
> **1798** Among the paints advertised by a Petersburg merchant was "Venetian Red." *Virginia Gazette and Petersburg Intelligencer.*
>
> **1808** In New Bern, James McKinlay wrote that "my house is built of the very best Materials. I imported the Brick from Philadelphia & painted it in the following manner Viz. 50 lbs of red lead mixed with 30 lbs of Venetian red. . . . if Venetian Red cannot be procured Spanish Brown will do but will not make quite so good a colour." Ernest Haywood Papers, SHC.

Venetian shutter   See **Venetian blind.**

Venetian window   A three-part window with a large central arched section flanked by narrower, square-headed ones. Generally, the whole is treated as an ensemble with columns or pilasters surmounted by an entablature. Associated with the works and writings of the Renaissance Italian architects Sebastiano Serlio and Andrea Palladio, the Venetian window is a hallmark of Palladian, design which flourished in Great Britain in the early and mid-18th century. By the middle of the century this window type began to appear in southern American architecture, chiefly as an adornment in the east end of Anglican church chancels. It was also used in other public buildings, such as the statehouse and exchange in Charleston, South Carolina, and in grander

Venetian window
Chancel, Pompion Hill Chapel, Berkeley County, S.C., 1765

gentry and merchant houses throughout the South until the early 19th century. The term *Palladian window* was not used in the early South.

> **1745** An estimate was made to install "A Venitian window on the Stairs" in Charles Pinckney's dwelling on Colleton Square in Charleston. Huger Smith, *Dwelling Houses of Charleston.*
>
> **1752** The builder John Ariss of Westmoreland County, Virginia, contracted to build a brick church in southern Maryland that was "to have a Window at the Altar piece after ye Venetian Fashion." Trinity Parish, Charles Co., Md., Vestry Book.
>
> **1802** The carpenter's accounts for the elegant Washington, D.C., house of wealthy Virginia planter John Tayloe included charges for "Venetian Sash and frame" and "Filling in studding to Venitian windows." Tayloe Papers, VHS.
>
> **1806** In remodelling the market house in Charles Town, Virginia, the builder was "to make a substantial jack arch over the front Door and also over the passage window opposite thereunto, which is to be in form of a venetion window." Jefferson Co., Va., Deed Book 1806–1808.

veranda (verandah) An open piazza or porch providing protection from the weather. The term did not come into use until the second quarter of the 19th century. See also **piazza, poarch, portico.**

> **1829** An English visitor noted that "what gives Charleston its peculiar character, however, is the verandah, or piazza, which embraces most of the houses on their southern side." Hall, *Travels in North America*, 3.

verdigris (verdegrease) A crystalline pigment used for interior painting, of either blue or green copper acetate. Verdigris was a product of a reaction between the vinegar of apples or grapes and sheets of copper or brass.

> **1764** "Verdigris is a rust or corrosion of copper formed by the action of some vegetable acid. . . . It is brought from France and Italy hither; and used in most kinds of painting, where green is required. Verditer makes a blue-green colour in paint: but it is generally used in yellow which by a proper mixture renders a true green." Dossie, *The Handmaid to the Arts.*
>
> **1798** A bill for repairs to the church of St. Helena's parish included charges for "Verdigrease" and "turpnt." St. Helena's Parish, S.C., Vestry Book.

verditer An inexpensive blue pigment, a by-product of the silver-refining process, precipitated using chalk, starch, or ashes. Due to its instability, its use was somewhat limited, the coloring of wallpapers being the most common application. A green verditer was derived from blue verditer.

> **1768** Before coming to Virginia, Governor Botetourt purchased "50lb of the Best Verditer" and "24lb of prussian blew" with which to color new wallpaper in the ballroom of the Governor' House in Williamsburg. Beaufort Papers, Gloucestershire Record Office.

vergeboard See **bargeboard.**

vermiculation See **rusticated.**

vestibule An entrance passage or lobby immediately inside a building serving as an antechamber for nearby rooms. The term had little currency in the South until the late 18th century. See also **lobby, hall.**

> **1760** An English visitor described the Governor's House in Annapolis as having "four large rooms on the lower floor, besides a magnificent hall, a staircase and a vestibule." Burnaby, *Travels Through the Middle Settlements in North-America.*
>
> **1798** "The main body" of the new capitol in Washington "is composed of two parts—a grand circular vestibule to the east, of 112 feet in diameter, both of full elevation—the first covered with a dome, the second with a temple." *Norfolk Herald.*

1817 At the museum in Richmond, "you enter into a vestibule, which communicates to the right and left, with two small apartments." *Richmond Enquirer.*
1817 At Hayes near Edenton, North Carolina, James C. Johnston ordered from New York an "oil floorcloth for the passage (10 feet 9 inches long), and another for the vestibule (19 feet 10 inches by 9 feet 5 inches)." Hayes Collection, SHC.
1821 Among the rooms listed in the inventory of Mrs. Lucretia Radcliffe's estate in Charleston were "a lower Vestibule" and one on each of the two floors above. Charleston Co., S.C., Inventory Book F.

vestry house, vestry room A freestanding structure, a room in a belltower, or a partitioned space in a church, where members of an Anglican parish governing body met to discuss parochial business such as the selection of ministers, construction and repair of churches and glebe buildings, and the administration of poor relief. At the end of the 17th and beginning of the 18th centuries, vestries in a number of parishes in Virginia and Maryland began to construct small, simply finished buildings in churchyards and other convenient locations for their monthly or bimonthly meetings. By the time of the Revolution a few scattered Anglican parishes in the lower South had also followed this practice. Other denominations may have followed a similar practice of erecting special buildings on church grounds. For example, by the second quarter of the 19th century, a number of Presbyterian congregations in North Carolina had erected session houses where governing members met to discuss church business.

1709 It was "order'd that there be a Vestry room built . . . [on] the Glebe land . . . by reason that the remoteness of Severall of the Vestry from Churches (the parrish being so Large and Extent) . . . [to be] fifteen feet Long and fifteen feet wide to be with an outside Chimney." All Faiths Parish, St. Mary's Co., Md., Vestry Book.
1722 A carpenter was hired "to Move the old Vestry house to the West End of the Church and to place it facing the West Door of the Church and to build an side Chimney." All Saints Parish, Calvert Co., Md., Vestry Book.
1738 A workman was paid "for the making a Vestry Room in the Bellfrey of the Church." St. Philip's Parish, Charleston, S.C., Vestry Book.
1774 The vestry agreed "to build a brick Vestry house at St. George's Chapel . . . Twenty four feet long and twenty feet wide from out side to out side, Eight feet pitch . . . to have a pine floor and to be lath and plaster." St. George's Parish, Harford Co., Md., Vestry Book.
1801 An application was made "to teach School in the Vestry house, which was Accordingly granted." St. Paul's Parish, Kent Co., Md., Vestry Book.

view The sight of the surrounding landscape. One of the most important considerations in choosing a site for a dwelling or garden was the overall relationship with nearby topography. See also **prospect.**

1760 The unfinished Governor's House in Annapolis was "situated very finely upon an eminence, and commands a beautiful view of the town and environs." Burnaby, *Travels Through the Middle Settlements in North-America.*
1787 In New Bern, the Governor's "palace is situated with one front to the River Trent and near the Bank, and commands a pleasing view of the Water." Attmore, *Journal of a Tour to North Carolina.*
1793 At Maycox in Prince George County, Virginia, "the pleasure grounds . . . contain about twelve acres, laid out on the banks of the James river . . . Beautiful vistas, which open as many pleasing views of the river." *Collections of the Massachusetts Historical Society,* 3.

view
Charles Fraser, A bench placed beneath the trees on a hill overlooking the tidal rice fields and the Cooper River at Rice Hope plantation in South Carolina

villa A secondary residence or estate, usually on the outskirts of a city. The term came into use in England in the 1720s and 1730s to describe residences erected in the Thames Valley just west of London. Constructed by successful merchants, professionals, and members of the gentry, they differed from the extensive ranges of great houses in their compactness and convenience. Comparatively speaking, the villas of the Thames Valley matched the size and ornamentation of the best dwellings erected by the gentry and merchants of the southern colonies. When the term came into use in America in the late colonial and early national period, it generally referred to a country seat of an individual who had his primary residence in a town. The plantation dwelling of a planter was rarely called a villa. Replicating the pattern of the Thames Valley, many of the wealthy of Baltimore erected villas on the outskirts of town in the very late 18th and early 19th centuries. In the center of these estates were modest but well-furnished brick and frame dwellings, surrounded by extensive pleasure grounds. See also **box** (2).

1765 Governor William Tryon of North Carolina was "desirous of not showing myself particularly partial to any particular Spot of the Country or people, I have hired three other houses. One at Wilmington to be at when I hold the Land Office . . . One at Newbern, where I hold the Genl Assembly and the Courts of Chancery, and a Small Villa within three Miles of Newbern, for the purpose or raising a little Stock and Poultry for use of the family." *The Correspondence of William Tryon,* 1.

1771 A notice read: "To be Lett . . . A PLANTATION on Ashley River, belonging to the reverand Mr. Martyn; a very agreeable and elegant Summer Retreat; about twelve Miles from Charlestown. . . . Though the Place is most proper for a gentleman's VILLA, yet it's Vicinity to the Market and many other Advantages would render it very profitable to an industrious Man." *South Carolina and American General Gazette.*

1796 Available "To Rent or Sell, [is] The remainder of a lease of that beautiful villa, late the property of Robert Adams, deceased, about a mile from town: there has been a great deal of money laid out on these premises—it would be an excellent situation for any gentleman wishing to retire from town, or for a place of public entertainment, being delightfully situated on the banks of the Potomack." *Alexandria Gazette.*

1803 Near Wilmington, North Carolina, was an "elegant and highly improved Villa called the Hermitage. . . . The Gardens and Pleasure Grounds equal to any in the United States." *Wilmington Gazette.*

vineyard The section of a garden or grounds devoted to the cultivation of grape vines.

1734 "To be let or SOLD an Island . . . which commands an entire prospect of the Harbor" of Charleston, containing "a piece of Garden-ground, where all the best kinds of Fruits and Kitchen Greens are produced, and . . . capable of being made a very good Vineyard." *South Carolina Gazette.*

1736 A plantation for sale at Goose Creek, South Carolina, had "a vineyard of about two years growth, planted with 1300 vines." *South Carolina Gazette.*

1811 "An Elegant Retreat" near Baltimore had "the most promising and productive small vineyard in this state. The cuttings, from which these vines are produced, were imported from France, Italy, and Germany." *Baltimore Whig.*

Virginia cabin Built throughout much of the upper South in the colonial and early national period were small, crudely constructed dwellings that some contemporaries referred to as *Virginia cabins.* The homes of frontier settlers, backwoods squatters, poor tenants, and slaves, most were fashioned out of round logs laid on top of one another without much skilled preparation. Many had *cabin roofs* and wood chimneys. See also **cabin.**

1780 "Here and there in the woods we saw Virginia cabins, built of unhewn logs and without windows." All functions were contained "in one room into which one enters when the house door opens. The chimney is built at the gable end, of unhewn logs looking like trees, or is omitted altogether." Mereness, *Travels in the American Colonies.*

Virginia house The name given to an earthfast wooden building whose simplified framing system could be constructed with an economy of labor and materials. Developed from various English framing methods by Chesapeake carpenters in the first half of the 17th century and employed by builders for more than two centuries, these earthfast structures were constructed with their posts, the principal framing members, anchored three or four feet into the ground or secured into ground-laid sills, and bound together at the eaves by wall plates. Above the plates and structurally independent of the wall frame rested a roof system composed of a series of common rafters. A covering of four- or five-foot-long riven clapboards provided structural rigidity for the wall and roof frames. This relatively light and simplified structural system eliminated much of the labor-intensive and complicated joinery of traditional English framing but resulted in a far inferior and less permanent building. By the third quarter of the 17th century, colonists in the Chesapeake began to use the term *Virginia house* as a shorthand reference for this distinctive building practice. See also **English frame.**

1647 It was decreed that every Virginia county was to have "sufficient prisons as are built according to the forme of Virginia houses, from which noe escape can be made without breaking or forcing some part of the prison house." Hening, *Statutes at Large*, 1.

1662 "Sufficient prisons should be built in each county, and that a house built after the forme of a Virginia house (our ability not extending to build stronger) should be accompted a sufficient prison." Hening, *Statutes at Large*, 2.

1692 At the end of his apprenticeship, a craftsman sued his master to secure "one sett of Carpenters tooles fitt for the building of a Virginia House." Charles Co., Md., Court Land Records Book 1690–1692.

1692 An agreement was made to build "one strong Substantiall Virga built house for a court house . . . Well Braced Above & below Studded double Joysts & Covered with four foot Boards." Middlesex Co., Va., Deed Book 1687–1750.

Virginia rail fence A type of fence composed of stacked, split rails describing in plan a series of interlocking angles. Traditionally associated with Virginia, but used throughout the Atlantic seaboard, especially in the middle and southern regions. For a more detailed description, see **worm fence.**

1789 An English traveller reported "from a mode of constructing these enclosures in zig-zag form, the New Englanders have a saying, when a man is in liquor, he is making 'Virginia Fences.'" Anburey, *Travels Through the Interior Parts of America*.

1828 "These Virginia fences, as they are called, have a strange appearance to an Englishman, being large trees split into four or five pieces of perhaps thirty feet long, and then piled upon each other at a sufficient angle, to make the upright forks almost needless." Beaufoy, *Tour Through Parts of the United States and Canada, by a British Subject*.

Virginia rail fence
Carter's Grove, James City County, Va.

vise (vice) An instrument with two jaws that are brought together by means of turning a screw, used to hold a piece of wood or the like in a tight grip. See also **cramp** (1).

vista (visto) A view or prospect, especially one seen through a long narrow opening through a wood. Vistas involved providing intentional viewpoints for surveying pleasing aspects of the surrounding landscape. Within a garden or pleasure ground, objects such as ornaments or small buildings were often erected to terminate a vista. Others opened up to broader topographical features such as mountains and rivers.

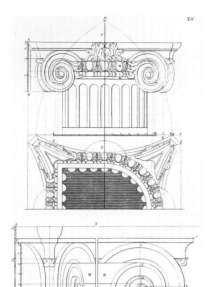

volute

voussoir
Mount Airy, Richmond County, Va.

1717 In Williamsburg, John Custis complained of Governor Spotswood's zeal in clearing trees from his property: "I happened to be at the Governors, and he was pleased to ask my consent, to cut down some trees that grew on my Land to make an opening, I think he called it a visto." Ludwell-Lee Papers, VHS.

1748 From the garden of Alexander "Singing Sandy" Gordon's dwelling in the Ansonborough section of Charleston, there "are several delightful Prospects into Cooper and Ashley-Rivers by Visto's; and lying open to the High-Road, has the Advantage of a Lane 18 feet wide into the same." *South Carolina Gazette.*

1785 At Mount Vernon, George Washington "began to open Vistas thro the Pine grove on the Banks of H. Hole." *Diaries of George Washington, 2.*

1804 Thomas Jefferson planned for "the spring of Montalto either to be brought to Monticello by pipes or to fall over the steps of stairs in cascade, made visible at Monticello through a vista . . . The ground between the upper & lower roundabouts to be laid out in lawns & clumps of trees, the lawns opening so as to give advantageous catches of prospect to the upper roundabout. Vistas from the lower roundabout to good portions of prospect walks." *Thomas Jefferson Landscape Architect.*

volute A spiral scroll forming the principal ornament on an Ionic capital. It is combined with acanthus leaves to form the major ornaments of the Composite capital. A smaller version appears beneath the abacus of the Corinthian capital, which 18th-century architectural books called a *caulicole, helix,* or *urella.* See also **caulicole, Ionic order.**

1734 "There are several Diversities in the Volute. In some the List or Edge is in the same Line or Plane throughout the Circumvolutions. . . . In others, the Spires or Circumvolutions fall back, and in others they project or stand out. Again, in some, the Circumvolutions are oval: in others, the Canal of one Circumvolution is detached from the List of another. . . . In others it seems to spring out of the Vase from behind the Ovum, and rises to the Abacus, as in most of the fine composite Capitals. Consoles, Modillions, and other Sorts of Ornaments, have likewise their Volutes." *Builder's Dictionary.*

1812 An Englishman visiting Washington, D.C., before it was torched by his countrymen observed that the White House "exterior looks well from its size and regularity but the style of architecture is by no means pure. The pilasters are Ionic but the volutes are heavy and ill executed." Foster, *Jeffersonian America.*

voussoir One of a series of wedge-shaped masonry blocks that form the face of an arch. The center voussoir is known as the *keystone.* See also **arch.**

wagon house A building or shed for the storage of a four-wheeled farm vehicle. See also **cart house.**

1773 On a farm called Sarah's Fancy Corrected stood a "wagon house 22 feet long and 10 feet wide." Queen Anne's Co., Md., Deed Book K.

wainscot (wainscoat, wenscott, winscott) Wood sheathing or panel work, used to line the walls of buildings. The term was used sometimes to describe the panel work of doors, pulpits, pews, and other pieces of joinery. Paneled wainscotting consists of stiles, rails, panels, base, and cap or surbase. Wainscotting came into fashion in the South in the second half of the 17th century as a decorative wall finish in the better dwellings and public buildings. Although the style and use of wainscotting varied, its popularity continued until the second quarter of the 19th century. During the colonial period, fireplace walls often received full height wainscotting, while some rooms were completely sheathed with pine and oak paneling. A much more modest use of this decorative element consisted of paneled dados, extending the height of the chair board with plastered walls above. In the second half of the 18th century, the term *modern wainscot* came into use to refer to a dado of flush sheathed boards. See also **panel work.**

> 1674 "The lower roome" of a courthouse in Charles County, Maryland, was "to be well wainscoted, the upper roome well daubed & sealed with morter white limed & sized, & the shead sealed & lined with riven boards." *Archives of Maryland*, 60.
> 1677 Specifications for Poplar Spring Church in Gloucester County, Virginia, included "2 wainscoate double pews one on each side of ye Chancell . . . 1 double pew above ye pulpitt & deske Joyninge to ye Scrime, all ye rest of ye pews on both sides of ye said church to be double, and all to bee done wth wainscoate Backs, the pulpit to be of wainscoate 4 foot diameter & made with 7 sides." Petsworth Parish, Gloucester Co., Va., Vestry Book.
> 1697 A workman was hired "to Wainscot the Church round about Six foot high with a Good Moulding, or Balecion on Top." St. Paul's Parish, Kent Co., Md., Vestry Book.
> 1737 A dwelling was to have "Good wainscott doors." Truro Parish, Fairfax Co., Va., Vestry Book.
> 1746 In Charles Pinckney's house in Charleston, the "Best Parlour 18 feet by 20-[is] to be wainscotted on the Chimney side." Smith, *Dwelling Houses of Charleston.*
> 1764 Writing to an English merchant, Henry Laurens of Charleston observed that "cypress is the best & Cheapest Wood with us for Wainscot, but your Oak is in my judgment infinitely preferable." *The Papers of Henry Laurens*, 4.
> 1766 A plantation for sale in Northampton County, North Carolina, contained "a good dwelling house 42 by 18, well finished, wainscoted chair board high." *Virginia Gazette.*
> 1783 "The walls" of the council room in the Governor's House in New Bern "are covered with modern wainscot with a Carved enrichment in the Base and Sur Base. . . . The dining room . . . is wainscoted with a plain moulding and flat pannel." Hawks Letter, Miranda Papers, Academia Nacional de la Historia, Caracas.

wainscot color A paint treatment simulating the color or grained appearance of oak. The color itself was composed of umber and white lead.

> 1727 "A Colour resembling new OAK TIMBER is made of Umber and white lead." *The Art of Painting in Oyl.*
> 1764 From Charleston, Henry Laurens wrote "I have painted one Room in my House Wainscot colour & pattern upon a coat of brown Plaister." *Papers of Henry Laurens*, 4.

walk A broad pathway of brick, flagstones, grass, oyster shells, or gravel in a garden, pleasure ground, or public area in a town such as a square, quay, or riverside. Walks were places of public and private exercises and social interaction. Using the layout of walks in English provincial towns in the 18th century as a model, a number of the larger cities in the South followed suit in the late 18th and early 19th centuries and planned walkways for public gathering and promenading. In private and public gardens, walks divided various components of the grounds, defining distinct areas and directing both sight and action. Often in pleasure grounds to make a walk look longer, the width would decrease as the walk led away from the main building. Gravel, oyster shell, and brick walks usually connected the dwelling to many of the domestic outbuildings.

> 1740 At Westover in Charles City County, Virginia, there were "new Gates, gravel Walks, hedges, and cedars finely twined." Bartram Papers, Historical Society of Pennsylvania.
> 1743 "From the backdoor" of the main dwelling at Crow-Field in South Carolina "is a spacious walk a thousand foot long; each side of which nearest the house is a grass plat ennamiled in a Serpentine manner with flowers." *Letterbook of Eliza Lucas Pinckney.*
> 1774 "The area of the Triangle made by the Wash-house, Stable, & School-House" at Nomini Hall in Westmoreland County, Virginia, "is perfectly level . . . laid out

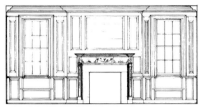

wainscot
Above: Dining Room, Peyton Randolph House, Williamsburg, Va.
Below: Blake Tenement, Charleston, S.C.

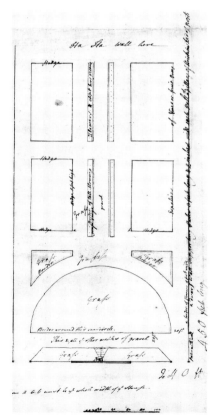

walk
Layout of gravel walks in a garden in Virginia

in rectangular Walks which are paved with Brick, & covered with Oyster-Shells." *Journal & Letters of Philip Vickers Fithian.*

1777 "At the front of the College" of William and Mary in Williamsburg "is a large Court Yard, ornamented with Gravel Walks, Trees cut into different Forms, & Grass." *VMHB*, 62.

1801 In a garden in Wilmington, North Carolina, "there are alcoves and summer houses at the termination of each walk." *Autobiography and Diary of Mrs. Elizabeth Clitherall.*

1803 An ordinance was passed by the city council of Savannah for "effectual protecting and preserving the trees in this City, and the turf, pavements, and other means which have been used to render the ground firm, and the walks pleasant to the Citizens, a number of posts have been erected and set up . . . for the purpose of preventing persons with carriages and horses from riding or driving within, or between the trees and posts so planted . . . and over the turf, pavements, or ways intended for foot passengers." *Columbian Museum and Savannah Advertiser.*

wallpaper   See **paperhanging.**

wall plate   A horizontal longitudinal timber placed on top of a masonry or timber frame wall, on which ceiling joists and, in some cases, roof trusses rest; a plate.   In timber framing, the upper ends of studs and posts are secured into this member. In early southern carpentry, studs were either lapped and nailed or mortised and tenoned into the wall plate. By the early 18th century, the term appears less often in Chesapeake documents. Most of the late colonial and early national period references simply call this principal framing member the *plate.* See also **false plate, plate, raising plate.**

> **1635** A parsonage house was to be built "forty foot long and eyghteene foot wyde and nine foot to the wall plates." *County Court Records of Accomack-Northampton, Virginia 1632–1640.*
>
> **1704** It was ordered that a "good English frame" courthouse have "one large sash window on each side of the house of three lights abrest to Reach from five foot high to ye wall plait." Middlesex Co., Va., Court Order Book 1694–1705.
>
> **1753** A carpenter was hired to build "two round Log Houses" in Augusta County, Virginia, "each twenty one feet Long and fifteen feet wide in the Clear to be eight Feet high under the joists which is to be square and three logs high above the joists beside the Wall plate." Preston Papers, VHS.

wall seat   A bench or form built into a wall, especially one located on the back or side walls in a gallery or ground floor of a church or meetinghouse, generally to provide seating for the poor, enslaved, or strangers.

> **1783** A motion was made "to have two Gallerys of 9 feet wide at the east and west end of the church for the accommodation of Negros and that the revenue of the church would be increased by having a south gallery, also of the same width, wherein ten convenient pews could be erected, besides a Wall seat for the use of poor white persons." Congregational Church, Charleston, S.C., Record Book.

walnut (wallnut)   A durable hardwood in the hickory family, the walnut grows extensively throughout the southeast. Because of its brown to dark brown color and its hardness, the black walnut was one of the most valuable timbers in early America. Joiners and cabinetmakers used it to make furniture, especially chairs, tables, and case pieces. Because of its value, walnut had only a limited use in building. In public buildings and domestic architecture, showpiece elements such as stair rails, balusters, wainscotting, and chimney pieces were fashioned out of walnut. In a number of churches, black walnut was the preferred material for pulpits, altarpieces, and communion rails and balusters. This hardwood timber resisted weather and rot well and was occasionally used for window sash, column bases, and sparingly, in a more prosaic manner, for shingles and fence posts. Some walnut planks were exported to Great Britain during the colonial period, but the trade was never extensive.

1698 Planter William Fitzhugh of Stafford County, Virginia, wrote to George Mason, an English merchant: "I shall never trouble Bristol Market more, with any Walnut plank, the reason of my sending this, was I hear you were your self building, I thought it might suite your conveniency, for Mr. Blaithwaite being building some where about your parts, has two Inch black Walnut plank from Capt. Brent, & the Governr who buys it for him pays six pence a foot here in the Country." William Blathwayt, Secretary of State, took a keen interest in the affairs of the American colonies. In the late 1690s, Blathwayt began work on Dyrham Park in Gloucestershire, where he incorporated much American timber in the stairs and other parts of the interior decoration. *William Fitzhugh and his Chesapeake World.*

1709 "The Walnut-Tree of *America* is call'd Black Walnut. . . . The Wood is very firm and durable, of which Tables and Chests of Drawers are made, and prove very well." Lawson, *A New Voyage to Carolina.*

1752 "The Pulpit Canopys Reading Desk and Communion Table Hand Rails and Ballasters [are] to be all of Black Wallnut Neatly done." Trinity Parish, Charles Co., Md., Vestry Book.

1806 A meetinghouse in Fayette County, Kentucky, was to have "sashes made of good walnut plank." *Kentucky Gazette and General Advertiser.*

1812 A two-story courthouse in Rutherford County, Tennessee, was to have a girder in the center of the ground-floor courtroom ceiling, "supported by two neat-turned walnut posts." *Nashville Whig.*

wardroom A closet or small storage space, often provided with chests and shelves, for clothing and bed linen.

warehouse A building or part of a building used for the storage of merchandise. Following the tobacco inspection acts passed in the Chesapeake colonies, a large number of warehouses were erected for the storage of hogsheads of tobacco at public landings. Most of these warehouses were one-story frame buildings measuring from 25 to 80 feet or more in length, with one or two sheds attached to the sides.   In the 17th and early 18th centuries, merchants often stored their wares in their dwellings, in lofts, cellars, or other storerooms. This practice continued through the early 19th century. In the late colonial period, specialized buildings began to be erected in larger southern port towns such as Charleston, Norfolk, Alexandria, and Baltimore. Two- and three-story warehouses, often containing counting rooms or offices, stood along the quaysides and wharfs filled with imported goods waiting for sale or redistribution to backcountry storekeepers. See also **bale house, counting room, inspection house, store.**

warehouse
Francis Guy, A warehouse in Baltimore, 1804

1638 Complaint of Virginians that "the erectinge and buildinge of generall warehouses and bringeinge our tobaccoe unto them will bee very chargeable and burthensome to the Colony." *Journals of the House of Burgesses,* 1.

1731 "Colonel George Harmonson agreed with the Court to build a warehouse for the Reception of Tobacco Forty foot long twenty foot wide ten foot pitch two shades eight foot wide four prizes with gallows and platforms and a wharf according to act of Assembly." Northampton Co., Va. Court Order Book 1729–1732.

1764 Advertised "To be SOLD . . . at BALTIMORE-TOWN . . . [is] A LARGE BRICK HOUSE . . . 45 Feet by 24, Two stories high, with a Brick Porch, having a good Cellar the whole length and Width of the Building, a Parlour, large Store Room and Warehouse, on the first Floor; Two Lodging Rooms, and a large Warehouse, on the second Floor, and a large Garret." *Maryland Gazette.*

1765 A notice read: "TO BE LETT . . . A large brick Warehouse, (late in the possession of Henry Laurens, Esq.) situate on the north end of the Bay, very convenient for trade; The back part is glazed, it has two fire-places, and a compting room, lathed and plaister'd." *South Carolina Gazette.*

warp   To bend or twist out of shape, especially from a flat or horizontal position. Green, unseasoned timber used in construction often bent as the moisture content decreased.

> 1800   Repairs to a courthouse included: "All the rotten fetheredge plank to be taken out and new put in where the plank is warped by the sun and nails drawn." Gates Co., N.C., County Accounts, NCA&H.
>
> 1807   A workman wrote to Thomas Jefferson that "you expressed a wish to have the sashes for Poplar Forest made of walnut. If you still desire it you will please to let me know that we may have the walnut got to kiln dry along with the plank. I would beg leave however to observe that I am afraid there is not to be had bout here what is so much give to warp that it will render it very unfit for that purpose." Coolidge Collection, Massachusetts Historical Society.

washboard
Battersea, Petersburg, Va.

washboard   A narrow board running along the floor at the base of a wainscotted or plastered wall. The washboard served as a protective and decorative finish. Of the three synonymous terms, *washboard*, *mopboard*, and *skirting*, the first was by far the most commonly used in the region through the early 19th century. After this time, the term *baseboard* came into vogue. See also **base (3), mopboard, skirting board.**

> 1737   A glebe house was to have "mouldings and washboards round the rooms." Truro Parish, Fairfax Co., Va. Vestry Book.
>
> 1793   Specifications for "Old East" at the University of North Carolina called for "a plain skirting or wash board about 4 inches broad & beaded on the upper edge." University Archives, UNC, Chapel Hill.
>
> 1816   An academy building in Hancock County, Georgia, had a "plain dado—chairboard high, including chairboard and wash-board above and below." *The News*.

wash house   A room or building in which clothes, linens, and other items are washed. Most wash houses were contained in outbuildings, often in association with kitchens. They contained a fireplace for heating water and large tubs for washing. The term appeared in the early 18th century in South Carolina. By the time of the Revolution, it was also being used in parts of Maryland and occasionally in Virginia, where the synonymous term *laundry* was more common. See also **laundry.**

> 1733   A plantation for sale near Goose Creek, South Carolina contained "a brick Kitchen and Wash-House." *South Carolina Gazette*.
>
> 1798   Located behind 198–206 King George Street in Annapolis was a "brick kitchen and wash house 24 by 16." U.S. Direct Tax, MSA.

washroom   A space where laundry is washed and cleaned, usually part of a kitchen or separate outbuilding. See also **wash house.**

> 1771   Among the outbuildings on a property for sale in Charleston was "a good Kitchen and Wash-Room." *South Carolina Gazette*.

watch box, watch house   A small building providing shelter for military or civil sentinels. Larger watch houses sometimes contained a lockup and various civic offices. Occasionally, fire engines were stored in watch houses or in contiguous sheds. In some of the larger towns, a number of small watch boxes were built in different locations to provide places of refuge for night patrols. See also **sentinel box.**

> 1747   It was "Resolved that a Prison and Watch house be built upon the Publick ground of the following dimensions 20 by 15 with a brick chimney eight foot pitch." Norfolk, Va., Common Hall Order Book 1736–1798.
>
> 1768   A contract was to be let for "a small House for the Watch to retire to, on the Public Land up Town, near the Market House." Norfolk, Va., Common Hall Order Book 1736–1798.

1797 The council decided "to have four watch boxes built and to affix them in such places and under such directions as they judge most beneficial for the public good." Fredericksburg, Va., City Council Minute Book 1782–1801.

water board A sloping plinth course used to cast water away from the foundation; a water table. See also **water table.**

1761 A stone church to be built in Winchester, Virginia, was to have a "24 Feet Pitch from the Water Board, and 2 1/2 feet from the Surface of the Earth, to the Water Board." *Maryland Gazette.*

water closet A small room fitted as a necessary or privy with a close stool fitted with a water supply to flush and discharge waste into a pipe. The use of water closets in the very late 18th and early 19th centuries was limited to only a handful of domestic and public structures. See also **necessary house.**

1803 President Jefferson complained that "the defectiveness of the pipes" in the White House "is rotting it fast at the water closets. Strong pipes will be wanting, and the water must be taken out from the cistern, not at the bottom, but at the sides by syphon going to the bottom." *The Correspondence and Papers of Benjamin Henry Latrobe,* 1.

1804 Although not called *water closets* but functioning as such, an exchange in Savannah was "to have two public and four private necessaries . . . to have a reservoir for the water from the roof- To have pipes to conduct the water to the necessaries and to have conductors or pipes from the necessaries to the river." *Columbian Museum and Savannah Advertiser.*

water leaf The stylized leaf of an aquatic plant, used as a decorative ornament in the late 18th and early 19th centuries. Occasionally it replaced acanthus leaves in carved capitals and also served as an enrichment in friezes and borders.

1800 Among the composition ornaments purchased by a John Steele from Lane Chapman and Wellford for his house in Rowan County, North Carolina, was "2 ft of Waterleaf fascia." John Steele Papers, SHC.

1805 In designing capitals for the Capitol in Washington, architect Benjamin Henry Latrobe noted that the carvings including "a high row of Raffle leaves, the lower a short circle of Water leaves." *The Correspondence and Miscellaneous Papers of Benjamin Henry Latrobe,* 2.

water mill A mill whose machinery is powered by a waterwheel. Water-driven mills were used to grind corn and wheat and to saw logs. Along with *windmills,* they appeared in the Chesapeake in the first half of the 17th century. They spread throughout the South wherever sufficient capital, a prospective local or coastwise market, and permission from local authorities to dam water courses converged. From the middle of the 18th century onward, a number of large commercial water mills in the Cape Fear Valley of North Carolina sawed yearly hundreds of thousands of board feet of lumber for export. See also **merchant mill, mill, waterwheel.**

1683 In St. Mary's County, Maryland, was "fifty acres of land called the Mill Dam with one Dwelling house, one Kitchen, one stable, one Water Mill house with two Grist Mills." *Archives of Maryland,* 70.

1736 A "Petition of Job Rogers to build a Grist Water Mill upon Deep Creek [is] granted." Bertie Co., N.C., Court Minute Book 1724–1739.

1755 An advertisement read: "To be SOLD . . . a VERY good Water-Mill, on the Head of South River, attended with a plentiful Stream of Water, is well situated for a Merchant Mill, and within nine miles of the City of Annapolis." *Maryland Gazette.*

1763 "Three very valuable WATER-MILLS on one Dam" were to be sold in Charles County, Maryland, "two of them in one House; the Stones are large, and of the best Cullen Grit; one of the Mills was built last Fall, and the other has been standing some Years, and is now thoroughly repaired." *Maryland Gazette.*

waterproof *(adj.)* Impermeable to water. *(n.)* Any substance used as a coating to prevent water from penetrating. *(v.)* To apply such a substance to a surface. The most common waterproofing used during the colonial and early national period was tar. Applied to roofs and walls, this resinous substance was believed to be the most effective way of preserving wooden surfaces. Putty and paint were also considered to have waterproofing capabilities. When exterior stuccoing came into fashion in the late 18th and early 19th centuries, a number of recipes were tried to render that material impermeable to water. See also **tar.**

> **1766** Church windows were "to be glazed with C[rown] glass, and puttied in with such puttie as will be proof against wind and water." All Faiths Parish, St. Mary's Co., Md., Vestry Book.
>
> **1807** A "receipt for a composition in imitation of Portland Stone . . . may be formed into shapes or used for water proof stuccoing" and was said to "possess the property of effectually preventing damps and wet from penetrating walls." *The Enquirer.*

water table
Carter's Grove, James City County, Va.

water table The sloping top of a plinth course in a masonry building used to cast water away from the foundation. Above this ledge, the masonry wall steps back two to three inches. To accentuate the break between the plinth and the upper wall of the building, water table bricks and stones were often molded or beveled to produce a decorative effect. See also **footlace, plinth.**

> **1662** Walls of a dwelling house in Virginia were "to be two brick thick to the water table, and a brick and a halfe thick above the water table to the roofe." Hening, *Statutes at Large*, 2.
>
> **1674** Walls of Maryland statehouse were "to be twenty eight inches thick from the bottom of the said foundacon to the water table which shall be three foote Cleere above ground and made shelving of." *Archives of Maryland 2.*
>
> **1734** "WATER TABLE is a Sort of Ledge left in Stone or Brick Walls, about 18 or 20 Inches from the Ground (more or less) from which Place the Thickness of the Wall is abated (or taken in) the Thickness of a Brick. In Brick Walls two Inches and a 1/4; thereby leaving that Ledge or Jutty that is call'd a Water Table." *Builder's Dictionary.*
>
> **1753** A church "foundation [is] to be laid three feet under the surface of the earth and the foundation to be five feet thick and three feet and half from the surface of the earth to the water table." Wicomico Parish, Northumberland Co., Va., Vestry Book.
>
> **1760** Foundations of a church were to be laid on "Solid Ground and three feet thick to the Sleepers or Water Tables." Augusta Parish, Augusta Co., Va., Vestry Book.

waterwheel A wooden wheel that is turned by the weight or momentum of water, used to operate the machinery of a mill. There were four types of vertical waterwheels in use in early America. The difference between the overshot, pitchback, breastshot, and undershot varieties was the point where the water, fed from a flume or sluice, struck the wheel. The overshot received water at the highest point and the undershot at the lowest, with the other two taking water at a intermediate point in the wheel. The waterwheel consisted of a shaft, arms, rims, drum boards, and partitions that formed buckets. Through a series of gears connected to the rotating shaft, the mill stones or saws were set into motion. See also **mill, water mill.**

> **1734** A "Grist Mill" to be sold in Delaware had "two Water Wheels. . . . there is a conveniency of Water Carriage from the Mills; it lies within a Mile of Christine Bridge." *Pennsylvania Gazette.*

1807 Adjoining the Hudson farm in southern Delaware was "a Grist Mill partly constructed to run two pair of Stones, but at this time is only furnished with one pair, said Mill is in tolerable repair excepting the water Wheel which is some defective, the waste gates to this mill requiring repairing at this time." Sussex Co., Del., Orphans Court Valuations K.

wattle (watle, watling) A thin, flexible branch, pole, or withe and, by extension, the coarse basketwork constructed with such materials. Wattle was used during the earliest years of settlement as an infilling between framing members. It was then covered with *daub*, a variable mixture of clay, mud or dung, and straw, and sometimes finished with plaster. Wattle or wattled fences were composed of groundset stakes around which the material was woven; wattle fences were never daubed. Such fences were favored for enclosing gardens, pens for smaller animals, and domestic yards from the 17th into the 19th century. Wattle represents a technique known to both European- and African-Americans, and its use appears to have been mutually reinforced in America.

1747 The walls of a church in Savannah were "to be watled betwixt the Studs with white Oak watling, and filled up on each Side with strong Plaister, that the Studs should be wholly covered at least three Quarters of an Inch, so that the Walls will be upwards of eight Inches thick." *Colonial Records of the State of Georgia*, 6.

1795 In Fairfax County, Virginia, a farm manager was "to drive stakes across [a gully] and wattle them at different distances, to catch and retain the trash that is swept down with the torrent.—They also serve to break the force of the water." *Writings of Washington*, 34.

1802 A plantation included "one old Wattled Garden." Sussex Co., Del., Orphans Court Valuations L.

wattle
The Quarter, Carter's Grove,
James City County, Va.

weatherboard Generally, any exterior sheathing enclosing the frame of a building and composed of a series of sawn or riven, lapped or flush-laid boards or planks laid horizontally. Most were lapped over one another or jointed, in order to shed water. Specifically, weatherboard was a lapped sheathing board, either rectangular in section or tapered with the upper edge feathered. The lower, exposed edge of such weatherboards was commonly beaded or molded on superior frame buildings in the South until the mid-19th century. Weatherboards were also used to sheath rough partition walls. See also **clapboard.**

1645 A workman was hired "to weatherboard the partition" of a dwelling. *County Court Records of Accomack-Northampton, Virginia 1640–1645.*

1721 Chapel built "for the ease and convenience of the frontire inhabitants" was to be "weather-boarded with good Clap-boards." Bristol Parish, Prince George Co., Va., Vestry Book.

1737 A North Carolina settler advised that "It is much better to Weatherboard with 3/4 boards and where ye Boards ly against ye Studs to dub it thin like ye feather edge so that so that between ye studs ye boards at ye upper edge remain 3/4 of an inch when nail'd on . . . which [prevents] them from splitting with ye heat of ye sun as ye feather edge, being generally thin generally does." Thomas Pollock Letterbook, NCA&H.

1741 A chapel was ordered "weatherboarded with featheredge plank nine inches broad with good lapps of two inches at the last." St. Paul's Parish, Chowan Co., N.C., Vestry Book.

1758 "The sides and ends" of a glebe house in Prince Edward County, Virginia, were "to be well weather Boarded with good featheredge Plank plained and beaded not to show more than six Inches nor less than two Inches lap." *W&MQ*, 2nd ser., 17.

1799 Craftsmen working on John Steele's house in Rowan County, North Carolina, were "to weatherboard the Same with three quarter inch plank quartered planed and beaded." John Steele Papers, SHC.

weatherboard
Beaded weatherboard, Smokehouse,
Bacon's Castle, Surry County, Va.

weathercock A vane, often in the form of a rooster that turns with its head to the wind. See also **vane.**

> 1726 Carpenter John Smith requested payment for "putting the . . . weather cock up" on the church in Annapolis. St. Anne's Parish, Anne Arundel Co., Md., Vestry Book.
> 1753 The vestry agreed "that the Weathercock be repaired and gilded." St. Philip's Parish, Charleston, S.C., Vestry Book.
> 1757 It was "Order'd that . . . the weather cock be painted Yellow and fixed on the Steeple." St. Helena's Parish, S.C., Vestry Book.

weather vane See **vane.**

weaving house A building in which to carry on textile manufacturing, generally found on the larger rural estates. These were multipurpose spaces, used for living as well as working, though some of the largest planters maintained dedicated weaving manufactories. Weaving provided a profitable outlet for surplus labor at certain times of the year. See **loom house, spinning house.**

> 1718 Appraisers listed a "weaveing house" among the buildings of Samuell Cornwell's plantation in Surry County, Virginia. Surry Co., Va., Deed and Will Book 1715–1730.
> 1768 Property for sale in Frederick County, Maryland, included "a Frame Weave Shop, where the Business is now carried on." *Maryland Gazette.*
> 1779 Landon Carter's "Weaving Manufactory" contained "2 looms and gear; 1 quil wheel; 1 cotton gin; 4 flax wheels; 5 great wheels; 7 pair cotton cards; 5 pair wool cards; 6 slays; 1 coam hackle; 2 pair of low cards; 1 pair clothier cards." Carter Papers, UVa.
> 1785 The Ellliott farm on the Eastern Shore of Maryland contained "one round log weaving house 14 feet square." Queen Anne's Co., Md., Guardian Bonds and Valuations SC.

wedge A piece of wood or metal, thick at one end and tapered to a thin edge at the other. When struck at the thick end with a blunt instrument, the thin edge of the wedge splits the wood, stone, or other material along the grain.

weight A piece of metal used to counterbalance window sash. Early sash weights were made of cast lead. By the early 19th century, ones fabricated of cast iron came into use. See also **lead** (2).

> 1735 John Sheppard of Charleston offered for sale "lead weights from 14 lbs. down." *South Carolina Gazette.*
> 1767 "The sashes of the Lower Windows" of a church were "to hang with weights and pullys." Fairfax Parish, Fairfax Co., Va., Vestry Book.
> 1803 Specifications for a church to be built on Johns Island near Charleston called for the "sashes [to be] hung with Cast Iron Weights." Johns Island Church Specifications, Library Society of Charleston.
> 1813 A court ordered that "iron weights [be] placed on the windows of the courthouse." Northampton Co., Va., Court Order Book 1806–1816.

weld The process of fusing metals with heat by an act such as hammering or compressing.

well 1. A deep, cylindrical pit, often lined with brick, stone, timber, or hogsheads, excavated to provide access to an underground spring.

> 1688 A craftsman was sued for failing to "brick up a well." Charles City Co., Va., Court Order Book 1687–1695.
> 1709 Richard Littlepage agreed "to make a Curb and Windless for the well, and a Shed over the Well." St. Peter's Parish, New Kent Co., Va., Vestry Book.

1763 On the Elliott estate was "one framed well." Queen Anne's Co., Md., Deed Book F.

1804 "A new well ougt to be dug and framed with white oak or with good Hogshead." Kent Co., Del., Orphans Court Valuations.

1804 In Savannah, "the practice of Washing Horses, Carriages, Clothes and other things at the public wells and pumps in the streets and squares of this city, and also allowing Hogs to go at large, tend to injure and impair the said wells and pumps and render the water contained therein less fit and proper for use." *Georgia Republican and State Intelligencer.*

2. A narrow framed opening between floors to provide access for a staircase or a chimney stack.

1680 A courthouse was to have "a fayre open well stare Casse up unto the Roofe." Talbot Co., Md., Judgments 1675–1682.

1746 Charles Pinckney's dwelling in Charleston was to have "proper wells for stairs chimneys as according to Plann." Huger Smith, *Dwelling Houses of Charleston.*

Welsh chimney (Welch, weltch chimney) In the 17th-century Chesapeake, a kind of wooden chimney based on a frame of ground-set corner posts. See also **chimney.**

1645 A dwelling house was to be built "twenty foot long with a welch Chimney in it besides and fifteen foote broade with a partition." *County Court Records of Accomack-Northampton, Virginia 1640–1645.*

1659 In Calvert County, Maryland, a directive was given to "putt up the Posts of the Welch Chimney" for a frame dwelling house. *Archives of Maryland,* 41.

Welsh stair A simply fashioned stair. Although the precise meaning of the term is unknown, it may have referred to a stair in the shape of a fixed ladder.

1668 In Charles County, Maryland, carpenter Thomas Alcocks sued George Thompson for payment for "Making a paire of welsh Staires, and taking downe of a welsh Chimney." *Archives of Maryland,* 60.

wharf (wharff, warfe) A substantial structure of timber or stone lying at the water's edge or projecting into a harbor or river, so that vessels can tie up alongside to load and unload their cargo. See also **landing (1), quay.**

1682 Charleston contained "wharfs for the Convenience of their Trade and Shipping." Salley, *Narratives of Early Carolina.*

1728 In Norfolk, "the Method of building Wharffs here is after the following Manner. They lay down long Pine Logs, that reach from the Shore to the Edge of the Channel. These are bound fast together by Cross-Pieces notcht into them, according to the Architecture of the Log-Houses in North Carolina. A wharff built thus will stand Several Years." Byrd, *History of the Dividing Line.*

1752 In Hampton, payment was made to John Bushell "for making a Tea & Crain to the Wharf." Elizabeth City Co., Va., Court Order Book 1747–1755.

1771 "To be Sold . . . in Charles Town . . . the LOT, HOUSE, and STORES on the Bay, now in the Occupation of Peter Leger & Company . . . . The Wharf fronting said House, containing in Front One Hundred and two Feet, and in Length from the Curtain Line to the head of the Wharf, four hundred feet, lately completed, whereon are sundry well built Stores. The Great extends One Hundred Feet farther than the Head of the Wharf." *South Carolina Gazette.*

1785 An advertisement read: "WHARF BUILDING, David Shaon, whose profession it is . . . recommends the driving of large piles on the outside walls of every wharf, which is the custom in Baltimore even in the Bason; but more peculiarly suitable here from the steepness with which the channel of Potomack is formed." *Virginia Journal and Alexandria Advertiser.*

1811 At Hampton, "the County Wharf contemplated to be built ought to be fully the width of the street leading thereto and raised even with the highest post now standing within the old wharf. We recommend the Wharf logs should be of pine and of a large size—the two upper courses to be good heart pine all the logs to have

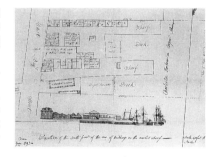

wharf
Row of buildings on the Market Wharf, Charleston, S.C., 1793

three square sides and the tie logs to be good heart—That the corners and abutments of the logs should be fastened with inch square Iron bolts and a proportion of the tie logs also fastened in the same manner—That the abutment of the wharf should extend up the street to the plank that forms the breast work across the street and from thence gradually sloped up the street to make the ascent easy for carriages, also that there should be six large cedar or locust posts fixed at regular and convenient distances in the wharf for fastening down vessels to and six large ring bolts drove in for the same purpose in front of the Wharf." Elizabeth City Co., Va., Deed and Will Book 1809–1818.

whetstone   A fine-grained stone used for giving a fine edge to cutting tools after they had been ground on a grindstone.

white lead   A white pigment commonly used in housepainting, either by itself or in combination with other coloring agents. A lead carbonate in the approximate formulation $2PbCO_3Pb(OH)_2$, it was a product of corrosion initiated by soaking lead sheets in vinegar or pressings left over from winemaking. The resulting pigment had very fine particles and therefore offered excellent coverage. White lead was generally regarded as an adulterated form of flake white or ceruse, being less pure and less white than either of these. Near the end of the 18th century, though, all three terms became more or less synonymous. Building accounts for the period generally refer to *white lead*. Through the colonial period, most of the material was imported from England and only supplanted by domestic manufacture in the early 19th century.

> 1734   "Ye doores and dorecases and window frames" of a church "to be twice primed first with Spanish brown then with white lead." Blisland Parish, James City and New Kent Cos., Va., Vestry Book.
> 1747   In a church, "the outside of the Doors & Door Cases, the outside of the window frames & Sashes the Cornish the Corner & Barge Boards [are] all to be well painted with white lead & oil." Albemarle Parish, Surry Co., Va., Vestry Book.
> 1759   A merchant in Savannah ordered from a firm in Bristol, England, a large quantity of "white lead ground in oyl in small kegs." *Collections of the Georgia Historical Society*, 13.
> 1764   Robert Dossie described flake white as "lead corroded by means of the pressings of the grape; and consequently in fact a ceruss prepared by the acid of grapes. It is brought here from Italy; and far surpasses, both with regard to the purity of its whiteness, and the certainty of its standing, all the ceruss or white lead, made here in common." Dossie, *The Handmaid to the Arts.*
> 1766   In a specification for construction of a new church, the vestry of All Faiths parish directed that the doors and windows "be painted three times over with white lead." All Faiths Parish, St. Mary's Co., Md., Vestry Book.

white lime   Whitewash. The term was used in the 17th century to describe a finish coat of lime and water applied to plaster, brick, and woodwork. By the early 18th century, the term was supplanted by *whitewash*. See also **lime, whitewash.**

> 1651   A plasterer was hired to "white lyme and wash over the dyning roome, the yellowe roome, & kitchinge, & chamber over the kitchinge." Norfolk Co., Va., Will and Deed Book 1646–1651.
> 1656   A description of a Chesapeake dwelling noted that "the rooms are large, daubed and white limed." Hammond, *Leah and Rachel.*
> 1674   The upper room of a courthouse in Charles County, Maryland, was to be "well daubed & sealed with morter white limed & sized." *Archives of Maryland*, 60.

whitewash   *(n.)* An architectural finish composed of slaked lime and water together with any one of a variety of additives, including salt, sugar, yellow ochre, or Spanish whiting. Inexpensive to make and easy to apply, whitewash was the earliest interior finish to see widespread use in the southern colonies. The scarcity of references to exterior whitewashing suggests that this finish was confined mostly to interior work. Period sources suggest that interiors were customarily whitened in the fall, covering over grease, dirt, and fly specks with a minimum of inconvenience. *(v.)* To apply a coating of whitewash, also referred to as *white liming*. See also **limewash, white lime.**

> 1677 Thomas Pate agreed to "plaister, lath and whitewash ye church at poplar springe." Petsworth Parish, Gloucester Co., Va., Vestry Book.
> 1710 In Baltimore County, Maryland, James Maxwell agreed with justices to build a courthouse at the towne of Joppa . . . the interior surface of the brick walls "to be plaistered and whitewashed." Baltimore Co., Md., Record Book B.
> 1737 Trustees of the Georgia colony agreed to solicit estimates for building a church in Georgia, "all to be rendered and white wash'd on the Inside." *Journal of the Earl of Egmont.*

whiting A chalk or calcium carbonate pigment and filler varying substantially in purity and whiteness. Deposits in this country are of poor quality, so it is probable that most whiting used in the South was imported. This material was often mixed with linseed oil to make glazier's putty. By the end of the 18th century, this material had become the leading adulterant of white lead, hence its occasional designation, *lead whiting.* See also **Spanish whiting.**

> 1756 William Lakey was paid 4/6 for "whiting and putty." Bertie Co., N.C., Court Records, New Actions, NCA&H.
> 1774 Accounts for the building of William Corbit's house in Odessa, Delaware, included charges for "Whiting" and "Lead Whiting." Sweeney, *Grandeur on the Appoquinimink.*
> 1807 A published recipe for making imitation Portland Stone called for "one and a half pecks of whiting." *The Enquirer.*

wicket A small door or gate within a larger door.

> 1756 At the College of William and Mary, "two new Locks" were to be added to "the Wicket Doors." *W&MQ*, 2d ser., 1.
> 1802 Carpenter Andrew McDonald charged John Tayloe for "2 1/2 in. 20 pannels coach house doors, with wicket" for use in the service buildings behind the Octagon in Washington, D.C. Tayloe Papers, VHS.

wigwam A Native American dwelling, often round or oval in shape, constructed of poles covered by bark, skins, or mats. See also **cabin** (1).

> 1705 "The manner the Indians have of building their Houses, is very slight and cheap; when they would erect a Wigwang, which is the Indian name for a House, they stick Saplins into the ground by one end, and bend the other at the top, fastening them together by strings made of fibrous Roots, the rind of Trees, or of the green Wood of the white Oak, which will rive into Thongs. The smallest sort of these Cabbins are conical like a Bee-hive; but the larger are built in an oblong form, and both are cover'd with the Bark of Trees, which will rive off into great flakes. Their Windows are little holes left open for the passage of Light. . . . Their Chimney, as among the true Born Irish, is a little hole in the top of the House, to let out the Smoak. . . . There's never more than one Room in a House, except some Houses of State, or Religion, where the Partition is made only by Mats, and loose Poles." Beverley, *The History of the Present State of Virginia.*

wilderness An ornamental grove of trees, thicket, or mass of shrubbery intentionally set in a remote area of a pleasure ground, penetrated by walks often in the design of a labyrinth.

> 1743 At Crow-Field near Charleston, a visitor was awed by "mounts, Wilderness, etc." *Letterbook of Eliza Lucas Pinckney.*

1785 George Washington spent time "in search of the sort of Trees I shall want for my Walks, groves, and Wildernesses." *Diaries of George Washington*, 2.
1806 "To diversify the scenery . . . a wilderness . . . [is] generally planted in close assemblages, with serpentine walks between; some leading in private meanders toward the interior parts, or braking out . . . some places being closely bordered with tall trees, to effect a gloominess and perfect shade: the different walks leading now and then into circular openings, each being surrounded with plantations as aforesaid; making the principal walks terminate in a grand opening in the centre of the wilderness, in which may be some edifice, or fine piece of water." M'Mahon, *The American Gardener's Calendar*.

wimble A tool used for boring; a brace. For a more detailed description, see **brace** (2).

windbeam A horizontal cross beam in a roof truss that ties a pair of rafters together at a level above the wall plate. See also **collar**.
1668 Carpentry work on a plantation included "wind-beaming a fourtie foot house." Charles Co., Md., Court Proceedings 1668.
1681 Framing a roof in a courthouse called for "the rafters to be sawn and three inches square to be coupled . . . the wind beams to be dovetayled." Northumberland Co., Va., Court Order Book 1678–1698.
1697 "Robert Norris doth oblige hemself to Arch the Church . . . fit for Plaistering . . . from the plate to the Wind beam, being about Seven foot Perpendicular." St. Paul's Parish, Kent Co., Md., Vestry Book.
1712 In a church with a principal rafter roof, "the principall wind beams be 5 by 7 inches square." Christ Church Parish, Middlesex Co., Va., Vestry Book.

winder A wedge-shaped step in a staircase. See also **stair**.

winder
Cupola House, Edenton, N.C.

windlass (windless) A device for raising objects, consisting of a horizontal member supported by two posts and turned by a crank or lever. A rope, cable, or chain was attached to the horizontal member at one end and a bucket, hook, or object at the other end. Windlasses were used in wells to raise water and in storehouses, barns, and other locations that required the movement of materials or objects from one level to another.
1709 "Capt. Richard Littlepage hath agreed . . . to make a Curb and Windless for the Well, and a Shed over the Well." St. Peter's Parish, New Kent Co., Va., Vestry Book.
1797 A notice read: "Valuable Slate Lands to be LEASED OR SOLD; LYING in the County of Buckingham. . . . A strata of Coal running through the same hills . . . going in a horizontal instead of a perpendicular direction . . . by which the dirt, water, and coal, may all be carried off by an easy and natural direction, instead of by pullies and windlesses." *Virginia Gazette and General Advertiser*.

windmill
Charles Fraser, A post mill, South Carolina

windmill Any one of various machines used for grinding or pumping, driven by the force of the wind acting upon a framework of sails that are connected by gears and shafts to a grindstone or pump. Windmills appeared in the South by the middle of the 17th century and continued to be used in a number of areas, including the eastern shore of Maryland and Virginia, through the 19th century. Perhaps the most common windmill was the *post mill*. The body of the mill containing the machinery stood on a large central post supported by large braces and could be rotated by moving a long tail pole to bring the wooden or canvas sails into the direction of the wind. A second type, known as a *smock mill* or *tower mill*, had a stationary body framed up from the ground and a cap with sails that was rotated to catch the wind. See also **mill, watermill**.

1642 On the eastern shore of Virginia, "Anthony Linny should build sett upp and finish a Wyndemill within the County of Accomack." *County Court Records of Accomack-Northampton, Virginia 1640–1645.*

1763 There was "TO BE LET . . . A LARGE well-built BRICK WIND-MILL, in Annapolis . . . situated by the side of the River Severn. . . . There are two Chimnies in it, and it is roomly enough for two or three Persons to live in with Comfort. The Stones are French burrs, 4 Foot over and 14 Inches deep." *Maryland Gazette.*

1805 Standing on Kent Island in Chesapeake Bay was "a very valuable WIND MILL, which is an object of importance in a place where there are no streams for water mills." *Republican Star or Eastern Shore General Advertiser.*

window frame 1. The structure of a window opening, either assembled as a prefabricated unit and set into a wooden or masonry wall, or built up within the wall frame with a sill and lintel demarcation the height of the opening and let into or nailed against vertical studs or posts. See also **frame, header, sill, lintel.**

2. The exposed, often molded, casing for window sash. From the 17th through the early 19th centuries, such finish was commonly applied to the structural elements of the window frame or cut directly into their surfaces. See also **architrave** (2).

window seat A flat surface between the interior face of a masonry wall and a window frame at a height suitable for sitting, or a paneled projection constructed for this purpose that formed a plinth below the architraves of the window opening.

1746 Charles Pinckney based the design of his "double cornice . . . surbase, window seats, & Jambs" in his best parlor after "Capt. Shubrick's dining room. . . . The back parlour, study and office with only surbase & skirting boards round, & plain window seats, with a beed and facings to the window Jambs." Huger Smith, *Dwelling Houses of Charleston.*

1811 The kitchen at Montpelier in Orange County, Virginia, had "3 plank window seats." Cocke Papers, UVa.

windowsill The lower part of a window frame. See **sill.**

wine room A space for the storage of casks or bottles of wine. Many larger houses had storage rooms, often in cellars, where wine, beer, cider, and other provisions were kept under lock and key.

1801 A property for sale in Charleston on the east side of Church Street contained a brick carriage house, and "over the carriage house is a wine-room." *City Gazette and Daily Advertiser.*

wing A part of a building projecting on one side or behind, or a separate, detached structure flanking the central or main section. See also **transept.**

1711 The vestry of Bruton Parish "received from the Honble Alexander Spotswood, a platt or draught of a church" in the city of Williamsburg "whose length 75 foot, and breadth 28 foot in the clear, with two wings on each side, whose width is 22 foot." *Records of Bruton Parish.*

1748 Permission was granted to build "a galerie in one of the crosses or wings of the church opposite to the front door." Upper Parish, Nansemond Co., Va., Vestry Book.

1787 The Governor's House in New Bern "is a large and elegant brick Edifice two Stories high, with two Wings for the offices, somewhat advanced in front towards the Road, these are also two Stories high but lower in height than the main building; these wings are connected with the principal Building by a circular arcade reaching from each of the front Corners to the Corner of the Wing." Attmore, *Journal of a Tour to North Carolina.*

1798 "The Capitol in the city of Washington . . . will contain a main body and two wings." *Norfolk Herald.*

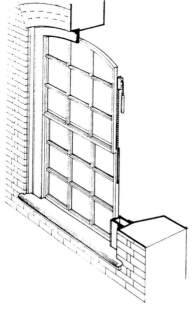

window frame (1)

winnowing house
Mansfield, Georgetown County, S.C.

winnowing house A building where grain is separated from the lighter particle of chaff by throwing it into the air and allowing the wind to blow away the impurities. See also **threshing floor.**

> **1733** A plantation near Goose Creek, South Carolina, contained "several Rice Mills, Mortars, &c., a winnowing House." *South Carolina Gazette.*

withdrawing room A chamber in a building for private conversation. The term was also used in a specialized sense the late 17th and early 18th centuries to refer to a magistrates' chamber in a courthouse, a place where justices retired to deliberate in private on public matters. In the late colonial period, the term was shortened to *drawing room* and the meaning changed to refer to a room where polite company was entertained. See also **drawing room.**

> **1689** A 40-by-20-foot courthouse was to be built with "a doore on one side of ye length into ye withdrawing Roome." Norfolk Co., Va., Deed Book 1686–1695.
> **1707** A courthouse was to have "handsome and ceil'd partitions above stairs for a withdrawing room for the Justices upon advisare volum or otherwise." Westmoreland Co., Va., Court Order Book 1705–1721.

within the walls A linear measurement of a building or part of a building exclusive of the enclosing walls; interior measurement. See also **in the clear, inside to inside.**

> **1733** It was "agreed with Mr. John Moore and Mr. Lewis Delony to build a Church in Blisland Parish as followeth Sixty feet long and twenty six foot wide within the walls." Blisland Parish, James City and New Kent Cos., Va., Vestry Book.

wooden chimney (wood chimney) The most common 18th- and early 19th-century term for a type of chimney constructed partially or totally of wooden materials, such as sawn or riven lumber, scantling, log, and wattle. For a more detailed description, see **chimney.**

> **1750** Specifications for a vestry house noted that it was to be "Sixteen feet Square framed work and Clapboarded the Covering boards to be Sapt and an Inside wooden chimney a plank floor and to be lofted with Clapboard and raised on blocks." Truro Parish, Fairfax Co., Va., Vestry Book.
> **1758** A new kitchen on Pasquotank River in North Carolina was built "with one small Brick Chimney in room of the old wood chimney." Secretary of State, Wills, NCA&H.
> **1772** On a plantation stood "one log quarter 20 by 16 wooden chimney burnt in the end." Queen Anne's Co., Md. Deed Book RT, No. 1.

wooden hinge A hinge made in the form of a hook and hinge but constructed of wood instead of iron. Oak is commonly riven for this purpose.

> **1728** "Most of the Houses in this Part of the Country are Log-houses, covered with Pine or Cypress Shingles, 3 feet long, and one broad. They are hung upon Laths with Peggs, and their doors too turn upon Wooden hinges and have wooden Locks to secure them, so that the Building is finisht without Nails or other Iron-Work." Byrd, *History of the Dividing Line.*

work A measure of the amount of workmanship on a piece such as a door or shutter that was to be exposed on both sides. In measuring the cost of a piece, craftsmen charged according to whether it was molded or raised on one or both sides. Pieces that were ornamented on one side were *single worked*, while those with moldings on both were *double worked*.

> **1790** An account for carpenter's work at Hampton near Baltimore listed "48 pannels in shutters double work @ 6/ . . . 44 ditto single work bead and flush @ 4/ pannel." *MHM*, 33.

1797 Work at a parsonage house noted "6 large double worked doors with Materials @ 71 . . . 7 Single worked doors with materials @ 60/." St. Michael's Parish, Charleston, S.C., Vestry Book.

workhouse **1.** A building or group of buildings erected to house the poor or vagrants of a parish, county, or corporation. In contrast to rural poorhouses, 18th-century urban workhouses had a less benevolent emphasis. Persons who committed petty offenses such as vagrancy or begging were forced into a workhouse. Most of these able-bodied paupers were expected to labor in exchange for shelter, medical attention, and other basic necessities. See also **almshouse, hospital (1), poorhouse.**

1735 "Whereas a number of Idle, Vagrant, and vitiously Inclined People either brought in by Shipping or . . . resorting hither from divers Parts of the Provinces And by Drinking and other sorts of Debauchery Speedily reducing themselves to Poverty and Diseases . . . And whereas the Parish officers are now often obliged to take up with very poor Accommodation of lodging &c. for sick persons . . . ye Petitioners humbly conceiv[e] that a Publick Workhouse & hospital under proper regulations will prove the most Effectual Remedies for these Evills." St. Philip's Parish, Charleston, S.C., Vestry Book.

1738 It was "ordered that all the Poor that are at present on the Parish, be removed from their several lodgings to the Work House immediately." St. Philip's Parish, Charleston, S.C., Vestry Book.

1751 "The Workhouse or Hospital erected for the use of the poor of this parish is not at present properly applyed for the use intended: And that in great measure owing to the opinion the poor people have contracted of the bad acconomy and ill treatment of the present warden to such degree that they choose rather to beg about the streets than take relief there." St. Philip's Parish, Charleston, S.C., Vestry Book.

1774 The North Carolina General Assembly passed an act "empowering vestries to build Workhouses to inflict corporal punishement on such poor under their care as shall behave refractorily." SPG Letterbook B, SPGFP.

1794 A "Workhouse 60 feet by 20 feet, two story high" was to be built. Norfolk, Va., Hustings Court-Order Book 1792–1795.

2. A building or shop where work is regularly performed. See also **workshop.**

1642 An inventory of an estate noted that "in the working house" were a variety of carpenter's tools. *County Court Records of Accomack-Northampton, Virginia 1640–1645.*

1774 Flanking the main house at Nomini Hall in Westmoreland County, Virginia, was "the Work-House." *Journal & Letters of Philip Vickers Fithian.*

1793 "James Moorman [is] charged with feloniously breaking & entering the shop or work house of Nathaniel Reynolds." Bedford County, Va., Court Order Book 1790–1795.

1801 On an Edgecombe County, North Carolina, plantation was "a work house 16 by 40 feet with a stack of chimnies." *The North Carolina Journal.*

workmanlike In the manner of or characteristic of a good workman; a general level of recognized craftsmanship and competence expected of any skilled artisan. The term was often included in articles of agreements between clients and undertakers in order that any deviance from that level of workmanship would not be tolerated. Generally, disagreements over this issue were resolved by arbitration. Outside craftsmen selected by each party viewed the work and rendered their decision.

1680 It was ordered that a courthouse "be substantially built workman like and that all the severall timbers ther to be good proportion and of such regular scantling as shall be reasonably advised by any good Archytecktare." Talbot Co., Md., Judgments 1675–1682.

1706 A complaint was made that Mathew Nichols had "not in a workmanlike manner . . . plasterurs work . . . a great deal had fallen downe." The court appointed

Thomas Everingham and William Edge, plasterers, to view the work. Accomack Co., Va., Court Order Book 1703–1709.

1742 "Mr. James Withers and Mr. Wood, who were appointed by a Rule of Court to decide the difference between the Gent. of the Vestry and John Meek, came to view the paving Work done by the said John Meek in & about the Belfry, Portico's and Church of St. Philip Charles Town, and were asked by the Vestry whether the same was done in a Workmanlike manner. Mr. Withers said it was not done in a Workmanlike manner, Mr. Wood said that a Mason would have done it better, but by the reason that the stones were rough & not squared Mr. Meek could not do it better." St. Philip's Parish, Charleston, S.C., Vestry Book.

1767 "The Consequence of this meeting was to receive of Messrs. Miller & Fullerton the Keys of the Parsonage House &c. as information we had of them that the same was Compleated in a Workmanlike Manner accordg. to agreement." St. Michael's Parish, Charleston, S.C., Vestry Book.

workmanship The amount of labor performed on a particular task; the amount of work executed by a craftsman.

1667 A committee was to "view the Middle Plantacon Church and make report to this vestry how much it is short of this church in Workmanship, and that allowance be made the undertaker accordingly." Christ Church Parish, Middlesex Co., Va., Vestry Book.

1734 "SAMUEL HOLMES of Charlestown Bricklayer undertakes and performs in workmanlike manner all sorts of Brickwork and Plaistering at reasonable Rates: He likewise if required draws Draughts of Houses and measures and values all sorts of Workmanship in houses or Buildings." *South Carolina Gazette.*

1769 "Vestry Agreed with Edward Davis to pay all Costs & Charges that said Davis Should be at on the Brick Church or Chapel of Ease in Benedict Hundred And Satisfie him for his Trouble & Workmanship on sd Church." Trinity Parish, Charles Co., Md., Vestry Book.

1804 Proposals were to be made "for doing by contract the whole workmanship requisite to the . . . enlargement of the Church." St. Michael's Parish, Charleston, S.C., Vestry Book.

workshop A place where a specific type of trade is carried on. See also **shop.**

1772 Property for sale in Prince George's County, Maryland, contained "a Dwelling House, with Two good Rooms which make Two good Workshops." *Maryland Gazette.*

1799 In Charleston, "J RICKETTS, Architect and Marble Mason, At his Work shop, corner of Governor's Bridge, INFORMS the Gentlemen of Charleston, and its vicinity, that he is returned to this city, with a CARGO of MARBLE, of the first quality." *Carolina Gazette.*

wormditch See **ditch.**

worm fence A type of fence composed of stacked, split rails describing in plan a series of interlocking angles. A worm fence might contain as few as five or as many as fourteen rails in a stack; a typical example included six to nine rails, five to eight feet high. Exceptionally durable woods like cedar and chestnut were preferred; locust, oak, and heart pine were also used. Worm fencing remained unpainted. The strength and stability of a worm fence depended entirely upon the angle at which one section of rails met another. The sharper or more acute the angle, the stronger the fence. The better built worm fences were buttressed with crossed stakes set at each angle and a heavy rail or rider resting on top. Such structures were often called stake and rider fences. Worm fences were easily built and readily dismantled, moved, and reassembled. They were favored for extensive fencing, such as enclosing cultivated fields and defining property boundaries. The variously named *worm, snake, zig-zag, Virginia rail,* and *stake and rider fence* was constructed from the 17th to the early 20th century. It appeared throughout the Southeast and mid-Atlantic, to a lesser degree in New England, and in more inland regions as western settlement progressed. Unlike all other kinds of fencing used in the early South, the *worm fence* was not part of the British building tradition; like log construction it may have been a product of Northern European building influences.

1685 At Jamestown were fences of "eight railes of Cloven timber about 9 foot long a piece wch pieces thus lie upon one another a lawfull fence is 8 railes high." Boyle Papers, Royal Society of London Archives.

1734 The trustees of the Georgia colony "have ordered the sum of 43.13.4 sterling to be applyed for inclosing the Glebe for the minister of Savannah . . . with a good worm fence six feet high." Christ Church Records, GHS.

1783 A 230-acre farm in Delaware included "about two thousand Pannels of Worm fence, the greater part Staked and ridered, and about One hundred and thirty Pannels about five Rails high, also." Sussex County, Del., Orphans Court Valuations D.

1787 George Washington noted that "at Dogue run" in Fairfax County, Virginia, workmen were "laying the worm of the New fence through the Woods." *Diaries of George Washington,* 5.

1789 An English traveler in Virginia observed "when they form an enclosure, these rails are laid so that they cross each other obliquely at each end, and are laid zig-zag to the amount of 10 or 11 rails in height. Then stakes are put against each corner, double across, with the lower ends drove a little into the ground, and about these stakes is placed a rail of double the size of the others, which is termed the rider, which, in a manner, locks up the whole and keeps the fence firm and steady." Anburey, *Travels Through the Interior Parts of America.*

wrench   A tool for turning nuts and bolts.

wrest (rest)   A tool with a flat, metallic blade interspersed with a series of slots, used for twisting or bending, especially the teeth of a saw. A wrest bent saw teeth at alternating angles, so that they could cut a kerf wider than the width of the blade and thus reduce friction.

wrought   Worked; a piece that has been shaped by hammering, carving, cutting, or planing.

1663 Courthouses were to be built with "good sufficient bricks, Lime and Timber and that the same be well wrought." *Journals of the House of Burgesses,* 2.

1714 "The floore of ye . . . Chappell [are to] be laid with pine plank one Inch & quarter when wrought." Christ Church Parish, Middlesex Co., Va., Vestry Book.

wrought iron   Iron that has been refined at a finery mill, producing a strong, malleable material used by blacksmiths to make a variety of objects such as tools, nails, locks, and hinges. Wrought iron differs from steel in that it contains very little carbon. See also **cast iron, forge, steel.**

1771 In Williamsburg, Robert Carter wrote to Clement Brooke at the Baltimore Furnace noting that "I send 2 patterns of wood to shew the sizes of grates to be made of wrought-iron . . . wanted for an hospital now building here for the reception of Lunaticks." Robert Carter Collection, MHS.

wrought nail   A metal fastener hammered into or through a piece in order to join one object with another; also, a hook on which to hang things. Wrought nails were forged from iron by blacksmiths and nailers in England and early America. The shanks of these nails can be distinguished from machine-cut nails by their taper on all four

wrought nail Types of wrought nails (*left to right*): rose, clasp, brad, headless brad, dog, clout, sprig, sprig (glazing point), tack, spike

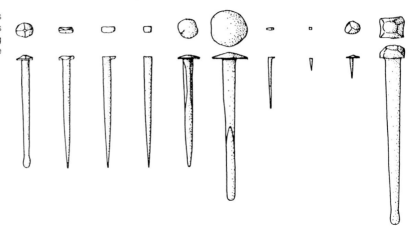

sides, instead of only two. Wrought nails were manufactured in a variety of sizes and forged with various types of heads and points, depending on their intended uses. A *rose head* nail had a distinctive head created by four strikes of a hammer, giving it the form of a four-leaf clover. It was the most common nail employed in rough framing and attaching exterior cladding. A *clasp head* nail was manufactured like a rose head nail but was struck an additional two times on the sides of the head. The resulting nail formed a T head and was used in trim work. *Brads* and *sprigs* were nails either with no heads, or a small lip on one side, and were used for trim work as well. A *dog* nail was used to secure door hinges. It had a large conical head that flattened out when driven against a metal hinge and helped secure the hinge close without disengaging the head. A *clout* nail was a large flat-headed nail used for fastening iron. A *spike* was a large nail, forged with either a round or square head, used to join large framing members or fasten planks. A *tack* was a short nail with a broad, flat head, often used to attach leather, fabric, or paperhangings to a wooden frame. A wrought nail is either pointed at the lower end of its shank, or flattened into a broad, spoon-shaped point. The term *wrought nail* was not used until the advent of *cut nail* manufacturing in the late 18th and early 19th centuries. It was then used to distinguish it from the new process. See also **brad, cut nail, flat point, nail, spike, sprig.**

1745 In an estimate of materials for a house, Charles Pinckney calculated that he needed "3 M 6d clouted nails at 2/10; 37 M rose head 4d nails 4p M; 12 M clasp head 10 d nails 13p M; 12 M clasp head nails 20d 20p per M; 5 M clasp head 12d Brads 17 pr M; 5 M 4d Batten." Huger Smith, *Dwelling Houses of Charleston*.

1790 Imported into Charleston from London and Liverpool were "clasp head, rose and clout nails of all sizes." *Columbian Herald*.

1795 Gabriel Manigault of Charleston ordered from London "400 M 20 penny Nails; 200 M 20 penny Flooring Brads; 400 M 6 penny rose head slender Nails; 50 M 6 penny Brads; 50 M 4 penny Brads." Manigault Papers, South Caroliniana Library.

1796 For sale in Fayetteville, North Carolina, were "a quantity of all kinds of wrought, and some cut NAILS." *North Carolina Minerva and Fayetteville Advertiser*.

1815 In an attempt to procure nails in Lynchburg, Thomas Jefferson requested "3000 nails of the length of the longest sample sent & 3000 of the shortest. Wrought nails would be preferred, but cut ones will do." Coolidge Collection, Massachusetts Historical Society.

x beam   See **cross beam.**

x cut saw   See **saw.**

x garnet   See **cross garnet.**

yard (yeard)   **1.** An area of uncultivated ground attached to, or enclosed by, a dwelling or building. On a domestic site, the yard contained service buildings and was used for associated activities. On urban sites in the South, the yard was often paved with brick, tile, or shells and was separated from kitchen and floral gardens by a fence or wall. In other contexts, the yard was the area adjacent to or surrounding a structure, generally enclosed by a wall or fence such as a churchyard, courtyard, or prison yard and was used for various purposes associated with it. A churchyard contained burials; a courtyard, the public buildings of a town or county; and a prison yard, the area where prisoners exercised.

> 1647   A tenant agreed to "maintain the old dwelling house and quartering houses and Tobacco houses in repair, as well as the pales about the yard and gardens." *W&MQ*, 1 ser., 5.
>
> 1686   At Green Spring, the former home of Governor William Berkeley in James City County, Virginia, a visitor wrote that the orchard was "well fenced in with Locust fence, which is as durable as most brick walls, a Garden, a hundred feet square, well pailed in, a Yeard where in is most of the foresaid necessary houses [domestic outbuildings], pallizado'd in with locust Punchens, which is as good as if it were walled in & more lasting than any of our bricks." *William Fitzhugh and his Chesapeake World.*
>
> 1743   A workman was hired to "rail in the Courthouse yard." Spotsylvania Co., Va., Order Book 1738–1749.
>
> 1753   A dwelling for sale in Prince William Parish, South Carolina, included "a garden at the south front, and yard lately paved in." *South Carolina Gazette.*
>
> 1771   Churchwardens were to have "the [church] yard secured so as to prevent the Cattle from going therein." St. Anne's Parish, Anne Arundel Co., Md., Vestry Book.

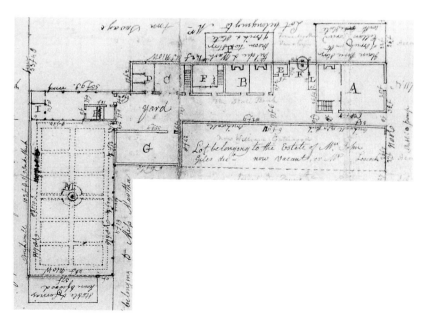

yard (1)   117 Broad Street, Charleston, S.C., 1797. (A) house of three stories with garret and cellars of brick, the lower story or floor occupied as a store and counting room, (B) kitchen and washroom, (C) carriage house, (D) stable, (E) pantry, (F) back store, (G) back store, (H) pigeon house, (I) shed and cowhouse, (K) well with two pumps, (L) cistern of water, (M) garden

1772 A plantation account noted the presence of "one new paled garden 150 feet by 100 in good repair with a paled yard between the dwelling house and garden in good repair." Queen Anne's County, Md., Deed Book K.

1774 "Mr. Carter observed that he much dislikes the common method of making Burying Yards round Churches, & having it almost open to every Beast." *Journal & Letters of Philip Vickers Fithian.*

1818 On a plantation in Cecil County, Maryland, time was spent "preparing for company, made cake, and had all the yards swept clean." *Diaries of Martha Ogle Forman.*

2. A cultivated area enclosed or attached to a dwelling often containing a flower garden, orchard, shade trees, or lawn. The meaning of the term in this sense grew out of the previous sense (1, above) and came into gradual use in the early 19th century to connote a pleasure ground or cultivated area, often reserved for flower beds, grass, fruit trees, and recreational exercise. See also **garden.**

1809 A traveler from South Carolina observed of Richmond that "every private yard is decorated with the handsomest shade trees which our Country boasts." *Journal of William D. Martin.*

1820 A tavern for sale at the Culpeper County, Virginia, courthouse included "a good garden and neat yard with trees &c. around the whole establishment." *Virginia Herald.*

3. A pen or fenced enclosure for animals or for the storage of feed, sometimes surrounded by farm buildings.

1763 A planter eagerly anticipated harvesting his crop and having "the Rice stacked in the Barn yard." *Papers of Henry Laurens*, 3.

1768 On a Fairfax County, Virginia, farm, the "Carpenters all . . . went to sawing railing for a goose yard." Anonymous Account in a 1768 Virginia Almanac, CWF.

1800 Behind a house for sale in Savannah was "a garden 34 by 45 feet, a cow yard 20 by 15 feet." *Columbian Museum and Savannah Advertiser.*

4. A piece of ground with or without buildings set apart for storage or for some specific activity or business.

1732 To be sold in Dorchester, South Carolina, was a "Tanyard." *South Carolina Gazette.*

1736 In Charleston was "a Timber-Yard kept in Bedon-street by Henry Bedon, where any Person may be supplied with all sorts of Boards, Scantling, Laths, Cedar Posts for Gardens, and Frames for Houses." *South Carolina Gazette.*

1786 For rent was "a BRICK-YARD about a mile from the Court-House [in Alexandria]; it has a case or wall built for burning bricks." *Virginia Journal and Alexandria Advertiser.*

1798 House frames and other material were available at a "Lumber yard" in Alexandria, Virginia. *Columbia Mirror and Alexandria Gazette.*

yellow poplar   A soft, fine-grained hardwood of the genus *Liriodendron tulipifera L.* with slight decay resistance. The heartwood ranges from a tan or yellowish brown to greenish brown. It was often called a tulip tree because of its flowering characteristics. Yellow poplar grows east of the Mississippi River. It was commonly used for framing, shingles, and weatherboards.

1752 In the Annapolis market house "the posts and rafters [are] to be of yellow poplar, and the weather-boarding to be feather edged yellow poplar." *Maryland Gazette.*

1772 A church was to be "covered with chestnut or yellow poplar, jointed shingles." Shelburne Parish, Loudoun Co., Va., Vestry Book.

zigzag fence   A type of fence composed of stacked, split rails describing in plan a series of alternating angles. For a more detailed description, see **worm fence.**

1793   In the vicinity of Winchester, Virginia, "the fields are so large, the tillage of them is so negligent, and the zigzag rail fences so remote from everything of rural elegance, that the country has by no means an inviting aspect." Toulmin, *The Western Country in 1793*.

zinc   A bluish-white metallic material rolled into sheets and used for roofing. First offered commercially in the early 19th century, zinc was touted as a cheaper alternative to copper or lead roof covering. It appeared in the South in the 1810s but never gained as widespread an acceptability as first expected, owing to the belief that it failed to withstand the effects of prolonged exposure to sulfuric and muriatic acids.

1819   A Norfolk hardware store advertised that it had "ZINC in Sheet, and NAILS for do. Zinc is used for sheathing Vessels, covering Houses, &c. &c. and is a great deal cheaper than Copper." *American Beacon and Norfolk & Portsmouth Daily Advertiser*.
1820   "PROPOSALS are desired for covering the Roof and Dome . . . of the Capitol of North Carolina, in a sound, tight, and effectual manner, with Zinc in sheets." *The Star and North Carolina Gazette*.

zocle   See **socle.**

zoophorus   A frieze or band bearing the carved or cast figures of animals and men.

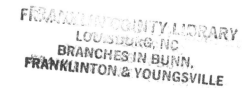

BIBLIOGRAPHY

Abbreviations used herein:
CWF = Colonial Williamsburg Foundation. GHS = Georgia Historical Society. MSA = Maryland State Archives. NCA&H = North Carolina Archives and History. SCA&H = South Carolina Archives and History. SPG = Society for the Propagation of the Gospel in Foreign Parts. VSL = Virginia State Library.

MANUSCRIPTS AND ARCHIVAL MATERIAL

Annapolis, Maryland

Maryland State Archives: Waring Collection; James Brice Ledger, 1767–1801; United States Federal Tax List, 1798.

Athens, Georgia

Hargrett Library, University of Georgia: Thomas Carr Accounts.

Austin, Texas

Church Historical Society: Francis Lister Hawks Collection.

Baltimore, Maryland

Maryland Historical Society: Charles Carroll Letterbook; Robert Carter Letterbooks; Robert Carter Papers; William Faris Diary; Riddell Accounts, Pleasants Papers.

Boston, Massachusetts

Massachusetts Historical Society: Coolidge Collection.

Bucks County, Pennsylvania

Bucks County Historical Society: John Mercer Ledger G.

Caracas, Venezuela

Academia Nacional de la Historia: Hawks Letter, Miranda Papers.

Chapel Hill, North Carolina

Southern Historical Collection, University of North Carolina: Cameron Papers; Juliana Margaret Conner Dairy; Cupola House Papers; Hawks Papers; Hayes Collection; Ernest Haywood Papers; Hubbard Papers; Susan Davis (Nye) Hutchinson Diary; Calvin Jones Papers; John Steele Collection.
University Archives: University Papers.

Charleston, South Carolina

Charleston Museum: William Drayton and William Izard, "Journal of a Tour by Sea and from Charleston to New York in 1786."
Library Society of Charleston: "Specifications for an Episcopal Church to Be Erected on Johns Island," folio 195.
South Carolina Historical Society: Ball Family Papers.

Charlottesville, Virginia

University of Virginia: Baylor Papers; Berkeley Family Papers; Burwell Manuscripts; Robert Carter Letterbooks; Robert Carter Papers; Cocke Papers; Jefferson Papers; Latane Papers; Pocket Plantation Papers; Joseph Prentis Garden Book; Randolph Papers; Charles Yates Letterbook, 1773–1783.

Columbia, South Carolina

Caroliniana Library, University of South Carolina: Papers of Gabriel Manigault.

Dover, Delaware

Delaware Bureau of Museums: John Dickinson Plantation Research Files.
Delaware Hall of Records: Dickinson Papers.

Durham, North Carolina

Perkins Library, Duke University: William Berkeley Papers, 1771–1800; Robert Carter Day Books and Letterbooks; Robert Carter Letterbooks; William Ellet's Arithmetic Book; Gardiner Papers; Hook Papers; Massie Papers.

Edinburgh, Scotland

Scottish National Record Office: Murraythwaite Collection.

Fairfax County, Virginia

Gunston Hall: "The Recollections of Gen. John Mason Pertaining to Gunston Hall."

Georgetown, District of Columbia

Georgetown University Library: James Carroll Day Book.

Gloucester, England

Gloucestershire Records Office: Beaufort Papers; Botetourt Papers from Badminton.

London, England

Lambeth Palace Library: Fulham Papers II; SPG Letterbook, A-B; SPG Papers.
Public Records Office: Colonial Office Papers.
Royal Society of London Archives: Boyle Papers.

Louisville, Kentucky

Filson Club: Jonathan Clark Notebook.

New York, New York

New York Public Library: William Beverley Letterbook, 1737–1744; Charles Carroll Letterbook.

Philadelphia, Pennsylvania

CIGNA Corporation Archives: INA Records.
Historical Society of Pennsylvania: Bartram Papers; Franklin Insurance Company Records.
Presbyterian Historical Society: James Madison Account Book, Shane Collection.

Raleigh, North Carolina

North Carolina Division of Archives and History: Thomas Henderson Letterbook; William Luten Ledger Book; Pattie Mordecai Papers; Thomas Pollock Letterbook; Skinner Estate Papers.

Richmond, Virginia

Virginia Historical Society: Robert Anderson Account Books; Letters of Robert Beverley, 1763–1774; Breckenridge Papers; Carter Family Papers, 1651–1861; Carter-Plummer Letterbook; Fairfax Papers; William Fitzhugh Letters; William Gooch Transcripts; Harrison Family Papers; Richard Bland Lee Occupational Papers; Ludwell-Lee Papers; Preston Papers; Tayloe Papers.

Virginia State Library: Malcolm Crawford Papers; Journal of Francis Jerdone; William Nelson Letterbook.

San Marino, California

Huntington Library: Robert Bolling Papers, Brock Collection; Charles Copeland Account Book; Jefferson Papers; Richard Henry Lee Memorandum Book.

Washington, D.C.

Library of Congress: Joseph Ball Letterbook; Compton Bassett Private Papers, Bassett Family Papers; Robert Beverley Letterbook; John Custis Letterbook, 1717–1741; James Hunt Account Book, 1775–1820; Izard Papers; Jefferson Papers; Jones Papers; Pocket Memorandum Book; Virginia Almanac, 1768; Washington Papers.

Williamsburg, Virginia

Colonial Williamsburg Foundation: James Anderson Account Book; Baylor Papers; Carter Family Papers from Shirley; Robert Carter Letterbooks; Dabney Family Papers; Joseph Freeman Papers, William Lightfoot Papers; Humphrey Harwood Ledger; Garret Minor Papers, 1776–1781; Randolph Inventory; Diary of Francis Taylor; William and Mary Research Report, Goodwin.

College of William and Mary: Armistead-Cocke Papers; Billups Papers; Cabell Papers; Francis Jerdone Account Book, 1750–1772; Skipwith Papers; Tucker Papers, Tucker-Coleman Collection; William and Mary Faculty Minutes, 1830–1836.

Wilmington, Delaware

Hagley Library: Longwood Manuscripts.

Worcester, Massachusetts

American Antiquarian Society: Diary of Robert Wormeley Carter.

STATE, COUNTY, AND CITY RECORDS

Delaware

Kent County Court Record Book, 1703–1718
Kent County Orphans Court Valuations, D-F
New Castle County Minutes of the Trustees of the Common, 1791–1869
New Castle County Orphans Court Valuations, D-I, K-O
New Castle County Tax List
New Castle County Trustees of the Poor, 1
Sussex County Orphans Court Valuations A, C-P

Maryland

Anne Arundel County Land Records Book, 1729–1730, 1737–1740, 1763–1768, 1803–1809
Anne Arundel County Prerogative Court Records, Inventories, 1718
Baltimore County Court Record Book IS
Baltimore County Land Records IS No. B
Calvert County Prerogative Court Records 40
Caroline County Court Minute Book No. 7
Charles County Court and Land Records Book, 1662–1665, 1676–1678, 1690–1692
Charles County Court Proceedings, 1668
Charles County Court Proceedings, Book 10, No. 1
Charles County Prerogative Court Records
Dorchester County Land Record Book, 1669–1683
Frederick County Land Records Book, 1767–1770
Frederick County Patents
Kent County Court Records
Maryland Patents Certificates and Warrants, 1637–1650, MSA
Maryland Prerogative Court, Inventories, MSA
Maryland Prerogative Court, Inventories and Accounts 2, MSA
Maryland Prerogative Court, Inventories and Accounts, 1716–1717, 1718, MSA
Maryland Prerogative Court Records, MSA
Maryland Prerogative Court, Wills, MSA
Maryland Provincial Court Proceedings, 1658–1662, MSA
Maryland Provincial Court Records, MSA
Maryland Testamentary Proceedings, 1666–1668, MSA
Prince George's County Record Book, 1734–1735
Queen Anne's County Deed Book, A-K
Queen Anne's County Guardian Bonds and Valuations SC
Talbot County Judgement Book, 1675–1682
Talbot County Land Records, 1692
Talbot County Land Records Book No. 12
Talbot County Land Records RF No. 12
Worcester County Orphans Court Proceedings, 1792–1797

North Carolina

Beaufort County Deed Book 1
Bertie County Court Minute Book, 1724–1739; 1740–1762
Bertie County Land Papers, 1736–1819
Bertie County New Court Actions
Capital Buildings Papers, Treasurer's and Comptroller's Papers, NCA&H
Carteret County Court of Pleas and Quarter Session Minute Book
Caswell County Court Minutes, 1823–1831
Caswell County Miscellaneous Court Records
Chowan County Accounts
Chowan County Civil Actions, 1760
Chowan County Court Minute Book, 1766–1772, 1780–1785
Chowan County Deed Book C
Chowan County Miscellaneous Court Accounts
Craven County Estate Papers
Craven County Treasurer of Public Building Accounts
Gates County, County Accounts
Gates County Miscellaneous Court Accounts
Hyde County Minute Book
Johnston County Court Minute Book, 1759–1766
Lincoln County Miscellaneous Court Papers
Northampton County Miscellaneous Court Records
North Carolina Legislative Papers, NCA&H
Onslow County Court Minute Book
Pasquotank County Accounts
Pasquotank County Miscellaneous Account
Pasquotank County Will Book, 1712–1722
Perquimans County Court Minute Book, 1755–1761
Perquimans County Deed Book A
Person County, County Accounts
Person County Miscellaneous Court Records

Randolph County Court Accounts
Secretary of State Records, NCA&H
Secretary of State Records, Chancery Proceedings and Wills, 1712–1754, NCA&H
Secretary of State Records, Council Minutes, Wills and Inventories, 1677–1701, NCA&H
Secretary of State Records, Inventories, 1728–1741, NCA&H
Secretary of State Records, Wills, NCA&H
Secretary of State Records, Wills, 1712–1722, 1722–1735, 1738–1752, NCA&H
Stokes County Miscellaneous Court Records
Wayne County Court Records
Wayne County Miscellaneous Court Records
Wilmington City Records

South Carolina

Accounts of the Public Treasurer, 1725–1730, SCA&H
Charleston City Council Ordinances
Charleston County Court Records
Charleston County Deed Book R
Charleston County Inventory Book, 1810–1818
Charleston County Inventory Book F
Charleston County Land Record Book, 1779–1781, 1787–1788
Charleston County Land Record Book, B9, R
Charleston County Will Book, 1724–1725, 1763–1767, 1776–1778, 1807–1818
Journal of the Commons House of Assembly, Nos. 34, 37, SCA&H
South Carolina General Tax Receipts and Payments, 1761–69, SCA&H
South Carolina Treasury Records, Ledger 1783–1791, SCA&H

Virginia

Accomack County Court Order Book 1666–1676, 1703–1709, 1744–1753, 1753–1763, 1774–1777, 1787–1790, 1793–1796, 1796–1798, 1798–1800, 1800–1804
Accomack County Deed, Will, and Order Book, 1663–1666
Accomack County Order and Will Book, 1671–1673
Accomack County Will, Deed, and Order Book, 1678–1682
Accomack County Will and Deed Book, 1676–1690
Accomack County Will and Order Book, 1682–1697
Alexandria Hustings Court Order Book, 1780–1787, 1796–1797
Alexandria Will Book, 1804–1807
Amelia County Court Order Book, 1735–1746, 1765–1767
Amelia County Court Minute Book, 1766–1769
Amelia County Deed Book, 1789–1791
Amelia County Loose Court Papers
Augusta County Court Judgments
Augusta County Court Order Book, 1729–1732, 1745–1747, 1748–1751, 1791–1793
Augusta County Deed Book No. 3
Bedford County Court Order Book, 1757–1758, 1763–1771, 1790–1795, 1795–1799
Bedford County Loose Court Papers, VSL
Bedford County Determined Cases, 1770
Berkeley County Will Book, 1796–1805
Brunswick County Court Order Book, 1745–1749
Caroline County Court Order Book, 1732–1740, 1740–1746, 1746–1754, 1755–1758, 1807–1809
Charles City County Court Order Book, 1656–1658, 1658–1661, 1672–1673, 1687–1695, 1823–1829
Charles City County Land Record Book, 1678–1680
Charlotte County Court Order Book, 1780–1784, 1786–1789, 1792–1794, 1797–1799

Culpeper County Court Order Book, 1798–1802, 1802–1803
Cumberland County Court Order Book, 1749–1751, 1774–1778
Elizabeth City County Court Order Book, 1731–1747, 1747–1755
Elizabeth City County Court Records, 1760–1769
Elizabeth City County Deed and Will Book, 1689–1699, 1737–1771, 1809–1818
Elizabeth City County Deed, Will, and Order Book, 1715–1721
Essex County Court Order Book, 1692–1695, 1703–1708, 1726–1729, 1738–1740, 1754–1757, 1812–1815, 1815–1817, 1821–1823
Essex County Will and Deed Book No. 10
Fairfax County Court Order Book, 1768–1770, 1770–1772
Fairfax County Deed Book, 1742–1746, 1774–1777
Fairfax County Will Book, 1742–1752, 1752–1767, 1767–1776, 1776–1782, 1783–1791
Fauquier County Court Order Book, 1759–1762, 1764–1768
Frederick County Court Order Book, 1743–1745, 1745–1748, 1748–1751, 1753–1754
Fredericksburg City Council Minute Book, 1782–1801, 1801–1829, 1829–1851
Giles County Court Order Book, 1806–1809
Goochland County Court Order Book, 1772–1778, 1797–1799, 1801–1803, 1810–1813, 1813–1819, 1825–1831
Halifax County Court Order Book, 1774–1779
Henrico County Court Order Book, 1678–1693
Henrico County Court Record Book, 1678–1693, 1688–1697
Henrico County Court Records, 1677–1692
Henrico County Deed and Will Book, 1677–1692
Henrico County Miscellaneous Court Records, 1650–1717
Henry County Court Minute Book, 1820–1827
Henry County Court Order Book, 1778–1782, 1792–1797, 1808–1811
Henry County Loose Court Papers
Isle of Wight County Court Order Book, 1747–1752
Isle of Wight County Inventory and Appraisement Book, 1726–1734
Isle of Wight County Will and Deed Book, 1662–1715
Isle of Wight County Will and Inventories Book, 1718–1729
Jefferson County Court Minute Book, 1803–1807
Jefferson County Deed Book, 1806–1808
Jefferson County Will Book, 1813–1816
King George County Court Order Book, 1721–1734, 1817–1822
King George County Deed Book, 1735–1744
King George County Inventory Book, 1721–1744
Lancaster County Court Order Book, 1652–1655, 1666–1680, 1680–1686, 1696–1702, 1702–1713, 1729–1743, 1770–1778, 1792–1799, 1799–1801, 1805–1808
Lancaster County Court Record Book, 1654–1666
Lancaster County Deed and Will Book, 1750–1758, 1758–1763
Lancaster County Deed Book, 1736–1743, 1812–1823
Lancaster County Inventory and Will Book, 1690–1709
Lancaster County Will and Deed Book, 1770–1783
Lancaster County Will and Inventory Book, 1709–1727
Loudoun County Court Order Book, 1757–1762, 1762–1765, 1765–1767, 1767–1770, 1776–1783, 1805–1806
Loudoun County Will Book, 1797–1802
Louisa County Court Order Book, 1774–1782
Lynchburg Common Council Minute Book, 1826–1838
Middlesex County Court Order Book, 1673–1680, 1680–1694, 1694–1705, 1710–1721, 1732–1737

Middlesex County Deed Book, etc., 1687–1750
Middlesex County Will Book, 1698–1713, 1713–1734, 1748–
1760, 1787–1793
Norfolk County Appraisement Book, 1755–1783, 1775–1800
Norfolk County Court Minute Book of Lower Norfolk Court
Norfolk County Court Order Book, 1710–1717, 1742–1746,
1771–1773, 1776–1779, 1786–1787, 1788–1790
Norfolk County Court Order and Will Book, 1723–1734
Norfolk County Deed Book, Nos. 9, 9A
Norfolk County Deed Book, 1637–1646, 1651–1656, 1675–
1686, 1686–1695, 1695–1703, 1733–1739, 1746–1750, 1764–
1765, 1786–1788
Norfolk County Deed and Will Book, 1666–1675, 1721–1725
Norfolk County Loose Court Papers
Norfolk County Miscellaneous Court Records, 1652–1748
Norfolk County Will and Deed Book, 1646–1651, 1651–1656,
1656–1666
Norfolk County Will Book, 1666–1675, 1755–1772, 1772–1788
Norfolk Common Hall Order Book, 1736–1798
Norfolk Hustings Court Order Book, 1788–1792, 1792–1795,
1802–1804
Northampton County Court Order Book, 1657–1664, 1664–
1674, 1689–1698, 1710–1716, 1716–1718, 1719–1722, 1729–
1732, 1777–1783, 1808–1816
Northampton County Court Order and Will Book, 1689–1698
Northampton County Deed and Will Book, 1655–1668
Northampton County Loose Court Papers
Northumberland County Court Order Book, 1652–1655, 1678–
1698, 1698–1713, 1713–1719, 1743–1749, 1749–1753, 1753–
1756, 1756–1758, 1844–1852
Northumberland County Court Record Book, 1652–1655,
1666–1672, 1710–1713, 1738–1743, 1743–1749, 1756–1758,
1766–1770, 1787–1793
Nottoway County Court Order Book, 1793–1797
Orange County Court Order Book, 1741–1743, 1747–1754,
1754–1763
Orange County Loose Court Papers
Orange County Will Book, 1744–1778
Petersburg City Council Minute Book, 1784–1811
Petersburg Deed Book No. 2
Petersburg Hustings Court Minute Book, 1791–1797
Portsmouth Town Minute Book, 1796–1821, 1822–1843
Powhatan County Loose Court Papers
Prince Edward County Court Order Book, 1754–1758, 1788–
1791, 1791–1793
Prince Edward County Will Book, 1754–1784
Prince Edward County Miscellaneous Court Papers
Prince William County Court Order Book, 1787–1791
Prince William County Deed Book, 1787–1791
Princess Anne County Court Minute Book, 1691–1709, 1717–
1728, 1737–1744, 1744–1753, 1762–1769
Princess Anne County Court Order Book, 1691–1709
Princess Anne County Deed Book, 1708–1714, 1770–1772,
1772–1773
Princess Anne County Loose Court Papers
Princess Anne County Will Book, 1795–1871
Rappahannock County Court Order Book, 1683–1686
Rappahannock County Deed Book, 1833–1835
Richmond County Account Book, 1724–1783
Richmond Common Council Minute Book, 1782–1793, 1793–
1806
Richmond County Court Order Book, 1692–1694, 1704–1708,
1711–1716, 1739–1746, 1746–1752, 1756–1762, 1769–1773,
1776–1784, 1822–1825, 1825–1832

Richmond County Miscellaneous Court Record Book
Richmond County Will Book, 1725–1753, 1753–1767, 1767–
1787
Richmond Hustings Court Order Book, 1808–1810
Richmond Hustings Deed Book, 1792–1799
Rockbridge County Court Order Book, 1778–1784
Rockbridge County Will Book 1
Rockingham County Court Order Book, 1791–1794
Russell County Court Order Book, 1813–1817
Shenandoah County Court Order Book, 1772–1774, 1795–1798,
1802–1805
Shenandoah County Will Book, 1783–1789
Southampton County Court Order Book, 1749–1754
Spotsylvania County Court Order Book, 1724–1730, 1730–1738,
1738–1749, 1749–1755, 1782–1786, 1787–1792
Spotsylvania County Will Book, 1722–1749, 1749–1759, 1772–
1798, 1798–1804, 1804–1810
Stafford County Court Order Book, 1664–1678, 1689–1693
Stafford County Will Book, 1748–1763
Staunton City Council Minute Book, 1801–1811
Surry County Court Order Book, 1671–1691, 1691–1713, 1713–
1718, 1754–1757
Surry County Deed, Order, and Will Book, 1645–1672
Surry County Deed and Will Book, 1652–1672, 1715–1730,
1783–1792
Sussex County Loose Court Papers
Virginia State Auditor's Papers, VSL
Virginia State Auditor's Papers, Vouchers 1777–1778, VSL
Westmoreland County Court Order Book, 1676–1689, 1690–
1698, 1705–1721, 1731–1739, 1739–1743, 1747–1750, 1819–
1823
Westmoreland County Deeds and Patents Book, 1665–1677
Westmoreland County Deed and Will Book, 1761–1768, 1814–
1819
Westmoreland County Deed, Will, and Patent Book, 1653–
1657
Westmoreland County Inventory Book, 1746–1752, 1752–1756
Westmoreland County Record Book, 1756–1767
Westmoreland County Records and Inventories, 1723–1746
Williamsburg Masonic Lodge Minute Book, 1773–1779
York County Claims for Losses, CWF
York County Court Judgments and Order Book, 1803–1814
York County Deed Book 1741–1754, 1755–1763, 1763–1769,
1769–1777
York County Deed, Order, and Will Book 1645–1649, 1657–
1662, 1665–1672, 1687–1691, 1691–1694, 1694–1698, 1698–
1702, 1709–1711, 1711–1714
York County Order and Will Book, 1716–1720
York County Will and Inventory Book, 1732–1740, 1745–1759,
1771–1782

CHURCH RECORDS

Georgia
Christ Church Parish, Savannah, Church Records, GHS

Maryland
All Faiths Parish, St. Mary's County, Vestry Book
All Saints Parish, Calvert County, Vestry Book
Chester Parish, Kent County, Vestry Book
Christ Church Parish, Calvert County, Vestry Book
King and Queen Parish, St. Mary's County, Vestry Book
St. Andrew's Parish, St. Mary's County, Vestry Book

St. Anne's Parish, Anne Arundel County, Vestry Book
St. George's Parish, Harford County, Vestry Book
St. James Parish, Anne Arundel County, Vestry Book
St. John's Parish, Queen Anne's County, Vestry Book
St. Luke's, Church Hill Parish, Queen Anne's County, Vestry Book
St. Paul's Parish, Kent County, Vestry Book
Third Haven Quaker Meeting, Minute Book 1
Tillotson Parish, Buckingham County, Vestry Book
Trinity Parish, Charles County, Vestry Book
William and Mary Parish, St. Mary's County, Vestry Book

North Carolina

St. Paul's Parish, Chowan County, Vestry Book
St. Paul's Parish, Edenton, Miscellaneous Vestry Papers

South Carolina

Christ Church Parish, Charleston County, Vestry Book
Congregational Church, Charleston, Record Book
Prince Frederick, Winyah Parish, Vestry Book
St. David's Parish, Craven County, Vestry Book
St. Helena's Parish, Vestry Book
St. John's, Berkeley Parish, Vestry Book
St. John's Lutheran Church, Charleston, Minute Book
St. John's Parish, Colleton County, Vestry Book
St. Michael's Parish, Charleston, Vestry Book
St. Paul's, Stono Parish, Vestry Book
St. Philip's Parish, Charleston, Vestry Book
St. Stephen's Parish, Berkeley County, Vestry Book

Virginia

Albemarle Parish, Surry County, Vestry Book
Antrim Parish, Halifax County, Vestry Book
Augusta Parish, Augusta County, Vestry Book
Blisland Parish, James City and New Kent Counties, Vestry Book
Bristol Parish, Prince George County, Vestry Book
Bruton Parish, Williamsburg, Records
Camden Parish, Pittsylvania County, Vestry Book
Chesterfield County, Baptist Church Minute Book
Christ Church Parish, Lancaster County, Vestry Book
Christ Church Parish, Middlesex County, Vestry Book
Cumberland Parish, Lunenburg County, Vestry Book
Cunningham Chapel Parish, Clarke County, Vestry Book
Dettingen Parish, Prince William County, Vestry Book
Elizabeth City Parish, Elizabeth City County, Vestry Book
Elizabeth River Parish, Norfolk County, Vestry Book
Fairfax Parish, Fairfax County, Vestry Book
Frederick Parish, Frederick County, Vestry Book
Fredericksville Parish, Louisa County, Indentures and Processioner Returns
Fredericksville Parish, Louisa County, Vestry Book
Kingston Parish, Gloucester County, Vestry Book
Lynnhaven Parish, Princess Anne County, Vestry Book
Newport Parish, Isle of Wight County, Vestry Book
Petsworth Parish, Gloucester County, Vestry Book
St. Andrew's Parish, Brunswick County, Vestry Book
St. George's Parish, Accomack County, Vestry Book
St. George's Parish, Spotsylvania County, Vestry Book
St. James, Northam Parish, Goochland County, Vestry Book
St. Mark's Parish, Culpeper County, Vestry Book
St. Mark's Parish, Cumberland County, Vestry Book
St. Patrick's Parish, Prince Edward County, Vestry Book
St. Paul's Parish, Hanover County, Vestry Book

St. Peter's Parish, New Kent County, Vestry Book
Shelburne Parish, Loudoun County, Vestry Book
Southam Parish, Cumberland County, Vestry Book
Stratton Major Parish, King and Queen County, Vestry Book
Suffolk Parish, Nansemond County, Vestry Book
Tillotson Parish, Buckingham County, Vestry Book
Truro Parish, Fairfax County, Vestry Book
Upper Parish, Nansemond County, Vestry Book
Wicomico Parish, Northumberland County, Vestry Book

NEWSPAPERS AND JOURNALS

Alexandria Advertiser and Commercial Intelligencer
Alexandria *Columbian Mirror and Alexandria Gazette*
Alexandria Daily Advertiser
Alexandria Daily Gazette, Commercial and Political
Alexandria Expositor, and the Columbian Advertiser
Alexandria Gazette
Alexandria Gazette and Daily Advertiser
Alexandria Herald
The Times. Alexandria Advertiser
The Times; and District of Columbia Daily Advertiser
The Virginia Gazette and Alexandria Advertiser
Virginia Journal and Alexandria Advertiser
Annapolis *Maryland Gazette*
Athens *Georgia Express*
Augusta Chronicle
Augusta Herald
The Augusta Chronicle and Gazette of the State
Baltimore *American and Commercial Daily Advertiser*
Baltimore *American Farmer*
Baltimore Daily Intelligencer
Baltimore Daily Repository
Baltimore Evening Post
Baltimore Evening Post and Daily Advertiser
Federal Gazette and Baltimore Daily Advertiser
Federal Republican and Baltimore Telegraph
Maryland Gazette: or, the Baltimore Advertiser
Maryland Journal and Baltimore Advertiser
Baltimore *The Telegraphe and Daily Advertiser*
Baltimore Whig
Boston *The Massachusetts Gazette*
Camden Gazette and Mercantile Advertiser
Charleston *The Carolina Gazette*
Charleston *City Gazette*
Charleston *City Gazette and Commercial Advertiser*
Charleston *The City Gazette, and the Daily Advertiser*
Charleston *The City Gazette and Daily Advertiser*
Charleston *The City Gazette, or the Daily Advertiser*
Charleston *Columbian Herald*
Charleston Courier
Charleston *The Gazette, of the State of South-Carolina*
Charleston Morning Post and Daily Advertiser
Charleston *South Carolina and American General Gazette*
Charleston *South Carolina Gazette*
Charleston *South Carolina Gazette and Country Journal*
Charleston *The South-Carolina Gazette, and Public Advertiser*
Charleston *South-Carolina State Gazette and Timothy & Mason's Daily Advertiser*
Charleston *The Times*
Charleston *State Gazette of South-Carolina*
Charlestown Gazette
Charlestown, Va., *Farmer's Repository*

Columbia, S.C., *The Telescope*
Darien Gazette
Easton *Maryland Herald and Eastern Shore Intelligencer*
Easton *The Republican Star and Eastern Shore General Advertiser*
Easton, Md., *Republican Star and General Advertiser*
Easton, Md., *The Republican Star or Eastern Shore General Advertiser*
Edenton, N.C., *Encyclopedian Instructor and Farmer's Gazette*
Fayetteville *Carolina Observer*
Fayetteville Gazette
The North-Carolina Minerva, and Fayetteville Advertiser
Fredericksburg *Political Arena*
Fredericksburg *The Virginia Herald*
The Virginia Herald and Fredericksburg Advertiser
Frederick-Town Herald
Fredericktown, Md., *Star of Federalism*
Georgetown, S.C., *Winyaw Intelligencer*
The Maryland Herald, and Hager's-Town Weekly Advertiser
Halifax *North Carolina Journal*
Leesburg *Genius of Liberty*
Lexington *Kentucky Gazette*
Lexington *Kentucky Gazette and General Advertiser*
Lexington, Ky., *The Reporter*
London Magazine
Louisville, Ky., *Western Courier*
Lynchburg Press
Lynchburg Press and Public Advertiser
Milledgeville *Georgia Journal*
Nashville *The Clarion and Tennessee Gazette*
Nashville *The Democratic Clarion and Tennessee Gazette*
Nashville *The Impartial Review and Cumberland Repository*
The Nashville Whig
Newbern Gazette
Newbern Herald
New Bern *North Carolina Gazette*
New York Daily Advertiser
New York Gazette, revived in the Weekly Post-Boy
American Beacon and Norfolk and Portsmouth Daily Advertiser
Norfolk *American Beacon and Commercial Diary*
Norfolk Gazette and Publick Ledger
Norfolk Herald
Virginia Chronicle and Norfolk and Portsmouth General Advertiser
Virginia Gazette, or Norfolk Intelligencer
Petersburg Intelligencer
The Intelligencer, and Petersburg Commercial Advertiser
Virginia Gazette and Petersburg Intelligencer
Philadelphia *The Pennsylvania Gazette*
Raleigh *The Minerva*
Raleigh Register
Raleigh Register, and North-Carolina Gazette
Raleigh Star
Raleigh *The Star*
Raleigh *The Star, and North-Carolina State Gazette*
Richmond and Manchester Advertiser
Richmond Commercial Compiler
Richmond Enquirer
Richmond *The Enquirer*
Richmond *The Observatory*
Richmond *Virginia Argus*
Richmond *The Virginia Gazette, and General Advertiser*
The Virginia Gazette. And Richmond and Manchester Advertiser
Richmond *Virginia Gazette and Weekly Advertiser*
Richmond *Virginia Gazette, or, the American Advertiser*
Richmond *The Virginia Independent Chronicle*

The North-Carolina Mercury, and Salisbury Advertiser
Columbian Museum and Savannah Advertiser
Savannah *Gazette of the State of Georgia*
Savannah *Georgia Gazette*
Savannah *Georgia Republican and State Intelligencer*
Savannah *Public Intelligencer*
The Savannah Republican
The Republican and Savannah Evening Ledger
City of Washington Gazette
Washington, D.C., *Daily National Intelligencer*
Washington Spy
Washington, Ga., *The Monitor*
Washington, Ga., *The News*
Williamsburg *Virginia Gazette*
Wilmington, N.C., *Cape Fear Recorder*
Wilmington, N.C., *The True Republican, or American Whig*
The Wilmington Centinel and General Advertiser
Wilmington Gazette

BOOKS, ARTICLES, AND UNPUBLISHED SOURCES

Abdy, Edward Strutt. *Journal of a Residence and Tour in the United States of North America, from April, 1833, to October, 1834.* 2 vols. London: J. Murray, 1835.

Aheron, John. *General Treatise of Architecture.* Dublin: Printed for the author by J. Butler, 1754.

Anburey, Thomas. *Travels through the Interior Parts of America.* 2 vols. New York: New York Times, 1969.

Archives of Maryland. 72 vols. Edited by William Hand Browne, Clayton Colman Hall, and Bernard Christian Steiner. Baltimore: Maryland Historical Society, 1883–1972.

Attmore, William. *Journal of a Tour to North Carolina* (1787). Edited by Lida Tunstall Rodman. The James Sprunt Historical Publications, vol. 17, no. 2. Chapel Hill: University of North Carolina, 1922.

Baily, Francis. *Journal of a Tour in Unsettled Parts of North America, in 1796 and 1797.* Edited by Jack D. L. Holmes. Carbondale: Southern Illinois University, 1969.

Banister, John. *John Banister and his Natural History of Virginia.* Edited by Joseph and Nesta Ewan. Urbana: University of Illinois Press, 1970.

Bartram, William. *Travels through North and South Carolina, Georgia, East and West Florida.* Savannah: Beehive Press, 1973.

[Beaufoy]. *Tour through Part of the United States and Canada. By a British Subject.* London: Longman, 1828.

Benjamin, Asher. *Architect, or, Practical House Carpenter.* New York: Dover Publications, 1988.

Bennett, William Wallace. *Memorials of Methodism in Virginia.* Richmond: author, 1871.

"Bernard Family." *William and Mary Quarterly*, 1st ser., 5 (Jul. 1986).

Beverley, Robert. *History and Present State of Virginia: A Selection.* Indianapolis: Bobbs-Merrill, 1971.

Birket, James. *Some Cursory Remarks Made by James Birket in His Voyage to North America, 1750–1751.* New Haven: Yale University Press, 1916.

Builder's Dictionary, or, Gentleman and Architect's Companion. 2 vols. London: 1734. Washington, D.C.: Association for Preservation Technology, 1981.

Burnaby, Reverend Andrew. *Travels through the Middle Settlements in North America in the Years 1759 and 1760, with Observations on the State of the Colonies.* Ithaca, NY: Great Seal Books, 1960.

Burt, Henry M. *The First Century of the History of Springfield: The Official Records from 1636 to 1736.* 2 vols. Springfield, Mass.: author, 1898–1899.

Byrd, William. *History of the Dividing Line and Other Tracts.* 2 vols. T. H. Wynne, ed. Richmond: 1866.

Byrd, William. *A Journey to the Land of Eden and Other Papers.* New York: Macy-Masius, 1928.

Byrd, William. *Secret Diary of William Byrd of Westover, 1709–1712.* Edited by Louis B. Wright and Marion Tinling. Richmond, Va.: The Dietz Press, 1941.

Caldwell, John Edwards. *A Tour through Part of Virginia in the Summer of 1808, also Some Account of the Islands of the Azores.* Edited by William M. E. Rachal. Richmond: Dietz Press, 1951.

Calendar of Virginia State Papers and other Manuscripts . . . Preserved in the Capitol at Richmond. 11 vols. Edited by William P. Palmer, et al. New York: Kraus Reprint Corp., 1968.

Calvert, Rosalie Stier. *Mistress of Riversdale: The Plantation Letters of Rosalie Stier Calvert, 1795–1821.* Edited by Margaret Law Callcott. Baltimore: Johns Hopkins University Press, 1991.

Candee, Richard. *Building Portsmouth: The Neighborhoods and Architecture of New Hampshire's Oldest City.* Portsmouth, N.H.: Portsmouth Advocates, Inc., 1992

Carter, Landon. *Diary of Colonel Landon Carter of Sabine Hall, 1752–1778.* 2 vols. Edited by Jack P. Greene. Charlottesville: University Press of Virginia for the Virginia Historical Society, 1965.

Carter, Robert. *Letters of Robert Carter, 1720–1727: The Commercial Interests of a Virginia Gentleman.* Edited by Louis B. Wright. San Marino, Calif.: The Huntington Library, 1940.

Castiglioni, Luigi. *Travels in the United States of North America, 1785–87.* Edited and translated by Antonio Pace. Syracuse, N.Y.: Syracuse University Press, 1983.

Chastellux, François Jean, Marquis. *Travels in North America: In the Years 1780, 1781 and 1782.* Edited and translated by Howard C. Rice, Jr. Chapel Hill: Published for the Institute of Early American History and Culture at Williamsburg, Va., by the University of North Carolina Press, 1963.

Christensen, John, and Charles Bohl. *McDowell Hall at St. John's College in Annapolis.* Annapolis: St. John's College Press, 1989.

"Church Building in Colonial Virginia." *Virginia Magazine of History and Biography* 3 (Apr. 1896).

Clitherall, Eliza Caroline Burgwin. *Autobiography and Diary of Mrs. Eliza Clitherall.* Vol. 2. Archives of the Lower Cape Fear Historical Society, Wilmington, North Carolina.

Colonial Panorama 1775: Dr. Robert Honyman's Journal for March and April. Edited by Philip Padelford. San Marino, Calif.: The Huntington Library, 1939.

Colonial Records of the State of Georgia. 25 vols. Edited by Allen Candler. Atlanta: Franklin Print and Publishing Company, 1904–1916.

Colonial Records of the State of Georgia. Vols. 20, 27–28. Edited by Kenneth Coleman and Milton Ready. Athens: University of Georgia Press, 1976–1984.

Colonial Records of the State of North Carolina. 10 vols. Edited by William L. Saunders. Raleigh: State of North Carolina, 1886–1890.

Conway, Moncure Daniel. "George Washington and Mount Vernon." *Memoirs of the Long Island Historical Society* 4 (1889).

Cooper, Thomas. *Some Information Respecting America.* London: Printed for J. Johnson, 1795.

Correspondence of Three William Byrds of Westover. Edited by Marion Tinling. Charlottesville: for the Virginia Historical Society by the University Press of Virginia, 1977.

"Correspondence Relating to Lord Botetourt." *Tyler's Quarterly Magazine* 3 (Jul. 1921).

County Court Records of Accomack-Northampton, Virginia, 1632–1640. Edited by Susie May Ames. Washington, D.C.: The American Historical Association, 1954.

County Court Records of Accomack-Northampton, Virginia, 1640–1645. Edited by Susie May Ames. Charlottesville: University Press of Virginia for the Virginia Historical Society, 1973.

Cresswell, Nicholas. *The Journal of Nicholas Cresswell, 1774–1777.* New York: Dial Press, 1928.

"The Diary of Frances Baylor Hill of Hillsborough, King and Queen County, Va." Edited by William K. Bottorff and Roy C. Flanagan. *Early American Literature Newsletter* 2 (Winter, 1967).

"The Diary of Mary Ambler, 1770." *Virginia Magazine of History and Biography* 45 (Apr. 1937).

Documents Relating to the Colonial, Revolutionary, and Post-Revolutionary History of the State of New Jersey. 42 vols. Newark: for the New Jersey Historical Society, 1880–1949.

Dorrington, Edward. *The Hermit, or, The Unparalled Sufferings and Surprising Adventures of Mr. Philip Quarll, an Englishman.* Westminster: T. Warner & B. Creake, 1727.

Dossie, Robert. *A Handmaid to the Arts.* 2 vols. London: Printed for J. Norse, 1758.

Douglass, Frederick. *My Bondage and My Freedom.* Edited by William L. Andrews. Urbana: University of Illinois Press, 1987.

Durand. *A Huguenot Exile in Virginia, or, Voyages of a Frenchman Exiled for His Religion, with a Description of Virginia and Maryland.* Edited by Gilbert Chinard. New York: The Press of the Pioneers, 1934.

"The Dwelling House on the Glebe Land in the Parish of St. Patrick in Prince Edward County." *William and Mary Quarterly*, 2d ser., 17 (Jul. 1937).

"Early Settlement of the Ohio Valley: Letters from Capt. Laurence Butler to Mrs. Joseph Cradock." *Magazine of American History* 1 (Jan. 1877).

Ecclesiastical Records of the State of New York, 1726–1736. Vol. 4. Albany: J. B. Lyon Company, 1902.

Eddis, William. *Letters from America.* Edited by Aubrey C. Land. Cambridge: Belknap Press of Harvard University Press, 1969.

Egmont, John Perceval. *The Journal of the Earl of Egmont: Abstract of the Trustees Proceedings for Establishing the Colony of Georgia, 1732–1738.* Edited by Robert G. McPherson. Athens: University of Georgia Press, 1962.

Enys, John. *American Journal of Lt. John Enys.* Edited by Elizabeth Cometti. Blue Mountain Lake, N.Y.: Adirondack Museum, 1976.

Executive Journals of the Council of Colonial Virginia, 1600–1775. 6 vols. Edited by H. R. McIlwaine. Richmond: D. Bottom, superintendent of public printing; Virginia State Library, 1925.

Faux, William. *Memorable Days in America, Being a Journal of a Tour to the United States.* London: W. Simpkin and R. Marshall, 1823.

Fessenden, Thomas. *The Register of the Arts.* Philadelphia: C. and A. Conrad & Company, 1808.

Finlay, Hugh. *Hugh Finlay Journal: A Colonial Postal History, 1773–1774.* U.S. Philatelic Classics Society, 1975.

Fisher, Sidney George. *Mount Harmon Diaries of Sidney George Fisher.* Edited by W. Emerson Wilson. Wilmington, Delaware: The Historical Society of Delaware, 1976.

Fithian, Philip Vickers. *Journal and Letters of Philip Vickers Fithian, 1773–1774: A Plantation Tutor of the Old Dominion.* Edited by Hunter Dickinson Farish. Williamsburg: Colonial Williamsburg, 1957.

Fitzhugh, William. *William Fitzhugh and His Chesapeake World, 1676–1701.* Edited by Richard Beale Davis. Chapel Hill: Published for the Virginia Historical Society by the University of North Carolina Press, 1963.

Fontaine, James. *Memoirs of a Huguenot Family.* Edited and translated by Ann Maury. Baltimore: Genealogical Publishing Company, 1967.

Forman, Martha Ogle. *Plantation Life at Rose Hill: The Diaries of Martha Ogle Forman, 1814–1845.* Edited by W. Emerson Wilson. Wilmington, Del.: The Historical Society of Delaware, 1976.

Foster, Augustus John. *Jeffersonian America: Notes on the United States of America Collected in the Years 1805–6–7 and 11–12.* Edited by Richard Beale Davis. San Marino, Calif.: The Huntington Library, 1954.

Gardiner, John, and David Hepburn. *The American Gardener.* Washington, D.C.: Samuel Smith, 1804.

Galt, John. *Lawrie Todd, or, The Settlers in the Woods.* 2 vols. New York: J & J Harper, printers, 1830.

Gerry, Elbridge, Jr. *Diary of Elbridge Gerry, Jr.* Edited by Claude Gernade Bowers. New York: Brentano's, 1927.

Gordon, Peter. *The Journal of Peter Gordon, 1732–1735.* Athens: University of Georgia Press, 1963.

Grove, William Hugh. "Virginia in 1732: The Travel Journal of William Hugh Grove." Edited by Gregory A. Stiverson and Patrick H. Butler III. *Virginia Magazine of History and Biography* 85 (Jan. 1977).

Halfpenny, William, and John Halfpenny. *Rural Architecture in the Chinese Taste.* London: Printed for R. Sayer, 1752.

Hall, Basil. *Travels in North America, in the Years 1827 and 1828.* Philadelphia: Carey, Lea & Carey, 1829.

Hall, Margaret Hunter. *The Aristocratic Journey, Being the Outspoken Letters of Mrs. Basil Written during a Fourteen Months' Sojourn in America, 1827–28.* Edited by Una Pope-Hennessy. New York: G. P. Putnam, 1931.

Hamilton, Alexander. *Gentleman's Progress: The Itinerarium of Dr. Alexander Hamilton, 1774.* Edited by Carl Bridenbaugh. Chapel Hill: University of North Carolina Press for the Institute of Early American History and Culture, 1948.

Hammond, John. *Leah and Rachel or the Two Fruitful Sisters Virginia and Maryland.* London: 1656.

Harris, Thaddeus M. *Journal of a Tour into the Territory Northwest of the Alleghany Mountains.* Boston: 1803.

Hazard, Ebenezer. "The Journal of Ebenezer Hazard in Virginia, 1777." Edited by Fred Shelley. *Virginia Magazine of History and Biography* 62 (Oct. 1954).

Hening, William Waller. *Statutes at Large, Being a Collection of All the Laws of Virginia, from the First Session of the Legislature in the Year 1619.* 13 vols. New York: Printed for the editor, 1819–1823.

Hening, William Waller. *Statutes at Large of Virginia, from October session 1792, to December session 1806 inclusive, in three volumes (new series), being a continuation of Hening. By Samuel Sheperd.* 3 vols. New York: AMS Press, 1970.

Hodgson, Adam. *Remarks during a Journey through North America.* New York: J. Seymour, Printer, 1823.

Honyman, Robert. "News of the Yorktown Campaign: The Journal of Dr. Robert Honyman, April 17–November 25,

1781." Edited by Richard K. MacMaster. *Virginia Magazine of History and Biography* 79 (Oct. 1971).

Hood, Graham. *Inventories of Four Eighteenth-Century Houses in the Historic Area of Williamsburg.* Williamsburg, Va.: Colonial Williamsburg Foundation, 1974.

Horry, Harriet Pinckney. *A Colonial Plantation Cookbook: The Receipt Book of Harriet Pinckney Horry, 1770.* Edited by Richard J. Hooker. Columbia, S.C.: University of South Carolina Press, 1984.

Huger Smith, Alice, and D. E. Huger Smith. *The Dwelling Houses of Charleston, South Carolina.* New York: Diadem Books, 1947.

Iredell, James. *Papers of James Iredell.* 2 vols. Edited by Don Higginbotham. Raleigh, N.C.: Division of Archives and History, Department of Cultural Resources, 1976.

Jefferson, Thomas. *Notes on the State of Virginia.* Philadelphia: Printed and sold by Prichard and Hall, 1788.

Jefferson, Thomas. *Thomas Jefferson's Farm Book: With Commentary and Relevant Extracts from Other Writings.* Edited by Edwin Morris Betts. Charlottesville: University Press of Virginia, 1987.

Jefferson, Thomas. *Thomas Jefferson's Garden Book.* Edited by Edwin Morris Betts. Philadelphia: The American Philosophical Society, 1944.

Jefferson, Thomas. *The Writings of Thomas Jefferson, 1743–1826.* 20 vols. Edited by Andrew A. Lipscomb and Albert E. Bergh. Washington D.C.: Issued under the auspices of the Thomas Jefferson Memorial Association of the United States, 1903–1904.

Jillson, Willard Rouse. *Tales of the Dark and Bloody Ground: A Group of Fifteen Original Papers on the Early History of Kentucky.* Louisville: Dearing Printing Co., 1930.

Jones, Hugh. *Present State of Virginia: From whence is Inferred a Short View of Maryland and North Carolina.* Edited by Richard L. Morton. Chapel Hill: Published for Virginia Historical Society by University of North Carolina Press, 1956.

"Journal of Josiah Quincy, Junior, 1773." Edited by Mark A. DeWolfe. *Proceedings of the Massachusetts Historical Society* 49 (1915–1916).

Journals of the House of Burgesses, 1619–1776. 13 vols. Edited by H. R. McIlwaine and John Pendleton Kennedy. Richmond: The Colonial Press, E. Waddey Co.: 1905–1915.

Keith, George. *A Journal of Travels from New-Hampshire to Caratuck on the Continent of North-America.* London: Printed by Joseph Downing for Brab. Aylmer, 1706.

Kennedy, John Pendleton. *Swallow Barn, or, A Sojourn to the Old Dominion.* Philadelphia: Lippincott, 1860.

Kimball, Fiske. *Thomas Jefferson, Architect: Original Designs in the Coolidge Collection of the Massachusetts Historical Society.* New York: DaCapo Press, 1968.

Lambeth, W. A., and Warren H. Manning. *Thomas Jefferson as an Architect and a Designer of Landscapes.* Boston: Houghton Mifflin Co., 1913.

Latrobe, Benjamin Henry. *The Correspondence and Miscellaneous Papers of Benjamin Henry Latrobe.* 2 vols. Edited by John C. Van Horne and Lee W. Formwalt. New Haven: Yale University Press for the Maryland Historical Society, 1984.

Latrobe, Benjamin Henry. *Virginia Journals of Benjamin Henry Latrobe, 1795–1798.* 2 vols. Edited by Edward C. Carter II. New Haven: Yale University Press for the Maryland Historical Society, 1977.

Latrobe, John H. B. *John H. B. Latrobe and His Times, 1803–1891.* Edited by John Semmes. Baltimore, Md.: The Norman, Remington Co., 1917.

Laurens, Henry. *Papers of Henry Laurens.* 9 vols. Edited by Philip M. Hamer, G.C. Rogers, Jr., and D. R. Chesnutt. Columbia: University of South Carolina Press for the South Carolina Historical Society, 1968–1980.

Lawson, John. *A New Voyage to Carolina.* Edited by Hugh Talmadge Lefler. Chapel Hill: University of North Carolina Press, 1967.

Le Jau, Francis. *Carolina Chronicle, 1706–1717.* Edited by Frank J. Klingberg. Berkeley: University of California Press, 1956.

"Letter of Col. John Banister, of Petersburg to Robert Bolling." *William and Mary Quarterly* 1st ser., 10 (Oct. 1901).

Leybourn, William. *Platform Guide Mate for Purchasers, Builders, Measurers.* 3 vols. London: Thomas Ratcliffe and Thomas Daniel, 1667–1668.

Lockwood, Alice B. *Gardens of Colony and State.* 2 vols. New York: Charles Scribner and Sons, 1931.

Logan, Martha Daniell. *The South-Carolina Almanack, for the Year of Our Lord 1756 with Directions for Managing a Kitchen-Garden Every Month in the Year. Done by a Lady.* Charleston, South Carolina, 1756.

"Lower Norfolk County Records, 1636–1646." *Virginia Magazine of History and Biography* 39 (Jan. 1931), 41 (Oct. 1933).

Martin, William. *The Journal of William D. Martin: A Journey from South Carolina to Connecticut in the Year 1809.* Charlotte, North Carolina: Heritage House, 1950.

McCoy, Elizabeth Francenia. *Early Wilmington Block by Block from 1783 On.* Wilmington, NC, 1805.

Millegen Johnston, George. *A Short Description of the Province of South-Carolina with an Account of the Air, Weather, and Diseases, at Charles-town.* London: Printed for J. Hinton, 1770.

"Minutes of the Council of General Court in Virginia, 1622–1629." *Virginia Magazine of History and Biography* 19 (Apr. 1911), 26 (Oct. 1918), 30 (Jan. 1922).

Mitchell, Elisha. *Diary of a Geology Tour by Dr. Elisha Mitchell in 1827 and 1828.* Edited by Kemp Battle. James Sprunt Historical Monograph, no. 6. Chapel Hill: University of North Carolina Press, 1905.

M'Mahon, Bernard. *American Gardener's Calendar.* Philadelphia: Printed by B. Graves for the author, 1806.

Moreau de Saint-Mery, M. L. E. *Moreau de St. Mery's American Journey, 1793–1798.* Edited and translated by Kenneth Roberts and Anna Roberts. Garden City, N.Y.: Doubleday and Co., Inc., 1947.

Morse, Jedidiah. *American Geography, or, The Present Situation of the United States of America.* London: printed for J. Stockdale, 1794.

Moxon, Joseph. *Mechanick Exercises, or, The Doctrine of Handyworks.* London: 1703. Scarsdale, N.Y.: Early American Industries Association, 1979.

M'Robert, Patrick. *A Tour through Part of the Northern Provinces of America.* Philadelphia: Historical Society of Pennsylvania, 1935.

Muhlenberg, Henry Melchior. *The Journals of Henry Melchior Muhlenberg.* 3 vols. Translated by Theodore G. Tappert and John W. Doberstein. Philadelphia: Evangelical Lutheran Ministerium of Pennsylvania and Adjacent States, 1942–1958.

Muller, John. *Treatise Containing the Elementary Part of Fortification, Regular and Irregular.* London: reprinted for C. Nourse, 1782.

Munford, William. *Poems, and Compositions in Prose on Several Occasions.* Richmond: Samuel Pleasants, Jr., 1798.

Narratives of Colonial America, 1704–1765. Edited by Howard Henry Peckham. Chicago: R.R. Donnelley, 1971.

Neve, Richard. *City and Country Purchaser, and Builder's Dictionary.* London: J. Nutt, 1703.

Nichols, Frederick Doveton, and Ralph E. Griswold. *Thomas Jefferson, Landscape Architect.* Charlottesville: University Press of Virginia, 1978.

North Carolina Higher-Court Records. 6 vols. Edited by Mattie Erma Parker (vols. 1–3), William L. Price, Jr. (vols. 4–5), and Robert J. Cain (vol. 6). In *Colonial Records of North Carolina,* 2d ser. Raleigh, N.C.: State Department of Archives and History, 1968–1981.

Norton, John, and Sons. *John Norton and Sons, Merchants of London and Virginia, Being the Papers from their Counting House for the Years 1750 to 1795.* Edited by Francis Norton Mason. New York: A. M. Kelley, 1968.

Nott, John. *The Cooks and Confectioners Dictionary* (1926). Reprinted with introduction and glossary by Elizabeth David. London: Lawrence Rivington, 1980.

Oldmixon, John. *British Empire in America* (1741). Reprint, New York: A. M. Kelley, 1969.

Oliver, William. *Eight Months in Illinois.* Ann Arbor: University Microfilms, 1966.

A Perfect Description of Virginia. London: 1649.

Perry, William Stevens. *Historical Collections Relating to the American Colonial Church.* 5 vols. New York: AMS Press, 1969.

Pilmore, Joseph. *Journal of Joseph Pilmore Methodist Itinerant, for the Years August 1, 1769 to January 2, 1774.* Edited by Frederick E. Maser and Howard T. Maag. Philadelphia: Message Publishing Company for the Historical Society of the Philadelphia Annual Conference of the United Methodist Church, 1969.

Pinckney, Eliza Lucas. *Letterbook of Eliza Lucas Pinckney, 1739–1762.* Edited by Elise Pinckney. Chapel Hill: University of North Carolina Press, 1972.

"Pleasants Murphy's Journal and Day Book." *William and Mary Quarterly,* 2d ser., 3 (Oct. 1923).

Radoff, Morris Leon. *Buildings of the State of Maryland at Annapolis.* Annapolis: Hall of Records Commission, 1954.

Randall, Henry Stephens. *The Life of Thomas Jefferson.* 3 vols. New York: Derby and Jackson, 1858.

Randolph, Mary. *The Virginia Housewife, or, Methodical Cook.* Philadelphia: E. H. Butler & Co., 1856.

Records of the Courts of Sussex County Delaware, 1677–1710. 2 vols. Edited by Craig W. Horle. Philadelphia: University of Pennsylvania Press, 1991.

Records of the Town of Braintree, 1640–1743. Edited by Samuel A. Bates. Randolph, Mass.: Daniel Huxford, Printer, 1896.

Records of the Virginia Company of London. 4 vols. Edited by Susan Myra Kingsbury. Washington, D.C.: GPO, 1906–1935.

Reynolds, Hezekiah. *Directions for House and Ship Painting.* Edited by Richard M. Candee. Worcester, Mass.: American Antiquarian Society, 1978.

Ridout, Orlando. *Building the Octagon.* Washington, D.C.: American Institute of Architects Press, 1989.

Rivoire, J. Richard. *Homeplaces: Traditional Domestic Architecture of Charles County, Maryland.* La Plata, Md.: Southern Maryland Studies Center, Charles County Community College, 1990.

Rose, Robert. *Diary of Robert Rose: A View of Virginia by a Scottish Colonial Parson, 1746–1751.* Edited by Ralph Emmett Fall. Verona, Va.: McClure Press, 1977.

Royall, Anne Newport. *Mrs. Royall's Southern Tour, or, Second Series of the Black Book.* 3 vols. Washington: 1830–1831.

Salley, A. S., Jr., ed. *Narratives of Early Carolina, 1650–1708.* New York: Barnes and Noble, 1967.

Salmon, William. *Palladio Londinensis, or, The London Art of Building.* London: 1755.

Schoepf, Johann David. *Travels in the Confederation, 1783–1784.* 2 vols. Translated and edited by Alfred J. Morrison. New York: B. Franklin, 1968. (Reise durch einige der mittlern und sudlichen Vereinigten Nordamerikanischen Staaten).

Shippen, Thomas Lee. *Westover Described in 1783: A Letter and Drawing Sent by Thomas Lee Shippen to His Parents in Philadelphia.* Richmond, Va.: William Byrd Press, 1952.

Smith, John. *The Art of Painting in Oyl.* London: Printed for A. Bettesworth, 1723.

Smith, John. *Complete Works of Captain John Smith.* 3 vols. Edited by Philip L. Barbour. Chapel Hill: University of North Carolina Press for the Institute of Early American History and Culture, 1986.

"Some Notes on he Four Forms of the Oldest Building of William and Mary College." Edited by E. G. Swem. *William and Mary Quarterly,* 2d ser., 8 (Oct. 1928).

Stalker, John, and George Parker. *Treatise of Japanning and Varnishing.* London: Alec Tiranti, 1971.

The State Records of North Carolina. 16 vols. (numbered 11–26). Edited by Walter Clark. Winston and Goldsboro: State of North Carolina, 1895–1906.

Stephens, William. *The Journal of William Stephens, 1743–1745.* Edited by Merton Coulter. Athens: University of Georgia Press, 1959.

Swan, Abraham. *The British Architect.* New York: Da Capo Press, 1967.

Sweeney, John A. H. *Grandeur on the Appoquinimink: The House of William Corbit at Odessa, Delaware.* Newark: University of Delaware Press, 1959.

Tailfer, Patrick. *True and Historical Narrative of the Colony of Georgia, by Pat. Tailfer and others. With Comments by the Earl of Egmont.* Edited by Clarence L. Ver Steeg, ed. Athens: University of Georgia Press, 1960.

Tatham, William. *Historical and Practical Essay on the Culture and Commerce of Tobacco.* London: Printed for Vernor & Hood, 1800.

Thatcher, James. *Military Journal of the American Revolution.* New York: New York Times, 1969.

Thomas Rasberry Letterbook, 1758–1761. Edited by Lilla Mill Hawes. In *Collections of the Georgia Historical Society* 13. Savannah: Georgia Historical Society, 1959.

"A Topographical Description of the County of Prince George in Virginia, 1793." In *The Collections of the Massachusetts Historical Society,* vol. 3 (1794).

Torrence, Clayton. *Old Somerset on the Eastern Shore of Maryland: A Study in Foundations and Founders.* Richmond, Va.: Whittet & Shepperson, 1935.

Touart, Paul Baker. *Somerset: An Architectural History.* Annapolis, Md.: Somerset County Historical Trust, 1990.

Toulmin, Harry. *Western Country in 1793: Reports on Kentucky and Virginia.* Edited by Marion Tinling and Godfrey Davies. San Marino, Calif.: Huntington Library, 1948.

Travels in the American Colonies. Edited by Newton Dennison Mereness. New York: Macmillan Company, 1916.

Trostel, Michael F. *Mount Clare, Being an Account of the Seat Built by Charles Carroll, Barrister, upon His Lands at Patapsco.* Baltimore: National Society of the Colonial Dames of America in the State of Maryland, 1981.

Tryon, William. *Correspondence of William Tryon and Other Selected Papers.* Edited by William S. Powell. Raleigh: Division of Archives and History, Department of Cultural Resources, 1980–1981.

Twining, Thomas. *Travels in America 100 Years Ago.* New York: Harper and Brothers, 1894.

Verral, William. *A Complete System of Cookery.* London: 1759. Reprinted as *The Cook's Paradise.* Introduction and appendices by R. L. Megroz. London: Sylvan Press, 1948.

Voyage to Virginia in 1609: Two Narratives, Strachey's "True Reportary" and Jourdain's Discovery of the Bermudas. Edited by Louis B. Wright. Charlottesville: Association for the Preservation of Virginia Antiquities by University Press of Virginia, 1964.

Wansey, Henry. *Henry Wansey and His American Journal, 1794.* Edited by David John Jeremy. Philadelphia: America Philosophical Society, 1970.

Ware, Isaac. *A Complete Body of Architecture, Adorned with Plans and Elevations from Original Designs.* London: T. Osborne and J. Shipton, 1756.

Warner and Hanna's Baltimore City Directory. Baltimore: 1801.

Washington, George. *The Diaries of George Washington.* 4 vols. Edited by John C. Fitzpatrick. New York: Houghton Mifflin Company, 1925.

Washington, George. *The Writings of George Washington from the Original Manuscript Sources, 1745–1799.* 39 vols. Edited by John C. Fitzpatrick. Washington: United States Government Print Office, 1931–1944.

Watkins, C. Malcolm. *Cultural History of Marlborough, Virginia.* Washington, D.C.: Smithsonian Institution Press, 1968.

Weld, Isaac. *Travels through the States of North America.* 2 vols. Edited by Martin Roth. New York: Johnson Reprint Corp., 1968.

Williams, George. *St. Michael's, Charleston, 1751–1951.* Columbia: University of South Carolina Press, 1951.

Woodmason, Charles. *The Carolina Backcountry on the Eve of the Revolution: The Journal and Other Writings of Charles Woodman, Anglican Itinerant.* Edited by Richard J. Hooker. Chapel Hill: for the Institute of Early American History and Culture at Williamsburg, Va., by the University of North Carolina Press, 1953.

Ye Countie of Albemarle in Carolina: A Collection of Documents, 1664–1675. Edited by William Stevens Powell. Raleigh: State Department of Archives and History, 1958.

Yetman, Norman R. *Life under the "Peculiar Institution": Selections from the Slave Narrative Collection.* New York: Holt, Rinehart, and Winston, 1970.

CREDITS

abacus Photograph no. CWF 92-CRL-965, 26A
acanthus Photograph no. CWF 92-CRL-337, 9s
air hole Photograph no. CWF 82-EAC-82-5318s
altarpiece Batty Langley, *City and Country Builder's and Workman's Treasury of Designs*, London, 1740, plate CX. No. 91-1603, CN
annulet Photograph no. CWF 92-CRL-337, 28s
anthemion Peter Nicholson, *The Princples of Architecture*, 1809, vol. III, plate 114. No. CWF 92-309, CN
arbor (1) Courtesy Gibbes Museum of Art, 38.36.1
arbor (2) Henry Howe, Historical Collections, c. 1845. No. CWF 88-474
arcade Photograph no. 92-CRL-333, 7s
arch (2) Drawing by Carl Lounsbury after Mark R. Wenger
architrave (2) Drawing by David Beatty after Jeffrey Bostetter
ashlar Photograph no. CWF 92-CRL-427, 14s
ashler Photograph no. CWF 91-CRL-1549, 2
avenue Courtesy South Carolina Historical Society
baluster Photograph no. CWF 92-CRL-354, 14s
banded architrave Photograph no. CWF 92-CRL-963, 9a
bar (2) Photograph no. CWF 92-CRL-453, 33s
barn Drawing by Bernard Herman and Margaret Mulrooney, Center for Historic Architecture and Engineering, Newark, Del.
base Isaac Ware, *A Complete Body of Architecture*, London, plate 19. No. CWF 92-127, CN
basement Courtesy Maryland Historical Society
batten Photograph no. CWF 85-EAC-1561, 1s
bead and reel Photograph no. CWF 92-CRL-967, 19s
bellflower Photograph no. CWF 93-CRL
binding joist, beam Batty Langley, *The Builder's Compleat Assistant*, 1738. No. CWF 91-1585, CN
blacksmith Moxon, *Mechanick Exercises*. CWF
bolection Drawing by Willie Graham
bond (a) Photograph no. CWF 91-CRL 1547, 1
  (b) Photograph no. CWF 84-EAC-5224
  (c) Photograph no. CWF 92-CRL-963, 22a
  (d) Photograph no. CWF 92-CRL = 335-32s
bounds Northampton County Deed and Will Book 1718-1725, p. 209
bow window Photograph by Susan Nash, c. 1930. No. CWF NA-1875
box (5) Courtesy South Carolina Historical Society
brace Drawing by David Beatty after Jeffrey Bostetter
bracket *(Above:)* Photograph no. CWF 91-CRL-1549, 37
(Below:) Photograph no. CWF 85-WJG-564-21
brickmaker, layer Moxon, *Mechanick Exercises*. CWF
Bristol stone Photograph no. CWF 90-WJG-863
buffet Photograph no. CWF 85-WJG-566, 14
button Photograph no. CWF 87-WJG-32, 18s
cabin roof Photograph no. CWF 89-CRL-277, 35s
cable, cabling Isaac Ware, *A Complete Body of Architecture*, London, plate 21. No. CWF 92-128, CN
capital Isaac Ware, *A Complete Body of Architecture*, London, plate 23
capitol *(Above:)* Bodleian Plate. No. CWF 78-654
(Center:) Illustration by William Goodacre, 1831. Courtesy Virginia State Library and Archives

(Below:) Drawing by B. H. Latrobe, 1811. Courtesy Library of Congress
carpenter Moxon, *Mechanick Exercises*. No. CWF 92-881, CN
cartouche Photograph no. CWF 92-CRL-83, 36s
casement From the Wharton Collection, photo courtesy of Carter Hudgins, Mary Washington College
cavetto Batty Langley, *Ancient Masonry, Both in the Theory & Practice*, 1737, plate C. No. CWF 91-1555, CN
chair board Photograph no. CWF 93-CRL
chamfer Drawing by David Beatty after Jeffrey Bostetter
chapel *(Exterior:)* Photograph no. CWF 86-WJG-6178, 1s
(Interior:) Photograph no. CWF 86-WJG-6176, 8s
(Plan:) Drawing by Carl Lounsbury
chimney Drawing by David Beatty after Jeffrey Bostetter
chimney back Photograph no. CWF C-90-55
chimney piece Batty Langley, *City and Country Builder's and Workman's Treasury of Designs*
Chinese Photograph no. CWF 85-WJG-1480, 9s
chink, chinking Photograph no. CWF 89-CRL-275, 33s
church Photograph no. CWF L-406
clapboard Photograph no. CWF 92-CRL-971, 9s
clapboard house, work Drawing by Cary Carson and Chinh Hoang, from *Winterthur Portfolio* 16 (1981)
closer Photograph no. CWF 84-WJG-356S
Coade stone Photograph no. CWF 92-CRL-970, 21s
colonnade Photograph no. CWF 92-CRL-333, 4s
column Photograph no. CWF 86-WJG-6183, 33s
common rafter Drawing by David Beatty after Jeffrey Bostetter
compass Photograph no. CWF 92-CRL-37, 33
Composite order Drawing by David Beatty after William Salmon, *Palladio Londinensis*, 1755
console Photograph no. CWF 92-CRL-37, 35
cope, coping (1) Photograph no. CWF 92-CRL-1055, 20s
Corinthian order Drawing by David Beatty after William Salmon, *Palladio Londinensis*, 1755
corner board Courtesy North Carolina Division of Archives and History, N-72-12-6035
cornhouse Drawing by David Beatty after Sharon Fleming
cornice (1) Drawing by David Beatty after Jeffrey Bostetter
courthouse *(Exterior:)* Photograph no. CWF 91-WJG-1348
(Plan:) Drawing by Carl Lounsbury
cove, coving Photograph no. CWF 85-WJG-567, 15s
cramp (1) Photograph no. CWF 92-CRL-1055, 8s
crossette Photograph no. CWF 92-CRL-453, 33s
cross garnet Photograph no. CWF 86-WJG-6171, 27s
cupola Photograph no. CWF 91-WJG-447, 16A
curtail step Photograph no. CWF 85-WJG-599, 10As
cut nail Drawing by David Beatty after Willie Graham
cyma Peter Nicholson, *The Principles of Architecture*, London, 1809, vol. II, plate 90. No. CWF 92-304, CN
dairy Drawing by David Beatty after Todd Tragash
dentil Photograph no. CWF 92-CRL-332, 22A
diamond (3) Photograph no. CWF 86-WJG-4146, 12s
dining room Courtesy Winterthur Museum
dome Courtesy Maryland Historical Society, 1897.1.3
doorcase James Gibbs, *Rules for Drawing*, plate XLII. No. CWF C87-709

Doric order Drawing by David Beatty after William Salmon, *Palladio Londinensis*, 1755

dovetail Photograph no. CWF 89-CRL-275, 21s

dragon beam Photograph no. CWF 91-CRL-1550, 10

drain Isaac Ware, *A Complete Body of Architecture*, plate 29-30. No. CWF 92-132, CN

draw (3) (a-b) Courtesy North Carolina Division of Archives and History, from British Public Record Office, N.77.9.2, N.77.9.4

(c) Westmoreland County, Va. Loose Court Papers

(d) Cabell Papers, College of William and Mary

drawing instruments William Salmon, *Palladio Londinensis*, plate 3. No. CWF 92-148, CN

Dutch roof Drawing by David Beatty

D window Photograph no. CWF 92-CRL-332, 1A

echinus Peter Nicholson, *The Principles of Architecture*, London, 1809, vol. III, plate 142. No. CWF 92-313, CN

egg and dart Photograph no. CWF 92-CRL-337, 18s

elevation (1) Courtesy Middleston Family Collection, College of Charleston

emboss Photograph no. CWF 93-CRL

enrich Photograph no. CWF 85-WJG-370, 10s

entablature Isaac Ware, *A Complete Body of Architecture*, plate 3. No. CWF 92-123, CN

escutcheon Photograph no. CWF 89-WJG-996, 25s

false plate Photograph no. CWF 84-WJG-2044, 19s

fanlight, sash Photograph no. CWF 92-CRL-429, 37s

festoon Photograph no. CWF 92-CRL-963, 13a

fill (1) *(Left:)* Photograph no. CWF 87-WJG-1386

(Right:) Photograph no. CWF 89-WJG-1554

fish pond Courtesy Gibbes Museum of Art, 38.36.71

floor, flooring *(Framing:)* Moxon, *Mechanick Exercises*. No. CWF 80-DS-2409

(Joint details:) Drawing by David Beatty after Jeffrey Bostetter

flue Courtesy Middleton Family Collection, College of Charleston

flute, fluting Peter Nicholson, *The Principles of Architecture*, London, 1809, vol. III, plate 204. No. CWF 92-330, CN

folding door Photograph no. CWF 85-WJG-1482,5s

font Photograph no. CWF 92-CRL-428, 20s

foot Photograph no. CWF 90-EAC-1275, 22s

foundation Photograph by Carter Hudgins

frame, framing Drawing by Jeffrey Bostetter and Carl Lounsbury

frank Drawing by David Beatty after Harold Bradley

French window Courtesy Middleton Family Collection, College of Charleston

fret William Salmon, *Palladio Londinensis*, plate M. No. CWF 92-168, CN

frieze Photograph no. CWF 92-CRL-333, 20s

frontispiece Photograph no. CWF 92-CRL-429-2s

gallery (1) Photograph no. CWF 90-WJG-869

garden *(Above:)* Courtesy Gibbes Museum of Art, 38.36.73

(Below:) Courtesy Mount Vernon Ladies' Association, no. 6506

gauge (2) Photograph no. CWF 85-WJG-1471, 31s

Gothic Photograph by Tim Buchman

grate (1) Photograph no. CWF 83-5117. WJG

grate (2) Photograph no. CWF 85-WJG-562-2

greenhouse 1930s photograph, no. CWF 85-506

guilloche Photograph no. CWF 93-CRL

ha ha Photograph no. CWF 92-CRL-1055, 28s

hall (2) Courtesy Library of Congress

hall (4) Photograph c. 1886 after an earthquake. Courtesy Charleston Library Society

hasp Photograph no. CWF 82-4876s. EAC

H hinge Photograph no. CWF 90-WJG-865

HL hinge Drawing by Jeffrey Bostetter

hook Drawing by Jeffrey Bostetter

hook and eye hinge Photograph no. CWF 82-3071s. EAC

hotel Henry Howe, *Historical Collections*, c. 1845. No. CWF 88-469

housebell Photograph no. CWF WJG

icehouse (1) Photograph c. 1930, no. CWF N2272, CN

impost Photograph no. CWF 92-CRL-332, 36a

intercolumniation Drawing by David Beatty

Ionic order Drawing by David Beatty after William Salmon, *Palladio Londinensis*, 1755

jamb Drawing by James F. Waite from Marcus Whiffen, *Eighteenth-Century Houses of Williamsburg*

jib door Photograph no. CWF 92-CRL-506, 9s

joiner Moxon, *Mechanick Exercises*. No. CWF 59-DW-658

joint Drawing by David Beatty after Jeffrey Bostetter and Cary Carson

joint (2) Drawings by David Beatty after Jeffrey Bostetter

joist Drawing by David Beatty after Jeffrey Bostetter

keystone, block Photograph no. CWF 92-CRL-428, 8s

king post Drawing by Jeffrey Bostetter

knee (2) Drawing By Jeffrey Bostetter

landscape Photgraph c. 1930, no. CWF N3497

lath Photograph no. CWF 86-WJG-5976, 14s

lathe Joseph Moxon, *Mechanick Exercises*, 3d ed., 1703. No. CWF 92-882 CN

lattice Photograph no. CWF 92-CRL-507, 4s

lightwood Photograph by Tim Buchman

lock Courtesy North Carolina Division of Archives and History

log construction Axonometric drawing by Jeffrey Bostetter

louver Photograph no. CWF 85-WJG-497, 11s

magazine Photograph no. CWF 91-CRL-587, 35a

mantelpiece Photograph no. CWF 93-CRL

marble Photograph no. CWF 85-WJG-1311, 7s

market house Drawing by Carl Lounsbury

meetinghouse *(Exterior:)* Photograph no. CWF 88-CRL-246, 6

(Plan:) Drawing by Carl Lounsbury

modillion Photograph no. CWF 91-CRL-1551, 27

molding Drawing by David Beatty after Jeffrey Bostetter

M roof Courtesy Maryland Historical Society

mullion Photograph no. CWF 82-3842s. EAC

muntin Photograph no. CWF 92-CRL-961, 31s

mutule Photograph no. CWF 92-CRL-332, 15a

necessary house *(Exterior:)* Photograph no. CWF 83-4608. EAC

(Plan:) Drawing by David Beatty after Doug Taylor

newel Photograph no. CWF 86-WJG-6549, 36s

niche Photograph no. CWF 92-CRL-427, 22s

notch Photograph no. CWF 85-WJG-500,5s

obelisk Courtesy Gibbes Museum of Art, no. 38.36.68

orchard Charleston County Register of Mesne Conveyance, plat no. 209

order Isaac Ware, *A Complete Body of Architecture*, plate 2. No. CWF 92-122 CN

outhouse Photograph no. CWF 92-WJG-455

oven *(Above:)* Photograph no. CWF 89-CRL-278, 16s

(Below:) Photograph no. CWF 85-WJG-581, 2a

ovolo Batty Langley, *Ancient Masonry, Both in the Theory & Practice*, 1737, plate C. No. CWF 91-1555, CN

oxeye window Photograph no. CWF 86-WJG-6178, 33s

pale Engraving after Peter Gordon. No. CWF C71-374

palisade Detail from a portrait of Mrs. Charles Carter by William Dering. No. CWF C77-940

panel (1) Drawing by David Beatty after Jeffrey Bostetter

paperhanging Photograph no. CWF 91-WJG-1121

papier mache Photograph no. CWF 85-WJG-562, 46

parapet (1) Photograph no. CWF 90-EAC-304, 27s

party wall Photograph by Susan Nash, c. 1930. No. CWF NA-969

passage (1) Photograph c. 1900-1920. No. CWF C-78-1044

pedestal Batty Langley, *The Builder's Benchmate*, 1747, plate 25. No. CWF C87-726

pediment Photograph no. CWF 92-CRL-429, 4s

penciling Photograph no. CWF 92-CRL-337, 30s

penitentiary Courtesy Virginia State Library and Archives

pew *(Above:)* Photograph no. CWF 86-WJG-6184, 18s
(Below:) Redrawn by Carl Lounsbury

piazza (1) Photograph no. CWF 92-CRL-425, 3s

piazza (2) *(Above:)* Courtesy Gibbes Museum of Art, 38.36.103
(Below:) Courtesy Maryland Historical Society

pier Photograph no. CWF 87-WJG-72, 12s

pigeon house Photograph by Singleton Moorhead, c. 1930. No. CWF 90-1267, CN

pilaster Photograph no. CWF 92-CRL-965, 33A

pillar Photograph no. CWF 92-CRL-427, 6s

pineapple Photograph no. CWF 92-WJG

plan (1) Courtesy Armistead-Cocke Papers, College of William and Mary

plank house Photograph by Tim Buchman

plaster *(Above:)* Photograph no. CWF WJG
(Below:) Photograph c. 1886 after an earthquake. Courtesy Charleston Library Society

plate Drawing by David Beatty after Jeffrey Bostetter

pleasure ground Courtesy Maryland Historical Society, 02.2.2

plinth (1) Photograph no. CWF 92-CRL-335, 8s

plinth (2) Photograph no. CWF 86-WJG-5950, 2s

plinth (3) Photograph no. CWF 85-WJG-2, 15

porch *(Above:)* Photograph no. CWF 92-CRL-426, 19s
(Below:) Photograph no. CWF 90-WJG-832

portico From *Gentleman's Magazine*, 1753. No. CWF C83-834

post in the ground *(Above:)* Photograph no. CWF 86-WJG-446, 6s
(Below:) Photograph no. CWF WJG

principal rafter, roof Drawing by David Beatty after Jeffrey Bostetter

prison Courtesy Southern Historical Collection

proportion William Salmon, *Palladio Londinensis*, plate A. No. CWF 92-146, CN

prostyle Henry Aldrich, *Elements of Civil Architecture*, 1824, tab. XVIII. No. CWF 91-1638, CN

pulpit Photograph no. CWF 90-WJG-862

quarry Courtesy Maryland Historical Society

quarter (1) Drawing by David Beatty after John Bernard

quarter (2) Photograph no. CWF 87-WJG-462, 15s

quirk Peter Nicholson, *The Principles of Architecture*, vol. II, 1809, plate 67. No. CWF 92-307, CN

quoin Photograph no. CWF 92-CRL-427, 9s

rabbet Courtesy Library of Congress

raising hinge Photograph no. CWF 86-WJG-6551, 16a

ramp Photograph no. CWF 73-FD-204

recess Photograph no. CWF 89-WJG-1566

reed, reeding Photograph no. CWF WJG

rim lock Photograph no. CWF 85-WJG-2, 18

rising joint Drawing by David Beatty after Edward Chappell

roof Drawing by David Beatty after Jeffrey Bostetter

rubbed Photograph no. CWF 92-CRL-428, 27s

rusticate, rustication Photograph no. CWF 92-CRL-965, 8a

scaffold, scaffolding J. Leadbeater, *The Gentleman and Tradesman's Compleat Assistant*, 1770. Courtesy Winterthur Library: Printed Book and Periodical Collection

scotia Drawing by David Beatty after Jeffrey Bostetter

screen Photograph by Susan Nash, c. 1930. No. CWF NA-1790

scroll Photograph no. CWF 92-CRL-965, 29a

section Courtesy Charleston Library Society

shed (1) Photograph no. CWF 82-5366s. WJG

shingle Photograph no. 90-EAC-929, 29s

shutter Photograph no. CWF 84-EAC-2182

sidelight Photograph no. CWF 89-WJG-1176

sill Drawing by David Beatty after Jeffrey Bostetter

single house *(Above:)* Photograph no. CWF 92-CRL-967, 11S
(Below:) Courtesy Charleston County Register of Mesne Conveyance, plat no. 519

sleeper Drawing by David Beatty after Jeffrey Bostetter

sliding door Photograph no. CWF 90-WJG-1251, 7s

smokehouse Drawing by David Beatty after Todd Tragash

soffit Photograph no. CWF 92-CRL-337, 25s

stack Photograph no. CWF 92-CRL-425, 0s

staircase Photograph no. CWF 90-WJG-831

stanchion Drawing by Jeffrey Bostetter

statehouse Drawing Mark R. Wenger

statue Courtesy North Carolina Archives and History, N.53.16.5164

steeple James Gibbs, *Book of Architecture*, 1728. No. CWF 57-CL-228

store Drawing by David Beatty after Charles Bergengren

storehouse Courtesy Gibbes Museum of Art, 38.36.91

stove (1) Photograph no. CWF 92-CRL-506, 36s

stove (2) Photograph no. CWF 87-WJG-1482

strut Photograph no. CWF 92-CRL-83, 18s

stucco (1) Courtesy Cook Collection, Valentine Museum, Richmond

stucco (2) Photograph no. CWF 88-WJG-1309, 18s

stud Drawing by David Beatty after Jeffrey Bostetter

sweep (1) Photograph no. CWF 87-WJG-463, 8s

swelling (1) Photograph no. CWF 92-CRL-335, 10s

swelling (2) Photograph no. CWF 85-WJG-582, 12a

tabby Photograph no. CWF 92-CRL-966, 4s

tavern *(Exterior:)* Photograph no. CWF WJG
(Plan:) Drawing by Carl Lounsbury

temple Photograph no. CWF WJG

tenement Photograph no. CWF 92-CRL-963, 16a

tenon Batty Langley, *The Builder's Compleat Assistant*, 1738. No. CWF 91-1585, CN

theater British Architectural Library, Royal Institute of British Architecture, London, 0244

tile *(Above:)* Photograph no. CWF 85-WJG-566, 42
(Center:) Photograph no. CWF 87-WJG-447, 10s
(Below:) Photograph no. CWF 86-WJG-6179, 27a

tobacco house *(Above:)* Photograph no. CWF 85-WJG-361, 8s
(Below:) CWF. Drawing by Willie J. Graham

tombstone Photograph no. CWF 92-CRL-83, 29s